ARCHAEOLOGY
WITHOUT BORDERS

ARCHAEOLOGY WITHOUT BORDERS

Contact, Commerce, and Change in the
U.S. Southwest and Northwestern Mexico

edited by
Laurie D. Webster and Maxine E. McBrinn

with

Mexican editor Eduardo Gamboa Carrera
INAH CENTRE, CHIHUAHUA

UNIVERSITY PRESS OF COLORADO

CONACULTA • INAH
CHIHUAHUA

© 2008 by the University Press of Colorado

Published by the University Press of Colorado
1624 Market Street, Suite 226
PMB 39883
Denver, Colorado 80202-1559

All rights reserved
First paperback edition 2023

 The University Press of Colorado is a proud member of the Association of University Presses.

The University Press of Colorado is a cooperative publishing enterprise supported, in part, by Adams State University, Colorado State University, Fort Lewis College, Metropolitan State University of Denver, University of Alaska Fairbanks, University of Colorado, University of Denver, University of Northern Colorado, University of Wyoming, Utah State University, and Western Colorado University.

ISBN 978-0-87087-889-9 (hardcover)
ISBN 978-1-64642-377-4 (paperback)
ISBN 978-0-87081-974-2 (ebook)

Library of Congress Cataloging-in-Publication Data

Archaeology without borders : contact, commerce, and change in the U.S. Southwest and northwestern Mexico / edited by Laurie D. Webster and Maxine E. McBrinn ; with Mexican editor, Eduardo Gamboa Carrera.
    p. cm.
  Includes bibliographical references and index.
  ISBN 978-0-87081-889-9 (hardcover : alk. paper) — ISBN 978-1-64642-377-4 (pbk : alk. paper) 1. Indians of North America—Commerce—Southwest, New. 2. Indians of Mexico—Commerce—Mexico, North. 3. Indians of North America—Southwest, New—Migrations. 4. Indians of Mexico—Mexico, North—Migrations. 5. Indians of North America—Southwest, New—History. 6. Indians of Mexico—Mexico, North—History. I. Webster, Laurie D., 1952– II. McBrinn, Maxine E.
  E78.S7.A73 2008
  979.004'97—dc22

2007039389

Support for the translation of papers in part three was provided by INAH.

Contents

List of Figures   ix

1. Creating an Archaeology without Borders   1
Maxine E. McBrinn and Laurie D. Webster

PART I: EARLY AGRICULTURAL ADAPTATIONS IN THE U.S. SOUTHWEST AND NORTHWESTERN MEXICO

2. The Transition to Agriculture in the Desert Borderlands: An Introduction   25
Gayle J. Fritz

3. The Setting of Early Agriculture in Southern Chihuahua   35
A. C. MacWilliams, Robert J. Hard, John R. Roney, Karen R. Adams, and William L. Merrill

4. Modeling the Early Agricultural Frontier in the Desert Borderlands   55
Jonathan B. Mabry and William E. Doolittle

5. Early Agriculture on the Southeastern Periphery of the Colorado Plateau: Diversity in Tactics   71
Bradley J. Vierra

6. A Method for Anticipating Patterns in Archaeological Sequences: Projecting the Duration of the Transition to Agriculture in Mexico—A Test Case   89
Amber L. Johnson

7. The Case for an Early Farmer Migration into
the Greater American Southwest   107
Steven A. LeBlanc

PART II: CONVERGING IDENTITIES: EXPLORING SOCIAL IDENTITY THROUGH MULTIPLE DATA CLASSES

8. Exploring Social Identities through Archaeological Data
from the Southwest: An Introduction   145
Linda S. Cordell

9. Archaeological Models of Early Uto-Aztecan Prehistory
in the Arizona-Sonora Borderlands   155
Jonathan B. Mabry, John P. Carpenter, and Guadalupe Sanchez

10. Interaction, Enculturation, Social Distance, and
Ancient Ethnic Identities   185
Patrick D. Lyons and Jeffery J. Clark

11. Networking the Old-Fashioned Way: Social and Economic Networks among
Archaic Hunters and Gatherers in Southern New Mexico   209
Maxine E. McBrinn

12. Architectural Metaphor and Chacoan Influence in
the Northern San Juan   227
Scott G. Ortman

13. Life's Pathways: Geographic Metaphors in Ancestral
Puebloan Material Culture   257
Kelley Hays-Gilpin

14. The Dynamic Nature of Cultural Identity during the Fourteenth
and Fifteenth Centuries in Central New Mexico   271
Suzanne L. Eckert

PART III: NEW RESEARCH FROM NORTHERN MEXICO: BORDERS, CONTACTS, LANDSCAPES, AND HISTORY

15. Avances del Norte de México (New Research from Northern Mexico)   285
Eduardo Gamboa Carrera

16. Imaginary Border, Profound Border: Terminological and Conceptual
Construction of the Archaeology of Northern Mexico   291
Francisco Mendiola Galván

17. Epic of the Toltec Chichimec and the Purépecha
in the Ancient Southwest   301
Patricia Carot and Marie-Areti Hers

18. Mesoamerican Influences in the Imagery of Northern Mexico   335
Arturo Guevara Sánchez

19. Turquoise: Formal Economic Interrelationships between
Mesoamerica and the North American Southwest   343
Phil C. Weigand

20. The Cultural Landscape of Cliff Houses in the
Sierra Madre Occidental, Chihuahua   355
Eduardo Gamboa Carrera and Federico J. Mancera-Valencia

21. All Routes, All Directions: The Prehistoric Landscape of Nuevo León   365
Moisés Valadez Moreno

22. Contributions of Walter W. Taylor to the
Archaeology of Coahuila, 1937–1947   373
Leticia González Arratia

23. Archaeology and Physical Anthropology: A Reflection on
Warfare in the Archaeological Vision   385
M. Nicolás Caretta

24. Pacification of the Chichimeca Region   393
Martha Monzón Flores

List of Contributors   405

Index   409

Figures

Figure 3.1. Map of Mexico and the southwestern United States. 38
Figure 3.2. Map of Chihuahua. 39
Figure 3.3. Map of southwestern Chihuahua, showing location of sites discussed in the text. 43
Figure 3.4. View of site A33-02, facing southeast. 47
Figure 3.5. Excavation profile of site A33-02. 48
Figure 5.1. Regional study areas: western San Juan Basin, northern San Juan Basin, and northern Rio Grande Valley. 73
Figure 5.2. Period 2 plant ubiquity in the western San Juan Basin. 74
Figure 5.3. Periods 1–3 plant ubiquity in the northern San Juan Basin. 75
Figure 5.4. Periods 1–3 plant ubiquity in the northern Rio Grande Valley. 76

Figures

Figure 5.5. Maize ubiquity by time period and region. 79
Figure 6.1. Global comparison of archaeological sequence durations by system state. 96
Figure 6.2. Map of projected duration of transition to agriculture for Mexico. 100
Figure 6.3. Projected sequence comparison for a few locations in Mexico. 101
Figure 11.1. Nested relationships between mobile hunters and gatherers. 211
Figure 11.2. Primary sandal elements. 212
Figure 11.3. Expected distribution of stylistic characteristics within the nested social organization of mobile hunters and gatherers. 213
Figure 11.4. Locations of sites cited in the text. 214
Figure 11.5. Cordage attributes. 215
Figure 11.6. Type 5 points. 216
Figure 11.7. Length versus proximal shoulder angle from Bat Cave (BC), Tularosa Cave (TC), Cordova Cave (CC), and Fresnal Shelter (FS). 217
Figure 11.8. Two-warp plain-weave sandal from Tularosa Cave. 218
Figure 11.9. Four-warp plain-weave sandal from Fresnal Shelter. 219
Figure 11.10. Four-warp scuffer-toe sandal from Fresnal Shelter. 220
Figure 11.11. Two-warp plain-weave sandal with fishtail heel from Fresnal Shelter. 221
Figure 12.1. The Northern San Juan region. 231
Figure 12.2. Pottery-band murals in kivas. 232
Figure 12.3. Pottery-band murals on storage rooms, and murals that blend landscape and container imagery. 233
Figure 12.4. Decorated kiva from site 42SA9310, southeastern Utah. 244
Figure 13.1. Four unfinished burden baskets with deliberate breaks in the banding line, Canyon del Muerto. 259
Figure 13.2. Homolovi Polychrome bowl with interior and exterior (in mirror) broken banding lines. 260
Figure 13.3. Pathways in petroglyphs. 262
Figure 13.4. Early painted pottery with design based on coiled basket. 264
Figure 13.5. Banding line on Jeddito Black-on-yellow bowl from Homol'ovi I with post-firing line break scratched in. 265
Figure 13.6. Close-up of triple line break at the rim of a bowl from Santo Domingo, probably early twentieth century. 266
Figure 14.1. Map of the Pueblo Southwest showing the location of Hummingbird Pueblo and Pottery Mound in the Lower Rio Puerco study area. 272
Figure 14.2. Map of Pottery Mound. 273
Figure 14.3. Map of Hummingbird Pueblo. 274
Figure 14.4. Interiors of four Pottery Mound Polychrome bowls and one bowl fragment from Pottery Mound showing examples of icons found on fourteenth- and fifteenth-century pottery in the study area. 276

Figures

Figure 17.1. Region referred to in the text as the Northwest, consisting of northwestern Mexico and the southwestern United States. 303

Figure 17.2. Cultures and chronological stages discussed in the text. 304

Figure 17.3. Partial view of the Loma Alta altar showing some of the sculptures. 305

Figure 17.4. The two sculptural traditions of the Loma Alta phase of Purépecha Culture and the Alta Vista–Vesuvio phase of the Chalchihuites Culture. 306

Figure 17.5. Fragment of a ritual vessel from Loma Alta decorated with post-firing painting in the stripped investment technique. 308

Figure 17.6. The Bird-Serpent, Loma Alta phase, site of Loma Alta. 311

Figure 17.7. Human-serpent composite figures from Loma Alta and the Chalchihuites area. 313

Figure 17.8. Figures with bows and arrows on ceramics and rock art. 319

Figure 18.1. (a) Engraving associated with the Ehécatl, the wind spirit in central Mexico, from San Quintín Canyon, Durango; (b) cruciform figure from a site in the Sierra Madre of Durango; (c) figure of Kokopelli from Piedra de Amolar; (d) butterfly-style hairdo found at Tepehuanes; (e) jar from La Ferrería, Durango, depicting a figure with only one leg. 336

Figure 18.2. (a) Dancers with braids and leather anklets similar to those worn by some groups in the southwestern United States; (b) polychrome sherd from the coastal cultures, found at La Ferrería, Durango; (c) hafted knife from Candelaria Cave; (d) spear guard from Candelaria Cave. 337

Figure 18.3. Major pre-Hispanic trade routes in the modern state of Durango, northern Mexico. 340

Figure 20.1. Map of northeastern Chihuahua, showing the distribution of cliff-house sites. 356

Figure 20.2. Profile of a 10.8-kilometer cut along the Río Sirupa, showing ecogeographical units. 360

Figure 20.3. Profile of the same cut along the Río Sirupa shown in Figure 20.2, showing the distribution of archaeological cultural materials identified from excavations in the cliff dwellings and features of the cultural and natural landscape. 361

Figure 20.4. Areas of Chihuahua where authors have applied the cultural landscape methodology. 362

1

CREATING AN ARCHAEOLOGY WITHOUT BORDERS

Maxine E. McBrinn and Laurie D. Webster

Pre-Hispanic contacts and cultural continuity between the southwestern United States and northwestern Mexico have commanded the interest of archaeologists since the earliest work in the region. Many of the founders and early practitioners of archaeological research in the Southwest, such as A. V. Kidder, Emil Haury, and Earl H. Morris, also spent time working in Mesoamerica. It was natural that they considered cultural continuity to extend over the international border into Mexico. Between the two world wars, E. B. Sayles (1936), Walter W. Taylor (2003; see also Gonzáles Arratia, Chapter 22), and other U.S. archaeologists conducted fieldwork in northern Mexico. Since then, the Instituto Nacional de Antropología e Historia (INAH) has become active in the archaeology of the northern borderlands, with Mexican-trained archaeologists now conducting most of the work in this region.

The Ninth Southwest Symposium was organized with the goal of sharing knowledge and increasing dialogue and collaboration between archaeologists in the U.S. Southwest and northwestern Mexico. (For the historical roots of this international meeting, see the introduction by Eduardo Gamboa Carrera, Chapter 15.) This volume presents the proceedings of the symposium held January 9–10, 2004, in Chihuahua City, Chihuahua, Mexico. This was the second Southwest Symposium held in Mexico; the first, in 1998, was in Hermosillo, Sonora. The 2004 conference was jointly planned by INAH and the board of the Southwest Symposium and was organized by Michael Whalen. It followed closely on the heels of the 2003 Pecos Conference, held at the important Chihuahuan site of Paquimé. This recent and rewarding trend of holding meetings in both the U.S. Southwest and northwestern Mexico underscores the deep historical and cultural connections that bind these regions into a broader culture area.

The theme of the 2004 Southwest Symposium was "Archaeology without Borders: Contact, Commerce, and Change in the U.S. Southwest and Northwestern Mexico." A primary goal of the conference was to offer participants a glimpse of the work being done by colleagues on the other side of the border. Convening the meeting in Mexico encouraged high participation by Mexican archaeologists working for INAH and others affiliated with Mexican academic institutions. Two of the four sessions were *a priori* dedicated to sessions organized by Mexican archaeologists, the other two by archaeologists from the United States. The themes of the Mexican sessions were "Identidad y Cultura" (Identity and Culture), moderated by Alejandro Martinez Muriel, and "Contacto y Comercio" (Contact and Commerce), moderated by Joaquín Garcia-Bárcena González. The themes of the U.S. sessions were "Variability in Agricultural Adaptations in the North American Southwest," organized by Robert J. Hard and John R. Roney, and "Converging Identities: Exploring Social Identity through Multiple Data Classes," organized by Maxine McBrinn and Laurie Webster. Simultaneous translations of all papers were provided.

ORGANIZATION OF THE VOLUME

This volume gathers together nineteen of the twenty-six papers presented at the symposium and incorporates one post-conference addition, Chapter 7 by Steven LeBlanc, included at the suggestion of the agricultural session organizers. Several presenters were unable to contribute to this publication because of time constraints or because their papers were being published in other venues.[1] As organizers of one of the sessions, we were invited by the Southwest Symposium board to edit the volume. We asked discussants Gayle Fritz (Chapter 2) and Linda Cordell (Chapter 8) to introduce the papers from their respective sessions and Eduardo Gamboa Carrera (Chapter 15) to contribute an introduction to the Mexican papers. In this introduction we focus on the general themes of the symposium.

Unlike the proceedings of the Hermosillo symposium (Villalpando 2002), which published some chapters in English and others in Spanish, the board decided to publish the proceedings of the Chihuahua symposium entirely in English. The exception is Eduardo Gamboa's introduction to the Mexican chapters (Chapter 15), presented in both languages for the benefit of Spanish-speaking readers. Following the symposium, most of the Mexican-session papers were translated into English by a Mexican translator working through the INAH office in Chihuahua. (The three chapters by Weigand, Carot and Hers, and Caretta were originally written in English.) We edited the papers to improve their readability and to reflect the conventions of scholarly writing in the United States. We are extremely pleased to make this Mexican research available to an English-speaking audience.

TOWARD AN ARCHAEOLOGY WITHOUT BORDERS

The international border between the United States and Mexico is a construct of the modern world. Pre-Hispanic cultural traditions did not change abruptly at the border, of course. Rather, the contemporary borderlands were once part of a great cultural continuum that stretched from north-central Mexico to the Great Basin and California and even beyond (see Reed 1964; McGuire 2002; LeBlanc, Chapter 7; Mabry, Carpenter, and Sanchez, Chapter 9). This broad area shares a number of geographical attributes, including an arid climate and significant topographical variation, which influenced the cultural traditions of peoples dependent on the resources of this vast region.

The name one applies to this region largely depends on the side of the border on which one resides. Most archaeologists from the United States know it as the Greater Southwest, whereas Mexican archaeologists refer to it as the Northwest, or La Gran Chichimeca. Although these terms approach the region from different perspectives (see Mendiola Galván, Chapter 16), all acknowledge the bi-directional exchange of people, goods, and ideas. The concept of the "Greater Southwest" culture area harkens back to the 1920s (Kroeber 1928), although the term itself was not coined until later (Beals 1943). Erik Reed (1964) famously used it to describe the region extending from Durango, Colorado, to Durango, Mexico, and from Las Vegas, Nevada, to Las Vegas, New Mexico. This term, however, conceptualizes the region from a U.S. perspective, not a Mexican one. Another term now popular with southwestern archaeologists, "North American Southwest," suffers from the same one-sided perspective, given that geographically the southwestern part of North America lies not in the United States but somewhere around Oaxaca, Mexico (McGuire 1997, 2002). Nevertheless, this term has the advantage of describing a geographical region rather than a culture area and thus avoids many a priori assumptions about cultural affiliation, linguistics, and historical connections linked to the "Greater Southwest" concept. (See McGuire 2002 for further discussion of this issue.)

U.S. visitors to Paquimé who study the map in the visitor center may be surprised to find the entire U.S. Southwest subsumed under the rubric of La Gran Chichimeca. This is the prevailing view from the south, however. This term is equally problematic because it represents a Mesoamerican perspective on the northern frontier (Mendiola Galván, Chapter 16; see also Gamboa Carrera, Chapter 15). This leaves northern Mexico somewhere in the middle, part of neither the U.S. Southwest nor Mesoamerica. Another term for this region—the western U.S.-Mexico borderlands—avoids these biases of perspective and defines the region in its own geographical terms (see also Vierra 2005) but seems rather narrow for an area that extends hundreds of miles north and south of the border. Others have settled on calling the region the Southwest/Northwest (McGuire 1997, 2002), an awkward but serviceable compromise.

The international border and the different concepts and perspectives used to describe this border region strongly influence our interpretations of the past. The presence of the border obscures the dynamic interplay of cultural influences and population movements that has characterized the U.S. Southwest and Northwest Mexico through time. It also reinforces an artificial partition of the region, giving archaeologists only a piecemeal view of broader cultural trends (Braniff 1997; Fish and Villalpando 1997; McGuire 2002). The division of this region into two separate countries also influences the field techniques, theoretical approaches, and research problems applied to the region as a whole. U.S. and Mexican archaeologists not only speak different languages, they also receive different academic training, acquire their funding from different sources, and follow different research priorities and mandates. (For detailed discussions of these issues, see McGuire 1997; Minnis and Whalen 2004; Newell 1999.) More prosaically, fieldwork in another country requires an extra layer of bureaucracy above and beyond that required for work in one's home country, necessitating work visas, passports, permits, and certification.

The same border that divides the two countries also hinders access to each others' work. A quick glance at the bibliographies from the Mexican chapters in this volume shows the large number of papers published internally by INAH, read as papers at meetings, or published in journals to which many academic U.S. libraries do not subscribe. This difficulty of access and a general lack of bilingualism have led to only superficial use of the Mexican literature by most English-speaking archaeologists. Although more Mexican archaeologists read English, they, too, have difficulties accessing the work of their U.S. colleagues, especially that published in the so-called gray literature.

A decade ago, Randall McGuire (1997) analyzed the citations made by authors who participated in a joint U.S.-Mexican symposium that addressed the international borderlands (Carpenter and Sanchez 1997). In that volume, 57 percent of the citations by Mexican authors were to literature written in English, whereas only 6 percent of the citations in the U.S. chapters were to literature written in Spanish. We conducted a similar analysis for this volume (excluding bibliographic references cited in this Introduction) and found a decline in the number of cross-language references cited.[2] Thirty-one percent of the citations in Part 3, the chapters on northern Mexico, are to literature published in English—roughly half the proportion noted by McGuire. But thirty-four of these fifty-six English citations were made by the three authors who submitted their chapters in English (Weigand, Carot and Hers, and Caretta), who are obviously more conversant in that language. Even more alarming, less than 1 percent of the citations by U.S. authors were to references written in Spanish. Thus, while it might have been hoped that scholars would have become more conversant with the research conducted by their international colleagues during the past ten years, the opposite appears to be true.

Although not encouraging, this situation is mitigated by several factors. Many of the theoretical issues of current interest to U.S. archaeologists presently lack parallels in the Mexican literature. Also, several of the U.S. chapters focus on research conducted on the Colorado Plateau, far north of the international border, where few Mexican archaeologists have worked or published. The fact that many of the Mexican authors cite their own publications shows that a large corpus of research has recently accumulated on the Mexican Northwest. Yet, whether as a result of language problems or lack of accessibility, virtually none of these references are cited by U.S. authors. This general unfamiliarity with the cross-border literature illustrates that scholarly dialogue and communication still have a long way to go before an "archaeology without borders" becomes a reality.

Differential access to research funding is another important concern. The U.S. Southwest enjoys international acclaim and high tourist dollars, with people from all over the world coming to visit such high-visibility sites as Mesa Verde, Chaco Canyon, and Casa Grande. Southwestern archaeology also attracts considerable financial support from both the public and private sectors. Many more archaeologists are employed in the southwestern United States than in northern Mexico, and research funding parallels this trend (McGuire 1997, 2002; Minnis and Whalen 2004:261–264). Northwestern Mexico is in the unenviable position of having to compete with the great pyramids and palaces of Mesoamerica for its research funding. As a result, much less is known about the archaeology of northwestern Mexico—and not because of a lack of intrinsic interest. Yet many archaeologists in Mexico, as well as the United States, have historically viewed northwestern Mexico as a peripheral region. Only recently has a major Mexican publication spurred renewed interest in this region as one with its own unique culture history (Braniff et al. 2001). More encouraging, INAH's recent investment in the new museum at Paquimé is a sign of Mexico's increased commitment to this region, and the designation of Paquimé as a World Heritage Site has raised its significance and visibility on an international scale.

Despite the many obstacles posed by the border, it is imperative that we share information. Archaeologists have long recognized that many cultural traditions entered the U.S. Southwest from the south, not just the triad of maize, beans, and squash but also ceramics (LeBlanc 1982), cotton and loom weaving (Teague 1998:98–101), the concept of ballcourts (Scarborough and Wilcox 1991), the Flower World ideological complex (Hill and Hays-Gilpin 1999), and other socio-religious concepts (Riley 2005), to name just a few. Other cultural traditions may have spread to the south, such as cliff-house architecture, rock art representations of the flute player, and the bow and arrow (Carot and Hers, Chapter 17; Guevara Sánchez, Chapter 18). Trade goods such as turquoise (Weigand, Chapter 19), macaws (Minnis et al. 1993), and copper bells (Vargas 2001) also moved across today's international border, but as Carot and Hers (Chapter 17) and Guevara Sánchez (Chapter 18) point out, these were a minor part of the larger exchange. The movements of people and ideas were far more influential. Without more detailed information about the intermediary points of transmission on both sides of the border, we are left to speculate about the processes, timing, and routes of these exchanges.

Questions of cultural continuity between the U.S. Southwest and Northwest Mexico are most fruitfully explored when U.S. and Mexican archaeologists work together. Fortunately, in recent years several successful collaborations have occurred between INAH and Mexican-trained archaeologists and those based in the United States or Canada. The Joint Casas Grandes Expedition (Di Peso, Rinaldo, and Fenner 1974) is one classic example, and Jane Kelley's Projecto Arqueología de Chihuahua (Kelley et al. 1999, 2004) and the INAH–Museum of New Mexico–University of New Mexico program led by Raphael Cruz Antillón, Timothy Maxwell, and Robert Leonard (Cruz Antillón et al. 2004) are others. Collaborative research has grown considerably in the past decade, especially in the states of Chihuahua and Sonora (e.g., Fish, Fish, and Villalpando in press; Hard, Zapata, and Roney 2001; McGuire and Villalpando 1993; McGuire et al. 1999; see also Foster and Gorenstein 2000; Jiménez Betts and Darling 2000). We applaud those archaeologists who have braved the bureaucracy of the border and eagerly await more collaborative projects.

As the joint projects mentioned earlier illustrate, dialogue and collaboration between Mexican and U.S. scholars are most successful when a topic is narrowly defined and of mutual thematic interest. One successful example was the 1994 symposium in Tucson that focused on the prehistory of the borderlands (Carpenter and Sanchez 1997). The participants were already familiar with each others' work and had, in many cases, participated in joint research, making the symposium a summation and continuation of ongoing dialogue. When a topic is of unequal interest or when theoretical approaches or methodologies are not shared, true dialogue is less likely. In our view, the sharing of information at future Southwest Symposia is most likely to be achieved when participants from both sides of the border are invited to participate in a single session with a tight topical focus rather than in sequential sessions of English- and Spanish-speaking presenters.

MAJOR THEMES OF THE NINTH SOUTHWEST SYMPOSIUM

Issues of identity, boundaries, and territory appear in various guises in all three sections of this book. As archaeologists, we are stymied by our inability to neatly categorize as we struggle with the issue of boundaries and scale. The diagnostic criteria we use to define societies privilege a fraction of the overall material culture, such as ceramics or architecture, producing culture areas that may not have existed in the past or do not conform to distinctions recognized at the time. This may be influenced by our modern lives within state-level societies, where absolute boundaries and territories are so politically important. More egalitarian societies probably had a very different cultural map and may not have felt the same need to subdivide the world. Certainly, they were interested in who was or was not a member of their group, but they may not have relied on absolute criteria. Lacking higher-level governing bodies to create boundaries, the line between near and far was probably more flexibly drawn, creating the smear of continuity we see in the archaeological record.

AGRICULTURAL ADAPTATIONS IN THE U.S.-MEXICO BORDERLAND

The chapters in Part 1 of this volume present new research on the introduction and adoption of agriculture in the U.S. Southwest and northwestern Mexico. The appearance of agriculture in this region is of perennial interest to most archaeologists working there, for many of the same reasons this question fascinates researchers working in Europe. Neither Europe nor the U.S. Southwest and northwestern Mexico are regions where important economic crops were first domesticated. In both regions, however, profound material and social changes accompanied or shortly followed the introduction of agriculture.

The adoption of agriculture in the U.S.-Mexico borderlands and other parts of the world has been an active area of study for decades. Still, fundamental questions remain. Did domesticated crops and knowledge of farming diffuse into existing populations from outside these regions, did migrants bring these crops and this knowledge with them, or did a combination of processes occur (see Mabry and Doolittle, Chapter 4; Johnson, Chapter 6; LeBlanc, Chapter 7; Mabry, Carpenter, and Sanchez, Chapter 9)? The answer is important because the appearance of agriculture ushered in a suite of cultural changes—increased sedentism, the introduction of ceramics, more durable architecture, expanding population densities, greater social complexity—that intensely altered the societies that followed. These developments were fundamental to creating the dominant societies in the region. The appearance of agriculture has also been theoretically linked to the introduction of new language groups, including Indo-European in Europe (Renfrew 1987) and Uto-Aztecan in the U.S. Southwest (Bellwood 1997; Hill 2001; LeBlanc, Chapter 7; Mabry, Carpenter, and Sanchez, Chapter 9). Of course, a number of differences are seen in the archaeological patterns of North America and Europe, including the temporal span of the transition and the nature of the material remains available for analysis. The commonalities, however, are instructive.

Initial research on early agriculture in the U.S. Southwest focused on the antiquity and forms of the earliest domesticated maize (Manglesdorf 1950, 1958, 1974; Dick 1965; Wills 1988, 1995) and the possible routes of its introduction (Haury 1962; Berry 1982; Wills 1988:2–3). This period is analogous to European research on the age and spread of the Linearbandkeramik Culture (Kossinna 1902) and the migration of Indo-Europeans into Europe (Childe 1926, 1950). More recent research in western North America and Europe has shown this transition to be considerably more diverse than originally thought and suggests that the best explanation may be early migration followed by cultural diffusion (e.g., Price, Gebauer, and Keeley 1995; Matson 1991; see also Mabry and Doolittle, Chapter 4, and Mabry,

Carpenter, and Sanchez, Chapter 9). Recently, European researchers have begun to examine the genetic diversity of both modern and ancient populations to critically examine the migration hypothesis, with results that suggest selective intermarriage between migrants and existing populations (Balter 2005; Haak et al. 2005). This approach holds much promise for American researchers as well (see LeBlanc, Chapter 7). These studies reveal that understanding the complex transition from foraging to farming in Europe and the U.S. Southwest and northwestern Mexico requires multiple lines of evidence from archaeology, linguistics, botany, and genetics.

As Linda Cordell has pointed out (1997:127-128), prior to the 1950s and 1960s no one felt it necessary to explain why people began to farm once this became a viable option. Given that farming permitted the creation of complex societies and our modern world, it was taken for granted that this was superior to a foraging lifeway. Not until ethnographic and archaeological research demonstrated that hunter-gatherers were at least as healthy as farmers did researchers become interested in the question: Why did people adapt agriculture? Today, this question forms the crux of current research and hypotheses, especially in the Southwest.

Models such as those offered by Mabry and Doolittle (Chapter 4) and Johnson (Chapter 6) explicate how and why peoples in the U.S. Southwest and Mexican Northwest incorporated agricultural practices into their subsistence systems. Mabry and Doolittle explore a wide range of farming niches and methods suitable for the region's arid environment, whereas Johnson's model predicts the pace of the transition from hunting and gathering to agriculture, based on environmental and climactic factors. Although these models differ widely in their goals and ambitions, both offer new ways to interpret the archaeological record.

Regional variation in the timing of and dependence on maize agriculture (Fritz, Chapter 2; Mabry, Carpenter, and Sanchez, Chapter 9) obscures easy answers to the fundamental questions of the appearance of agriculture in the region. Why did some groups continue to follow a hunter-gatherer lifeway, supplementing wild resources with maize and tending their gardens as part of their yearly rounds (Wills 1988), while others quickly took advantage of the stability farming provided (Mabry 2002; Roney and Hard 2002; Mabry and Doolittle, Chapter 4)? Some groups took much longer than others to commit to this new subsistence method (MacWilliams et al., Chapter 3; Vierra, Chapter 5). In other cases, migrating groups may have brought their agricultural knowledge and methods with them (LeBlanc, Chapter 7). Some researchers have suggested the presence of a well-defined agricultural frontier, with maize grown behind a line and "pure" hunters and gatherers ahead of it (Carpenter, Sanchez, and Villalpando 2002; Geib and Spurr 2002; Matson 1991). Although with more data we may yet find a better-defined agricultural frontier, the research reported here does not support this notion.

Temporal and geographical variation in the commitment to agriculture raises questions about our use of terminology. As MacWilliams and colleagues point out (Chapter 3), although chronologically we may be dealing with the Middle or Late Archaic periods, by that time some groups were no longer practicing an "archaic" subsistence pattern. These authors and others prefer the term "Early Agricultural" to describe the period of transition, reserving the terms "Middle Archaic" and "Late Archaic" for specific chronological periods (see also Huckell 1995, 1996).

Recently, archaeologists have begun to explore the possibility that agriculture was introduced to some parts of northwestern Mexico and the U.S. Southwest by Uto-Aztecan speakers from central Mexico (Hill 2001; LeBlanc, Chapter 7; Mabry, Carpenter, and Sanchez, Chapter 9). LeBlanc's chapter offers a valuable summary of the linguistic, genetic, and archaeological data in support of this hypothesis and also some ways to test it. The Uto-Aztecan migration hypothesis mirrors ideas about the spread of early farming in Africa, Europe, and the Middle East and offers the potential to find global patterns, as well as local variability, in the spread and adoption of agriculture.

ARCHAEOLOGICAL APPROACHES TO SOCIAL IDENTITY

Part 2 of this volume focuses on questions of social identity. The assignment of identity to archaeological remains has been a primary goal of archaeology since its inception (Jones 1997). Archaeologists cannot speak of past peoples without assigning some name to each group, even if that name is derived from a prominent artifact class, such as the Beaker People, the Clovis Culture, or the Basketmakers (Cordell 1997; Kossinna 1902). Although these assignments may not represent social divisions of the past, such terms are useful and easy. Unfortunately, even when archaeologists understand the limitations of the terminology, their use reifies its meanings. Only recently have archaeologists begun to appreciate the complex and multilayered nature of social identity. One result is the decreasing use of the term "ethnicity," which implies a single, static group identity, as opposed to fluid and nested identities that may be internally or externally defined.

The idea that social identity cannot always be defined objectively is articulated by Michael Moerman (1965), who pointed out that an individual's assignment to a particular social group (in his case, "Lue") is situational. Frederik Barth (1969) consciously used a subjective definition of ethnicity and suggested that an objective definition was impossible. In his view, a man was "Pathan" because he identified himself as "Pathan." The idea that social identity is situational and not uniform within the bounds of space and time makes these social distinctions difficult to address through the medium of material culture alone. Without the benefit of living informants, what tools are available to archaeologists to interpret social identity (see Ferguson 2004; Mills 2004:3–11)?

Practice theory, the idea that enculturation is visible in the material record, offers one approach (Bourdieu 1977, 1990; see also Lemonnier 1986). Although technological style was first used in Europe to examine contemporary and historical social differences, archaeologists soon realized that this approach also offered a window into the prehistoric past. Since then, concepts of technological style, social boundaries, and social agency have proven to be effective archaeological tools for exploring social identity (Dobres 2000; Dobres and Hoffman 1999; Hegmon 1992, 1998; Jones 1997; Stark 1998).

At about the time practice theory was becoming a standard method in archaeology, researchers in the U.S. Southwest began seeking new ways to infer social groups and patterns of migration from the archaeological record (e.g., Bernardini 2002, 2005; Clark 2001; Duff 2002; Eckert 2003, see also Chapter 14; Lyons 2001, 2003; McBrinn 2002, 2005; Stone 2003). Jeffery Clark (2001; see also Lyons and Clark, Chapter 10), building on the work of Christopher Carr (1995) and others, developed concepts of acculturation, interaction, and technological style to examine migration in the Southern Southwest. Others used oral histories from contemporary Pueblo groups to structure their models (e.g., Bernardini 2002, 2005; Lyons 2001, 2003), testing them with evidence from architecture, ceramics, rock art, or other material classes to interpret the timing and routes of migrations. Such studies, coupled with renewed interest in cultural affiliation as a result of the Native American Graves Protection and Repatriation Act of 1990 (e.g., Ferguson and Loma'omvaya 1999), have energized archaeological research in the Southwest and provided archaeologists with new conceptual tools for exploring questions of cultural and social identity.

Another recent approach for investigating social identity in the archaeological record is the study of conceptual metaphors embodied in various classes of human behavior, such as architecture, ceramic and textile designs, mural decorations, and language (Ortman 2000, see also Ortmann, Chapter 12; Hays-Gilpin, Chapter 13; Sekaquaptewa and Washburn 2004, 2006). These researchers draw from the fields of cognitive psychology, linguistics, and symmetry studies (e.g., Fauconnier 1997; Lakoff 1993; Lakoff and Johnson 1980; Washburn and Crowe 1988) to explore the contextual use of designs and other media at varying scales, using these patterns to infer shared metaphorical meanings as a window into the mental constructs of past social groups. This approach is especially effective when native consultants are involved and cultural continuity is assumed.

The chapters in Part 2 examine social identity for a wide range of groups and time periods in the U.S. Southwest. They demonstrate that social identity in the Southwest, as elsewhere, is rarely clear-cut or well defined. Modern Pueblo people derive their identities from a complex web of village, clan, moiety, or sodality affiliations and universal identifiers such as kin, sex, and status. Membership in any one of these groups can be signaled in different ways. When we graft onto this complex situation a long tradition of migrations and periods of consolidation and dispersal, even a general term like "Puebloan" is of indeterminate meaning (see Lyons and Clark, Chapter 10, for an example of "Puebloan" peoples moving into a new area and adopting local traditions). Mapping group histories into the past is extraordinarily difficult and requires significant assumptions on the part of the researcher (Ferguson 2004). Mapping groups forward from a point in the past is also fraught with difficulty (e.g., Irwin-Williams 1979; Ford, Schroeder, and Peckham 1972). The most successful attempts may be those conducted at the village or tribal scale that integrate oral histories into their models (e.g., Bernardini 2005; Lyons and Clark, Chapter 10).

Although the authors in this section use a variety of means to examine social identity, common issues emerge. All lead back to the basic notion that social identity is situational and negotiated and exists at both conscious and unconscious levels. The scale of identity matters in these kinds of studies and influences the kinds of material culture considered. Researchers concerned with the negotiation of identity by individuals or close kin groups (e.g., Mabry, Carpenter, and Sanchez, Chapter 9; McBrinn, Chapter 11) employ different kinds of evidence than those who explore identity on a clan or tribal level (Eckert, Chapter 14; Hays-Gilpin, Chapter 13; Lyons and Clark, Chapter 10; Ortman, Chapter 12). For example, as described by McBrinn (2002, 2005, see also Chapter 11), the manufacture of cordage would have been a common, perhaps even a daily, activity. Material produced at this level of frequency might show the results of enculturation (*habitus* and practice) to a greater degree than an activity conducted more intermittently. To borrow from Lyons and Clark (Chapter 10), because cordage is created by craftspeople working at a smaller social distance than people building new room blocks, cordage and architecture are likely to reflect different aspects of social identity.

This leads to a second set of considerations. The more evidence from different media and social contexts one can incorporate into a study, the more social distinctions (or identities) one is likely to discern. Just as a comparison of gender or ranking is impossible if only artifacts made by high-ranking males are considered, so inferences about social distinctions are only possible if a variety of material classes are used. Fortunately, the outstanding preservation of perishable artifacts in many parts of the southwestern United States and northwestern Mexico extends the range of artifacts available for study in this region, making it a superb area to conduct this kind of cross-media research.

CONTACTS, LANDSCAPES, AND THE HISTORY OF ARCHAEOLOGICAL PRACTICE

Part 3 presents chapters from the two symposium sessions organized by Mexican archaeologists. Discussing new research from the states of Durango, Zacatecas, Nuevo León, Coahuila, and Chihuahua, these chapters address three basic themes: cultural contacts, cultural landscapes, and the history of archaeological practice and discourse. Cultural interaction is a common concern of many authors. Questions of contacts between the southwestern United States and northern Mexico, as well as the flow of goods and ideas, have long captured the interest of archaeologists on both sides of the border (e.g., Bradley 1993; Braniff 1995; Carot 2000; Haury 1945, 1962; Hedrick, Kelley, and Riley 1974; Kelley 1966; Pohl 2001; Weigand and García de Weigand 2001; Woosley and Ravesloot 1993). Several chapters in the volume emphasize the social, ideological, or economic linkages between these regions and other parts of Mexico. The scale of these studies ranges from Phil Weigand's (Chapter

19) analysis of the long-distance exchange of turquoise between Mesoamerica and the U.S. Southwest, to a summary of Walter Taylor's concern with connections between Coahuila and West Texas (Gonzáles Arratia, Chapter 22), to Gamboa Carrera and Mancera-Valencia's (Chapter 20) study of economic and social relations within the Casas Grandes regional system.

The focus of analysis varies as well. Guevara Sánchez (Chapter 18) uses the medium of rock art to investigate stylistic relationships and possible contacts among groups in Durango, Zacatecas, Chihuahua, and the U.S. Southwest. The study by Carot and Hers (Chapter 17) has a broader focus, employing multiple lines of evidence (architecture, ceremonial and funerary practices, ceramics, iconography) to explore the bi-directional movements of people and ideas across what the authors conceptualize as a mutual cultural "bridge" linking the Toltec Chichimec and Purépecha (Tarascan) cultures of north-central Mexico with the Hohokam and ancestral Pueblos of the southwestern United States. Their research underscores the fluid and dynamic nature of the boundaries between these regions over time. Monzón Flores (Chapter 24) uses a different form of evidence—early Spanish texts—to critique sixteenth-century encounters between Spanish interests and nomadic groups in the Chichimeca region. Although this perspective, by its nature, is almost entirely one-sided, Monzón Flores's study expands our understanding of post-conquest dynamics and consequences for indigenous groups in what is now northern Mexico (see also Pailes and Reff 1985; Spicer 1963).

The archaeology of cultural landscapes is of considerable interest to Mexican archaeologists, just as it is in other parts of the world (e.g., Ashmore and Knapp 1999). Gamboa Carrera and Mancera-Valencia (Chapter 20) draw from the models of Carl Sauer and other cultural geographers and introduce a new interpretive model they call "archaeogeography" to interpret the natural and cultural landscapes of Paquimé and nearby cliff dwellings of the Sierra Madre Occidental. Their analysis finds close ties between the cliff dwellings and the ritual city of Paquimé expressed through shared iconography, architectural features, and a communication system based on roads and watchtowers. Their work augments recent studies of interaction in the Casas Grandes regional system (VanPool et al. 2000; Whalen and Minnis 2001). Cultural landscapes of the sacred are the focus of Valadez Moreno's (Chapter 21) study of hunter-gatherer societies in Nuevo León, which considers how rock art, rituals, and the ordering of ceremonial space structured social relations. Citing the importance of caves and prominent topographical features as prime ritual spaces (cf. Taube 1986), Valadez Moreno explores the metaphorical meaning of imagery related to hunting, the veneration of water, and human and animal fertility.

Finally, several authors focus on the history of archaeological research and discourse in the borderlands region. González Arratia (Chapter 22) makes extensive use of contemporary archival sources in her critique of Taylor's research in Coahuila between 1937 and 1947. Discussing Taylor's theoretical concern with relationships between the cultures of Coahuila and those of West Texas and Mesoamerica, González offers a year-by-year account of his fieldwork, collections, and interpretations and addresses reasons much of his work remained unpublished until after his death (e.g., Taylor 2003).

Philosophical and epistemological reflections on archaeological methods and discourse structure the contributions by Caretta (Chapter 23) and Mendiola Galván (Chapter 16). Caretta expounds upon the problem of inferring pre-Hispanic warfare from archaeological remains and urges physical anthropologists to become more involved in these analyses. Mendiola Galván calls for increased epistemological vigilance by archaeologists in their use of archaeological labels and terms. His insightful critique into the historiography of such concepts as Mesoamerica, Greater Southwest, and Gran Chichimeca illustrates how these concepts have produced ambiguities and obscured the cultural diversity of northern Mexico.

The recent publication of *La Gran Chichimeca* (Braniff et al. 2001) has forged a new appreciation for this region. In promoting the rich archaeological heritage of northern Mexico in much the same way Mesoamerica and the U.S. Southwest have been presented to the public, the volume affirms the significance of the region, its outstanding cultural resources, and its diverse cultural past. Increasing work in northern Mexico by Mexican, U.S., and Canadian scholars, new avenues of funding, an increased commitment by INAH, and greater international collaboration are signs that, while we are not there yet, we are finally approaching an archaeology without borders.

Acknowledgments. We express our appreciation to our two reviewers, Randall McGuire and an anonymous reviewer, for their detailed and insightful comments on our Introduction and the other chapters in this volume. We found their comments extremely helpful, and we incorporated most of their suggestions. This volume is a much better product because of their input. We also thank Darrin Pratt, our editor at the University Press of Colorado, for his exceptional guidance and patience during this process. Michael Whalen and the Southwest Symposium board offered us the opportunity to edit this volume and encouraged us as we worked through the process. We thank them for their confidence and support.

NOTES

1. The following papers were presented at the symposium but do not appear in this volume:

K. Renne Barlow, *Understanding Variability in Time Spent Farming Maize: Examples from the Fremont and the Tarahumara*

Roy Bernard Brown, Patricia Fornier García, and Alfonso Rosales López, *Contacto y Comercio: un Acercamiento Arqueológico a los Pobladores de El Paso del Norte, Pueblos y Parajes*

Rafael Cruz Antillón and Tim Maxwell, *La Turquesa en el Sistema Regional de Casas Grandes*

Edgar K. Huber and Heather J. Miljour, *Early Maize on the Colorado Plateau: New Dates from West-Central New Mexico*

Viviane Jaenicke-Després, Edward Buckler, Bruce Smith, John Doebley, and Svante Pääbo, *Analysis of Key Genes in the Domestication of Maize from Archaeological Maize Cobs*

Peter Jiménez Betts, Humberto Medina González, and Enrique Garcia, *Riptide on the Chichimec Sea: Perspectives on Ritual Landscapes of Northern and Central Mesoamerica*

Laurie Webster, *Early Mogollon Social Identity: Evidence from Clothing, Containers, and Ritual* (an expanded version of this paper appears in the volume *Zuni Origins: Anthropological Approaches on Multiple Americanist and Southwestern Scales*, ed. David A. Gregory and David R. Wilcox. University of Arizona Press, Tucson, in press.)

2. These tallies were generated from the original manuscripts, before additional cross-language citations were added at the suggestion of reviewers.

REFERENCES CITED

Ashmore, Wendy, and Arthur B. Knapp (editors)
1999   *Archaeologies of Landscape: Contemporary Perspectives*. Blackwell, Oxford.

Balter, Michael
2005   Ancient DNA Yields Clues to the Puzzle of European Origins. *Science* 310:964–965.

Barth, Frederik
1969   Introduction. In *Ethnic Groups and Boundaries: The Social Organization of Cultural Differences*, ed. Frederik Barth, 9–38. Little, Brown, Boston.

Beals, Ralph L.
1943   Cultural Relations between Northern Mexico and the Southwest United States: Ethnologically and Archaeologically. In *El Norte de México y El Sur de Estados Unidos: Tercera Reunión de Mesa Redonda sobre Problemas Antropológicos de México y Centro América*, ed. Rafael García Granados, 191–199. Sociedad Exicana de Antropología, México.

Bellwood, Peter
1997   Prehistoric Cultural Explanations for Widespread Linguistic Families. In *Archaeology and Linguistics: Aboriginal Australia in Global Perspective*, ed. P. McConvell and N. Evans, 123–134. Oxford University Press, Melbourne.

Bernardini, Wesley
2002   *The Gathering of the Clans: Understanding Ancestral Hopi Migration and Identity*, A.D. 1275–1400. Ph.D. dissertation, Department of Anthropology, Arizona State University, Tempe. ProQuest, Ann Arbor.
2005   *Hopi Oral Tradition and the Archaeology of Identity*. University of Arizona Press, Tucson.

Berry, Michael S.
1982   *Time, Space, and Transition in Anasazi Prehistory*. University of Utah Press, Salt Lake City.

Bourdieu, P.
1977   *Outline of a Theory of Practice*. Cambridge University Press, Cambridge.
1990   *The Logic of Practice*. Polity, Cambridge, England.

Bradley, Ronna J.
  1993   Marine Shell Exchange in Northwest Mexico and the Southwest. In *The American Southwest and Mesoamerica: Systems of Prehistoric Exchange*, ed. Jonathan E. Ericson and Timothy G. Baugh, 121-158. Plenum, New York.

Braniff, Beatriz
  1995   Diseños Tradicionales Mesoamericanos y Norteños. Ensayo de Interpretación. In *Arqueología del Occidente y Norte de México; Homenaje a J. Charles Kelley*, ed. Barbro Dahlgren and Ma. de los Dolores Soto de Arechavaleta, 181-209. Instituto de Investigaciones Antropológicas, Universidad Nacional Autónoma de México, México.
  1997   Comentarios. In *Prehistory of the Borderlands*, ed. John Carpenter and Guadalupe Sanchez, 129-130. Arizona State Museum Archaeological Series 186. University of Arizona Press, Tucson.

Braniff, Beatriz, Linda S. Cordell, María de la Luz Gutierrez, Marie-Areti Hers, and Elisa Villalpando.
  2001   *La Gran Chichimeca: El Lugar de los Rocas Secas*. Conaculta y Jaca Books, México y Milano.

Carot, Patricia
  2000   Las Rutas al Desierto: de Michoacán a Arizona. In *Nómadas y Sedentarios en el Norte de México: Homenaje a Beatriz Braniff*, ed. Marie-Areti Hers, José Luis Mirafuentes, Ma. De los Dolores Soto, and Miguel Vallebueno, 91-112. Instituto de Investigaciones Antropológicas, Estéticas, e Históricas, Universidad Nacional Autónoma de México, México.

Carpenter, John P., and Guadalupe Sanchez (editors)
  1997   *Prehistory of the Borderlands*. Arizona State Museum Archaeological Series 186. University of Arizona Press, Tucson.

Carpenter, John P., Guadalupe Sanchez, and Maria Elisa Villalpando
  2002   Of Maize and Migration: Mode and Tempo in the Diffusion of *Zea mays* in Northwest Mexico and the American Southwest. In *Traditions, Transitions, and Technologies: Themes in Southwestern Archaeology*, ed. Sarah H. Schlanger, 245-256. University Press of Colorado, Boulder.

Carr, Christopher
  1995   A Unified Middle-Range Theory of Artifact Design. In *Style, Society, and Person: Archaeological and Ethnological Perspectives*, ed. Christopher Carr and Jill E. Neitzel, 171-258. Plenum, New York.

Childe, V. G.
  1926   *The Aryans: A Study of Indo-European Origins*. Kegan Paul, Trench, Trubner, and Co., London.
  1950   *Prehistoric Migrations in Europe*. Aschehoug, Oslo.

Clark, Jeffery J.
  2001   *Tracking Prehistoric Migrations: Pueblo Settlers among the Tonto Basin Hohokam*. Anthropological Papers of the University of Arizona 65. University of Arizona Press, Tucson.

Cordell, Linda
  1997   *Archaeology of the Southwest*, 2nd ed. Academic, New York.

Cruz Antillón, Rafael, Robert D. Leonard, Timothy D. Maxwell, Todd L. VanPool, Marcel J. Harmon, Christine S. VanPool, David A. Hyndman, and Sydney S. Brandwein
    2004   Galeana, Villa Ahumada, and Casa Chica: Diverse Sites in the Casas Grandes Region. In *Surveying the Archaeology of Northwest Mexico*, ed. Gillian E. Newell and Emiliano Gallaga, 149–176. University of Utah Press, Salt Lake City.

Dick, Herbert
    1965   *Bat Cave*. School of American Research Monograph 27, Santa Fe.

Di Peso, Charles C., John B. Rinaldo, and Gloria Fenner
    1974   *Casas Grandes: A Fallen Trading Center of the Gran Chichimeca*, Volume 4. Amerind Foundation, Dragoon, Ariz., and Northland Press, Flagstaff, Ariz.

Dobres, Marcia-Anne
    2000   *Technology and Social Agency: Outlining a Practice Framework for Archaeology*. Blackwell, Oxford.

Dobres, Marcia-Anne, and Christopher R. Hoffman (editors)
    1999   *The Social Dynamics of Technology: Practice, Politics and World Views*. Smithsonian Institution Press, Washington, D.C.

Duff, Andrew I.
    2002   *Western Pueblo Identities: Regional Interaction, Migration, and Transformation*. University of Arizona Press, Tucson.

Eckert, Suzanne L.
    2003   *Social Boundaries, Immigration, and Ritual Systems: A Case Study from the American Southwest (New Mexico)*. Ph.D. dissertation, Department of Anthropology, Arizona State University, Tempe. ProQuest, Ann Arbor.

Fauconnier, Giles
    1997   *Mappings in Thought and Language*. Cambridge University Press, Cambridge.

Ferguson, T. J.
    2004   Academic, Legal, and Political Contexts of Social Identity and Cultural Affiliation Research in the Southwest. In *Identity, Feasting, and the Archaeology of the Greater Southwest*, ed. Barbara J. Mills, 27–41. University Press of Colorado, Boulder.

Ferguson, T. J., and Micah Loma'omvaya
    1999   *Hoopoq'uaqam niqw Wukoskyavi (Those Who Went to the Northeast and Tonto Basin): Hopi-Salado Cultural Affiliation Study*. Report on file at the Hopi Cultural Preservation Office, Kykotsmovi, Ariz.

Fish, Paul Robert, and Maria Elisa Villalpando
    1997   Introduction. In *Prehistory of the Borderlands*, ed. John Carpenter and Guadalupe Sanchez, xv–xvi. Arizona State Museum Archaeological Series 186. University of Arizona Press, Tucson.

Fish, Suzanne K., Paul R. Fish, and Elisa Villalpando (editors)
    In press   *Enduring Borderlands Traditions: Trincheras Sites in Time, Space, and Society*. University of Arizona Press, Tucson.

Ford, Richard I., Albert H. Schroeder, and Stewart L. Peckham
    1972   Three Perspectives on Puebloan Prehistory. In *New Perspectives on the Pueblos*, ed. Alfonso Ortiz, 19–39. University of New Mexico Press, Albuquerque.

Foster, Michael, and Shirley Gorenstein
2000 Greater Mesoamerica: The Archaeology of West and Northwest Mexico. University of Utah Press, Salt Lake City.

Geib, Phil R., and Kimberly Spurr
2002 The Forager to Farmer Transition on the Rainbow Plateau. In Traditions, Transitions, and Technologies: Themes in Southwestern Archaeology, ed. Sarah H. Schlanger, 224-244. University Press of Colorado, Boulder.

Haak, Wolfgang, Peter Forster, Barbara Bramanti, Shuichi Matsumura, Guido Brandt, Marc Tänzer, Richard Villems, Colin Renfrew, Detlef Gronenborn, Kurt Werner Alt, and Joachim Burger
2005 Ancient DNA from the First European Farmers in 7500-Year-Old Neolithic Sites. Science 310:1016-1018.

Hard, Robert J., José E. Zapata, and John R. Roney (editors)
2001 Una Investigación Arqueológica de los Sitios Cerros con Trincheras del Arcaico Tardío en Chihuahua, México. Informe al Consejo de Arqueología, Instituto Nacional de Antropología e Historia. Center for Archaeological Research, University of Texas at San Antonio, Special Report 27-S, San Antonio.

Haury, Emil W.
1945 The Problem of Contacts between the Southwestern United States and Mexico. Southwestern Journal of Anthropology 1(1):55-74.
1962 The Greater American Southwest. In Courses toward Urban Life: Archeological Considerations of Some Cultural Alternatives, ed. Robert J. Braidwood and Gordon R. Willey, 106-131. Viking Fund Publications in Anthropology 32, New York.

Hedrick, Basil C., J. Charles Kelley, and Carroll L. Riley (editors)
1974 The Mesoamerican Southwest: Readings in Archaeology, Ethnohistory, and Ethnology. Southern Illinois University Press, Carbondale.

Hegmon, Michelle
1992 Archaeological Research on Style. Annual Review of Anthropology 21:517-536.
1998 Technology, Style, and Social Practices: Archaeological Approaches. In The Archaeology of Social Boundaries, ed. Miriam T. Stark, 264-279. Smithsonian Institution Press, Washington, D.C.

Hill, Jane H.
2001 Proto-Uto-Aztecan: A Community of Cultivars in Central Mexico? American Anthropologist 103(4):913-934.

Hill, Jane, and Kelley A. Hays-Gilpin
1999 The Flower World in Material Culture: An Iconographic Complex in the Southwest and Mesoamerica. Journal of Anthropological Research 55:1-37.

Huckell, Bruce B.
1995 Of Marshes and Maize: Preceramic Agricultural Settlements in the Cienega Valley, Southeastern Arizona. Anthropological Papers of the University of Arizona 59. University of Arizona Press, Tucson.
1996 The Southwestern Archaic: Scale and Perception of Preceramic Hunter-Gatherers. In Interpreting Southwestern Diversity: Underlying Principles and Overarching Patterns, ed. Paul R. Fish and J. Jefferson Reid, 7-15. Anthropological Research Paper 48. Arizona State University, Tempe.

Irwin-Williams, Cynthia
    1979   Post-Pleistocene Archaeology, 7000-2000 B.C. In *Handbook of North American Indians, Volume 9, Southwest*, ed. Alfonso Ortiz, 31-42. Smithsonian Institution Press, Washington, D.C.

Jiménez Betts, Peter, and J. Andrew Darling
    2000   Archaeology of Southern Zacatecas: The Malpaso, Juchipila, and Valparaiso-Bolaños Valleys. In *Greater Mesoamerica: The Archeology of West and Northwest Mexico*, ed. Michael Foster and Shirley Gorenstein, 155-180. University of Utah Press, Salt Lake City.

Jones, Sîan
    1997   *The Archaeology of Ethnicity: Constructing Identities in the Past and Present*. Routledge, New York.

Kelley, J. Charles
    1966   Mesoamerica and the Southwestern United States. In *Archaeological Frontiers and External Connections: The Handbook of Middle American Indians*, Volume 4, ed. Gordon Ekholm and Gordon R. Willey, 95-110. University of Texas Press, Austin.

Kelley, Jane H., Joe D. Stewart, Art C. MacWilliams, and Karen R. Adams
    2004   Recent Research in West-Central Chihuahua. In *Identity, Feasting, and the Archaeology of the Greater Southwest*, ed. Barbara J. Mills, 295-310. University Press of Colorado, Boulder.

Kelley, Jane H., Joe D. Stewart, Art C. MacWilliams, and Loy C. Neff
    1999   A West-Central Chihuahuan Perspective on Chihuahua Culture. In *The Casas Grandes World*, ed. Joe D. Stewart and Carroll L. Riley, 63-77. University of Utah Press, Salt Lake City.

Kossinna, G.
    1902   Die Indogermanishe Frage Archäologish Beantwortet. *Zeitshrift fur Ethnologie* 34:161-222.

Kroeber, Alfred L.
    1928   Native Culture of the Southwest. *University of California Publications in American Archaeology and Ethnology* 23, 375-398. University of California Press, Berkeley.

Lakoff, George
    1993   The Contemporary Theory of Metaphor. In *Metaphor and Thought*, 2nd ed., ed. Andrew Ortony, 202-251. Cambridge University Press, Cambridge.

Lakoff, George, and Mark Johnson
    1980   *Metaphors We Live By*. University of Chicago Press, Chicago.

LeBlanc, Steven A.
    1982   The Advent of Pottery in the Southwest. In *Southwestern Ceramics: A Comparative Review*, ed. A. H. Schroeder, 27-52. Arizona Archaeologist 15. Arizona Archaeological Society, Phoenix.

Lemonnier, Pierre
    1986   The Study of Material Culture Today: Toward an Anthropology of Technical Systems. *Journal of Anthropological Archaeology* 5(2):147-186.

Lyons, Patrick D.
  2001 *Winslow Orange Ware and the Ancestral Hopi Migration Horizon*. Ph.D. dissertation, Department of Anthropology, University of Arizona, Tucson. ProQuest, Ann Arbor.
  2003 *Ancestral Hopi Migrations*. Anthropological Papers of the University of Arizona 68. University of Arizona Press, Tucson.

Mabry, Jonathan B.
  2002 The Role of Irrigation in the Transition to Agriculture and Sedentism in the Southwest: A Risk Management Model. In *Traditions, Transitions, and Technologies: Themes in Southwestern Archaeology*, ed. Sarah H. Schlanger, 178-199. University Press of Colorado, Boulder.

Manglesdorf, Paul C.
  1950 The Mystery of Corn. *Scientific American* 183:20-29.
  1958 Ancestor of Corn. *Science* 128:1313-1320.
  1974 *Corn*. Belknap, Cambridge, Mass.

Matson, R. G.
  1991 *The Origins of Southwestern Agriculture*. University of Arizona Press, Tucson.

McBrinn, Maxine E.
  2002 *Social Identity and Risk Sharing among the Mobile Hunters and Gatherers of the Archaic Southwest*. Ph.D. dissertation, Department of Anthropology, University of Colorado, Boulder. ProQuest, Ann Arbor.
  2005 *Social Identities among Archaic Mobile Hunters and Gatherers in the American Southwest*. Arizona State Museum Archaeological Series 197. University of Arizona Press, Tucson.

McGuire, Randall H.
  1997 Crossing the Border. In *Prehistory of the Borderlands*, ed. John Carpenter and Guadalupe Sanchez, 130-137. Arizona State Museum Archaeological Series 186. University of Arizona Press, Tucson.
  2002 The Meaning and Limits of the Southwest/Northwest: A Perspective from Northern Mexico. In *Boundaries and Territories: Prehistory of the U.S. Southwest and Northern Mexico*, ed. M. Elisa Villalpando, 173-183. Anthropological Research Papers 54. Arizona State University, Tempe.

McGuire, Randall H., and Maria Elisa Villalpando
  1993 *An Archaeological Survey of the Altar Valley, Sonora, Arizona*. Arizona State Museum Archaeological Series 184. University of Arizona Press, Tucson.

McGuire, Randall H., Maria Elisa Villalpando, Victoria Vargas, and Emiliano Gallaga M.
  1999 Cerro de Trincheras and the Casas Grandes World. In *The Casas Grandes World*, ed. Curtis Schaafsma and Carrol Riley, 134-148. University of Utah Press, Salt Lake City.

Mills, Barbara J.
  2004 Identity, Feasting, and the Archaeology of the Greater Southwest. In *Identity, Feasting, and the Archaeology of the Greater Southwest*, ed. Barbara J. Mills, 1-23. University Press of Colorado, Boulder.

Minnis, Paul E., and Michael E. Whalen
    2004   Forty Years after the Joint Casas Grandes Project: An Introduction to Chihuahuan Archaeology. In *Identity, Feasting, and the Archaeology of the Greater Southwest*, ed. Barbara J. Mills, 261-275. University Press of Colorado, Boulder.

Minnis, Paul E., Michael E. Whalen, Jane H. Kelley, and Joe D. Stewart
    1993   Prehistoric Macaw Breeding in the North American Southwest. *American Antiquity* 58(2):270-275.

Moerman, Michael
    1965   Ethnic Identification in a Complex Civilization: Who Are the Lue? *American Anthropologist* 67(5):1215-1230.

Newell, Gillian E.
    1999   American and Mexican Archaeology: Differences in Meaning and Teaching. *SAA Bulletin* 17(5):29-31.

Ortman, Scott G.
    2000   Conceptual Metaphor in the Archaeological Record: Methods and an Example from the American Southwest. *American Antiquity* 65(4):613-645.

Pailes, Richard A., and Daniel T. Reff
    1985   Colonial Exchange Systems and the Decline of Paquimé. In *The Archaeology of West and Northwest Mexico*, ed. Michael Foster and Philip Weigand, 353-363. Westview, Boulder.

Pohl, John M.D.
    2001   Chichimecatlalli: Strategies for Cultural and Commercial Exchange between Mexico and the American Southwest, 1100-1521. In *The Road to Aztlan: Art from a Mythic Homeland*, ed. Virginia M. Fields and Victor Zamudio-Taylor, 86-101. Los Angeles County Museum of Art, Los Angeles, and University of New Mexico Press, Albuquerque.

Price, T. Douglas, Anne Birgitte Gebauer, and Lawrence H. Keeley
    1995   The Spread of Farming into Europe North of the Alps. In *Last Hunters–First Farmers: New Perspectives on the Prehistoric Transition to Agriculture*, ed. T. Douglas Price and Anne Birgitte Gebauer, 95-126. School of American Research Press, Santa Fe.

Reed, Erik K.
    1964   The Greater Southwest. In *Prehistoric Man in the New World*, ed. Jesse D. Jennings and Edward Norbeck, 175-193. University of Chicago Press, Chicago.

Renfrew, Colin
    1987   *Archaeology and Language: The Puzzle of Indo-European Origins*. Cambridge University Press, New York.

Riley, Carroll
    2005   *Becoming Aztlan: Mesoamerican Influence in the Greater Southwest, A.D. 1200-1500*. University of Utah Press, Salt Lake City.

Roney, John R., and Robert J. Hard
    2002   Early Agriculture in Northwestern Chihuahua. In *Traditions, Transitions, and Technologies: Themes in Southwestern Archaeology*, ed. Sarah H. Schlanger, 160-177. University Press of Colorado, Boulder.

Sayles, E. B.
   1936   An Archaeological Survey of Chihuahua, Mexico. Medallion Paper 22. Gila Pueblo, Globe, Ariz.

Scarborough, Vernon L., and David R. Wilcox (editors)
   1991   The Mesoamerican Ballgame. University of Arizona Press, Tucson.

Sekaquaptewa, Emory, and Dorothy Washburn
   2004   They Go Along Singing: Reconstructing the Hopi Past from Ritual Metaphors in Song and Image. American Antiquity 69(3):457–486.
   2006   Metaphors of Meaning in Mural Paintings, Pottery and Ritual Song. Plateau 3(1): 26–47.

Spicer, Edward
   1963   Cycles of Conquest. University of Arizona Press, Tucson.

Stark, Mariam T.
   1998   The Archaeology of Social Boundaries. Smithsonian Institution Press, Washington, D.C.

Stone, Tammy
   2003   Social Identity and Ethnic Interaction in the Western Pueblos of the American Southwest. Journal of Archaeological Theory and Method 10(1):31–67.

Taube, Karl A.
   1986   The Teotihuacan Cave of Origin: The Iconography and Architecture of the Emergence in Mesoamerica and the American Southwest. RES: Anthropology and Aesthetics 29–30:31–82.

Taylor, Walter W.
   2003   Sandals from Coahuila Caves with an Introduction to the Coahuila Project, Coahuila, Mexico: 1937–1941, 1947, ed. Nicholas J. Demerath, Mary C. Kennedy, and Patty Jo Watson. Studies in Pre-Columbian Art and Archaeology 35. Dumbarton Oaks, Washington, D.C.

Teague, Lynn S.
   1998   Textiles in Southwestern Prehistory. University of New Mexico Press, Albuquerque.

VanPool, Todd L., Christine S. VanPool, Rafael Cruz Antillón, Robert D. Leonard, and Marcel J. Harson
   2000   Flaked Stone and Social Interaction in the Casas Grandes Region, Chihuahua, Mexico. Latin American Antiquity 11:163–174.

Vargas, Victoria D.
   2001   Mesoamerican Copper Bells in the Pre-Hispanic Southwestern United States and Northwestern Mexico. In The Road to Aztlan: Art from a Mythic Homeland, ed. Virginia M. Fields and Victor Zamudio-Taylor, 196–211. Los Angeles County Museum of Art, Los Angeles, and University of New Mexico Press, Albuquerque.

Vierra, Bradley J. (editor)
   2005   The Late Archaic across the Borderlands: From Foraging to Farming. University of Texas Press, Austin.

Villalpando, Maria Elisa
   2002   Boundaries and Territories: Prehistory of the U.S. Southwest and Northern Mexico. Anthropological Research Papers 54. Arizona State University, Tempe.

Washburn, Dorothy K., and Donald W. Crowe
    1988   *Symmetries of Culture: Theory and Practice of Plane Pattern Analysis.* University of Washington Press, Seattle.

Weigand, Phil C., and Acelia García de Weigand
    2001   A Macroeconomic Study of the Relationships between the Ancient Cultures of the American Southwest and Mesoamerica. In *The Road to Aztlan: Art from a Mythic Homeland*, ed. Virginia M. Fields and Victor Zamudio-Taylor, 184–195. Los Angeles County Museum of Art, Los Angeles, and University of New Mexico Press, Albuquerque.

Whalen, Michael E., and Paul E. Minnis
    2001   *Casas Grandes and Its Hinterland: Prehistoric Regional Organization in Northwest Mexico.* University of Arizona Press, Tucson.

Wills, W. H.
    1988   *Early Prehistoric Agriculture in the American Southwest.* School of American Research Press, Santa Fe.
    1995   Archaic Foraging and the Beginning of Food Production in the American Southwest. In *Last Hunters–First Farmers: New Perspectives on the Prehistoric Transition to Agriculture*, ed. T. Douglas Price and A. B. Gebauer, 215–242. School of American Research Press, Santa Fe.

Woosley, Anne I., and John C. Ravesloot (editors)
    1993   *Culture and Contact: Charles C. Di Peso's Gran Chichimeca.* Amerind Foundation, Dragoon, Ariz., and University of New Mexico Press, Albuquerque.

Part I

Early Agricultural Adaptations in the U.S. Southwest and Northwestern Mexico

2

THE TRANSITION TO AGRICULTURE IN THE DESERT BORDERLANDS

An Introduction

Gayle J. Fritz

This is an exciting and challenging time to be studying the transition to agriculture in the Desert Borderlands (northwestern Mexico and the southwestern United States). Such an explosion of new information has occurred in recent years that it is difficult to keep up-to-date, even with the World Wide Web and electronic mail. The opportunities to serve as discussant during the session on Early Agriculture at the 2004 Southwest Symposium in Chihuahua City and to adapt those comments for publication in this volume have been valuable learning experiences. As an archaeologist who knows more about transitions to agriculture in eastern North America than in Mexico or the U.S. Southwest, I bring something of an outsider's perspective to this region and only hope this has sufficient value to offset its drawbacks.

Archaeologists have barely had time to absorb all the recent discoveries that make it necessary to remodel the dynamics of early agriculture in the Desert Borderlands. Evidence includes solid documentation of 4,000-year-old maize (Diehl 2005; Huber and Miljour 2004; Huckell 2005), 3,000-year-old irrigation canals (Damp, Hall, and Smith 2002; Mabry 2006), and 3,000- to 3,500-year-old village-like habitation sites with ubiquitous remains of maize associated with structures and storage

Gayle J. Fritz

pits (Hard and Roney 1998, 2005; Mabry 2005; Roney and Hard 2002). Fewer than ten years ago, we doubted dates on maize older than 3,200 to 3,500 years B.P., and the majority view held that crops were integrated gradually into the subsistence systems of mobile hunter-gatherers who either needed additional resources to offset shortages caused by demographic or ecological stress or simply recognized the advantages of growing moderate amounts of maize to reduce the risks of foraging in a variable and unpredictable environment (Cordell 1997; Minnis 1992; Wills 1988, 1995). Even though the inhabitants of recently investigated early agricultural settlements such as Milagro (Huckell, Huckell, and Benedict 2002), Los Pozos (Gregory and Diehl 2002), and Cerro Juanaqueña (Hard and Roney 1998; Roney and Hard 2002) might not have been fully sedentary in the sense of living in fixed households for twelve months of the year, a new scenario of less gradual abandonment of residential mobility than previously envisioned is clearly necessary for parts of the Greater Southwest.

The chapters covering early agriculture exemplify several traditional strengths of southwestern archaeology: solid theoretical foundations, a clear focus on key issues, and careful analysis of data using innovative methods. A number of recurring themes run through the chapters. One is the problem of distinguishing migration of farming populations from adoption of crops by local hunter-gatherers. A second is recognizing optimal geographic or ecological conditions for early crop cultivation. Related to this is the task of assessing factors that would lead occupants of the larger region or of particular subregions to add maize to their diet or move to new places to plant crops. Finally, the authors are keenly aware of distinct geographic and cultural variations within northwestern Mexico and the southwestern United States that enable discussion of multiple transitions from foraging to farming rather than relying on a single explanation for the spread of agriculture.

A recurring lament by northern Mexican and U.S. scholars of early agriculture in this region has been the spottiness of fieldwork targeting Late Archaic sites in northwestern Mexico. Although gaps are still large, recent projects including the work described by MacWilliams and colleagues in Chapter 3 are rapidly contributing essential information. This chapter combines old and new information from southern Chihuahua, a region likely to have been crossed by maize and other domesticated plants when early agriculture spread from more southerly parts of Mexico. Environmental and historical overview sections are thorough and very useful, but the most interesting section is the presentation of results from recent archaeological survey and test excavations at a series of sites in both the Sierra Tarahumara and the Basin and Range Province to the east. These researchers tested three rockshelter sites with artificial terraces built up behind D-shaped stone walls, all near arable fluvial terraces, finding abundant occupation debris dating to the Middle and Late Archaic periods along with more recent material. Maize from these sites was directly dated to the mid-first millennium A.D. rather than the Archaic period, but clearly the potential exists for investigating the initial transition from foraging to farming. Work at terraced hill sites (*cerros de trincheras*) in southeastern Chihuahua yielded limited evidence for early farming, including direct radiocarbon maize dates of 3410 ± 40 B.P. and 1950 ± 50 B.P. Most of the occupation at these southern Chihuahuan *cerros de trincheras*, however, seems to belong to the Ceramic period.

Both D-shaped terrace sites and *cerros de trincheras* indicate labor investment at particular locations, which is taken to represent logistic settlement strategies on the part of hunter-gatherers who were in the right places at the right time and seem to have been "fortuitously organized to receive maize agriculture." More work will be needed (and is currently being carried out by this team, with National Science Foundation funding) to uncover subsistence remains and artifacts that can take us beyond this point. MacWilliams and colleagues describe the diversity of environmental zones in this far-from-barren region and correctly point out that even before 4000 B.P., maize probably "had wide tolerances, allowing radiation across an array of environmental settings." Although this chapter reports initial phases of fieldwork, there is clearly much to be learned from the spottily studied mountains, valleys, and basins of northwestern Mexico.

One of several issues addressed in Chapter 4, by Jonathan Mabry and William Doolittle, is whether the first farmers in the Desert Borderlands were agricultural colonists or indigenous hunter-gatherers who adopted crop production. This discussion is a good precursor to later chapters, including Chapter 7 by LeBlanc and Chapter 9, in the section on Converging Identities, by Mabry, Carpenter, and Sanchez. Although LeBlanc describes Mabry (2005) as seeming "to have a rather equivocal position on the migration model," I can appreciate the balanced approach and consideration of alternatives. In Mabry and Doolittle's view, "migration versus diffusion is a false contrast" because both processes probably came into play on the early agricultural frontier. They propose a plausible scenario for the introduction of maize into the Desert Borderlands beginning between 5000 and 4000 B.P., with Uto-Aztecan speakers moving in from both the north and the south prior to the introduction of maize. These groups might well, according to the authors, have manipulated and managed locally occurring "weedy" plants such as chenopods, amaranths, and large-seeded grasses to the point of cultivation and relied on the "indigenous development of plant husbandry" to supplement harvested and hunted foods. Maize is seen as making its way northward beginning about 4000 B.P. and being adopted by the hunter-gatherer-cultivators (termed "forager-farmers"), who then expanded into "new agricultural niches." Subsequently (3,000–2,500 B.P.), crops including pepo squash, bottle gourd, and kidney beans were passed up from the south and incorporated into existing mixed subsistence systems, possibly along with an immigration of Mexican farmers. This resulted in "localized increases in agricultural dependence" within a wide sphere of interacting social groups.

The possibility of pre-maize husbandry of indigenous plants in the Desert Borderlands has been discussed for decades, in part because of the significance it might have for tethering foragers to suitable patches of plant resources and for establishing sets of tools and behaviors into which non-native domesticates could be incorporated. Increasing reliance on harvested plant foods can be seen throughout

Gayle J. Fritz

the Archaic, as can the manufacture of seed-processing tools amenable for grinding hard kernels of maize along with other grasses. Intensified interactions between wild plants and people might be expected to carry both people and plants along the continuum to domestication. Still, we need actual archaeobotanical evidence for husbandry that goes beyond basic harvesting before much weight can be placed on pre-maize horticulture in the Greater Southwest. In eastern North America, where the Eastern Agricultural Crop Complex includes sunflower (*Helianthus annuus* var. *macrocarpus*), sumpweed (*Iva annua* var. *annua*), the eastern squash (*Cucurbita pepo* ssp. *ovifera* var. *ovifera*), a thin-coated chenopod *(Chenopodium berlandieri* ssp. *jonesianum),* maygrass *(Phalaris caroliniana),* and other suspected crops, signs of domestication include seed size increase (for sunflower, sumpweed, and ovifera squash), reduction of seed coat thickness (chenopod), and presence of stored seeds outside the natural range of the species (maygrass) (Smith 2006; Smith and Cowan 2003). Gary Nabhan and colleagues (Nabhan and de Wet 1984; Nabhan et al. 1981) have demonstrated that both Sonoran panic grass (*Panicum sonorum*) and Devil's Claw (*Proboscidea parviflora*) were domesticated in the Sonoran Desert region, and Suzanne Fish (2000) has documented extensive cultivation of agaves in the Hohokam region of southern Arizona. Vorsila Bohrer (1991) makes a strong case for cultivation of several other indigenous southwestern plants. None of the solid evidence, however, predates the introduction of maize, and discussion of pre-maize plant husbandry in this region remains highly speculative.

Perhaps the most significant contribution of Mabry and Doolittle's chapter is how distinctly it highlights the advantages of water-table and flood farming for early farmers in the Desert Borderlands, redirecting archaeologists' attention away from such distinctions as upland versus lowland agriculture to widely distributed micro-niche settings in both uplands and lowlands where productivity and energy efficiency could be high and both risk and labor requirements would be low. The potential value of concentrating attention on sites near springs, other places where water tables are naturally high (or were, before modern environmental degradation), or where mesa-top runoff, overbank flooding, and other variants of "ak chin" farming could be practiced is not lost on other authors in this volume, including MacWilliams and colleagues and Vierra.

Bradley Vierra's chapter (Chapter 5) is an insightful synthesis of relevant data from Late Archaic sites in the northern Rio Grande Valley and the western and northern reaches of the San Juan Basin, beginning at 1260 B.C., with newly reported Accelerator Mass Spectrometry (AMS) dates on maize from Jemez Cave, up until the middle of the first millennium A.D. The database includes archaeobotanical evidence (399 samples) and other information from 53 habitation sites where 101 structures were excavated. Archaeobotanical comparisons are based primarily on ubiquities (percentage of samples in which an item occurs) of maize, chenoams, *Cucurbita* rind or seeds, Indian ricegrass seeds, and dropseed grass seeds. The information comes mostly from chapters in the gray literature of cultural resource management reports that are sometimes difficult to obtain. Several key plant types including squash rind were reexamined to check for potential wild versus domesticated status.

Vierra sees no evidence for initial migration of early farmers but rather a geographically uneven addition of crops into existing foraging economies, followed by long stretches when the archaeobotanical indices show relatively low-level use of maize until after A.D. 500. This is supported by groundstone tool types and by architectural and storage pit features. Late Archaic food producers across the southeastern Colorado Plateau periphery region were attracted to well-watered spots where crops could be grown in proximity to stands of piñon and juniper or places where fall plant resources were especially abundant. This chapter is an extremely valuable synthesis, but archaeologists would benefit from additional details including volumes of soil processed by flotation (which Vierra notes were not always available), total seed counts, frequencies, and ratios such as maize-to-wood charcoal counts and weights. Ubiquity is a useful measure, but because a taxon is increasingly likely to be represented as sample size (soil volume) increases, comparison of unequal volumes is problematic, and analysts need to take that into account.

Amber Johnson's contribution (Chapter 6) is an ambitious, global-level comparison of the durations of three general types of adaptation (intensified hunting-gathering, the transition to agriculture, and intensified agriculture) set in an environmental frame of reference. After explaining key elements of the model, Johnson looks more closely at regions within the modern boundaries of Mexico. Of particular interest to southwestern scholars is the focus on how long the periods of intensified hunting-gathering and transition to agriculture lasted there, as well as in other regions characterized by comparable climatic and biotic regimes. The general goal is to develop an analytical strategy capable of elevating debates about indigenous adoption of crops versus site unit intrusion of farmers above the current level by establishing "unambiguous criteria for recognizing the impact of migration versus indigenous adoption of new economic strategies." A shorter-than-expected duration of agricultural transition in northwestern Mexico might, for example, potentially point to an in-migration of farmers.

This is an excellent goal, and Johnson's chapter, although in her words a "first step" or a "provocative first pass," provides much stimulation for further refinement and discussion. I would like to see a fuller, more detailed application to Chihuahua, Sonora, Arizona, and New Mexico in light of recent archaeological discoveries. In note 4 we learn that the northern Mexican projections do not include "unearned water, that is, water that fell as precipitation somewhere else, which may be flowing through an area in a river." Future incorporation of this factor, which Johnson states is forthcoming, would be especially important given current attention to early agricultural sites located in places where high water tables and floodwaters, including water from through-flowing rivers, existed.

As an eastern North Americanist, I question the assumption resulting in the long "observed" duration (5,500 years) assigned to intensified hunting-gathering in the Illinois Valley and the correspondingly short (400 years) "observed" duration allowed for the transition to agriculture in that region. Johnson does not use chronological dates in her tables or text, but if we agree that the transition to agriculture in Illinois ended at 1000 B.P. with the intensification of maize, that would mean the cutoff between intensified hunting-gathering and transitional agriculture would fall at 1400 B.P. This ignores decades of paleoethnobotanical research documenting the presence of indigenous cultigens in west-central Illinois as far back as 4500 B.P. and the economic significance of a developed pre-maize Eastern Agricultural Crop Complex in the Illinois River Valley beginning no later than 2200 B.P. (Asch and Asch 1985; Smith and Cowan 2003). Recent research in northern Japan shows a similar inclusion of domesticated plants into a mixed fishing-hunting-gathering economy far earlier than previously known (Crawford 1997). In many parts of the world it may well be true, as Johnson hypothesizes, that a heightened focus on aquatic resources resulted in prolonged intensified hunting-gathering and shortened agricultural transitions. In Illinois, however, and evidently also in parts of Japan, both aquatic *and* terrestrial resources were intensified, allowing low-level food-producing systems with varying amounts of cultivated and domesticated plants to persist for centuries or even millennia (Smith 2001). This underscores the crucial process of evaluating and interpreting data prior to their incorporation into models such as Johnson's, but it does not lessen the potential value of her conceptual approach.

Steven LeBlanc's presentation (Chapter 7) of the case for a northward Uto-Aztecan farmer migration complements nicely, without too much redundancy of data, the earlier and later chapters coauthored by Mabry in this volume. Considerable attention has recently been focused on farmer migration models as a result of a global-scale treatment by Peter Bellwood (2005) and collaborations between Bellwood and Jared Diamond (Diamond and Bellwood 2003) and Bellwood and Colin Renfrew (2003). Bellwood (2005:174) takes the position that in the Southwest, "agricultural introduction occurred with population movement from Mexico, an assumption supported by new interpretations of the Uto-Aztecan language family." This view contrasts sharply with responses I received from prominent U.S.-based Southwest archaeologists when I asked for their opinions on the subject. Some rejected outright any plausibility of demic diffusion, whereas others were trying to be open-minded but struggled with a lack of hard evidence for site-unit intrusions. LeBlanc confronts the debate head-on, contributing a lucid, in-depth discussion that clarifies a number of key issues for readers who (like me) have been taken aback by strong, conflicting statements by advocates on both sides. He concludes that the linguistic, genetic, and material culture evidence "provide[s] a fairly good case for a Uto-Aztecan–speaking farmer spread resulting in the wide distribution of a language family." Still, he points out that we are hindered by the fact that the northward spread of maize predated pottery and that "there is really no evidence one way or the other to show whether sites in northern Chihuahua and Sonora or northern Arizona relate to those farther south in any meaningful way." Along with Mabry, Carpenter, and Sanchez (Chapter 9), LeBlanc discusses the likelihood that indigenous foragers in parts of the U.S. Southwest began planting maize and other crops centuries after the movement of Uto-Aztecan "immigrants" into southern Arizona and, from there, into that part of the Colorado Plateau known as Western Basketmaker territory.

The situation clearly calls for continuing efforts to integrate material culture with environmental parameters (as addressed by the authors of Chapters 3-6); close scrutiny of archaeobotanical, lithic, and other archaeological correlates of food production (as accomplished especially admirably by Vierra); more work in poorly studied and geographically key areas (as MacWilliams and colleagues are doing); and comprehensive understanding of how subregions fit into broader schemes of agricultural transitions in the Desert Borderlands and surrounding areas.

The theoretical sophistication and knowledge represented in these chapters reflect decades of extremely hard work in the field, laboratory, and library. My appreciation is particularly directed to these and other archaeologists and paleoethnobotanists who have taken pains to make flotation and archaeobotanical analysis integral components of their research designs in spite of the added costs incurred. I thank all the authors, the conference organizers, and the volume editors for allowing me to participate in this stage of the process of furthering knowledge about early agriculture in northwestern Mexico and the southwestern United States.

REFERENCES CITED

Asch, David L., and Nancy B. Asch
    1985   Prehistoric Plant Cultivation in West-Central Illinois. In *Prehistoric Food Production in North America*, ed. Richard I. Ford, 149-203. Anthropological Papers 75. Museum of Anthropology, University of Michigan, Ann Arbor.

Bellwood, Peter
    2005   *First Farmers: The Origins of Agricultural Societies*. Blackwood, Malden, Mass.

Bellwood, Peter, and Colin Renfrew (editors)
    2003   *Examining the Farming/Language Dispersal Hypothesis*. McDonald Institute for Archaeological Research, Cambridge, England.

Bohrer, Vorsila L.
    1991   Recently Recognized Cultivated and Encouraged Plants among the Hohokam. *Kiva* 56:227-236.

Cordell, Linda
    1997   *Archaeology of the Southwest*, 2nd ed. Academic, San Diego.

Crawford, Gary W.
    1997   Anthropogenesis in Prehistoric Northeastern Japan. In *People, Plants, and Landscapes: Studies in Paleoethnobotany*, ed. Kristen J. Gremillion, 86-103. University of Alabama Press, Tuscaloosa.

Damp, Jonathan E., Stephen A. Hall, and Susan J. Smith
    2002   Early Irrigation on the Colorado Plateau near Zuni Pueblo, New Mexico. *American Antiquity* 67:665-676.

Diamond, Jared M., and Peter Bellwood
  2003   Farmers and Their Languages: The First Expansions. *Science* 300:597–603.
Diehl, Michael W.
  2005   Morphological Observations on Recently Recovered Early Agricultural Period Maize Cob Fragments from Southern Arizona. *American Antiquity* 70:361–375.
Fish, Suzanne K.
  2000   Hohokam Impacts on Sonoran Desert Environment. In *Imperfect Balance: Landscape Transformations in the Precolumbian Americas*, ed. David L. Lentz, 251–280. Columbia University Press, New York.
Gregory, David A., and Michael W. Diehl
  2002   Duration, Continuity, and Intensity of Occupation. In *Traditions, Transitions, and Technologies: Themes in Southwestern Archaeology*, ed. Sarah H. Schlanger, 200–244. University Press of Colorado, Boulder.
Hard, Robert J., and John R. Roney
  1998   A Massive Terraced Village Complex in Chihuahua, Mexico, 3000 Years Before Present. *Science* 279:1661–1664.
  2005   The Transition to Farming on the Rio Casas Grandes and in the Southern Jornada Mogollon Region. In *The Late Archaic across the Borderlands*, ed. B. J. Vierra, 141–186. University of Texas Press, Austin.
Huber, E. K., and H. J. Miljour
  2004   Early Maize on the Colorado Plateau: New Dates from West-Central New Mexico. Paper presented at the Ninth Southwest Symposium, Chihuahua City, Chihuahua, Mexico.
Huckell, Bruce B., Lisa W. Huckell, and Karl K. Benedict
  2002   Maize Agriculture and the Rise of Mixed Farming-Foraging Economies. In *Traditions, Transitions, and Technologies: Themes in Southwestern Archaeology*, ed. Sarah H. Schlanger, 137–159. University Press of Colorado, Boulder.
Huckell, Lisa W.
  2005   Early Maize from LA 137258, Catron County, New Mexico. In *Fence Lake Project: Archaeological Data Recovery in the New Mexico Transportation Corridor and First Five-Year Permit Area, Fence Lake Coal Mine Project, Catron County, New Mexico, Volume 3*, ed. E. K. Huber and C. R. Van West, 30.1–30.18. Technical Series 84. Statistical Research, Inc., Tucson.
Mabry, Jonathan B.
  2005   Changing Knowledge and Ideas about the First Farmers in Southeastern Arizona. In *The Late Archaic across the Borderlands*, ed. B. J. Vierra, 41–83. University of Texas Press, Austin.
Mabry, Jonathan B. (editor)
  2006   *Las Capas: Early Agriculture and Sedentism in a Southwestern Floodplain*. Anthropological Papers 28. Center for Desert Archaeology, Tucson (draft).
Minnis, Paul E.
  1992   Early Plant Cultivation in the Desert Borderlands of the American West. In *The Origins of Agriculture: An International Perspective*, ed. C. W. Cowan and P. J. Watson, 121–141. Smithsonian Institution Press, Washington, D.C.

Nabhan, Gary P., and Jan J. de Wet
    1984   *Panicum sonorum* in Sonoran Desert Agriculture. *Economic Botany* 38:65–82.

Nabhan, Gary P., Alfred Whiting, Henry Dobyns, Richard Hevly, and Robert Euler
    1981   Devil's Claw Domestication: Evidence from Southwestern Indian Fields. *Journal of Ethnobiology* 1(1):135–164.

Roney, John R., and Robert J. Hard
    2002   Early Agriculture in Northwestern Chihuahua. In *Traditions, Transitions, and Technologies: Themes in Southwestern Archaeology*, ed. Sarah H. Schlanger, 163–180. University Press of Colorado, Boulder.

Smith, Bruce D.
    2001   Low Level Food Production. *Journal of Archaeological Research* 9:1–43.
    2006   Eastern North America as an Independent Center of Plant Domestication. *Proceedings of the National Academy of Sciences* 103(33):12223–12228.

Smith, Bruce D., and C. Wesley Cowan
    2003   Domesticated Crop Plants and the Evolution of Food Production Economies in Eastern North America. In *People and Plants in Ancient Eastern North America*, ed. Paul E. Minnis, 105–125. Smithsonian Institution Press, Washington, D.C.

Wills, W. H.
    1988   *Early Prehistoric Agriculture in the American Southwest*. School of American Research Press, Santa Fe.
    1995   Archaic Foraging and the Beginning of Food Production in the American Southwest. In *Last Hunters, First Farmers*, ed. D. Price and A. B. Gebauer, 215–242. School of American Research Press, Santa Fe.

3

THE SETTING OF EARLY AGRICULTURE IN SOUTHERN CHIHUAHUA

A. C. MacWilliams, Robert J. Hard, John R. Roney,
Karen R. Adams, and William L. Merrill

The history and details of how agriculture spread and became entrenched over vast areas are difficult to elucidate. In this chapter, physiographic, environmental, and recently acquired archaeological information from southern Chihuahua is used to contextualize the arrival of maize agriculture in the region sometime between ca. 4000 and 1500 B.C. The purpose of doing so is to better understand settlement patterns and other aspects of adaptation in the region during the interval when agriculture arrived and to build a foundation for further research.

Southern Chihuahua presents unique opportunities for investigating early agriculture because its intermediate geographic location may provide data relevant to the spread of agriculture from central Mexico into northwestern Mexico and the southwestern United States. Much of the landscape remains intact, including many locations that are reasonable prospects for evidence of early agriculture. The varied landscape provides many settings that can be sampled to understand where early agriculture may have been adopted. Although some problems exist, the general visibility of preceramic sites is good.

In the southwestern United States, the Early Agricultural period is defined as the preceramic interval during which agriculture was introduced and widely accepted.

A. C. MacWilliams, Robert J. Hard, John R. Roney, Karen R. Adams, and William L. Merrill

This interval is proving to be complex, varied, and dynamic. In reviving this term from dormancy, Bruce Huckell (1995:16) is explicit about the Early Agricultural period defining preceramic agriculturalists. He suggests that the Early Agricultural period began around 1500-1200 B.C. and lasted until A.D. 200, equivalent to the dates of the Late Archaic period. Rapidly accumulating data from the Tucson Basin suggest modifications to this scheme may be needed. Currently, the widespread use of ceramics is initially placed at A.D. 150 (Gregory 2001:253; Gregory and Diehl 2002:204; Mabry 1998:18), although their appearance occurred several centuries earlier (Heidke 1999). Pottery and figurine fragments appear to be associated with two 2000 B.C. direct dates on maize from the Tucson Basin (Jonathan Mabry, personal communication, 2003). Edgar Huber (2005) demonstrates that maize arrived on the Colorado Plateau by 2100 B.C., during the late Middle Archaic period. The dynamic qualities of research on this period make establishment of strict definitions difficult. Extrapolating the term and concept of the Early Agricultural period to southern Chihuahua will likely show that this term refers to a time-transgressive process as Early Agricultural sites are discovered. If agriculture is not demonstrated to be present, Huckell (1995) recommends retaining the term "Late Archaic period." For these reasons, in discussing southern Chihuahua archaeology, we will continue to refer to the Middle and Late Archaic periods as purely chronological units and use the Early Agricultural period to refer to the general period during which farming was adopted in northwestern Mexico and the southwestern United States.

The earliest directly dated maize, which comes from Oaxaca, dates to 4300 cal B.C., but molecular evidence suggests maize was first domesticated along the Río Balsas of Michoacán and Guerrero somewhat earlier (Piperno and Flannery 2001:2102). More controversial pollen, phytolith, and starch grain evidence from the tropical lowlands on the Gulf Coast of Tabasco, the Panamanian tropical forest, and northern South America suggests an even earlier initial date for maize, ca. 5500-3000 B.C. (e.g., Piperno and Flannery 2001:2103; Pope et al. 2001:1373). The earliest cluster of redundant maize dates in the intensively studied southwestern United States, where agriculture ultimately underpinned mid-level societies, is 2100 B.C. (Huber 2005). This leaves a broad window of 2,000 years (ca. 4000-2000 B.C.) during which maize agriculture can reasonably be expected to have arrived in and passed through southern Chihuahua and minimally another 2,000 years (ca. 2000 B.C.-A.D. 1) comparable to the Early Agricultural period of the southwestern United States.

The general idea of an Early Agricultural period includes two important conditions: the introduction of agriculture into southern Chihuahua and the entrenchment of agriculture. The introduction of agriculture, by whatever means, is defined as the time when people first had access to domesticated seeds, such as maize, and some information regarding how to produce a harvest. During this introductory period, referred to as "incipient agriculture" by Bruce Smith (1997), agriculture was maintained at a modest level. At this level, in the southwestern United States and presumably in northwestern Mexico, no agriculture-driven major changes occurred in settlement or population, and farming efforts contributed a relatively minor portion of the diet (e.g., Minnis 1992). Incipient agriculture may, however, have been important in reducing risks or enhancing access to nondomesticated resources (Wills 1988). Entrenched agriculture is the condition at which settlement, seasonal movement, social organization, and material culture changed to accommodate agriculture to the extent that they were ill suited to hunter-gatherer adaptations.

In southern Chihuahua, we should expect to find two general classes of early agricultural sites: those that reflect the introduction of agriculture and are not immediately distinguishable from pre-agricultural sites and those that exhibit evidence of entrenched agriculture. Among some groups in southern Chihuahua, rapid agricultural entrenchment should be most apparent through increased proximity to optimal farmland such as fluvial terraces, more substantial habitation sites, and more task camps as people become seasonally tethered to their farmlands. Particularly in marginal settings but near optimal farmland as well, agricultural sites of any age may reflect the incipient or introductory strategy. The underlying conditions that bring about either strategy are likely far more complex than simply potential farming productivity (e.g., Binford 2001; Hard and Roney 2005).

SOUTHERN CHIHUAHUA

Southern Chihuahua divides into three general zones based on physiography, modern environment, and vegetation (Figures 3.1 and 3.2). From east to west, these are the low Basin and Range country, the higher Basin and Range country, and the Sierra Madre Occidental. The Chihuahuan Desert of southeastern Chihuahua ranges from 1,400–1,700 m in elevation, excluding mountain ranges. Mean annual precipitation in Chihuahua, which primarily comes from summer monsoons, increases toward the south and west. Southeastern Chihuahua receives only about 300–350 mm modern mean annual precipitation, and mean June high temperatures normally exceed 26°C. The only perennial water other than isolated springs is in saline lakes such as Laguna de Palomas. Vegetation is desert scrub often dominated by mesquite. Even today, this part of Chihuahua is sparsely inhabited. Artifact scatters of many ages are widespread (González Arratia 1992; Marrs 1949), and small roasting pits are abundant in some areas, but no known evidence indicates that residents ever departed from hunter-gatherer subsistence in this region.

The higher-elevation Basin and Range Province of central southern Chihuahua, located roughly between the Pan American Highway or nearby Río Florida and the Río Balleza, is considerably more hospitable. Valley elevations are 1,600–1,800 m, whereas mountain peaks often reach 2,000 m. The valleys of perennial rivers such as the Río San Pedro, Río Conchos, and many tributaries contain wide floodplains and well-defined fluvial terraces. Modern mean annual precipitation is in the range of 400–450 mm per year, and average temperatures are several degrees lower than in southeastern Chihuahua. The area is mapped as Plains and Semidesert

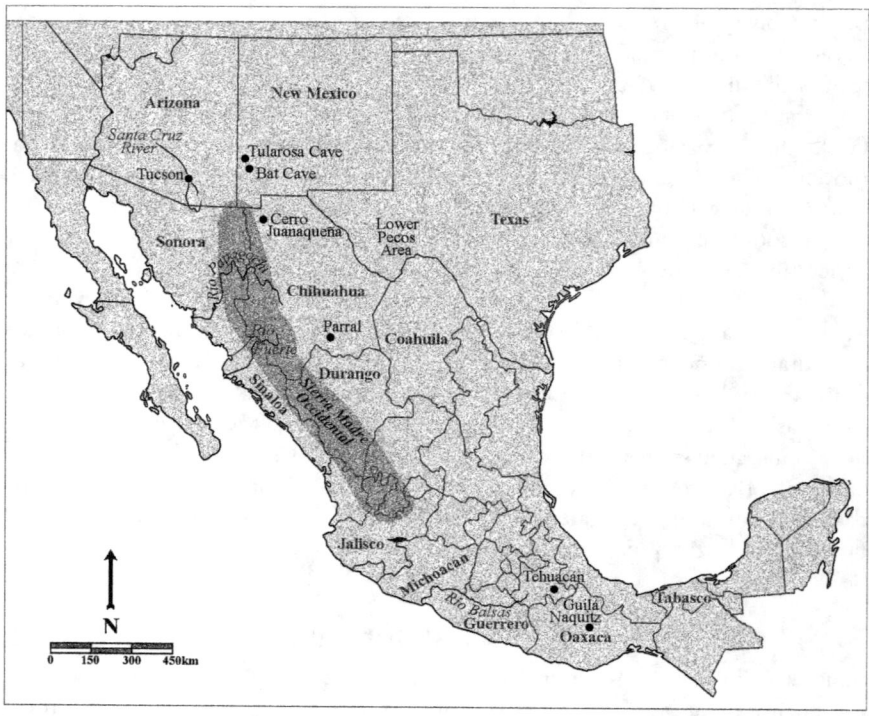

Figure 3.1. Map of Mexico and the southwestern United States.

Grassland (Brown and Lowe 1980) and is now a mix of Chihuahuan desert scrub and grasslands. Dry farming is practiced in better locations, and irrigation farming is widespread.

The Sierra Madre Occidental of southern Chihuahua (referred to hereafter as the Sierra Tarahumara) is somewhat higher in elevation, and the topography and climate are appreciably different from the higher Basin and Range Province. Elevations range from 1,800–2,800 m, and mean annual rainfall is 600–850 mm. The landscape is predominantly rhyolite plateau dissected by deep canyons (*barrancas*). Mesas are also common landforms. There are perennial rivers, such as the Río Urique, and many perennial tributary streams. The Sierra Tarahumara is largely mapped as Madrean Evergreen Woodland and Petran Montane Conifer Forest biotic communities (Brown and Lowe 1980) and is prevalently pine and oak forest. In the *barrancas*, semi-tropical vegetation offers many alternative resources to the forest and woodlands. Arable plots are generally located on narrow river floodplains, such as the Río Urique, and more frequently on medium-size and small side drainages. The Tarahumara use dry farming techniques with animal and chemical fertilizers to farm small upland valley bottoms. There are a few small seep fields that also require

The Setting of Early Agriculture in Southern Chihuahua

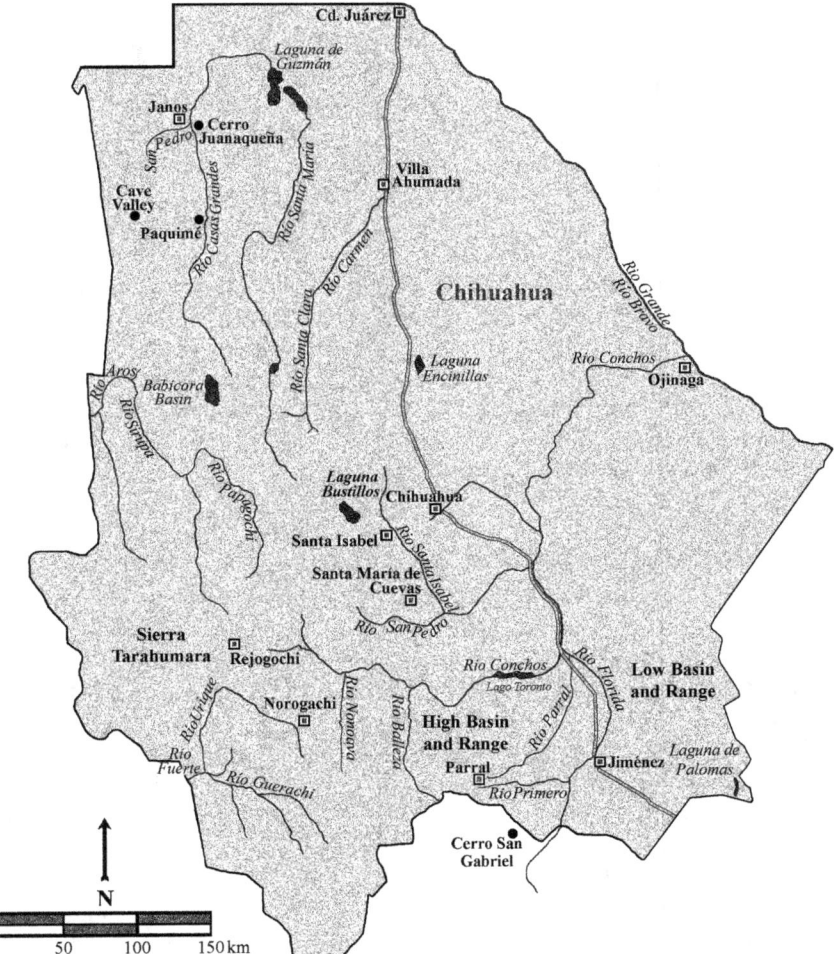

Figure 3.2. Map of Chihuahua.

fertilizing, limited slash-and-burn bean farming, and some plowing on steep slopes (Bennett and Zingg 1935; Hard and Merrill 1992).

Which physiographic and climatic parameters are judged to be ideal for early agriculture depends on what is believed about the earliest strains of maize and the diverse habitats containing them. Guilá Naquitz, in Oaxaca, is about 1,900 m in elevation and has modern average precipitation of 600 mm annually. In contrast, the Río Balsas watershed, at 1,000–1,500 m elevation, is far warmer and wetter, receiving 1,200–1,600 mm of annual precipitation (Piperno and Flannery 2001:2101). By circa 5,500 years ago, maize was present in the Tehuacán Valley, with a climate more similar to that of Oaxaca (Long et al. 1989:1037). In other words, maize was viable in disparate settings at least 1,500–2,000 years before its first known appearance in the southwestern United States or northwestern Mexico. Restricted corridors for the spread of agriculture was once a popular view (Haury 1962; Lister 1958), but it now seems more plausible that early maize had wide tolerances, allowing radiation across an array of environmental settings, much as Bruce Benz (1999:29) suggests.

That being the case, many settings in southern Chihuahua are reasonable for the successful practice of subsistence agriculture. However, the Chihuahuan Desert of southeastern Chihuahua remains an improbable setting for subsistence agriculture under any semblance of present conditions. In the central portion of southern Chihuahua, archaeology takes on a much different feel. It is becoming clear that there are widespread sites of many forms and ages that include more than hunter-gatherer bands. Farther west in the Sierra Tarahumara, where subsistence agriculture remains the backbone of survival, there is also a previously unrecognized diversity of archaeological remains.

PREVIOUS RESEARCH ON EARLY AGRICULTURE IN CHIHUAHUA

Traditionally, the topic of early agriculture in Chihuahua has been approached in terms of what it means for the southwestern United States. As Paul Mangelsdorf (1958:98) framed the issue, referring to excavated maize from Cave Valley in northwestern Chihuahua, "This, in itself, is not proof that the maize of the American Southwest originated in northwestern Mexico, but there is a strong presumption that this is the case." Encouragement for the once-popular view that the Sierra Madre Occidental of Chihuahua was a conduit for maize agriculture has come from two principal sources within Chihuahua. The first is work by Robert Zingg (1940), who excavated three caves (in two sites) in the Sierra Tarahumara of southern Chihuahua during 1931 (Figure 3.2). At Zingg's "Cave A," located 2 km northeast of Norogachi, the lowest excavation levels contained lithics without ceramics. He did not report maize from these lower levels. This did not deter Zingg (1939:212) from concluding that a local sequence began with "Rio Fuerte Basketmaker" cave inhabitants who farmed maize but lacked beans and pottery.

Robert Lister (1958) excavated in Swallow Cave and four other Cave Valley sites at an elevation of about 2,000 m in the Sierra Madre Occidental of northwestern Chihuahua. In the lower strata of Swallow Cave, Lister found only a few lithics and three maize cobs in strata about 1 m below the ceramic-bearing levels. In the absence of radiocarbon dates, the age of these lower deposits remains uncertain. Charles Di Peso and colleagues (1974) estimated the age of the lower levels at Swallow Cave dug by Lister to be about 2500 B.C. Lister's work provides qualified evidence that maize agriculture extended into the Sierra Madre Occidental fairly early, fostering the idea that the Sierra Madre Occidental was a corridor through which agriculture spread north. This view is complemented by the upland settings of Bat Cave and Tularosa Cave, among the first early agricultural sites discovered in the southwestern United States (Haury 1962).

In the vastness of Chihuahua's Basin and Range country east of the Sierra, archaeologists have typically focused on much later Ceramic-period sites to the exclusion of practically all else. Information about early agriculture did not reemerge until the 1990s with work at Cerro Juanaqueña and related sites near Janos (Hard and Roney 1998, 2004; Roney and Hard 2004). These thirteen *cerros de trincheras* (hills with constructed terraces) are located mostly in the Río Casas Grandes watershed, with a few in the Río Santa María Valley of Chihuahua. These optimal settings for agriculture have perennial rivers and broad floodplains with elevations of about 1,400–1,600 m. The hill sites are located along the river floodplains in a region mapped as Semidesert Grassland (Brown and Lowe 1980), now suffering from overgrazing and historic shrub invasion. Over four field seasons, four of these sites were partially excavated, with most work directed at Cerro Juanaqueña. This 150-m-high hill is by far the largest of the northwest Chihuahua *cerros de trincheras*, containing about 550 terraces constructed of stone and sediment. Over 300 projectile points from this site are almost entirely Late Archaic forms. Close to 650 complete and broken, deeply worn basin metates were recorded at Cerro Juanaqueña. In a region renowned for its pottery, there are only a few sherds from the surface of this preceramic site, a pattern that also holds for the other *cerros de trincheras*.

Radiocarbon dates from the four *trincheras* sites suggest two episodes of occupation: the first, and by far the largest, at about 1250 B.C., and the second around 200 B.C. These are sizable sites that must have accommodated dozens or, in the case of Cerro Juanaqueña, a couple of hundred people (Roney and Hard 2002). The presence of substantial quantities of maize and probable domesticated amaranth and the largely sedentary nature of a settlement of this scale leave no doubt about a major role for entrenched agriculture during these early times (Hard and Roney 1998, 2004; Hard et al. 1999; Roney and Hard 2002). Construction of these *cerros de trincheras* by agriculturalists is linked to increased conflict among groups by 3,200 years ago (Roney and Hard 2002). Dependence on entrenched maize agriculture likely required protecting harvests and land. Results from Cerro Juanaqueña contradict the long-standing view that maize was invariably only a minor component of what were essentially forager economies throughout the region until the end of the Early Agricultural period. To what extent it is coincidental or consequential that this same area is the central setting of a major mid-level society (Casas Grandes or Paquimé) more than two millennia later remains open to discussion.

CURRENT RESEARCH IN SOUTHERN CHIHUAHUA

Since 2002, we have been recording and testing sites in the Basin and Range Province and the Sierra Tarahumara of southern Chihuahua for the purpose of identifying Early Agricultural sites and, more broadly, acquiring information that contextualizes early agriculture in southern Chihuahua. In regard to the latter purpose, we

A. C. MacWilliams, Robert J. Hard, John R. Roney, Karen R. Adams, and William L. Merrill

have located sites with late Middle Archaic- and Late Archaic-period remains in several settings. In the Basin and Range Province these settings are fluvial terraces, rockshelters and caves, *bajadas*, and *cerros de trincheras*. Work to date has focused on two distinct groups of Basin and Range sites: those constructed with D-shaped terraces, and *cerros de trincheras*.

D-Shaped Terrace Sites

A phenomenon first noted by Richard Brooks (1971:169) in the Basin and Range country of southern Chihuahua is the widespread presence of rockshelter sites with built-up terraces behind D-shaped walls, which he referred to as "platform shelter sites." He did not suggest an age for these sites but commented that they were comparable to sites seen in the Chalchihuites area of Durango. We recorded three of these sites in the Parral area and a fourth near Santa Isabel (Figure 3.3). These sites share several distinct traits. The terraces generally follow cliff bases for 20 to 25 m, defining the straight side of an uppercase D, and arc outward about 10 to 15 m from the cliffs. The sites are invariably within 1.5 km of fluvial terraces suitable for agriculture. Surface assemblages at three of the sites include a mixture of Archaic to recent materials, whereas the fourth site, Sitio Pienso (A47-05), shows abundant surface lithics and little else.

We tested three of the terrace sites. At Cueva de los Indios (C75-01) near Santa Isabel, terrace deposits extended to 2.3 m below the surface, although the terrace surface is overlain by roughly 15 cm of overburden. This multicomponent site has a wide range of materials. The oldest are a basalt Plainview lance base and, from 20 cm deeper in the excavation, a radiocarbon date of 9120 ± 50 (8440–8250 cal B.C., Beta-185635) from charcoal.[1] At least half of the almost fifty whole and broken projectile points recovered from this site closely or fully resemble late Middle Archaic and Late Archaic forms. Bifacial reduction is heavily represented in the abundant flaked stone. More recent materials, which are concentrated in upper levels, include arrow points, plain ware, one Mimbres Black-on-white sherd, and closer to the surface some green-glaze pottery. The faunal assemblage is remarkable both for its quantity of over 300 individual specimens (NISP) and because 80 percent of the identified elements found throughout the deposit are tortoise and turtle (Schmidt 2004). Maize samples found in the same excavation level as a late Middle Archaic Arenosa point and one plain ware sherd date to the early Ceramic period (1400 ± 40, cal A.D. 600–680, Beta 182383; 1310 ± 40, cal A.D. 655–780, Beta 182384). The terrace deposits at this site are somewhat mixed as a result of both construction of the terrace and subsequent disturbance by rodents. The relative abundance of typed artifacts suggests that prevalent use of the site was during the late Middle Archaic and Late Archaic periods. In spite of this problem, C75-01 remains interesting because of the abundance of artifacts that coincide with the interval when maize spread north and its proximity to excellent terraces along the Río Santa Isabel.

The Setting of Early Agriculture in Southern Chihuahua

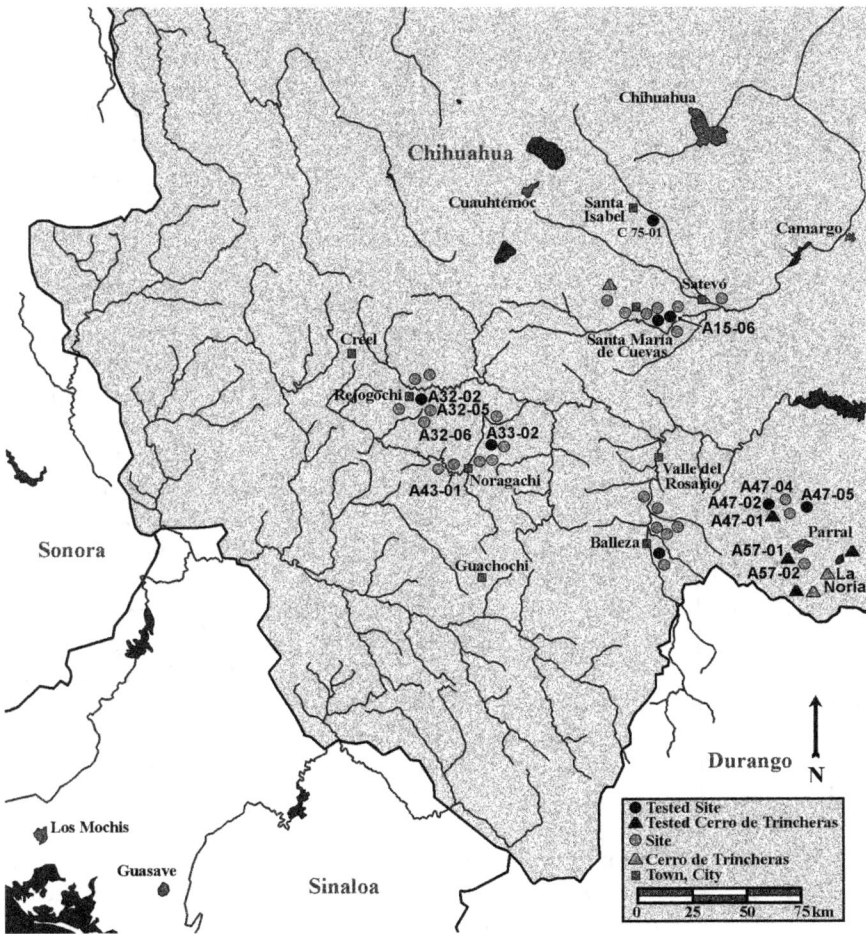

Figure 3.3. Map of southwestern Chihuahua, showing location of sites discussed in the text.

Site A47-02 consists of two D-shaped terraces and several smaller features beneath shallow overhangs in volcanic conglomerate cliffs northwest of Parral. A small test unit indicated terrace deposits were badly mixed, although the one projectile point found at this site is a Middle to Late Archaic Charcos point (Turner and Hester 1993:90). Nearby rockshelter A47-04 was not tested but also has a mixed surface assemblage that includes several late Middle Archaic to Late Archaic dart points.

Sitio Pienso (A47-05) is another D-shaped terrace site located in the same drainage. The generally recognized time interval for over one dozen projectile points from this site embraces the late Middle Archaic to Latest Archaic periods. A 1 ×

43

2 m excavation produced over 4,000 pieces of flaked stone, much of it from biface reduction, and not one sherd. A diverse faunal assemblage includes turtle, tortoise, jackrabbit, cottontail, and mule deer (Schmidt 2004). Cobble manos, a small grinding slab, charcoal, and fire-cracked rock are also present. A recent radiocarbon date of 170 ± 40 (Beta 185632, four calibration intercepts span A.D. 1650–1950) is obviously intrusive and has nothing to do with the site age, whereas an older date of 2770 ± 40 (1000–825 cal B.C., Beta 182382) is in line with the site assemblage. Neither radiocarbon sample was from maize, which was not found in our limited excavations at A47-05 during 2003.

By all indications, these four rockshelters with D-shaped terraces were heavily used habitation sites, with considerable labor invested in terrace construction and with substantial assemblages, including cobble manos, ample flaked stone debris, and faunal material. Based on replicative experiments at Cerro Juanaqueña (Hard et al. 1999), we estimate that these terraces required five person-days or more to construct. Metates are absent from excavations, except for a single grinding slab from Sitio Pienso. The only time span shared by the four site assemblages is the late Middle Archaic to Late Archaic, which we believe imprecisely dates terrace construction. Based largely on Texas chronologies and types, the projectile point assemblages suggest initial Archaic-period occupations no earlier than 2500–2000 B.C., with continued use through the Late Archaic period. None of these four sites provides direct evidence of preceramic agriculture from limited testing, but they remain pertinent to the discussion. If initial occupation of these sites predates the arrival of agriculture in the area, which is presently a possibility of unknown likelihood, they at least connote a predisposition to accept agriculture. According to W. H. Wills (1988:41), predisposition involves repetitive seasonal movement, limited geographic movement, and resource storage capacity. Suzanne and Paul Fish (1994:86) have suggested that experience with manipulation of wild plants may be an important pre-agricultural adaptation. The investment in terrace construction and the dense assemblages are more congruent with logistically organized settlement, as the rockshelters are far from typical forager camps (sensu Binford 1980). Such a strategy may imply plant intensification and decreased residential mobility (Binford 2001). Proximate locations to fluvial terraces may be related to the use of wild or domestic resources or both. In the case of the Parral area, the volcaniclastic cliffs contain abundant, high-quality chert cobbles that provide much of the chert in assemblages. The generalization that hunter-gatherers will move to the least portable resource and reach the others with task groups (Binford 1980; Wills 1988:43) may be applicable in this instance.

Cerros de Trincheras

There are also *cerros de trincheras* in southern Chihuahua, and at least some of these hills have evidence, albeit limited, for early agriculture. Deric Nusbaum (1940) was the first to identify *cerros de trincheras* in southern Chihuahua and in nearby northern Durango. Nine of these hill sites are now known from the central Basin and Range Province in southern Chihuahua. Gerry Raymond (2001; Raymond et al. 2003) tested three southern Chihuahua *cerros de trincheras* during 2000 in affiliation with the Cerro Juanaqueña project. We have since returned to one of these sites, Cerro Prieto de Santa Bárbara (A57-01), mapped another site, and both mapped and tested three additional *cerros de trincheras* sites in the region. One of Raymond's samples from Cerro Prieto de Santa Bárbara (Terrace 5, Level 7) produced a maize radiocarbon date of 3410 ± 40 (1770-1620 cal B.C., Beta 174996), and another one from Cerro La Noria (Terrace 1, Level 4) produced a maize date of 1950 ± 50 (50 cal B.C.-cal A.D. 140, Beta 174994) (Raymond et al. 2003). However, unlike *cerros de trincheras* in northwestern Chihuahua, those in the south have substantial Ceramic-period occupations. So far, we have been unable to isolate an earlier component on any of these terraced hills.

The southern *cerros de trincheras* each have from five to forty terrace walls made with stacked rocks and have closely arranged round rock outlines, presumably of structures, on top. These outlines are typically about 3 to 3.5 m in diameter. Several of these sites have saddles that are cleared of rocks and enclosed by stone walls, an arrangement not seen in northwestern Chihuahua. Assemblages from these hills are variable and include brown to buff plain ware with infrequent red ware. The only metate fragments seen are basin and slab varieties. On the hills with sizable samples of lithics, extensive bifacial reduction is evident. This is particularly true of Cerro las Flojeras (A47-01), located within direct sight of three of the D-shaped terrace sites. At four of the five sites tested in 2003, at least one dart point indistinguishable from known and well-defined Archaic dart points from Arizona, New Mexico, and Texas was found. In addition, more recent arrow points and ceramics were recovered. Eight radiocarbon dates from six of these sites, including two tested by Raymond, fall primarily into the interval A.D. 500-1000, which probably reflects the major period of occupation, given the ubiquity of ceramics in the test units. Whether probable Early Agricultural-period components of these hills are scaled-down variants of northwestern Chihuahua *cerros de trincheras* remains unclear but seems quite possible. Present evidence for this distills down to two early maize radiocarbon dates, projectile points, lithics not at all characteristic of the Ceramic period in the greater region, and the northwestern Chihuahua precedent.

Other Basin and Range sites of note include an extensive artifact scatter (A57-02) on the *bajada* beside Cerro Prieto de Santa Bárbara that has several late Middle Archaic dart points. Only two sherds were found in this sprawling site. The Los Pilares site (A15-06) is on a fluvial terrace along the Río San Pedro and includes an aceramic buried component of unknown extent and age. In summary, sites or components that likely date to the window when agriculture arrived are widespread in the higher Basin and Range country of Chihuahua. These sites occur in diverse settings and in most instances imply some stabilization in settlement.

A. C. MacWilliams, Robert J. Hard, John R. Roney, Karen R. Adams, and William L. Merrill

The Sierra Tarahumara

Fieldwork in two areas of the Sierra Tarahumara also produced evidence of habitation during the later mid-Holocene. Limited survey along Arroyo Caliente near Rejogochi produced one site (A32-06) with a dart much like or the same as late Middle Archaic Gypsum/Almagre points (see Justice 2002) and another (A32-05) comparable to Late Archaic Shumla points (Turpin 1991:32–33). A third open site (A43-01), on a terrace of the Río Urique near Norogachi, had one dart comparable to Chiricahua points. This is a widespread type also dated to the later Middle Archaic period in the southwestern United States. The ages of these points are extrapolated and not directly verified, and we lack excavation data from these three sites. Nonetheless, they are important for simply adding to very scarce evidence that the Sierra Tarahumara was inhabited coincident with an interval of rapidly spreading maize agriculture several thousand years ago.

Additional evidence has come from two cave sites tested during 2003. The first montane cave tested is in a moderately remote location near Rejogochi. Sowérare (translates as Swallow Place), or A32-02, is a rockshelter perched below the base of one cliff and above a lower cliff in the Río Urique watershed. This small cave has been thoroughly plundered, but intact deep midden deposits remain in front of the cave. We dug a single 1 m unit in the midden to a depth of over 120 cm below the surface. Underneath spoil from the looted cave, the actual midden deposits contained dense lithics, rare ground stone, and charcoal. No maize was found, but two samples of wood charcoal yielded radiocarbon dates of 2660 ± 40 (880–790 cal B.C., Beta 185630) and 3500 ± 40 (1920–1725 cal B.C., Beta 182381). These samples are in stratigraphic order and are chronologically consistent with the midden assemblage and dart points from the site. Based on such a small excavation sample, it would be premature to rule out the presence of maize.

The second cave is located about 1 km west of Zingg's Cave A, near Norogachi, and was almost certainly recorded by Zingg. In this sizable cave site known as Ganóchi (Place of the Giant, A33-02; Figure 3.4), a single 1 × 1 m excavation replicated the pattern seen at Swallow Cave, of lithics and maize below ceramics, in deep cave fill. The upper 80 cm contained abundant artifacts, including pottery, and bits of cord and basketry, with remnants of a mud and grass container (Figure 3.5). Lithics, although moderately scarce, continued to approximately 130 cm below the surface. Organic artifacts continued to bedrock at more than 200 cm below the surface. A maize sample from 180 cm below the surface produced a radiocarbon date of 2280 ± 40 (400–350 cal B.C. and 310–210 cal B.C., Beta 185631).

At this point, it is reasonable to argue that people expanded into the Sierra Tarahumara no later than the late Middle Archaic period. Sites are widely distributed in both areas of the Sierra we have worked in and are in locations presently well suited to small-scale subsistence agriculture. In our limited work there is no indication of *cerros de trincheras* or the D-shaped terrace sites in the Sierra Tarahumara. Overall, sites in the mountains are small, even by the modest standards of southern Chihuahua.

Figure 3.4. View of site A33-02, facing southeast.

CONCLUSIONS AND DISCUSSION

Our present results allow us to make several conclusions. There are many locations in diverse settings across southern Chihuahua west of the Río Florida where subsistence agriculture is feasible. Southwestern Chihuahua was widely inhabited during the later mid-Holocene, by which time people were distributed over the entire landscape. In the Basin and Range country of central southern Chihuahua, there are indications of increased settlement stability on a modest scale from the late Middle Archaic period. Maize agriculture minimally dates to ca. 1600 B.C. in the upper Basin and Range region and to 300 B.C. in the Sierra Tarahumara.

A marked increase in visible archaeology is seen beginning with the late Middle Archaic period, ca. 2500–2000 B.C., based on extrapolation from well-dated sites in the United States. It is not clear if this increase precedes or coincides with the arrival of maize agriculture. Coincidence would mean the same people who made San José, Langtry, and Pedernales dart points were at least introduced to agriculture. There is no precedent for this farther north, although there need not be, particularly given the direction of agriculture's spread. Interestingly, Thomas Hester (1989:59) describes the "late phase" of the Middle Archaic period in Texas, where agriculture is not a factor, as "perhaps the most distinctive and dominant occupational period in the Lower Pecos in terms of the sheer amount of cultural refuse." No evidence points to mass departure from the Sierra Tarahumara at any time to populate the Basin and Range country. Growth of an indigenous population in an area favorable to hunter-gatherers is left as the strong possibility. The settlement

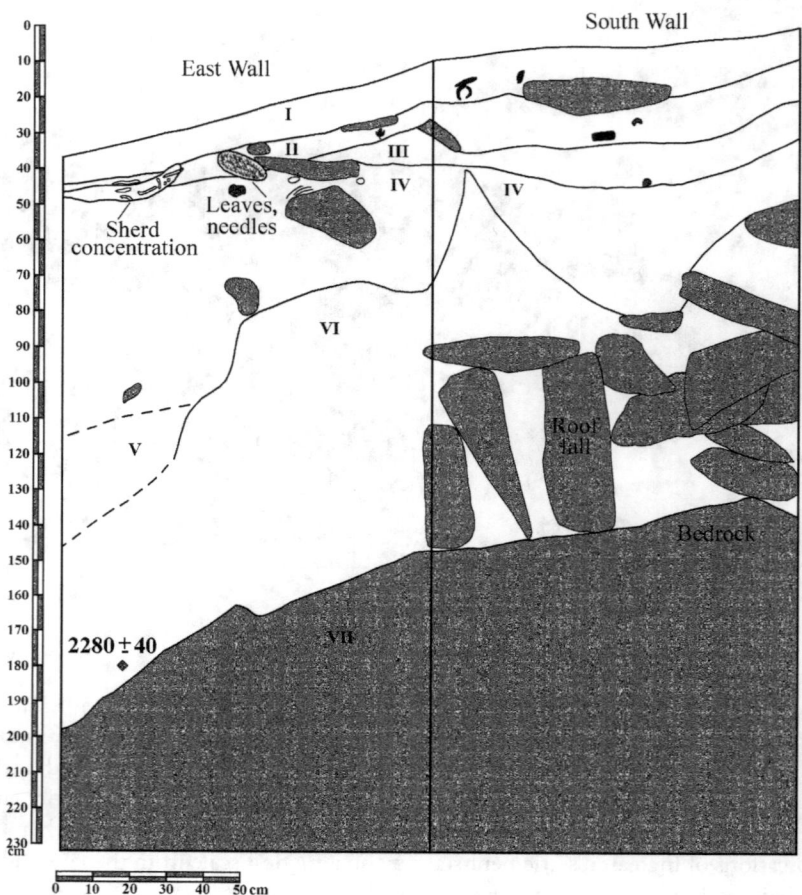

Figure 3.5. Excavation profile of site A33-02.

information briefly presented here might reveal the development of more conspicuous logistical hunter-gatherer sites created by populations fortuitously organized to receive maize agriculture (see Binford 1980; Fish and Fish 1994; Wills 1988:41).

Entrenched agriculture, as defined here, is implied for the southern *cerros de trincheras*. Although these are modest efforts in comparison with many larger *cerros de trincheras*, and as exclusively preceramic sites they may have been even smaller, the labor investment in building even a few terraces cannot be discounted. The D-shaped terrace sites also reveal a departure from forager settlement, although the presence of maize from preceramic contexts in these sites remains unproven.

The Sierra Tarahumara presents a similar picture of widespread remains from the late Middle Archaic period onward, but with an important difference. The few sites known to have Archaic materials are relatively small. The deep deposits at both cave sites we tested probably reflect repeated, but not populous, occupation. Lister's (1958) work in the Sierra Madre Occidental left little to no doubt about early agriculture of some scale in the mountains. Results from the Ganóchi Cave substantiate this with a maize radiocarbon date exceeding 2,000 years—long before metal tools and goat dung fertilizer, presently so vital to Tarahumara agriculture, were available (Hard and Merrill 1992).

A final point to ponder is the relationship among the introduction of agriculture, entrenchment, and the long-term consequences of entrenchment. A well-known pattern in the history of the southwestern United States is the cycle of agricultural intensification, population increase, aggregation, and political complexity, although considerable disagreement exists on the underlying causal relationships (e.g., Boserup 1965; Cordell, Doyel, and Kintigh 1994; Leonard and Reed 1993; Stone and Downum 1999). Southwestern Chihuahua is an exception to this generalization. It has been long recognized that nothing resembling the dynamic mid-level regional polities of the southwestern United States or northern Chihuahua and nothing evoking Mesoamerican elaboration ever developed in southern Chihuahua. The possible emergence of *cerros de trincheras* during the Early Agricultural period, and their certain use between ca. A.D. 500–1000, suggest a foundation for a growing society, but evidently little came of it. Undated Ceramic-period sites of many forms are widespread. The apparent paradoxical absence of both agricultural intensification and significant aggregation in southwestern Chihuahua deserves more research because understanding why this cycle did not occur may provide insight into the underlying dynamics of growth and aggregation both to the north and south. It appears that entrenchment of agriculture occurred, but with only limited pressure toward aggregation and intensification of food production. Whether the structure of domestic and wild resources influenced this developmental trajectory remains to be examined. This issue and the other uncertainties recognized in this chapter await new research.

Acknowledgments. This work was supported by a grant from the Committee for Research and Exploration, National Geographic Society, and the National Science Foundation (0220292). We greatly appreciate the support of the Consejo de Arqueología, Instituto Nacional de Antropología e Historia (INAH), and Ing. Joaquín García-Barcena González, president, as well as the assistance of Centro INAH Chihuahua and Antrop. Elsa Rodriguez Garcia, director. Lic. Ranferi Juárez Silva deserves special recognition for his tireless help in the field and Arq. Rafael Cruz Antillón for his extensive logistical assistance The people of the many communities we visited were always helpful, including those of Balleza, Norogachi, Parral Rejogochi, and Sta. Maria de las Cuevas. Cultural anthropologist Dr. Felice Wyndham took us to sites in the Rejogochi area, including Sowérare, and we greatly appreciate her interest and support.

A. C. MacWilliams, Robert J. Hard, John R. Roney, Karen R. Adams, and William L. Merrill

NOTES

1. All radiocarbon dates reported here are based on a half life of 5,568 years, are corrected for isotopic fractionation, and are calibrated [cal] at 2 sigma, as reported by Beta Analytic. If more than one calibration range is listed, all are given unless otherwise noted. All samples not identified as maize are wood charcoal.

REFERENCES CITED

Bennett, Wendell C., and Robert M. Zingg
    1935   *The Tarahumara: An Indian Tribe of Northern Mexico.* University of Chicago Press, Chicago.

Benz, Bruce F.
    1999   On the Origin, Evolution, and Dispersal of Maize. In *Pacific Latin America in Prehistory: The Evolution of Archaic and Formative Cultures,* ed. Michael Blake, 25–38. Washington State University Press, Pullman.

Binford, Lewis R.
    1980   Willow Smoke and Dogs' Tails: Hunter-Gatherer Settlement Systems and Archaeological Site Formation. *American Antiquity* 45:4–20.
    2001   *Constructing Frames of Reference: An Analytical Method for Archaeological Theory Building Using Ethnographic and Environmental Data Sets.* University of California Press, Berkeley.

Boserup, Ester
    1965   *The Conditions of Agricultural Growth: The Economics of Agrarian Change under Population Pressure.* G. Allen and Unwin, London.

Brooks, Richard H.
    1971   Lithic Traditions in Northwestern Mexico, Paleo-Indian to Chalchihuites. Unpublished Ph.D. dissertation, Department of Anthropology, University of Colorado, Boulder.

Brown, David E., and Charles H. Lowe
    1980   *Biotic Communities of the Southwest.* USDA Forest Service General Technical Report RM-78 (map). Rocky Mountain Forest and Range Experiment Station, Fort Collins, Colo.

Cordell, Linda S., David E. Doyel, and Keith W. Kintigh
    1994   Processes of Aggregation in the Prehistoric Southwest. In *Themes in Southwest Prehistory,* ed. George J. Gumerman, 109–134. School of American Research Press, Santa Fe.

Di Peso, Charles C., John B. Rinaldo, and Gloria Fenner
    1974   *Casas Grandes: A Fallen Trading Center of the Gran Chichimeca.* 8 vols. Amerind Foundation Series 9. Amerind Foundation, Dragoon, Ariz., and Northland Press, Flagstaff, Ariz.

Fish, Suzanne K., and Paul R. Fish
    1994   Prehistoric Desert Farmers of the Southwest. *Annual Review of Anthropology* 23:83–108.

González Arratia, Leticia
  1992   La Población Prehispánica Cazadora-Recolectora y el Desierto de Chihuahua. In *Historia General de Chihuahua: Geología, Geografía y Arqueología*, ed. Arturo Márquez-Alameda, 163–185. Universidad Autónoma de Ciudad Juárez, Ciudad Juárez.

Gregory, David A.
  2001   An Evaluation of Early Agricultural Period Chronology in the Tucson Basin. In *Excavations in the Santa Cruz River Floodplain: The Early Agricultural Period Component at Los Pozos*, ed. David A. Gregory, 237–254. Anthropological Papers 21. Center for Desert Archaeology, Tucson.

Gregory, David A., and Michael W. Diehl
  2002   Duration, Continuity, and Intensity of Occupation at a Late Cienega Phase Settlement in the Santa Cruz River Floodplain. In *Traditions, Transitions, and Technologies: Themes in Southwestern Archaeology*, ed. Sarah H. Schlanger, 200–223. University Press of Colorado, Boulder.

Hard, Robert J., and William L. Merrill
  1992   Mobile Agriculturalists and the Emergence of Sedentism: Perspectives from Northern Mexico. *American Anthropologist* 94:601–620.

Hard, Robert J., and John R. Roney
  1998   A Massive Terraced Village Complex in Chihuahua, Mexico, 3000 Years Before Present. *Science* 279(5337):1661–1664.
  2004   Late Archaic Period Hilltop Settlements in Northwestern Chihuahua, Mexico. In *Identity, Feasting, and the Archaeology of the Greater Southwest*, ed. Barbara Mills, 276–294. University Press of Colorado, Boulder.
  2005   The Transition to Farming on the Rio Casas Grandes and in the Southern Jornada Mogollon Region. In *The Late Archaic across the Borderlands: Foraging to Farming*, ed. Bradley J. Vierra, 141–186. University of Texas Press, Austin.

Hard, Robert J., José E. Zapata, Bruce K. Moses, and John R. Roney
  1999   Terrace Construction in Northern Chihuahua, Mexico: 1150 B.C. and Modern Experiments. *Journal of Field Archaeology* 26:129–146.

Haury, Emil W.
  1962   The Greater American Southwest. In *Courses toward Urban Life*, ed. Robert J. Braidwood and Gordon R. Willey, 106–131. Viking Fund Publications in Anthropology 32. Wenner-Gren Foundation for Anthropological Research, New York.

Heidke, James M.
  1999   Cienega Phase Incipient Plainware from Southeastern Arizona. *Kiva* 64(3):311–338.

Hester, Thomas R.
  1989   Chronological Framework for Lower Pecos Prehistory. *Bulletin of the Texas Archeological Society* 59:53–64.

Huber, Edgar K.
  2005   Early Maize at the Old Corn Site (LA 137258). In *Fence Lake Project, Archaeological Data Recovery in the New Mexico Transportation Corridor and First Five-Year Permit Area, Fence Lake Coal Mine Project, Catron County, New Mexico, Volume 4, Synthetic*

Studies and Summary, ed. Edgar K. Huber and Carla R. Van West, 36.1–36.33. Statistical Research Technical Series 84, Tucson.

Huckell, Bruce B.
1995 Of Marshes and Maize: Preceramic Agricultural Settlements in the Cienega Valley, Southeastern Arizona. Anthropological Papers 59. University of Arizona Press, Tucson.

Justice, Noel D.
2002 Stone Age Spear and Arrow Points of the Southwestern United States. Indiana University Press, Bloomington.

Leonard, Robert D., and Heidi E. Reed
1993 Population Aggregation in the Prehistoric American Southwest: A Selectionist Model. American Antiquity 58:648–661.

Lister, Robert H.
1958 Archaeological Excavations in the Northern Sierra Madre Occidental, Chihuahua and Sonora, Mexico. In Archaeological Excavations in the Northern Sierra Madre Occidental, Chihuahua and Sonora, Mexico, ed. Robert H. Lister, 1–95. University of Colorado Studies, Series in Anthropology 7. University of Colorado Press, Boulder.

Long, Austin, B. F. Benz, D. J. Donahue, A.J.T. Jull, and L. J. Toolin
1989 First Direct AMS Dates on Early Maize from Tehuacán, Mexico. Radiocarbon 31:1035–1040.

Mabry, Jonathan B.
1998 Introduction. In Archaeological Investigations of Early Village Sites in the Middle Santa Cruz Valley: Analyses and Synthesis, ed. Jonathan B. Mabry, 1–29. Anthropological Papers 19. Center for Desert Archaeology, Tucson.

Mangelsdorf, Paul C.
1958 Archaeological Evidence on the Evolution of Maize in Northwestern Mexico. In Archaeological Excavations in the Northern Sierra Madre Occidental, Chihuahua and Sonora, Mexico, ed. Robert H. Lister, 96–119. University of Colorado Studies, Series in Anthropology 7. University of Colorado Press, Boulder.

Marrs, Garland J.
1949 Problems Arising from the Surface Occurrence of Archaeological Material in Southeastern Chihuahua, Mexico. Unpublished master's thesis, Department of Anthropology, University of New Mexico, Albuquerque.

Minnis, Paul E.
1992 Earliest Plant Cultivation in the Desert Borderlands of North America. In The Origins of Agriculture: An International Perspective, ed. C. Wesley Cowan and Patty Jo Watson, 121–141. Smithsonian Institution Press, Washington, D.C.

Nusbaum, Deric
1940 Gila Pueblo Detail Sheet for GP U:13:2 (CHIH). Document on file, Arizona State Museum Archives, Tucson.

Piperno, D. R., and K. V. Flannery
2001 The Earliest Archaeological Maize (Zea mays L.) from Highland Mexico: New Accelerator Mass Spectrometry Dates and Their Implications. Proceedings of the National Academy of Science 98:2101–2103.

Pope, Kevin O., Mary E.D. Pohl, John G. Jones, David L. Lentz, Christopher von Nagy, Francisco J. Vega, and Irvy R. Quitmyer
    2001   Origin and Environmental Setting of Ancient Agriculture in the Lowlands of Mesoamerica. *Science* 292:1370–1373.

Raymond, Gerry R.
    2001   La Investigación de Algunos Sitios al Sur de Chihuahua. In *Una Investigación Arqueológica de los Sitios Cerros con Trincheras del Arcaico Tardío en Chihuahua, México*, ed. Robert J. Hard, José E. Zapata, and John R. Roney, 37–44. Informe al Consejo de Arqueología, Instituto Nacional de Antropología e Historia. Center for Archaeological Research, University of Texas at San Antonio, Special Report 27-S, San Antonio.

Raymond, Gerry R., John R. Roney, A. C. MacWilliams, Robert J. Hard, Karen R. Adams, and William L. Merrill
    2003   Looking for Early Maize between the Southwest and Mesoamerica: A Field Report from Southwest Chihuahua, Mexico. Paper presented at the 68th Annual Meeting of the Society for American Archaeology, Milwaukee, Wis.

Roney, John R., and Robert J. Hard
    2002   Early Agriculture in Northwestern Chihuahua. In *Traditions, Transitions, and Technologies: Themes in Southwestern Archaeology*, ed. Sarah Schlanger, 163–180. University Press of Colorado, Boulder.
    2004   A Review of Cerros de Trincheras in Northwestern Chihuahua. In *Surveying the Archaeology of Northwest Mexico*, ed. Gillian E. Newell and Emiliano Gallaga, 127–148. University of Utah Press, Salt Lake City.

Schmidt, Kari M.
    2004   Faunal Remains from Test Excavations at Early Agricultural Sites in Southern Chihuahua, Mexico. Manuscript on file, Center for Archaeological Research, University of Texas, San Antonio.

Smith, Bruce D.
    1997   Reconsidering the Ocampo Caves and the Era of Incipient Cultivation in Mesoamerica. *Latin American Antiquity* 8:342–383.

Stone, Glenn D., and Christian E. Downum
    1999   Non-Boserupian Ecology and Agricultural Risk: Ethnic Politics and Land Control in the Arid Southwest. *American Anthropologist* 101:113–128.

Turner, Ellen Sue, and Thomas R. Hester
    1993   *A Field Guide to Stone Artifacts of Texas Indians*. Gulf, Houston.

Turpin, Solveig A.
    1991   Time Out of Mind: The Radiocarbon Chronology of the Lower Pecos River Region. In *Papers on Lower Pecos Prehistory*, ed. Solveig A. Turpin, 1–49. Studies in Archeology 8. Texas Archeological Research Laboratory, University of Texas, Austin.

Wills, W. H.
    1988   *Early Prehistoric Agriculture in the American Southwest*. School of American Research Press, Santa Fe.

A. C. MacWilliams, Robert J. Hard, John R. Roney, Karen R. Adams, and William L. Merrill

Zingg, Robert M.
- 1939 *A Reconstruction of Uto-Aztecan History*. University of Denver Contributions to Ethnography II. G. E. Stechert, New York.
- 1940 *Report on Archaeology of Southern Chihuahua*. Contributions of the University of Denver, Center of Latin American Studies, Denver.

4

Modeling the Early Agricultural Frontier in the Desert Borderlands

Jonathan B. Mabry and William E. Doolittle

In 1998 excavations near Tucson in southern Arizona along the path of a highway construction project uncovered a series of canals dating between about 3,000 and 2,400 years ago (in uncalibrated radiocarbon years) (Mabry 2006b). This confirmed the earlier discovery of canals about as old at a nearby site in the same floodplain (Ezzo and Deaver 1998). Shortly thereafter, some Basketmaker II canals of almost the same age were found near Zuni Pueblo in northwestern New Mexico (Damp et al. 2000). This new and unexpected evidence for very early irrigated farming in both the southern and central parts of southwestern North America led Mabry to search the literature to find out if these canals were truly anomalous. A surprisingly wide variety of different types of farming can be identified or inferred for the Early Agricultural period, including most of those documented historically in southwestern North America (see Doolittle 2000).

This recognition of diversity, in turn, led Mabry (2005) to consider how recent approaches to the transition to agriculture in southwestern North America (including northwestern Mexico) tend to assume as the primary motivation either energy maximization (e.g., Barlow 2002; Diehl 1997) or risk minimization (e.g., Huckell 1990; Minnis 1992) and how these models calculate the labor, yield, and predictability of a single "generic" type of early agriculture—either rain-fed farming or flood farming. These models—based on the optimization of a single characteristic of a single kind of agriculture—now seem too simplistic because early agriculture in this region was actually quite diverse, and these different types of early farming strategies would have had widely varying productivities, risks, labor requirements, and energy efficiencies.

Mabry (2005) attempted to identify the differences between the various early "farming systems" using ethnographic and experimental data, and on the basis of these differences he developed a predictive model of how the early agricultural landscape of southwestern North America initially filled and changed in response to environmental and demographic cycles. This model applies to what is now the southwestern United States and the borderlands of northwestern Mexico (northern Sonora and Chihuahua). As defined in that study and here, "farming systems" are combinations of crop complexes, agricultural technologies, and cultivation techniques.

CROP COMPLEXES

Revising previous models on the basis of paleobotanical evidence and currently available direct radiocarbon dates on cultigens, Mabry identified three prehistoric crop complexes in southwestern North America and raised the possibility of a fourth. The possible fourth one is an indigenous Early Southwestern Crop Complex that may have included native weedy and seedy annuals and large-seeded perennial grasses that were protected, encouraged, and possibly cultivated in naturally disturbed, damp alluvial soils between about 5000 and 4000 B.P. In the continuum of people-plant relationships, these forms of manipulation (done either consciously or not) fall between the gathering of wild plants and what is normally thought of as agriculture (Doolittle 2000).

In addition to this possible native crop complex, early southwestern farming was based on an Early Mesoamerican Crop Complex that included Central American tropical domesticates from varied upland and lowland habitats and that arrived at different times: maize by at least 3700 B.P. and probably as early as 4000 B.P., pepo squash and possibly cotton by 3000 B.P., and common bean and bottle gourd by 2500 B.P. A Late Mesoamerican Crop Complex included tropical domesticates from hot, humid Central American habitats that arrived between about 1500 and 900 B.P.: another variety of cotton, maiz de ocho, jackbean, cushaw squash, butternut squash, and domesticated tobacco. A Late Southwestern Crop Complex included several Sonoran Desert natives locally domesticated between about 1500 and 900 B.P.: tepary bean, agave, little barley, Mexican crucillo, panic grass, and Devil's Claw.

EARLY AGRICULTURAL TECHNOLOGIES

The agricultural technologies used by early southwestern farmers were comparable to those of Formative and Neolithic farmers in other parts of the world and included fire, structures, and tools. Historically, many native southwestern farmers used fire to clear fields of woody species, to stimulate regeneration of wild seed-bearing plants after harvest, and to return plant nutrients back to the soil (Dobyns 1981). At some Hohokam sites, high proportions of pollen from weeds that pioneer burned grasslands as well as concentrations of charcoal and ash may indicate deliberate burning to promote grasses and cool-season annuals during late prehistory (Bohrer 1992).

Physical traces of a variety of technologies for landscape modification and water control by early southwestern farmers have been identified at archaeological sites, and some related features, although not preserved, can be inferred. While silted-up ditches and canals have been identified archaeologically, historic practices suggest that stone and brush weirs were also built to divert water from springs, streams, and rivers into these artificial channels. It is also likely that canyon floods were slowed and spread by earthen berms built on alluvial fans where canyons opened onto *bajadas*. Rock terraces were built on hillsides to slow runoff, trap sediments, and create level planting surfaces. Large pits, including bell-shaped and slab-lined types commonly found at early farming sites in the Southwest, were presumably used for storage of maize surpluses; their appearance in the archaeological record of each region correlates with the transition to maize agriculture.

Examples of the tools early farmers used for digging canals, preparing fields, and planting, harvesting, and processing seeds are preserved at archaeological sites. Stone tools for milling seeds (metates, manos, mortars, pestles) are commonly found at the habitation sites of early farmers. Stone hoes have been recovered from some early farming settlements (e.g., Turnbow 2000). Digging sticks, trowels made of bark and wood, seedbeater sticks, and woven parching trays have been found in Basketmaker II caves in northeastern Arizona (Guernsey and Kidder 1921) and southwestern Utah (Nusbaum 1922) and in late preceramic levels containing maize and sometimes also squash and bottle gourd in several caves in southwestern and west-central New Mexico (Cosgrove 1947; Hough 1914; Martin et al. 1952). However, many of these tools were already being used by local hunter-gatherer groups, some of whom were probably cultivating native plants before the Early Mesoamerican Crop Complex arrived.

Additional information about early farming technology in the Southwest is gained from linguistic data. The Proto-Uto-Aztecan lexicon includes words traditionally associated with intensive use of wild seeds but that can also be understood to be associated with early agriculture. These include words for "digging stick," "to plant," "to grind," "metate," and "mano" (Hill 2001). A common heritage among northern and southern Uto-Aztecan languages has also been identified in the "way of speaking" about the manipulation of water for agriculture, including cognates and semantic parallels for the words "canal," "dam," and "to irrigate"; this implies that irrigation was practiced in the Southwest prior to the breakup of the Proto-Uto-Aztecan speech community between 3000 and 2500 B.P. (Hill 2001).

Jonathan B. Mabry and William E. Doolittle

EARLY CULTIVATION TECHNIQUES

Although not all cultivation techniques—such as fallowing, staggered planting, intercropping, and multiple cropping—are archaeologically visible, several different early cultivation techniques can be identified or inferred from physical traces. These include the locations of early farming settlements and fields on specific landforms and soils favorable for agriculture, built structures and surface modifications that enhanced and directed runoff, canals that diverted perennial river flows, and signs of the use of fire to clear weeds and brush from fields and canals.

A literature search produced evidence of varied forms of dry farming, runoff farming, flood farming, water-table farming, and irrigated farming in use by early maize farmers in several parts of southwestern North America between 3750 and 3000 B.P. (Mabry 2005). The definitions of these types of farming follow those in Doolittle (2000), with the addition of water-table farming:

- Flood farming: location of fields in naturally flooding areas (includes overbank flood farming and "ak chin" farming without water spreaders)
- Water-table farming: location of fields in areas with high water tables ("sub-irrigation")
- Runoff farming: modification of surface gradients to slow runoff in field locations, and diversion of runoff or seasonal stream flows to fields
- Irrigated farming: diversion of perennial flows from rivers, streams, or springs to fields
- Dry farming: location of fields in areas with moisture-retaining soils
- Rain-fed farming: location of fields in areas with adequate and properly timed rainfall (rare)

On the basis of the archaeological and historical evidence (e.g., Adams and Peterson 1999; Arbolino 2001), we believe rain-fed farming was practiced only rarely throughout prehistory and historic times and only at higher elevations that had both adequate rainfall and long enough growing seasons. Except for dry farming, all early types of farming were focused specifically on alluvial landforms with naturally replenished soil nutrients. However, replenishment from natural floods was sporadic, and deposition was often spotty. The most regular and spatially uniform fertilization with sediments and organic detritus occurred in irrigated fields and was therefore artificial. Flood farming, runoff farming, and water-table farming were all permanent, fixed-plot, sustainable systems. In contrast, dry farming and irrigated farming probably required shifting field locations and fallow cycles to restore soil fertility and, in irrigated systems, to reduce waterlogging and salinization (Ackerly 1988; Huckleberry 1992). Swidden dry farming on upland mesas and mountains did not develop until after 1800 B.P., and new forms of runoff and dry farming developed after 1000 B.P. These included water storage in reservoirs, use of recently deposited volcanic ash as mulch, use of artificial rock piles and gravel layers as mulches, and gridded gardens. Unlike the earlier forms of farming, all of these later types were unsustainable because of exhaustion and nonrenewal of soil nutrients. The several early cultivation techniques were not entirely discrete but were overlapping modes. Each group of early farmers probably practiced multiple types simultaneously and shifted emphasis when necessary. However, some groups likely specialized in certain types.

CHARACTERISTICS OF EARLY FARMING SYSTEMS ON THE AGRICULTURAL FRONTIER

Modeled characteristics of early maize farming systems include productivities, risks, labor requirements, and energy efficiencies.

Productivities

The productivities of different cultivation techniques can be estimated from ethnographic and experimental data (see references in Mabry 2005). However, no data are available for water-table farming or overbank flood farming (other than recession farming along the lower Colorado River and in southern Sonora and northern Sinaloa; see references in Doolittle 2000; Mabry 2005). North of the U.S.-Mexico border, historical maize yields among Native American groups in the Southwest ranged between 2,350 to 130 kilograms/hectare (kg/ha) in this order, from highest to lowest: flood (recession type), irrigated, runoff/ak chin, dry, rain-fed. However, yields within each type of cultivation technique varied by elevation: historic data show that runoff yields were relatively higher above about 5,500 feet (1,676 m) because of higher rainfall, and irrigated yields were relatively higher below 5,500 feet because of longer growing seasons (Arbolino 2001).

Based on their smaller ear sizes, early Mexican and southwestern maizes probably had one-quarter to one-third the yields of historic varieties (Diehl 1997; Kirkby 1973). Mabry (2005) used this method to estimate the productivities of early maize under different cultivation techniques: (1) take average historic yields, (2) calculate normal yield ranges (two-thirds of year-to-year variation) from coefficients of variation, (3) multiply by a constant of one-third (Kirkby's estimated ratio of productivity), (4) round the upper and lower limits to the nearest 25 kg/ha.

In the absence of historical or experimental data, yields for overbank flood farming and water-table farming must be estimated differently: relative differences are projected by considering likely effects of elevation and growing season length, recurring destructive floods, and lengths of time water is available to crop root zones. Estimates for average yields of early southwestern maize under different cultivation techniques range from 50 to 525 kg/ha, with normal year-to-year variations between 15 and 60 percent (Mabry 2005).

Estimated yields of rain-fed and dry farming were very marginal, probably only occasionally viable and then only at higher elevations. This fits with the historical pattern that rain-fed farming on the Colorado Plateau was often unsuccessful below about 6,000 feet (1,829 m) elevation (Adams and Peterson 1999; Arbolino 2001).

Jonathan B. Mabry and William E. Doolittle

The yields of runoff, ak chin, and overbank flood farming were better, but only at higher elevations. Irrigated farming had higher and more stable yields, reaching its maximum potential at lower elevations. Floodplain farming had higher but less stable yields and also was best at lower elevations. Water-table farming had the most consistently high yields at all elevations. Ranked in order from highest to lowest average yield at all elevations: water-table, irrigated, overbank flood, runoff and ak chin, dry, rain-fed. This is the same order Anne Kirkby (1973) observed for traditional systems in Oaxaca.

Risks

Risk can be measured in terms of probability of crop loss and year-to-year variance. The rankings of early farming systems from highest to lowest variance were mostly the opposite of the order for productivity, except for overbank flood farming, which had both high average yields and high variation. Droughts had the greatest impacts on dry farming and runoff farming, while floods had the greatest impacts on flood farming and irrigated farming. Water-table farming had the lowest risks because, during all but the worst droughts, subsurface water was present in the root zones of crops; if the source of the high water table was a spring rather than a river, the fields were relatively less vulnerable to floods as well. Ranked in order from lowest to highest risk at all elevations: water-table farming, irrigated farming, runoff and ak chin farming, dry farming, floodplain farming, and rain-fed farming.

Labor Requirements

Experiments conducted in central Mexico on the labor requirements of different maize cultivation techniques without modern tools or draft animals (Logan and Sanders 1976) show that the ranking of techniques from highest to lowest labor requirements is largely the same as that for lowest to highest risk. That is, in general there is an inverse correlation between labor inputs and risk: as labor inputs increase, risks decrease. The data also show a direct general correlation between increased labor inputs and increased productivity. Although not part of this experiment, calculations indicate that an exception is water-table farming, in which relatively low labor inputs are associated with low risks (Mabry 2005).

Energy Efficiencies

Conversions to kilocalories allow calculations of ratios of outputs to inputs, which can be used as measures of energy efficiency. In the experimental data, dry farming had the lowest energy efficiency. In this model, the greatest energy efficiencies were found in water-table farming almost always, floodplain farming in good years, and irrigated farming at lower elevations.

In terms of the relationship between labor inputs and energy returns, in general there is a direct correlation between increased labor and decreased energy returns, as Ester Boserup's (1965) model predicts. The exceptions are found at the extremes of labor inputs: in a good year, flood farming can have high energy returns for relatively little labor, and irrigated farming typically has both high labor inputs and high energy returns. The calculated energy returns for some early maize cultivation techniques show significant differences between pre-processing and post-processing energy returns because of the relatively high energy costs of grinding maize into flour—sometimes double or triple the energy costs of field labor.

Compared with the energy returns for wild plant food staples, the pre-processing returns of several maize cultivation techniques—especially water-table farming, floodplain farming in a good year, and irrigated farming at lower elevations—ranked above the top wild plant resources (saguaro fruit, mesquite pods, acorns, and piñon nuts). However, if the maize yields were completely processed into flour, energy returns would have dropped below the top wild plant foods.

Mabry (2005) hypothesized that because of the significant decreases in energy returns resulting from processing, it seems likely that only small portions of early maize yields were ground into flour. If, instead, early maize was mostly prepared for consumption by roasting the green ears (as was done with historical maize varieties above 6,000 feet elevation in northern New Mexico; Snow 1991) and popping and parching the mature kernels (as evident from parching trays preserved in dry caves), then the "pre-processing" energy return rates are the relevant estimates.

Minimal processing in these ways would explain the very high ubiquities of maize remains at early agricultural sites in the region (75–100 percent of flotation samples), usually in the form of carbonized ears and kernels, and the relatively inefficient designs of metates at these sites (cf. Adams 1999). The abundance of chewed maize stalks in preceramic levels of caves in northern Chihuahua and Sonora (Lister 1958), presumably for their sugar content (cf. Iltis 2000:36 and quoted in Crosswhite 1982; Smalley and Blake 2003), may also be explained by a minimal processing strategy of maize use during this period.

This also provides a behavioral ecology explanation for the spread of maize agriculture in southwestern North America. Based on the energy optimization principle of the diet-breadth model, maize was added to the diet because—under certain cultivation techniques and when only minimally processed—it yielded equal or higher energy returns than those of existing wild plant foods (Mabry 2005). Only with the later spread of more productive, floury varieties of maize and the development of more efficient metates did grinding begin to make sense in energy terms (see also Adams 1999).

THE ORDER OF NICHE FILLING ON
THE AGRICULTURAL FRONTIER

It seems clear that while all models are simple by definition, optimization models that emphasize just one characteristic of farming systems, such as risk or energy efficiency, are too simplistic. If the various early maize cultivation techniques are compared in terms of the multiple characteristics discussed here, we can see that some techniques are relatively more optimal than others in terms of each characteristic. These differences in risk, labor, productivity, and efficiency all would have influenced subsistence decisions.

However, this model does not assume consistently rational behavior. Cross-cultural data have shown that decisions by non-industrial farmers are often reactionary or opportunistic and are made with imperfect knowledge and short-term vision (Plattner 1981). On the other hand, ethnological data also show that the general subsistence goals of non-industrial farmers include a balance between minimization of risk and labor and maximization of yield and efficiency (Wilken 1987). Assuming that these were also the general goals of early southwestern farmers, the model predicts the order of development of agricultural niches on the landscape.

The model predicts that water-table farming, with its relatively low risks, low labor requirements, high yields, and high energy efficiency, would have tended to be practiced first in each region of what is now the southwestern United States and the northwestern borderlands of Mexico. Overbank flood farming, with somewhat higher risks but low labor requirements and potentially high yields and energy returns, also would have been practiced early in the sequence. Dry farming was marginal in terms of risks, yields, and energy returns and was successful only at higher elevations; this agricultural niche would have been developed only after the more optimal niches were filled. Especially in the desert lowlands, rain-fed farming was a truly marginal niche for the very desperate or for those who had other cultivation systems in operation and could afford this low-labor gamble.

Initially, early southwestern farmers probably leapfrogged from one area of constantly damp, regularly inundated alluvium to the next closest one until the settings most favorable for water-table farming and flood farming were fully occupied. Jane Hill (2001) presents this leapfrogging scenario for early maize farmers, but we argue that this process was begun by groups cultivating indigenous plants in these same settings prior to the arrival of maize.

Farmers then spread to other settings and developed different cultivation techniques, creating new, less optimal agricultural niches that required increasing labor inputs to obtain adequate yields and increasing reliance on foraging of wild foods to offset rising risks. The agricultural landscape was filled when the least optimal agricultural niches approached the risks, labor costs, and energy returns of pure hunting-and-gathering strategies.

In some regards, this scenario resembles Doolittle's (1980) model of agricultural expansion in which, over time, a growing agricultural population exploits decreasingly optimal lands with decreasingly efficient labor techniques. The model presented here adds the prediction that as more marginal lands came under cultivation, the farming systems would also have become increasingly risky.

During droughts the order of abandonment would have tended to be the opposite, but with water-table farming sometimes continuing uninterrupted. After a drought ended, the cycle of niche filling would repeat. This predicted sequence of niche filling and abandonment is the same as was observed during the twentieth century among peasant farmers in Oaxaca (Kirkby 1973) and on agricultural frontiers in West Africa (Stone 1986), except that rain-fed farming was also a viable type in these subtropical regions. Niche-filling sequences that began with water-table farming are also inferred for Formative-period agricultural development in the Valley of Oaxaca (Flannery et al. 1967) and the Basin of Mexico (Flannery et al. 1967; Neiderberger 1979).

The model first presented by Mabry (2005), and expanded here, also predicts that farming groups would shift between cultivation techniques, adjust their relative emphases on agriculture and foraging, and even revert completely to hunting and gathering as environmental conditions, population densities, and competition for agricultural resources altered the relative costs and benefits of different niches.

CULTURAL PROCESSES ON THE AGRICULTURAL FRONTIER

Recent excavations by Mabry (2006a) in the Santa Cruz floodplain near downtown Tucson have uncovered information relevant to understanding the processes involved in the spread of maize to the Desert Borderlands of the United States and Mexico. In this location Mabry found maize radiocarbon dated to about 3700 B.P. (uncalibrated, or ca. 2100 B.C. calibrated). This maize was recovered from a pithouse settlement, in association with pottery (!) and a southwestern Middle Archaic dart point type called Armijo. Research has turned up other sites across the Southwest with apparent or possible associations of maize with this indigenous point type.

The implications are clear and significant: the association in Tucson, and possible associations elsewhere, of the earliest maize with an indigenous southwestern Archaic dart point type whose genealogy extends back to the Middle Holocene (its shape evolved somewhat over time, and earlier variants are called San Jose; see Mabry, Carpenter, and Sanchez, Chapter 9) mean that maize diffused among local hunter-gatherer groups—some of which were probably already cultivators of indigenous plants—prior to any migration from the south. Of course, this makes sense as the first stage on an agricultural frontier, and it also makes sense that both diffusion and migration processes were at work on this frontier (migration versus diffusion is a false contrast).

This does not mean there was not a Proto-Uto-Aztecan migration (or more than one) from the south or that maize was not cultivated in the Proto-Uto-Aztecan community, as Hill (2001) concludes from the linguistic evidence. But it may support the idea that the Uto-Aztecan migration occurred at the end of the Middle Holocene Altithermal *before* maize arrived in this region, concurrent with movements of remnants of earlier indigenous populations back into the Southwest's desert lowlands from Altithermal refugia on the Colorado Plateau and the eastern Great Basin. (Unlike the Arizona-Sonora lowlands, the archaeological records of these areas show continuous development through the Middle Holocene Altithermal.)

This scenario of an earlier arrival of Proto-Uto-Aztecans in the Southwest is supported by archaeological evidence of their arrival in the southwestern Great Basin and the southern California coast between 5000 and 4000 B.P. (see references in Mabry, Carpenter, and Sanchez, Chapter 9). Although it probably represents technological diffusion across linguistic and cultural boundaries, the distribution of the contracting stem Gypsum point and its adhesive-based hafting technique between 5000 and 4000 B.P. indicates the development of a large continuum of interaction extending from central Mexico to the Great Basin and from the southern California coast to the Colorado Plateau (Chapter 9). During this same interval, some foraging groups would have begun intensively harvesting and then manipulating indigenous plants in their natural habitats.

Between about 4000 and 3500 B.P., maize would have spread like wildfire across an already established continuum of local foraging groups with overlapping territories and regular contacts with each other through networks for mating, trading, and sharing information about resources and new hunting technologies. Some of these groups were probably already skilled at plant husbandry; significantly, during the growing season they were also occupying the most optimal niches for farming.

The San Pedro phase in the Desert Borderlands, with its Formative Mesoamerican traits such as bell-shaped pits, and the subsequent arrival of other Mesoamerican cultigens may represent later migrations, diffusions, or both. In our opinion, immigrations of farmers into the region are less likely because the most optimal agricultural niches would have already been filled.

In summary, the arrival of tropical cultigens in the desert lowlands of the Arizona-Sonora borderlands may fit better with current archaeological evidence in terms of this sequence:

ca. 5000 B.P.	Migrations from both north and south at the end of the Altithermal; indigenous development of plant husbandry in optimal niches
ca. 4000 B.P.	Diffusion of maize from the south; adoption by local forager-farmers; expansion into new agricultural niches
ca. 3000–2500 B.P.	Diffusions of pepo squash, common bean, bottle gourd, cotton (?) from the south; adoption by local farmer-foragers; possible immigrations from the south; localized agricultural intensification; localized increases in agricultural dependence

The social processes involved on the early agricultural frontier in the U.S.-Mexico borderlands and the rest of southwestern North America should be reconceptualized as including both diffusions and migrations and both hunter-gatherers with their own knowledge of native plant husbandry and farmers introducing domesticated cultigens into new environmental settings. We also argue that the addition of maize to indigenous subsistence strategies, the development of new farming systems, the intensification of agriculture through increased labor, and the sequence of niche filling and abandonment on the agricultural landscape of the Southwest can each be predicted on the basis of differences in risk, labor, productivity, and energy efficiency—all of which influenced subsistence choices.

THE DEMOGRAPHIC DIMENSION OF THE AGRICULTURAL FRONTIER

Population density changes would have been an additional variable affecting the rates of niche filling and abandonment. In particular, population growth played an important role during transitions to agriculture. In traditional societies around the world, farmers have higher average fertility than hunter-gatherers (Bentley, Jasienka, and Goldberg 1993; Sellen and Mace 1997), and sudden and exponential increases in birth rates probably accompanied transitions to agriculture in each region when they occurred. In Europe this "Neolithic demographic transition" is reflected in the sudden increase in immature (child and young adult) skeletons in Neolithic burial populations, indicating significantly higher birth rates than in Mesolithic populations (Bocquet-Appel 2002). In hunter-gatherer and agriculturalist skeletal samples from North America, this transition is reflected in a shift from forager mortality curves that rise rapidly with increasing age to farmer mortality curves that are much flatter (Buikstra and Konigsberg 1985).

Some researchers attribute this higher fertility among farmers to shorter birth spacing as a result of earlier weaning made possible by a combination of (1) a diet high in starches and dairy products; (2) improved ceramic vessels and cooking techniques that made available soft, easily digestible foods; and (3) a strong division of labor between genders (Bocquet-Appel 2002; Buikstra, Konigsberg, and Bullington 1986; Sellen 2001). However, others point to the effects on fertility of consuming domesticated grains, all of which are high-glycemic carbohydrates that trigger insulin production, which in turn promotes fat storage. After women of childbearing age cross a certain threshold of body fat, a complex series of hormonal responses occurs—including increased estrogen production—leading to increased ovulation and a higher birth rate (Kakos 2003).

In this positive-feedback situation, Formative-Neolithic populations that quickly adopted grain-centered diets experienced immediate and rapid population growth that accelerated the rates of niche filling on the agricultural landscape. However, after this initial stage of demographic change lasting perhaps 500–1,000 years, the detrimental effects of agricultural diets on health, combined with increased transmission of pathogens among dense, sedentary populations (Armelagos, Goodman, and Jacobs 1991; Cohen and Armelagos 1984; Larsen 1995), often led to increases in mortality that returned populations to an equilibrium or a slower growth rate (Bocquet-Appel 2002).

These effects on fertility and mortality would have been less dramatic in populations that gradually incorporated grains into their diets and initially had relatively small aggregations, as appears to have occurred in the Southwest. But sooner or later, even slowly growing populations would have neared niche carrying capacities. If these capacities were not, or could not be, increased through labor intensification (as Boserup 1965 predicted) or the populations did not or could not expand into more marginal lands (as Doolittle 1980 predicted), they became more vulnerable to environmental stresses such as droughts and floods. This would have sometimes resulted in short-term increases in mortality or temporary abandonment of those niches. Clearly, such fluctuations in population density must have played an important role in how the Southwest's agricultural landscape initially filled and subsequently evolved.

REFERENCES CITED

Ackerly, Neal W.
    1988   False Causality in the Hohokam Collapse. *Kiva* 55(4):305–319.

Adams, Jenny L.
    1999   Refocusing the Role of Food-Grinding Tools as Correlates for Subsistence Strategies in the U.S. Southwest. *American Antiquity* 64(3):475–498.

Adams, Karen R., and Kenneth L. Peterson
    1999   Environment. In *Colorado Prehistory: A Context for the Southern Colorado River Basin*, ed. W. D. Lipe, M. D. Varien, and R. H. Wilhusen, 14–50. Colorado Council of Professional Archaeologists, Denver.

Arbolino, Risa D.
    2001   *Agricultural Strategies and Labor Organization: An Ethnohistoric Approach to the Study of Prehistoric Farming Systems in the Taos Area of Northern New Mexico.* Unpublished Ph.D. dissertation, Department of Anthropology, Southern Methodist University, Dallas.

Armelagos, George J., Alan H. Goodman, and Kenneth H. Jacobs
    1991   The Origins of Agriculture: Population Growth during a Period of Declining Health. *Population and Environment* 13(1):9–22.

Barlow, K. Renee
    2002   Predicting Maize Agriculture among the Fremont: An Economic Comparison of Farming and Foraging in the American Southwest. *American Antiquity* 67(1):65–88.

Bentley, G. R., G. Jasienka, and T. Goldberg
    1993   Is the Fertility of Agriculturalists Higher Than That of Nonagriculturalists? *Current Anthropology* 34:778–785.

Bocquet-Appel, Jean-Pierre
    2002   Paleoanthropological Traces of a Neolithic Demographic Transition. *Current Anthropology* 43(4):637–650.

Bohrer, Vorsila L.
    1992   New Life from Ashes II. The Tale of Burnt Brush. *Desert Plants* 10(3):122–125.

Boserup, Ester
1965 *The Conditions of Agricultural Growth: The Economics of Agrarian Change under Population Pressure.* Aldine, New York.

Buikstra, J. E., and L. W. Konigsberg
1985 Paleodemography: Critiques and Controversies. *American Anthropologist* 87:316-333.

Buikstra, J. E., L. W. Konigsberg, and J. Bullington
1986 Fertility and the Development of Agriculture in the Prehistoric Midwest. *American Antiquity* 51:528-546.

Cohen, Mark N., and George J. Armelagos (editors)
1984 *Paleopathology at the Origins of Agriculture.* Academic, New York.

Cosgrove, C. B.
1947 *Caves of the Upper Gila and Hueco Areas in New Mexico and Texas.* Papers of the Peabody Museum of American Archaeology and Ethnology 24(2). Harvard University, Cambridge, Mass.

Crosswhite, Frank C.
1982 Corn (*Zea mays*) in Relation to Wild Relatives. *Desert Plants* 3:193-202.

Damp, Jonathan E., James W. Kendrick, Donovan Quam, Jeffery Waseta, and Jerome Zunie
2000 *Households and Farms in Early Zuni Prehistory: Settlement, Subsistence, and the Archaeology of Y Unit Draw, Archaeological Investigations at Eighteen Sites along New Mexico State Highway 602.* Zuni Cultural Resource Enterprise Report 593. Pueblo of Zuni, N.M.

Diehl, Michael W.
1997 Rational Behavior, the Adoption of Agriculture, and the Organization of Subsistence during the Late Archaic Period in the Greater Tucson Basin. In *Rediscovering Darwin: Evolutionary Theory and Archaeological Explanation,* ed. C. Michael Barton and Geoffrey A. Clark, 251-265. Archaeological Papers of the American Anthropological Association 7. American Anthropological Association, Arlington, Va.

Dobyns, Henry F.
1981 *From Fire to Flood: Historic Human Destruction of Sonoran Desert Riverine Oases.* Ballena Press Anthropological Papers 20. Ballena, Socorro, N.M.

Doolittle, William E.
1980 Aboriginal Agricultural Development in the Valley of Sonora, Mexico. *Geographical Review* 70(3):328-342.
2000 *Cultivated Landscapes of Native North America.* Oxford University Press, Oxford.

Ezzo, Joseph A., and William L. Deaver
1998 *Watering the Desert: Late Archaic Farming at the Costello-King Site.* Technical Series 68. Statistical Research, Tucson.

Flannery, Kent V., Anne V.T. Kirkby, Michael J. Kirkby, and Aubrey W. Williams Jr.
1967 Farming Systems and Political Growth in Ancient Oaxaca. *Science* 158(3800):445-454.

Guernsey, Samuel J., and Alfred V. Kidder
　1921　Basket-Maker Caves of Northeastern Arizona. Papers of the Peabody Museum of American Archaeology and Ethnology 12, no. 1, Cambridge, Mass.

Hill, Jane H.
　2001　Proto-Uto-Aztecan: A Community of Cultivators in Central Mexico? *American Anthropologist* 103(4):913–934.

Hough, Walter
　1914　*Culture of the Ancient Pueblos of the Upper Gila River Region, New Mexico and Arizona.* United States National Museum Bulletin 87. U.S. Government Printing Office, Washington, D.C.

Huckell, Bruce B.
　1990　*Late Preceramic Farmer-Foragers in Southeastern Arizona: A Cultural and Ecological Consideration of the Spread of Agriculture into the Arid Southwestern United States.* Unpublished Ph.D. dissertation. Arid Lands Resource Sciences, University of Arizona, Tucson.

Huckleberry, Gary
　1992　Soil Evidence of Hohokam Irrigation in the Salt River Valley, Arizona. *Kiva* 57(3): 237–249.

Iltis, Hugh H.
　2000　Homeotic Sexual Translocations and the Origin of Maize (*Zea mays*, Poaceae): A New Look at an Old Problem. *Economic Botany* 54(1):7–42.

Kakos, Peter J.
　2003　Living in the Zone: Basketmaker Food Packages, Hormonal Responses, and the Effects on Population Growth. In *Anasazi Archaeology at the Millennium: Proceedings of the Sixth Occasional Anasazi Symposium*, ed. Paul F. Reed, 35–47. Center for Desert Archaeology, Tucson.

Kirkby, Anne V.T.
　1973　*The Use of Land and Water Resources in the Past and Present Valley of Oaxaca, Mexico.* Memoirs of the Museum of Anthropology, University of Michigan 5, Ann Arbor.

Larsen, Clark S.
　1995　Biological Changes in Human Populations with Agriculture. *Annual Review of Anthropology* 24:185–213.

Lister, Robert H.
　1958　*Archaeological Excavations in the Northern Sierra Madre Occidental, Chihuahua and Sonora, Mexico.* University of Colorado Studies, Series in Anthropology 7. University of Colorado Press, Boulder.

Logan, Michael H., and William T. Sanders
　1976　The Model. In *The Valley of Mexico: Studies in Pre-Hispanic Ecology and Society*, ed. Eric R. Wolf, 31–58. School of American Research Advanced Seminar Series. University of New Mexico Press, Albuquerque.

Mabry, Jonathan B.
　2005　Diversity in Early Southwestern Farming Systems and Optimization Models of Transitions to Agriculture. In *Subsistence and Resource Use Strategies in Early Agri-*

cultural Communities in Southern Arizona, ed. Michael W. Diehl, 113–152. Anthropological Papers 34. Center for Desert Archaeology, Tucson.

2006a Radiocarbon Dating of Early Occupations. In *Rio Nuevo Archaeology Program, 2000-2003: Investigations at the San Agustin Mission and Mission Gardens, Tucson Presidio, Tucson Pressed Brick Company, and Clearwater Site*, ed. J. Homer Thiel and Jonathan B. Mabry. Pp. 19.1–19.5. Technical Report 2004-11. Center for Desert Archaeology, Tucson.

Mabry, Jonathan B. (editor)
2006b *Las Capas: Early Irrigation and Sedentism in a Southwestern Floodplain*. Anthropological Papers 28. Center for Desert Archaeology, Tucson (draft).

Martin, Paul S., John B. Rinaldo, Elaine Bluhm, Hugh C. Cutler, and Roger Grange Jr.
1952 *Mogollon Cultural Continuity and Change: The Stratigraphic Analysis of Tularosa and Cordova Caves*. Fieldiana: Anthropology 40. Field Museum of Natural History, Chicago.

Minnis, Paul E.
1992 Earliest Plant Cultivation in the Desert Borderlands of North America. In *The Origins of Agriculture, an International Perspective*, ed. C. W. Cowan and P. J. Watson, 121–141. Smithsonian University Press, Washington, D.C.

Neiderberger, Christine
1979 Early Sedentary Economy in the Basin of Mexico. *Science* 203(4376):131–142.

Nusbaum, Jesse L.
1922 *A Basket-Maker Cave in Kane County, Utah*. Indian Notes and Monographs 29. Museum of the American Indian, Heye Foundation, New York.

Plattner, Stuart
1981 Food for Thought in Agricultural Decision Making. *Reviews in Anthropology* 8(4): 393–408.

Sellen, D. W.
2001 Relationship between Fertility, Mortality, and Subsistence: Results of Recent Phylogenetic Analyses. In *Humanity from African Naissance to Coming Millennia*, ed. P. V. Tobiaas, M. A. Rath, J. Moggi-Cecchi, and G. A. Doyle, 51–64. University of Florence Press, Florence, Italy.

Sellen, D. W., and R. Mace
1997 Fertility and Mode of Subsistence: A Phylogenetic Analysis. *Current Anthropology* 38:878–889.

Smalley, John, and Michael Blake
2003 Sweet Beginnings: Stalk Sugar and the Domestication of Maize. *Current Anthropology* 44(5):675–703.

Snow, David H.
1991 Upland Prehistoric Maize Agriculture in the Eastern Rio Grande and Its Peripheries. In *Farmers, Hunters, and Colonists: Interaction between the Southwest and the Southern Plains*, ed. K. A. Spielman, 71–88. University of Arizona Press, Tucson.

Stone, Glen D.
1986 The Cultural Ecology of Frontier Settlement. Paper presented at the Annual Meeting of the Society for American Archaeology, New Orleans, La.

Turnbow, Christopher A. (editor)
   2000   *A Highway through Time: Archaeological Investigations along NM 90.* TRC Technical Report 2000-3, Albuquerque.

Wilken, Gene C.
   1987   *Good Farmers: Traditional Agricultural Resource Management in Mexico and Central America.* University of California Press, Berkeley.

5

EARLY AGRICULTURE ON THE SOUTHEASTERN PERIPHERY OF THE COLORADO PLATEAU

Diversity in Tactics

Bradley J. Vierra

The recent discovery of Late Archaic irrigation features in the Zuni area has raised questions about current arguments that attempt to explain the dispersal of maize across the Colorado Plateau (Damp, Hall, and Smith 2002). These arguments include the northward expansion of farming communities (Berry 1982, 1985; Elyea 1999) versus the integration of maize into local foraging economies (Irwin-Williams 1973; Minnis 1992; Vierra 1994a, 1996; Wills 1988). Others disagree as to whether cultivation initially occurred in lowland (Matson 1991) versus upland settings (Ford 1985; Vierra and Foxx 2002). Finally, some researchers suggest that economies dependent on maize agriculture were present in the region during the first millennium B.C. (Damp, Hall, and Smith 2002), and others believe it did not arrive until the sixth or seventh century A.D. (Vierra 1993a, 1996).

Recent excavations of numerous Late Archaic habitation sites in the southeastern periphery of the Colorado Plateau, including the San Juan Basin and the northern Rio Grande Valley, are providing an emerging picture of the rise of early agriculture from circa 1000 B.C. to A.D. 500. This database will be used to evaluate the contrasting perspectives that attempt to explain the dispersal of maize across the region. I suggest that maize was differentially integrated into local foraging economies across the region and that early maize cultivation occurred in a variety of lowland and upland settings. Indeed, the initial timing and period leading to the dependence on this cultigen could be quite variable.

METHODS

The excavation of these Late Archaic habitation sites has yielded a wealth of archaeobotanical data. This study will focus on these flotation samples and the ubiquity of maize across the study area. Data were also collected on the ubiquity of *cucurbita* and beans, as well as wild species such as cheno-ams, Indian ricegrass, and dropseed grasses, also common in Late Archaic sites. However, none of the samples contained any evidence of beans, and *cucurbita* was identified at only three sites.

The sample consists of 53 Late Archaic habitation sites that contain structures and extramural features. These sites are divided into three areas: the western San Juan Basin (n=4), the northern San Juan Basin (n=23), and the northern Rio Grande Valley (n=26) (Figure 5.1). Data were collected on a total of 399 flotation samples, with 50 percent from the northern San Juan Basin, 30 percent from the northern Rio Grande Valley, and 20 percent from the western San Juan Basin sites. Overall, 101 structures have been excavated, with 61 percent of the flotation samples retrieved from interior versus exterior contexts.

To study the pattern of long-term change, the sample has been divided into three periods: Period 1 (ca. 1000–500 B.C.), Period 2 (ca. 500–1 B.C.), and Period 3 (ca. A.D. 1–500). This temporal framework was used to avoid any reference to local culture-historical chronologies. Of the 399 flotation samples, about half (49%) were derived from Period 2 contexts, with 26 percent from Period 1 and 25 percent from Period 3.

I begin by discussing the ubiquity of maize and other plant species by area and time period. I then contrast these data with information about Late Archaic site structure, including habitation structures and internal features. Finally, I contrast these Late Archaic maize ubiquity data with information from Ceramic-period sites in each area. Together, the data provide a current perspective on the timing of and dependence on maize agriculture across the three areas.

MAIZE UBIQUITY

Plant species ubiquity indices are a rough indirect measure of a plant's contribution to the diet. Although quantitative data as parts per liter may represent a more accurate measure of plant abundance, these data are not always presented in reports. Plant collection, processing, and storage techniques can all affect their presence in the archaeological record. Luckily, charred cupules and kernels are often present when maize is used because the cobs were commonly burned for fuel. Maize ubiquity varies by time, being low during Period 1 (18%; n=105) and increasing during Period 2 (38%; n=196) and Period 3 (32%; n=98). This represents the total sample

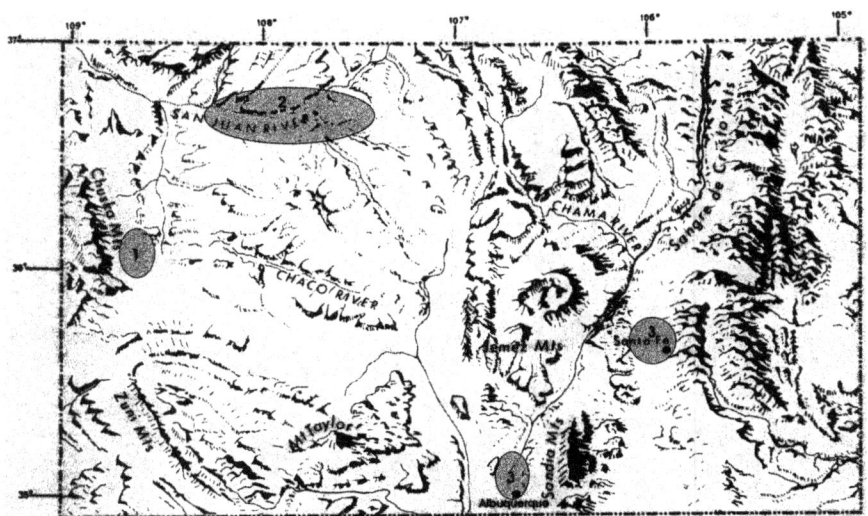

Figure 5.1. Regional study areas: western San Juan Basin (1), northern San Juan Basin (2), and northern Rio Grande Valley (3). Adapted from Williams and McAllister (1979).

size (n) and the percentage (%) of samples containing maize. The question is, does this pattern vary by area?

The Western San Juan Basin

Pipeline excavations in the western San Juan Basin provided some of the first evidence of early agriculture in the region. A single Period 1 structure (LA 6444) contains the earliest date for maize in the area, with a calibrated intercept of 788 B.C. Both flotation samples from this structure yielded maize (Freuden 1998). Three Period 2 sites represent a complementary settlement system for the area. These are site 423-158, a possible winter habitation site; LA 6444, which contains a series of structures presumably situated near agricultural fields; and LA 6448, a field cache site with numerous large storage pits (Freuden 1998; Hammet 1994a; Kearns, Kugler, and Stirniman 1998; Redd, Wellman, and Burgett 1994). Because the flotation samples from the oldest dated structure at 423-158 had not been previously analyzed, I asked Pamela McBride to study these samples for the current research project.

Figure 5.2 illustrates the ubiquity of plant species for these Period 2 sites. Of the sixty-nine flotation samples, 90 percent contained cheno-ams, 78 percent maize, 30 percent Indian ricegrass, 10 percent *cucurbita*, and none contained any dropseed. A variety of maize parts, including kernel, cupule, glume, and cob fragments, is present at the two sites located near agricultural fields. *Cucurbita* rind fragments were also recovered from the field cache site. Spring snowmelt and summer rains

73

Bradley J. Vierra

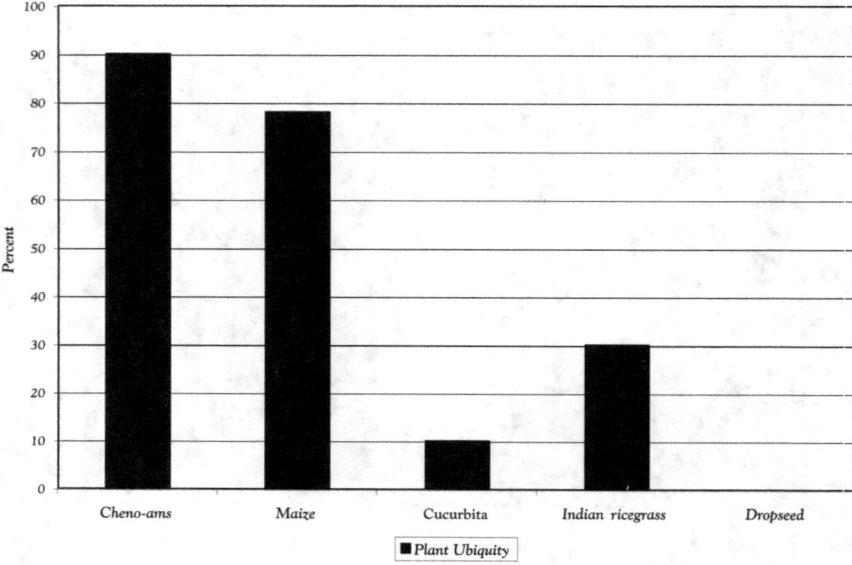

Figure 5.2. Period 2 plant ubiquity in the western San Juan Basin.

from the slopes of the Chuska Mountains would have provided an excellent source of moisture for floodwater and playa farming. The field cache site is situated near a playa that would have acted as a catch basin for this water. Thirty-two large storage pits are present on the site, some of which contained the remains of twelve individuals. This presumably reflects the repeated use of the site and territorial marking of the area for agricultural use. Marine shell artifacts recovered from the burials reflect long-distance exchange relationships.

Only a single Period 3 site has been excavated in the area (Burgett, Neff, and Sale 1994; Hammet 1994b). One of three samples taken from the structure contained maize and cheno-ams. Ceramics were also found on the floor. However, unpublished notes on file at Eastern New Mexico University indicate that the Anasazi Origins Project also excavated a Period 3 site near Grants with multiple structures, storage pits, maize, and a burial. I conducted an isotopic analysis of these human remains that indicates a diet heavy in C4 plants, with a carbon isotope value of -10. This corresponds to the large amount of cheno-ams and maize present in the western San Juan Basin Late Archaic samples.

The Northern San Juan Basin

Late Archaic habitation sites situated in the northern San Juan Basin are primarily distributed in upland areas around Farmington and the Navajo Reservoir

Early Agriculture on the Southeastern Periphery of the Colorado Plateau

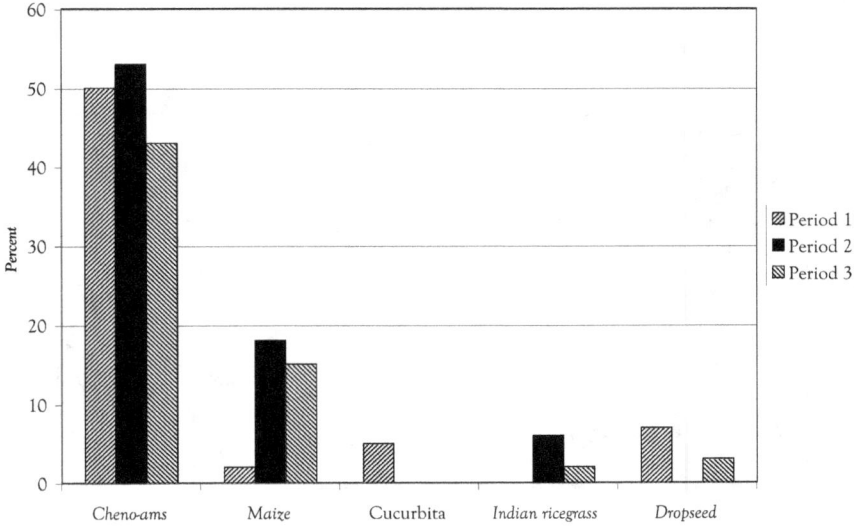

Figure 5.3. Periods 1–3 plant ubiquity in the northern San Juan Basin.

(Arms 1999; Brown 1991; Dean 1993; Elyea and Hogan 1993; Henderson 1983; Honeycutt and Fetterman 1994; Horn, Fetterman, and Honeycutt 2003; Hovezak and Sesler 2002a, 2002b). This mesa country is dissected with shallow canyons that drain into the Animas and San Juan rivers. The area has recently witnessed a marked increase in excavation work and therefore has the largest sample of sites from all three periods. The earliest directly dated maize is from LA 70667, which yielded a date of 505 B.C. However, maize is also associated with a charcoal date of 1140 B.C. from an earlier component at the same site and maize pollen with a charcoal date of 1350 B.C. from an associated mano and floor surface at LA 81172.

Figure 5.3 illustrates the ubiquity of plant species by time period. Cheno-ams show a consistent presence of about 50 percent during all three periods (50%, 53%, and 43%, respectively). In contrast, maize is very low for Period 1 (2%) and increases during Periods 2 (18%) and 3 (15%). Early maize agriculture could have been practiced in well-watered settings such as the heads of side canyons that had both spring and summer runoff from the mesa tops.

Cucurbita is present in only two samples from a Period 1 structure (LA 81172; Honeycutt and Fetterman 1994). Because this is one of the earliest documented examples of *cucurbita* in the region, I asked Pamela McBride and Mollie Toll to review the seed and two rind fragments. They concluded that the rind fragments are too small and the seed too eroded to positively identify them as domesticated squash. In addition, a squash seed has been directly dated to 950 B.C. from a rockshelter and maize to 770 B.C. from a small field cache site near Chaco Canyon. This maize

75

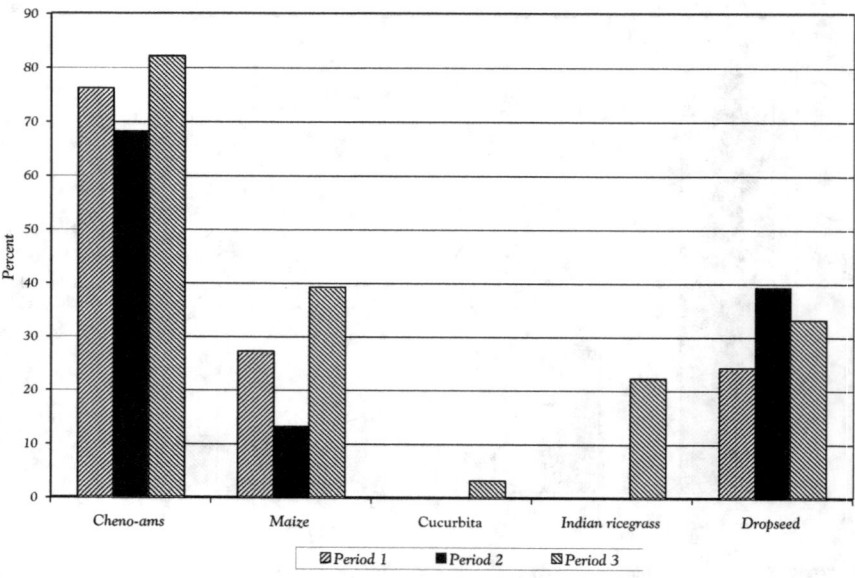

Figure 5.4. Periods 1–3 plant ubiquity in the northern Rio Grande Valley.

sample was not corrected for isotopic fractionation, so a corrected date might be closer to 970 B.C. (Simmons 1986).

The presence of grass seeds is low in all samples, with Indian ricegrass present in Periods 2 and 3 (6% and 2%, respectively) and dropseed in Periods 1 and 3 (7% and 2%, respectively). This, of course, contrasts with campsites located within the lowland areas of the basin where grass seeds dominate the samples and presumably reflect summer occupations (Toll and Cully 1994).

The Northern Rio Grande Valley

Late Archaic habitation sites in the northern Rio Grande Valley are primarily located in the Albuquerque area near Rio Rancho and Zia Pueblo and in the Santa Fe area (Acklen 1995; Bargman, Gerow, and Elyea 1999; Brandi and Dilley 1998; Elyea and Sheppard 1999; Gerow and Bargman 1999; Kennedy 1998; Lakatos, Post, and Murrell 2001; Lent 1991; Post 1996, 2000; Schmader 1994a, 2001; Seymour, Hokanson, and Cunningham 1997; Walth 1999). Most of the Albuquerque area sites represent Period 1 and 2 occupations, versus mostly Period 3 occupations in the Santa Fe area. Figure 5.4 illustrates that the percentage of cheno-ams is very high for all three periods (68–82%), with dropseed also ubiquitous for these periods (24–39%). In contrast, Indian ricegrass (22%) and *cucurbita* (3%) are only present in the Period 3 samples, thereby indicating greater plant diversity during this later period. Maize ranges from 13 to 39 percent for Periods 1–3; however, a review of early maize sites in the area by Richard Ford and me indicates that some of the Period 1 specimens are not maize (e.g., at LA 107577 [Seymour, Hokanson, and Cunningham 1997] and Ojala Cave [Foxx 1982]). Indeed, the carbon isotope value of the dated sample from LA 107577 is -24.5, indicating that it is a C3 and not a C4 plant. Therefore, the presence of maize is actually somewhat lower in Period 1.

The early charcoal dates of 1400–1200 B.C. for maize at LA 110946 stand out in marked contrast to the other dated maize sites in the Rio Grande Valley (e.g., A.D. 200 at the Chama Alcove site; Vierra 1998). However, Richard Ford and I recently dated two maize specimens from Jemez Cave to circa 1260 B.C., thereby supporting the early dates at LA 110946. The high ubiquity of maize at LA 110946 compares with that observed at the sites in the western San Juan Basin, where floodwater and playa farming was presumably practiced. This contrasts with the situation at Jemez Cave, where Richard Ford (1985) suggests that maize was planted in the mud flats adjacent to the Soda Dam lake in a piñon-juniper setting. This indicates that early maize cultivation was occurring in both lowland and upland settings at the same time. Finally, LA 110946 also contains an older component that dates to circa 1700–1500 B.C. This component lacks maize but contains cheno-ams, dropseed, and some Indian ricegrass, indicating that the site was already occupied during the summer growing season prior to the use of maize.

The presence of maize during Periods 1 and 3 is biased toward two sites. If we remove these sites, most of the remaining samples do not contain maize. The majority of the remaining Period 3 samples are from habitation sites in the Santa Fe area. Indeed, Matthew Schmader (1994a) excavated two habitation sites near Santa Fe that were similar to other Late Archaic structures, except that they were radiocarbon dated to ca. A.D. 870 and 895. The lack of maize from habitation sites and the late dates for maize in this area have prompted Schmader, Stephen Post, and me to suggest that maize played a minor subsistence role in this northern area of the Rio Grande Valley until much later (Schmader 1994a; Post 2002; Vierra 1998).

SITE STRUCTURE

A review of these Late Archaic habitation structures indicates that they are often fairly similar. That is, they are shallow, oval-shaped depressions about 3 to 4 m in diameter. The fill is often charcoal-stained soil that represents the burned remains of the superstructure. There is a hearth and possibly a few other features on an unprepared floor encircled with postholes, reflecting a brush wickiup-like structure. Additional features may be present outside the dwelling, including a hearth, a roasting pit with fire-cracked rock, or some other generalized pit features. Most often, one to three contemporaneous structures are present on a site.

The previous discussion of maize ubiquity indicates a general pattern of a low reliance on agriculture during Period 1, followed by an increased reliance during

Periods 2 and 3. However, this appears to vary by area and environmental setting. How does Late Archaic site structure compare with these ubiquity data?

Mean structure size is similar for Periods 1 and 2 (3.9 m, sd=1.3; 3.5 m, sd=1.1) but increases somewhat during Period 3 (4.3 m, sd=1.5). The latter standard deviation is slightly larger because of a wider range of sizes, including seven Period 3 structures that have diameters of about 7 m. With respect to internal features, hearths are consistently present during all three periods, but formal collared hearths appear for the first time during the later part of Period 3. More notable is an increase in the number of internal versus external features through time, from Period 1 (49%, n=51) to Period 2 (60%, n=118) and Period 3 (77%, n=75). In addition, the number of internal storage pits greater than about 50 cm in depth also increased markedly from Period 1 (0%, n=25) to Period 2 (11%, n=43) to Period 3 (33%, n=35). The botanical evidence indicates that maize, cheno-ams, and grass seeds were all stored in these pits.

Substantial roof support systems also appear during Period 3. During Period 1 the evidence solely indicates simple brush structures with postholes along the perimeter, with only a single structure (2%) during Period 2 having a four-post support system. By Period 3, 34 percent (n=12) of the structures have four to six main roof supports.

In summary, the site structure data appear to reflect an increase in the length of site occupation(s), storage, and presumably a reliance on agriculture during Period 3. In addition, significant changes in technology were also occurring during the later part of Period 3 (ca. A.D. 400–500), including the addition of ceramics and the bow and arrow. The former marks significant changes in food preparation and storage and the latter a higher hunting return rate for a wider range of medium and small game. Nonetheless, much of this changing Period 3 site structure pattern is limited to the Navajo Reservoir area, with only a single site containing this evidence in the Northern Rio Grande.

LONG-TERM AGRICULTURAL DEPENDENCE

What about the long-term pattern of increasing agricultural dependence from Late Archaic- through Ceramic-period times? McBride's (1994:456–457) study of flotation samples from Late Archaic and Pueblo sites in the San Juan Basin and Upper Puerco area for the ENRON pipeline project indicates that about 40 percent of the Late Archaic features contain maize versus over 80 percent of the Pueblo I features dating to circa A.D. 700–900. Carolyn Brandt's (2002) analysis of flotation samples from the Fruitland Project also identified a marked increase in the ubiquity of maize from Late Archaic to Pueblo I contexts. That is, 11 percent of the Period 1 and 2 (Archaic; n=16) and 16 percent of the Period 3 (Basketmaker; n=9) samples contain maize, versus 84 percent of samples from the sites dating to circa A.D. 700–900 (Pueblo I; n=43) (Figure 5.5; left). Mollie Toll's (1993) study of sites dating to circa A.D. 500–900 in Chaco Canyon indicates a slightly lower maize ubiquity of 53

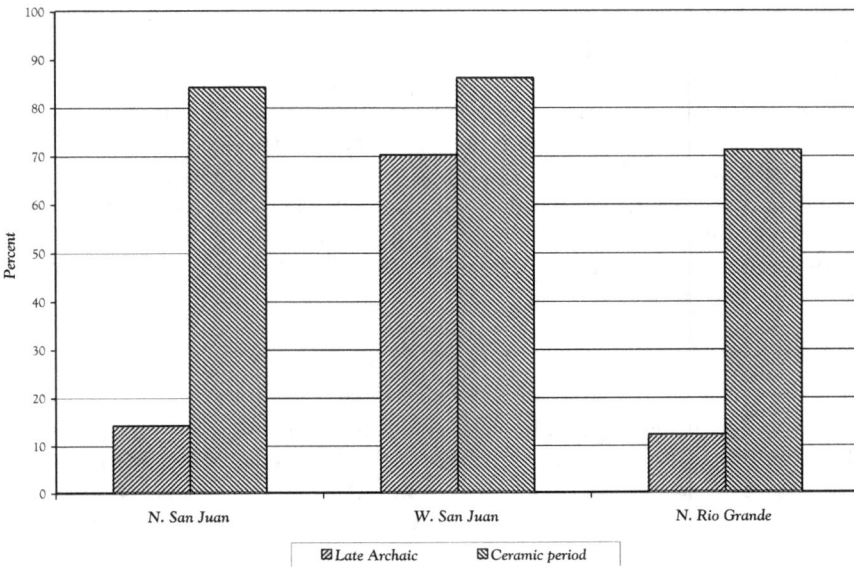

Figure 5.5. Maize ubiquity by time period and region.

percent. As Wirt (Chip) Wills and Thomas Windes (1989) have argued, the large habitation site of Shabik'eschee Village, dating to circa A.D. 500-700, probably represents episodic site aggregation during periods of increased agricultural and piñon crop productivity that provided a surplus of stored foods.

These data appear to contrast with studies of habitation sites dating to circa A.D. 450-700 along the Chuska slope, which continue to show a marked emphasis on maize cultivation (Reed 2000). For example, Timothy Kearns and colleagues' (2000) study of sites for the El Paso Natural Gas pipeline project identified pithouse villages with maize ubiquity of 78-94 percent. This compares with the Period 2 figure of 70 percent for the two habitation sites (Figure 5.5; center).

Finally, in the Albuquerque area, Schmader points out that the first pit structures with early Puebloan attributes—that is, deep, functionally varied structures with four-post roof supports, collared hearths, and southeast-facing ventilators—do not appear until about A.D. 650 (Schmader 1994b:460). This architectural form changed little over the next 250 years (Schmader 1994b:461). Maize ubiquity at the River's Edge sites, dating to circa A.D. 650-900, is 71 percent (n=114; Brandt 1991a, 1991b), a marked increase over most Late Archaic sites (Figure 5.5; right).

In summary, except for the western San Juan Basin where floodwater and playa farming continued in importance, there appears to be a marked increase in the presence of maize by circa A.D. 600-900. Maize ubiquity increases over cheno-ams, with squash and beans present in all of the areas by this time period. In addition, long-term changes in the ground stone and chipped-stone assemblages are generally similar to the maize ubiquity pattern found in these areas (Hovezak and Sesler 2002c; Torres 2000; Vierra 1993a, 1993b, 1994b). It should also be pointed out that not all cobs are equal. That is, cob size does increase through time (Adams 1994). Finally, pit-structure architecture is generally believed to represent a higher degree of seasonal mobility than standing-wall architecture (Gilman 1983, 1987). Questions remain as to whether these pithouse villages actually represent long-term occupation (Reed 2000) or multiple occupational episodes (Wills and Windes 1989; Gregory and Diehl 2002). I would also expect these residential patterns to vary across the region.

CONCLUSION

In conclusion, I suggest that the regional variability identified in this study is not the result of farmers moving into the area, as has been suggested by Michael Berry and Janette Elyea. In addition, Patrick Hogan's (1994) argument that the San Juan Basin was segregated by foragers to the west and farmers to the east during the Late Archaic is not supported. The evidence indicates a pattern of long-term changes in maize production and site complexity from circa 1000 B.C. to A.D. 500. More important, there appears to be regional variation in the timing of and dependence on maize agriculture, occurring earlier in the western San Juan Basin and later in other parts of the basin and the northern Rio Grande Valley. That is, Period 2 maize ubiquity is over 70 percent in the western basin, versus less than 20 percent in the other two areas.

Although R. G. Matson's (1991) contention that early agriculture on the Colorado Plateau occurred in floodwater settings is partially supported by these data, it appears that maize cultivation occurred in both lowland and upland contexts. On the other hand, the Colorado Plateau and adjacent northern Rio Grande Valley is a topographically and environmentally diverse place. Given Renee Barlow's (2002) recent arguments concerning the higher return rate of floodwater farming over collecting wild seeds, we should think about the implications of this research in respect to my study.

The diet-breadth model ranks various species based on a cost-benefit analysis of foraging return rates (Kelly 1995:78–90; MacArthur and Pianka 1966; Stephens and Krebs 1986:17–24). Large game is generally considered to have the greatest return, succulents and wild seeds the lowest. Floodplain and high water-table farming is also considered a low investment and high return strategy (Barlow 1997, 2002; Dering 1999; Mabry 2003; Simms 1987). Given the environmental diversity of the study area, I suggest that early agriculture also occurred in well-watered micro-niche settings that have lower return rates but are situated adjacent to piñon-juniper woodlands and fall plant resource areas. This would have reduced any seasonal scheduling conflicts and provided a backup strategy for natural resource shortfalls (Vierra and Foxx 2002; also see Minnis 1985). This was probably the case at Jemez Cave, where

Ford (1985) has determined that maize was consumed both green and ripe. Other potential locales for cultivation would include springs and areas with mesa-top runoff. In addition, hunting would also have been productive in these upland settings.

I would therefore expect greater maize cultivation when and where floodwater and playa farming was more productive than harvesting wild seed plants (including piñon nuts, weedy annuals, and grasses). However, this cost-benefit relationship will vary by local environmental setting and annual resource productivity. The lower costs associated with smaller distances between upland and lowland resource areas and the diminished potential for floodwater and small micro-niche farming might explain the increased dependence on hunting and gathering over cultivation in some parts of the study area, including the northern Rio Grande Valley. The opposite situation would explain the importance of maize cultivation and the presence of cache sites located near agricultural fields along the Chuska slope in the western San Juan Basin.

Finally, I agree with Jonathan Mabry's and William Doolittle's arguments (Mabry 2003; Mabry and Doolittle, Chapter 4, this volume) that high water-table settings were important for early agriculture and that the use of floodwater farming has probably been overemphasized. Other potential locales for cultivation would include areas adjacent to playas, ponds, springs or seeps, and mesa-top runoff. Later, during the Ceramic period, the high water-table areas along the margins of large river valleys were probably used near these early villages. Indeed, in the Northern Rio Grande, hunter-gatherers may have continued the planting of maize in upland micro-niche settings while agriculturalists used the adjacent lowland river valleys until the twelfth century A.D. time period.

Acknowledgments. This chapter would not have been possible without the help of friends and colleagues who provided me with unpublished data, printer galleys, or reports hot off the press. My thanks to Jerry Fetterman, Steve Fuller, Tim Hovezak, Pamela McBride, and Mollie Toll.

REFERENCES CITED

Acklen, John
    1995   *Data Recovery at LA 100419 and LA 100420, Albuquerque International Airport Expansion, Bernalillo County, New Mexico.* Technical Report 11288-0020. TRC Mariah Associates, Albuquerque.

Adams, Karen
    1994   Regional Synthesis of Zea Mays in the Prehistoric American Southwest. In *Corn and Culture in the Prehistoric New World,* ed. Sissel Johannessen and Christine A. Hastorf, 273–302. Westview, Boulder.

Arms, George
    1999   LA 111589. In *Data Recovery along the 1995 MAPCO Four Corners Pipeline: Artifact Analysis for Sites in the San Juan Basin/Colorado Plateau, Sandoval, San Juan and*

McKinley Counties, New Mexico, comp. K. Brown, 47-64. Office of Contract Archeology, University of New Mexico, Albuquerque.

Bargman, Byrd, Peggy Gerow, and Janette Elyea
 1999 LA 110946, San Luis de Cabezon Site. In *Data Recovery along the 1995 MAPCO Four Corners Pipeline: Artifact Analysis for Sites in the San Juan Basin/Colorado Plateau, Sandoval, San Juan and McKinley Counties, New Mexico*, comp. K. Brown, 11-64. Office of Contract Archeology, University of New Mexico, Albuquerque.

Barlow, Renee
 1997 *Foragers That Farm: A Behavioral Ecology Approach of Corn Farming for the Fremont.* Ph.D. dissertation, Department of Anthropology, University of Utah, Salt Lake City.
 2002 Predicting Maize Agriculture among the Fremont: An Economic Comparison of Farming and Foraging in the American Southwest. *American Antiquity* 67:65-88.

Berry, Michael
 1982 *Time, Space and Transition in Anasazi Prehistory.* University of Utah Press, Salt Lake City.
 1985 The Age of Maize in the Greater Southwest: A Critical Review. In *Prehistoric Food Production in North America*, ed. Richard Ford, 279-308. Anthropological Papers 75. University of Michigan, Ann Arbor.

Brandi, James, and Michael Dilley
 1998 *Archaeological Investigation of Fourteen Sites in Unit 22, Rio Rancho, New Mexico.* Rio Grande Consultants, Albuquerque.

Brandt, Carolyn
 1991a The River's Edge Archaeobotanical Analysis: Patterns in Plant Refuse. In *At the River's Edge: Early Puebloan Settlement in the Middle Rio Grande Valley*, ed. Matthew Schmader. Rio Grande Consultants, Albuquerque. Unpaginated addendum.
 1991b The River's Edge Archaeobotanical Analysis: Phase II Data Recovery. In *At the River's Edge: Early Puebloan Settlement in the Middle Rio Grande Valley. Phase 2 Report: Results of the 1989 Field Season*, ed. Matthew Schmader. Rio Grande Consultants, Albuquerque. Unpaginated addendum.
 2002 Macrobotanical Remains. In *Archaeological Investigations in the Fruitland Project Area: Late Archaic, Basketmaker, Pueblo I and Navajo Sites in Northwestern New Mexico. Material Culture, Bioarchaeological and Special Studies*, ed. Timothy Hovezak and Leslie Sesler, 307-336. Research Papers 4. La Plata Consultants, Dolores, Colo.

Brown, Gary
 1991 *Archaeological Data Recovery at San Juan Coal Company's La Plata Mine, San Juan County, New Mexico.* Technical Report 355. Mariah Associates, Albuquerque.

Burgett, Galen, Louis Neff, and Mark Sale
 1994 Site 442-3. In *Excavation and Interpretation of Aceramic and Archaic Sites*, Volume 14, ed. Tim Burchett, Bradley Vierra, and Kenneth Brown, 177-198. Office of Contract Archeology, University of New Mexico, Albuquerque.

Damp, Jonathan, Steven Hall, and Susan Smith
 2002 Early Irrigation on the Colorado Plateau Near Zuni Pueblo, New Mexico. *American Antiquity* 67:665-676.

Dean, Glenna
 1993 Archeobotanical Studies. In *Data Recovery at Three Archaic Sites in the Bolack Land Exchange*, ed. Janette Elyea and Patrick Hogan, 7.1–7.25. Office of Contract Archeology, University of New Mexico, Albuquerque.

Dering, Phil
 1999 Earth Oven Plant Processing in Archaic Period Economies: An Example from a Semi-Arid Savannah in South-Central North America. *American Antiquity* 64:659–674.

Elyea, Janette
 1999 Archaic Foragers and Early Farmers in the Jemez and Puerco Valleys. In *Data Recovery along the 1995 MAPCO Four Corners Pipeline: Artifact Analysis for Sites in the Jemez and Las Huertas Drainages, Sandoval County, New Mexico*, comp. K. Brown, 143–154. Office of Contract Archeology, University of New Mexico, Albuquerque.

Elyea, Janette, and Patrick Hogan (editors)
 1993 *Data Recovery at Three Archaic Sites in the Bolack Land Exchange*. Office of Contract Archeology, University of New Mexico, Albuquerque.

Elyea, Janette, and J. Sheppard
 1999 LA 25864. In *Data Recovery along the 1995 MAPCO Four Corners Pipeline: Artifact Analysis for Sites in the Jemez and Las Huertas Drainages, Sandoval County, New Mexico*, comp. K. Brown, 43–138. Office of Contract Archeology, University of New Mexico, Albuquerque.

Ford, Richard
 1985 Re-Excavation of Jemez Cave. *Awanyu* 3:13–27.

Foxx, Teralene
 1982 Vegetative Study. In *Bandelier Excavations in the Flood Pool of Cochiti Reservoir*, ed. Lyndi Hubbell and Diane Traylor, 382–431. National Park Service, Southwestern Regional Resources Center, Santa Fe.

Freuden, Charles
 1998 LA 6444: Insulator Site. In *Pipeline Archaeology 1990–1993: The El Paso Natural Gas North System Expansion Project, New Mexico and Arizona, Volume II*, comp. Timothy M. Kearns and Janet L. McVickar, 223–300. Western Cultural Resource Management, Farmington, N.M.

Gerow, Peggy, and Byrd Bargman
 1999 LA 110942. In *Data Recovery along the 1995 MAPCO Four Corners Pipeline: Artifact Analysis for Sites in the Jemez and Las Huertas Drainages, Sandoval County, New Mexico*, comp. K. Brown, 139–152. Office of Contract Archeology, University of New Mexico, Albuquerque.

Gilman, Patricia
 1983 *Changing Architectural Forms in the Prehistoric Southwest*. Ph.D. dissertation, Department of Anthropology, University of New Mexico, Albuquerque.
 1987 Architecture as Artifact: Pit Structures and Pueblos in the American Southwest. *American Antiquity* 52:538–564.

Gregory, David, and Michael Diehl
  2002   Duration, Continuity, and Intensity of Occupation at a Late Cienega Phase Settlement in the Santa Cruz River Floodplain. In *Traditions, Transitions, and Technologies: Themes in Southwestern Archaeology*, ed. Sarah H. Schlanger, 200–223. University Press of Colorado, Boulder.

Hammet, Julia
  1994a   Paleoethnobotanical Analysis (423-158). In *Excavation and Interpretation of Aceramic and Archaic Sites*, Volume 14, ed. Tim Burchett, Bradley Vierra, and Kenneth Brown, 147–148. Office of Contract Archeology, University of New Mexico, Albuquerque.
  1994b   Paleoethnobotanical Analysis (442-3). In *Excavation and Interpretation of Aceramic and Archaic Sites*, Volume 14, ed. Tim Burchett, Bradley Vierra, and Kenneth Brown, 195. Office of Contract Archeology, University of New Mexico, Albuquerque.

Henderson, Ruth
  1983   H-26-56. In *Cultural Resource Investigations on Gallegos Mesa: Excavations in Blocks VIII and IX, and Testing Operations in Blocks X and XI, Navajo Indian Irrigation Project, San Juan County, New Mexico*, ed. Lawrence Vogler, 338–407. Navajo Nation Papers in Anthropology 24, Window Rock, Ariz.

Hogan, Patrick
  1994   Foragers to Farmers: The Adoption of Agriculture in the Northern Southwest. In *Archaic Hunter-Gatherer Archaeology in the American Southwest*, ed. Bradley Vierra, 155–184. Contributions in Anthropology 13. Eastern New Mexico University, Portales.

Honeycutt, Linda, and Jerry Fetterman
  1994   *Excavations along the Arkansas Loop Pipeline Corridor, Northwestern New Mexico.* Woods Canyon Archaeological Consultants, Yellow Jacket, Colo.

Horn, Jonathan, Jerry Fetterman, and Linda Honeycutt
  2003   *The Rocky Mountain Expansion Loop Pipeline Data Recovery Project.* Woods Canyon Archaeological Consultants, Yellow Jacket, Colo.

Hovezak, Timothy, and Leslie Sesler
  2002a   *Archaeological Investigations in the Fruitland Project Area: Late Archaic, Basketmaker, Pueblo I, and Navajo Sites in Northwestern New Mexico. The Archaic Sites*, Volume 2. Research Papers 4. La Plata Archaeological Consultants, Dolores, Colo.
  2002b   *Archaeological Investigations in the Fruitland Project Area: Late Archaic, Basketmaker, Pueblo I, and Navajo Sites in Northwestern New Mexico. The Basketmaker and Pueblo I Sites*, Volume 3. Research Papers 4. La Plata Archaeological Consultants, Dolores, Colo.
  2002c   Prehistoric and Protohistoric Lithic Technologies in the Fruitland Study Area. In *Archaeological Investigations in the Fruitland Project Area: Late Archaic, Basketmaker, Pueblo I, and Navajo Sites in Northwestern New Mexico. Material Culture, Bioarchaeological and Special Studies*, Volume 5, ed. Timothy Hovezak and Leslie Sesler, 49–186. Research Papers 4. La Plata Archaeological Consultants, Dolores, Colo.

Irwin-Williams, Cynthia
  1973   *The Oshara Tradition: Origins of Anasazi Culture.* Contributions in Anthropology Series 5(1). Eastern New Mexico University, Portales.

Kearns, Timothy, Chris Kugler, and Paul Stirniman
    1998   The Dog Leg Site (LA 6448): A Basketmaker II Cache Locale in the Southern Chuska Valley, New Mexico. In *Pipeline Archaeology 1990–1993: The El Paso Natural Gas North System Expansion Project, New Mexico and Arizona, Volume II*, comp. Timothy M. Kearns and Janet L. McVickar, 301–476. Western Cultural Resource Management, Farmington, N.M.

Kearns, Timothy, Janet McVickar, and Lori Stephens Reed
    2000   The Early and Late Basketmaker III Transition in Tohatchi Flats, New Mexico. In *Foundations of Anasazi Culture: The Basketmaker-Pueblo Transition*, ed. Paul F. Reed, 115–144. University of Utah Press, Salt Lake City.

Kelly, Robert
    1995   *The Foraging Spectrum: Diversity in Hunter-Gatherer Lifeways*. Smithsonian Institution Press, Washington, D.C.

Kennedy, Michael
    1998   *Archaeological Investigation of Five Sites in the Santa Fe National Cemetery, Santa Fe, New Mexico*. Rio Grande Consultants, Albuquerque.

Lakatos, Steven, Stephen Post, and J. Murrell
    2001   *Data Recovery Results from Two Archaeological Sites along North Ridgetop Road, Santa Fe County, New Mexico*. Archaeology Notes 290. Office of Archaeological Studies, Museum of New Mexico, Santa Fe.

Lent, Steven
    1991   *The Excavation of a Late Archaic Pit Structure Near Otowi, San Ildefonso Pueblo, New Mexico*. Archaeology Notes 52. Office of Archaeological Studies, Museum of New Mexico, Santa Fe.

Mabry, Jonathan
    2003   Diversity in Early Southwestern Farming Systems and Optimization Models of Transition to Agriculture. Paper presented at the 68th Annual Meeting of the Society for American Archaeology, Milwaukee, Wis.

MacArthur, Robert, and Eric Pianka
    1966   On Optimal Use of a Patchy Environment. *American Naturalist* 100:603–609.

Matson, R. G.
    1991   *The Origins of Southwestern Agriculture*. University of Arizona Press, Tucson.

McBride, Pamela
    1994   Description of Anasazi Archeobotanical Remains. In *Across the Colorado Plateau: Anthropological Studies for the Transwestern Pipeline Expansion Project, Volume 15, Subsistence and Environment*, ed. Joseph C. Winter, 443–457. Office of Contract Archeology, University of New Mexico, Albuquerque.

Minnis, Paul
    1985   Domesticating People and Plants in the Greater Southwest. In *Prehistoric Food Production in North America*, ed. R. Ford, 309–340. Anthropological Paper 75. Museum of Anthropology, University of Michigan, Ann Arbor.
    1992   Earliest Plant Cultivation in the Desert Borderlands of North America. In *The Origins of Agriculture: An International Perspective*, ed. C. Wesley Cowan and Patty Jo Watson, 121–142. Smithsonian Institution Press, Washington, D.C.

Post, Stephen
    1996   *Las Campanas de Santa Fe, Sunset Golf Course, and Estates IV, Estates V and Estates VII Excavations.* Archaeology Notes 193. Office of Archaeological Studies, Museum of New Mexico, Santa Fe.
    2000   *Archaic Seasonal Camps and Pueblo Farming in the Piedmont: Excavation of Two Small Sites, LA 61315 and LA 61321, along the Santa Fe Relief Route State Road 599 (Phase 3), Santa Fe, New Mexico.* Archaeology Notes 277. Office of Archaeological Studies, Museum of New Mexico, Santa Fe.
    2002   Emerging from the Shadows: The Archaic Period in the Northern Rio Grande. In *Traditions, Transitions, and Technologies: Themes in Southwestern Archaeology*, ed. Sarah H. Schlanger, 33–48. University Press of Colorado, Boulder.

Redd, Ingrid, Kevin Wellman, and Galen Burgett
    1994   Site 423-158 (LA 88526). In *Excavation and Interpretation of Aceramic and Archaic Sites*, Volume 14, ed. Tim Burchett, Bradley Vierra, and Kenneth Brown, 125–156. Office of Contract Archeology, University of New Mexico, Albuquerque.

Reed, Paul F.
    2000   Introduction. In *Foundations of Anasazi Culture: The Basketmaker-Pueblo Transition*, ed. Paul F. Reed, 3–18. University of Utah Press, Salt Lake City.

Schmader, Matthew
    1994a   *Archaic Occupations of the Santa Fe Area: Results of the Tierra Contenta Archaeology Project.* Rio Grande Consultants, Albuquerque.
    1994b   *Early Puebloan Site Structure and Technological Organization in the Middle Rio Grande Valley, New Mexico.* Ph.D. dissertation, Department of Anthropology, University of New Mexico, Albuquerque.
    2001   *Gimme Shelter: Uncovering Archaic Structures in Rio Rancho and Santa Fe, New Mexico.* Rio Grande Consultants, Albuquerque.

Seymour, Deni, Jeffrey Hokanson, and Vicky Cunningham
    1997   *Excavations at Lru-Kish Kachreu and Other Sites at the Sandoval Landfill.* Report 15. Lone Mountain Archaeological Services, Albuquerque.

Simmons, Alan
    1986   New Evidence for the Early Use of Cultigens in the American Southwest. *American Antiquity* 51(1):73–88.

Simms, Steven
    1987   *Behavioral Ecology and Hunter-Gatherer Foraging.* BAR International Series 381. British Archaeological Reports, Oxford.

Stephens, David, and John Krebs
    1986   *Foraging Theory. Monographs in Behavior and Ecology.* Princeton University Press, Princeton, N.J.

Toll, Mollie
    1993   *Botanical Indicators of Early Life in Chaco Canyon: Flotation Samples and Other Plant Materials from Basketmaker and Early Puebloan Occupations.* National Park Service, Southwestern Region, Santa Fe.

Toll, Mollie, and Anne Cully
    1994   Archaic Subsistence and Seasonal Population Flow in Northwest New Mexico. In *Archaic Hunter-Gatherer Archaeology in the American Southwest*, ed. Bradley Vierra,

103-120. Contributions in Anthropology 13. Eastern New Mexico University, Portales.

Torres, John
  2000 Changing Lithic Technology during the Basketmaker-Pueblo Transition: Evidence from the Anasazi Heartland. In *Foundations of Anasazi Culture: The Basketmaker-Pueblo Transition*, ed. Paul F. Reed, 221-230. University of Utah Press, Salt Lake City.

Vierra, Bradley
  1993a Technological Variation and Subsistence Strategies: Explaining Changes in Stone Tool Technology. Paper presented at the Fifth Occasional Anasazi Symposium, Farmington, N.M.
  1993b Explaining Long-Term Changes in Lithic Procurement and Reduction Strategies. In *Architectural Studies, Lithic Analysis, and Ancillary Studies*, Volume 17, ed. Bradley J. Vierra, 139-380. Office of Contract Archeology, University of New Mexico, Albuquerque.
  1994a Archaic Hunter-Gatherer Mobility Strategies in Northwestern New Mexico. In *Archaic Hunter-Gatherer Archaeology in the American Southwest*, ed. Bradley J. Vierra, 121-154. Contributions in Anthropology 13(1). Eastern New Mexico University, Portales.
  1994b A Study of Basketmaker II Lithic Technology. In *Excavation and Interpretation of Aceramic and Archaic Sites*, Volume 14, ed. Tim Burchett, Bradley Vierra, and Kenneth Brown, 413-424. Office of Contract Archeology, University of New Mexico, Albuquerque.
  1996 Late Archaic Settlement, Subsistence and Technology: An Evaluation of Continuity vs. Replacement Arguments for the Origins of Agriculture in the Northern Southwest. Paper presented at the Conference on the Archaic Prehistory of the North American Southwest, Albuquerque.
  1998 *Results of the 1993-94 Excavations Conducted at the Chama Alcove Site, Rio Arriba County, New Mexico*. Center for Archaeological Research, University of Texas at San Antonio.

Vierra, Bradley, and Teralene Foxx
  2002 Archaic Upland Resource Use: The View from the Pajarito Plateau, New Mexico. Paper presented at the 67th Annual Meeting of the Society for American Archaeology, Denver, Colo.

Walth, Cherie
  1999 LA 109129. In *Data Recovery along the 1995 MAPCO Four Corners Pipeline: Artifact Analysis for Sites in the Jemez and Las Huertas Drainages, Sandoval County, New Mexico*, comp. K. Brown, 71-130. Office of Contract Archeology, University of New Mexico, Albuquerque.

Williams, Jerry, and Paul McAllister (editors)
  1979 *New Mexico in Maps*. University of New Mexico Press, Albuquerque.

Wills, Wirt
  1988 *Early Prehistoric Agriculture in the American Southwest*. School of American Research, Santa Fe.

Wills, Wirt, and Thomas Windes
   1989   Evidence for Population Aggregation and Dispersal during the Basketmaker III Period in Chaco Canyon, New Mexico. *American Antiquity* 54:347–369.

6

A Method for Anticipating Patterns in Archaeological Sequences

Projecting the Duration of the Transition to Agriculture in Mexico—A Test Case

Amber L. Johnson

Discussions of early agriculture have long been synonymous with historical arguments about the timing of migration of farmers or the diffusion of crops and technology from centers of domestication, as well as interpretive arguments about whether the spread of new subsistence strategies was more likely the result of the migration of farming people or the adoption of new strategies by local populations. Yet there are no good arguments about the conditions under which people *do not* migrate or crops and technology *do not* diffuse. Therefore, we have many interpretive arguments that accommodate what is known and tell a nice story but little development of the theoretical principles that allow us to specify the conditions under which we do and do not expect to find agriculture. Developing the generalizations that could form the foundation of this kind of theory requires fairly substantial knowledge of variability both in the archaeological record of early agriculture and in the hunting-gathering adaptations such as those that regularly precede food-producing economies. Lewis Binford's (2001:363–399) long-term research on the environmental and demographic factors that impact hunter-gatherer subsistence and settlement strategies provides one foundation for this research. Recent archaeological research on early agriculture provides another.

Within the last decade, archaeological research in the large and diverse geographic region that includes the U.S. Southwest and Mexican borderlands has greatly expanded our knowledge of the variability in the timing of intensive plant utilization and mix of resources included in the earliest horticultural adaptations in this region. Several of the authors included in this volume have made significant contributions to the documentation and synthesis of data on a variety of intensively used native plants and earlier dates on water control features and maize across this region (also see Doolittle and Mabry 2006:109–110). The growing body of evidence indicates (1) intensive use of wild plants long before the earliest maize is present, (2) considerable variety within individual sites combined with considerable variance among sites in the types of plants present even after maize is present, (3) earlier dates for the presence of maize across this region, and (4) earlier dates on water control features in this arid region than in the tropical regions of Mesoamerica.

This new knowledge of the archaeological record relating to early agriculture challenges what Doolittle and Mabry (2006:110–111) refer to as "The Simplistic Paradigm"—the conventional model of a "relatively sudden shift from hunting and gathering to agriculture" that occurred by either diffusion or migration. Further, they argue, "No longer is it useful or realistic to assume that Southwestern agriculture began with maize, or that there was initially a single kind of early farming that spread across the Southwest prior to the development of other cultivation techniques. Rather than thinking in simple, specific, single-process, single-event terms, our thinking about the early history of maize in the greater Southwest should be framed in the context of complex, diverse, and evolutionary processes over an extended period of time" (Doolittle and Mabry 2006:118).

The most common research strategy to develop our knowledge of such processes is continued fieldwork combined with periodic synthesis. Together, these further increase the archaeological data available to researchers. Another productive research strategy is to continue to develop knowledge of the specific subsistence options available and their relative cost-benefit to people living in different environmental settings and under different demographic conditions (e.g., Barlow 2002:70–84). These strategies produce and synthesize increasingly detailed knowledge of particular places at particular times and thus contribute to significant increases in specific knowledge of the archaeological record at local and regional scales of comparison. However, as such detailed knowledge accumulates for multiple regions around the world, it becomes increasingly difficult to compare large-scale patterns of change in subsistence and settlement systems. Thus, there is also a need to develop generalizations that can be applied globally to allow us to learn how these "complex, diverse, and evolutionary processes" compare from one region of the world to another.

The primary goal of this chapter is to develop general theoretical principles regarding the conditions under which hunter-gatherer subsistence strategies are expected to change into horticultural subsistence strategies. Such generalizations can provide a global framework for anticipating variance in basic features of the archaeological record related to the transition to agriculture. Results of a preliminary attempt to work with archaeological data at this global scale of comparison are reported and then used to illustrate a method for anticipating variability in durations of basic subsistence adaptations across Mexico. That is, generalizations based on knowledge of hunter-gatherer subsistence and patterns of subsistence change in archaeological sequences around the world are used to predict where in Mexico the earliest and the latest horticultural strategies are expected. It is unlikely that these predictions are absolutely accurate. However, having predictions based on current knowledge will put the field in a productive posture to learn what else we might need to know.

THE TRANSITION TO AGRICULTURE

Although in the archaeological literature the end point of the transition to agriculture has received much greater attention than the beginning point, any explanation for the process of becoming dependent upon agriculture must start with knowledge of variability in the initial conditions of hunting-gathering adaptations. Binford (2001) has recently demonstrated just how variable hunting-and-gathering adaptations are. Ecological variables and both population density and residential group sizes all contribute significantly to the range of observed hunter-gatherer system states (Binford 2001:164-174, 382-387). In regions of the world where agriculture does become an important subsistence strategy, the change from hunting and gathering to agricultural subsistence may be very early or very late in actual date and very rapid or very slow in its pace.

Variability in the transition to agricultural subsistence provides an opportunity to learn about cultural processes at many different scales. In global perspective, why does food production become the main subsistence strategy in many regions but not others? Where food production does become important, why is the transition to agriculture in some regions very early but rather slow while in others it is very late but rather fast? Why is there so much variation within a region in both the timing and the organization of subsistence strategies during this transition? At a smaller scale, what can we learn from local variability in settlement patterns and site context about the cultural context in which food production becomes important? How can we learn enough from what we already (think we) know about global-scale patterning in archaeological sequences to be able to say something about what we would expect to see in a region where we have less archaeological knowledge?

Given what we know about the broad range of variability in basic subsistence and settlement patterns, as well as in the organization of marriage, politics, trade, warfare, and many other aspects of hunter-gatherer systems, variation is expected in the timing, duration, and details of both the transition to agricultural subsistence and the organization of those systems once established. Even if the process governing the transition to agriculture is similar in most parts of the world, the way it operates should vary as the initial conditions it operates upon vary. If we can establish generalizations that, other things being equal, allow us to anticipate variability in a broad range of archaeological sequences, we will be in a position to evaluate claims that something (for example, the mode of introduction of agriculture) was not equal. If we can use Binford's environmental frame of reference to calculate an ecologically informed (and thus variable) expected duration for the transition to agriculture, observations that deviate from that expected value can be treated analytically to determine what other factors contribute to the variance. As an example, Binford's frames of reference is used to calculate expected durations for three distinct phases of archaeological sequences, and these equations are then used to project expected values onto Mexico, using the calculated frames of reference for weather station locations in that country. A comparison of projected sequences demonstrates how much variability in sequence patterns is expected to exist based on variance in local conditions alone.

I begin by briefly reviewing the method Binford used to construct his environmental and hunter-gatherer frames of reference that are central to this research. Next, I summarize global patterns relating to the duration of archaeological phases leading up to the transition to agriculture and place Mexico in a global perspective. That is, I use generalizations at the global scale to see how various locations in this region would be expected to pattern, given what we know about the transition elsewhere. Following a discussion of these global patterns, in which I explore the general cultural processes underlying variability in the duration of unintensified hunting and gathering, intensified hunting and gathering, and the transition to agriculture in a variety of settings, I then explore the potential use of this analytical strategy for developing a method for recognizing patterns that would not be expected to arise out of local conditions alone.

FRAMES OF REFERENCE

This research uses both the environmental and hunter-gatherer frames of reference described in Binford's 2001 *Constructing Frames of Reference* as a framework for exploring archaeological variability. Briefly, the environmental frame of reference is calculated on the basis of simple geographical and climate data (latitude, elevation, distance to the nearest coast, soil type, mean monthly temperature, and rainfall). In all, there are about fifty-five annual summary values ranging from the mean annual temperature (CMAT) to such variables as the percentage of months during the growing season with a water deficit (PERWDEF), standing plant biomass (BIO5), and net aboveground plant productivity (NAGP). Several of these variables measure the same property of the environment in subtly different ways, and nearly all are derived from either data or equations extant in the ecological literature. The advantages of this environmental frame of reference are that (1) it can be calculated for any location for which basic weather station data are available, (2) the results are directly comparable because the calculations are standardized, and (3) it can be used to calculate multiple regression equations for other properties we might be interested in projecting elsewhere.

Using Binford's standard calculations, two types of data have been projected using regression equations calculated from environmental variables. The first is a value for expected prey biomass (EXPREY) based on measured ungulate biomass from 104 locations around the globe. The second is the hunter-gatherer frame of reference, including values for expected population density (WDEN); percentage subsistence dependence on hunting (WHUNTP), gathering (WGATHP), and aquatic resources (WFISHP); number of moves (EXNOMOV) and distance moved per year (EXDMOV); and several other continuous variables recorded in Binford's 339-case hunter-gatherer data set. These projections make it possible to characterize the organizational variability that would be expected if the world were populated by hunter-gatherers like those known ethnographically. These projections are not analogies based on only a few cases thought to be relevant in a given region, nor are they intended to represent a "true" picture of the past; rather, they are based on relationships developed from data on most of the documented hunter-gatherers around the world. As such, they offer a baseline for comparing both the distributions of archaeological materials and the properties of archaeological sequences over large areas. They are especially relevant to the question of variability in the transition to agriculture, since the demographic and organizational variability of hunter-gatherer groups provides the initial conditions for variability in the transition to agriculture.

Of course, archaeologists are well aware that neither environments nor human adaptations remain constant over time. In the best of all possible worlds, there would be a standardized and reliable strategy for modeling paleoclimates that would provide mean monthly temperature and precipitation values that could serve as the basis for calculating a dynamic environmental frame of reference for a given location over the span of the archaeological record (for one potential strategy, see Bryson and Bryson 1995).[1] Because this type of modeling strategy is not yet fully developed, I use the frames of reference calculated for the modern period as a tool for exploring variability in archaeological sequences. It is understood, then, that this environmental frame of reference is more directly applicable to our pattern recognition goals in regions and during time periods in which environments have not changed dramatically. Regions or time periods for which this is not the case should be treated with caution. Whereas the absolute values for environmental variables cannot be expected to be accurate for all archaeological time periods across the Greater Southwest, the strong influence of geography on environmental patterning ensures that mountains will get relatively more rainfall and have relatively cooler temperatures than neighboring lowlands. Thus, the geographic patterns within a region are expected to be germane even to periods in the past, when the absolute values of environmental variables would have been different. In short, while the current frame of reference is not the best data we can imagine for archaeological research, it is the best we have right now, so let us see what happens when we use it.

Amber L. Johnson

A GLOBAL COMPARISON OF ARCHAEOLOGICAL SEQUENCE DURATIONS

The patterns of change recorded in archaeological sequences around the world are fascinating for both the similarities in pattern among widely separated places and the differences in pattern within a limited area. I have recently begun to organize archaeological information in such a way as to make direct comparison of archaeological sequences possible at a global scale of analysis. The first step is to partition sequences into broadly comparable adaptations—unintensified hunting and gathering, intensified (broad-spectrum) hunting and gathering, transition to agriculture, and agriculture. Each sequence is based on the current summary literature for a region to establish dates for such things as earliest regular occupation, earliest use of seed-grinding equipment, fishhooks or fishnets, pottery vessels, house types, settlement sizes, mortuary practices, and the earliest evidence of domesticates. In general, intensified hunting and gathering is marked by either a shift in plant-processing equipment (for example, the introduction of plant-grinding equipment or a shift in the prevalence or surface area of grinding equipment) or investment in equipment for accessing aquatic resources (for example, fishhooks, fishnets, or harpoons). The transition to agriculture is marked at the early end by the earliest evidence of cultivars or domesticates (usually as one component of a mostly hunting-and-gathering adaptation) and at the later end by the apparent dominance of agriculture in the economy and subsistence of a region (indicated by change in settlement pattern or artifacts such as hoes).

To date, I have assembled a very preliminary data set based on fairly well-documented sequences from sixteen locations around the world (Table 6.1).[2] Whereas the sequences themselves are developed using the most accurate dates available, the data are recorded as durations of each broad phase of adaptation. This makes it possible to directly compare sequences with dramatically different starting dates in terms of the length of time it takes to get from one transition to another. For example, using a standard historical method of comparison, we might comment on how much earlier agriculture emerged in the Near East (ca. 10,000 B.P.) than in Mesoamerica (ca. 7000 B.P.). However, if we compare durations of time from initial occupation to the emergence of agriculture, we are struck by how much more quickly things happened in Mesoamerica (only 4,800 years of strictly hunting and gathering) compared to the Near East (at least 9,500 years of strictly hunting and gathering). Interestingly, the basic *pattern* of change from unintensified to intensified hunting and gathering and through the transition to agriculture to a dominantly agricultural economy is very similar for both the Near East and the Valley of Oaxaca. In these sequences, the relative durations for intensified hunting and gathering and the transition to agriculture are very similar—that is, they take up roughly equal portions of the overall archaeological sequence. In contrast, sequences from Japan and the Illinois and Ohio valleys have much longer durations of intensified hunting and gathering and very rapid transitions to agriculture.

A Method for Anticipating Patterns in Archaeological Sequences

Table 6.1 Comparison of observed and expected archaeological sequence durations in years used for global comparison

	Unintensified Hunting and Gathering		Intensified Hunting and Gathering		Transition to Agriculture	
Location of Sequence	observed	expected[§]	observed	expected[§]	observed	expected[§]
Tasmania	12,000	–	8,000	6,136	N/A	–
Seward Peninsula, Alaska	3,000	2,297	5,500	4,763	N/A	–
Central European plain*	N/A	–	2,500	3,817	0.01	–
Honshu, Japan*	7,600	–	9,900	11,419	0.01	–
Illinois Valley	5,000	5,486	5,500	4,814	400	278
Baltic	2,500	–	4,800	4,398	500	362
Eastern Sahara[#]	N/A	–	2,200	2,813	500	–
Khartoum	N/A	–	4,000	2,328	600	934
Southern Arizona	5,500	6,865	1,800	3,312	900	1,100
Ohio Valley	5,500	5,029	3,800	4,463	1,200	1,077
Mountains of Peru	4,000	4,019	0	2,139	2,000	2,339
Basin of Mexico	4,800	3,918	2,000	1,666	2,100	1,817
Near East	7,000	–	2,500	4,430	2,500	2,662
Colorado Plateau	4,200	4,911	800	(0)[†]–1,519	2,500	2,736
Coast of Peru	N/A	–	4,000	2,865	3,000	3,100
Tehuacán and Oaxaca valleys	900	2,335	3,900	3,223	3,200	2,722

* System states change extremely rapidly with introduction of agriculture; no archaeological measure of duration of transition.

\# Sequence is punctuated by periods of occupational hiatus as a result of hyperaridity; "agriculture" in this case marks the advent of highly mobile mixed sheep/goat and cattle pastoralism.

§ Expected values are adjusted predicted values calculated while running linear regression utility in SPSS (v 11.5). See Note 3 for equations and statistical description of each equation.

† Since negative temporal durations are impossible to imagine, predicted values less than zero are set equal to zero.

The contrast between sequences with relatively long durations of the transition to agriculture and those with relatively long durations of intensified hunting and gathering are clearly represented in Figure 6.1, which shows a global comparison of archaeological sequence durations in years sorted by length of the growing season. In locations characterized by a twelve-month growing season, the pattern of shorter intensified hunting and gathering and a longer transition to agriculture, as described for the Near East and the Valley of Oaxaca, is fairly common. Variance among sequences with twelve-month growing seasons may be related to seasonality conditioned by precipitation; for example, the eastern Sahara, Khartoum, and southern Arizona all have somewhat shorter transitions to agriculture than other sequences with twelve-month growing seasons, and all are located in arid settings with highly seasonal rainfall patterns. Where the growing season is shorter than twelve months, as, for example, in the Illinois Valley and Japan, this pattern is reversed, with longer durations of the intensified hunting-and-gathering phase and much shorter durations for the transition to agriculture. The only exception to the longer duration for intensified hunting and gathering among these sequences is

Amber L. Johnson

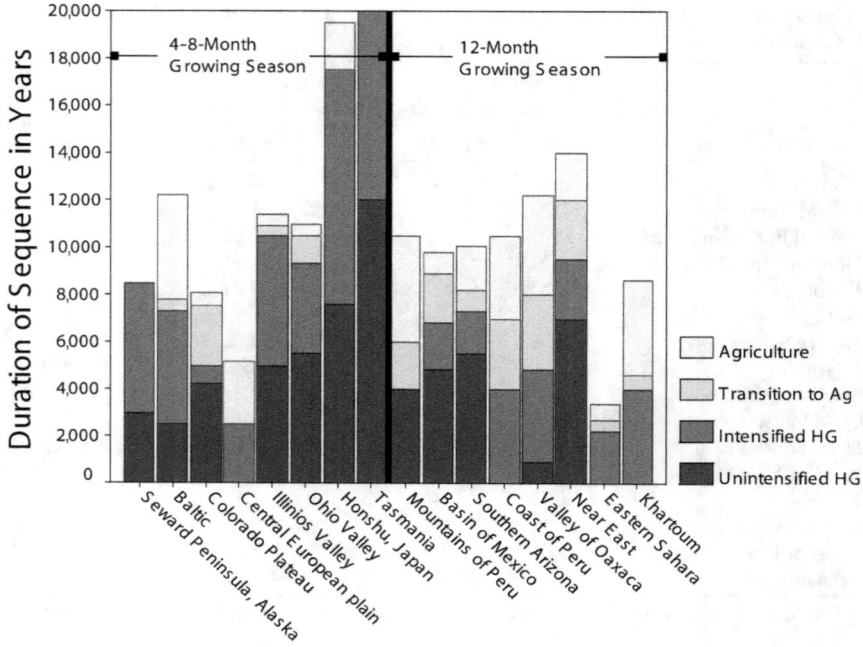

Figure 6.1. Global comparison of archaeological sequence durations by system state. Duration data are presented in Table 6.1. Sequences are sorted by length of growing season.

derived from the Colorado Plateau, the only such region among those with short growing seasons with little potential for intensifying on aquatic resources. The next step toward developing generalizations that would allow us to predict the basic structure of archaeological sequences in the absence of existing archaeological data is to determine the ecological conditions under which longer or shorter durations of unintensified hunting and gathering, intensified hunting and gathering, and the transition to agriculture occur.

GENERALIZATIONS REGARDING ECOLOGICAL CONTEXT

How can we learn about the ecological context conditioning the variable durations of these three distinct phases of archaeological sequences? A good place to start is to summarize the basic relationships suspected to condition much of the archaeological variability on the hunting-and-gathering end of archaeological sequences. All scientific generalizations are prefaced by the phrase "other things being equal" to acknowledge that we cannot address all sources of variability simultaneously or be certain of every boundary condition that must be specified.

- Generalization 1: Other things being equal, the duration of unintensified hunting and gathering (generally with high mobility and focused on terrestrial resources) is longer in regions where the initial intensification is on terrestrial plants rather than aquatic resources. Why should the duration of unintensified hunting and gathering, emphasizing residential mobility to access resources, be longer in such cases? There is a strong relationship between the length of the growing season and hunter-gather subsistence and intensification options. Where growing seasons are longer, unintensified hunter-gatherers are mostly dependent on terrestrial plants and more likely to intensify on plants. Where growing seasons are shorter, unintensified hunter-gatherers are mostly dependent on terrestrial animals and more likely to intensify on aquatic resources. Since it takes more space, thus lower population densities, to depend on terrestrial animals than on either terrestrial plants or aquatic resources, Binford (1990:148) has argued that where aquatic resources are an option, they are often associated with specific points of access (such as a beach) and therefore reduce mobility costs. Thus, unintensified hunter-gatherers shifting from hunting to aquatic resources may begin to intensify at lower population densities than unintensified hunter-gatherers mostly dependent on terrestrial plants may intensify their use of those plants.

- Generalization 2: Other things being equal, the higher the terrestrial model density,[3] the shorter the duration of unintensified hunting and gathering. Terrestrial model density indicates the population density of culturally unaided humans (that is, those not using technology to process inedible foods or to access inaccessible foods) that could be supported based simply on the accessibility and abundance of edible plants and animals (Binford 2001:160–205). This model value is expected to predict not hunter-gatherer densities but rather the density of an acultural generalist feeder built like us and dependent only on terrestrial resources. Nevertheless, places with higher terrestrial model densities have more abundant and accessible resources, thus they probably supported higher population densities of unintensified hunter-gatherers from early in the sequence. Other things being equal, hunter-gatherer populations in areas of high terrestrial model densities have more room to grow before they put population pressure on terrestrial resources than those in areas of low terrestrial model densities. High terrestrial model densities may also foster higher rates of population growth, although this is still speculation. As these more densely populated regions experience population growth (even at an average rate), they become packed much more quickly than neighboring regions with lower initial population densities. Unlike population pressure or carrying capacity, concepts that focus on the balance between population densities and available resources, packing is a mechanical effect of increasing population densities (Binford 1983:203–213). At some point, hunter-gatherers who use residential mobility to access resources reach a population density such that there is already one foraging group in each foraging area. For terrestrial plant–dependent hunter-gatherers, Binford (2001:229–234) has modeled this population density as just over nine people per 100 square kilometers (about twenty-one people per 225 square kilometers of foraging area). Regardless of the abundance of terrestrial resources, packing ensures some form of intensification as it becomes necessary to feed more people in less space and thus brings an early end to unintensified hunting and gathering. The local structure of resources (presence and scale of aquatic habitats, types, diversity and abundance of terrestrial plants) conditions the general intensification options available.

- Generalization 3: Other things being equal, access to aquatic resources increases the duration of intensified hunting and gathering. In addition to providing a subsistence opportunity with fewer mobility costs, aquatic resources support higher hunter-gatherer population densities than do either terrestrial animal- or terrestrial plant-based adaptations (see Binford 2001:214). Therefore, aquatic resources may extend the duration of intensified hunting and gathering on both ends by providing a way to cut mobility costs early on and by supplementing higher regional population densities than a strictly terrestrial adaptation does. However, once aquatic dependent groups switch to agriculture, they tend to switch much more quickly. Durations of the transition to agriculture are generally very short.

- Generalization 4: Other things being equal, in areas where hunter-gatherers intensify first on terrestrial plants, some form of plant cultivation is likely to occur, and the duration of the transition to agriculture is relatively long compared with areas where the first intensification is on aquatic resources. A comparison of hunter-gatherer subsistence adaptations above and below the packing threshold (Binford 2001:375), that is, 9.098 persons per 100 square kilometers, demonstrates that below this population density there are a fair number of hunter-gatherer groups dominantly dependent on terrestrial animals, especially in environments above about 40 degrees latitude. Above this population density, there are no hunter-gatherer groups dominantly dependent on terrestrial animals. Above 40 degrees latitude, most hunter-gatherers with packed populations are dominantly dependent on aquatic resources, whereas below 40 degrees latitude, they are dominantly dependent on terrestrial plants. Thus, there is a strong geographically correlated suite of expectations as to which pattern of intensification we should expect to see in an archaeological sequence.

EXPECTATIONS FOR MEXICO

In global perspective, most of Mexico would be expected to support hunter-gatherers dominantly dependent on terrestrial plants, with relatively low terrestrial model densities in the arid north and much higher terrestrial model densities in the tropical regions in the south. Therefore, we would expect moderate to long durations for unintensified terrestrial hunting and gathering in the north and shorter durations for unintensified hunting and gathering in the tropics. Once intensification begins, we would expect relatively long durations of intensified hunting and gathering and relatively short transitions to agriculture near the coasts, where aquatic resources would be more available, and the opposite pattern of relatively short durations of intensified hunting and gathering and relatively long durations of the transition to agriculture in the interior, where aquatic resources are less available.[4] Let us see what happens when we project values for sequence duration from equations run on the global sequences onto Mexico.

I have linked the locations of the archaeological sequences used for global comparison to the environmental frame of reference to use environmental variables to calculate regression equations for the duration of (1) unintensified hunting and gathering, (2) intensified hunting and gathering, and (3) the transition to agriculture. Some archaeological sequences are eliminated from the regression analyses to maintain as much consistency as possible in the data. The equation for the duration of unintensified hunting-gathering was run only on the New World sequences because of the difficulty of determining when to begin a modern hunting-gathering adaptation in many Old World sequences, which are complicated by the presence of previous hominins and archaic modern humans. The equation for the duration of intensified hunting-gathering uses all available sequences. The equation for the duration of the transition to agriculture uses only those sequences where there is an archaeologically visible transition to agriculture (Tasmania, Seward Peninsula, Central European plain, and Japan are eliminated by this criteria—they either have no agricultural component or are clearly instances of rapid introduction of and economic dependence on already domesticated plants) and a continuous occupation of the region across the transition from hunting-gathering to agriculture (eastern Sahara is omitted because of occupational hiatus). The resulting equations[5] are then used with data collected from 254 Mexican weather stations to project the durations of each of these phases onto locations not used to derive the original equations (with the exception of the Valley of Oaxaca and Basin of Mexico). Figure 6.2 maps the variability in projected duration for the transition to agriculture over all of Mexico, given what we know about the relationships between environmental variables and the duration of the transition to agriculture in eleven locations around the world. Values calculated strictly from environmental variables project a wide range of variability, with some locations expected to make the transition in much less than 600 years, whereas others are expected to take longer than 3,600 years.

With these calculated values for expected duration of unintensified hunting and gathering, intensified hunting and gathering, and the transition to agriculture, it is possible to develop expectations for differences in overall patterns of sequence variability across the study region. Figure 6.3 compares these projected sequences for several locations in Mexico. Note the dramatic difference between projected sequences where hunter-gatherers are expected to be either less than or greater than 30 percent dependent on aquatic resources (WFISHP). Although this variable (WFISHP) is not used in any of the equations to calculate sequence durations, the projected durations are distributed according to expectations derived from the global-scale generalizations with respect to aquatic dependence outlined earlier. Longer durations for intensified hunting and gathering are projected for locations where hunter-gatherers would be expected to depend largely on aquatic resources. If the

Amber L. Johnson

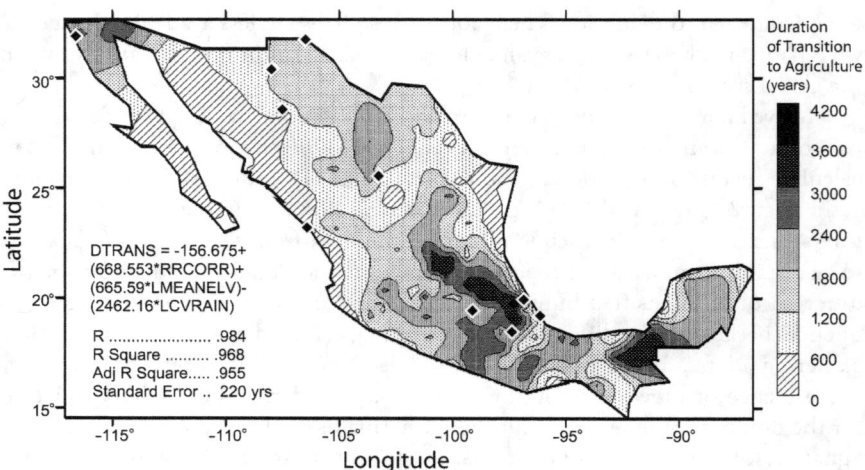

Figure 6.2. Map of projected duration of transition to agriculture for Mexico. Shading represents values of expected duration of transition to agriculture (DTRANS) projected from an equation using a measure of seasonality of rainfall (RRCORR), $\log_{10}$ of elevation (LMEANELV; ft), and $\log_{10}$ of the coefficient of variability in mean monthly rainfall (LCVRAIN). (See note 5 for further discussion of equation.) Diamonds mark locations of weather stations used for the projected sequence comparison in Figure 6.3. From north to south, they are Enseñada, Juarez, Casas Grandes, Guerrero, Matamoros, Mazatlan, Misantla, Mexico City, Veracruz, and Tehuacán.

initial resident population was established at roughly the same time across the study area, these expected durations carry implications about where adaptations should change earlier or later across the region. For example, based on the established relationships, if Misantla and Guerrero had the same date for initial occupation, we would anticipate the beginning of intensified hunting and gathering at Misantla at approximately the same time as the end of the transition to agriculture at Guerrero. Assuming some areas are occupied earlier than others, yet another layer of information is necessary to draw implications about the date at which changes are expected to occur across the region.

The research strategy discussed here has allowed me to develop specific expectations for the durations of various phases in archaeological sequences even for a region of which I have little direct archaeological knowledge. If these expectations are reasonably accurate, we will have learned something about the factors that condition variability in archaeological patterning at a global scale. If they are not, by demonstrating how they are not, we are in a position to learn something more about the variability in the archaeological record and probably about the importance of working at multiple scales (for further discussion of shifting scales and controlling variability, see Johnson 2004).

A Method for Anticipating Patterns in Archaeological Sequences

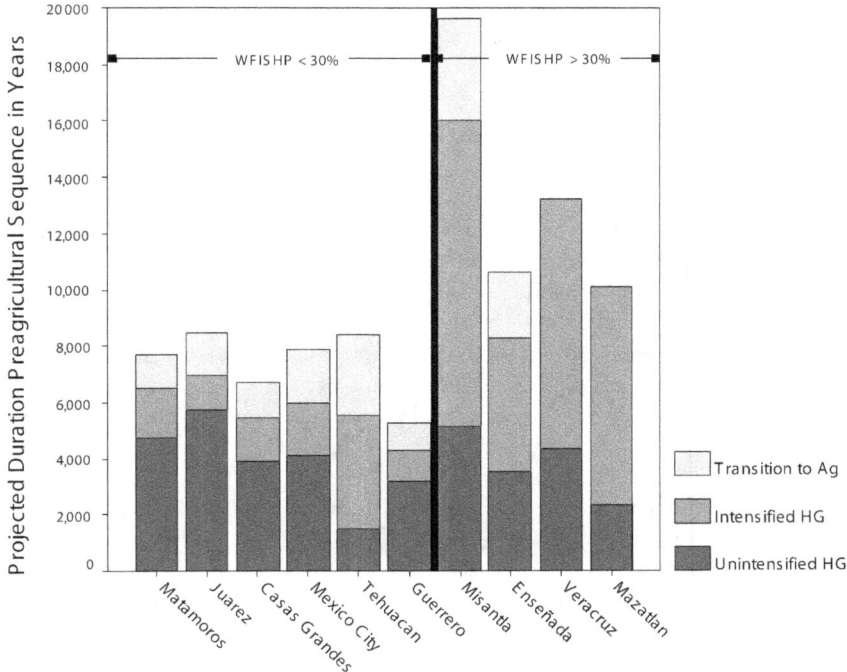

Figure 6.3. Projected sequence comparison for a few locations in Mexico. Durations of unintensified hunting and gathering, intensified hunting and gathering, and the transition to agriculture are projected from equations derived from global data (note 5) and are stacked to provide a picture of the projected pre-agricultural sequence for ten locations in Mexico. Stations are sorted by projected hunting-and-gathering dependence on aquatic resources (WFISHP). Locations were chosen to represent a wide range of variability in projected hunter-gatherer adaptations.

DISCUSSION

I began this chapter by establishing a research goal that should put us in a better position to evaluate arguments regarding the transition from hunting and gathering to agriculture. The primary goal was to develop general theoretical principles regarding the conditions under which hunter-gatherer subsistence strategies are expected to change into horticultural subsistence strategies. This was accomplished by combining data recorded for archaeological sequences around the globe with Binford's (2001) environmental frame of reference and generalizations derived from his study of variability in hunter-gatherer system states.

We have seen that when archaeological sequences are compared at a global scale of analysis, there are numerous regularities in the pattern of these sequences. These regularities can be generalized as follows: other things being equal, (1) the duration of unintensified hunting and gathering is longer where the initial intensification is on terrestrial plants rather than aquatic resources; (2) the higher the terrestrial model density, the shorter the duration of unintensified hunting and gathering; (3) access to aquatic resources increases the duration of intensified hunting and gathering; and (4) in areas where hunter-gatherers intensify first on terrestrial plants, some form of plant cultivation is likely to occur, and the duration of the transition to agriculture is relatively long compared with areas where the first intensification is on aquatic resources. Combining these generalizations regarding the process of intensification with Binford's discussion of intensification related to population packing (Binford 2001:363–399), transitions to agriculture are expected to develop based on local conditions where these conditions hold: (1) hunter-gatherer population densities exceed the packing threshold, decreasing the area within which a local group can exercise residential mobility for accessing resources, thus increasing the need for intensification; and (2) plants are the most likely targets for intensification. There is likely to be further variability in the timing of what we recognize as agriculture related to the types of plants intensified. For example, I would expect agriculture to arise earlier where intensification is on annuals (e.g., grains) than where it is on perennials (e.g., nuts).[6]

Given that a predictable intensification process is operating to produce transition from hunting and gathering to agriculture, there is no reason to believe the "invention" or "origin" of agriculture was a rare event or that knowledge of this subsistence strategy had to spread out from the centers of domestication through either diffusion or migration. Under similar local conditions of increasing population density and the possibilities for intensifying on plants, plant cultivation and domestication would be expected to occur in many different places without relying on migration of farming populations to bring the knowledge with them. The growing archaeological record of plant intensification preceding the introduction of maize across the Mexican borderlands and the U.S. Southwest confirms this part of the argument.

Nevertheless, some crops, like maize, have well-documented, fairly narrow geographic origins. When these crops begin to be found across a larger region, we would like unambiguous criteria for diagnosing the mode of transmission. Thus, a secondary goal of this chapter was to develop analytical tools that allow us to predict the pattern of culture change we would expect to see if there were no external pressure on the system. Analytical exploration of the divergence between the observed archaeological sequence and these expectations serves as a first step toward developing unambiguous criteria for recognizing cases where there is external pressure (for example, migrations of successful farmers) from the archaeological record. To accomplish this goal, I used data recorded for sixteen globally distributed archaeological sequences to calculate equations that can be used to project expected values for the duration of various phases of archaeological sequences anywhere modern weather station data are available. This strategy allows us to use existing archaeological information as leverage for further knowledge growth.

Let us consider the equation projecting the duration of the transition to agriculture (see note 5). Given the strength of the relationship between the duration of the transition to agriculture and environmental variables, if the transition is thought to be influenced significantly by migration, then either migration must respond predictably to the environmental setting or cultural changes must be more strongly influenced by local developments than by external influences.

Of the sixteen sequences used in the global comparison, only eleven were used to calculate this equation. In two locations—Tasmania and the Seward Peninsula in Alaska—there was no archaeologically recorded transition to agriculture. Rather, intensified hunting and gathering continues to the end of the sequence. In two other locations—Honshu, Japan, and the Central European plain—the transition to agriculture is not measurable in the archaeological record because the change from hunting and gathering to agricultural economies was too rapid for this transition to appear as a distinct archaeological system state. One *could* argue that this was the result of migration, diffusion, or, following Binford (1999), niche filling when some new combination of resources became available. In any case, these are exceptional patterns and were not used to generate the equations. Finally, the data from the eastern Sahara were eliminated from this equation because of an occupational hiatus between the transition to agriculture and fully agricultural phases, indicating that the duration of the transition to agriculture in the larger region must have been longer than that recorded at Nabta Playa (Wendorf and Schild 2001), and because agriculture is an inaccurate description of the mobile, pastoral adaptation that caps this sequence. Thus, the equation for the duration of the transition to agriculture relies only on data from archaeological sequences where there is a clear, continuous, archaeologically measurable transition from hunting and gathering to agriculture. This, then, is one of the boundary conditions that must be equal for the projected value to be accurate. Therefore, we could use the projected value as a model of what we would expect if the transition to agriculture were based on local conditions alone. If the archaeological sequences in some region were to demonstrate significant deviation from this projected value, migration would be one possible explanation for this unexpected pattern of change.

The key to being able to evaluate arguments about migration lies in understanding what the pattern should look like in the absence of migration. The method developed here is a first step toward doing this. It could be further developed by using relevant criteria for adding sequences to the global comparison and for partitioning data for archaeological sequences where migrations are known to occur and there is no suspicion of a migration. The point of this discussion is that the debate regarding the importance of migration in transitions to agricultural economies need not remain a matter of debate. There are analytical strategies that could be used to develop unambiguous criteria for recognizing the impact of migration versus indigenous adoption of new economic strategies.

CONCLUSION

This study demonstrates how we can develop intellectual tools that allow us to ground our analysis of change in human adaptive strategies documented in the archaeological record. It is a first step, based on a preliminary comparison of a global sample of archaeological sequences. Nevertheless, the strategy of projecting actual values for expected durations of distinct system-states using an environmental frame of reference has real potential for putting us in a position to further our ability to explain variability in the archaeological record at many different scales of analysis. Whether the projections are used within a region to guide research design and choice of field locations for further study, or whether these global patterns are used as a frame of reference for arguing about the likelihood of migration as a contributing factor in what seems a rapid pattern of culture change, the greatest learning opportunities come when our observations about the archaeological record fail to match our expectations. Should significant differences between observed and expected values be found, the next challenge is figuring out what we must know to explain the variability. Regions such as the Mexican borderlands and the U.S. Southwest, where rigorous fieldwork is rapidly contributing new knowledge about local and regional variability in adaptations throughout an intensification sequence, provide ideal settings for developing these methods further.

NOTES

1. The modeling strategy developed by Reid Bryson and colleagues (1995) has the potential to become such a strategy. While temperature models are firmly grounded in knowledge of factors contributing to patterns of climate change, precipitation models are simply fitted using modern monthly variability as a model for interannual variability over the last several thousand years. Further, no standardized method is available for calculating the models; therefore, considerable room exists for fitting the model to other known paleoenvironmental indicators. My own work testing models developed by the Bryson strategy using pollen data has yielded considerable support for temperature models and very little support for rainfall models. There are likely to be regions where this strategy works well as currently designed and others where it does not. At this time, this strategy does not meet the criteria for a globally applicable, standardized modeling strategy, although it does yield mean monthly temperature and rainfall estimates as output.

2. There is insufficient space in this chapter to fully document the development of these sequences. Readers with questions about the durations or their documentation are encouraged to contact the author.

3. Binford (2001:chapter 6) developed the terrestrial model density to estimate the number of culturally unaided people the environment could support to serve as a baseline against which to measure the population densities achieved by hunter-gatherers.

4. Projections for northern Mexico are based on the most basic suite of input variables, which do not allow us to anticipate the presence of unearned water, that is, water that fell as precipitation elsewhere, which may be flowing through an area in a river. There are likely spots in the interior where some aquatic resources would have been available in sources of unearned water. With a bit more work measuring the lengths of drainages and the distance

of particular locations from the headwaters, we will be able to use equations to project subsistence dependence that do take such resources into consideration. This will yield a more accurate picture of likely adaptations, which, in turn, will revise our expectations for durations of the phases of intensification. Thus, these projections should be considered a provocative first pass rather than a best possible final result.

5. Duration of unintensified hunting and gathering (HG) is calculated from an equation run using only the New World sequences (see Table 6.1) because of the difficulty in determining when to begin a modern HG adaptation in many of the Old World sequences. For this equation: R=0.950, R2=0.902, Adj. R2=0.863. The standard error of the predicted value is 570 years.

> DUNINHG2=10,145.643 - (1,870.561*REVEN) - (128.940*BAR5)
>
> Where, REVEN measures evenness of rainfall throughout the year and
> BAR5 measures biomass accumulation ratio (in addition to standing biomass from new growth).

Duration of intensified HG is an equation run on all sequences in Table 6.1: R=0.921, R2=0.849, Adj R2=0.811. The standard error of the predicted value is 1,112 years.

> DINTNSHG=7,128.24 - (1,312.075*LWATD) - (0.715*ELEV)+(1,130.312*TERMG2)
>
> Where, LWATD = log10 of annual water deficit measured in millimeters,
> ELEV = elevation in feet, and

TERMG2 = number of culturally unaided people per hundred square kilometers who could be supported by available and accessible plant foods (from Binford's terrestrial model; Binford 2001:chapter 6).

Duration of transition to agriculture is an equation run on all sequences where there is an archaeologically visible transitional phase (Tasmania, Seward Peninsula, Central European plain, and Japan are omitted from analysis) and a continuous occupation of the region across the transition from HG to agriculture (eastern Sahara omitted from analysis). For this equation: R=0.984, R2=0.968, AdjR2=0.955. The standard error of the predicted value is 220 years.

> DTRANS= -156.675 + (668.553*RRCORR2) + (665.59*LMEANELV) - (2,462.16*LCVRAIN)
>
> Where, RRCORR2 = the number of months separating peak temperatures and peak rainfall,
> LMEANELV = log (10) of elevation, measured in feet, and
> LCVRAIN = log (10) of the coefficient of variation of precipitation, measured in millimeters.

6. Current research, including collaborations with Robert Hard, University of Texas–San Antonio, and Adolfo Gil, CONDORCET, Argentina, explores these ideas further.

REFERENCES CITED

Barlow, K. R.
    2002   Predicting Maize Agriculture among the Fremont: An Economic Comparison of Farming and Foraging in the American Southwest. *American Antiquity* 67(1): 65–88.

Binford, L. R.
    1983   *In Pursuit of the Past: Decoding the Archaeological Record*, 1st ed. Thames and Hudson, New York.

Amber L. Johnson

- 1990 Mobility, Housing and Environment: A Comparative Study. *Journal of Anthropological Research* 46:119–152.
- 1999 Time as a Clue to Cause? *Proceedings of the British Academy* 101:1–35.
- 2001 *Constructing Frames of Reference: An Analytical Method for Archaeological Theory Building Using Hunter-Gatherer and Environmental Data Sets*, 1st. ed. University of California Press, Berkeley.

Bryson, R. A., and R. U. Bryson
- 1995 *An Archaeoclimatology Workbook: High-Resolution, Site-Specific Climate Modeling for Field Scientists* 1.1.4. Center for Climatic Research, University of Wisconsin-Madison, and Department of Geology and Geophysics, University of Minnesota, Minneapolis.

Doolittle, W. E., and J. B. Mabry
- 2006 Environmental Mosaics, Agricultural Diversity, and the Evolutionary Adoption of Maize in the American Southwest. In *Histories of Maize: Multidisciplinary Approaches to the Prehistory, Linguistics, Biogeography, Domestication, and Evolution of Maize*, ed. J. E. Staller, R. H. Tykot, and B. F. Benz, 109–121. Elsevier-Academic, Boston.

Johnson, A. L.
- 2004 On Niche Breadth, System Stability, and the Importance of a Phrase. In *Processual Archaeology: Exploring Analytical Strategies, Frames of Reference, and Culture Process*, ed. A. L. Johnson, 261–296. Praeger, Westport, Conn.

Wendorf, F., and R. Schild
- 2001 *Holocene Settlement of the Egyptian Sahara*, Volume 1: *The Archaeology of Nabta Playa*. 2 vols. Kluwer Academic/Plenum, New York.

7

THE CASE FOR AN EARLY FARMER MIGRATION INTO THE GREATER AMERICAN SOUTHWEST

Steven A. LeBlanc

Humans are fascinated with humans. Our fascinations include: How did we get where we are? How did we fill up the earth? Why and how did we become farmers? Why do we speak so many languages, or perhaps, why do we speak so few? Addressing these and similar questions helps us place ourselves in the world. Sometimes the answers come in small pieces; sometimes they are what we expect. In other cases, however, unexpected insights change our perceptions markedly, and the answers are far from what we predicted. The unexpected nature of the behavior in the wild of our close relatives, the chimpanzees, is a classic case in point. Perhaps not of that scale, but certainly paradigm breaking, is the idea that farming was invented only a handful of times in a handful of places, and it was the farmers themselves who rapidly spread farming to much of the world from these core places. We have long thought about the significance of the initial adoption of agriculture, yet the story of its spread may be every bit as fascinating.

This chapter was not presented at the 2004 Southwest Symposium and is a later addition to the volume. It is included here at the suggestion of the organizers of the Agricultural Adaptations session.

Steven A. LeBlanc

Closely linked to the idea of a rapid spread of farmers from a few initial core areas of domestication is the thought that this process was accompanied by the spread of these farmers' languages, which led to vast areas of the globe being populated by peoples speaking a few related languages. Today, only a few places on earth are filled with a patchwork of small, unrelated, or distantly related language families. The idea that many of the language distributions seen in the world today are the result of the initial spread of agriculture has added a fascinating component not only to the debate on language evolution and distributions but also to the distribution of genetic markers. Perhaps most important, it has added a new dimension to our understanding of the transition from foraging to farming—a seminal transformation in human history. If the joint spread of farmers and languages is correct in its broad form, then the way most of the world became farmers is quite different from what was proposed, at least indirectly, forty years ago (e.g., Binford 1968).

Most of the interest in and arguments about this farmer spread model in its variant forms have focused on the Old World, in particular the spread of farmers from the Middle East, Southeast Asia, and West Africa. Only much more recently has a comparable model been suggested for the Americas, in particular for the spread of farmers from central Mexico. Interestingly, the proposal for a farmer spread from Mexico was first made by Peter Bellwood (1994, 1997), not by a New World archaeologist or linguist. Most recent ideas about the Old World patterns are well summarized in Bellwood (2001, 2004), Diamond and Bellwood (2003), Renfrew (1996), Bellwood and Renfrew (2003), and Hill (2001); and comparisons have been made between the Old World and New World patterns by LeBlanc (2003b). My purpose here is not to rehash these arguments; the bigger picture only concerns us in a few comparative ways.

The focus here is on the possible spread of early farmers from Mesoamerica into the American Southwest. The model proposed for Mesoamerica can be summarized as follows: agriculture, in particular maize agriculture (but not necessarily limited to maize), developed in central or west-central Mesoamerica and became a viable subsistence strategy sometime around 3000–2500 B.C. At some point prior to 2500 B.C., farmers who spoke an early form of Uto-Aztecan (UA) began to spread north in either a wave of advance or a leapfrogging process, ultimately reaching the desert areas of southern Arizona, southern New Mexico, northern Sonora, and northern Chihuahua. From there, after a pause of some time, the farmers spread farther north into the Four Corners region of northeastern Arizona and southeastern Utah, where they are known archaeologically as Western Basketmaker II. Ultimately, some of their descendants moved into the Great Basin and desert California, where they stopped farming but continued to be speakers of UA.

It has also been proposed that in parallel with the situation in the Near East and perhaps Southeast Asia, there were multiple radiations out of the original core area of domestication in Mesoamerica (Diamond and Bellwood 2003). This would have involved the spread of Mayan speakers to the Gulf of Mexico and the Yucatán. In parallel with the Middle East, some linguistic groups, especially the Oto-

Manguean, did not spread much at all. That is, the northern spread of UA-speaking farmers was only one part of a process of the adoption and spread of agriculture out of the Mesoamerican core area.[1]

My purpose here is to review the evidence, both pro and con, for a UA-speaking farmer spread into the American Southwest. It is hoped that this will stimulate research where we have information and help with the derivation of new ways of testing the model. This is not intended as a review of the history of these ideas or to build a case for a particular interpretation. Instead, the goal is to look at the various lines of evidence that have been or could be advanced to confirm or refute the model and to see where they stand at present.

BACKGROUND

The process of the spread of farmers in the overall model has received various names and been met with controversy. The original formulation by Albert Ammerman and Luca Cavalli-Sforza (1979) used the term "wave of advance" to describe the process. This idea predicted that farmers on and near the boundary between farmers and foragers would increase in number, and these groups would hive off and found new communities in the former territory of the foragers. This was proposed to be a fairly regular process, resulting in a movement of the dividing line between foragers and farmers of a fairly constant average number of kilometers per year. It was soon pointed out that such farmers would have selected certain soil types and other physiographic features to found new settlements, and the boundary line would have been more of a blotchy zone than an actual line. This process has been given several names, including leapfrogging or "salutatory jumps" (van Andel and Runnels 1995). Moreover, some areas might have been avoided altogether by the initial farmers, ultimately leaving large pockets of foragers surrounded by farmers (e.g., Scarre 2002). In the case of the New World, in the more arid region north of Mesoamerica the process may have been to jump from the optimal farming zone of one river valley north to the optimal zone of the next river valley. Only over time would the growing population of the initial river valley expand into all the possible farming niches in that valley.

This model, regardless of how it might be nuanced, is very different from one that considers the movement of only domesticates and technology—that is, a diffusion model without significant movement of people. Of course, even if migration were the most significant factor, we would expect reality to be more complex, with some diffusion and some migration. In particular, it would appear that where foragers had high population densities, the diffusion of farming technology was much more likely than a migration of farmers into these foragers' territories. The adoption of agriculture by foragers in what is now Scandinavia is considered an example of such a process (Price, Gebrauer, and Keeley 1995; Price 2000). Such examples by no means negate the importance of migration to the process of farming spread, as long as such diffusion was relatively restricted in space.

Steven A. LeBlanc

The wave of advance, or some version of this theory, can be contrasted with block, long-distance, or coordinated migrations, where large numbers of people move en masse to new locations, often moving through the territories of others or otherwise ignoring large intervening spaces. Examples of this include the waves of nomads that swept through Europe or the movement of Athapaskan speakers from Canada into the Southwest, with none of the migrants remaining in the intervening territory. No one has proposed such a block migration for the initial spread of agriculture, although it remains a distinct possibility for the proposed movement from the low desert to the Four Corners area of the Southwest by the Western Basketmakers.

A key aspect of the farmer spread model is that it was the result of rapid population growth by sedentary farmers. This growth would have been much more rapid for the farmers than for the foragers whose lands were encroached upon. That is, low-density, stable population foragers were at a competitive disadvantage against sedentary farmers and were either replaced by the farmers violently (LeBlanc 2003a, 2003b) or were partially absorbed into the farmer societies, as considered in a later section.

The Western Basketmaker II population is a particularly important part of this model because we have so much information about them, more than for any other relevant cultural group. Before I present the evidence for and against the overall model, I outline the situation for the Western Basketmakers because it interweaves with the general model in many ways.

THE PARTICULAR CASE OF BASKETMAKER II

It has been proposed that the last stage in this spread of farmers into the American Southwest from Mesoamerica consisted of what are now termed Western Basketmaker II groups moving north from the low desert around Tucson and adjacent areas to the Four Corners region of Arizona and Utah. This particular case is of special interest, in part because it is in an area better known archaeologically for the relevant time periods than any of the areas to the south. It was Richard Wetherill, discoverer of Mesa Verde, who apparently first used the term Basketmaker (Blackburn and Williamson 1997). The first solid information about the Basketmakers was recovered in the 1910s (Kidder and Guernsey 1919; Guernsey and Kidder 1921). For these and other reasons discussed later, the Basketmaker II (referred to hereafter as just Basketmaker) situation is worth consideration in more detail, even though it represents only a small portion of the proposed geographic range of the UA speaker spread.[2]

The Basketmaker situation has an interesting nuance. A number of people have proposed that there were two types of Basketmakers. This has been proposed by Morris and Burgh (1954), Irwin-Williams (1967), and Berry and Berry (1986) but is fully laid out, championed, and synthesized by Matson (1991, 2001, 2003b; Matson and Dohm 1994). One division, termed the Western Basketmakers, is made up of the proposed migrant maize farmers, spreading from the southern Arizona area into what is today northeastern Arizona and southeastern Utah. In turn, it has been proposed that members of an indigenous population of former foragers living in northwestern New Mexico (Eddy 1961, 1966) and southwestern Colorado (Morris and Burgh 1954; Reed and Kainer 1978) were not swamped and replaced by the encroaching farmers but adopted farming themselves and are known as the Eastern Basketmakers.[3]

In sum, it is proposed that there were two populations of farmers dating from the middle of the last millennium B.C. and the first few centuries A.D. in the Plateau country of the Northern Southwest (see Smiley 1994 for a review of the relevant dates). Neither group made pottery, hence the name Basketmakers. However, the argument goes that they were ethnically very distinct. Some of these differences have long been recognized; others have only been discovered subsequent to and as a response to the proposed migration model. Prior to the Basketmaker period and contemporary with it to the north in the Great Basin were indigenous foragers known as the Archaic. It has been proposed that the Eastern Basketmakers derived from some of these Archaic peoples. I do not deal with these indigenous foragers here; Bruce Huckell (1996), however, provides an excellent overview of current knowledge about them.

The evidence that these two archaeological cultures were distinct is substantial and compelling, although a number of avenues of research have not been well explored, and some ambiguities remain. What follows is only a brief discussion of the relevant differences. The two types of Basketmakers made their baskets, sandals, cradle boards, and pithouses differently (Matson 2003b).[4] They had distinct forms of projectile points (side notched versus corner notched) and different methods and tools for chipping them (Geib 2002). They buried their dead in different orientations (Mowrer 2003).[5] Also, the Western Basketmaker migrants made cordage almost exclusively from yucca, while it appears the indigenous Eastern Basketmakers used yucca, Indian hemp (Apocynum), and milkweed (Haas 2003), although how commonly these fibers were used is unclear.[6]

Another, more tentative difference also exists. The Western Basketmakers took trophy heads and, in particular, removed the skin from the victim's head and carefully painted and sewed the skin into a trophy. This is attested to by numerous examples from rock art and from actual recovered skins (Cole 1984; Kidder and Guernsey 1919). In contrast, nothing like this is known from the Eastern Basketmaker area or from the more northern Archaic people, who resemble the Eastern Basketmaker in a variety of ways. These people, in turn, possibly had a distinctive behavior of taking scalps and stretching them on a special type of open-weave basket (Howard and Janetski 1992).[7] As for many potential Eastern Basketmaker traits, it is unclear how common these scalp baskets were. It is possible that both groups had traditions of taking trophies from defeated enemies, but they did so in different and distinctive ways. Other tantalizing differences include the presence of dog burials among Western but not Eastern Basketmakers and the use of red ochre or hematite in burials—about 8 percent among Western Basketmakers (if one ignores the aberrant Cave 7 burials) and none for the Eastern Basketmakers (Mowrer 2003).

A major difference also appears to exist in the rock art of the two areas. The western area has numerous examples of the dramatic style termed San Juan Anthropomorphic (Schaafsma 1980, 1994; Cole 1984, 1990). No similarly dramatic style is known from the Eastern Basketmaker area. However, some figures mimic the broad-shouldered, narrow-waisted figures from the west (Schaafsma 1963). Unfortunately, these are not well dated and may be from the Basketmaker III period. This may account for the differences in headdresses, arms, and feet between the broad-shouldered figures in the two areas; the eastern examples may derive from the earlier Basketmaker II figures from the west. Overall, there is less rock art in the eastern area than in the west, making good comparisons difficult. Some scholars see antecedents of the San Juan style in the preceding Barrier Canyon Archaic style, while in other ways they seem distinctly different. If antecedents are present, it would not negate the differences between the two areas but would argue against the Western Basketmakers being migrants.

As I discuss in the upcoming archaeological evidence section, some similarities are seen between the Western Basketmaker San Juan style and pictographs in northern Chihuahua, which do not fit with the idea of a San Juan style derivation from the Barrier Canyon style. This topic needs to be further explored with the migration model explicitly in mind, but at present, rock art seems to demonstrate a tightly interacting Western Basketmaker system (Robins 1995). It provides little support for differences between Eastern and Western Basketmaker or a southern link to the Western Basketmaker population. Other possible cultural differences may turn out to be significant after further work. In all, given the similarities in the environment around the Four Corners area and how hard it is to recognize the kinds of material cultural traits that might reflect ethnic differences, the number of differences between Western and Eastern Basketmaker that have been found is remarkable, if not overwhelming.[8]

A final warning note on the Basketmaker situation is in order. Strong evidence indicates that the Western Basketmakers were committed farmers, based on settlement patterns, midden remains, stable isotopes, coprolites, and dental caries (Chisholm and Matson 1994; Martin 1999; Matson 2003a; Matson and Chisholm 1991; Schollmeyer and Turner 2004; but see Wills 2001).[9] However, we have only settlement pattern data that suggest the Eastern Basketmakers were also such committed farmers. Until equally strong evidence is provided for them, we need to be cautious about this conclusion and the models we derive from it.

While the differences are considerable, linking the Western Basketmakers (the proposed migrants) to the pre-pottery-making farmers—variously termed Pre-pottery Neolithic, San Pedro Cochise, and Pre-pottery Formative—of the lower desert in southern Arizona is less strong. Until recently, it was not realized that there were substantial numbers of farmers by 1000 B.C. or earlier in this southern zone. Several projects and overviews, discussed in the archaeological evidence section, have radically changed our understanding.

We lack the quantities of perishable remains in southern Arizona to compare with the abundant remains in the Four Corners region. Some links, however, do exist. P. G. Matson (personal communication) and Laurie Webster (in press) feel the McEuen Cave material is very similar overall to Western Basketmaker. It is not clear if Huckell and colleagues (1999) are of the same mind. Matson also suggested that the Mogollon rockshelters are transitional between the San Pedro and Western Basketmaker. Webster (in press, note 3) has identified several possible Early Agricultural perishable assemblages from undated caves in the southern Mogollon region that could be compared to Western Basketmaker. While some Western Basketmaker sandals and baskets are similar to those of the San Pedro Cochise, I know of no one who has looked to see if there are similarities in cordage fibers. Western Basketmaker projectile points do look like southern San Pedro points, although I have been unable to determine whether the San Pedro points were made with the same special tools and methods of the Western Basketmakers.[10]

Relationships between projectile points are far more complex than considered here (see Chapter 9 for a more nuanced discussion). It has been suggested that contracting stem points appeared earlier in Mesoamerica than in the Southwest (Berry and Berry 1986; Mabry 1998b), that Cortaro bifaces may be associated with initial farmers (Roth and Huckell 1992), and that San Pedro points evolved somewhat later (Carpenter, Sanchez, and Villalpando 2002). Cortaro bifaces seem to be a local southwestern development, however. Mabry and colleagues make a good case that they were made prior to and after farming began (Chapter 9). They do not seem very relevant to the migration issue. The relationships between point types from central Mexico to the Four Corners region warrant further analysis, but presently they do not seem to provide much support for or against the migration model.

Pithouses from the low desert are different from those of either of the Basketmakers but are more similar to the earliest ones from Western Basketmaker and quite different from Eastern Basketmaker forms. Both the Western Basketmaker and low desert pithouses lack vestibules, often have bell-shaped storage pits in the floor, and have vertical peripheral roof supports instead of the horizontal or cribbed roofs found in Eastern Basketmaker structures. Burial orientations are rather variable for the fairly small southern desert sample, as are burial orientations today among modern indigenous southwestern populations. The majority of the broadly contemporary La Playa burials from Sonora are described as oriented to the west (Montero et al. 2004; also discussed later in this chapter), which fits neither the Western nor Eastern Basketmakers, although the excavators noted that numerous burials had red ochre associated with them, which does match the Western Basketmaker pattern. Burials of maize farmers with red ochre from the same time span were also found in the Cienega Valley of southern Arizona (Minturn and Lincoln-Babb 1995), so this trait is worth further study. In a similar vein, dog burials are found in both the La Playa and Western Basketmaker burial contexts, and the distribution of this behavior may have cultural significance.

Also, there does not seem to be a continuum of early farmers between the low desert and the Western Basketmaker area. What have been termed Basketmaker II sites are found along the Little Colorado River (Gumerman 1966). McEuen Cave apparently has material that fits well with a link between the low desert sites and Western Basketmaker II (Huckell, Huckell, and Shackley 1999). Even if both these localities are evidence of early migrant farmers, which is far from demonstrated for the Little Colorado sites, that still leaves a good 175-kilometer gap with no good evidence one way or the other. Whether this is the result of a lack of good cave deposits from the intervening area, a result of leapfrogging behavior, or evidence against the migration model is unclear; this issue has been little considered.

We also know that maize farming was not ubiquitous in the 500 B.C.–A.D. 500 time range in the Southwest. Around two dozen rather amorphous pit structures dating to this period have been excavated from almost as many different sites along the western side of the Rio Grande Valley near Albuquerque. In spite of considerable flotation analysis, no maize has been recovered from them (Schmader 2001; see also Post 2002).

Further complicating matters, it is possible that maize agriculture diffused to southern Arizona, and only at that point was there a migration of farmers to the Four Corners area, leading to the two different Basketmaker societies. That is, the documentation of a migration at the very end of the range of maize farming does not demonstrate the existence of a significant migration over the entire range being discussed. On the other hand, as will be considered, the fact that today the farming population in the former Western Basketmaker range speaks UA and it is believed that the later residents of the more easterly area did not provides interesting support for this longer migration scenario.

EVIDENCE FOR A UTO-AZTECAN MIGRATION INTO THE SOUTHWEST

Having laid out the basic model of a Uto-Aztecan–speaking farmer spread and the special case of the Basketmakers, I now examine several lines of linguistic, genetic, and archaeological evidence. Factors that do not support such a model also need to be considered. Finally, I discuss other possible models that could account for some of the supportive evidence and some of the negatives. This is a fairly complicated mosaic to discuss and analyze, so it is presented in several parts.

Linguistic Evidence

Some background is required to understand the current linguistic evidence for an early Uto-Aztecan speaker spread. UA, in some form, is spoken from southern Mesoamerica to Idaho and from California to the Plains. In particular, UA speakers form an almost continuous chain from the northern part of central Mexico (Aztec and related languages) to Huichol and Cora farther north. From there, a large area of UA Tepiman and Piman speakers extends up into the area around Tucson and Phoenix (with a gap between closely related Tepiman and Piman occupied by UA speakers, the Opata, Tarahumara, and others). Then there is a gap from the Pima north to the Hopi of northern Arizona. From there, the entire Great Basin into southern Idaho spoke closely related UA languages, lumped into a subfamily termed Numic—including Shoshonean, Ute, Paiute, and, out onto the Plains, Comanche. Peoples in southern California spoke Takic and related UA languages. Neither the Numic speakers nor the southern California UA speakers practiced farming in any meaningful way. It is this enormous expanse of UA—from central Mexico to Idaho—that makes it such a good candidate for a farmer spread, if one accepts other worldwide cases of the process.

In Mesoamerica, one branch of Uto-Aztecan is found, obviously including Nahua, the language spoken by the Aztecs. However, three other language families also occur there: Mayan, Oto-Manguean, and Mixe-Zoquean, as well as some minor or isolated languages. Within Mesoamerica, UA did not cover a particularly large area, nor was it highly differentiated. Mayan and Oto-Manguean covered reasonably large areas within Mesoamerica, whereas Mixe-Zoquean was rather restricted in space.

Also relevant is the linguistic situation in the Greater Southwest at the time of European contact, involving four ancient language families and the more recent Athapaskan speakers. As noted, UA speakers are represented by Piman speakers of southern Arizona and Sonora, the extinct Concho of northern Chihuahua, the Hopi of northern Arizona, and the Numic speakers of the Great Basin (Paiutes, Shoshone, Utes, and other tribes). The Rio Grande Pueblos are Tanoan speakers (Tewa, Tiwa, and Towa, as well as now-extinct languages). It has been postulated that Tanoan is very distantly related to UA, but any common language would have existed far earlier than the posited spread of UA into the Southwest and can be ignored (see Hill, in press). In addition, there are speakers of Zuni and Keres (the latter spoken by Acoma and some Rio Grande Pueblos, such as Santo Domingo and Cochiti). At this point, Zuni and Keres are considered unrelated to any other languages, certainly any others in the Southwest (Hale and Harris 1979).

The southwestern picture is further complicated because of the sharp decline in the number of polities, and presumably languages, in the Southwest since the A.D. 1200s. There are no obvious linguistic descendants of the peoples archaeologically known as the Mogollon (LeBlanc 1989; Wheat 1955). The Zuni have often been proposed as such descendants, but recent thought on the subject provides little support for this. It is unclear whether the Hohokam, the archaeological entity that succeeded the early farmers of the low desert, were the ancestors of the present-day Pima or whether the Hohokam greatly declined in numbers and were partially or totally supplanted or absorbed by Piman speakers, who then spread north into the Hohokam heartland (see Shaul and Hill 1998 for a good perspective on this).[11] Furthermore, a number of polities on the Colorado Plateau (roughly twenty-four of twenty-seven) have become extinct since the A.D. 1200s. It is extremely unlikely that no languages were lost in this process. Thus, what we see today as linguistic isolates and gaps in language distributions may be the result of events in late prehistory. The historic situation may not well reflect the situation a thousand or more years ago (LeBlanc 1999, 2000).

To complicate matters even further, little, if any, consensus exists as to what languages were spoken by which archaeological entities. (The best syntheses are still the now-dated Ford, Schroeder, and Peckham 1972 and Irwin-Williams 1967.) For example, it has been proposed that the people of Mesa Verde spoke some form of either Keres or Tanoan. It is generally agreed that the present-day Hopi are an amalgam of peoples (the Hopi define them as clans) from a wide area, with the amalgamation taking place in late prehistory, most likely in the A.D. 1200s or later, or at least after the breakup of Chaco in the A.D. 1100s. It is unlikely that all these groups spoke the same language before migrating to the Hopi area. A common language could have resulted from each new group adopting Hopi after its arrival (if it had not spoken it previously), or, alternatively, one large group could have moved in and its language became dominant, even though the previous inhabitants did not speak Hopi. Although the slow assimilation of people (clans) with no language shift is more likely, other possibilities do exist. That is, because of the process of the formation of present-day Hopi society, the original language spoken earlier by people in the immediate area was not necessarily Hopi, although most likely it was.

Jane Hill has been the leading linguistic proponent of a northern spread of UA along with farming, and a brief summary of her work follows (Hill 2001, 2002, 2003, in press). In short, she proposes that the earlier idea that UA originated in the southern United States and northern Mexico and from there spread south into central Mexico is not supported by any substantial evidence. This contradicts a long and widely held view (e.g., Campbell 1977; Fowler 1983; Hale and Harris 1979; Lamb 1958). So although her case appears strong to the non-linguist, it is controversial. Of particular importance, Hill has reconstructed a number of terms (about ten) for maize, maize farming, and maize processing from the original UA, termed Proto-Uto-Aztecan. Interestingly, both Proto-Maya and Proto-Mixe-Zoque in central Mexico also had agricultural terms in their proto-vocabulary.[12] (Importantly, Tanoan, a presumed indigenous southwestern language, did not). The implication is that an early form of each of these language families was spoken in Mesoamerica at the time agriculture was developed, and all became farmers roughly simultaneously. Of note, Hill cannot reconstruct Proto-Uto-Aztecan terminology for beans, which, based on archaeological evidence, were added to the farming complex at a later date than the proposed initial farming spread (but see Mabry 2005). Hill argues that UA spread north and then differentiated, first into a northern and southern branch, then the northern branch split further. One split took place as some farmers moved into areas that did not support farming. Alternatively, UA speakers may have moved beyond the Southwest as farmers, but because of climate change these areas later no longer supported farming, and the UA speakers reverted to a forager lifestyle.

The fact that not all UA speakers were farmers in the recent past has been used to argue against them having been farmers initially. This seems to bother linguists. I cannot envision an archaeologist believing this provides any strong evidence against an initial farmer model as it is known to have happened elsewhere. Hill does a good job of demolishing the logic of rejecting a southern origin for UA based on the presence of UA speakers who were not farmers. She goes on to look at the proposed dates for these linguistic divisions and finds them broadly compatible with the migration model from central Mesoamerica. Although she admits that several aspects of the linguistic evidence are still unclear or possibly contradictory, it generally fits with what we know, and she believes there is no strong contradictory evidence (although see Campbell 2003 and Carpenter, Sanchez, and Villalpando 2002 for other views).

In addition, Hill has shown that linguistic borrowing between UA and Tanoan is just what would be expected if northern UA was spoken by migrant farmers in the Southwest and Tanoan was the language of indigenous foragers who adopted agriculture. She argues that about 3,000 years ago, the two proto-groups exchanged vocabularies. The speakers of the precursor to the modern Tanoan languages obtained a number of words relating to cultivated plants from northern UA speakers, while the early northern Uto-Aztecan speakers obtained a number of words for indigenous plants of the Colorado Plateau from Tanoan speakers (Hill 2002, in press).

There are still other linguistic lines of evidence to pursue in the future. These include terminology for pottery and cooking with pottery, which was not part of the initial farming complex and should not reconstruct to Proto-Uto-Aztecan. Supportive evidence would include terminology that involved other aspects of the initial farming complex besides maize that could be reconstructed to Proto-UA. It must be remembered that a rapid farmer spread is a very new idea, not just to archaeologists but also to linguists. Both, as late as the mid-1980s, assumed that Uto-Aztecan speakers were Archaic foragers who spread from the Greater Southwest well into Mexico and the Great Basin and had not migrated north (e.g., Wilcox 1986). Because the migration model and a southern origin for UA are such new ideas, many avenues of linguistic research relevant to a migration model have yet to be explored.

Again, while the evidence in favor of Proto-Uto-Aztecan speakers having been farmers is good, this does not automatically support the full migration model. A migration could have extended only part of the way north, after which diffusion took hold, and only later did UA speakers move farther north, resulting in the apparent isomorphism between initial farmers and present-day UA speakers. That is, the linguistic evidence is compelling, but it is only one of many lines of evidence that must be considered in demonstrating the validity of the model.

Biological Evidence

Biological evidence for a possible UA speaker migration comes from several sources. First and strongest is direct genetic evidence. This comes primarily from living peoples in both Mexico and the Southwest, but ancient DNA data are available from the Southwest as well. Evidence in the form of skeletal traits (including dental traits) also exists. DNA-genetic data fall into three categories: mitochondria (mtDNA), Y-chromosome, and autosomal. Of these, mtDNA, which derives only from the female line, is currently of the most interest and utility. Considerable variability exists within human mtDNA that is not believed to be under selection and so provides good evidence for historic relationships. mtDNA variants are usually lumped into larger groupings called haplogroups. Depending on how they are defined, there are dozens or hundreds worldwide, but as we shall see, the number of different major haplogroups in the Americas is very limited, presumably because of a small number of people in the initial colonizing group(s).

The genetic data are in their early stages of collection and interpretation, especially those from the New World. In fact, it is not always obvious how to interpret the data at hand. So it is useful to draw upon what we know about the genetics in an area where we have both much more genetic data and much better archaeological data, namely the Middle East and Europe. I deal with these data first to build a framework for interpreting the New World genetic data.

Middle Eastern and European mtDNA. Current understanding of events in the Middle East and Europe is that agriculture developed in the Fertile Crescent, especially in the Levantine (western) part of the arc. It then spread to the Anatolian Plateau, beginning in the 7000s B.C., and ceramics were added to the toolkit soon thereafter. From there, it spread west into the Balkans by land and into eastern Greece, especially Thessaly and Macedonia, possibly by sea as well as by land. Farming or farmers spread from there into Western Europe, finally reaching the British Isles around 4000 B.C. It has been proposed that these early farmers spoke Indo-European (Renfrew 1987). This story has far too many nuances to consider here, but one aspect is particularly revealing: the initial farmer spread into northern Greece.

It is widely, but perhaps not universally, accepted that the earliest farmers in Greece were migrants from Asia (Perles 2001; Runnels 2001, 2003; van Andel and Runnels 1995). Extensive archaeological survey in northern Greece has found little evidence for preceding Mesolithic foragers, and their population must have been low. The sudden phenomenal increase in population, the founding of dozens of farming village sites, and a host of close material correlates of these farmers with those of Western Asia point to a substantial migration around 6800 B.C. So although other aspects of a farmer spread through Europe may be debated (see Zvelebil and Lillie 2000 and other chapters in Price 2000), the case for a farmer migration to Greece is compelling. Thus, this case serves as an instructive example of the resultant genetic makeup of modern populations derived in part from such farmer spreads. That is, Greece is a case where we reasonably know what happened, so what do the genetics look like in such a situation?

Relevant data have been presented in various papers, including Bellwood and Renfew (2003) and especially Richards (2003) and Richards et al. (1996). According to Richards and others (2000), who, incidentally, seems strongly against a Neolithic migration of any consequence (see Richards 2003), the mtDNA (female) contribution of Middle Eastern Neolithic migrants in Greece (actually southeastern Europe because his sample of 166 individuals includes 42 Albanians, with the remainder from northern Greece) is about 20 percent. However, the Middle Eastern sample includes Iran, the Arabian Peninsula, and the Fertile Crescent, as well as Turkey (in spite of considerable effort, I cannot find the basic data for just Turkey and Greece). Thus, it seems fair to argue that genetic analysis shows a Neolithic migrant contribution to the northern Greece gene pool of 20-25 percent using standard methods and assumptions.[13]

The upshot is that there is much less genetic evidence than one might expect for the clearly large-scale movement of early farmers into an almost empty area. Why? There are several possible reasons. Not all of Greece was empty in 6800 B.C. While Thessaly may have been colonized, foragers in other areas may have switched to farming and sustained enough population growth to resist being completely replaced by the descendants of the migrants. Second, the farmers may have incorporated foragers into their gene pool, especially women, the rationale for and mathematics of which I discuss later. Third, about half the genetic diversity in both Greece and Anatolia seems to be the result of later population movements and gene flows. So even if the late Neolithic population of Greece had 20 percent indigenous and 80 percent migrant mtDNA, the modern ratios of the mtDNA would be only 10 percent and 40 percent, with the other 50 percent mtDNA derived from later events.

Still other factors are at work, however. Importantly, the presumption is that the DNA of the migrants can be differentiated from those of the indigenous foragers. However, the farmers in the not-too-distant past had been foragers themselves, and the founding farming population must have had some gene flow with foragers in Anatolia.[14] Just how different were the forager genes between Greece and the Fertile Crescent? Certainly, there must have been some differences, but equally they should not be expected to have been completely different. That is, a founding population of farmers, wherever they are from—a core area or an area they colonized previously—will not be completely genetically distinct from any indigenous foragers they displace or do not displace. Thus, any measure of a migrant farmer genetic contribution must underestimate their actual proportion in the early stages of colonization.

When we look at Greece, the seeming paradox of archaeological evidence for a clear migration of farmers from Anatolia, and the estimate of only approximately 20 percent of the mtDNA genes and approximately 25 percent of the Y-chromosome genes in modern Greece being from such Neolithic farmers, is not a paradox at all. It is simply the result of all these factors combined. We should not expect there to be much more genetic trace of such migrations in any other instances. That is, 20-25 percent of exotic farmer genes is evidence not of a minor migration of farmers and primarily evidence of agricultural diffusion but the opposite.[15] These frequencies represent the effect of a relatively massive migration of farmers displacing relatively small numbers of indigenous foragers. We should interpret the evidence from the New World with this example in mind.

Before proceeding, there is another aspect of Neolithic farmer behavior that we must model: the nature of farmer-forager interaction along the boundary zone between encroaching farmers and indigenous foragers. Based on what we know about such interaction among foragers and farmers/herders and what we know about warfare and conflict in the past (LeBlanc 2003a), we can expect that farmers will incorporate forager females into the farmer gene pool but much less rarely forager males. The encroaching farmers should be expected to have come into conflict with the foragers.[16] In such conflict situations, the greater numbers and reproductive capacity of the farmers should mean they would win out most of the time. In other situations, tribally organized farmers kill men and often children while capturing women, especially those of reproductive age. Even without conflict, we would expect there to have been differential incorporation of female genes into the farmer gene pool. For example, in Southern Africa, Bantu-speaking herders incorporate !Kung forager women, especially women in their reproductive prime, into the Bantu herder gene pool but not men. We would expect the same for the Neolithic forager-farmer interaction. As the farmers spread, they would have incorporated women into their social systems. And since this would have been a one-directional process, such incorporation would have had a dilutive effect on the farmer mtDNA genes. Each generation, as the farmers advanced, some forager genes would have been included in the gene pool, so that the proportion of farmer genes would have declined generation by generation. This would have been true whether the interaction was peaceful or competitive. In either case, forager women would have been brought into farmer societies.

Although small per generation, the cumulative effect of this process would have been significant. For example, assume that 2 percent of the women along the edge of an advance were captured or incorporated as foragers every generation, and they had an mtDNA haplogroup not present among the farmers (that is, for every 100 farmer women, 2 forager women were incorporated into the farmers). If this process was repeated for forty generations (1,000 years), the initial farmer mtDNA along the edge of the advance would be diluted to less than half.[17] Such a rate of incorporation does not seem unreasonable. Of course, as the farming population grew, the number of foragers that would be incorporated would have declined proportionally, so such a rate would only be maintained along the leading edge of an advance.

In summary, a massive Neolithic migration of farmers into Greece resulted in a residual effect of only 25 percent demonstrably Neolithic genes introduced into the modern Greek gene pool.

mtDNA evidence for a Uto-Aztecan Speaker Migration. With this background, we can examine the current relevant DNA evidence for the spread of Uto-Aztecan.

The Case for an Early Farmer Migration into the Greater American Southwest

There is recent useful information on Mexican mtDNA as the result of a massive project by Brian Kemp and associates (Kemp 2006; Kemp, Resender, and Smith 2005), who have systematically sampled UA speakers from central Mexico into Chihuahua. There is also a fair amount of mtDNA data from modern southwestern peoples, including UA-speaking Pima, Paiute, and related groups, and smaller numbers from Tanoan and Zuni speakers. There is also a good mtDNA sample from Athapaskan speakers, who entered the Southwest long after the events we are interested in, but given that the gene flow between them and historic Pueblo and Piman peoples has the potential for obscuring underlying patterns, they need to be incorporated into our thinking. Finally, there is a small but interesting amount of ancient mtDNA from Anasazi populations, including a small number of published and unpublished Basketmaker II samples. These include both skeletal and non-skeletally derived mtDNA. There is also ancient mtDNA from the Great Basin. There are no useful Keres speaker samples, and the Hopi sample is extremely small. This is unfortunate when one looks to relationships among the Basketmaker populations. Moreover, no ancient mtDNA samples exist from early farmers from southern Arizona or Sonora. Finally, there are not enough Y-chromosome data to discuss in any meaningful way.

The peoples of the Americas have four basic mtDNA haplogroups, termed A, B, C, and D. There is also a rare haplogroup X, but it is hard to detect. It is inconsistently reported (see Smith et al. 1999) and appears to be rare in the Southwest, so at present it is best only to consider differences among the basic four haplogroups. Within these haplogroups, there is additional variability in what is termed the hyper-variable region of the mtDNA. Such hyper-variable region data are used extensively in Europe and the rest of the world. Little use of them has been made in the Americas, however, and so, unfortunately, they are ignored here.

Overall, high frequencies of A and moderate B and low D seems a generalized pattern for modern-day central Mesoamerica, the purported point of origin for the spreading farmers. This includes Maya (and Mixe) speakers, with 32–63 percent A and 0–12 percent D; Oto-Manguean speakers (Mixtec and Zapotec), with 33–93 percent A and very low D, 0–6 percent. Of greater relevance are mtDNA frequencies from Uto-Aztecan speakers from central Mexico. Two modern samples of Nahua speakers have 38–63 percent A and just a trace (1–2%) of D. An archaeological sample from Tlatelolco (in the Aztec capital of Tenochtitlán) shows a similarly high A (65%) and a higher D (17%). At the time, this was a very cosmopolitan city, and much of the population may not have been of Uto-Aztecan extraction, which might account for the high D (data aggregated in Lorenz and Smith 1996 and greatly increased and summarized by Kemp 2006).

There are also data from three Uto-Aztecan–speaking communities that span the gap between central Mexico and the Southwest: Tarahumara, Huichol, and Cora. These have 18–25 percent A, 21–49 percent B, and 0–5 percent D. The Uto-Aztecan (Piman) speakers of southern Arizona have about 5 percent A, 49 percent B, and a very low D of 0.5 percent. It has been suggested that since the prehistoric period, modern Piman speakers have had significant gene flow with non-Uto-Aztecan–speaking Yumans. The Piman speakers can be characterized as having low A as a result of a clinal decline in Uto-Aztecans as one moves north, further diluted by long-term interaction with Yuman speakers who have extremely low A. The Hopi have 17 percent A and 83 percent B, but the sample size is only six individuals.

Thus, there seems to be a cline in the level of A among UA speakers as one moves north. Haplogroup A goes from 50 percent or more in central Mexico to around 25 percent in very northern Mexico. Overall, this is in contrast to mtDNA in the American Southwest, where Puebloan A is very low and the region is dominated by haplogroup B (ignoring the small Hopi sample). The exception is the Athapaskan speakers, who may have been fixed or almost fixed on A when they reached the Southwest. They presently have about 58–64 percent A, presumably lowered by admixture with Puebloan and Pimans. I return to the Athapaskan speakers later.

The mtDNA of Numic speakers of the Great Basin is interpretively difficult. The current idea is that northern UA speakers moved into southern California and from there radiated into the Great Basin. They have even lower A than other UA speakers but high D (Northern Paiute/Shoshoni A=0, B=42%, D=48%). Also relevant are some mtDNA from farther west. Kaestle and Smith (2001) report 12 percent A and 44 percent D for a small sample of California Penutian and 46 percent A and 27 percent D for Central Coast Hokan. That is, aboriginal California seems to have high D. One is tempted to see the Numic high levels of D as a result of admixture with Californians prior to their expansion into the Great Basin. We would expect them to have picked up some A as well, although they could have admixed with people resembling the Washo, who live on the boundary between the Great Basin and California and have no A, 54 percent B, and 11 percent D (Lorenz and Smith 1996). With all these possibilities, it is difficult to make sense of the Numic data (and the Fremont, discussed later). Although they are relevant to our discussion as UA speakers, they do not seem to shed any light on the issues at hand.

The Tanoans, who today occupy the Rio Grande Valley but who may have been related to the Eastern Basketmakers, have no A, B=89 percent, and no D. The only other modern sample of relevance is Zuni, with A=15 percent, B=77 percent, and no D (data from Lorenz and Smith 1996). Some of the Zuni A could be the result of admixture with Athapaskan, but Kemp and colleagues (2005) nicely demonstrate that this is not always the case, based on sequencing the hyper-variable region. Some of this A is indigenous A and not Athapaskan A. Since Zuni is not Uto-Aztecan but may well have incorporated some Hohokam or Mogollon groups (at least the former are assumed to have been UA speakers; Shaul and Hill 1998) into its polity (Smith, Woodbury, and Woodbury 1966; Matson, in press), this would explain the presence of indigenous A mtDNA.

Two samples are useful for trying to define a non-UA baseline for the Southwest. First is the modern Tanoan speaker sample from the Rio Grande area. As previously stated, several lines of evidence suggest they may derive in part from indigenous foragers who took up farming. As mentioned, they have no A, with B=89 percent, and no D. A second sample is the ancient Fremont, who occupied part of the Great Basin north of what was the Western Basketmaker II territory up to the A.D. 1200s, when they disappear from the archaeological record. One idea is that they were Anasazi who expanded north when the climate was favorable. Others would have them as descendants of the original Archaic population. Most likely they were multiethnic, with some perhaps derived from Anasazi and others probably descended from various different Archaic populations. In any case, based on mtDNA extracted from archaeological specimens, they have very low D and A and low C: A=0 percent, B=61 percent, C=13 percent, D=6 percent (O'Rourke, Parr, and Carlyle 1999).[18] The pattern looks similar, but not identical, to the Tanoans, and both may be representative of the ancestral Archaic peoples of the Plateau and Great Basin.

Ancient Basketmaker II mtDNA. Recently, the study of Basketmaker II mtDNA has taken a new turn. It has been possible to extract DNA from ancient quids and aprons from Basketmaker caves. The haplogroups represented by thirteen quids from Boomerang Shelter have been determined (LeBlanc et al. 2007). In addition, haplogroup data have been recovered from bone from eight individuals from Canyon de Chelly (del Muerto) and Marsh Pass in Arizona and Grand Gulch and Cottonwood Canyon in southeastern Utah (Carlyle et al. 2000; Carlyle 2003). Each data set shows roughly the same pattern, and when combined, the sets provide a spatially diverse sample of twenty-one determinations. The Western Basketmaker quids from Boomerang Cave have 15 percent A and no D. The Western Basketmaker bone samples have 12.5 percent A and again no D. In combination, Western Basketmaker II has A=14 percent, B=81 percent, C=5 percent, D=0 percent. Carlyle (2003) also produced a later Anasazi sample spanning the area from southeastern Utah to near Zuni, dating from Basketmaker III through PIII. It has 9 percent A, 65 percent B, and again no D. However, this sample size is only twenty-three individuals, and the temporal and geographic spans are considerable.

In summary, there is a cline in the amount of haplogroup A among UA speakers as one moves north from central Mexico. The Western Basketmaker II sample, with its mid-level of A, slight C, and no D, is consistent with an original population from central Mexico that incorporated indigenous populations as it spread north. That is, it could be argued that the level of haplogroup A was diluted, but not to the extent seen in later southwestern Uto-Aztecan speakers or non-UA speakers like the Tanoans.[19] The low C and low D of the Western Basketmakers is also what one would expect before these increased with admixture over the ensuing two millennia. It is very difficult to explain these data by arguing that the Western Basketmaker II population was indigenous with similar mtDNA frequencies as the rest of the Southwest at 2000–1500 B.C. and simply converted to maize farming through diffusion. One can see the lack of A among the Numic speakers of the Great Basin as the end of the haplogroup A cline.

Steven A. LeBlanc

We can interpret this decline in the frequency of A as one moves north out of central Mexico as dilution of the frequency of A as indigenous, non-A-bearing forager women were added to the farmer gene pool. As noted, such a cline is observed in European mtDNA as one moves from the Middle East. For Mesoamerica and the Southwest, we would expect early Uto-Aztecan–speaking farmers, including Western Basketmakers, to have values of A somewhat lower than the Uto-Aztecan–speaking Tarahumara (25%) but higher than the 7 percent of some Piman speakers. We would expect D to be very low, and this is just what we find. Clearly, the sample sizes for all these groups are very small (more than ten times smaller than those usually analyzed for Europe). Some key populations have no samples at all, and almost no work has been done on the hyper-variable region. Thus, these data should be taken with considerable skepticism. Nevertheless, there are patterns to the data, and they provide some, although limited, support for the Uto-Aztecan migration model.

Other Genetic Evidence

Additional genetic evidence falls into two categories: that from other direct genetic traits besides mtDNA and that from indirect measures, such as dental or morphological traits. The most relevant other direct genetic data are from Smith and colleagues (2000). A rare mutational variant of the albumin gene termed Albumin Mexico (AL*Mexico) occurs in both Mesoamerica and the Southwest. It is present in low frequencies in all major language groups in Mexico and so would seem to have a deep history there. In the United States, it is limited to the Southwest and is found at about 5 percent in the UA-speaking Pima but is very rare among the Numic of the Great Basin (0.5%). No useful information on the Hopi exists. It was previously reported among the Zuni, but Smith and colleagues (2000) did not find it in a sample of 202 Zuni, so if present, it is very rare. It is not found among the Tanoan speakers. It occurs in low frequencies among the Yuman speakers and Apache. It can be argued that it is present among the Yumans because of their close and long interaction with the Pima and among the Apache because of similar, but more recent, gene flow. Thus, AL*Mexico seems to be derived in the Southwest from UA speakers and was present early enough that it made it into the Numic gene pool, although at low levels. Given its presence among most of the language families of Mesoamerica, the mutation must have occurred in Mesoamerica and moved north, not the reverse. This would support the Hill model for the origins of UA in Mesoamerica and the northern spread of UA. However, it would be helpful to have knowledge about its distribution among UA speakers between the Pima and Mesoamerica and a better sample from the Hopi before drawing more inferences from these data.

Measuring indirect genetic traits, such as dentition, has all the sampling problems inherent in ancient mtDNA studies, compounded by imperfect correspondence to underlying genetics. Conversely, these traits can be, and have been, applied to large samples, and they reflect autosomal genes, so they present a useful complement to the direct genetic data, as long as their limitations are recognized.

Unfortunately, an ongoing study on Basketmaker skull morphology is not complete, although the investigators believe there are strong morphological differences between Eastern and Western Basketmakers (Doug Owsley, personal communication, 2004). These researchers are not planning to compare Basketmakers with relevant populations from Mexico or southern Arizona in the near future, so this line of evidence will be of limited utility for some time. There are also considerable discrete dental-trait data on Basketmaker and comparative samples (Turner 1993). These have been interpreted as supporting an Eastern versus Western Basketmaker difference, with the Western Basketmakers much more Mesoamerican-like than the Eastern Basketmakers (e.g., Matson 2003b). Recently, however, additional dental data have been collected, and the earlier data have been re-tabulated because the earlier work did not directly address the Western versus Eastern Basketmaker or UA speaker questions. Moreover, some Basketmaker III individuals were commingled with the Basketmaker II samples in the initial study, potentially mixing populations inappropriately. The new data show that the Eastern and Western Basketmaker populations were very different, about as different as any pair of samples in the Southwest from later periods. Thus, they strongly support the difference between the two Basketmaker populations and provide very tentative supportive evidence that the Western Basketmaker population was related to UA speakers (LeBlanc, Turner, and Morgan, in press). However, the Eastern Basketmaker sample is still quite small, and until a larger sample can be scored, the implications of these data must be viewed with caution.

Archaeological Evidence

The relevant archaeological record is far better understood for the Southwest than for either northwestern Mexico or central Mexico. Central Mexico has evidence for a long sequence of the domestication of maize and other crops (relevant information on maize is summarized by Carpenter, Sanchez, and Villalpando 2002). Much of this information is from caves. Early farming villages are not well-known before the use of pottery about 1600–1400 B.C. (see Clark and Cheetham 2002 for a regional synthesis). There are two possibilities. One is that we should expect reasonably sized farming villages that date prior to the use of pottery. Any UA-speaking migrants presumably spread out of the core area prior to this time because the spread of agriculture (either through migration or diffusion) was not accompanied by pottery. Clark and Cheetham (2002) point out that at around 2500 B.C. there seems to be a notable shift in subsistence and land-use patterns and dependence on cultigens. Perhaps more relevant to us is their finding of indirect evidence of swidden agriculture and a significant impact on the environment all across the lowlands about 3000–2500 B.C. This timing is also supported by Pope and colleagues (2001). If the dates are correct, this would be evidence of significant population growth and the situation that I would expect to prompt a wave of advance spread. In this scenario, the conditions that would have prompted a spread of UA-speaking farmers to the north would have been met at or before 2500 B.C., that is, 1,000 years or more before pottery was in general use in Mesoamerica.

Conversely, an alternative argument is that early maize was grown for its sweet, sugary stems and not its cobs (Smalley and Blake 2003), and it was not until circa 1500 B.C. that selection in Mesoamerica resulted in a valuable, storable seed crop, and farmers growing maize for its cobs spread only after that date; this would have been closely coincident with the use of ceramics. That is, maize grown for its stems would not have provided the basis for a commitment to agriculture. Such maize might have reached the Southwest through diffusion and been used by foragers who dabbled in farming. In turn, cob maize would have enabled a commitment to agriculture, and a migration of farmers would only have taken place after cob maize had evolved. This would be reflected in the jump in population size seen in southern Arizona around 1000 B.C., when we might expect such late migrants to have reached there. David Webster and colleagues (2005) argue for a late circa 1500 B.C. transition to seed-maize growing for the Mayan area, supporting this alternative. While the sugar maize–cob maize distinction may account for early maize dates and later substantial villages in the Southwest, more evidence seems to favor an earlier migration, but a later date for an actual migration is a real possibility. Our lack of knowledge of the early farmers in the core area in terms of architecture and other material culture makes looking for evidence of a migration under either scenario more difficult than it otherwise would be. It certainly makes it harder than is the case in other areas of the world where the migration model has been proposed.

We understand even less about the archaeology between the core area and the Greater Southwest than we do of the critical time period in Mesoamerica. Preceramic villages or even cave sites are not known, except for a handful of very poorly reported examples, until one reaches Sonora or northern Chihuahua. Most of what is known has come to light very recently, radically altering our understanding for this period. In the case of Sonora, the La Playa site has a large number of burials and baking ovens from the relevant time period, but no actual village site has been discovered or excavated (Carpenter, Sanchez, and Villalpando 2005; Montero et al. 2004). In the case of Chihuahua, hilltop habitation sites, some of substantial size such as Cerro Juanaqueña (Hard and Roney 1999, 2005; Roney and Hard 2002), are known.[20] We do not know if all such sites were on hilltops (*trincheras* sites) or if there were river-edge villages like those in southern Arizona discussed later. The terracing of hilltops, from which the term *trincheras* is derived, is not restricted to Chihuahua. There are *trincheras* sites in Sonora, at least one of which has preceramic dates. However, the largest one, Cerro de Trincheras, which gave its name to the others (Sauer and Brand 1931), dates much later. Some *trincheras* are also known from southwestern New Mexico, although there is no evidence that they date before A.D. 200 (Roney 1999). There are also *trincheras* sites in Arizona. Although some were certainly used in the late prehistoric period, there is a B.C. date from one (Fish et al. 1986). Because later ceramic-producing occupation of such sites would mask earlier use, many of the *trincheras* may have been originally occupied in the Late Archaic, unbeknown to us. One possibility is that the *trincheras* were used in concert with sites along the floodplains, with the hills used for storage and defense while many daily activities, especially roasting-pit cooking, were done on the flats. The fact that the floodplain sites essentially disappear when silted over because of the absence or near absence of pottery, just as almost all large habitations sites were hidden in southern Arizona, makes this possibility more likely than we might expect.

It is in southern Arizona where the archaeological picture has recently changed most dramatically and our knowledge has increased significantly (see especially Gregory 2001; Huckell 1996; Huckell and Huckell 1984; Mabry 1998b, 2005). Much of this new material is nicely summarized in an issue of *Archaeology Southwest* devoted to early agriculture (Gregory 1999). The information comes from a series of river-edge habitation sites, such as Los Pozos, Milagro, Santa Cruz Bend, and Stone Pipe, dating to the first millennium B.C. (especially 800–400 B.C.). The decision of just what to call these habitations is in a state of flux. The generic term would be the Early Agricultural period or, as Bill Lipe has proposed, the Pre-pottery Formative. In southern Arizona the habitation sites have been assigned to the San Pedro and Cienega phases and, for the whole low desert area, the San Pedro stage of the Cochise Culture. Most of the larger sites are Cienega phase and date more recently than 800 B.C. Only with these sites in the Tucson Basin (and, to a lesser extent, elsewhere) do we get a good sense of architecture and other elements, but we have little with which to compare them. What we can say is that a number of sites have large numbers of pithouses, sometimes in the hundreds. It is not clear, however, whether they represent large aggregates of people or reuse and rebuilding in the same locality over long periods by a small number of people at any one time. Based on data from the Tucson sites and those in the Cienega Valley (Huckell 1995), a good case can be made that these were committed farmers. There is ample evidence of maize and large storage facilities.

The Sonoran site of La Playa has produced from only a fraction of the area about 160 burials that date from this same early period (Carpenter, Sanchez, and Villalpando 2002, 2005). This also implies a much larger population than that from the prior foraging period. Thus, what seems to be the case for both Sonora and the Tucson area is that the farmer population was substantially larger than what preceded it. Numerous defensive sites in northern Chihuahua on hilltops adjacent to good floodplain farmland, also dating to around 1000 B.C., seem to imply the same thing, especially that the numbers were large enough to create competition for good farmland. The apparent sudden appearance of farmers has also been proposed based on changes in perishables, settlement patterns, and maize for the low-elevation areas around El Paso, but there is much less information there than for southern Arizona (Hyland and Adovasio 2000; O'Laughlin 1980).

It has yet to be demonstrated that all the San Pedro–like societies in this large desert area shared the same culture or were descendants of UA-speaking migrants.

However, nothing substantial points to any of them being indigenous people converting to farming, as has been proposed for Eastern Basketmaker. The similarity in timing, in projectile points, and in *trincheras* sites on both sides of the Sierra and the area occupied in later periods by UA speakers would seem to support a wave of advance migration along both sides of the mountain chain (Roney and Hard 2004).

Moreover, the majority opinion among those who have focused on the Tucson and southern Arizona area is that there seems to be a cultural break with what preceded these sites. There is no strong evidence for continuity in cultural tradition in Sonora, northern Chihuahua, or El Paso either. That is, in none of these places do the early farmers seem to be essentially the same indigenous Archaic people who just added maize to their subsistence base.

A final factor, as noted elsewhere, is what a migration rate might have been between the Mesoamerican core area and the Tucson area. If this spread took 500–700 years, which seems to fit with either of the two start dates discussed earlier, then a rate of advance of about 2.5–3.7 kilometers per year is within the range found for some proposed Old World farmer migrations (LeBlanc 2003b). Although this does not demonstrate such a movement, it shows that it is well within the realm of possibility. Conversely, there is no evidence one way or the other to show whether the sites in northern Chihuahua and Sonora or southern Arizona relate to those farther south in any meaningful way because we do not know enough about sites deeper into Mexico. In sum, the archaeology from the Mesoamerican core area, northwestern Mexico, and the Southern Southwest is compatible with a migration of farmers but is not particularly supportive at this time.

The Basketmaker evidence from the Northern Southwest is a bit clearer. The difference between Eastern and Western is clear and strong. There are less strong but still significant links between Western Basketmaker and the low desert San Pedro farmers just discussed. One intriguing piece of evidence is rock art. The Candelaria style of art in Chihuahua seems far more similar to the Western Basketmaker San Juan Anthropomorphic style than can be ascribed to chance alone (Schaafsma 1997). The Candelaria style also seems to date to the right time interval. However, I know of no similar rock art between Chihuahua and the Four Corners area, which points out the outstanding issue of a substantial geographical gap between the early farmers of the low desert and those of the Four Corners. Is there really a gap in their distribution, merely a lack of relevant data for the area in-between, or have existing data not been carefully evaluated for similarities or differences? I believe these questions and the overall level of similarity between these groups can be addressed with the data at hand. They just need to be reevaluated with these questions in mind.

ALTERNATIVE MODELS

This discussion of the primary evidence for a linguistic-farmer spread has been presented with only minor reference to alternative models or negative evidence. Many different aspects of the migration model have alternatives. Several of these issues are discussed here.

The traditional and alternative models for both the introduction of maize into the Southwest and the observed differences in Western and Eastern Basketmakers is one of in situ adoption of maize and local differentiation of indigenous peoples. The traditional model has maize, not people, reaching the Southwest from Mexico. This model is most clearly articulated by Wirt (Chip) Wills (1988) and Paul Minnis (1992). In this scenario, maize (and squash), once it reached the Southwest, did not allow for a rapid shift from foraging to farming and was simply incorporated into a modified forager lifeway. Slowly over time, these foragers evolved into societies ever more dependent on farming, and only well into the A.D.s did they really become committed farmers. However, there seems to have been a commitment to farming in the Basketmaker area at least by a few centuries B.C. and in the Tucson area several hundred years before. A middle ground seems to be exemplified by Jonathan Mabry (2005), who sees less of a sharp break than scholars like R. G. Matson see between the earliest maize growers and Archaic populations. Mabry (2005) seems to have a rather equivocal position on the migration model. As noted earlier, it might be that sugar maize reached the Southwest via diffusion and was used by Archaic foragers, and it was only later that cob maize–growing farmers migrated into the area. Moreover, there is the old idea that there may have been a much later migration of farmers from the south who made ceramics and had other cultural traits found in the earliest Hohokam and Mogollon phases (Haury 1976; see also LeBlanc 1982). If such a migration took place, it might be responsible for the modern distribution of Uto-Aztecan.

An alternative explanation for the differences between the Eastern and Western Basketmakers is that both could have been ethnically different foragers who adopted maize farming. They were culturally different before they adopted maize and had both genetic and cultural interaction prior to and after its adoption, but not enough to erase the prior existing differences between them. It can also be argued that we happen to have archaeological samples from the eastern and western parts of the Basketmaker range that are reasonably far apart and little information about the people who lived in the middle, so there may have been more of a gradient than it appears. However, the large territories we would expect for such foragers would argue against this scenario. There is no reason the entire Northern Southwest would have been homogeneous for various cultural traits or genes prior to the introduction of maize, and such differences alone do not demonstrate a migration from the south of Western Basketmakers. The problem with such models is how to test them. Many of the tests seem to rely on negative evidence. Some carefully thought-out tests for in situ transitions would be very helpful.

CONCLUSION

Although the proposed Uto-Aztecan farmer spread would have taken place around 4,000 years ago, we have a surprising amount of relevant information, and it should be possible to generate a great deal more. Now that we have a concrete model to test, additional tests should be rapidly forthcoming. At present, these various lines of evidence provide a fairly good case for a Uto-Aztecan–speaking farmer spread resulting in the wide distribution of a language family. There is supporting evidence from genetics, linguistics, and material culture remains. Each major line of evidence also has independent lines of evidence. There is no compelling line of evidence that refutes the migration model. However, the evidence for a substantial difference between the Western and Eastern Basketmakers is stronger than that for a Uto-Aztecan farmer migration into the Southwest. We must not let the evidence for differences between the Basketmakers substitute for support for a movement of people from central Mesoamerican into the southern Southwest.

As is often the case with archaeology, what actually happened is far more intriguing than what we first envisioned. If the farmer spread idea is correct, the trajectory for the Southwest was not one of slow and gradual change. Rather, a key and critical step was a rapid and dramatic change in lifestyle caused by a major migration. Moreover, the biological and ethnic composition of the Southwest would have been both different and more diverse from what has often been portrayed. Over the last 3,000 years, the people and traditions converged and merged rather than differentiated. If this model holds up, much of the subsequent history of the Southwest will need to be reevaluated in its light.

In many ways, this farmer-spread migration fits a worldwide pattern seen on other continents, but the validity of each case needs to be tested on its own. At this point, it is hard to believe there is nothing to all these data: that there was no migration of significance and the spread of Uto-Aztecan had nothing to do with the spread of agriculture. Conversely, it is also hard to believe the actual process is as simple as we currently see it. We must remember that the overall model of major language ranges being the result of initial farmer spreads is only about twenty years old. Even more relevant, the idea of a Uto-Aztecan farmer spread is less than ten years old. Few archaeological research projects are deliberately focused on this issue, and the process of reevaluating the extant archaeological data is just beginning (e.g., Haas 2003; Mowrer 2003). This is equally true for genetic and linguistic studies (e.g., Carlyle 2003; Kemp 2006). Although attempts, such as this one, to synthesize what is known are useful to make clear the gaps in our knowledge, this is little more than a crude attempt at true synthesis. These studies will not be at the level we wish for another decade, if we are lucky.

NOTES

1. The Middle East example has been claimed to involve the spread of Indo-European into Europe, Semetic into North Africa, and Elamite-Dravidian into the Indus Valley.

2. The proper term for this period is Basketmaker II. The standard Anasazi sequence terms the period that followed (ca. A.D. 500–700) Basketmaker III, in spite of the fact that these people made pottery. The present discussion is focused solely on Basketmaker II. To simplify terminology, the II is dropped.

3. The boundaries of these two types of Basketmakers are not as clear as might be assumed. The range of the Eastern Basketmaker is considered to extend from the La Plata River on the west to Hidden Valley and Vallecito Reservoir along the north, from the Pine River and Navajo Reservoir on the east to around the confluence of Blanco Canyon, Largo Canyon, and Carrizo Canyon in the southeast, and just south of the San Juan River as a southern boundary. However, the Basketmaker II sites on the La Plata are not clearly Eastern or Western Basketmaker (e.g., Foster 1983; Railey and Acklen 1999; Reed and Horn 1988). So just where the boundary between Eastern and Western Basketmaker lies is unclear. In addition, the cultural affiliation of those who lived south of the San Juan is also unclear. Were the temporal equivalents of Basketmaker II in the Chaco area or along the Little Colorado River also Western Basketmaker, or were they as-yet poorly defined different entities? Similar issues surround some of the other boundaries.

4. A considerable number of Basketmaker II pithouses have been excavated in the La Plata Mine area, including those at LA 61848, LA 61896, Kin 'Atsá (LA 49498), and the Sundance site (LA 61915) (Brown 1991; Railey and Acklen 1999; Reed and Horn 1988). These pithouses are for the most part rather amorphous, and how they relate to either Western or Eastern Basketmaker is not obvious based on their shapes and presumed roofing methods. The Sundance site does have a pithouse with an antechamber, but the beams do not seem to form a crib. Just what is taking place architecturally between the core areas of West and East is far from worked out.

5. Eastern Basketmaker II orientations of a sample N=57 are S=5 percent, E-W=17 percent, N=72 percent, and S=6 percent. Western Basketmaker II orientations with an N=14 are S=30 percent, E-W=15 percent, N=20 percent, and S=49 percent, excluding Cave 7.

6. It has been proposed (Matson 2003b and elsewhere) that Eastern and Western Basketmakers twisted their cord differently, Z twist versus S twist. This turns out not to be the case because of incorrect terminology in one study (see Haas 2003 for a nice job of sleuthing this out). However, the fact that both groups are roughly the same in this regard is not of significance. There is a 50 percent probability they would be the same by chance alone, and if there is any human tendency to twist the same way (e.g., Z twist is more natural), they are even more likely to be the same.

7. Although Farmer (1997) notes the existence of these behaviors among Basketmakers, he does not recognize the patterning. One is tempted to link the head taking and skinning to Mesoamerican behaviors and to see the scalping as a more generic widespread North American behavior, further linking the Western Basketmakers to the south.

8. There was both temporal and spatial variability in Western Basketmaker Culture, with at least Lolomai, Grand Gulch, and White Dog variants. As important as these are, they are beyond the present scope.

9. Schollmeyer and Turner (2004) conflate Basketmaker II and Basketmaker III, so just what is being compared is not as clear as it might be.

10. It is a bit shocking that despite ample material to work with, no one seems to have looked at this very interesting and important behavior in the southern area.

11. Shaul and Hill argue that the Hohokam were linguistically diverse, with both Zuni and Yuman speaker participants, and that the original area for Piman (actually Tepiman) was close to isomorphic with the Hohokam area. However, this is based to some degree on the term for Saguaro cactus without demonstrating that the term may have applied to some other large cactus, of which there are many in Mexico.

12. Information provided by Jane Hill.

13. The Greek population sampled is from north of the best-known area of early Neolithic settlements. Why there has been no attempt to sample the more relevant area based on the archaeology is a mystery to me. I believe this is evidence for geneticists working very independently from archaeologists. The Y-chromosome data (Richards 2003:fig. 6) show about a 19 percent difference between Turkey and Greece for Neolithic lineages derived from the Middle East (although the overall Middle East component is about 44%). It is generally accepted for Europe that the Y-chromosome component shows a greater Middle East contribution than mtDNA, so this result is not surprising. As we have only mtDNA for UA speakers, the Y-chromosome data are not very relevant.

14. In this case, we know there were Mesolithic groups capable of voyaging to the Aegean Islands (to obtain obsidian and probably to fish and hunt seabirds). So there could have been gene flow not only by land but also by sea during the Mesolithic.

15. In fact, Bentley and colleagues (2003) and Dupanloup and colleagues (2004) have interpreted these same data as providing evidence for a much greater Neolithic genetic component in Europe than Richards and others conclude.

16. There is evidence to this effect along the boundary between foragers and farmers in Neolithic northern Europe (Keeley and Cahen 1989), although there has been little search for such evidence elsewhere.

17. Found by (the frequency of the mtDNA being diluted)/(1+% forager females being incorporated) × the power of the number of generations.

18. Slightly different values were reported by Parr and colleagues (1996) based on preliminary analysis of this same sample.

19. A second pool of high A existed in present-day western Canada and Alaska, which is not really relevant to the migration model. This is clearly a differently derived pool of haplotype A than that of central Mexico. Haplotype A is not universally high in the northern part of North America, the home of the Athapaskan speakers, but the very high levels seem to be restricted to Athapaskans (e.g., Dogrib with A=100%, Haida A=94%). Other northern people have significant A, such as the Ojibwa with 64 percent A, while the Sioux have 56 percent A, the Cheyenne-Arapaho 34 percent A, and the Chippewa of Wisconsin only 28 percent A. None of these frequencies is nearly as high as those among Athapaskans (data from or summarized by Malhi et al. 2003 and Lorenz and Smith 1996).

20. There is considerable evidence for the use of maize on these sites. Domesticated amaranth may also have been grown, and it may have been part of the new crop complex (Hard and Roney 2005). However, if amaranth was a local domesticate, it suggests the possibility that there was an agricultural tradition that preceded the spread of maize agriculture in the Southwest.

REFERENCES CITED

Ammerman, A. J., and L. L. Cavalli-Sforza
    1979   The Wave of Advance Model for the Diffusion of Early Farming in Europe. In *Transformations: Mathematical Approaches to Culture Change*, ed. C. Renfrew and K. L. Cooke, 275–294. Academic, New York.

Bellwood, P.
    1994   An Archaeologist's View of Language Macrofamily Relationships. *Oceanic Linguistics* 33:391–406.

1997	Prehistoric Cultural Explanations for Widespread Language Families. In *Archaeology and Linguistics: Aboriginal Australia in Global Perspective*, ed. P. McConvell and N. Evans, 123-134. Oxford University Press, Melbourne.
2001	Early Agriculturalist Population Diasporas? Farming, Languages, and Genes. *Annual Review of Anthropology* 30:181-207.
2004	*First Farmers: The Origins of Agricultural Societies.* Blackwell, Oxford.

Bellwood, P., and C. Renfrew (editors)
- 2003   *Examining the Farming/Language Dispersal Hypothesis.* McDonald Institute for Archaeological Research, Cambridge, England.

Bentley, R. A., L. Chikhi, and T. D. Price
- 2003   The Neolithic Transition in Europe: Comparing Broad Genetic and Local Isotopic Evidence. *Antiquity* 77:63-66.

Berry, C., and M. S. Berry
- 1986   Chronological and Conceptual Models of the Southwestern Archaic. In *Anthropology of the Desert West: Essays in Honor of Jesse D. Jennings*, ed. C. J. Condie and D. D. Fowler, 253-327. University of Utah Anthropology Papers 110. University of Utah Press, Salt Lake City.

Binford, L.
- 1968   Post-Pleistocene Adaptations. In *New Perspectives in Archaeology*, ed. S. R. Binford and L. R. Binford, 313-341. Aldine, Chicago.

Blackburn, F. M., and R. A. Williamson
- 1997   *Cowboys and Cave Dwellers: Basketmaker Archaeology in Utah's Grand Gulch.* School of American Research Press, Santa Fe.

Brown, G. M.
- 1991   *Archaeological Data Recovery at San Juan Coal Company's La Plata Mine, San Juan County, New Mexico.* Technical Report 335. Mariah Associates, Albuquerque.

Campbell, L.
- 1997   *American Indian Languages: The Historical Linguistics of Native America.* Oxford University Press, Oxford.
- 2003   What Drives Linguistic Diversification and Language Spread? In *Examining the Farming/Language Dispersal Hypothesis*, ed. P. Bellwood and C. Renfrew, 49-64. McDonald Institute for Archaeological Research, Cambridge, England.

Carlyle, S. W.
- 2003   *Geographical and Temporal Lineage Stability among the Anasazi.* Ph.D. dissertation, Department of Anthropology, University of Utah, Salt Lake City. ProQuest, Ann Arbor.

Carlyle, S. W., R. L. Parr, G. Hayes, and D. H. O'Rourke
- 2000   Context of Maternal Lineages in the Greater Southwest. *American Journal of Physical Anthropology* 113:85-101.

Carpenter, J. P., G. Sanchez, and M. E. Villalpando
- 2002   Of Maize and Migration: Mode and Tempo in the Diffusion of *Zea mays* in Northwest Mexico and the American Southwest. In *Traditions, Transitions, and Technologies*, ed. S. H. Schlanger, 245-258. University Press of Colorado, Boulder.

Steven A. LeBlanc

   2005   The Late Archaic/Early Agricultural Period in Sonora, Mexico. In *The Late Archaic across the Borderlands: From Foraging to Farming*, ed. B. J. Vierra, 13-40. University of Texas Press, Austin.

Chisholm, B., and R. G. Matson
   1994   Carbon and Nitrogen Isotopic Evidence on Basketmaker II Diet at Cedar Mesa, Utah. *Kiva* 60:239-256.

Clark, J. E., and D. Cheetham
   2002   Mesoamerica's Tribal Foundations. In *The Archaeology of Tribal Societies*, ed. W. A. Parkinson, 278-339. International Monographs in Prehistory, Ann Arbor.

Cole, S. J.
   1984   Analysis of a San Juan (Basketmaker) Style Painted Mask in Grand Gulch, Utah. *Southwestern Lore* 50(1):1-6.
   1990   *Legacy on Stone: Rock Art of the Colorado Plateau and Four Corners Region*. Johnson, Boulder.

Diamond, J. M., and P. Bellwood
   2003   Farmers and Their Languages: The First Expansions. *Science* 300:597-603.

Dupanloup, I., G. Bertorelle, L. Chikhi, and G. Barbujani
   2004   Estimating the Impact of Prehistoric Admixture on the Genome of Europeans. *Molecular Biology and Evolution* 21(7):1361-1372.

Eddy, F. W.
   1961   *Excavations at Los Pinos Phase Sites in the Navajo Reservoir District*. Museum of New Mexico Papers in Anthropology 4, Santa Fe.
   1966   *Prehistory in the Navajo Reservoir District, Northern New Mexico*. Museum of New Mexico Papers in Anthropology 15, Santa Fe.

Farmer, J. D.
   1997   Iconographic Evidence of Basketmaker Warfare and Human Sacrifice: A Contextual Approach to Early Anasazi Art. *Kiva* 62(4):391-420.

Fish, P. R., S. K. Fish, A. Long, and C. Miksicek
   1986   Early Corn Remains from Tumamoc Hill, Southern Arizona. *American Antiquity* 51(3):563-572.

Ford, R. I., A. H. Schroeder, and S. L. Peckham
   1972   Three Perspectives on Puebloan Prehistory. In *New Perspectives on the Pueblos*, ed. A. Ortiz, 19-40. University of New Mexico Press, Albuquerque.

Foster, M. S.
   1983   *Archaeological Investigation of Five Sites within the Cortez CO2 Project Corridor Near La Plata, New Mexico*. Nickens and Associates, Montrose, Colo.

Fowler, C.
   1983   Some Lexical Clues to Uto-Aztecan Prehistory. *International Journal of Linguistics* 49(3):224-257.

Geib, P. R.
   2002   Basketmaker II Horn Flaking Tools and Dart Point Production: Technological Change at the Agricultural Transition. In *Traditions, Transitions, and Technologies: Themes in Southwestern Archaeology*, ed. S. H. Schlanger, 272-306. University Press of Colorado, Boulder.

Gregory, D. A. (editor)
    1999   *Archaeology Southwest* 13(1). Center for Desert Archaeology, Tucson.
    2001   *Excavations in the Santa Cruz River Floodplain: The Early Agricultural Period Component at Los Pozos*. Center for Desert Archaeology Anthropological Papers 21, Tucson.

Guernsey, S. J., and A. V. Kidder
    1921   *Basket-Maker Caves of Northeastern Arizona: Report on the Explorations, 1916–1917*. Papers of the Peabody Museum of American Archaeology and Ethnology 8(2). Harvard University, Cambridge, Mass.

Gumerman, G. J.
    1966   Two Basketmaker II Pithouse Villages in Eastern Arizona: A Preliminary Report. *Plateau* 39:80–87.

Haas, W. R.
    2003   *The Social Implications of Basketmaker II Cordage Style Distribution*. Unpublished M.A. thesis, Department of Anthropology, Northern Arizona University, Flagstaff.

Hale, K., and D. Harris
    1979   Historical Linguistics and Archeology. In *Handbook of North American Indians: Southwest*, Volume 9, ed. A. Ortiz, 170–177. Smithsonian Institution Press, Washington, D.C.

Hard, R. J., and J. R. Roney
    1999   A Massive Terraced Village Complex in Chihuahua, Mexico, Dated to 3000 Years Before Present. *Science* 279:1661–1664.
    2005   The Transition to Farming on the Rio Casas Grandes and in the Southern Jornada Mogollon Region. In *The Late Archaic across the Borderlands: From Foraging to Farming*, ed. B. J. Vierra, 141–186. University of Texas Press, Austin.

Haury, E. W.
    1976   *The Hohokam, Desert Farmers and Craftsmen: Excavations at Snaketown, 1964–1965*. University of Arizona Press, Tucson.

Hill, J. H.
    2001   Proto-Uto-Aztecan: A Community of Cultivators in Central Mexico? *American Anthropologist* 103(4):913–934.
    2002   Toward a Linguistic Prehistory of the Southwest: "Azteco-Tanoan" and the Arrival of Maize Cultivation. *Journal of Anthropological Research* 58:457–475.
    2003   Uto-Aztecan Cultivation and the Northern Devolution. In *Examining the Farming/Language Dispersal Hypothesis*, ed. P. Bellwood and C. Renfrew, 331–340. McDonald Institute for Archaeological Research, Cambridge, England.
    In press   Northern Uto-Aztecan and Kiowa-Tanoan: Evidence of Contact between the Proto-Languages? *International Journal of American Linguistics*.

Howard, J., and J. C. Janetski
    1992   Human Scalps from Eastern Utah. *Utah Archaeology* 5(1):125–132.

Huckell, B. B.
    1995   *Of Marshes and Maize: Preceramic Agricultural Settlements in the Cienega Valley, Southeastern Arizona*. Anthropology Papers of the University of Arizona 59. University of Arizona Press, Tucson.

Steven A. LeBlanc

    1996   The Archaic Prehistory of the North American Southwest. *Journal of World Prehistory* 10(3):305-373.

Huckell, B. B., and L. W. Huckell
    1984   *Excavations at Milagro, a Late Archaic Site in the Eastern Tucson Basin.* Cultural Resource Management Section, Arizona State Museum, University of Arizona, Tucson.

Huckell, B. B., L. W. Huckell, and M. S. Shackley
    1999   McEuen Cave. *Archaeology Southwest* 13(1):12. Center for Desert Archaeology, Tucson.

Hyland, D. C., and J. M. Adovasio
    2000   The Mexican Connection: A Study of Sociotechnical Change in Perishable Manufacture and Food Production in Prehistoric New Mexico. In *Beyond Cloth and Cordage: Archaeological Textile Research in the Americas*, ed. P. B. Drooker and L. D. Webster, 141-159. University of Utah Press, Salt Lake City.

Irwin-Williams, C.
    1967   Prehistoric Cultural and Linguistic Patterns in the Southwest Since 5000 B.C. Paper presented at the 32nd Annual Meeting of the Society for American Archaeology, Ann Arbor.

Kaestle, F. A., and D. G. Smith
    2001   Ancient Mitochondrial DNA Evidence for Prehistoric Population Movement: The Numic Expansion. *American Journal of Physical Anthropology* 115:1-12.

Keeley, L. H., and D. Cahen
    1989   Early Neolithic Forts and Villages in Northeastern Belgium: A Preliminary Report. *Journal of Field Archaeology* 16:157-176.

Kemp, B. M.
    2006   *Mesoamerica and Southwest Prehistory, and the Entrance of Humans into the Americas: Mitochondrial DNA Evidence.* Ph.D. dissertation. Department of Anthropology, University of California, Davis.

Kemp, B. M., A. Resender, and D. G. Smith
    2005   Mitochondrial DNA Variation among Uto-Aztecan Speakers. Paper presented at the 104th Annual Meeting of the American Anthropological Association, Washington, D.C.

Kidder, A. V., and S. J. Guernsey
    1919   *Archaeological Explorations in Northeastern Arizona.* Bureau of American Ethnology Bulletin 65. Government Printing Office, Washington, D.C.

Lamb, S.
    1958   Linguistic Prehistory in the Great Basin. *International Journal of Linguistics* 24:95-100.

LeBlanc, S. A.
    1982   The Advent of Pottery in the Southwest. In *The Development of Southwestern Ceramic Patterns: A Comparative Review*, ed. A. Schroeder, 27-52. Arizona Archaeologist 15. Arizona Archaeological Society, Phoenix.

1989	Cultural Dynamics in the Southern Mogollon Area. In *Dynamics of Southwestern Prehistory*, ed. L. S. Cordell and G. J. Gumerman, 179–207. Smithsonian Institution Press, Washington, D.C.
1999	*Prehistoric Warfare in the American Southwest*. University of Utah Press, Salt Lake City.
2000	Regional Interaction and Warfare in the Late Prehistoric Southwest. In *The Archaeology of Regional Interaction: Religion, Warfare, and Exchange across the American Southwest and Beyond*, ed. M. Hegmon, 41–70. University Press of Colorado, Boulder.
2003a	*Constant Battles*. St. Martin's, New York.
2003b	Conflict and Language Dispersal: Issues and a New World Example. In *Examining the Farming/Language Dispersal Hypothesis*, ed. P. Bellwood and C. Renfrew, 357–365. McDonald Institute for Archaeological Research, Cambridge, England.

LeBlanc, S. A., L. S. Cobb Kreisman, B. M. Kemp, F. E. Smiley, A. N. Dhody, and T. Benjamin
    2007   Quids and Aprons: Ancient DNA from Artifacts from the American Southwest. *Journal of Field Archaeology* 32(2):161–175.

LeBlanc, S. A., C. Turner, and M. Morgan
    In press Genetic Relationships Based on Discrete Dental Traits: Basketmaker II and Mimbres. Manuscript submitted to *International Journal of Osteoarchaeology*.

Lorenz, J. G., and D. G. Smith
    1996   Distribution of Four Founding mtDNA Haplogroups among Native North Americans. *American Journal of Physical Anthropology* 101:307–323.

Mabry, J. B.
    1998a   Archaic Complexes of the Late Holocene. In *Paleoindian and Archaic Sites in Arizona*, ed. J. B. Mabry, 73–88. Technical Report 97-7. Center for Desert Archaeology, Tucson.
    2005   Changing Knowledge and Ideas about the First Farmers in Southeastern Arizona. In *The Late Archaic across the Borderlands: From Foraging to Farming*, ed. B. J. Vierra, 41–83. University of Texas Press, Austin.

Mabry, J. B. (editor)
    1998b   *Archaeological Investigations of Early Village Sites in the Middle Santa Cruz Valley: Analyses and Synthesis*. Center for Desert Archaeology Anthropological Papers 19, Tucson.

Malhi, R. S., H. M. Mortensen, J. A. Eshleman, B. M. Kemp, J. G. Lorenz, F. A. Kaestle, J. R. Johnson, C. Gorodezky, and D. G. Smith
    2003   Native American mtDNA Prehistory in the American Southwest. *American Journal of Physical Anthropology* 120:108–124.

Martin, S. L.
    1999   Virgin Anasazi Diet as Demonstrated through the Analysis of Stable Carbon and Nitrogen Isotopes. *Kiva* 64(4):495–514.

Matson, R. G.
    1991   *The Origins of Southwestern Agriculture*. University of Arizona Press, Tucson.
    2001   Basketmaker II Origins: The Evidence for Migration. Paper presented at the 66th Annual Meeting of the Society for American Archaeology, New Orleans, La.

2003a What Is Basketmaker II? Paper presented at the 68th Annual Meeting of the Society for American Archaeology, Milwaukee, Wis.
2003b The Spread of Maize Agriculture in the U.S. Southwest. In *Examining the Farming/Language Dispersal Hypothesis*, ed. P. Bellwood and C. Renfrew, 341–356. McDonald Institute for Archaeological Research, Cambridge, England.
In press The Archaic Origins of the Zuni: Preliminary Explorations. In *Zuni Origins: Anthropological Approaches on Multiple Americanist and Southwestern Scales*, ed. D. A. Gregory and D. R. Wilcox. University of Arizona Press, Tucson.

Matson, R. G., and K. Dohm (editors)
1994 Anasazi Origins: Recent Research on the Basketmaker II. *Kiva* 60(2).

Matson, R. G., and B. Chisholm
1991 Basketmaker II Subsistence: Carbon Isotopes and Other Dietary Indicators from Cedar Mesa, Utah. *American Antiquity* 56:444–459.

Minnis, P. E.
1992 Earliest Plant Cultivation in the Desert Borderlands of North America. In *The Origins of Agriculture: An International Perspective*, ed. C. W. Cowan and P. J. Watson, 121–142. Smithsonian Institution Press, Washington, D.C.

Minturn, P. D., and L. Lincoln-Babb
1995 Bioarchaeology of the Donaldson Site and Los Ojitos. In *Of Marshes and Maize: Preceramic Agricultural Settlements in the Cienega Valley, Southeastern Arizona*, ed. B. B. Huckell, 106–116. Anthropological Papers of the University of Arizona 59. University of Arizona Press, Tucson.

Montero, C., J. P. Carpenter, E. Barnes, A. H. Rohn, and J. Watson
2004 Early Agriculture Period Burials at La Playa (SON F:10:03), Sonora, Mexico: Further Preliminary Results. Paper presented at the 69th Annual Meeting of the Society for American Archaeology, Montreal, Canada.

Morris, E. H., and R. F. Burgh
1954 *Basket Maker II Sites Near Durango, Colorado*. Carnegie Institution Publication 604. Carnegie Institution of Washington, Washington, D.C.

Mowrer, K.
2003 *Basketmaker II Mortuary Practices: Social Differentiation and Regional Variation*. Unpublished M.A. thesis, Department of Anthropology, Northern Arizona University, Flagstaff.

O'Laughlin, T. C.
1980 *The Keystone Dam Site and Other Archaic and Formative Sites in Northwest El Paso, Texas*. El Paso Centennial Museum Publications in Anthropology 8. University of Texas, El Paso.

O'Rourke, D. H., R. L. Parr, and S. W. Carlyle
1999 Molecular Genetic Variation in Prehistoric Inhabitants of the Eastern Great Basin. In *Prehistoric Lifeways in the Great Basin Wetlands: Bioarchaeological Reconstruction and Interpretation*, ed. B. E. Hemphill and C. S. Larsen, 84–102. University of Utah Press, Salt Lake City.

Parr, T. L., S. W. Carlyle, and D. H. O'Rourke
  1996 Ancient DNA Analysis of Fremont Amerindians of the Great Salt Lake Wetlands. *American Journal of Physical Anthropology* 99:507–518.

Perles, C.
  2001 *The Early Neolithic in Greece*. Cambridge University Press, Cambridge.

Pope, K. O., M. D. Phol, J. G. Jones, D. L. Lentz, C. von Nagy, F. J. Vega and I. R. Quitmeyer
  2001 Origin and Environmental Setting of Ancient Agriculture in the Lowlands of Mesoamerica. *Science* 292:1370–1373.

Post, S. S.
  2002 Emerging from the Shadows: The Archaic Period in the Northern Rio Grande. In *Traditions, Transitions, and Technologies: Themes in Southwestern Archaeology*, ed. S. H. Schlanger, 33–48. University Press of Colorado, Boulder.

Price, T. D. (editor)
  2000 *Europe's First Farmers*. Cambridge University Press, Cambridge.

Price, T. D., A. B. Gebrauer, and L. H. Keeley
  1995 The Spread of Farming into Europe North of the Alps. In *Last Hunters–First Farmers: New Perspectives on the Prehistoric Transition to Agriculture*, ed. T. D. Price and A. B. Gebrauer, 95–126. School of American Research Press, Santa Fe.

Railey, J. A., and J. C. Acklen
  1999 *La Plata Archaeology Investigations at Six Sites in BHP's La Plata Mine*. TRC Mariah Associates, Albuquerque.

Reed, A. D., and J. C. Horn
  1988 *Archaeological Investigations of Kin 'Atsa" (LA 49498): A Late Archaic–Basketmaker Transition, Basketmaker II, and Dinetah Phase Navajo Habitation Site in San Juan County, New Mexico*. Nickens and Associates, Montrose, Colo. Prepared for BHP-Utah International, San Juan Coal Company, La Plata Mine.

Reed, A. D., and R. E. Kainer
  1978 The Tamarron Site: A Basketmaker II Site in Southwestern Colorado. *Southwestern Lore* 44(1–2):1–47.

Renfrew, C.
  1987 *Archaeology and Language: The Puzzle of Indo-European Origins*. Cambridge University Press, New York.
  1996 Language Families and the Spread of Farming. In *The Origins and Spread of Agriculture and Pastoralism in Eurasia*, ed. D. Harris, 70–92. UCL Press, London.

Richards, M.
  2003 The Neolithic Invasion of Europe. *Annual Review of Anthropology* 32:135–162.

Richards, M., H. Corte-Real, P. Forster, V. Macaulay, H. Wilkinson-Herbots, A. Demaine, S. Papiha, R. Hedges, H.-J. Brandelt, and B. Sykes
  1996 Paleolithic and Neolithic Lineages in the European Mitochondrial Gene Pool. *American Journal of Human Genetics* 59:185–203.

Richards, M., and others (more than twenty)
  2000 Tracing European Founder Lineages in the Near Eastern mtDNA pool. *American Journal of Human Genetics* 67:1251–1276.

Robins, M. R.
    1995   Modeling the San Juan Basketmaker Socio-Economic Organization: A Preliminary Study in Rock Art and Social Dynamics. In *Early Farmers in the Northern Southwest: Papers on Chronometry, Social Dynamics, and Ecology*, ed. F. E. Smiley and M. R. Robins, 73-120. Animas-La Plata Archaeological Project Research Paper 7. United States Department of the Interior, Bureau of Reclamation, Upper Colorado Region, and Northern Arizona University, Flagstaff.

Roney, J. R.
    1999   Canador Peak, an Early Pithouse-Period Cerro de Trincheras in Southwestern New Mexico. In *La Frontera: Papers in Honor of Patrick H. Beckett*, ed. M. S. Duran and D. T. Kirkpatrick, 173-184. Archaeological Society of New Mexico, Albuquerque.

Roney, J. R., and R. J. Hard
    2002   Early Agriculture in Northwestern Chihuahua. In *Traditions, Transitions, and Technologies: Themes in Southwestern Archaeology*, ed. S. H. Schlanger, 160-177. University Press of Colorado, Boulder.
    2004   A Review of Cerros de Trincheros in Northwestern Chihuahua. In *Surveying the Archaeology of Northwestern Mexico*, ed. G. E. Newell and E. Gallaga, 127-147. University of Utah Press, Salt Lake City.

Roth, B. J., and B. B. Huckell
    1992   Cortaro Points and the Archaic of Southern Arizona. *Kiva* 57(4):353-370.

Runnels, C. N.
    2001   The Stone Age of Greece from the Paleolithic to the Advent of the Neolithic. In *Aegean Prehistory: A Review*, ed. T. Cullen, 225-258. Archaeological Institute of America, Boston.
    2003   First Farmers in Europe. In *Ancient Europe 8000 B.C.-A.D. 1000: Encyclopedia of the Barbarian World*, ed. P. Bogucki and P. J. Crabtree, 218-226. Charles Scribner's Sons, Farmington Hills, Mich.

Sauer, C. O., and D. D. Brand
    1931   Prehistoric Settlements of Sonora, with Special Reference to Cerros de Trincheras. *University of California Publications in Geography* 5(3):67-148. Berkeley.

Scarre, C.
    2002   Pioneer Farmers? The Neolithic Transition in Western Europe. In *Examining the Farming/Language Dispersal Hypothesis*, ed. P. Bellwood and C. Renfrew, 395-407. McDonald Institute for Archaeological Research, Cambridge, England.

Schaafsma, P.
    1963   *Rock Art in the Navajo Reservoir District*. Museum of New Mexico Papers in Anthropology 7. Museum of New Mexico Press, Santa Fe.
    1980   *Indian Rock Art of the Southwest*. School of American Research, Santa Fe, and University of New Mexico Press, Albuquerque.
    1994   *The Rock Art of Utah*, rev. ed. University of Utah Press, Salt Lake City.
    1997   Rock Art Sites in Chihuahua, Mexico. Archaeology Notes 171. Museum of New Mexico, Office of Archaeological Studies, Santa Fe.

Schmader, M. F.
  2001 Gimme Shelter: Uncovering Archaic Structures in Rio Rancho and Santa Fe, New Mexico. Paper presented at the 66th Annual Meeting of the Society for American Archaeology, New Orleans, La.

Schollmeyer, K. G., and C. G. Turner II
  2004 Dental Caries, Prehistoric Diet and the Pithouse to Pueblo Transition in Southwestern Colorado. *American Antiquity* 69(4):569–582.

Shaul, D., and J. Hill
  1998 Tepimans, Yumans, and Other Hohokam. *American Antiquity* 63:375–396.

Smalley, J., and M. Blake
  2003 Sweet Beginnings: Stalk Sugar and the Domestication of Maize. *Current Anthropology* 44(5):675–703.

Smiley, F. E.
  1994 Agricultural Transition in the Northern Southwest: Patterns in the Current Chronometric Data. *Kiva* 60(2):165–189.

Smith, D. G., J. G. Lorenz, B. K. Rolfs, R. L. Bettinger, B. Green, J. Eshleman, B. Schultz, and R. S. Malhi
  2000 Implications of the Distribution of Albumin Naskapi and Albumin Mexico for New World Prehistory. *American Journal of Physical Anthropology* 111:557–572.

Smith, D. G., R. S. Malhi, J. Eshleman, J. G. Lorenz, and F. A. Kaestle
  1999 Distribution of mtDNA Haplogroup X among Native North Americans. *American Journal of Physical Anthropology* 110:271–284.

Smith, W., R. B. Woodbury, and N.F.S. Woodbury
  1966 *The Excavation of Hawikuh by Frederick Webb Hodge: Report of the Hendricks-Hodge Expedition, 1917–1923*. Museum of the American Indian, Heye Foundation, New York.

Turner II, C. G.
  1993 Southwest Indian Teeth. *National Geographic Research and Exploration* 9(1):32–53.

van Andel, T. H., and C. N. Runnels
  1995 The Earliest Farmers in Europe. *Antiquity* 69:481–500.

Webster, D., D. Rue, and A. Traverse
  2005 Early *Zea* Cultivation in Honduras: Implications for the Iltis Hypothesis. *Economic Botany* 59(2):101–111.

Webster, L. D.
  In press Mogollon and Zuni Perishable Traditions and the Question of Zuni Origins. In *Zuni Origins: Anthropological Approaches on Multiple Americanist and Southwestern Scales*, ed. D. A. Gregory and D. R. Wilcox. University of Arizona Press, Tucson.

Wheat, J. B.
  1955 *Mogollon Culture Prior to A.D. 1000*. American Anthropological Association Memoir 82, Menasha, Wis.

Wilcox, D. R.
  1986 The Tepiman Connection: A Model of Mesoamerican-Southwestern Interaction. In *Ripples in the Chichimec Sea: New Considerations of Southwestern-Mesoamerican*

Interactions, ed. F. J. Mathien and R. H. McGuire, 135–154. Southern Illinois University Press, Carbondale.

Wills, W. H.
- 1988 *Early Prehistoric Agriculture in the American Southwest*. School of American Research Press, Santa Fe.
- 2001 Pithouse Architecture and the Economics of Household Formation in the Prehistoric American Southwest. *Human Ecology* 29(4):477–500.

Zvelebil, M., and M. Lillie
- 2000 Transition to Agriculture in Eastern Europe. In *Europe's First Farmers*, ed. T. D. Price, 57–92. Cambridge University Press, Cambridge.

Part II

Converging Identities: Exploring Social Identity through Multiple Data Classes

8

Exploring Social Identities through Archaeological Data from the Southwest

An Introduction

Linda S. Cordell

Social identity refers to the various ways people identify themselves in relation to their membership in diverse social groups. The use of the term "social identity," as opposed to gender, clan, ethnicity, class, nationality, or religion, recognizes the nested and mutable identities individuals espouse as well as individual choice in affiliation. A single individual in any society will have several social identities, such as household member, kin relation, participant in a religious group, hunter, and speaker of a particular language. The social identities of individuals change throughout their lives, as they assume, often by choice, roles in diverse groups. Making inferences about the social identities of people in the past is critical to contemporary archaeology in the United States, for both academic and legal reasons (Ferguson 2004). Discussions relating to social identity are at the core of questions about ancient migrations, the formation of alliances, and maintenance of social boundaries of inclusion and exclusion that have been central to southwestern archaeology since its inception. Today, in order to implement the Native American Graves Protection and Repatriation Act, archaeologists are also required to make determinations of cultural affiliation, which is construed to include social identity.

Linda S. Cordell

Examining past social identities was one of three key topics included in the Eighth Southwest Symposium held in Tucson, Arizona, in 2002 (Mills 2004). At that symposium, social identity was explored primarily through ethnographic (Fowler 2004; Webster and Loma'omvaya 2004), historic (Levine 2004), and linguistic (Hill 2004) data. For the Ninth Southwest Symposium, convened in Chihuahua City in January 2004, Laurie Webster and Maxine McBrinn assembled a session that built upon its predecessor yet differed from the previous symposium session in two important ways. First, contributors were asked to examine social identity with purely archaeological data. Second, participants were asked to explore social identity in more than one class of archaeological data, such as ceramics *and* architecture. Revised papers from that session are included here.

The chapters that follow explore various theoretical perspectives and invoke historic or ethnographic examples, yet the focus in each is explicitly on issues in southwestern archaeology and archaeological data. The classes of data examined are those that are accessible to archaeologists, including ceramics, lithics, wall paintings, pictographs and petroglyphs, architecture, and fiber artifacts. The time period of interest in these chapters extends from about 3,500 years ago to about 500 years ago. Even in chapters where the sources of inference are ethnographic, for example, Hays-Gilpin's (Chapter 13) work on visual metaphors in Hopi material culture, the interpretations are applied to data available for archaeological scrutiny (ceramics, basketry, petroglyphs). In addition to addressing their inquiries to archaeological data, presenters were asked to examine evidence for social identity in more than one class of data. Therefore, Mabry, Carpenter, and Sanchez (Chapter 9) looked at projectile points, fiber artifacts, water control technologies, and cultigens; McBrinn (Chapter 11) at projectile points and fiber artifacts; Ortman (Chapter 12) at kiva architecture and wall paintings; Hays-Gilpin (Chapter 13) at pottery, basketry, and rock art; and Eckert (Chapter 14) at architecture, ceramics, kiva murals, and fauna.

The order of the chapters here differs from the chronological order of their subject matter, which was the way they were presented in Chihuahua City. This section begins with a chapter by Mabry, Carpenter, and Sanchez (Chapter 9), which evaluates Jane Hill's (2001) model of migration of Uto-Aztecan-speaking farmers into the Southwest. Although Mabry, Carpenter, and Sanchez focus on discerning the social identity of these early farming peoples, their chapter is also relevant to the discussions in Part 1 of this book concerning the initial spread of agriculture into the Southwest. By placing their chapter at the beginning of the contributed chapters in Part 2, we hope to facilitate comparison with those in Part 1, particularly Steven LeBlanc's discussion in Chapter 7 that reviews the same linguistic model from a different perspective.

Lyons and Clark (Chapter 10) provide an introduction to some of the more general intellectual positions that underlie archaeological discussions of social identity and how these, in turn, influence directions of inquiry and interpretations in southwestern archaeology. They explore a number of conceptual dichotomies useful in untangling the literature relating to social identity. The most basic contrast they describe is between interactionist approaches to identity and enculturationist perspectives. Interactionists view style, including technological style, or the choices made during the course of material culture production (Lechtman 1977; Lemonnier 1986), as primarily active, largely intentional signaling. For example, from this perspective a potter would consciously decide to use a particular color scheme to signal identity with others producing pottery decorated with the same colors. In this interactionist context, style has function, and that function is to signal affiliation. In the literature of southwestern archaeology, interactionist interpretations of stylistic similarity have been used to suggest the existence of alliances that may also be marked by the frequent exchange of goods within the alliance structure (Plog 1983, 1984; Upham 1982). These alliances and exchanges may, in turn, serve to buffer shortfalls in subsistence production, which would make them particularly useful in the relatively unpredictable environments of the Southwest (Braun and Plog 1982).

According to Lyons and Clark, an enculturationist view, by contrast, emphasizes the "unconscious or passive stylistic variation" often reflected in objects of low physical and contextual visibility. These similarities in unconsciously selected attributes of low visibility are interpreted as reflecting a common enculturative background (Clark 2001; Lyons and Clark, Chapter 10). These attributes are often used to infer ethnicity or culture of origin and are therefore helpful in recognizing ethnically heterogeneous settlements and, within regions, the presence of intrusive migrant groups. Lyons and Clark list a series of dichotomous concepts that more or less follow from the differences between interactionist and enculturationist perspectives, including instrumentalism versus essentialism, instrumentalist versus primordialist, ethnic identity versus cultural identity, and agency versus structure. Recognition of these distinctions is helpful for understanding current literature in southwestern archaeology, including much of the literature on alliances, exchange, and migration.

Lyons and Clark also discuss approaches drawn from a variety of sources that may bridge the structure (culture) and agency dichotomy. They pay particular attention to Richard Jenkins's (1997) social constructionist model of ethnic identity, which focuses attention on the contexts within which different kinds of markers of social identity are employed. Examples of the kinds of contexts Jenkins describes are instances of demographic stability or instability, interacting populations of like or unlike size, interacting populations with more or less equal or unequal access to power, and so forth. Lyons and Clark propose that these contextual parameters suggest different strategies that would be employed to signal social identity. For example, under conditions of more or less equal access to power among groups, individuals might use markers of social identity that are both flexible and easily emphasized or deemphasized. Understanding the demographic and political contexts of identity formation and marking would be especially useful to archaeologists in differentiating processes such as migration from emulation or exchange.

As Barbara Mills (2004:4) points out, however, social theorists from Anthony Giddens (1979, 1984) and Pierre Bourdieu (1977, 1990) to Frederick Barth (1969) and others have recognized that identity is multifaceted, situational, negotiated, and expressed at various scales (i.e., age, gender, residence, ethnicity). Further, each of these ways of expressing identity is variously constructed in each society. For these reasons alone, inferring identity from archaeological data poses a number of challenges. Other challenges arise as well because virtually all of these theorists accept Barth's (1969) model of ethnic identity as the social organization of cultural difference.

Barth's (1969) classic statement about ethnic groups continues to be a touchstone for subsequent theorists, including Lyons and Clark. Barth defined an ethnic group as a population (1) that is largely biologically self-perpetuating, (2) that shares fundamental cultural values realized in overt cultural forms, (3) that makes up a field of communication and interaction, and (4) whose membership identifies itself and is identified by others as constituting a category distinguishable from other categories of the same order (Barth 1969:10-11). The necessary component of the definition is the last, which entails self-ascription. Barth concluded that the sum of objectively different features is not necessarily important. Rather, for Barth, identification of an ethnic group is limited to those features seen by the actors themselves as significant. It is this most crucial part of the definition with which archaeologists have the most difficulty. Barth's approach is ethnographic, entailing access to individuals who can express their identities and affiliations. Archaeologists generally do not have access to people who can tell them whether an object, or an attribute of an object, is significant and carries meaning.

Lyons and Clark note that interactionists follow agency theory, which views people as mindful participants. Thus interactionists conceive of style as primarily *intentional* signaling, whereas enculturationists view style as *unconscious* or *passive* variation. Interactionist perspectives require that the intentions of the individual be known. Adopting this perspective does not seem useful for archaeology. Rather, it would be helpful for archaeologists to use some of the implications of practice theory (Bourdieu 1977), which is less concerned with knowing individuals' intentions. Whereas practice theory acknowledges the active choices of participants in any society, practice theory does not focus as closely on individual intent as it does on outcomes (Dobres and Robb 2000). Individual choice matters in both agency and practice frameworks. Practice consists of a series of choices; however, these choices may be conscious, subconscious, or unconscious. Nevertheless, their implementation leaves material manifestations that reflect multiple levels of group identity (Stark 2006).

Without living people to tell us that they identify themselves as a group in contrast to other groups, we as archaeologists cannot pursue a purely Barthian approach to identity. If we try, we run the risk of extending our data too far. Diacritica of social identity not only change over time but may move from markers that are material, hence potentially available to archaeologists, to markers that leave no trace in the archaeological record. For example, as Lyons and Clark note, markers that once took material forms that are potentially visible archaeologically, such as dress or pottery forms, may be replaced by the archaeologically invisible, such as spoken or unwritten language. How are these and other markers of social identity recognized? Living people use them and notice them and tell others, including ethnologists, that they mark group identity and sometimes what they symbolize. Those of us who work in the Southwest are privileged to work among the indigenous descendant peoples (Pueblos, Seri, O'Odham, Yaqui, and others) of those whose material remains we study and who can tell us who they are in relation to others. Yet what of markers that changed over time, and what of the millennia of pre-agricultural southwestern hunter-and-gatherer occupations? What also of the social markers that existed, for example, in Chacoan and other times when the social landscapes of the Southwest did not mirror those known in modern times?

The distinction between passive style and active style is not particularly useful for archaeology because generally archaeologists cannot detect the intentions of past actors from the material record available for study. We will probably never know whether the end products of the choices we see reflected in artifacts were conscious or not. Practice theory, which does not entail knowing the intention of social agents, seems to offer a more productive approach to this particular aspect of inferring social identity. Among the chapters in this section, two that provide especially useful insights into the dilemma of reading identities from artifacts are those of McBrinn (Chapter 11) and Mabry, Carpenter, and Sanchez (Chapter 9). They do so because they focus on practice theory and on technological style (Lechtman 1977; Lemonnier 1986) and because they examine hunter-gatherer populations in time periods remote from our own, when social maps of the Southwest were unlike those with which we are familiar.

McBrinn's (Chapter 11, 2005) study of Archaic hunters and gatherers in southern New Mexico admits the difficulty of seeing diacritics of ethnicity in remnant "stones and bones." Rather, she uses existing models of hunter-gatherer behavior and ethnographic research to suggest that Archaic hunters and gatherers participated in at least two different kinds of networks of interaction. One of these is networks of learning and enculturation. Learning and enculturation networks are developed through face-to-face interactions, hence they may be fairly spatially localized. The other kind of network McBrinn distinguishes is an economic network of risk sharing that will include people who interact infrequently and potentially over considerable distances. Each of these kinds of networks, McBrinn notes, should be reflected in different kinds of attributes of artifacts.

McBrinn links the two types of networks to two different kinds of stylistic variation James Sackett (1986, 1990) refers to as isochrestic and iconological. McBrinn suggests that attributes reflecting isochrestic style are learned through kinship networks or networks of enculturation and are generally not visible in the finished product. It does not matter if isochrestic style is conscious or not. Those attributes that are not visible in finished objects cannot function as signals—of affiliation or anything else. Iconological style, on the other hand, can signal affiliation by being visible to others within networks whose members may or may not be in day-to-day interaction. In her example, the same class of artifacts—sandals or projectile points—will be composed of attributes reflecting both kinds of style and both kinds of networks. McBrinn's work shifts the focus of analysis from the type to the attribute. Attributes are expected to reflect participation, learning, and choice in different kinds of social networks. The distributions of these different kinds of attributes should form different spatial patterns reflecting the size and shape of the social groups within which they operate. McBrinn's approach has two very important consequences. It frees archaeologists from having to know what was in the minds of individuals in the past, and it focuses on networks of social interaction rather than on bounded groups. Being able to define bounded groups would require analysis at a different (larger) scale.

Mabry, Carpenter, and Sanchez (Chapter 9) bring together archaeological data on lithics, fiber artifacts, radiocarbon dates on cultigens, and aspects of agricultural technology to evaluate a model of migration based on linguistic reconstruction. Jane Hill (2001) proposed that speakers of Proto-Uto-Aztecan, originating in the central Mexican highlands, introduced maize agriculture into the Southwest. Hill's model provided a catalyst for studies that examine how we might think about migration for time periods lacking ceramics and settlement layout, our usual archaeological markers. Mabry, Carpenter, and Sanchez eschew the "points equal people" approach. Like McBrinn, they focus on attributes of projectile points, elements of hafting design not visible when the point is in use, to reflect choices learned during enculturation. Mabry, Carpenter, and Sanchez give us a great deal to think about, and their conclusions do not fully support Hill's model. Again, I find two lessons from this chapter particularly important for archaeologists. First, the authors encourage us not to privilege language but to see language as one of many potential social markers that may or may not be activated in particular circumstances. Second, I believe we need to stop thinking like Americans. Many people in the world are bilingual or multilingual; they use language situationally. There is no reason to dismiss this possibility for temporally remote hunter-gatherers.

Although addressing a time period—the fifteenth century—that is very distant from the Archaic hunter-gatherers and early agriculturalists of McBrinn's and Mabry, Carpenter, and Sanchez's chapters, Eckert (Chapter 14) also examines attributes that reflect different kinds of social interaction. In the Pueblo Southwest, the fifteenth century was a time of migration and population aggregation. Among other locations, very large settlements were founded at the sites of Hummingbird and Pottery Mound in central New Mexico. Eckert uses different data classes and specific ceramic attributes to argue that those who founded these two communities participated in a regional, integrating ritual system and also maintained identities reflecting their different origins and migration histories. Of particular importance here is the notion of nested social identities. Individuals participate in more than one social network and have more than one social identity. Eckert uses theoretical insight provided by Patricia Crown's (1994) study of ritual integration reflected in thirteenth-century Salado polychrome pottery and Miriam Stark's (2006) presentation of communities of practice to discern different social networks reflected in technological style. The notion that technological style relates to networks of learning and enculturation is similar to the discussions of isochrestic style in the chapters concerning hunters and gatherers. Here, however, these attributes are visible and are thought to signal social boundaries within each of the aggregated villages. Eckert's data are rich, and I find her argument compelling. At the same time, I hope her ideas stimulate further development of theory that will assist us in understanding the contexts within which social boundaries are maintained and signaled. These could well follow the bridging arguments discussed by Lyons and Clark.

The remaining chapters explore identity in terms of the structure of attributes seen in more than one class of archaeological data. For Ortman (Chapter 12) and Hays-Gilpin (Chapter 13), it is visual metaphor. These authors use metaphor theory to address social interaction reflected in symbols. As I understand it, metaphor theory, like analysis of symmetry classes, brings a perspective from cognitive psychology. As Hays-Gilpin points out, some symbols are human universals. Although these are interesting to note, if we are interested in social identity we should focus on variations within these universals, the presence or absence of visual metaphors in specific archaeological contexts, or both. Both Hays-Gilpin and Ortman indicate that the meanings of these metaphors—visual, architectural, or both—can be deciphered through language, and such metaphors can be used as social markers. Hays-Gilpin's look at "LIFE IS A PATHWAY" depends upon ethnographic and ethnohistoric data as well as discussions with Native Hopi speakers. Ortman's observations about architectural metaphors in Chacoan and Northern San Juan Ancestral Pueblo worlds employ a code-breaking procedure that does not depend upon access to Native speakers. Both chapters strike me as exciting and productive, in part because they focus on some of the most attractive (pottery, architecture, wall paintings) and intractable (symbols) of the archaeological remains.

Metaphor theory examines the same visual metaphors in different classes of material culture, such as a specific line break woven into basketry or painted on a bowl. If we, as archaeologists, must actually know the meaning of the symbol to the Native speaker, I suspect this will be an impossible task. The meanings attached to symbols change over time within single linguistic or cultural traditions and, of course, vary among cultural traditions, regardless of whether the traditions are historically related. That is the nature of symbols. We need theory and, I suspect, a great deal of controlled cross-cultural analysis to help us sort out what might be a period of changing metaphor rather than cultural interaction or a period of changes in affiliation. Ortman begins to develop necessary middle-range theory in proposing very specific procedures to decipher metaphorical meanings of architectural features among Ancestral Pueblos. I find his approach intriguing and his use of it masterful.

Linda S. Cordell

The topic of "identity" continues to be tremendously important in anthropology, sociology, political science, philosophy, and, increasingly, archaeology (Mills 2004). The chapters in this section provide stimulating and innovative approaches to this important and complicated issue. As a group, the chapters provide new directions for research and new insights into variation in archaeological data. They point to the need to continue to develop theory—at different levels—that will be useful in linking attributes of artifacts to networks of social interaction and in understanding the general conditions under which networks change. The laboratory afforded by the archaeology of the Southwest and the history of its vibrant Native peoples should continue to be sources of ideas about the dynamics of social identity that are useful to diverse academic disciplines and to all who wish to better understand the world in which we live.

REFERENCES CITED

Barth, Frederick
    1969   Introduction. In *Ethnic Groups and Boundaries*, ed. Frederick Barth, 9–38. Little, Brown, Boston.

Bourdieu, Pierre
    1997   *Outline of a Theory of Practice*. Cambridge University Press, New York.
    1990   *The Logic of Practice*. Polity, Cambridge, England.

Braun, David P., and Stephen Plog
    1982   Evolution of "Tribal" Social Networks: Theory and Prehistoric North American Evidence. *American Antiquity* 47(3):504–525.

Clark, Jeffery J.
    2001   *Tracking Prehistoric Migrations: Pueblo Settlers among the Tonto Basin Hohokam*. Anthropological Papers of the University of Arizona 65. University of Arizona Press, Tucson.

Crown, Patricia L.
    1994   *Ceramics and Ideology: Salado Polychrome Pottery*. University of New Mexico Press, Albuquerque.

Dobres, Marcia-Anne, and John E. Robb
    2000   Agency in Archaeology: Paradigm or Platitude? In *Agency in Archaeology*, ed. Marcia-Anne Dobres and John E. Robb, 3–18. Routledge, London.

Ferguson, T. J.
    2004   Academic, Legal, and Political Contexts of Social Identity and Cultural Affiliation in the Greater Southwest. In *Identity, Feasting, and the Archaeology of the Greater Southwest: Proceedings of the 2002 Southwest Symposium*, ed. Barbara J. Mills, 27–41. University Press of Colorado, Boulder.

Fowler, Catherine S.
    2004   Material Culture and the Marking of Southern Paiute Ethnic Identity. In *Identity, Feasting, and the Archaeology of the Greater Southwest: Proceedings of the 2002 Southwest Symposium*, ed. Barbara J. Mills, 107–123. University Press of Colorado, Boulder.

Giddens, Anthony
    1979   *Central Problems in Social Theory*. Cambridge University Press, New York.
    1984   *The Constitution of Society: Outline of the Theory of Structuration*. Polity, Cambridge, England.

Hill, Jane H.
    2001   Proto-Uto-Aztecan: A Community of Cultivars in Central Mexico? *American Anthropologist* 103(4):913-934.
    2004   Two Styles of Language and Social Identity among the Tohono O'Odham. In *Identity, Feasting, and the Archaeology of the Greater Southwest: Proceedings of the 2002 Southwest Symposium*, ed. Barbara J. Mills, 124-138. University Press of Colorado, Boulder.

Jenkins, Richard
    1997   *Rethinking Ethnicity*. Sage, London.

Lechtman, Heather
    1977   Style in Technology: Some Early Thoughts. In *Material Culture, Style, Organization, and Dynamics of Technology*, ed. Heather Lechtman and Robert S. Merrill, 3-20. West, New York.

Lemonnier, Pierre
    1986   The Study of Material Culture Today: Towards an Anthropology of Technical Systems. *Journal of Anthropological Archaeology* 5:147-186.

Levine, Frances
    2004   Surviving Extinction: The Legacy of Pecos Pueblo. In *Identity, Feasting, and the Archaeology of the Greater Southwest: Proceedings of the 2002 Southwest Symposium*, ed. Barbara J. Mills, 93-106. University Press of Colorado, Boulder.

McBrinn, Maxine E.
    2005   *Social Identities among Archaic Mobile Hunters and Gatherers in the American Southwest*. Arizona State Museum Archaeological Series 197. University of Arizona Press, Tucson.

Mills, Barbara J.
    2004   Identity, Feasting, and the Archaeology of the Greater Southwest. In *Identity, Feasting, and the Archaeology of the Greater Southwest: Proceedings of the 2002 Southwest Symposium*, ed. Barbara J. Mills, 1-23. University Press of Colorado, Boulder.

Plog, Fred
    1983   Political and Economic Alliances on the Colorado Plateau, A.D. 400-1450. In *Advances in World Archaeology*, Volume 2, ed. Fred Wendorf and Angela E. Close, 289-330. Academic, New York.
    1984   Exchange, Tribes, and Alliances: The Northern Southwest. *American Archaeology* 4(3):217-223.

Sackett, James R.
    1986   Isochrestism and Style: A Clarification. *Journal of Anthropological Archaeology* 5:26-77.
    1990   Style and Ethnicity in Archaeology: The Case for Isochrestism. In *The Uses of Style in Archaeology*, ed. Margaret Conkey and Christine Hastorf, 32-43. Cambridge University Press, Cambridge.

Stark, Miriam T.
  2006   Glaze Ware Technology, the Social Lives of Pots, and Communities of Practice in the Late Prehistoric Southwest. In *The Social Lives of Pots: Glaze Wares and Cultural Transformation in the Southwest AD 1250–1680*, ed. Judith A. Habicht-Mauche, Suzanne L. Eckert, and Deborah L Huntley, 17–33. University of Arizona Press, Tucson.

Upham, Steadman
  1982   *Polities and Power: An Economic and Political History of the Western Pueblo*. Academic, New York.

Webster, Laurie D., and Micah Loma'omvaya
  2004   Textiles, Baskets, and Hopi Cultural Identity. In *Identity, Feasting, and the Archaeology of the Greater Southwest: Proceedings of the 2002 Southwest Symposium*, ed. Barbara J. Mills, 74–92. University Press of Colorado, Boulder.

9

ARCHAEOLOGICAL MODELS OF EARLY UTO-AZTECAN PREHISTORY IN THE ARIZONA-SONORA BORDERLANDS

Jonathan B. Mabry, John P. Carpenter, and Guadalupe Sanchez

A number of researchers have attempted to follow a trail of linguistic clues back to the origins of the Uto-Aztecan language family, unusual both for its large north-south geographical range spanning the boundary between tropical and temperate environments and for the large variety of subsistence adaptations and social structures represented among its contemporary speakers. But while some linguistic detectives are convinced the Arizona-Sonora borderlands at the juncture of the southwestern United States and northwestern Mexico were the homeland of foragers who were the first speakers of the ancestral Uto-Aztecan "proto-language" (Campbell 1977; Fowler 1983; Hale and Harris 1979; Lamb 1958; Miller 1983b; Romney 1957; Suárez 1979), others argue that this region was a frontier of northward expansion by the original Uto-Aztecan speakers, who may have been the first farmers in the highlands of Mexico (Bellwood 1997, 1999; Hill 1996, 2001, 2003).

For archaeologists, these linguistic models of culture history are intriguing, but they raise a perennial question in their own field of study: How can a pre-literate culture, its members speaking a common language, be recognized in the archaeological record? The assumption that sets of material culture traits represent "cultures" and the postulation of migrations to explain the appearance of new sets of traits in the archaeological record were givens for generations of archaeologists emphasizing cultural-historical classification (Willey and Sabloff 1982). These conventions have come under criticism as overly simplistic in the correlation of ethnicity with material remains and as underestimating the role of internal cultural changes (Thompson 1958; Adams, Van Gerven, and Levy 1978; but see Anthony 1990). The result of these reappraisals is a growing recognition among archaeologists that while some material traits will cluster in relation to ethnicity, it is not certain which traits might do so in a particular case (Sutton 1991).

In this chapter we evaluate linguistic models of early Uto-Aztecan history in the light of archaeological data, focusing on evidence from the critical region of the Arizona-Sonora borderlands. We interpret temporal-spatial patterns in the archaeological record in terms of material culture "complexes" representing, simultaneously, cultural traditions and communication networks (Mabry 1998). In this perspective a set of artifact styles and feature types overlapping in time and space to form a complex could have spread through (1) migration, involving an actual movement of people; (2) diffusion, involving slow transmission across cultural-linguistic boundaries or rapid dispersal within a cultural-linguistic continuum; or (3) a combination of migration and diffusion processes. On the basis of ethnographic and historical studies, we assume that certain aspects of material culture, particularly "passive styles" and "technological styles," are useful cultural markers because they unconsciously represent cultural identity. Here, we focus on these aspects of style expressed by projectile points, direct radiocarbon dates on cultigen remains, and other archaeological data to infer (1) the diffusion of maize to indigenous cultural groups either before or after the arrival of Proto-Uto-Aztecan peoples in the Arizona-Sonora borderlands; (2) a series of subsequent diffusions, migrations, or both from the south that introduced other Mesoamerican cultigens and material culture traits; (3) the extent of the Proto-Uto-Aztecan continuum prior to its breakup into northern and southern groups; and (4) the timing of that divergence. (Editor's note: Interested readers are also referred to LeBlanc [Chapter 7] for a different approach to this topic.)

LINGUISTIC MODELS

Uto-Aztecan is one of the largest and most widely distributed language families in the Americas, extending from the Shoshoneans in southern Idaho south to the Pipil in Nicaragua. Based on more than 100 sets of cognates that exhibit sound correspondence and similarities in meaning, the numerous linguistic members of the Uto-Aztecan family have been demonstrated to comprise a genetic unit, meaning that in the remote past there existed a single linguistic community in which a common ancestral language, Proto-Uto-Aztecan (PUA), was spoken. Suggestions for the center of origin for Uto-Aztecan languages—the PUA homeland—vary widely, although most scholars support a northern origin in western North America, ranging anywhere from the Columbia Plateau (Hopkins 1965), northern California (Nichols 1981), the Great Basin (Goss 1977), or the northern Rockies (Taylor 1961) south to the foothills of the Mogollon Highlands and the Sierra Madre (Fowler 1983; Romney 1957), the deserts of the Arizona-Sonora borderlands (Lamb 1958), or southern California (Miller 1995). Catherine Fowler (1983) identified twenty-seven cognates for plants and animals that were presumably part of the folk biological knowledge of PUA and that she suggested placed them in the mid-elevation, mixed woodland-grassland zone of the northern Sierra Madre foothills in northern Mexico and the Basin and Range Province of southern Arizona and southwestern New Mexico. Jane Hill (2003) argues for a PUA homeland somewhere at the northwestern edge of Mesoamerica, in an upland region where the set of flora and fauna reconstructed by Fowler (1983) can be found, as in the present-day Mexican states of Jalisco, Nayarit, Durango, Zacatecas, and Aguascalientes.

Linguistic geography and degree of internal differentiation suggest that Uto-Aztecan is younger than Hokan, Penutian, or Algic in western North America but nevertheless indicative of considerable antiquity. Glottochronological analyses have arrived at estimates ranging between 8,000 and 3,000 years to account for the degree of internal differentiation in the Uto-Aztecan stock. Romney (1957) estimated the time depth of the PUA community at about 3,000 years, although the data on which his estimate was based remain unpublished. Later studies yielded estimates of 4,000 years (Hale 1958) and 4,700 years (Swadesh 1960). Fowler (1983) uses a figure of 5,000 years as a minimum age for the Proto-Uto-Aztecan dialect chain. The figure of 6000 B.C. that appeared in a widely cited publication by Miller (1983b) is almost certainly a misprint (i.e., it should probably be B.P.), as the author elsewhere referred to 5,000 (Miller 1984) and 4,000 (Miller 1995) years of time depth. Most linguists today accept 5,000 to 6,000 years as a minimum age for the proto-language, thus establishing a baseline between approximately 4000-3000 B.C.

Hale (1958) and Voegelin and colleagues (1962) suggested that the Proto-Uto-Aztecan stock subsequently split into northern and southern substocks, the northern developing into the Shoshonean and Sonoran branches and the southern into the Nahuatlán branch. Today, many place the Sonoran languages in the southern group (Campbell and Longacker 1978; Fowler 1983; Heath 1977; Hill 1996; Manaster Ramer 1992), with the Tepiman languages representing the northernmost subgroup (Shaul and Hill 1993).

Bascom's (1965) reconstruction of Proto-Tepiman includes a cognate for saguaro cactus, which is not found in other Uto-Aztecan languages. This suggests to Fowler (1983) that Tepehuan speakers spread southward from a Proto-Tepiman homeland in the Sonoran Desert; she attributes the locations of the Tarahumara and Cahitan groups that interrupt the distribution of Piman languages to subsequent movements of these groups toward the west Mexican coast. This contrasts with her earlier suggestion that the southern languages began to diverge from PUA in the Sonoran foothills of the Sierra Madre, perhaps in the Río Sonora and Río Yaqui basins (Fowler 1972). Shaul and Hill (1993) argue that Proto-Tepiman was in contact with Yuman languages and thus forward a northern center of development for this subgroup of the southern Uto-Aztecan languages.

Jonathan B. Mabry, John P. Carpenter, and Guadalupe Sanchez

We have previously followed the borderlands homeland model in arguing that the introduction of maize into northwestern Mexico and the southwestern United States could be attributed either to (1) the movement of agricultural Proto-Southern-Uto-Aztecans (PSUA) out of a presumed homeland in the coastal plain, the *serrana* of the Sierra Madre Occidental surrounding the region where Sonora, Chihuahua, Durango, and Sinaloa merge, or both (Carpenter, Mabry, and Sanchez 2001; Carpenter, Sanchez, and Villalpando 2002, 2005), or to (2) diffusion across a previously established continuum of Proto-Uto-Aztecan speakers spanning these regions (Mabry 2005a; see also Mabry and Doolittle, Chapter 4, this volume). As part of the first model, we have also suggested that the timing of the initial bifurcation of Uto-Aztecan into northern and southern branches (circa 6000 B.P.) could be explained by the abandonment of the Sonoran Desert region as a result of changing climatic conditions during the Middle Holocene interval of higher temperatures (the Altithermal period). Likewise, the subsequent diversification of PSUA beginning at approximately 4000–3000 B.P. could be attributed to the re-population of the desert areas (which remained a largely empty niche) by agricultural peoples following a return to more amenable conditions with the onset of the Late Holocene. In the second model, PUA groups first arrived in the thinly populated borderlands at the beginning of the Late Holocene, before the arrival of maize, and all this linguistic diversification occurred subsequently.

Recently, Hill (2001) has challenged some of the conventional linguistic models of Uto-Aztecan prehistory (which she herself had long upheld)—both the one that envisioned PUA speakers to be foragers who later adopted agriculture and the one that held that their homeland was in the Arizona-Sonora borderlands. Based on linguistic data, with some references to radiocarbon dates on cultigens from archaeological sites, Hill elaborated on Bellwood's (1997, 1999) model that agriculture was introduced to the U.S. Southwest by a migration of Uto-Aztecan speakers from central Mexico. Specifically, Hill's (2001) major propositions are that (1) maize was introduced to the Southwest by a single northward migration of Proto-Uto-Aztecan agriculturalists who originated in central Mexico, (2) the PUA community included the domesticators of maize, (3) the initial expansion of Proto-Uto-Aztecans into the Southwest occurred between about 4,000 and 3,000 years ago, (4) the PUA expansion into the Southwest occurred in a leapfrog pattern from oasis to oasis, (5) the PUA community practiced irrigation, (6) the PUA community began to break up between the arrival of maize and beans, and (7) the historically non-agricultural Uto-Aztecan peoples in the extreme north abandoned agriculture during prehistoric time. This new model is important because of its fresh perspective and breadth of interpretation, and it has forced both linguists and archaeologists to rethink their positions on early Uto-Aztecan prehistory. In the rest of this chapter, we explore whether the linguistic and archaeological data converge to provide a coherent picture of early Uto-Aztecan speakers in the Arizona-Sonora borderlands, including their role in the arrival of agriculture in this region.[1]

POSSIBLE ARCHAEOLOGICAL EVIDENCE OF THE ARRIVAL OF EARLY UTO-AZTECANS IN THE SOUTHWEST

Projectile Points

To identify the material traces of a population movement from a specific homeland during the pre-pottery period of prehistory, we first turn to projectile points, "the only artifacts that are routinely discovered at Archaic sites that have the potential to inform us about the movement of information, ideas, and perhaps even people over the landscape that is now the Southwest" (Huckell 1996:3). But like pots, points do not necessarily equal peoples. The types of variations in projectile points that are most likely related to cultural identities need to be identified on the basis of ethnoarchaeological, historical, and technological studies.

An ethnoarchaeological study in southwestern Africa has shown that variations in the shapes of projectile point blades may consciously express social differences within the same ethnic group and so are examples of "active style" (Weissner 1983). This conscious expression of difference is often related to the need to mark boundaries between groups that are in constant contact, even among those that are culturally and linguistically related. Among nineteenth-century Numic-speaking bands in the Great Basin, variations in arrow shaft decorations, rather than arrowhead shapes, were expressions of different group identities, and shaft decoration varied the most between closely interacting groups (Sinopoli 1991). Decorated Basketmaker dart foreshafts and mainshafts found in caves in the Southwest (Cosgrove 1947) and the Great Basin (Harrington 1933) display great variability in decorative elements and may be similar expressions of group identities among a population using the same hafting technique. Clearly, active style variations in projectile point blades, foreshafts, and mainshafts may be useful signs of differences between cultural subgroups and possibly between unrelated cultures, but they are not necessarily markers of cultural differences.

In contrast, the less visible, more conservative, and largely unconscious variations in projectile designs are examples of "passive style" and reflect shared enculturative backgrounds even more strongly (Weissner 1983). What, then, are the aspects of passive style represented in the designs of Archaic and Early Agricultural projectiles of the southwestern United States and Mexico? Hafting designs, the techniques used to attach points to shafts, may or may not be related to cultural identities. Rather, they represent "technological traditions" that may have crossed cultural boundaries (Musil 1988). The temporal-spatial distribution of a particular hafting design represents a time and an area of shared technology that was a product of information flow among groups in frequent contact because they were exploiting the same environment (Holmer 1986). However, the geographical limits and temporal continuities of such technological traditions allow some conclusions about whether they are indigenous or introduced.

The best examples of passive style in projectile points are the less visible variations within each hafting design tradition: the variations in the shapes and dimensions of projectile point stems, bases, notches, and necks. These were largely obscured from direct view by sinew bindings and may have been unconscious reflections of cultural identity because they were culturally specific, alternative solutions to the same technological problems. Here, several dart point types representing different hafting technological traditions and their passive style variations are discussed in terms of their possible associations with the earliest farming cultures between the borderlands and central Mexico.

POINT TYPES REPRESENTING DISTINCT HAFTING DESIGNS

Contracting stem points. The contracting stem dart point represents a unique hafting design that may have originated in Mexico. Based on the residues found on a large proportion of contracting stem points in the Southwest and the Great Basin, it has been suggested that these points were glued into the socketed or split ends of foreshafts with adhesives such as asphaltum and pine pitch and that this is a hafting tradition that originated south of the other hafting traditions in North America, probably in Mesoamerica (Holmer 1986). Known by various names, contracting stem points appeared between about 5000 and 4000 B.P. in the lower Rio Grande and Pecos valleys (Almagre and Langtry types) (Marmaduke 1978), the Southwest (Gypsum Cave, Agustín, and Pelona types) (Berry and Berry 1986), and the southern Great Basin (Elko Contracting Stem and Gatecliff Contracting Stem) (Holmer 1986; Thomas 1981). Similar points (including examples with adhesive residues) appeared along the southern California coast and the Channel Islands (Harrington 1933:117–118; Koerper and Drover 1983:10; Orr 1968) as early as 4500 B.P. (Justice 2002:194). However, the contracting stem point variants in southern coastal California may have developed independently from earlier leaf-shaped points (Justice 2002:194).

Similarly shaped points appeared in the central highlands of Mexico, within the Coxcatlán phase in the Tehuacán Valley (MacNeish, Nelken-Terner, and Johnson 1967), associated with maize radiocarbon dated to about 4700 B.P. (circa 3500 B.C. calibrated) (Long et al. 1989). This is among the earliest maize yet identified in the central highlands, although maize dating to about 5400 B.P. (circa 4200 B.C. calibrated) has been found in the southern highland region of Oaxaca (Piperno and Flannery 2001). Similar contracting stem point types have also been reported from non-agricultural sites in Coahuila and Tamaulipas in northeastern Mexico, estimated to date between roughly 6000 and 3500 B.P. (circa 4900–1800 B.C. calibrated) (MacNeish 1958; Taylor 1966).

At only two sites north of Mexico has this point type been found in association with possible maize remains. At the Keystone Dam site near El Paso, contracting stem points were found in a stratum bracketed by charcoal dates between 4100 and 3300 B.P. (circa 2600–1600 B.C. calibrated) and containing small, circular pit structures, storage pits, roasting pits, fire-cracked rock hearths, grinding tools, and probable maize pollen (O'Laughlin 1980). In Bat Cave, contracting stem points occur together with expanding stem Bat Cave points and side-notched Chiricahua points in the deepest stratum (Dick 1965), which has provided a maize radiocarbon date of 3740 ± 70 B.P. (circa 2150 B.C. calibrated) (Wills 1988). When this date was published, it was suggested that it may be unreliable because of possible contamination with a preservative, but that was an attempt to explain a data outlier that seemed implausible at the time. Today, this date closely matches the earliest direct dates on maize in several parts of the Southwest (see references in Mabry 2005b).

Expanding stem points. Representing a different, probably indigenous southwestern hafting design are expanding stem points, of which the best known are the San Jose variants. These have narrow, usually serrated blades and either a straight stem with a concave base (sometimes with shoulders) or an expanding stem with concave sides and base. Both forms were included in the original definition of the San Jose complex (Bryan and Toulouse 1943), but Irwin-Williams (1973) called the first San Jose and the second Armijo and believed the latter developed from the former. Obsidian hydration dates support this interpretation (Moore 1994). A variant of the Pinto point resembles the first variant, which has sometimes been referred to as San Jose–Pinto (Bayham et al. 1986; Berry and Berry 1986; Huckell 1996). The Bat Cave point (Dick 1965:fig. 23c-h) appears to be an unserrated, straight-based version of the second variant (Justice 2002).

These variants, glossed here as expanding stem points, are found only in the Southwest, in both possible and definite associations with maize. In northwestern New Mexico, San Jose points were found in association with maize pollen at two sites in Chaco Canyon; hearths containing maize pollen yielded four charcoal dates between 3985 and 3560 B.P. (circa 2500-1900 B.C. calibrated) (Simmons 1982, 1986). In this same region, charcoal dates of 3480 ± 95 and 3390 ± 120 B.P. (circa 1800 B.C. and 1700 B.C. calibrated) were obtained from a stratum containing San Jose points and maize pollen in En Medio Shelter (Irwin-Williams and Tompkins 1968). Also in this region, at Atlatl Cave, San Jose–Pinto Basin points were found in the same levels as maize remains (cob fragments?), with an associated charcoal date of 4240 ± 70 B.P. (circa 2900 B.C. calibrated) (Berry and Berry 1986). In southern Arizona, unserrated points with narrow blades, including two tip fragments and a complete example with an expanding stem with a straight base and broad, shallow side notches, were associated with maize dates of 3690 ± 40 and 3650 ± 40 B.P. (circa 2100 B.C. calibrated) at the Clearwater site (Mabry 2006b). Points similar to the complete example from the Clearwater site have been variously called San Jose (Huckell 1977), Bat Cave (Dick 1965), Armijo (Irwin-Williams 1973), Concho (Plog 1981), and Armijo-Concho (Parry, Smiley, and Burgett 1994).

Radiocarbon dates are also known from contexts with expanding stem points but no maize. These include dates between about 4300 and 4000 B.P. (circa 3300 B.C. and 2500 B.C. calibrated) from the Buried Dune site in southern Arizona (Bayham et al. 1986) and a date of 3520 ± 60 B.P. (circa 1800 B.C. calibrated) from the Laguna Salada site in the Little Colorado River Valley in northeastern Arizona (Martin and Rinaldo 1960). At sites with these point types, pit structures and storage pits are known at sites both with maize (Clearwater) (Mabry 2006b) and without maize (Collier Dunes) (Irwin-Williams 1973, 1979).

The oldest radiocarbon dates associated with expanding stem points (but not maize) are from northwestern New Mexico and indicate that the time span of this point type on the Colorado Plateau extends back into the Middle Holocene, prior to the arrival of maize. Charcoal dates of 6770 ± 240 and 6060 ± 180 B.P. (circa 5600 B.C. and 5000 B.C. calibrated) are reported from San Jose strata at Armijo Tank Shelter in Arroyo Cuervo (Berry and Berry 1986), and charcoal dates of 5680 ± 180 and 5660 ± 270 B.P. (circa 4500 B.C. calibrated) are reported from San Jose sites in the San Juan Basin (Del Bene and Ford 1982). A charcoal date of 6880 ± 200 B.P. (circa 5700 B.C.) from Grants Arroyo Site 1 is from a hearth in a dune deposit containing both San Jose and leaf-shaped, parallel-flaked Yuma points (Agogino and Hester 1958); either both point types were made by the same cultural group (Agogino and Hester 1958), or this date is related to an earlier occupation associated with the leaf-shaped points (possibly resharpened Bajada points; Justice 2002).

Expanding stem points may have an even deeper lineage in the Southwest. While a number of archaeologists have treated the San Jose point as a southwestern variant of the Pinto point of the Great Basin, both Irwin-Williams (1973, 1979) and Justice (2002) have argued that the San Jose type evolved independently from the Bajada point of the Middle Holocene in the Southwest. The Bajada type is reported to date between about 6800 and 5200 B.P. (circa 5600–4000 B.C. calibrated) in northwestern New Mexico (Irwin-Williams 1979) and between about 7800 and 6400 B.P. (circa 6600–5300 B.C. calibrated) in south-central New Mexico (MacNeish 1993). However, its distribution is largely confined to the Colorado Plateau, at elevations above 6,000 feet (Mabry 1998). In northeastern Arizona, San Jose points (including an unserrated variant) were found together with Bajada points at the Hastqin site (Huckell 1977) and at AZ D:11:3063 on Black Mesa (Parry and Smiley 1990); radiocarbon dates on charcoal from hearths at both sites cluster near 8000 B.P. (circa 7000 B.C. calibrated).

The temporal priority of expanding stem points in sequences of point types associated with early maize (except possibly the temporally overlapping Chiricahua point, discussed later) is demonstrated in some cave and floodplain sequences. San Jose points occur by themselves in the earliest occupational strata at En Medio Shelter (Irwin-Williams and Tompkins 1968) and Harbison Cave in northern Arizona (Jennings 1971) and then are followed stratigraphically by Armijo, Basketmaker, and San Pedro notched point types in those cave sequences. Bat Cave points co-occur with contracting stem points (Augustin, Pelona, and other varieties) and triangular and leaf-shaped bifaces in the earliest occupation level at Bat Cave (the top of the Buff Sand) and then appear with these types and also with Chiricahua and Datil points in the next-higher level (Level VI) (Dick 1965). Between about 3700 and 2000 B.P. (circa 2100–50 B.C.) in the floodplain of the middle Santa Cruz Valley in southern Arizona, there was possibly a local evolution from the expanding stem Armijo/Bat Cave–like point, to the straight-stemmed Empire points, then to the side- to corner-notched San Pedro point, the side-notched Western Basketmaker point, and the corner-notched Cienega point series, with some temporal overlaps between these types and variants (Jane Sliva, personal communication 2006).

Straight-stem points. The Empire point, with a straight stem and long, narrow triangular blade, dates to the early San Pedro phase, and its known distribution includes south-central Arizona and northwestern Sonora (Stevens and Sliva 2002). At the Las Capas site in the middle Santa Cruz Valley of southern Arizona, Empire points were found together with San Pedro points in a stratum containing maize radiocarbon dated to 3050-2950 B.P. (circa 1250-1150 B.C. calibrated) (Hesse and Foster 2005; Sliva 2005). At a nearby site in the same valley, a similar point type, but with a shorter and more convex-based stem and resembling the Datil point, has been found in association with San Pedro points and maize radiocarbon dated to 3080-2970 B.P. (circa 1300-1200 B.C. calibrated) (Wöcherl 2005). Jane Sliva (personal communication 2006) has suggested that these stemmed Empire point variants led to a shallow side-notched variant and then to the notched San Pedro, Western Basketmaker, and Cienega point types.

Side-notched points. The Chiricahua point was originally identified as "intrusive" in the type-site assemblages of the Chiricahua stage in southeastern Arizona, bracketed between 9,000 and 4,500 years old by geoclimatic correlations (Sayles and Antevs 1941). Since then, this point type has been found at sites radiocarbon dated between about 4800 and 3900 B.P. (circa 3600-2400 B.C. calibrated) and no earlier in this region (Bayham et al. 1986; Huckell 1996). Its currently known distribution, while concentrated in southeastern Arizona, extends to every part of the Southwest except the northern and western Colorado Plateau and the lower Colorado Valley (Huckell 1996) and into northern Sonora and Chihuahua (Irwin-Williams 1967). Huckell (1996) and others have noted similarities among the Chiricahua point, the Northern Side-notched point, and other side-notched types of the Colorado Plateau and eastern Great Basin dating to the Middle Holocene and the initial part of the Late Holocene.

The presence of maize cobs in strata that yielded Chiricahua points (along with other Middle Archaic types) and radiocarbon dates on charcoal of about 5900 and 5600 B.P. (circa 4800-4400 B.C. calibrated) in Bat Cave in west-central New Mexico (Dick 1954, 1965) and the presence of maize pollen in a stratum that contained a single Chiricahua point at the Cienega Creek site in southeastern Arizona (Martin and Schoenwetter 1960) have been cited by many (e.g., Haury 1962; Dick 1965; Hunter-Anderson 1986; Sayles 1983) as evidence of the arrival of agriculture in the Mogollon Highlands during the Chiricahua stage. However, the identification of maize pollen in the deepest cultural layer at Cienega Creek is equivocal (Berry 1982), and re-dating of several charcoal samples with the CO_2 method bracket this deposit between about 3000 and 2400 B.P. (circa 1200-400 B.C. calibrated) (Wills 1988:137-141). On the other hand, the earliest maize from Bat Cave, thought by

Wills (1988) to date no earlier than 3100 B.P. (circa 1300 B.C. calibrated), may be as old as 3740 B.P. (circa 2150 B.C. calibrated) if the oldest direct date is not rejected. Several maize radiocarbon dates averaging about 3700 B.P. (circa 2100 B.C. calibrated) have been obtained from contexts containing Chiricahua points in McEuen Cave in the Gila Mountains of southeastern Arizona (Huckell, Huckell, and Shackley 1999; Steven Shackley, personal communication 2003).

Later notched point types definitely associated with early agricultural sites in the Arizona-Sonora borderlands include the San Pedro, Western Basketmaker, and Cienega points. Rather than developing from the earlier Chiricahua point, with its apparent affinities to earlier notched types to the north, these later notched types appear to have evolved locally in the southern Arizona–northern Sonora region from a series of stemmed point types (Jane Sliva, personal communication 2006). The San Pedro point—with a triangular blade, straight to convex base, and shallow side or corner notches—dates to the San Pedro and Cienega phases (3000–2000 B.P.) (circa 1200 B.C.–A.D. 50 calibrated) and has been found in southern and western Arizona, western New Mexico, and northern Sonora (Lorentzen 1998). The Western, or San Juan, Basketmaker II point—with a triangular blade, straight to convex base, and deep side or corner notches—dates to about 2800–1600 B.P. (circa 1000 B.C.–A.D. 400 calibrated) and has been found on the southern and central Colorado Plateau in northeastern Arizona, southeastern Utah, and northwestern New Mexico (Justice 2002); it has also been found recently at sites in the Tucson Basin in Late San Pedro- and Early Cienega-phase contexts (Mabry 2006b). The Cienega point series—with triangular blades (sometimes serrated, slightly concave, or both), expanding to straight stems, convex stem bases, and deep, wide corner notches—dates to about 2600–1800 B.P. (circa 800 B.C.–A.D. 200 calibrated) and is found in southeastern Arizona, southwestern New Mexico, and northern Sonora; a small early variation is probably an arrowhead, representing the introduction of the bow and arrow to the Southwest (Sliva 1999).

Cortaro biface. At the Clearwater (Mabry 2006b) and Buried Dune (Bayham et al. 1986) sites in southeastern Arizona, Armijo/Bat Cave points co-occur with the triangular, concave-based biface type formerly referred to as the Cortaro point, which is now thought to be a multifunctional tool type (Jane Sliva, personal communication 2003). The distribution of Cortaro bifaces includes northernmost Sinaloa and Sonora, southeastern Arizona, and southwestern New Mexico (Carpenter, Sanchez, and Villalpando 2005; Roth and Huckell 1992). In southeastern Arizona they are associated with Armijo/Bat Cave points at the Clearwater site in the Tucson Basin (with maize dates of 3690 and 3650 B.P., or circa 2100 B.C. calibrated; Mabry 2006a) and possibly in McEuen Cave in the middle Gila Valley (with several maize dates averaging about 3700 B.P., or circa 2100 B.C. calibrated; Steve Shackley, personal communication 2003). Cortaro bifaces also co-occur with later San Pedro and Cienega points in the borderlands (Sliva 2005). Two possibilities are apparent: (1) Cortaro bifaces represent a long, Late Holocene technological tradition among both hunting-and-gathering groups and early farming groups in the Arizona-Sonora borderlands and northwestern Mexico; or (2) they are associated with the initial arrival of maize-bearing Uto-Aztecan–speaking peoples in the borderlands (Carpenter, Sanchez, and Villalpando 2002, 2005).

Atlatls

Like projectile point hafting designs, the general designs of atlatls represent Archaic technological traditions that probably spread across linguistic and cultural boundaries. However, Ferg and Peachey (1998:188) have noted that the known distribution of "male-type" atlatls, with cylindrical shafts and raised spurs, in the southern Baja Peninsula and mainland Mexico corresponds in part to the geographic distribution of the "Hokaltecan" languages, while the distribution of "mixed-type" atlatls, with troughed flat boards and flush or only slightly raised spurs, corresponds well with the distribution of the Uto-Aztecan languages. Within a set of fifty-six mixed-type whole or partial atlatls found at twenty-nine sites in the U.S. Southwest and northwestern Mexico, flush spurs are the primary type found in the Southwest, while slightly projecting spurs predominate in northwestern Mexico, with an area of overlap in the border area of southern New Mexico, northern Chihuahua, and westernmost Texas (Ferg and Peachey 1998:191, fig. 8).

Fiber Artifacts

The appearance of new manufacturing techniques for cordage, basketry, sandals, and other woven items in a region may represent migration, diffusion events, or both. The appearances of bundle-foundation coiled basketry, twill plaiting, final S-twist cordage, and four-warp wickerwork sandals between 3000 and 2500 B.P. (circa 1200–700 B.C. calibrated) in the Jornada Basin of south-central New Mexico are synchronous with the appearance of tropical cultigens in the region (Hyland, Adovasio, and Taylor 1998; Hyland and Adovasio 2000). These new techniques and forms of northern Mexican origin were added to older ones and did not replace them. The retention and addition of technological styles may represent one or more migration and hybridization events, characterized by a merging of immigrant farmers and indigenous hunter-gatherers (Hyland, Adovasio, and Taylor 1998; Hyland and Adovasio 2000).

Relevant to future studies of possible clues about cultural identities in the Southern Southwest during the transition to agriculture are the presence of both two-rod-and-bundle foundations and one-rod foundations among the coiled basketry in the cremations at the Cienega Creek site (Haury 1957), now dated to about 2400–1900 B.P. (circa 1200–400 B.C. calibrated) (Wills 1988:137-141). Likewise, the differences in initial direction of cordage spin and in sandal warp and foot-tie treatments among specimens from levels containing early cultigen remains in Fresnal Shelter in the Tularosa Basin of south-central New Mexico (predominately Z-spin cordage and sandal warps that are knotted off) and in Bat Cave, Tularosa Cave, and Cordova Cave in west-central New Mexico (all mostly S-spin cordage and sandal warps that become ties) may indicate ethnic differences (McBrinn 2002, 2005).

Water Control Technologies

A common heritage among northern and southern Uto-Aztecan languages has also been identified in the way of speaking about the manipulation of water for agriculture, including cognates and semantic parallels for the words "canal," "dam," and "to irrigate." This implies that irrigation was practiced in the Southwest prior to the breakup of the Proto-Uto-Aztecan speech community between 3,000 and 2,500 years ago (Hill 2001).

This scenario is supported by recent discoveries of irrigation canals dating between 1500–500 B.C. at Early Agricultural–period sites in the Tucson Basin (Ezzo and Deaver 1998; Mabry 1999, 2006a, 2006b; Mabry, Holmlund, and Nials 2002) and canals dating as early as 1200 B.C. at Basketmaker II sites on the southern Colorado Plateau (Damp et al. 2000). These earliest known canals in the Southwest, which diverted perennial river flows, are older and more complex than the earliest known canals in Mesoamerica—ditches for runoff diversion and drainage built in Guerrero, Oaxaca, Veracrúz, the Basin of Mexico, Guatemala, and Belize during the Early Formative period between 1200–800 B.C. (Doolittle 1990; Neely 2005). Therefore, it seems likely that early southwestern farmers developed irrigation independently, after the arrival of maize and squash from Mexico.

Cultigens

Like technologies and styles, cultigens can also be introduced to new regions by diffusion and migration processes. Current evidence of the timing of cultigen arrivals and dispersals also suggests there was more than one migration or diffusion event that introduced tropical cultigens to the Southwest (Doolittle and Mabry 2006; Mabry 2005b). The currently available direct dates (see references in Mabry 2005b) suggest that both maize and squash arrived in the southern Basin and Range Province between 4000 and 3700 B.P. (circa 2500–2100 B.C. calibrated). Maize spread rapidly northward, reaching the Mogollon Highlands and the southern Colorado Plateau by 3800–3750 B.P. (circa 2200 B.C. calibrated). Maize did not spread east of the middle Rio Grande Valley until 2900 B.P. (circa 1100 B.C. calibrated), and dispersal farther northward and eastward on the Colorado Plateau did not occur until between 2500 and 2000 B.P. (circa 750–50 B.C. calibrated). Pepo squash reached the Mogollon Highlands and the southern Colorado Plateau between 3000–2900 B.P. (circa 1200–1100 B.C. calibrated). Bottle gourd and common bean arrived in the southern Basin and Range Province between 3000 and 2500 B.P. (circa 1200–750 B.C. calibrated). These currently available data indicate that maize and pepo squash were the first tropical cultigens to arrive (possibly together, as a crop complex) and that they spread rapidly to all parts of the Southwest, while common bean and bottle gourd arrived about a millennium later and spread gradually northward.

DISCUSSION

Marmaduke (1978:248) attributes the distribution of the contracting stem point type and its glued hafting design as representing the transmission of a cultural idea (i.e., diffusion of a technological tradition), but Berry and Berry (1986) argue that it indicates population movements from Mesoamerica northward. Holmer (1994) suggests that this point type was part of the Proto-Numic (Proto-Northern-Uto-Aztecan) material culture assemblage, which appeared in the archaeological record of the southwestern Great Basin by 5000 B.P. (circa 3800 B.C. calibrated). He interprets radiocarbon dates associated with this point type as indicating its spread north and east, reaching southern Utah by 4400 B.P. (circa 3000 B.C. calibrated) and western Colorado by 3800 B.P. (circa 2200 B.C. calibrated), a pattern he attributes to the expansion of the Numic peoples.

The range of this hafting technological tradition in northwestern Mexico and western North America does generally coincide with the distribution of Uto-Aztecan languages, and it is possible that this hafting technology diffused northward along with maize cultivation (Carpenter, Sanchez, and Villalpando 2005). However, the appearance of this hafting design in northeastern Mexico as early as 6000 B.P. (circa 4900 B.C. calibrated) indicates that either this technological tradition was transmitted across ethnic/linguistic boundaries or there was an initial migration of Proto-Uto-Aztecans into this region that left no historical linguistic traces. It seems likely that the broad spread of this hafting design in Mexico and western North America between about 6000–4000 B.P. (circa 4900–2500 B.C. calibrated) primarily represents diffusion of a new technology across cultural and linguistic boundaries and among both foraging and farming groups (akin to the later diffusion of bow-and-arrow technology, for example) rather than primarily a migration or series of population movements of a specific cultural group at such an enormous scale.

However, within this hafting tradition, minor variations in stems (for example, among Gypsum, Agustín, Pelona, Elko Contracting Stem, and Gatecliff Contracting Stem types) may represent passive stylistic variation between different cultural groups. For example, some Great Basin groups may have adapted this new point type to an indigenous split-end foreshaft design, resulting in a hybrid technology. In the central Great Basin, the Gatecliff Contracting Stem and Gatecliff Split Stem types (which resemble the bifurcate-stemmed Pinto Shouldered type), perhaps representing socketed and split-end foreshaft designs, respectively, co-occur in strata bracketed by charcoal radiocarbon dates between about 5000 and 3300 B.P. (circa 3800–1500 B.C. calibrated) (Thomas 1981). The Gypsum series B and Langtry varieties, with slightly indented bases, which appeared in the southeastern Great Basin by 3600 B.P. (circa 1900 B.C. calibrated) (Fowler, Madsen, and Hattori 1973) and in the lower Rio Grande Valley by 4500 B.P. (circa 3300 B.C. calibrated) (Turner and Hester 1985), may also be modifications to better seat the points in a split-end foreshaft (Justice 2002).

Perhaps the most important implication of the wide diffusion of this new hafting technology is that it demonstrates that after a long break in contact in the desert lowlands of the U.S.-Mexico borderlands during the Altithermal of the Middle Holocene, populations came into contact with each other over a continuous area extending from central Mexico to the central Great Basin and from the southern California coast to the Colorado Plateau. Similarly, the broad distribution of mixed-type atlatls across the southwestern U.S. and northern Mexico (Ferg and Peachey 1998) indicates contacts during the early portion of the Late Holocene. Significant to the arguments here is that this return to the Desert Borderlands and establishment of contacts prior to 4000 B.P. (circa 2500 B.C. calibrated) preceded the spread of tropical cultigens northward and that the spread of the glued hafting design through those contacts therefore reflects a combination of migration and diffusion processes.

In contrast to the new hafting design of the contracting stem point, expanding stem points and side-notched points represent older hafting designs initially used during the Middle Holocene by indigenous hunting-and-gathering groups on the Colorado Plateau and in the Great Basin. Through migration or diffusion or both processes, these hafting designs spread southward into the desert lowlands at the beginning of the Late Holocene. The simplest explanation is that hunting-and-gathering populations from the Colorado Plateau (and possibly the eastern Great Basin) expanded southward as environmental conditions improved in the lowlands, and there some of them adopted maize agriculture after contacts with Proto-Uto-Aztecan farmers in northern Mexico. Then, through regular contacts among groups using these hafting designs, maize rapidly diffused northward to the Mogollon Highlands and the Colorado Plateau.

The sequence of dart point styles found at early agricultural sites in southern Arizona suggests continuity between early southwestern cultivators using expanding stem (and possibly side-notched points) and subsequent early farming groups using other notched point types. The Late Holocene appearance of the Cortaro biface, whose distribution is limited to the borderlands region, may represent local development of a new general-purpose tool by the first farmers of this region.

Most of the known atlatl specimens in northwestern Mexico and the southwestern United States are not well dated, but the few that have been radiocarbon dated (Ferg and Peachey 1998; Moreno 2000) or dated by their association with temporally diagnostic artifacts were manufactured during the Late Holocene, after the arrival of maize. Therefore, the northern and southern distributions of two slightly different variations in spur designs on mixed-type atlatls may represent passive stylistic variation reflecting ethnic differences between subgroups of Uto-Aztecans (northern and southern?) that developed after the arrival of Mesoamerican agriculture.

Linguistic data suggest the chronology of tropical cultigen arrivals in the Southwest. Many of the surviving Native American languages of the Southwest and Mexico belong to the Uto-Aztecan family of languages, and shared word roots and similarities in grammatical and semantic structures allow linguists to trace these related languages back to a common ancestral language of several thousand years ago. Fowler (1994) and Hill (2001) have shown that maize was cultivated during the time of the Proto-Uto-Aztecan speech community because there is a shared vocabulary for the cultivation and processing of maize between northern Uto-Aztecan languages, such as Hopi (and probably Numic), and the southern languages in this family (such as Nahuatl, the language of the Aztecs). Words for "squash" also show similarities that indicate that this cultigen spread before the breakup of the dialect continuum, while differences in words for "bean" show that it diffused among Uto-Aztecan speech communities after the breakup. The timing of this breakup is therefore bracketed by the initial dates of squash and bean in the Southwest (Hill 2001), currently 3700 and 2500 B.P. (circa 2100 and 750 B.C. calibrated), respectively.

The timing of the appearances of tropical cultigens in the southwestern archaeological record can be reconciled with Hill's (2001) linguistic model by several alternate scenarios: (1) a northward expansion of people who spoke the PUA language brought maize and squash to the Southwest, and then other tropical cultigens spread after the breakup of this PUA speech community; (2) an expansion of PUA speakers (from either north or south) occurred prior to the spread of agriculture as the climate improved at the beginning of the Late Holocene, and then these cultigens diffused in two or more waves across a continuum of linguistically and culturally related hunting-and-gathering groups; or (3) both diffusion and migration processes were at work on the early agricultural frontier in the Southwest, and early agriculturalists in this region included speakers of both the PUA language and indigenous languages (Hokan and possibly Penutian).

The rapid dispersal of maize and pepo squash to the Mogollon Highlands and the southern Colorado Plateau may have been a result of either the existence of such an established linguistic-cultural continuum or of northward migrations of farmers from the desert lowlands. The latter scenario best fits the relatively sudden appearance on the central Colorado Plateau of the Western (or White Dog-phase) Basketmaker II archaeological complex (1000 B.C.?–A.D. 500) with maize and pepo squash and provides an explanation for similarities in the material cultures of the Western Basketmaker II and San Pedro complexes (1200–800 B.C.) of the southwestern U.S./northwestern Mexico borderlands.

In comparing the assemblage of perishable materials in San Pedro–phase levels of Ventana Cave in southern Arizona with similar materials in Western Basketmaker II cave occupations in the Four Corners area, R. G. Matson (1991, 1999) has argued that these two complexes also have in common some sandal types and coiled basketry with two-rod-and-bundle foundation and uninterlocked stitch. Mabry (2006b) noted that some elements of the San Pedro complex overlap with the Western Basketmaker II complex: Western Basketmaker points, San Pedro points, bone dice, bulbous stone pipes. These shared elements of both nonperishable and perishable materials appear to support models proposing that the sudden appearance of the Western Basketmaker II complex on the Colorado Plateau represents a migration of San Pedro-phase farmers between 850 and 500 B.C. (Berry and Berry 1986; Matson 1991, 1999). This scenario would also account for the spread of the PUA language community to the Northern Southwest before 500 B.C., as reconstructed with linguistic data by Hill (2001, 2003).

The long delays in maize dispersal north of the Colorado and San Juan rivers, on the other hand, may have been a result of these rivers becoming the boundaries between PUA farmers and indigenous hunter-gatherer groups who later adopted agriculture (cf. Geib 1996). In contrast to maize and squash, both common bean and bottle gourd spread more slowly from south to north, probably because of their preferences for warm temperatures and long growing seasons and because they had to cross emerging cultural boundaries after the breakup of the PUA speech community.

If Proto-Uto-Aztecans brought agriculture with them, or if agriculture spread among them after their arrival in western North America, why did it not persist into historic times among the speakers of northern Uto-Aztecan languages? Romney (1957) was the first to suggest that the historically non-agricultural Uto-Aztecan peoples in the extreme north had abandoned agriculture, referring to archaeological evidence of agriculture in the area of the Great Basin occupied by Shoshoneans, historical evidence of irrigation of wild plants by the Owens Valley Paiute, and the documented practice of broadcast sowing of wild plant seeds by several groups in the basin. Could these features be interpreted as remnants of a past agricultural tradition among Shoshonean people? Hill (2001) reiterated this possibility to explain the presence of agriculture-related word cognates in some northern Uto-Aztecan languages.

The irrigation canals recently found at early farming sites in the Southwest, the prehistoric maize cobs and possible canal found in dunes near Lovelock, Nevada (Jensen 1976), and the historical practice of irrigating maize fields in southwestern Nevada (Steward 1938) all suggest that the historical irrigation of wild plants by the Owens Valley Paiute and broadcast sowing of wild plant seeds by other Ute and Shoshonean groups in the western Great Basin represent remnants of an ancient horticultural complex in a region ultimately too marginal for tropical cultigens. Then again, Great Basin agricultural strategies may also be explained by diffusion from adjacent agricultural traditions to the east. The high degree of correspondence between the distribution of Uto-Aztecan language and agriculture, together with the ethnohistoric cultivation practices documented by Steward and others and the linguistic evidence cited by Hill (2001), suggest that agriculture may have been abandoned after the PUA expansion into the Great Basin. However, this does not inform on whether agriculture arrived in the Great Basin by diffusion or migration.

The dating of possible archaeological evidence of the arrival of Proto-Uto-Aztecans in regions beyond the Southwest may help bracket their earlier arrival in the Southwest. The arrival of Uto-Aztecan, Takic-speaking peoples on the southern California coast (the so-called Shoshonean wedge that split the previous continuum of Hokan [Yuman]-speaking peoples) is generally associated with regional settlement and subsistence changes that occurred between about 3500 and 3000 B.P. (circa 1800-1200 B.C. calibrated) (Erlandson 1997; Mason, Koerper, and Langenwalter 1997; Moratto 1984) and the appearance of cremations about this time (King 1981). However, it has also been variously proposed that the Uto-Aztecan arrival on the southern California coast is marked by the appearances of flexed inhumations by 6400 B.P. (circa 5400 B.C. calibrated) (Drover and Spain 1972), of *Olivella* grooved rectangular beads at about 5000 B.P. (circa 3800 B.C. calibrated) (Howard and Raab 1993; King 1990; Vellanoweth 1995), of contracting stem dart points about 4500 B.P. (circa 3300 B.C. calibrated) (Harrington 1933), and of clockwise-coiled basketry about 3800 B.P. (circa 2200 B.C. calibrated) (Bleitz 1991).

In the southwestern Great Basin, the arrival of Proto-Uto-Aztecans has been attributed to the appearance of contracting stem dart points about 5000 B.P. (circa 3800 B.C. calibrated) (Holmer 1994), while the apparent continuity in material culture and subsistence strategy in the central Great Basin since about 5000-4500 B.P. (circa 3800-3300 B.C. calibrated) until historic time has been cited as evidence of the long presence of Uto-Aztecans (Aikens and Witherspoon 1986).

Although arrivals of Proto-Uto-Aztecans on the southern California coast between 3500 and 3000 B.P. (circa 1800-1200 B.C. calibrated) would fit with a circa 4000 B.P. (circa 2500 B.C. calibrated) arrival of PUA agriculturalists in the Arizona-Sonora borderlands region, a date of 5000 B.P. (circa 3800 B.C. calibrated) or earlier for reaching either the Great Basin or the Pacific Coast would imply an arrival in the Southwest prior to the arrival of Mesoamerican cultigens. Acceptance of such a scenario would strengthen the case for a pre-agricultural northward expansion of PUA speakers or would require revisiting the models of PUA origins in the Great Basin or farther north rather than to the south.

Regarding Fowler's (1983) newer position that the locations of Tarahumara and Cahitan groups that interrupt the distribution of Piman languages are a result of subsequent movements of these groups toward the west Mexican coast, we believe both linguistic and ethnographic data demonstrate they have been in place for at least 2,000 years, if not more. The Cahitan-speaking groups of the coastal plain have traditionally been considered late arrivals, descending from the Sierra Madre Occidental and displacing presumably Tepiman-speaking peoples (Beals 1932:145; Braniff 1992:217; Sauer 1934:82; Wilcox 1986). However, as discussed by Miller (1983a:333), this interpretation seems to have been based solely on geographical appearances. In considering the linguistic data, Miller and others (1983a, 1983b; D. Shaul, personal communication 1993) have suggested that the Cahitans may have been established on the coastal plain near the beginning of the Christian era. In turn, the Tepimans may likely represent a late (circa twelfth-century) intrusion, perhaps from the north (Hill 1996; Fowler 1980; Miller 1983a:333, 1983b; Shaul and Hill 1993).

Long-term in situ development for the lowland Cahitans is also supported by the ethnographic data. Sixteenth-century population estimates indicate an extremely high density, with figures ranging from 70,000 souls and 5.2 persons per square kilometer for the Tahue to 60,000 Opata with a projected density of 1.5 persons per square kilometer (Sauer 1935:5). Extensive *temporal* agriculture was carried out along the floodplains of the major drainages, reportedly producing up to three harvests per year for a wide range of cultigens that included maize, beans, squash, cotton, peppers, eggplant, and guavas (Sauer and Brand 1932:52). Some groups also reflect well-developed maritime exploitation of both littoral and deep-water resources (Pérez de Ribas 1944; Sheridan 1981). In contrast, the Lower Pimans are often described in contact-period documents as occupying largely marginal lands, practicing little or no agriculture, and with little exploitation of coastal resources (Tom Sheridan, personal communication 1993).

SUMMARY

We argue that current archaeological evidence does not reconcile neatly with Hill's (2001) linguistic model of a Proto-Uto-Aztecan migration from central Mexico that brought Mesoamerican agriculture to the Southwest. Some archaeological data point to the possibility of a pre-agricultural expansion of PUA speakers into the Southwest, creating a linguistic-cultural continuum across which maize and pepo squash later spread. However, a variety of archaeological evidence suggests that the Arizona-Sonora borderlands were reoccupied from both the south and the north at the end of the Middle Holocene and that maize and other early tropical cultigens arrived and spread across the Southwest through a combination of diffusion and migration processes. The implication is that some early farmers in the Southwest spoke indigenous languages while others spoke Proto-Uto-Aztecan. As with maize and squash agriculture, irrigation spread across the Southwest before the breakup of the PUA community, and the historical practice of irrigating wild plants by some Paiute groups in the western Great Basin may reflect a remnant of that early irrigated-farming complex. However, irrigation technology (and most likely ceramics) probably represents independent innovations by early southwestern farmers.

NOTE

1. Bellwood (1997, 1999) and Hill (2001) referred to the "rake-like" structure of the Uto-Aztecan language family as an indication of the rapid divergences that would occur with migration and rapid agricultural colonization. However, such a structure could also develop with increasing sedentism and loss of contact between groups and with other processes of ethnogenesis. Miller (1984:20-21) suggested that because the ancestral PUA community was composed of hunter-gatherers in contact with a small number of other groups, a "wave principle" operated, a situation in which there is "a dialect continuum which dissolves into distinct languages and in which newly budded languages reflect the earlier dialect relationships."

With the shift to agriculture and the resulting greater population density and increased sedentism, the geographic area of mutual influence was reduced, but the network included more people. This may have functioned to minimize the wave principle and to maximize a "family tree principle" (which Miller preferred) or a rake principle (favored by Bellwood and Hill), in which multiple splits occur in quick succession within a parent language. While the linguistic evidence for multiple splits in rapid succession within Uto-Aztecan presented by Bellwood and Hill represent a rake-like principle, it is possible that the process of language change shifted to this principle *after* the diffusion of agriculture and increasing sedentism.

REFERENCES CITED

Adams, William Y., Dennis P. Van Gerven, and Richard S. Levy
    1978   The Retreat from Migrationism. *Annual Review of Anthropology* 7:483-532.

Agogino, George, and J. Hester
    1958   Comments on the San Jose Radiocarbon Date. *American Antiquity* 24(2):187-188.

Aikens, C. Melvin, and Younger T. Witherspoon
    1986   Great Basin Numic Prehistory: Linguistics, Archaeology, and Environment. In *Anthropology in the Desert West: Essays in Honor of Jesse D. Jennings*, ed. C. Condie and D. D. Fowler, 7-20. University of Utah Anthropological Papers 110. University of Utah Press, Salt Lake City.

Anthony, David W.
    1990   Migration in Archaeology: The Baby and the Bathwater. *American Anthropologist* 92(4):895-914.

Bascom, B. W.
    1965   *Proto-Tepiman (Tepehuan-Piman)*. Unpublished Ph.D. dissertation, Department of Anthropology, University of Washington, Seattle.

Bayham, Frank E., Donald H. Morris, and M. Steven Shackley (editors)
    1986   *Prehistoric Hunter Gatherers of South Central Arizona: The Picacho Reservoir Archaic Project*. Anthropological Field Studies 13. Department of Anthropology, Arizona State University, Tempe.

Beals, Ralph
    1932   *The Comparative Ethnology of Northwestern Mexico Before 1750*. Ibero-Americana 2. University of California Press, Berkeley.

Bellwood, Peter
    1997   Prehistoric Cultural Explanations for Widespread Linguistic Families. In *Archaeology and Linguistics: Aboriginal Australia in Global Perspective*, ed. P. McConvell and N. Evans, 123-134. Oxford University Press, Melbourne.
    1999   Austronesian Prehistory and Uto-Aztecan Prehistory: Similar Trajectories? University of Arizona Department of Anthropology Lecture Series, Tucson, January 27.

Berry, Claudia F., and Michael S. Berry
    1986   Chronological and Conceptual Models of the Southwestern Archaic. In *Anthropology of the Desert West: Essays in Honor of Jesse D. Jennings*, ed. C. J. Condie and D.

D. Fowler, 253-327. Anthropological Papers 110. University of Utah Press, Salt Lake City.

Berry, Michael S.
1982   Time, Space, and Transition in Anasazi Prehistory. University of Utah Press, Salt Lake City.

Bleitz, Dana
1991   A Discussion Concerning Evidence of Coiled Basketry from SNI-11 on San Nicolas Island, California. *California Anthropologist* 18(1):25-27.

Braniff, Beatriz
1992   *La Frontera Protohistórica Pima-Opata en Sonora, México: Proposiciones Arqueológicas Preliminares*, Volume I. Collección Científica, INAH, México.

Bryan, Kirk, and Joseph H. Toulouse Jr.
1943   The San Jose Non-Ceramic Culture and Its Relation to a Puebloan Culture in New Mexico. *American Antiquity* 8(3):269-280.

Campbell, Lyle
1977   *American Indian Languages: The Historical Linguistics of Native America*. Oxford University Press, New York.

Campbell, Lyle, and Ronald Longacker
1978   Proto-Aztecan Vowels. Parts I, II, III. *International Journal of American Linguistics* 44:85-102, 197-210, 262-279.

Carpenter, John P., Jonathan Mabry, and Guadalupe Sanchez
2001   Arqueología de los Grupos Yuto-Aztecas Tempranos. In *Avances y Balances de las Lenguas Yuto-Aztecas: Homenaje a Wick R. Miller*, ed. Jose Luis Moctezuma and Jane H. Hill, 359-374. Colección Científica 438. INAH-Conaculta, México.

Carpenter, John P., Guadalupe Sanchez, and Elisa Villalpando
2002   Of Migration and Maize: Mode and Tempo in the Diffusion of Zea mays into Northern Mexico and the American Southwest. In *Traditions, Transitions, and Technologies: Themes in Southwestern Archaeology*, ed. Sarah H. Schlanger, 245-258. University Press of Colorado, Boulder.

2005   The Late Archaic/Early Agricultural Period in Sonora, Mexico. In *The Late Archaic across the Borderlands*, ed. B. J. Vierra, 13-40. University of Texas Press, Austin.

Cosgrove, C. Burton
1947   *Caves of the Upper Gila and Hueco Areas in New Mexico and Texas*. Papers of the Peabody Museum of American Archaeology and Ethnology 24(2), Cambridge, Mass.

Damp, Jonathan E., James W. Kendrick, Donovan Quam, Jeffery Waseta, and Jerome Zunie
2000   *Households and Farms in Early Zuni Prehistory: Settlement, Subsistence, and the Archaeology of Y Unit Draw, Archaeological Investigations at Eighteen Sites along New Mexico State Highway 602*. Zuni Cultural Resource Enterprise Report 593. Pueblo of Zuni, N.M.

Del Bene, Terry A., and Dabney Ford
1982   *Archaeological Excavations in Blocks VI and VII, Navajo Indian Irrigation Project, San Juan County, New Mexico*. Navajo Nation Papers in Anthropology 13. Navajo Tribal Cultural Resource Management Program, Window Rock, Ariz.

Dick, Herbert W.
　1954　The Bat Cave Corn Complex: A Note on Its Distribution and Archaeological Significance. *El Palacio* 61:139–144.
　1965　*Bat Cave*. School of American Research Monograph 27, Santa Fe.

Doolittle, William E.
　1990　*Canal Irrigation in Prehistoric Mexico: The Sequence of Technological Change*. University of Texas Press, Austin.

Doolittle, William E., and Jonathan B. Mabry
　2006　Environmental Mosaics, Agricultural Diversity, and the Evolutionary Adoption of Maize in the American Southwest. In *Histories of Maize*, ed. John E. Staller, Robert H. Tykot, and Bruce F. Benz, 109–122. Academic, Amsterdam.

Drover, Christopher E., and James N. Spain
　1972　An Early, Articulated Inhumation from 4-ORA-64: A Discussion. *Pacific Coast Archaeological Society Quarterly* 8(4):35–44.

Erlandson, Jon
　1997　The Middle Holocene along the California Coast. In *Archaeology of the California Coast during the Middle Holocene*, ed. J. M. Erlandson and M. A. Glassow, 1–10. Perspectives in California Archaeology, Volume 4. Institute of Archaeology, University of California, Los Angeles.

Ezzo, Joseph A., and William L. Deaver
　1998　*Watering the Desert: Late Archaic Farming at the Costello-King Site*. Technical Series 68. Statistical Research, Tucson.

Ferg, Alan, and William D. Peachey
　1998　An Atlatl from the Sierra Pinacate. *Kiva* 64(2):175–200.

Fowler, Catherine S.
　1972　Some Ecological Clues to Proto-Numic Homelands. *University of Nevada Desert Research Institute Publications in the Social Sciences* 8:105–121.
　1980　Some Lexical Clues to Uto-Aztecan Prehistory. Paper presented at the Uto-Aztecan Historical Symposium, Linguistics Institute, University of New Mexico, Albuquerque.
　1983　Some Lexical Clues to Uto-Aztecan Prehistory. *International Journal of American Linguistics* 49(3):224–257.
　1994　Corn, Beans, and Squash: Some Linguistic Perspectives from Uto-Aztecan. In *Corn and Culture in the Prehistoric New World*, ed. S. Johannessen and C. A. Hastorf, 445–467. Westview, Boulder.

Fowler, Don D., David B. Madsen, and Eugene M. Hattori
　1973　*Prehistory of Southeastern Nevada*. Desert Research Institute Publications in the Social Sciences 6. Desert Research Institute, Reno, Nev.

Geib, Phil R.
　1996　AMS Dating of Plain-Weave Sandals from the Central Colorado Plateau. *Utah Archaeology* 9(1):35–53.

Goss, James A.
　1977　Linguistic Tools for the Great Basin Prehistorian. In *Models in Great Basin Prehistory*, ed. Don D. Fowler, 49–70. Desert Research Institute Publications in the Social Sciences 12. Desert Research Institute, Reno, Nev.

Hale, Kenneth
  1958   Internal Diversity in Uto-Aztecan I. *International Journal of American Linguistics* 24: 101-107.

Hale, Kenneth, and David Harris
  1979   Historical Linguistics and Archeology. In *Handbook of North American Indians*, Volume 9, *Southwest*, ed. Alfonso Ortiz, 170-177. Smithsonian Institution Press, Washington, D.C.

Harrington, Mark R.
  1933   *Gypsum Cave, Nevada*. Southwest Museum Papers 8, Los Angeles.

Haury, Emil W.
  1957   An Alluvial Site on the San Carlos Indian Reservation, Arizona. *American Antiquity* 23(1):2-27.
  1962   The Greater American Southwest. In *Courses toward Urban Life: Archeological Considerations of Some Cultural Alternatives*, ed. Robert J. Braidwood and Gordon R. Willey, 106-131. Viking Fund Publications in Anthropology 32. Aldine, Chicago.

Heath, Jeffry
  1977   Uto-Aztecan Morphophonemics. *International Journal of American Linguistics* 43:27-36.

Hesse, S. Jerome, and Michael S. Foster (editors)
  2005   *Investigations of Middle Archaic and Early Agricultural Period Components at Las Capas: The Treatment Plant Locus*. SWCA Cultural Resources Report 05-165. SWCA, Tucson.

Hill, Jane H.
  1996   The Prehistoric Differentiation of Uto-Aztecan Languages and the Lexicon of Early Southwestern Agriculture. Paper presented at the 61st Annual Meeting of the Society for American Archaeology, New Orleans, La.
  2001   Proto-Uto-Aztecan: A Community of Cultivars in Central Mexico? *American Anthropologist* 103(4):913-934.
  2003   Uto-Aztecan Cultivation and the Northern Devolution. In *Examining the Farming/Language Dispersal Hypothesis*, ed. P. Bellwood and C. Renfrew, 331-340. McDonald Institute for Archaeological Research, Cambridge, England.

Holmer, Richard N.
  1986   Common Projectile Points of the Intermountain West. In *Anthropology of the Desert West: Essays in Honor of Jesse D. Jennings*, ed. C. J. Condie and D. D. Fowler, 89-115. Anthropological Papers 110. University of Utah Press, Salt Lake City.
  1994   In Search of the Ancestral Northern Shoshone. In *Across the West: Human Population Movement and the Expansion of the Numa*, ed. D. B. Madsen and D. Rhode, 179-187. University of Utah Press, Salt Lake City.

Hopkins, Nicholas A.
  1965   Great Basin Prehistory and Uto-Aztecan. *American Antiquity* 31:48-60.

Howard, William J., and L. Mark Raab
  1993   Olivella Grooved Rectangle Beads as Evidence of a Mid-Holocene Southern Channel Islands Interaction Sphere. *Pacific Coast Archaeological Society Quarterly* 29(3):1-11.

Huckell, Bruce B.
- 1977 *The Hastqin Site: A Multicomponent Site Near Ganado, Arizona.* Contribution to Highway Salvage Archaeology in Arizona 61. Arizona State Museum, University of Arizona, Tucson.
- 1996 Style and Substance: Projectile Points, the Cochise Culture, and the Archaic Prehistory of the Southern Deserts in the American West. Paper presented at the 61st Annual Meeting of the Society for American Archaeology, New Orleans, La.

Huckell, Bruce, Lisa W. Huckell, and M. Steven Shackley
- 1999 McEuen Cave. *Archaeology Southwest* 13(1):12. Center for Desert Archaeology, Tucson.

Hunter-Anderson, Rosalind L.
- 1986 *Prehistoric Adaptation in the American Southwest.* Cambridge University Press, Cambridge.

Hyland, David C., and James M. Adovasio
- 2000 The Mexican Connection: A Study of Sociotechnical Change in Perishable Manufacture and Food Production in Prehistoric New Mexico. In *Beyond Cloth and Cordage: Archaeological Textile Research in the Americas*, ed. Penelope Ballard Drooker and Laurie D. Webster, 141–159. University of Utah Press, Salt Lake City.

Hyland, David C., James M. Adovasio, and R. E. Taylor
- 1998 Corn, Cucurbits, Cordage, and Colonization: An Absolute Chronology for the Appearance of Mesoamerican Domesticates and Perishables in the Jornada Basin, New Mexico. Paper presented at the 63rd Annual Meeting of the Society for American Archaeology, Seattle, Wash.

Irwin-Williams, Cynthia
- 1967 Picosa: The Elementary Southwestern Culture. *American Antiquity* 32(4):441–457.
- 1973 *The Oshara Tradition: Origins of Anasazi Culture.* Eastern New Mexico University Contributions in Anthropology 5(1), Portales.
- 1979 Post-Pleistocene Archaeology, 7000–2000 B.C. In *Handbook of North American Indians*, Volume 9, *Southwest*, ed. Alfonso Ortiz, 31–42. Smithsonian Institution Press, Washington, D.C.

Irwin-Williams, Cynthia, and S. Tompkins
- 1968 *Excavations at En Medio Shelter, New Mexico.* Eastern New Mexico University Contributions in Anthropology 1(2), Portales.

Jennings, Calvin H.
- 1971 *Early Prehistory of the Coconino Plateau, Northwestern Arizona.* Ph.D. dissertation, Department of Anthropology, University of Colorado, Boulder.

Jensen, A.
- 1976 Lovelock Dune Corn Cob: A Preliminary Report. In *Nevada Archaeological Survey Reporter*, 13–17. Nevada Archaeological Survey, University of Nevada, Reno.

Justice, Noel D.
- 2002 *Stone Age Spear and Arrow Points of the Southwestern United States.* Indiana University Press, Bloomington.

King, Charles
- 1981 The Evolution of Chumash Society: A Comparative Study of Artifacts Used in System Maintenance in the Santa Barbara Channel Region Before A.D. 1804. Ph.D. dissertation, Department of Anthropology, University of California, Davis.
- 1990 Evolution of Chumash Society. Garland, New York.

Koerper, Henry C., and Christopher E. Drover
- 1983 Chronology Building for Coastal Orange County: The Case from CA-Ora-119-A. Pacific Coast Archaeological Society Quarterly 19(2):1-33.

Lamb, Sydney M.
- 1958 Linguistic Prehistory in the Great Basin. International Journal of American Linguistics 24:95-100.

Long, Austin, Bruce F. Benz, D. J. Donahue, A.J.T. Jull, and L. J. Toolin
- 1989 First Direct Dates on Early Maize from Tehuacán, Mexico. Radiocarbon 31(3): 1035-1040.

Lorentzen, Leon
- 1998 Common Paleoindian and Archaic Projectile Points of Arizona. Appendix in Paleoindian and Archaic Sites in Arizona, by J. B. Mabry, 137-151. State Historic Preservation Office, Arizona State Parks, Phoenix.

Mabry, Jonathan B.
- 1998 Paleoindian and Archaic Sites in Arizona. State Historic Preservation Office, Arizona State Parks, Phoenix.
- 1999 Las Capas and Early Irrigation Farming. Archaeology Southwest 13(1):14. Center for Desert Archaeology, Tucson.
- 2005a Changing Knowledge and Ideas about the First Farmers in Southeastern Arizona. In The Late Archaic across the Borderlands: From Foraging to Farming, ed. Bradley J. Vierra, 41-83. University of Texas Press, Austin.
- 2005b Diversity in Early Southwestern Farming Systems and Optimization Models of Transitions to Agriculture. In Subsistence and Resource Use Strategies of Early Agricultural Communities in Southern Arizona, ed. Michael W. Diehl, 113-152. Anthropological Papers 34. Center for Desert Archaeology, Tucson.
- 2006a Radiocarbon Dating of Early Occupations. In Rio Nuevo Archaeology Program, 2000-2003: Investigations at the San Agustin Mission and Mission Gardens, Tucson Presidio, Tucson Pressed Brick Company, and Clearwater Site, ed. J. Homer Thiel and Jonathan B. Mabry, 191-195. Technical Report 2004-11. Center for Desert Archaeology, Tucson.

Mabry, Jonathan B. (editor)
- 2006b Las Capas: Early Irrigation and Sedentism in a Southwestern Floodplain. Anthropological Paper 28. Center for Desert Archaeology, Tucson (draft).

Mabry, Jonathan B., James P. Holmlund, and Fred Nials
- 2002 Early Canals in Southwestern North America. Paper presented at the 67th Annual Meeting of the Society for American Archaeology, Denver, Colo.

MacNeish, Richard S.
- 1958 Preliminary Archaeological Investigations in the Sierra de Tamaulipas, Mexico. Transactions of the American Philosophical Society 48:Part 6.

1993 Preliminary Investigations of the Archaic in the Region of Las Cruces, New Mexico. Cultural Resources Management Program, Historic and Natural Resources Report 9. Directorate of Environment, United States Army Air Defense Artillery Center, Fort Bliss, Tex.

MacNeish, Richard S., Antoinette Nelken-Terner, and Irmgard W. Johnson
1967 *The Prehistory of the Tehuacan Valley,* Volume 2. *Nonceramic Artifacts.* University of Texas Press, Austin.

Manaster Ramer, A.
1992 Tubatulabal Aman and the Sub-classification of Uto-Aztecan. *California Linguistic Notes* 23(2):30–31.

Marmaduke, William S.
1978 *Prehistoric Culture in Trans-Pecos Texas: An Ecological Explanation.* Unpublished Ph.D. dissertation, Department of Anthropology, University of Texas, Austin.

Martin, Paul S., and John B. Rinaldo
1960 Excavations in the Upper Little Colorado Drainage, Eastern Arizona. *Fieldiana* 51(1):1–127. Field Museum of Natural History, Chicago.

Martin, Paul S., and James Schoenwetter
1960 America's Oldest Cornfield. *Science* 132:33–34.

Mason, Roger D., Henry C. Koerper, and Paul E. Langenwalter II
1997 Middle Holocene Adaptations on the Newport Coast of Orange County. In *Archaeology of the California Coast during the Middle Holocene,* ed. J. M. Erlandson and M. A. Glassow, 35–60. Perspectives in California Archaeology, Volume 4. Institute of Archaeology, University of California, Los Angeles.

Matson, R. G.
1991 *The Origins of Southwestern Agriculture.* University of Arizona Press, Tucson.
1999 The Spread of Maize to the Colorado Plateau. *Archaeology Southwest* 13(1):10–11.

McBrinn, Maxine E.
2002 *Social Identity and Risk Sharing among the Mobile Hunters and Gatherers of the Archaic Southwest.* Ph.D. dissertation, Department of Anthropology, University of Colorado, Boulder.
2005 *Social Identities among Archaic Mobile Hunters and Gatherers in the American Southwest.* Arizona State Museum Archaeological Series 197. University of Arizona Press, Tucson.

Miller, Wick R.
1983a A Note on Extinct Languages of Northwest Mexico of Supposed Uto-Aztecan Affiliation. *International Journal of American Linguistics* 49:328–334.
1983b Uto-Aztecan Languages. In *Handbook of North American Indians,* Volume 10, *Southwest,* ed. Alfonso Ortiz, 113–124. Smithsonian Institution Press, Washington, D.C.
1984 The Classification of the Uto-Aztecan Languages Based on Lexical Evidence. *International Journal of American Linguistics* 50(1):1–24.
1995 Prehistoria de las Lenguas Indígenas del Noroeste de México. In *Sonora: Origen y Destino. XIX Simposio de Historia y Antropología de Sonora. Instituto de Investigaciones*

Historicas de la Universidad de Sonora, Hermosillo, Sonora, Febrero de 1994, Volume 2, 163-171. Universidad de Historia y Antropología, Universidad de Sonora, Hermosillo.

Moore, Roger A.
1994 Archaic Projectile Point Typology/Chronology in Northern New Mexico and the Four Corners. In *Archaic Hunter and Gatherer Archaeology in the American Southwest*, ed. B. J. Vierra, 456-475. Eastern New Mexico University Contributions in Anthropology 13. Eastern New Mexico University, Portales.

Moratto, Michael J.
1984 *California Archaeology*. Academic, Orlando, Calif.

Moreno, Teresa K.
2000 Accelerator Mass Spectrometry Dates from McEuen Cave. *Kiva* 65(4):341-360.

Musil, Robert R.
1988 Functional Efficiency and Technological Change: A Hafting Tradition Model for Prehistoric North America. In *Early Human Occupation in Far Western North America*, ed. J. A. Willig, C. M. Aikens, and J. L. Pagan, 373-387. Anthropological Papers 21. Nevada State Museum, Carson City.

Neely, James A.
2005 Mesoamerican Formative Period Water Management Technology: An Overview with Insights on Development and Associated Method and Theory. In *New Perspectives on Formative Mesoamerican Cultures*, ed. T. G. Powis, 127-146. BAR International Series 1377. Archeopress, Oxford.

Nichols, M.J.P.
1981 Old California Uto-Aztecan. In *Reports from the Survey of California and Other Indian Languages*, ed. A. Schlichter, W. L. Chafe, and L. Hinton, 1:5-41. The Survey of California and Other Indian Languages, Berkeley.

O'Laughlin, Thomas C.
1980 The Keystone Dam Site and Other Archaic and Formative Sites in Northwest El Paso, Texas. *Publications in Anthropology* 8. El Paso Centennial Museum, University of Texas, El Paso.

Orr, Phil C.
1968 *Prehistory of Santa Rosa Island*. Santa Barbara Museum of Natural History, Santa Barbara, Calif.

Parry, William J., and Francis E. Smiley
1990 Hunter-Gatherer Archaeology in Northeastern Arizona and Southeastern Utah. In *Perspectives on Southwestern Prehistory*, ed. Paul E. Minnis and Charles L. Redman, 47-67. Westview, Boulder.

Parry, William J., Francis E. Smiley, and Galen R. Burgett
1994 The Archaic Occupation of Black Mesa, Arizona. In *Archaic Hunter-Gatherer Archaeology in the American Southwest*, ed. B. J. Vierra, 185-230. Contributions in Anthropology 13(1). Eastern New Mexico University, Portales.

Pérez de Ribas, Andrés
1944 *Historia de los Triunfos de Nuestra Santa Fe entre Gentes las Más Bárbaras y Fieras del Nuevo Orbe (1645)*. Tres volúmenes. Editorial Layac, México.

Piperno, Dolores R., and Kent V. Flannery
  2001 The Earliest Archaeological Maize (Zea mays L.) from Highland Mexico: New Accelerator Mass Spectrometry Dates and Their Implications. *Proceedings of the National Academy of Science* 98(4):2101–2103.

Plog, Fred
  1981 *Cultural Resources Overview: Little Colorado Area, Arizona*. USDA Forest Service, Southwestern Region, Phoenix.

Romney, A. Kimball
  1957 The Genetic Model and Uto-Aztecan Time Perspective. *Davidson Journal of Anthropology* 3:35–41.

Roth, Barbara J., and Bruce B. Huckell
  1992 Cortaro Points and the Archaic of Southern Arizona. *Kiva* 57(4):353–370.

Sauer, Carl O.
  1934 *The Distribution of Aboriginal Tribes and Languages in Northwestern Mexico*. Ibero-Americana 5. University of California Press, Berkeley.
  1935 *Aboriginal Population of Northwestern Mexico*. Ibero-Americana 10. University of California Press, Berkeley.

Sauer, Carl O., and Donald Brand
  1932 *Aztatlán, Prehistoric Mexican Frontier on the Pacific Coast*. Ibero-Americana 1. University of California Press, Berkeley.

Sayles, Edwin B.
  1983 *The Cochise Cultural Sequence in Southeastern Arizona*. Anthropological Papers of the University of Arizona 42. University of Arizona Press, Tucson.

Sayles, Edwin B., and Ernst Antevs
  1941 *The Cochise Culture*. Medallion Papers 29. Gila Pueblo, Globe, Ariz.

Shaul, David L., and Jane H. Hill
  1993 Pimans and the Hohokam. Paper presented in the Department of Anthropology, University of Arizona, Tucson.

Sheridan, Thomas E.
  1981 Prelude to Conquest: Yaqui Population, Subsistence and Warfare during the Protohistoric Period. In *The Protohistoric Period in the North American Southwest*, ed. D. R. Wilcox and W. B. Masse, 71–93. Anthropological Research Papers 24. Arizona State University, Tempe.

Simmons, Alan H.
  1982 Chronology. In *Prehistoric Adaptive Strategies in the Chaco Canyon Region, Northwestern New Mexico, Volume 3: Interpretation and Integration*, assemb. A. H. Simmons, 807–824. Navajo Nation Papers in Anthropology 9. Navajo Nation, Window Rock, Ariz.
  1986 New Evidence for the Early Use of Cultigens in the American Southwest. *American Antiquity* 51:73–88.

Sinopoli, Carla M.
  1991 Style in Arrows: A Study of an Ethnographic Collection from the Western United States. In *Foragers in Context*, ed. Preston T. Miracle, Lynn E. Fisher, and Jody Brown, 63–87. Michigan Discussions in Anthropology, Volume 10. University of Michigan, Ann Arbor.

Sliva, R. Jane
    1999   Cienega Points and Late Archaic Period Chronology in the Southern Southwest. *Kiva* 64(3):339–367.
    2005   Developments in Flaked Stone Technology during the Transition to Agriculture. In *Material Cultures and Lifeways of Early Agricultural Communities in Southern Arizona*, ed. R. Jane Sliva, 47–98. Anthropological Papers 35. Center for Desert Archaeology, Tucson.

Stevens, Michelle N., and R. Jane Sliva
    2002   Empire Points: An Addition to the San Pedro Phase Lithic Assemblage. *Kiva* 67(3): 326.

Steward, Julian H.
    1938   *Basin-Plateau Aboriginal Sociopolitical Groups*. Bureau of American Ethnology Bulletin 120. Smithsonian Institution, Washington, D.C.

Suárez, Jorge
    1979   *The Mesoamerican Languages*. Cambridge University Press, Cambridge.

Sutton, Mark Q.
    1991   Approaches to Linguistic Prehistory. *North American Archaeologist* 12(4):303–324.

Swadesh, Morris
    1960   *Estudios sobre Lengua y Cultura*. Acta Antropológica, segunda época 2(2). Escuela Nacional de Antropología y Historia, Sociedad de Alumnos, México.

Taylor, Walter W.
    1961   Archaeology and Language in Western North America. *American Antiquity* 27:71–81.
    1966   Archaic Cultures Adjacent to the Northeastern Frontiers of Mesoamerica. In *Archaeological Frontiers and External Connections*, ed. Robert Wauchope, 59–94. Handbook of Middle American Indians, Volume 4. University of Texas Press, Austin.

Thomas, David Hurst
    1981   How to Classify the Projectile Points from Monitor Valley, Nevada. *Journal of California and Great Basin Anthropology* 3:7–43.

Thompson, Raymond H. (editor)
    1958   *Migrations in New World Culture History*. University of Arizona Social Science Bulletin 27, Tucson.

Turner, Ellen Sue, and Thomas R. Hester
    1985   *A Field Guide to Stone Artifacts of Texas Indians*. Texas Monthly Press, Austin.

Vellanoweth, René L.
    1995   New Evidence from San Nicolas Island Concerning the Distribution and Manufacture of Olivella Grooved Rectangular Beads. *Pacific Coast Archaeological Society Quarterly* 31:13–22.

Voegelin, Charles F., Florence M. Voegelin, and Kenneth Hale
    1962   *Typological and Comparative Grammar of Uto-Aztecan: I (Phonology)*. Indiana University Publications in Anthropology and Linguistics, Memoir 17 of the International Journal of American Linguistics. Waverly, Baltimore.

Weissner, Polly
    1983   Style and Social Information in Kalahari San Projectile Points. *American Antiquity* 48:253–276.

Wilcox, David
    1986   The Tepiman Connection: A Model of Mesoamerican-Southwestern Interaction. In *Ripples in the Chichimec Sea: New Considerations of Southwestern-Mesoamerican Interactions*, ed. Frances Joan Mathien and Randall H. McGuire, 135–154. Southern Illinois University Press, Carbondale.

Willey, Gordon R., and Jeremy A. Sabloff
    1982   *A History of American Archaeology*. W. H. Freeman, San Francisco.

Wills, W. H.
    1988   *Early Prehistoric Agriculture in the American Southwest*. School of American Research Press, Santa Fe.

Wöcherl, Helga (editor)
    2005   *Archaeological Investigations at the El Taller, AZ AA:12:92 (ASM), and Rillito Fan, AZ AA:12:788 (ASM), Sites along Eastbound I-10 between Sunset and Ruthrauff Roads, as Part of the I-10 Frontage Roads Project, Pima County, Tucson, Arizona*. Technical Report 2003-08. Desert Archaeology, Tucson.

10

INTERACTION, ENCULTURATION, SOCIAL DISTANCE, AND ANCIENT ETHNIC IDENTITIES

Patrick D. Lyons and Jeffery J. Clark

Noting abundant evidence of ancient migrations in the American Southwest, a number of researchers have recently called for the development of more sophisticated models of ancient identity and interaction (e.g., Bernardini 2002; Clark 2001; Duff 2002; Lyons 2003; Stone 2003; see also Blake 2004; Jones 1997; Lilley 2004; Meskell 2002). Current approaches can typically be characterized as either "interactionist" or "enculturationist" in emphasis. The interactionist perspective privileges agency, whereas the enculturationist perspective emphasizes structure.

In this chapter we describe the interactionist and enculturationist programs, demonstrate that this dichotomy reflects old theoretical schisms, and argue that attempts to bridge the two perspectives in sociocultural anthropology have much to offer archaeologists. Recognizing the importance of considering both structure and agency in archaeological models of group identity, and based on lessons derived from an ethnographic case study, we suggest a theoretical and methodological focus on social distance. We argue that social distance is a key bridging concept, linking the best of what interactionist and enculturationist perspectives have to offer.

Patrick D. Lyons and Jeffery J. Clark

THE CULTURE HISTORY APPROACH TO ANCIENT SOCIAL GROUPS

The culture area methodology employed by early ethnologists was built on the premise that cultural differences were primarily attributable to ecological factors related to subsistence. Although these researchers conceived of cultures as bounded entities indicated by trait distributions, they cautioned that boundaries between groups were usually indistinct, that trait distributions often overlapped, and that historical factors such as migration and diffusion accounted for some spatial patterns (see, e.g., Holmes 1914; Kroeber 1939; Wissler 1926). Archaeologists working within the culture history paradigm (e.g., Colton 1939; Gladwin and Gladwin 1934; McKern 1939), which was derived from the culture area approach, used spatial and temporal patterns in material culture to define ancient social groups.

Early practitioners of the New Archaeology criticized culture historians for their neglect of process and urged their colleagues to focus on why cultural systems developed, how they functioned, and how they changed through time (e.g., Binford 1962). Recently, a new set of criticisms has been leveled. Andrew Duff (2002), for example, has warned that demographic and historical factors affect the degree to which material culture variability reflects social boundaries. This critique is an outgrowth of an old theoretical tension in anthropology, between structure (i.e., shared norms, values, ways of making and doing things) and agency (i.e., strategic and situational manipulation of social capital and identities by individuals or groups).

Advances in method and theory over the last thirty years, which include recognizing the dynamics of structure and agency (e.g., Bourdieu 1977; Giddens 1979, 1984; Ortner 1984; Sewell 1992) and the development of communication-based models of style (e.g., Wobst 1977), have resulted in two reactions to the culture history approach. The first is manifest in the literature as the interactionist perspective, an alternative that emphasizes agency over structure. The second is labeled here the enculturationist perspective, a refined, sophisticated restatement of the culture history model that emphasizes structure over agency.

THE INTERACTIONIST PERSPECTIVE

The interactionist approach recognizes humans as actors or agents who negotiate identities within a complex milieu of social resources and constraints (see Stone 2003). Archaeologists working from an interactionist perspective model group boundaries and shared identities based on evidence of regular interaction, assuming that such behavior reflects intentional, strategic action (e.g., Braun and Plog 1982; Duff 2002; Hantman and Plog 1982; Plog 1980; Upham 1982; Upham, Lightfoot, and Feinman 1981). The interactionist perspective, in most cases, entails a particular approach to stylistic variation in the archaeological record and lends itself to a focus on exchange as a measure of interaction.

Style, Interaction, and Group Boundaries

As Michelle Hegmon (1992) has shown, there are nearly as many definitions of style as there are archaeologists studying this phenomenon. Definitions differ mainly in terms of their relative emphasis on the communicative aspect of style (Wobst 1977). Some archaeologists conceive of style largely as a passive reflection of social groups encoded through interaction (e.g., Sackett 1982), whereas others see it as an active means of "messaging"—of communicating or negotiating group membership (e.g., Wiessner 1984), statuses (e.g., Ferguson 1991; Miller 1982, 1985; Pauketat and Emerson 1991), and worldview (e.g., Wyckoff 1990) or of reinforcing group norms (e.g., David, Sterner, and Gavua 1988). It is probably best to view style—including technological style (see Lechtman 1977; Lemonnier 1986)—as multifaceted and multifunctional. Some aspects of style may be "active," and simultaneously others may be "passive" (Carr 1995a, 1995b; David, Sterner, and Gavua 1988; Friedrich 1970; Hegmon 1992).

As noted by Christopher Carr (1995a), isochrestic (Sackett 1982), emblemic (Wiessner 1983), and assertive (Wiessner 1983) styles may be combined in the same medium or even in the same object, with each corresponding to one or more aspects of technology, design structure, or decorative execution. The interactionist perspective proceeds from this premise and emphasizes active, intentional stylistic variation over passive stylistic variation that results from differences in learning frameworks, for example.

Early proponents of this approach sought to combat the assumptions that underlay earlier models of southwestern socioeconomic and political organization (Braun and Plog 1982; Hantman and Plog 1982; Plog 1980). They asserted that previous work had proceeded from two faulty premises: (1) that each ancient village in the American Southwest was economically self-sufficient, and (2) that spatial patterns in the distribution of styles and artifact types most often reflected episodes of migration, diffusion, or both.

Instead, these researchers built on models of style developed by Lewis Binford (1965) and H. Martin Wobst (1977). They argued that (1) style is a functional aspect of artifact variability in that it has adaptive implications; (2) the messages communicated through artifacts are constrained by the social distance between the actors involved; (3) communication is constrained by artifact visibility; (4) to be effective, messages should be invariant and recurrent; and (5) messages (or "secondary functional variation," sensu Binford 1965:206; also "ideo-function" and "socio-function," sensu Rathje and Schiffer 1982) are constrained by the social contexts of the producer and consumer and the context of an object's use or uses.

Given these propositions, interactionists derive expectations regarding spatial patterns of stylistic similarity and difference. They argue that social groups should seek to create and maintain connections with other social groups as a buffer against environmental unpredictability (Braun and Plog 1982; Plog 1980). Accordingly, regional integration should increase as regional uncertainty increases, and increasing connectedness will be marked by increasing stylistic similarity.

Exchange as a Marker of Group Boundaries

By the early 1980s, some Southwesternists had begun modeling social group boundaries and social organization in terms of exchange. Two key concepts underlying the models that emerged during this period are spheres of exchange (Bohannon 1955; see also Appadurai 1986; Kopytoff 1986) and social distance (Sahlins 1968; Wobst 1977).

David Braun and Stephen Plog (1982) presented expectations regarding the relationship between exchange and social boundaries within a model of the links between stylistic similarity and social integration. They argued that more intense social connectedness should be marked by increased stylistic similarity and exchange. The types of exchanges involved, in this case, should be those associated with actors characterized by close social relationships: "[A]s the social distance between the confronting parties decreases . . . the exchanged goods become less costly, less standardized, or made of relatively less scarce raw materials and are often more utilitarian and/or consumable" (Braun and Plog 1982:511).

Jeffrey Hantman and Stephen Plog (1982) added to the discussion by noting that patterns of stylistic similarity and difference need not necessarily correspond with patterns in commodity exchange. They argued that these two phenomena can reveal different scales of simultaneous interaction, that is, social boundaries, when each is considered. Citing Steadman Upham (1982), they pointed out that stylistic similarity may not necessarily reflect intensity of interaction but may instead be a symbol of group identity or affiliation. Further, they argued that patterns of stylistic similarity and commodity exchange are related to population size and density, settlement pattern, and information distribution networks and reflect sociopolitical organization and the organization of craft production.

Upham (1982; see also Upham, Lightfoot, and Feinman 1981; Upham, Crown, and Plog 1994), Fred Plog (1983, 1984), and others have proposed the use of "alliances" as units of archaeological analysis. They define alliances as economic and political organizations that crosscut units of analysis associated with culture history. Traces of alliances are manifest in the archaeological record, they argue, as patterned variation in the distribution of exotic commodities.

Upham's (1982; Upham, Lightfoot, and Feinman 1981) basic argument is that Pueblo IV-period multisite communities in the Northern Southwest were stratified sociopolitically—elites with centralized power managed the production and distribution of prestige goods to create and maintain intracommunity status and intercommunity alliances. Upham sought to prove the existence of hierarchical social organizations in terms of evidence of elite control over the production and distribution of polychrome pottery. According to Upham, the presence and proportion of polychrome pottery within a given assemblage constitute a function of site size—a correlate of sociopolitical power—because such objects are labor-intensive symbols of wealth and leadership that circulated within a network of "prestige chain exchange" (see Feinman, Upham, and Lightfoot 1981; Upham, Lightfoot, and Feinman 1981; see also Renfrew 1972). In this way, Upham's model linked interaction patterns to the nature of intraregional sociopolitical organization and interregional social boundaries. The empirical foundation of Upham's case study, however, has been undercut by more recent research (Adams, Stark, and Dosh 1993; Downum 1987; Lyons 2001, 2003).

THE ENCULTURATIONIST PERSPECTIVE

The enculturationist perspective, like the interactionist approach, is a reaction to the culture history approach. Unlike the interactionist perspective, however, the enculturationist approach represents a conscious refinement of the earlier paradigm and emphasizes largely unconscious, or passive, stylistic variation (see Stone 2003).

Early Enculturationist Approaches: Learning Frameworks and Normative Culture

Initially, enculturationists offered an explicit model of stylistic variation built on a normative view of culture (i.e., all of culture is shared and homogeneous within groups) and the assumption of "general continuity in learning and enculturation" (Binford 1963:91–92; see also Plog 1980:115–122). Accordingly, regular face-to-face interaction in the context of learning frameworks was identified as the key process that transmitted styles through time and space (Hill 1970; Longacre 1970). Given this foundation, early enculturationists proceeded from the premise that spatial discontinuities in style were caused by natural barriers to social interaction, social and cultural boundaries, or both (Plog 1980:115–116). Plog (1980:115–122) and Hegmon (1992:526–527) identified the so-called ceramic sociology school associated with the early New Archaeology as a prime example of this approach.

Recent Enculturationist Approaches: Recognizing the Effects of Culture and Ethnicity

Current practitioners of the enculturationist program take a step back from patterns in the archaeological record, asking and answering how one is to distinguish among the residues of exchange, emulation, and migration. Following Binford (1965), Hegmon (1992), and Carr (1995a, 1995b), we assert that style in artifacts can both consciously (e.g., Wiessner 1983, 1984; Wobst 1977) and unconsciously (e.g., Sackett 1982) express group identity, bridging a gulf between two camps of earlier theorists who favored one or the other position.

We start from the premise that patterns produced as a result of ethnicity are purposeful, unstable, and conditional, whereas those associated with enculturation are relatively stable and unconscious. Following Carr (1995a, 1995b; see also Wobst 1977), we link the purposeful communication of ethnicity to objects with high physical and contextual visibility and posit that enculturation is reflected in objects of low physical and contextual visibility:

> High visibility attributes are . . . more likely to be emulated . . . by other groups and can be distributed widely without migration. Thus they often are not reliable indicators of population movement. . . . [A]ttributes with low physical and contextual visibility can be assumed to have little message potential . . . [and] are inherently more stable through time than their visible counterparts because they are less subject to careful scrutiny and . . . reflection . . . [and] they are less likely to be imitated. Stylistic similarities in low visibility attributes . . . reflect . . . a common enculturative background . . . [whereas] differences in these attributes are the result of stylistic or cultural drift [among] noninteracting groups. (Clark 2001:12)

These important tenets were tested by Jeffery Clark (2001) through a cross-cultural analysis of ethnographically and ethnoarchaeologically recorded population movements. Based on sixty-one cases spanning five continents, Clark (2001:18) found domestic spatial organization, foodways, and technological styles reflected in the nondecorative production steps of ceramic vessels, textiles, walls, and domestic installations most useful in tracking immigrants.

In an archaeological case study, Clark documented evidence of Puebloan immigrants in the eastern Tonto Basin, Arizona, by contrasting (1) indigenous and foreign patterns in domestic spatial organization, village construction sequence, and aggregation; (2) wall construction methods; (3) wood species selection for architectural elements; and (4) distributional patterns associated with corrugated pottery and polished red ware pottery. An important complement to Clark's reconstruction is Miriam Stark and colleagues' (1998:227–228; see also Miksa and Heidke 1995) use of ceramic sourcing to document the local production of a foreign technological style (i.e., corrugation as a surface treatment and the thinning of vessels by scraping as opposed to paddle and anvil) and their ability to associate evidence of corrugated pottery production with architectural indicators of the presence of immigrants (Stark, Clark, and Elson 1995:237).

Learning Frameworks Revisited: The Effects of Enculturation on Decorative Layouts

As previously noted, many discussions of ceramic decorative and technological style assume that assemblage-scale stylistic patterns are created as a result of the differential transmission of information between potters (e.g., Carlson 1970:109; Hill 1970; Longacre 1970; Washburn 1977). A number of researchers have attempted to test this assumption by observing interaction among groups of living potters, whether on the basis of kinship, residence, or other kinds of ties (e.g., Friedrich 1970; Stanislawski and Stanislawski 1978; Hardin 1984; Hayden and Cannon 1984; Herbich 1987). Margaret Hardin's (1984; see also Friedrich 1970) work on ceramic decorative style suggests that some aspects are passive reflections of socialization. According to Hardin (Friedrich 1970; Hardin 1984), styles are learned, stored, viewed, and transmitted in terms of group-specific mental stylistic "grammars." Such grammars, Hardin (1984:592) suggests, represent significant "barriers to visual communication" with outsiders. Hardin argues that styles or elements thereof may be borrowed and manipulated, but the act of manipulation usually entails reference to the borrower's repertoire. This is the case because, she insists, styles are cognitively based and are analyzed differently by different groups. Hardin (Friedrich 1970) notes that whereas design elements or configurations (what others call "pattern," cf. Carlson 1970:85; Pomeroy 1974:5) may be transmitted from potter to potter or from pot to potter with a minimum of interaction, their specific ("precisely correct") uses and the decorative division of space are not easily transmitted.

The results of such studies (e.g., Friedrich 1970; Hardin 1984; Washburn and Crowe 1988) indicate that social boundaries are marked by differences in the organization of decorative space, much in the same way such boundaries are often marked by differences in the organization of domestic space. Both Hardin (1984; see also Friedrich 1970) and Dorothy Washburn (1977, 1978; see also Washburn and Crowe 1988) specifically suggest that group membership is reflected in the rules of design composition. Given the results of Hardin's and Washburn's work, it seems wise to conceive of the rules of decorative division of space (i.e., layout) as reflective of the process of enculturation. This is an especially powerful approach when coupled with fine-grained knowledge of ceramic production and distribution, as well as recovery context (Shepard 1985:336–347, table 11; see also Montgomery and Reid 1990; Triadan 1997:60–78, 80–81; Zedeño 1994:18–21, table 3.1).

The use of the enculturationist approach, bolstered by sourcing data, enabled Patrick Lyons (2001, 2003) to establish that Winslow Orange Ware represents an expression of the ceramic tradition of the Hopi Mesas and that the builders and inhabitants of the Homol'ovi villages, near Winslow, Arizona, were predominately immigrants from the north (most likely the Hopi Mesas). Furthermore, based on (1) associations between evidence of northern immigrants and traces of local production of Roosevelt Red Ware (also known as Salado polychrome pottery) (Crown 1994) and (2) the dominance of northern layout styles throughout the Roosevelt Red Ware sequence, Lyons has been able to build on Patricia Crown's (1994) research to argue that northern groups were responsible for not only the origin but also the spread of so-called Salado ceramics throughout Arizona, New Mexico, and northern Mexico.

The enculturationist perspective emphasizes unconscious stylistic variation and entails a two-phase approach to ancient identity: establishing the presence of divergent cultural traditions—the raw material of ethnicity—before examining interaction across social boundaries. The bridging opportunities made possible by this approach are discussed in the sections that follow. But first, we trace the roots of the interactionist-enculturationist schism in anthropology and sociology and discuss recent attempts to move beyond it.

Patrick D. Lyons and Jeffery J. Clark

THE ROOTS OF THE PROBLEM

Many contemporary researchers (e.g., Stone 2003) trace the origin of the structure-agency dichotomy in studies of social (ethnic) identity to a key paper by Fredrik Barth (1998a) and a volume he edited, *Ethnic Groups and Boundaries: The Social Organization of Culture Difference* (Barth 1998b). Some (e.g., Duff 2002) also point to Michael Moerman's (1965) classic paper subtitled "Who Are the Lue?" as a seminal work (see also Leach 1954). Two important points must be made regarding Barth, Moerman, and the tension between structure and agency. First, Barth and Moerman, although proposing apparently novel models of ethnic identity that focused on the production, reproduction, and symbolic communication of difference, were addressing a theoretical and methodological enigma with much deeper roots. Second, both Barth and Moerman recognized the importance of cultural factors, or structure, in the production and reproduction of ethnic boundaries by social actors.

Key Oppositions (Dichotomies)

The theoretical tension between culture and ethnicity highlighted by Moerman (1965) and Barth (1998a), most recently manifested in the dichotomy between enculturationist and interactionist perspectives, can be traced back to these oppositions (Bentley 1987; Jenkins 1996, 1997; see also Hegmon 1998): culture versus society, cultural identity versus ethnic identity, primordialism (essentialism) versus instrumentalism, and structure versus agency.

Indeed, more than forty years ago, Binford (1965:206) warned that stylistic variation "may arise from a traditional way of doing things within a family or a larger social unit, or it may serve as a conscious expression of between-group solidarity." Twenty-five years ago, this observation was repeated by Braun and Plog (1982:510), who called for analytical separation between "the social context in which a person learned his or her decorative repertoire" (i.e., structure) and "social constraints on the choosing of alternative decorative options during the act of decoration" (i.e., agency), although they privileged the latter. The enculturationist program, as we have discussed, urges the same analytical split but emphasizes the former.

Anthropological Models of Ethnicity: "The Baby and the Bathwater"

David Anthony's (1990) use of the proverbial "baby thrown out with the bathwater" image called attention to the fact that archaeologists of the late twentieth century had gone too far in rejecting migration as an important and interesting subject of study. We are tempted to employ the same metaphor in decrying the fact that stylistic variation born of enculturation has been too strongly deemphasized recently in models of ethnicity (Jenkins 1996, 1997; see also Hegmon 2003). This neglect of culture (structure, enculturation, learning frameworks), in our opinion, is a result of intense focus on the processes of self-ascription and boundary maintenance (agency). Richard Jenkins (1997:107) makes the same point:

> Barth ... argued that the focus for the investigation of ethnicity should be "the ethnic boundary that defines the group, not the cultural stuff that it encloses."
> ... It is an argument that must remain at the center of our thinking. In insisting that there is no simple equation between cultural variation and the discontinuities of ethnic differentiation, it prevents us from mistaking the morphological enumeration of cultural traits for the analysis of ethnicity. However, this argument might also be construed as suggesting that the cultural stuff out of which that differentiation is arbitrarily socially constructed is somehow irrelevant, and this surely cannot be true.

Tammy Stone (2003) echoes Jenkins's critique, arguing that recent interactionist studies ignore or devote too little attention to cultural variation in the quest to document and understand ethnic interaction and differentiation. Stone, like us, urges a synthetic approach that makes use of patterns reflecting enculturation as well as interaction. In the next section, we discuss attempts by anthropologists and sociologists to fashion such an approach.

SOCIOLOGICAL AND ANTHROPOLOGICAL ATTEMPTS TO BRIDGE STRUCTURE AND AGENCY

Practice Theory

Practice theory (Ortner 1984; Sewell 1992) consists of a group of perspectives that attempt to bridge structure and agency. Its main proponents include anthropologist Pierre Bourdieu and sociologist Anthony Giddens. According to Sherry Ortner, the key premise of practice theory is that humans, as agents, make strategic choices in the context of constraining cultural systems, or structure.

Bourdieu's (1977) critical contributions in this arena include the concepts of *habitus* and practice. Habitus is defined as a system of durable dispositions—ways of being, tendencies, propensities, inclinations (Bourdieu 1977:72, 214 n.1). G. Carter Bentley (1987:27) characterizes habitus as "dispositions . . . not normally open to conscious apprehension." Practice is action that produces and reproduces structure.

Giddens (1979, 1984) labels his approach to uniting structure and agency "structuration theory." A central premise of Giddens's model is the notion of the "duality of structure," that structure is "both the medium and outcome" of social interaction (Giddens 1979:5). As noted by Marcia-Anne Dobres and Christopher Hoffman (1994:224), "[P]ractice theory accepts the normative aspects of a cultural 'system' but sees them as a set of background meaning-structures, or 'habitus,' in which social activities are conducted and different interests worked out." This is similar to the notion that ethnic identity is created from the raw material of cultural differences.

These ideas were not lost on Bentley (1987), who seized on Bourdieu's concept of habitus as a means of mediating primordialist (structure-based) and instrumentalist (agent-based) conceptions of ethnic identity. Bentley (1987:35) argued that "ethnic identity derives from situationally shared elements of a multidimensional habitus." Kevin Yelvington (1991) later criticized Bentley's equating of ethnicity and habitus as too restrictive, noting that this approach overemphasized structure and left too little room for agency. In addition, Yelvington (1991:160–161) echoed Ortner's (1984:146) litany of critical questions regarding Bourdieu's theory of practice: How is structure produced and reproduced? How has a given structure changed in the past? How will a given structure change in the future?

Jenkins's Social Constructionist Model of Ethnicity

Yelvington's major contribution to the debate was to suggest moving beyond practice theory to the use of what Jenkins (1996, 1997) refers to as a social constructionist model of ethnicity and ethnic identity. Jenkins (1996, 1997) argues that the schism between structure and agency, as it relates to ethnic identity, is bound up in other basic theoretical and methodological oppositions in the social sciences, such as the choice between emphasizing the individual or the group. He urges researchers to appreciate and build upon the "dialectic of identification" between similarity and difference that manifests itself in the relationship between the internal (self-ascription) and the external (categorization by others) (Jenkins 1996:20, 1997:13).

Jenkins labels his model of ethnic identity "social constructionist" and traces its roots through Barth, back to sociologists Max Weber (1978) and Everett Hughes (Coser 1994). His model is best summarized as ten related premises (Jenkins 1997:13–14, 40, 47–58, 64):

1. Primary (initial) ethnic identification is internalized during childhood socialization along with cultural markers of group membership, including language, religion, nonverbal behavior, and similar markers. Children know who they are (to which group they belong) because their parents tell them.

2. Ethnicity is "centrally concerned with culture" but is also rooted in social interaction.

3. Ethnicity is primary but not primordial. Although ethnic identity can have a strong impact on social interaction (rights and responsibilities), it is not immutable.

4. Ethnicity is not necessarily fixed and unchanging, but it is not infinitely variable, malleable, or negotiable. Ethnicity is a product of history (time, place, and process).

5. Ethnicity can be salient and durable.

6. Ethnicity is not something one has but is what one does. Ethnicity is performed, and claims of ethnicity may be rejected by group members or others based on performance. (This premise is an obvious point of potential linkage

with artifact-based and receiver-oriented communication theory developed by Michael Schiffer and Andrea Miller [1999]).

7. Depending upon power relations, identities, including ethnic identities, may be imposed by outsiders.
8. Ethnicity is simultaneously collective and individual.
9. Cultural differences do not equate with ethnic group boundaries, but cultural differences are the raw materials from which such boundaries are constructed.
10. Groups choose relevant ethnic symbols based on the context of their interaction and their histories.

Jenkins's premises reinforce the importance of giving equal consideration to structure and agency when modeling ancient social identities. The ethnographic case study that follows illustrates many of Jenkins's points and frames our discussion of the dynamics of social distance.

THE CASE OF THE ARIZONA TEWA

The Arizona Tewa, also known as the Hopi-Tewa, Tewa-Hopi, or First Mesa Tewa, may represent the most important southwestern ethnographic analog for migration and ethnic dynamics (Dozier 1951, 1954, 1966; Fewkes 1894, 1899, 1900; Freire-Marreco 1914; Kroskrity 1993; Parsons 1925, 1926; Stanislawski 1979; Yava 1978). Upon arriving at First Mesa to live among the Hopi in 1696, this group brought with it, from the Rio Grande Valley, a series of interrelated cultural traditions, reflected in distinctive language, religion, and artifacts.

Paul Kroskrity (1993) reports that, over time, the social distance between the Arizona Tewa and the Hopi changed. Initially, there was a marriage proscription, the Arizona Tewa were organized principally in terms of patrilineal moieties, and their religion emphasized curing and warfare over weather control. Now, intermarriage is common, the Arizona Tewa are organized in terms of Hopi-style matrilineal clans, and they have added to their ritual calendar many Hopi-style religious ceremonies concerned with weather control. Kroskrity (1993:25) suggests that adopting Hopi clan organization facilitated intermarriage and legitimized Arizona Tewa land claims in the eyes of the Hopi.

Kroskrity argues that as social relations increased (and social distance decreased) between the Arizona Tewa and the Hopi, the former became more culturally similar to the latter, and the Arizona Tewa seized upon a core of distinctive traits—including the Arizona Tewa language and an emphasis on military prowess and war-related ritual—as a badge of ethnic identity. Following Barth (1998a:14, 31; see also Jenkins 1997), Kroskrity refers to these cultural traits as "diacritica of ethnicity." The lessons here for archaeologists are that:

1. Ethnicity, as social agency, can be durable, even in the face of more than 300 years of close contact, cooperation, co-residence, and intermarriage.

2. Diacritica of ethnicity can change through time as social contexts change, that is, as social distance decreases and overall cultural similarity increases.
3. Diacritica of ethnicity that once took material form, such as hairstyles (Ningsheng 1989), dress, pottery forms and decorations, and similar markers, may fall away, but other badges of identity, such as language and religion, may remain or become galvanized over time.
4. Time depth is required to trace ethnic dynamics and changes in diacritica of ethnicity that reflect social distance.
5. Decreasing examples and saliency of material diacritica of ethnicity (increasing cultural similarity) may reflect decreasing social distance.
6. Knowledge of distinct cultural traditions is prerequisite to understanding ethnic identity and dynamics.

Although some may perceive the Arizona Tewa case as nothing more than a "cautionary tale," we argue that it has much to offer in terms of how archaeologists might model change and persistence in group identity. In the next section, we offer some preliminary steps in that direction.

CONCLUSION: INTERACTION, ENCULTURATION, SOCIAL DISTANCE, AND ANCIENT ETHNIC IDENTITIES

A bridging approach based on theory and method forged by Carr can only get one so far. Identifying distinct cultural traditions first and then documenting interaction between culture-bearing groups represents meaningful progress in archaeological theory and method. We know, however, that ethnic groups are not simply culture-bearing groups and that similarity in material culture may mask variability in ethnic identity. Likewise, we know that ethnic identity can accommodate cultural variability. Fortunately, we have as a foundation Barth's model of ethnic identity as the "social organization of cultural difference." Ethnicity always coincides in some way with culture. However, we cannot yet, based on current method and theory, predict the specific diacritica of ethnicity that will be chosen as a basis for integration and differentiation (Barth 1998a:14).

Up to this point, our research has been guided by this question: Which classes of material culture or aspects thereof are most likely to passively reflect enculturation (structure) as opposed to actively communicating ethnicity (agency)? Recent theoretical developments and the Arizona Tewa case study raise a different overarching question, however: Under what conditions might we expect certain classes of diacritica of ethnicity to be employed?

Barth's work, the Arizona Tewa case study, and others in the literature (as well as archaeological case studies; see Stone 2003) suggest that (1) under conditions of demographic stability and rough numerical similarity, and (2) within the context of relatively equal power relations, diacritica of ethnicity will take many forms. These include very public, physically and contextually visible badges of group membership, such as hairstyle, clothing, and exterior aspects of architecture, as well as more subtle, flexible, and less materially traceable symbols of affiliation and differentiation, such as language.

Conversely, under conditions of demographic imbalance or crisis, severe power differential, or both, the diacritica employed for self-ascription, as opposed to categorization by others, will be limited to those of a more flexible variety—phenomena easily emphasized or deemphasized according to situational advantage or disadvantage. Arizona Tewa code switching between the Arizona Tewa and Hopi languages comes to mind as an excellent example of a persistent and yet flexible boundary marker. By the same token, under conditions of demographic crisis, continuity in distinct cultural traditions is threatened as a result of the breakdown of learning frameworks (Ezell 1963; Shennan 2000).

As archaeologists, we have, of necessity, usually limited ourselves to a narrow consideration of cultural differences with material traces—artifacts, architecture, and settlement patterns. One of our key foci has been the visibility of different aspects of artifacts and architecture, but ethnographic examples teach us that vital, durable ethnic symbols are to be found in language and elements of kinship and social organization that leave no residues in the archaeological record. Religious practices often leave material traces, but interpreting them requires reference to another body of method and theory (e.g., Walker 1995a, 1995b).

Barth (1998a:16) reminds us that ethnic "interaction requires and generates a congruence of codes and values—in other words, a similarity or community of culture . . . [and also] a structuring of interaction which allows the persistence of cultural differences." In such situations, systematic rules—sets of prescriptions and proscriptions—develop. In this process, domains of interaction, convergence, and congruence are defined and other areas of social life are held off-limits in terms of interchange.

From this perspective, we can move beyond discussions of the communication potential of objects, architecture, and human bodies to consider the meaning of shared learning frameworks among ancient groups. We may be unable, presently, to address ancient ethnicity directly, but we can approach social distance. Interactionists (e.g., Braun and Plog 1982:510-512) have made good use of the concept of social distance in relation to the concept of spheres of commodity exchange (Bohannon 1955; Sahlins 1968, 1972) and information exchange (Wobst 1977). David Abbott (2000:130-132, 134-142, 157-170) has recently offered a bridging perspective that integrates increasing similarity in the technological style of plain ware among groups and increasing intergroup exchange as products of decreasing social distance. In this way, he is able to posit changes in social affiliation over time based on residues of enculturation and interaction.

Social distance is a powerful and attractive concept. It is inherent or implicit in enculturationist models because learning frameworks, by definition, are composed of socially close individuals, whether they interact on the basis of residence, descent, or some other tie. Enculturationists, of late, have tended to think about learning frameworks in the singular or to compare and contrast them, but, as Abbott has shown, much is to be gained by considering the simple fact that changes in social relations (changes in social distance) will create new learning frameworks and, in turn, affect material culture traditions. Abbott's study also underscores the importance of multiple lines of evidence in such arguments. He is able to draw on patterns in enculturation and interaction that relate to distinct organizations of production (household versus specialist) and to different spheres of exchange. This perspective is made possible by two important theoretical advances attributable to interactionists: (1) rejection of the model of the isolated, economically self-sufficient ancient southwestern village (e.g., Plog 1980; Braun and Plog 1982), and (2) the idea that spatial distance is not always a good indicator of social distance (see also Cameron 1992; Chernela 1992; Kramer and Douglas 1992).

The concept of social distance is also appealing on an entirely different level in that it evokes process, change, and scale. These are much more agreeable notions than the connotation of permanence associated with the concept of boundary. It seems useful to accept the premise that a reduction in social distance, as measured in terms of material culture similarity (in the context of the dynamics of demography and power), may relate to a reconfiguring of identity or of levels thereof. Such patterns may reflect the fact that two or more groups have come to see themselves as a unity or the fact that one group has come to see itself as a unit of a larger entity.

Barth's model of group dynamics posits structured interaction, defined in terms of domains. Under certain conditions, more interaction domains may be opened to interchange, resulting in the development of new or more similar traditions (shared ways of making and doing). It stands to reason that frequent, sustained, pervasive interaction, involving multiple domains, will significantly affect preexisting cultural traditions.

The rules of interaction between different social groups on the Hopi Mesas during the late pre-Hispanic and protohistoric periods apparently involved interchange in many domains, requiring similarity in most physically and contextually visible aspects of material culture (such as ceramics and architecture), and delimited the ritual arena as the domain of complementarity and competition. Today, intragroup differences, related to distinct origins and histories, are maintained, displayed, and indeed celebrated in this ritual context. For example, past homelands and unique ceremonial traditions are key elements of Hopi clan and phratry identity.

Barth (1998a:17-26) argues that ethnic identities persist so long as there is a basis for interaction along these lines. He theorizes that complementarity in ecological, economic, or social niches provides such opportunities. Further, he argues that groups and individuals maintain or alter such identifications largely based on perceived benefits (see also Atkinson 1989; Stahl 1991). For the Arizona Tewa of long ago, adopting aspects of Hopi social and religious organization allowed them tangible benefits: intermarriage, legitimized access to land, and integration within the Hopi political system. We argue that, in general, with decreasing social distance, archaeologists should expect to find more congruence, that is, more domains of interaction, and less opportunity for integration and differentiation along ethnic lines as the result of a lack of complementary niches.

REFERENCES CITED

Abbott, David R.
    2000   *Ceramics and Community Organization among the Hohokam*. University of Arizona Press, Tucson.

Adams, E. Charles, Miriam T. Stark, and Deborah S. Dosh
    1993   Ceramic Distribution and Exchange: Jeddito Yellow Ware and Implications for Social Complexity. *Journal of Field Archaeology* 20(1):3-21.

Anthony, David W.
    1990   Migration in Archaeology: The Baby and the Bathwater. *American Anthropologist* 92(4):895-914.

Appadurai, Arjun
    1986   Introduction: Commodities and the Politics of Value. In *The Social Life of Things: Commodities in Cultural Perspective*, ed. Arjun Appadurai, 3-63. Cambridge University Press, Cambridge.

Atkinson, Ronald R.
    1989   The Evolution of Ethnicity among the Acholi of Uganda: The Precolonial Phase. *Ethnohistory* 36(1):19-43.

Barth, Fredrik
    1998a   Introduction. In *Ethnic Groups and Boundaries: The Social Organization of Culture Difference*, ed. Fredrik Barth, 9-38. Waveland, Prospect Heights, Ill. Originally published in 1969 by Little, Brown, Boston.

Barth, Fredrik (editor)
    1998b   *Ethnic Groups and Boundaries: The Social Organization of Culture Difference*. Waveland, Prospect Heights, Ill. Originally published in 1969 by Little, Brown, Boston.

Bentley, G. Carter
    1987   Ethnicity and Practice. *Comparative Studies in Society and History* 29(1):24-55.

Bernardini, Wesley
    2002   *The Gathering of the Clans: Understanding Ancestral Hopi Migration and Identity*, A.D. 1275-1400. Ph.D. dissertation, Department of Anthropology, Arizona State University, Tempe. ProQuest, Ann Arbor.

Binford, Lewis R.
    1962   Archaeology as Anthropology. *American Antiquity* 28(2):217-225.
    1963   "Red Ocher" Caches from the Michigan Area: A Possible Case of Cultural Drift. *Southwestern Journal of Anthropology* 19(1):89-108.
    1965   Archaeological Systematics and the Study of Culture Process. *American Antiquity* 31(2, part 1):203-210.

Blake, Emma
    2004   Space, Spatiality, and Archaeology. In *A Companion to Social Archaeology*, ed. Lynn Meskell and Robert W. Preucel, 230-254. Blackwell, Malden, Mass.

Bohannon, Paul
  1955　Some Principles of Exchange and Investment among the Tiv. *American Anthropologist* 57(1, part 1):60–70.

Bourdieu, Pierre
  1977　*Outline of a Theory of Practice*, trans. Richard Nice. Cambridge University Press, Cambridge.

Braun, David P., and Stephen Plog
  1982　Evolution of "Tribal" Social Networks: Theory and Prehistoric North American Evidence. *American Antiquity* 47(3):504–525.

Cameron, Catherine M.
  1992　An Analysis of Residential Patterns and the Oraibi Split. *Journal of Anthropological Archaeology* 11(2):173–186.

Carlson, Roy L.
  1970　*White Mountain Redware: A Pottery Tradition of East-Central Arizona and Western New Mexico*. University of Arizona Anthropological Papers 19. University of Arizona Press, Tucson.

Carr, Christopher
  1995a　Building a Unified Middle-Range Theory of Artifact Design: Historical Perspectives and Tactics. In *Style, Society, and Person: Archaeological and Ethnological Perspectives*, ed. Christopher Carr and Jill E. Neitzel, 151–170. Plenum, New York.
  1995b　A Unified Middle-Range Theory of Artifact Design. In *Style, Society, and Person: Archaeological and Ethnological Perspectives*, ed. Christopher Carr and Jill E. Neitzel, 171–258. Plenum, New York.

Chernela, Janet M.
  1992　Social Meaning and Material Transaction: The Wanano-Tukano of Brazil and Colombia. *Journal of Anthropological Archaeology* 11(2):111–124.

Clark, Jeffery J.
  2001　*Tracking Prehistoric Migrations: Pueblo Settlers among the Tonto Basin Hohokam*. Anthropological Papers of the University of Arizona 65. University of Arizona Press, Tucson.

Colton, Harold S.
  1939　*Prehistoric Culture Units and Their Relationships in Northern Arizona*. Museum of Northern Arizona Bulletin 17. Northern Arizona Society of Science and Art, Flagstaff.

Coser, Lewis A. (editor)
  1994　*Everett C. Hughes: On Work, Race, and the Sociological Imagination*. University of Chicago Press, Chicago.

Crown, Patricia L.
  1994　*Ceramics and Ideology: Salado Polychrome Pottery*. University of New Mexico Press, Albuquerque.

David, Nicholas, Judy Sterner, and Kodzo Gavua
  1988　Why Pots Are Decorated. *Current Anthropology* 29(3):365–389.

Dobres, Marcia-Anne, and Christopher R. Hoffman
  1994   Social Agency and the Dynamics of Prehistoric Technology. *Journal of Archaeological Method and Theory* 1(3):211-258.

Downum, Christian E.
  1987   Potsherds, Provenience and Ports of Trade: A Review of the Evidence from Chavez Pass. Revised version of a paper presented at the Fourth Mogollon Conference, Tucson, Ariz., 1986.

Dozier, Edward P.
  1951   Resistance to Acculturation and Assimilation in an Indian Pueblo. *American Anthropologist* 53(1):56-66.
  1954   The Hopi-Tewa of Arizona. *University of California Publications in American Archaeology and Ethnology* 44(3):257-376.
  1966   *Hano: A Tewa Indian Community in Arizona.* Holt, Rinehart, and Winston, Fort Worth.

Duff, Andrew I.
  2002   *Western Pueblo Identities: Regional Interaction, Migration, and Transformation.* University of Arizona Press, Tucson.

Ezell, Paul H.
  1963   Is There a Hohokam-Pima Cultural Continuum? *American Antiquity* 29(1):61-66.

Feinman, Gary M., Steadman Upham, and Kent G. Lightfoot
  1981   The Production Step Measure: An Ordinal Index of Labor Input in Ceramic Manufacture. *American Antiquity* 46(4):871-884.

Ferguson, Leland
  1991   Struggling with Pots in Colonial South Carolina. In *The Archaeology of Inequality*, ed. Randall H. McGuire and Robert Paynter, 28-39. Basil Blackwell, Oxford.

Fewkes, Jesse Walter
  1894   The Kinship of a Tanoan-Speaking Community in Tusayan. *American Anthropologist* (o.s.) 7(2):162-167.
  1899   The Winter Solstice Altars at Hano Pueblo. *American Anthropologist* 1(2):251-276.
  1900   Tusayan Migration Traditions. In *Nineteenth Annual Report of the Bureau of American Ethnology, 1897-1898* (part 2), 573-633. Government Printing Office, Washington, D.C.

Freire-Marreco, Barbara
  1914   Tewa Kinship Terms from the Pueblo of Hano, Arizona. *American Anthropologist* 16(2):269-287.

Friedrich, Margaret Hardin
  1970   Design Structure and Social Interaction: Archaeological Implications of an Ethnographic Analysis. *American Antiquity* 35(3):332-343.

Giddens, Anthony
  1979   *Central Problems in Social Theory: Action, Structure and Contradiction in Social Analysis.* University of California Press, Berkeley.
  1984   *The Constitution of Society: Outline of the Theory of Structuration.* University of California Press, Berkeley.

Gladwin, Winifred, and Harold S. Gladwin
  1934   A Method for Designation of Cultures and Their Variations. Medallion Papers 15. Gila Pueblo, Globe, Ariz.

Hantman, Jeffrey L., and Stephen Plog
  1982   The Relationship of Stylistic Similarity to Patterns of Material Exchange. In *Contexts for Prehistoric Exchange*, ed. Jonathon E. Ericson and Timothy K. Earle, 237–263. Academic, New York.

Hardin, Margaret A.
  1984   Models of Decoration. In *The Many Dimensions of Pottery: Ceramics in Archaeology and Anthropology*, ed. S. E. van der Leeuw and A. C. Pritchard, 573–607. University of Amsterdam Press, Amsterdam.

Hayden, Brian, and Aubrey Cannon
  1984   Interaction Inferences in Archaeology and Learning Frameworks of the Maya. *Journal of Anthropological Archaeology* 3(4):325–367.

Hegmon, Michelle
  1992   Archaeological Research on Style. *Annual Review of Anthropology* 21:517–536.
  1998   Technology, Style, and Social Practices: Archaeological Approaches. In *The Archaeology of Social Boundaries*, ed. Miriam T. Stark, 264–279. Smithsonian Institution Press, Washington, D.C.
  2003   Setting Theoretical Egos Aside: Issues and Theory in North American Archaeology. *American Antiquity* 68(2):213–243.

Herbich, Ingrid
  1987   Learning Patterns, Potter Interaction and Ceramic Style among the Luo of Kenya. *African Archaeological Review* 5:193–204.

Hill, James N.
  1970   *Broken K Pueblo: Prehistoric Social Organization in the American Southwest.* Anthropological Papers of the University of Arizona 18. University of Arizona Press, Tucson.

Holmes, W. H.
  1914   Areas of American Culture Characterization Tentatively Outlined as an Aid in the Study of Antiquities. *American Anthropologist* 16(3):413–446.

Jenkins, Richard
  1996   *Social Identity*. Routledge, London.
  1997   *Rethinking Ethnicity*. Sage, London.

Jones, Siân
  1997   *The Archaeology of Ethnicity: Constructing Identities in the Past and the Present.* Routledge, London.

Kopytoff, Igor
  1986   The Cultural Biography of Things: Commoditization as a Process. In *The Social Life of Things: Commodities in Cultural Perspective*, ed. Arjun Appadurai, 64–91. Cambridge University Press, Cambridge.

Kramer, Carol, and John E. Douglas
  1992   Ceramics, Caste, and Kin: Spatial Relations in Rajasthan, India. *Journal of Anthropological Archaeology* 11(2):187–201.

Kroeber, Alfred L.
  1939 Cultural and Natural Areas of Native North America. *University of California Publications in American Archaeology and Ethnology* 38:1-242.

Kroskrity, Paul V.
  1993 *Language, History, and Identity: Ethnolinguistic Studies of the Arizona Tewa.* University of Arizona Press, Tucson.

Leach, Edmund R.
  1954 *Political Systems of Highland Burma: A Study of Kachin Social Structure.* London School of Economics, London.

Lechtman, Heather
  1977 Style in Technology—Some Early Thoughts. In *Material Culture: Styles, Organization, and Dynamics of Technology,* ed. Heather Lechtman and Robert S. Merrill, 3-20. West, St. Paul.

Lemonnier, Pierre
  1986 The Study of Material Culture Today: Toward an Anthropology of Technical Systems. *Journal of Anthropological Archaeology* 5(2):147-186.

Lilley, Ian
  2004 Diaspora and Identity in Archaeology: Moving Beyond the Black Atlantic. In *A Companion to Social Archaeology,* ed. Lynn Meskell and Robert W. Preucel, 287-312. Blackwell, Malden, Mass.

Longacre, William A.
  1970 *Archaeology as Anthropology: A Case Study.* Anthropological Papers of the University of Arizona 17. University of Arizona Press, Tucson.

Lyons, Patrick D.
  2001 *Winslow Orange Ware and the Ancestral Hopi Migration Horizon.* Ph.D. dissertation, Department of Anthropology, University of Arizona, Tucson. ProQuest, Ann Arbor.
  2003 *Ancestral Hopi Migrations.* Anthropological Papers of the University of Arizona 68. University of Arizona Press, Tucson.

McKern, W. C.
  1939 The Midwestern Taxonomic Method as an Aid to Archaeological Culture Study. *American Antiquity* 4(4):301-313.

Meskell, Lynn
  2002 The Intersection of Identity and Politics in Archaeology. *Annual Review of Anthropology* 31:279-301.

Miksa, Elizabeth J., and James M. Heidke
  1995 Drawing a Line in the Sands: Models of Ceramic Temper Provenance. In *The Roosevelt Community Development Study,* Volume 2, *Ceramic Chronology, Technology, and Economics,* ed. James M. Heidke and Miriam T. Stark, 133-205. Anthropological Papers 41. Center for Desert Archaeology, Tucson.

Miller, Daniel
  1982 Structures and Strategies: An Aspect of the Relationship between Social Hierarchy and Cultural Change. In *Symbolic and Structural Archaeology,* ed. Ian Hodder, 89-98. Cambridge University Press, Cambridge.

1985   *Artefacts as Categories: A Study of Ceramic Variability in Central India.* Cambridge University Press, Cambridge.

Moerman, Michael
    1965   Ethnic Identification in a Complex Civilization: Who Are the Lue? *American Anthropologist* 67(5, part 1):1215-1230.

Montgomery, Barbara K., and J. Jefferson Reid
    1990   An Instance of Rapid Ceramic Change in the American Southwest. *American Antiquity* 55(1):88-97.

Ningsheng, Wang
    1989   Ancient Ethnic Groups as Represented on Bronzes from Yunnan, China. In *Archaeological Approaches to Cultural Identity*, ed. Stephen J. Shennan, 195-206. Routledge, London.

Ortner, Sherry B.
    1984   Theory in Anthropology Since the Sixties. *Comparative Studies in Society and History* 26(1):126-166.

Parsons, Elsie Clews
    1925   *A Pueblo Indian Journal, 1920-1921.* Memoirs of the American Anthropological Association 32. Collegiate, Menasha, Wis.
    1926   The Ceremonial Calendar of the Tewa of Arizona. *American Anthropologist* 28(1):208-229.

Pauketat, Timothy R., and Thomas E. Emerson
    1991   The Ideology of Authority and the Power of the Pot. *American Anthropologist* 93(4):919-941.

Plog, Fred
    1983   Political and Economic Alliances on the Colorado Plateaus, A.D. 400-1450. In *Advances in World Archaeology*, Volume 2, ed. Fred Wendorf and Angela E. Close, 289-330. Academic, New York.
    1984   Exchange, Tribes, and Alliances: The Northern Southwest. *American Archeology* 4(3):217-223.

Plog, Stephen
    1980   *Stylistic Variation in Prehistoric Ceramics: Design Analysis in the American Southwest.* Cambridge University Press, Cambridge.

Pomeroy, John A.
    1974   A Study of Black-on-White Painted Pottery in the Tonto Basin, Arizona. *Southwestern Lore* 39(4):1-34.

Rathje, William L., and Michael B. Schiffer
    1982   *Archaeology.* Harcourt Brace Jovanovich, New York.

Renfrew, Colin
    1972   *The Emergence of Civilization: The Cyclades and the Aegean in the Third Millennium B.C.* Methuen, London.

Sackett, James R.
    1982   Approaches to Style in Lithic Archaeology. *Journal of Anthropological Archaeology* 1(1):59-112.

Sahlins, Marshall D.
  1968 *Tribesmen.* Prentice-Hall, Englewood Cliffs, N.J.
  1972 *Stone Age Economics.* Aldine, New York.

Schiffer, Michael B., with Andrea R. Miller
  1999 *The Material Life of Human Beings: Artifact, Behavior and Communication.* Routledge, London.

Sewell, William H.
  1992 A Theory of Structure: Duality, Agency, and Transformation. *American Journal of Sociology* 98(1):1-29.

Shennan, Stephen J.
  2000 Population, Culture History, and the Dynamics of Culture Change. *Current Anthropology* 41(5):811-835.

Shepard, Anna O.
  1985 *Ceramics for the Archaeologist.* Braun-Brumfield, Ann Arbor. Originally published in 1956 as Carnegie Institution Publication 609. Carnegie Institution, Washington, D.C.

Stahl, Ann B.
  1991 Ethnic Style and Ethnic Boundaries: A Diachronic Case Study from West-Central Ghana. *Ethnohistory* 38(3):250-275.

Stanislawski, Michael B.
  1979 Hopi-Tewa. In *Handbook of North American Indians,* Volume 9, *Southwest,* ed. Alfonso Ortiz, 587-602. William C. Sturtevant, general ed. Smithsonian Institution Press, Washington, D.C.

Stanislawski, Michael B., and Barbara Stanislawski
  1978 Hopi and Hopi-Tewa Ceramic Tradition Networks. In *The Spatial Organization of Culture,* ed. Ian Hodder, 61-76. University of Pittsburgh Press, Pittsburgh.

Stark, Miriam T., Jeffery J. Clark, and Mark D. Elson
  1995 Causes and Consequences of Migration in the 13th Century Tonto Basin. *Journal of Anthropological Archaeology* 14:212-246.

Stark, Miriam T., Mark D. Elson, and Jeffery J. Clark
  1998 Social Boundaries and Technical Choices in Tonto Basin Prehistory. In *The Archaeology of Social Boundaries,* ed. Miriam T. Stark, 208-231. Smithsonian Institution Press, Washington, D.C.

Stone, Tammy
  2003 Social Identity and Ethnic Interaction in the Western Pueblos of the American Southwest. *Journal of Archaeological Theory and Method* 10(1):31-67.

Triadan, Daniela
  1997 *Ceramic Commodities and Common Containers: Production and Distribution of White Mountain Red Ware in the Grasshopper Region, Arizona.* Anthropological Papers of the University of Arizona 61. University of Arizona Press, Tucson.

Upham, Steadman
  1982 *Polities and Power: An Economic and Political History of the Western Pueblo.* Academic, New York.

Upham, Steadman, Patricia L. Crown, and Stephen Plog
  1994   Alliance Formation and Cultural Identity in the American Southwest. In *Themes in Southwest Prehistory*, ed. George J. Gumerman, 183-210. School of American Research Press, Santa Fe.

Upham, Steadman, Kent G. Lightfoot, and Gary M. Feinman
  1981   Explaining Socially Determined Ceramic Distributions in the Prehistoric Plateau Southwest. *American Antiquity* 46(4):822-833.

Walker, William H.
  1995a   *Ritual Prehistory: A Pueblo Case Study.* Ph.D. dissertation, Department of Anthropology, University of Arizona, Tucson. University Microfilms, Ann Arbor.
  1995b   Ceremonial Trash? In *Expanding Archaeology*, ed. James M. Skibo, William H. Walker, and Axel E. Nielsen, 67-79. University of Utah Press, Salt Lake City.

Washburn, Dorothy K.
  1977   *A Symmetry Analysis of Upper Gila Area Ceramic Design.* Papers of the Peabody Museum of Archaeology and Ethnology, Vol. 68. Harvard University, Cambridge, Mass.
  1978   A Symmetry Classification of Pueblo Ceramic Designs. In *Discovering Past Behavior: Experiments in the Archaeology of the American Southwest*, ed. Paul Grebinger, 101-121. Gordon and Breach, London.

Washburn, Dorothy K., and Donald W. Crowe
  1988   *Symmetries of Culture: Theory and Practice of Plane Pattern Analysis.* University of Washington Press, Seattle.

Weber, Max
  1978   *Economy and Society: An Outline of Interpretive Sociology.* Ed. Guenther Roth and Claus Wittich. University of California Press, Berkeley. Originally published in 1922 as *Wirtschaft und Gesellschaft*, Mohr, University of Tübingen, Tübingen.

Wiessner, Polly
  1983   Style and Social Information in Kalahari San Projectile Points. *American Antiquity* 48(2):253-276.
  1984   Reconsidering the Behavioral Basis for Style: A Case Study among the Kalahari San. *Journal of Anthropological Archaeology* 3(3):190-234.

Wissler, Clark
  1926   *The Relation of Nature to Man in Aboriginal America.* Oxford University Press, New York.

Wobst, H. Martin
  1977   Stylistic Behavior and Information Exchange. In *For the Director: Research Essays in Honor of James B. Griffin*, ed. Charles E. Cleland, 317-342. Anthropological Papers of the Museum of Anthropology 61. University of Michigan, Ann Arbor.

Wyckoff, Lydia L.
  1990   *Designs and Factions: Politics, Religion, and Ceramics on the Hopi Third Mesa.* University of New Mexico Press, Albuquerque.

Yava, Albert
  1978   *Big Falling Snow: A Tewa-Hopi Indian's Life and Times and the History and Traditions of His People.* Ed. and annotated Harold Courlander. Crown, New York.

Yelvington, Kevin A.
    1991   Ethnicity as Practice? A Comment on Bentley. *Comparative Studies in Society and History* 33(1):158–168.

Zedeño, María Nieves
    1994   *Sourcing Prehistoric Ceramics at Chodistaas Pueblo, Arizona: The Circulation of People and Pots in the Grasshopper Region.* Anthropological Papers of the University of Arizona 58. University of Arizona Press, Tucson.

11

Networking the Old-Fashioned Way

Social and Economic Networks among Archaic
Hunters and Gatherers in Southern New Mexico

Maxine E. McBrinn

Social identity is difficult to see archaeologically. Finding those differences in material culture that signify social differences, as language often does, has proven a formidable task. Most efforts in this area have looked for material differences in peoples of the recent past (Croes 1987; Grosball 1987; Patterson 1987; Rogers 1995) or even in the present (David et al. 1991), when we know ethnographically that differences existed. How much more difficult, then, is it to ask this question outside of the period when text can inform us? We figuratively shrug our shoulders and give up when the people being studied are far enough in the past. When we look at the Archaic or Paleoindian periods, archaeologists use terminology that equates projectile points with culture, as when we blithely speak of the "Clovis people" or the "Cochise Culture" (see LeTourneau 1998:67–71 for a discussion on the applicability of the use of Folsom points to define an analytic unit). But when pressed, few of us would claim that we know how or when projectile points indicate social or cultural differences, and there is no theory that explains such a linkage. When "stones and bones" are what remain, we have no recourse but to use what we have. Additionally, there are no systematic models to explain the social organization of mobile hunters and gatherers beyond the band, although we recognize that modern hunter-gatherers have many social contacts outside their residential group. I propose here that there are two interband social groups that may be seen archaeologically and that while it may be possible to see these groups by examining a single artifact class, they are easier to identify when artifacts from multiple classes are used in the analysis.

As suggested, social identity is inherently difficult to define and apply. Cultural anthropologists, who can ask their informants to identify themselves, have found that the answer to "Who are you?" varies depending on the context (Barth 1969; Jones 1997; Wolf 1982). Every individual has a number of identities that minimally reflect his or her varying roles as a family member, friend, neighbor, business partner, or stranger. Each of these roles contributes only a part of that person's identity, and which role dominates at any time depends on the context, including where that person is at that time, to whom he or she is speaking, what he or she is doing, and the people nearby. Because social identity is inherently multidimensional (Barth 1969; Jones 1997; Wolf 1982), it is difficult to recognize and parse in contemporary societies or to decode which material markers identify any given aspect of identity.

Identifying social identity solely through material culture is even more difficult. Archaeologically, social identity not only consists of entangled layers, such as kinship and language, and discrete values, such as sex, but also rests on material markers that we may not recognize as having the same significance or value as in the past. Before starting on any quest to discover identity through material culture or to examine distributions of social identity, archaeologists must be careful to acknowledge the intrinsic social richness present in each society and to consider and clearly define what kinds of social identity we hope to find. No single artifact class should or could be expected to reflect the full diversity of social identity that exists in every society (Croes 1987; David et al. 1991; Grosball 1987; Patterson 1987; Rogers 1995). I suggest that by examining different classes of material culture, particularly artifacts made and used in varying social contexts, it may be possible to tease out some of the multiple social identities that existed in the past.

This chapter examines social identity among mobile hunters and gatherers during the Late Archaic period in southern New Mexico (McBrinn 2002, 2005). It builds on the geographic distribution of different style categories to suggest that craft-training networks existed within a larger economic sphere. Three kinds of artifacts were used in this study: projectile points, cordage, and sandals. These were chosen in part for the sample sizes available from sites of the appropriate period but also because they represent objects I assume were made and used in different contexts. Projectile points were used to hunt and were often carried outside residential sites. Cordage is ubiquitous, since it is used in composite objects as well as by itself and thus is unlikely to carry deliberate stylistic meaning. Sandals were worn beyond camp confines but have hidden attributes that may reflect craft training.

At least two distinct kinds of identity may be visible in the artifacts of the Archaic Southwest (McBrinn 2002, 2005). Based on existing models (Dyson-Hudson and Smith 1978; Kelly 1995; MacDonald and Hewlett 1999; Winterhalder 1986, 1997;

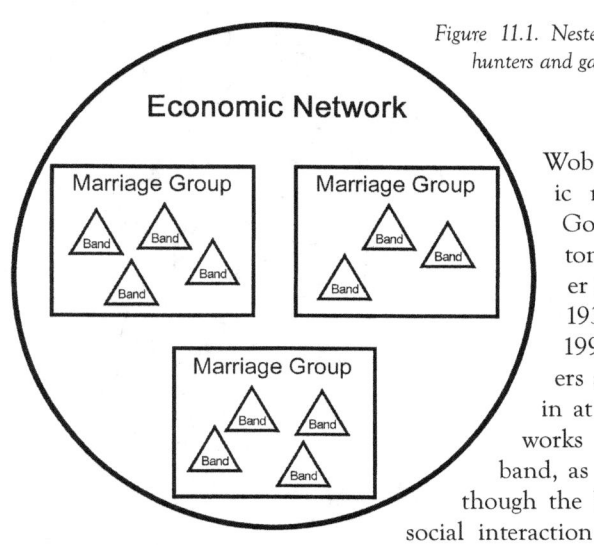

Figure 11.1. Nested relationships between mobile hunters and gatherers.

Wobst 1974) and ethnographic research (Cashdan 1985; Gould 1982, 1991; Hamilton 1982a, 1982b; Silberbauer 1994; Smith 1988; Steward 1938; Wiessner 1983, 1984, 1997), mobile arid-lands hunters and gatherers participated in at least two interaction networks beyond their residential band, as shown in Figure 11.1. Although the band is the basic unit of social interaction for mobile hunters and gatherers, it is not visible archaeologically except as a single site component. The transience of a band's membership, as a result of individual and family movement between bands, and the general dependence of a band's territory on the exact membership make it difficult or impossible to recognize a band's presence at different sites across the landscape. Add a lack of chronometric precision to this inherent fluidity in band personnel and territory, even when Accelerator Mass Spectrometry (AMS) radiocarbon dates are possible, and we clearly need to look for social identity at a scale larger than the band.

The social group above the band level is the marriage group. This group, also called the maximal band (MacDonald and Hewlett 1999; Wobst 1974), is where most members find their mates. Because this group includes most or all of an individual's extended kin, it also provides craft training for its members. By craft training, I refer to the mundane matters of everyday life, such as flint knapping, basket making, spinning, and woodwork, and do not include more esoteric knowledge, such as religious or supernatural training. It is possible and perhaps even likely that specialists from outside the family or even outside the marriage group provided more advanced religious training.

An even larger group, the economic network, allows people to mitigate the risk of living in an unpredictable environment through resource-sharing relationships with people beyond their extended kin (Cashdan 1985; Gould 1982, 1991; Hamilton 1982a, 1982b; Myers 1982; Silberbauer 1994; Smith 1988; Wiessner 1982, 1984). These relationships are informal and are negotiated separately by bands, nuclear families, or even individuals. The result is that not all members of a marriage group will necessarily share all economic partners. Despite the way it is depicted in Figure 11.1, the economic network is not a monolithic entity but is flexible, tailored to the needs of its members.

Figure 11.2. Primary sandal elements (adapted from Martin et al. 1952:261).

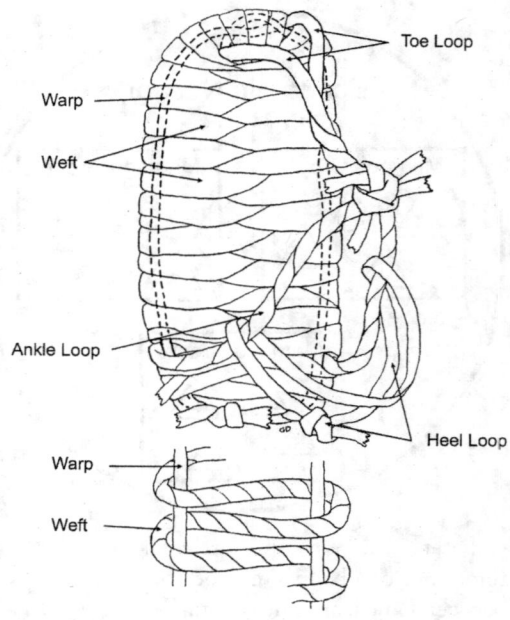

These latter two kinds of social groups, the marriage group and the economic network, may be seen in the material record as patterning in the geographic distribution of style. Before continuing this line of reason, it is important to define the terms *iconological* and *isochrestic* style (Hegmon 1992; Sackett 1986, 1990). Both kinds of style are visible in Figure 11.2, a schematic diagram of a sandal from Tularosa Cave. First note the general shape, the distinctive foot attachment mechanism, and the overall look of the sandal. These are all examples of iconological style, the very visible variation in material culture. A square heel or the use of a different weaving technique would make this sandal look distinctively different and would be examples of iconological variation. Now note that the warps are hidden beneath the wefts in the complete sandal. If the warps were made from a bundle of whole yucca leaves rather than from the shredded and spun yucca found in this sandal, that difference would be invisible to all but the most inquisitive viewer. Warp construction, then, is an example of isochrestic, or technological, variation. Isochrestic stylistic choices are hidden in the final artifact, made, then covered or obliterated in the complete construction process.

These distinctive kinds of style can be mapped onto hunter-gatherer social groups, as shown in Figure 11.3. The marriage group, because of its role in craft training, is visible through isochrestic stylistic choices. Fiber artifacts like cordage and sandals, because they are made and used locally, are especially likely to reflect this training (Maslowski 1996; Minar 2000, 2001; Newton 1974; Petersen 1996; Petersen and Wolford 2000). Research has shown that once craftspeople have learned a technique, they are unlikely to change it (Minar 2000). Even more, ethnographers have shown that making basic changes to craft techniques is sometimes seen as unlucky and is discouraged. This conservative practice ensures consistency in the material record.

In contrast, the economic network should be visible in shared iconological style, particularly in artifacts seen and used outside the residential camp (McBrinn 2002, 2005; Wiessner 1984). Projectile point morphology and easily visible char-

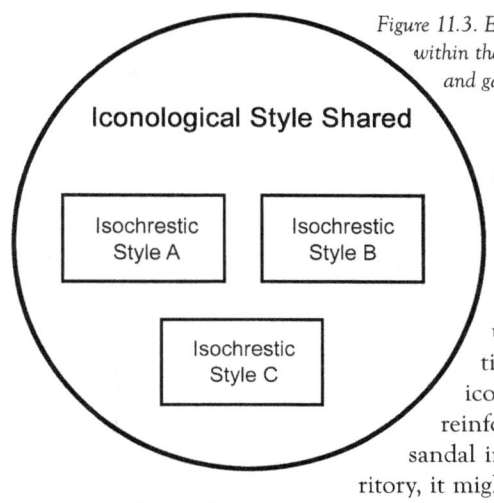

Figure 11.3. Expected distribution of stylistic characteristics within the nested social organization of mobile hunters and gatherers.

acteristics of sandals, such as overall shape, communicate participation in this network. I am not necessarily proposing that members of an economic network consciously used iconological style to signal participation. Rather, the use of similar iconological style likely was passively reinforced. If a strange projectile point or sandal impression was found in a given territory, it might alarm the owners, such that nonowner members of the economic network using that land would be discouraged from leaving behind traces that were obviously foreign.

As an example of how this simple use of style might indicate social groups, I (McBrinn 2002, 2005) examined cordage, sandals, and projectile points from three sites in the Mogollon Highlands (Bat Cave, Tularosa Cave, and Cordova Cave) and from one site in the Tularosa Basin (Fresnal Shelter). As shown in Figure 11.4, these sites form two clusters, separated by the Rio Grande. All the site components used in my sample date to the Late Archaic period, making them roughly contemporaneous. Because of the proximity of the three Mogollon Highland sites, well within most estimates of the territory required for mobile hunter-gatherers in this environment (McBrinn 2002, 2005), I assume that members of the same marriage group created all these sites. In contrast, I assume that Fresnal Shelter, in the northern Tularosa Basin, is likely to have been used by members of a different marriage group. The distance between these two clusters of sites, combined with the existence of the river dividing them, makes it very unlikely that a single marriage group used both areas. The people who used Fresnal Shelter, however, were probably members of the same larger economic network as the Mogollon Highland peoples.

Because of space limitations, I present only a sample of the total results here, but they should suffice to illuminate this technique and identify the two different kinds of social networks created and used by the peoples of the Late Archaic. It is hoped that these results show the power of this approach.

CORDAGE

Initial spin direction, or the way a craftsperson first spins yarns in making rope or string (Figure 11.5), is one attribute that may have varied between the two areas in the analysis (McBrinn 2002, 2005). This attribute is an example of isochrestic

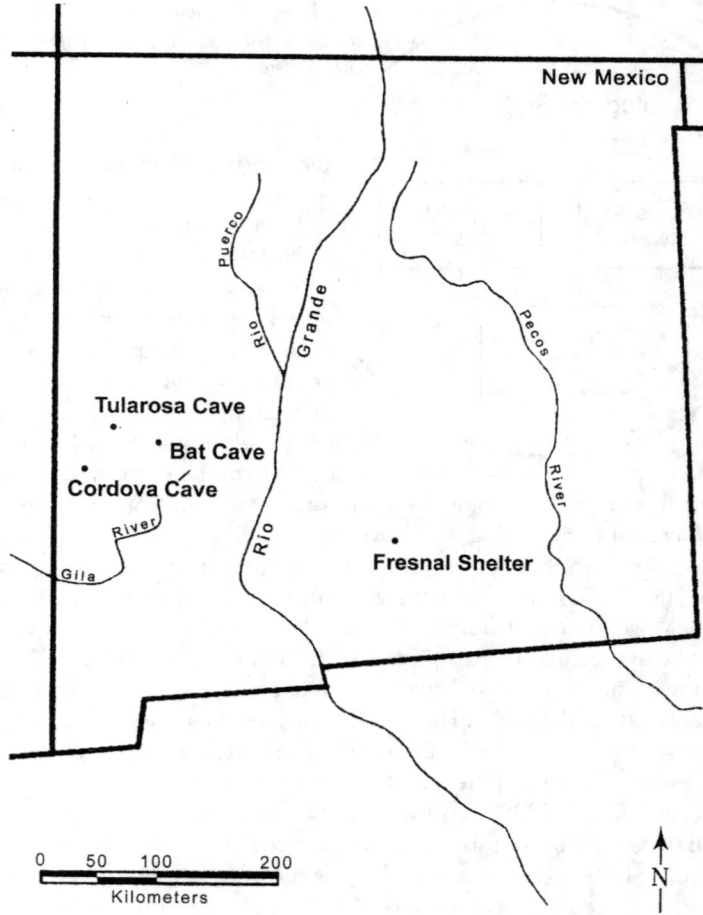

Figure 11.4. Locations of sites cited in the text. Map drawn by Andrew Jordan.

style because it reflects craft-training practices and is essentially invisible to a casual viewer. Ethnographic and archaeological research in the eastern United States and elsewhere has shown that cordage spin direction sometimes shows cultural differences when other artifacts do not (Maslowski 1996; Newton 1974; Petersen 1996; Petersen and Wolford 2000). In addition, studies with modern spinners show that people are unlikely to rethink spin direction after learning the craft and that they overwhelmingly replicate the motion and actions of their teachers (Minar 2000, 2001).

I analyzed a total of 475 pieces of cordage, 226 from Fresnal Shelter and 249 from the combined Mogollon Highland sites (McBrinn 2002, 2005). As shown

Table 11.1. Initial spin direction results

	Mogollon Highland Sites		Fresnal Shelter	
	Number	Percent	Number	Percent
S-Spin	145	58	34	15
Z-Spin	104	42	192	85
Total	249	100	226	100

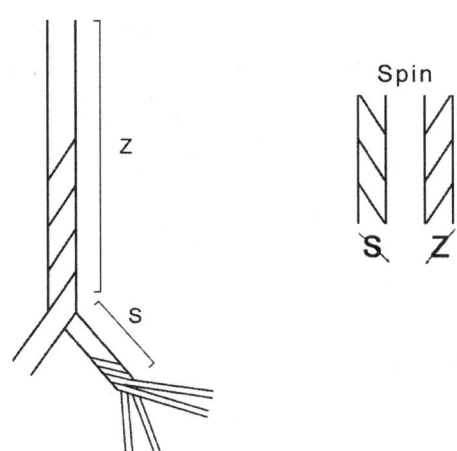

Figure 11.5. Cordage attributes. Left: initial spin (lower) and final plying twist (upper). Right: S and Z spin directions. Illustration by Andrew Jordan.

in Table 11.1, the initial spin directions in the two areas are markedly different. Whereas the peoples using the Mogollon sites generally chose an S-wise initial spin direction, the cordage at Fresnal Shelter was overwhelmingly initially spun Z-wise. Supporting this, the cordage from each of the three Mogollon sites shows essentially no difference in spin structure. This variance in spin between the cordage from the Mogollon Highlands and the Tularosa Basin persists even when controlled for differences in raw material.

PROJECTILE POINTS

Projectile points from the Mogollon Highland sites and Fresnal Shelter show a markedly different pattern (McBrinn 2002, 2005). Generally, the projectile point morphology from the four sites shows a use of iconological style consistent with an outward display of affiliation. Four projectile point types were numerous enough in the Late Archaic site components of both areas that they could be statistically analyzed. All four types produced a similar pattern as that shown for the Type 5 points, corner-notched triangular points named by Herbert Dick (1965) in his Bat Cave typology. Figure 11.6 shows examples of Type 5 points from three of the sites used in this study. As can be seen, there is a large morphological variability in this type, even within a single site.

I made thirteen measurements of each point to generate a cluster analysis of this point type. The expectation was that if there were differences among these points, they would form two distinct clusters, one from the Mogollon sites and another from Fresnal Shelter. When I forced the two clusters, however, each

Maxine E. McBrinn

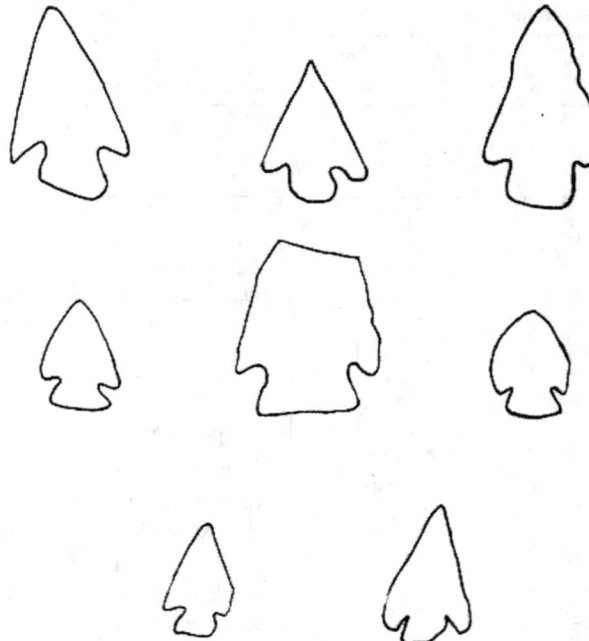

Figure 11.6. Type 5 points. From top to bottom: *Fresnal Shelter*, *Bat Cave*, and *Tularosa Cave*.

contained points from both areas. I then considered the possibility that this group of points would best be described by four clusters, each containing the points found at a single site. But again, none of the four clusters I created contained all the points from a given site. In other words, the points did not naturally cluster by geographic provenience.

To examine the problem from another perspective, I mapped the relationship between the total length of each point to its proximal shoulder angle (PSA). I chose length as an indication of overall size, since most morphological measurements varied proportionally. The PSA, a measurement of the notching angle, showed the greatest variation irrespective of the size of the projectile points and could potentially differentiate the points by provenience. As seen in Figure 11.7, there is high variability in both sets of measurements, but the projectile points from Fresnal Shelter fit nicely with those from the Mogollon.

One possible explanation for some of the variability in length seen in Type 5 points is that some of them may be the result of a broken point reworked into a new, shorter point, a variation that would be purely functional in nature. To test this idea, an identical analysis was conducted examining the relationship between neck width (instead of total length) and PSA. The results were very similar to those shown in Figure 11.7. In fact, there is considerable heterogeneity within the point

Type 5

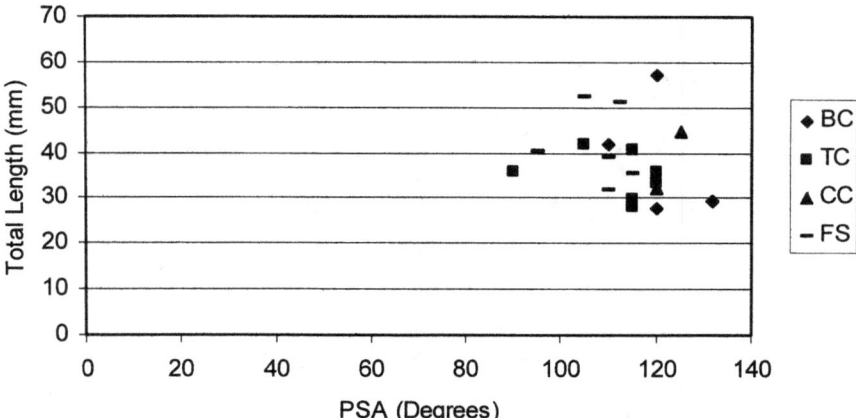

Figure 11.7. *Length versus proximal shoulder angle from Bat Cave (BC), Tularosa Cave (TC), Cordova Cave (CC), and Fresnal Shelter (FS).*

type from each site but an overall homogeneity in point morphology among sites and between the Mogollon Highlands and the Tularosa Basin.

In other words, all the Type 5 points examined from both areas are best described as a single population. This collection forms one statistical cluster and does not vary meaningfully in morphology between those points found at the Mogollon sites and those found at Fresnal Shelter. This may indicate that either the people who used these points accepted a wide range of execution of the mental template for this point type or that the projectile points were traded among different marriage groups within the same economic network (McBrinn 2002, 2005). Because of the large numbers of visibly different cherts used to make these points, it seems likely that points were traded among the members of an economic network. This hypothesis needs to be tested in the future.

SANDALS

The sandal analysis yielded more complex results than were seen in the projectile points or the cordage, displaying stylistic attributes shared across all four sites while also showing isochrestic differences between the sandals from the Mogollon sites and those from the Tularosa Basin (McBrinn 2002, 2005). Sandals from the Archaic components of all four sites were either two-warp plain weave, as shown in Figures 11.2 and 11.8, or four-warp plain weave, as shown in Figure 11.9 (Deegan 1993, 1995). These major construction techniques are iconological stylistic attributes, as are the other commonalities shared among all the sandals examined: toe

Maxine E. McBrinn

Figure 11.8. Two-warp plain-weave sandal from Tularosa Cave. © The Field Museum of Natural History catalog number 260675. Photo by Maxine McBrinn.

and heel silhouettes and the treatment of the very visible weft. Each of these sandal attributes would be visible in not only the physical sandal but also in footprints left by the sandals. These footprints can linger a relatively long time in the arid climate of the Southwest (Hays-Gilpin 1998). Note that all sandals examined from each of

Networking the Old-Fashioned Way

Figure 11.9. Four-warp plain-weave sandal from Fresnal Shelter. Eastern New Mexico University Museum catalog number 01.D25.203. Photo by Maxine McBrinn.

the sites are weft-dominant, which means the composition of the warp would be hidden from all but the most determined viewers.

Some of the less visible construction techniques in the sandals, however, show isochrestic choices that differ between the two areas of interest. First, while all the sandals from Fresnal Shelter in the Tularosa Basin used whole yucca leaves for warp manufacture, the sandals from the Mogollon sites, as shown in Figure 11.2, often used shredded and sometimes spun yucca to make the warps. In addition, the warps in the Mogollon sandals were simply twisted at the toe and then emerged to form the toe loop of the sandal tie system (Figure 11.2). This was not true in any of the Tularosa Basin sandals examined, despite the obvious utility of this structure. Instead, the toe loops were independently attached in the Fresnal Shelter sandals (Figure 11.10), and the warps were finished at the toe in a variety of methods.

I would argue that these isochrestic stylistic differences between the Mogollon sandals and those from the Tularosa Basin probably indicate that the craft-training traditions in these two areas were distinct and confirm that their makers were members of two different marriage groups. The iconological similarities in all sandals from both areas show that these people were part of the same economic networks, those larger risk-sharing affiliations.

This pattern repeats those already discussed for cordage and projectile points. However, a few of the sandals from Fresnal Shelter differ from those from the Mogollon area in another dimension. A small number of the sandals from that site

Maxine E. McBrinn

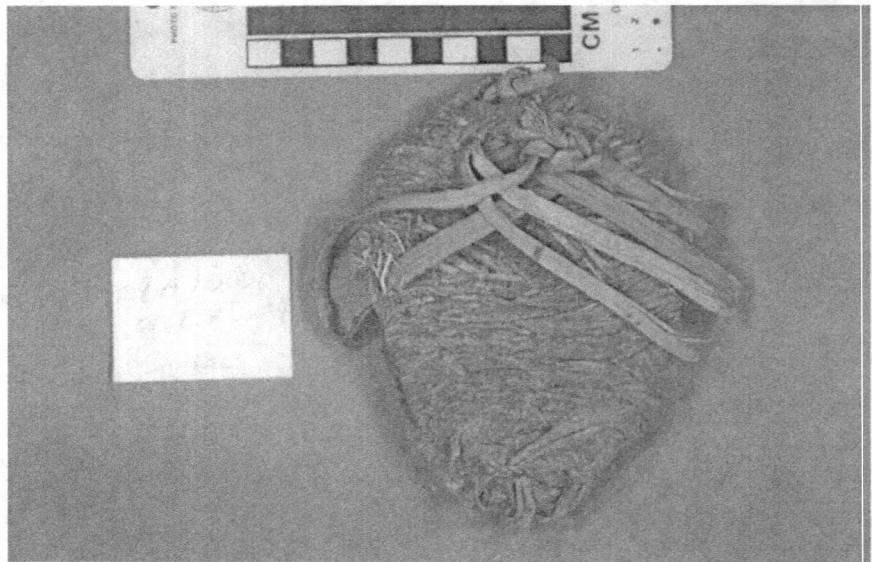

Figure 11.10. Four-warp scuffer-toe sandal from Fresnal Shelter. Eastern New Mexico University Museum catalog number 01.E25.129. Photo by Maxine McBrinn.

are scuffer-toe (Cosgrove 1947) or partial foot sandals, as shown in Figure 11.10. Another small subset of the Fresnal Shelter sandals has fishtail heels (Cosgrove 1947), formed by allowing the bases of the whole yucca-leaf warps to extend past the sandal body, as shown in Figure 11.11. Both of these sandal attributes, the scuffer-toe size and shape and the fishtail heel, seem to be southern traits, appearing earlier at more southern sites (Cosgrove 1947; McBrinn 2002, 2005). Neither attribute is common in sandals from the Mogollon area during the Archaic period. These clearly iconological choices in a small subset of the sandals from Fresnal Shelter may indicate that the people who used that site included southern peoples in their economic network. Since each local group would have negotiated its own economic network, depending on its territory and that of its neighbors, it is reasonable to believe the peoples of the Tularosa Basin would have included the northern Chihuahuan people immediately to the south in their risk-sharing network.

SUMMARY

This study illustrates how isochrestic stylistic choices in the cordage and sandals made and used in the Mogollon area differ from those found in the northern Tularosa Basin at Fresnal Shelter. These stylistic choices would have been invisible unless an observer either closely examined the artifacts or watched them being

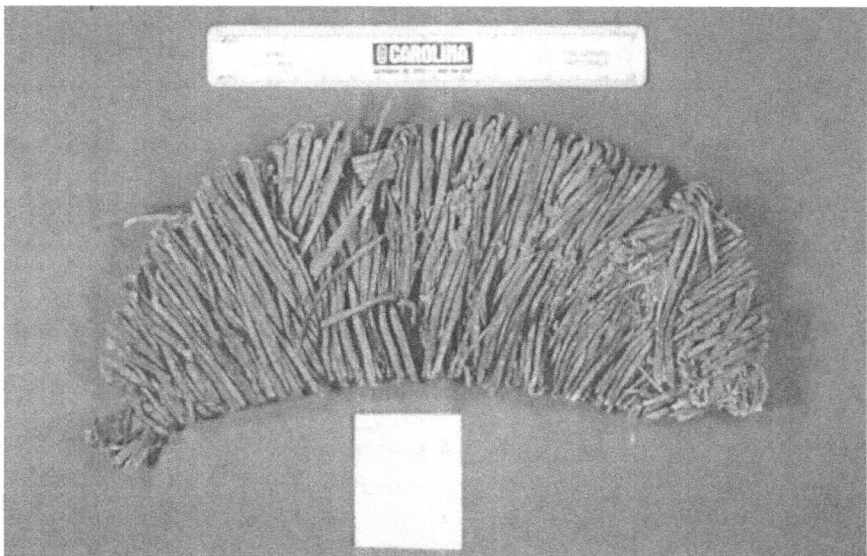

Figure 11.11. Two-warp plain-weave sandal with fishtail heel from Fresnal Shelter. Eastern New Mexico University Museum catalog number 01.C25.3. Photo by Maxine McBrinn.

made. The differences in these isochrestic attributes indicate different craft-training practices and traditions between these two areas. Assuming that craft training is done within a kinship group, we can infer that these differences also indicate the existence of different marriage groups. Given the distance between these areas and their separation by the Rio Grande, this would be expected.

How, then, do we explain the similarities in projectile point types and morphologies and in visible sandal attributes between these two areas? If we accept the argument that certain isochrestic stylistic choices reflect different marriage groups, then how do we explain the lack of iconological stylistic differences in projectile points? I believe these similarities in projectile point and sandal morphology reflect the existence of a larger social group, that of a risk-sharing economic network. Materials created to be used within the context of the larger economic network used style to show affiliation with others in the same network. This use of style, however, was probably unconscious. There were good reasons not to create projectile points or sandals that were obviously different from those made by economic partners. This lack of difference reinforced the unity of the separate groups within the network and minimized the difficulty of using an economic network partner's resources when required.

The creators of the artifacts I examined used style, consciously or not, to indicate affiliation and belonging rather than to mark territorial or social boundaries between peoples. Thus the material culture shows us people reaching out to each other across the boundaries that are so prominent in ethnographies and in the cultural ecology models of human behavior. Materially, we see affiliation rather than boundary marking. We see people living and learning among their extended kin, and neighbors who could be relied upon in times of need. The variations in style in the artifacts I have described illustrate the existence of different kinds and levels of social networks and social identity. They show the marriage network, where craft training was provided, and a larger economic network, where neighbors extended aid when needed. If I had limited my research to a single artifact class, either lithics or fiber artifacts, I would never have been able to see the existence of these two different kinds of social identity. By carefully considering different kinds of style in a range of artifact classes, we can begin to see in material culture some of the social complexity we know exists in even the least complex societies.

REFERENCES CITED

Barth, Frederik
    1969   Introduction. In *Ethnic Groups and Boundaries: The Social Organization of Cultural Differences*, ed. Frederik Barth, 9–38. Little, Brown, Boston.

Cashdan, Elizabeth A.
    1985   Coping with Risk: Reciprocity among the Basarwa of Northern Botswana. *Man* 20:454–474.

Cosgrove, Cornelius Burton
    1947   *Caves of the Upper Gila and Hueco Areas in New Mexico and Texas*. Papers of the Peabody Museum of American Archaeology and Ethnology 24(2). Harvard University, Cambridge, Mass.

Croes, Dale
    1987   Locarno Beach at Hoko River, Olympic Peninsula, Washington: Wakashan, Salishan, Chimakuan or Who? In *Ethnicity and Culture: Proceedings of the Eighteenth Annual Conference of the Archaeological Association of the University of Calgary*, ed. Reginald Auger, Margaret F. Glass, Scott MacEachern, and Peter H. McCartney, 259–283. University of Calgary, Calgary, Alberta.

David, Nicholas, Kodzo Gavua, A. Scott MacEachern, and Judy Sterner
    1991   Ethnicity and Material Culture in North Cameroon. *Canadian Journal of Archaeology* 15:171–177.

Deegan, Ann Cordy
    1993   Anasazi Fibrous Sandal Terminology. *Kiva* 59:49–64.
    1995   Anasazi Sandal Features: Their Research Value and Identification. *Kiva* 61:57–69.

Dick, Herbert W.
    1965   *Bat Cave*. School of American Research Monograph 27. University of New Mexico Press, Albuquerque.

Dyson-Hudson, Rada, and Eric Alden Smith
    1978   Human Territoriality: An Ecological Reassessment. *American Anthropologist* 80:21–41.

Gould, Richard A.
　1982　To Have and Have Not: The Ecology of Sharing among Hunter-Gatherers. In *Resource Managers: North American and Australian Hunter-Gatherers*, ed. Nancy M. Williams and Eugene S. Hunn, 69-91. AAAS Selected Symposium 67. Westview, Boulder.
　1991　Arid-Land Foraging as Seen from Australia: Adaptive Models and Behavioral Realities. *Oceania* 62:12-33.

Grosball, Sue
　1987　Ethnic Boundaries within the Inca Empire: Evidence from Huanuco, Peru. In *Ethnicity and Culture, Proceedings of the Eighteenth Annual Conference of the Archaeological Association of the University of Calgary*, ed. Reginald Auger, Margaret F. Glass, Scott MacEachern, and Peter H. McCartney, 115-124. University of Calgary, Calgary, Alberta.

Hamilton, Annette
　1982a　The Unity of Hunting-Gathering Societies: Reflections on Economic Forms and Resource Management. In *Resource Managers: North American and Australian Hunter-Gatherers*, ed. Nancy M. Williams and Eugene S. Hunn, 229-247. AAAS Selected Symposium 67. Westview, Boulder.
　1982b　Descended from the Father, Belonging to Country: Rights to Land in the Australian Western Desert. In *Politics and History in Band Societies*, ed. Eleanor Leacock and Richard Lee, 85-108. Cambridge University Press, Cambridge.

Hays-Gilpin, Kelley A.
　1998　Epilogue: This Sandal Business. In *Prehistoric Sandals from Northeastern Arizona: The Earl H. Morris and Ann Axtell Morris Research*, ed. Kelley Ann Hays-Gilpin, Ann Cordy Deegan, and Elizabeth Ann Morris, 121-126. Anthropological Papers of the University of Arizona 62. University of Arizona Press, Tucson.

Hegmon, Michelle
　1992　Archaeological Research on Style. *Annual Review of Anthropology* 21:517-536.

Jones, Siân
　1997　*The Archaeology of Ethnicity: Constructing Identities in the Past and Present*. Routledge, New York.

Kelly, Robert L.
　1995　*The Foraging Spectrum: Diversity in Hunter-Gatherer Lifeways*. Smithsonian Institution Press, Washington, D.C.

LeTourneau, Philippe
　1998　The "Folsom Problem." In *Unit Issues in Archaeology: Measuring Space, Time, and Material*, ed. Ann F. Romenofsky amd Anastasia Steffen, 52-73. University of Utah Press, Salt Lake City.

MacDonald, Douglas H., and Barry S. Hewlett
　1999　Reproductive Interests and Forager Mobility. *Current Anthropology* 40(4):501-523.

Martin, Paul S., John B. Rinaldo, Elaine A. Bluhn, Hugh C. Cutler, and Roger Grange Jr.
　1952　*Mogollon Cultural Continuity and Change: The Stratigraphic Analysis of Tularosa and Cordova Caves*. Fieldiana:Anthropology 40. Field Museum of Natural History, Chicago.

Maslowski, Robert F.
1996 Cordage Twist and Ethnicity. In *A Most Indispensable Art: Native Fiber Industries from Eastern North America*, ed. James B. Petersen, 88-99. University of Tennessee Press, Knoxville.

McBrinn, Maxine E.
2002 Social Identity and Risk Sharing among the Mobile Hunters and Gatherers of the Archaic Southwest. Ph.D. dissertation, Department of Anthropology, University of Colorado, Boulder.
2005 Social Identities among Archaic Mobile Hunters and Gatherers in the American Southwest. Arizona State Musuem Archaeological Series 197. University of Arizona Press, Tucson.

Minar, C. Jill
2000 Spinning and Plying: Anthropological Directions. In *Beyond Cloth and Cordage: Archaeological Textile Research in the Americas*, ed. Penelope Ballard Drooker and Laurie D. Webster, 85-99. University of Utah Press, Salt Lake City.
2001 Motor Skills and the Learning Process: The Conservation of Cordage Final Twist Direction in Communities of Practice. *Journal of Anthropological Research* 57:381-405.

Myers, Fred R.
1982 Always Ask: Resource Use and Land Ownership among Pintupi Aborigines of the Australian Western Desert. In *Resource Managers: North American and Australian Hunter-Gatherers*, ed. Nancy M. Williams and Eugene S. Hunn, 173-195. AAAS Selected Symposium 67. Westview, Boulder.

Newton, Dolores
1974 The Timbira Hammock as a Cultural Indicator of Social Boundaries. In *The Human Mirror*, ed. Miles Richardson, 231-251. Louisiana State University Press, Baton Rouge.

Patterson, Thomas C.
1987 Tribes, Chiefdoms and Kingdoms in the Inca Empire. In *Power Relations and State Formation*, ed. Thomas C. Patterson and Christine W. Gailey, 117-127. American Anthropological Association, Washington, D.C.

Petersen, James B.
1996 Fiber Industries from Northern New England: Ethnicity and Technological Traditions during the Woodland Period. In *A Most Indispensable Art: Native Fiber Industries from Eastern North America*, ed. James B. Petersen, 100-119. University of Tennessee Press, Knoxville.

Petersen, James B., and Jack A. Wolford
2000 Spin and Twist as Cultural Markers: A New England Perspective on Native Fiber Industries. In *Beyond Cloth and Cordage: Archaeological Textile Research in the Americas*, ed. Penelope Ballard Drooker and Laurie D. Webster, 101-117. University of Utah Press, Salt Lake City.

Rogers, Rhea J.
1995 Tribes as Heterarchy: A Case Study from the Prehistoric Southeastern United States. In *Heterarchy and the Analysis of Complex Societies*, ed. Robert Ehrenreich, Carole L. Crumbley, and Janet E. Levy, 7-16. Archaeological Papers of the Amer-

ican Anthropological Association 6. American Anthropological Society, Arlington, Va.

Sackett, James R.
- 1986 Isochrestism and Style: A Clarification. *Journal of Anthropological Archaeology* 5: 266-277.
- 1990 Style and Ethnicity in Archaeology: The Case for Isochrestism. In *The Uses of Style in Archaeology*, ed. Margeret Conkey and Christine Hastorf, 32-43. Cambridge University Press, Cambridge.

Silberbauer, George B.
- 1994 A Sense of Place. In *Key Issues in Hunter-Gatherer Research*, ed. Ernest S. Burch and Linda Ellanna, 119-143. Berg, Oxford.

Smith, Eric Alden
- 1988 Risk and Uncertainty in the "Original Affluent Society": Evolutionary Ecology of Resource-Sharing and Land Tenure. In *Hunters and Gatherers 1: History, Evolution and Social Change*, ed. Tim Ingold, David Riches, and James Woodburn, 222-251. Berg, Oxford.

Steward, Julian H.
- 1938 *Basin-Plateau Aboriginal Sociopolitical Groups.* Bureau of American Ethnology Bulletin 120. Smithsonian Institution, Washington, D.C.

Wiessner, Polly
- 1982 Risk, Reciprocity and Social Influences on !Kung San Economics. In *Politics and History in Band Societies*, ed. Eleanor Leacock and Richard Lee, 61-84. Cambridge University Press, New York.
- 1983 Style and Social Information in Kalahari San Projectile Points. *American Antiquity* 48:253-276.
- 1984 Reconsidering the Behavioral Basis for Style: A Case Study among the Kalahari San. *Journal of Anthropological Archaeology* 3:190-234.
- 1997 Seeking Guidelines through an Evolutionary Approach: Style Revisited among the !Kung San (Ju/'hoansi) of the 1990s. In *Rediscovering Darwin: Evolutionary Theory and Archaeological Explanation*, ed. C. Michael Barton and Geoffrey A. Clark, 157-176. Archeological Papers of the American Anthropological Association 7. American Anthropological Association, Arlington, Va.

Winterhalder, Bruce
- 1986 Diet Choice, Risk, and Food Sharing in a Stochastic Environment. *Journal of Anthropological Archaeology* 5:369-392.
- 1997 Gifts Given, Gifts Taken: The Behavioral Ecology of Nonmarket, Intragroup Exchange. *Journal of Archaeological Research* 5(2):121-168.

Wobst, H. Martin
- 1974 Boundary Conditions for Paleolithic Social Systems: A Simulation Approach. *American Antiquity* 39:147-178.
- 1977 Stylistic Behavior and Information Exchange. In *For the Director: Research Essays in Honor of James B. Griffin*, ed. Charles E. Cleland, 317-341. Anthropological Papers, Museum of Anthropology, University of Michigan, Ann Arbor.

Wolf, Eric R.
- 1982 *Europe and the People without History.* University of California Press, Berkeley.

12

ARCHITECTURAL METAPHOR AND CHACOAN INFLUENCE IN THE NORTHERN SAN JUAN

Scott G. Ortman

In the fall of 1928, a group of elders from Acoma Pueblo decided to visit the capital of their new nation in Washington, D.C. During their visit, one of them worked with anthropologists from the Bureau of American Ethnology to record the origin story he learned when he was initiated into the Koshari society as a young man. The early episodes of this narrative (published in Stirling 1942) describe the beginning of time, before the Acomas emerged from the fourth world below to begin their life in this world. As is common in origin stories (e.g., Littleton 1982), the Acoma man's narrative provides a social charter for the society in which he lived, in that it explains the origins of leadership positions and medicine societies, spells out their roles and duties, and establishes the basis of their authority. The narrative also lays out the basic tenets of Acoma religion and worldview by explaining what the nonhuman world is, how it came to be, and how the Acomas were to honor and regulate it through their ritual practices.

The most important episode for the purposes of this chapter is the one in which Iatiku, the mother of the Acomas, gave Oak Man instructions on how to build the first kiva (Stirling 1942:18–20). According to Iatiku, the kiva was to be called "underworld house" in ceremonial language and represented the place where the Acomas lived with the corn mothers before their emergence from the North. The roof hatch, through which the light from above could be seen when inside, represented *shipapu*, the path of emergence; the walls represented the dome of the sky; the roof timbers, the Milky Way; and the ladder, the rainbow. There were "fog seats" for spirits to sit on; the hearth was called "bear"; and the small circular pit that archaeologists call the *sipapu* was the "doorway to the powers that rule," including the cardinal mountains, the sun, and the moon.

This narrative presents a conception of the underworld as a place that was similar to this world and presents the kiva as a microcosm of this world by blending together terms applied to both the kiva and the environment. The world is conceived as a building when the narrative speaks of a "doorway" to the sun and moon and refers to the Milky Way as "way above earth beam." Likewise, the kiva is presented as a microcosm when the hearth is called "bear" and the ladder is called "rainbow."

This narrative about the first kiva illustrates a phenomenon cognitive scientists call *conceptual projection* (Fauconnier 1997). In this case, entities and properties of the kiva are projected onto the world writ large, and relationships among elements of the kiva are used to explain how corresponding elements of the world relate to each other. That is, the world is conceptualized as a kiva, and the kiva is a microcosm of this world. These architectural metaphors, expressed through idioms, the names of parts of buildings, and the form and decoration of buildings, reveal the significance of architecture for cultures all over the world. However, the specific metaphors that make architecture meaningful vary from place to place. In West Africa, for example, the Batammaliba house does not have a "rainbow" or "fog seats" but does have a stomach, womb, eyes, nose, mouth, and so forth (Blier 1987:122). So in this culture, the house is conceptualized as a person in addition to being a microcosm like the Acoma kiva.

Architectural metaphors can also become deeply embedded within a culture and highly resistant to change. For example, the Southern Tiwa, who today live about seventy miles east of Acoma near Albuquerque, New Mexico, call the kiva or pithouse *túła*, a word that varies from *tuła*, "cottonwood tree," only in the stress on the initial vowel (Harrington n.d.:29). Cottonwoods grow rapidly where there is groundwater, and Southern Tiwa people say they emerged into this world from *ship'aphun'ai*, or "eye-water black place," a lake to the north (the direction for which the associated color is black among Southern Tiwas) at the headwaters of the Rio Grande (Harrington n.d.:1). This conceptual imagery is very similar to that of their linguistic cousins, the Rio Grande Tewa, who call the kiva *te'e*, a word that also varies from *te*, "cottonwood," only in the stress on the initial vowel (Harrington 1916), and say they emerged from *p'okwin*, a lake in the north (Ortiz 1969). In addition, the Tewa refer to the emergence path as *p'okwik'oji*, or "lake roof-hole." All of this suggests that both the Rio Grande Tewa and the Southern Tiwa imagine the lake of emergence as a pithouse or kiva with roof entry. This architectural metaphor is probably part of their common inheritance (S. Tiwa *túła*, "pithouse," and *tuła*, "cottonwood," are likely cognate with Tewa *tequa*, "house," and thus with *te*, "cottonwood," and *te'e*, "kiva"), despite the fact that these two Tanoan languages have probably been separate for about 1,000 years (Davis 1959). The Tanoan image of the emergence lake as a kiva is different from that of the Acomas, who use the kiva to conceptualize the underworld overall.

These examples illustrate that architectural metaphors can reveal some of the concepts that define cultural identities and make them distinctive, meaningful, and traditional. Architectural metaphors are widespread in the ethnographic record (Parker Pearson and Richards 1994:note 1) and are probably at least as old as the Paleolithic caves of Europe (Lewis-Williams 2002:chapter 9), so they have likely been part of the human imagination for most of our history. These metaphors are obvious in the earlier examples because they are expressed through figurative language, but for archaeologists the critical question is whether we can decipher such metaphors from archaeological evidence alone, without recourse to ethnographic analogy or linguistic reconstruction. I believe we can if we ground our method in generalizations on the structure of figurative thought and follow a code-breaking procedure similar to that used in decipherment of ancient scripts (see Ortman 2000:616–621).

In this chapter I use this middle-range theory of the mind (after Cowgill 1993) to decipher some architectural metaphors of Ancestral Pueblo people who lived in the Northern San Juan region of southwestern Colorado and southeastern Utah between A.D. 1020 and 1280. I argue that these people conceived of buildings as containers and also as microcosms of a world that was container-like. I then examine the extent to which these concepts are expressed in sites associated with Chaco Canyon to determine whether these architectural metaphors could have spread into the Northern San Juan by way of the Chacoan regional system. I argue that several "Chaco outlier" great houses in the Northern San Juan materialized local metaphors not expressed in Chaco Canyon. This, in turn, suggests that even if "Chacoan influence" involved the introduction of new architectural traits to the Northern San Juan, it did not involve the replacement of local architectural metaphors by Chacoan worldview concepts.

DECIPHERING ARCHITECTURAL METAPHORS

In my previous work, I proposed that conceptual metaphors can be deciphered from archaeological evidence using methods derived from cognitive research on figurative speech, especially the work of George Lakoff (1987, 1993; Lakoff and Johnson 1980, 1999), Gilles Fauconnier (1997; Fauconnier and Turner 1994), Raymond Gibbs (1994), and others (Croft and Cruse 2004:chapter 8; Kövecses 2002). From a review of this literature, I have identified six properties of metaphor that characterize human cultural cognition (Table 12.1; also see Ortman 2000). These generalizations are critical because they provide something like "grammatical" rules for figurative expressions in material culture. In other words, expressions of a

Scott G. Ortman

Table 12.1. Six properties of conceptual metaphor (from Ortman 2000:616–619).

1. Directionality principle:	Metaphor is a point-for-point mapping of image-schematic structure from a concrete source domain to an abstract target domain.
2. Superordinate principle:	Conceptual metaphors exist at the superordinate level of classification but are expressed using concrete imagery.
3. Invariance principle:	Image-schematic properties of the source that contradict properties of the target are not mapped.
4. Constitutive principle:	Metaphors do more than express the results of thinking; they actually represent conventionalized ways of thinking and reasoning.
5. Blending principle:	Multiple source domains can be combined for mapping onto a single target if they share image-schematic structure.
6. Experiential principle:	Metaphors derive from the concrete, bodily experiences of individuals in specific physical and social contexts.

proposed metaphor should follow these rules if we have a large enough corpus of material culture to study and if the metaphor really was part of the culture of an ancient social group rather than invented by the analyst.

The logic of metaphor analysis is quite different from traditional hypothesis testing, where the data are supposed to be independent of the hypothesis under consideration. Instead, in metaphor analysis, as in decipherment, the hypothesis to be tested actually determines what the data are. This aspect of my approach makes some archaeologists uncomfortable, but it is in fact the way epigraphers have worked from the time of Napoleon to the present day (Pope 1999). When deciphering an ancient script, there is no way to assign phonetic values to signs until one has developed a model of the type of writing system represented (alphabetic, syllabic, logographic) and the language expressed by it. It is therefore not practical to test numerous working hypotheses on how a writing system works because each hypothesis leads to a different assessment of what the signs of the script represent and thus to separate analyses of the "data." It is more efficient to pursue the hypothesis that appears most promising to determine whether a script produces plausible utterances when the signs are interpreted according to this hypothesis.

I suggest that metaphor analysis works the same way. Figurative thought is, in fact, highly structured and follows the "grammatical" rules identified in cognitive linguistic research that are summarized in Table 12.1. These rules are analogous to the concept that complete sentences have a subject, object, and verb. If one interprets a corpus of material culture in terms of a given metaphor hypothesis and determines that the resultant "data" have a structure consistent with the rules of figurative thought, then it can be said that one has supported a metaphor hypothesis. A researcher can also reject this hypothesis if new data that clearly contradict this structure come to light. In short, I believe metaphor analysis can produce stable knowledge of the past that is every bit as justified as reconstructed settlement patterns, climate cycles, or interaction networks.

In this chapter I pursue the decipherment of architectural metaphors. These can be materialized in any number of ways, including the form and construction of

Architectural Metaphor and Chacoan Influence in the Northern San Juan

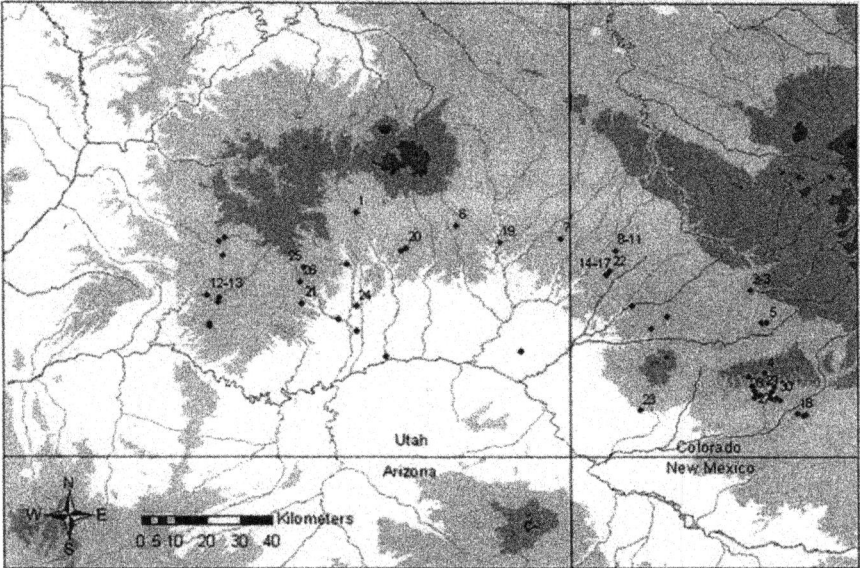

Figure 12.1. The Northern San Juan region. Diamonds indicate locations of sites containing decorated buildings. Numbers indicate locations of murals cataloged in Table 12.2. © Crow Canyon Archaeological Center.

buildings, the ritual uses of architectural spaces, and the decoration of architectural surfaces. I focus primarily on decorative treatment and include observations on form and construction that relate to architectural metaphors suggested by decoration. Through a combination of site visits and literature reviews, I have compiled a database of painted and engraved compositions on the walls of buildings in the Northern San Juan region (Figure 12.1). My sample includes ninety-two compositions in eighty-three structures from fifty-four different sites. Most are from cliff dwellings, but decorated walls are also preserved in open sites, including kiva murals from four "Chaco outlier" great houses—Lowry Ruin, Haynie Ruin, the Hedley Site Complex, and the Bluff Great House. In these pages I adduce evidence that several architectural metaphors were expressed through these wall decorations.

Buildings Are Containers

The oldest decorated building in my database is a subrectangular pit structure exposed by looting in Harness Cave, in Allen Canyon, Utah (Figure 12.2a). Although it has not been tree-ring dated, its subrectangular shape, the absence of masonry pilasters, the presence of Mancos Black-on-white pottery, and the absence of later types on the surface of the site suggest it dates to the first half of the A.D.

231

Scott G. Ortman

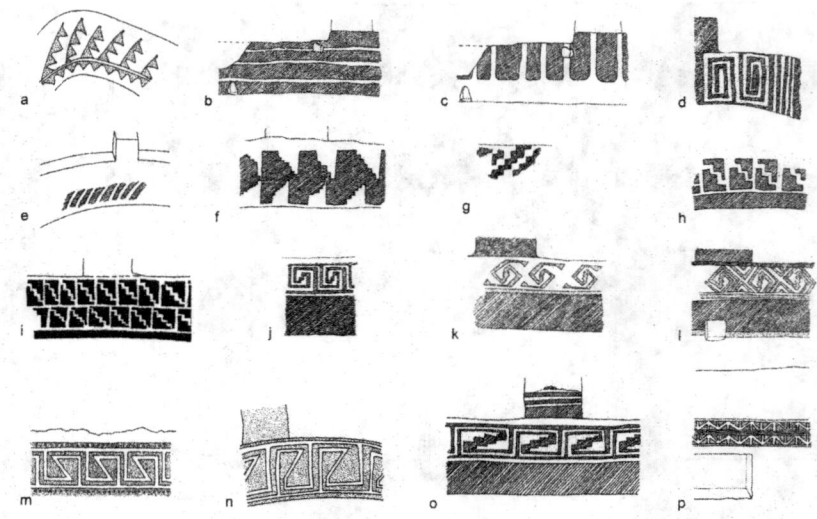

Figure 12.2. Pottery-band murals in kivas: (a) Mural 1, Harness Cave, adapted from author photo; (b) Mural 2, 5MT5498, adapted from Rohman 2003:fig. 12-31; (c) Mural 3, 5MT5498, adapted from Rohman 2003:fig. 12-31; (d) Mural 5, Haynie Ruin, adapted from author photo; (e) Mural 6, Alkali Ridge Site 11, adapted from Brew 1946:fig. 87d, (f) Mural 8, Lowry Ruin, adapted from Martin 1936: plate LXI; (g) Mural 9, Lowry Ruin, adapted from Martin 1936:plate LXII; (h) Mural 10, Lowry Ruin, adapted from Martin 1936:plate LXIII; (i) Mural 11, Lowry Ruin, adapted from Martin 1936: plate LXIV; (j) Mural 14, Knobby Knee Stockade, adapted from Morris 1991:fig. 3.39; (k) Mural 15, Knobby Knee Stockade, adapted from Morris 1991:fig. 3.42; (l) Mural 16, Knobby Knee Stockade, adapted from Morris 1991:fig. 3.44; (m) Mural 19, Dibble site, adapted from Smith 1952:fig. 7h; (n) Mural 20, Westwater 5 Kiva Ruin, adapted from author photo; (o) Mural 22, Roundtree Pueblo, adapted from Morris 1991:fig. 5.24; (p) Mural 27, Long House, adapted from Cattanach 1980:fig. 66. Scale varies. Renderings by Scott Evans, © Crow Canyon Archaeological Center.

1000s. The painted mural in this structure is a band design that covered the entire lining wall and is exposed on two walls and appears to run continuously around all four. The motifs and layout of this mural are also identical to designs commonly found on Mancos Black-on-white pottery. I have identified twenty-seven additional compositions in nineteen additional sites dating between A.D. 1060 and 1280 that consist of geometric band-design murals (Figure 12.2, 12.3g, h; Table 12.2). Following the logic of decipherment, I have assumed that these murals are representations of pottery designs and have recorded details of their form and context based on the hypothesis that they express a metaphorical conceptualization of buildings as containers. Using these data, combined with information on kiva roof construction, I have identified archaeological patterns that illustrate all six properties of conceptual metaphor. This suggests that BUILDINGS ARE CONTAINERS was an architectural

Architectural Metaphor and Chacoan Influence in the Northern San Juan

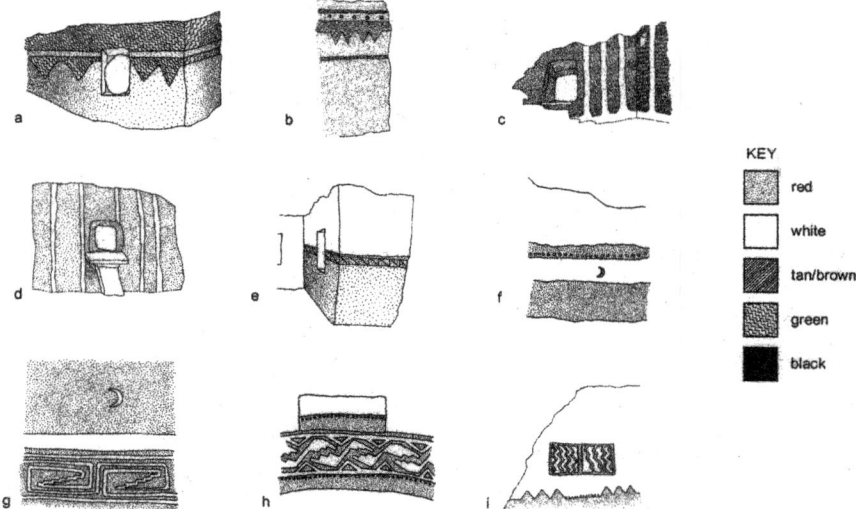

Figure 12.3. Pottery-band murals on storage rooms, and murals that blend landscape and container imagery: (a) Mural 12, Green House; (b) Mural 13, Green House; (c) Mural 18, Hoy House; (d) Mural 21, Moon House; (e) Mural 25, Polychrome House; (f) interior of Moon House, Room I; (g) Mural 24, Fishmouth Canyon Ruin; (h) Mural 26, Painted Kiva site; (i) Mural 30, Cliff Palace. Scale varies. All adapted from author photos except for g, adapted from author photo and BLM site file photos. Renderings by Scott Evans, © Crow Canyon Archaeological Center.

metaphor of the Northern San Juan. (Small caps are used to denote conceptual metaphors, following the convention established by Lakoff and Johnson [1980].) In the following paragraphs I review these six properties and discuss patterns that illustrate them in this corpus of data.

The first property, the *directionality principle*, states that conceptual projection usually proceeds from a relatively structured source to a more abstract target. This is why *Time Is Space* but space is not time; *spring* can be just around the corner, you can be *sitting* just around the corner, but you cannot be sitting *spring* from me. The pottery-band murals illustrate this principle because several details of pottery decoration are mapped onto structure walls, but details of architecture are never mapped onto pottery. For example, nineteen kivas in the database are decorated with band designs identical to those found on pottery bowls, but I have never seen a pottery bowl on which kiva floor features were represented in paint.

In addition, the designs mapped onto structure walls follow the chronological development of both pottery designs and weaving processes. In my previous work, I found that Northern San Juan pottery designs were based on the metaphor POTTERY IS A TEXTILE and documented that innovations in pottery decoration closely followed innovations in weaving processes over time (see Ortman 2000:table 6). This

Table 12.2. Pottery-band and container/landscape murals in the Northern San Juan region.

Map Reference	Site Name	Site Number	Structure Number	Structure Type	Mural Loc
Pottery-band murals					
1	Harness Cave	—	Pit structure	Kiva	Interior w
2–3	—	5MT5498	Structure 6	Kiva	Interior w
4	Site 875	5MV875	Kiva B	Kiva	Interior w
5	Haynie Ruin	—	Kiva	Kiva	Interior w
6	Site 11, Alkali Ridge	—	Kiva	Kiva	Interior w
7	Hedley Main Ruin	42SA22760	Structure 3005	Kiva	Interior w
8–11	Lowry Ruin	5MT1566	Kiva A, B, D	Kivas	Interior w
12–13	Green House	—	Rooms	Granaries?	Exterior w
14–17	Knobby Knee Stockade	5MT2525	Pit structure 6	Kiva	Interior w
18	Hoy House (Porcupine House)	5MTUMR2150	Rooms 41, 43, 45, 47, 49	Granaries?	Exterior w
19	Dibble site	—	Kiva	Kiva	Interior w
20	Westwater 5-Kiva Ruin	42SA14	Kiva	Kiva	Interior w
21	Moon House	42SA5005	M-1, Room B5	Granary?	Exterior w
22	Roundtree Pueblo	5MT2544	Pit structure 6	Kiva	Interior w
23	Cowboy Wash	5MT9541	Feature 12	Kiva	Interior w
Compositions that blend container and landscape imagery					
24	Fishmouth Canyon Ruin	42SA8817	Square Kiva, F2	Kiva	Interior w
25	Polychrome House	42SA1732	Rooms	Granary	Exterior w
26	Painted Kiva site	42SA9310	West Kiva	Kiva	Interior w
27	Long House	5MV1200	Kiva E	Kiva	Interior w
28	Kodak House	5MV1212	Kiva B	Kiva	Interior w
29	Spruce Tree House	5MV640	Room 47	Tower	Interior w
30	Cliff Palace	5MV625	Room 11	Tower	Interior w
31	Red Kiva site	42SA23910	Kiva	Kiva	Interior w

Note: 1. Crow Canyon Archaeological Center.

(A.D.)	Number of Compositions	Description	Reference(s)
-1060	1	Coiled basket motif band design	Author site visit, 10/5/03
-1140	2	Framing pattern (coiled basketry texture) underneath a non-loom band design	Rohman 2003:fig. 12-31
-1100	1	Geometric, possible non-loom band design	Lister 1965:plate 9
-1140	1	Non-loom band design	Village Project large site files, CCAC[1] archive
-1140	1	Twill-rib texture (striped-twill) band design	Brew 1946:fig. 87d
-1140	1	Indeterminate geometric band design	Ortman et al. 2000; unpublished field notes on file, CCAC
-1140	4	Four plain-tapestry band designs	Martin 1936:plates LXI, LXII, LXIII, LXIV; Ahlstrom, Breternitz, and Warren 1985
-1180	2	Two coiled basket motif band designs	Author site visit, 7/2001
-1225	4	One plain-tapestry band, two twill-tapestry bands, and one twill-tapestry band inside a framing pattern (coiled basketry texture)	Morris 1991:figs. 3.39, 3.42, 3.44
-1225	1	Non-loom band design	Nickens 1981:fig.3; Author site visit 7/3/03
-1260	1	Plain-tapestry band design	Smith 1952:figure 7h
-1260	1	Plain-tapestry band design	Author site visit, 10/5/03
-1260	1	Non-loom band design	Bloomer 1989:98
-1260	1	Plain-tapestry band inside a framing pattern (coiled basketry texture)	Morris 1991:fig. 5.24
-1260	1	Plain-tapestry band design	Martin, p.c., 2004
-1260	1	Plain-weave band design with framing line, with crescent on west wall and disc on east wall above band design	Gunckel 1892:562; Utah State site form; Author site visit, 10/5/03
-1280	1	Bichrome with etched, plain-weave band design at upper boundary of red field	Author site visit, 6/2001; Utah State site form
-1280	1	Twill-tapestry band design on lower lining wall; horizon scene on pilasters	Author site visit, 6/2000; Utah State site form
-1280	1	Twill-weave band design with framing lines, with mountain sheep in white field above band design	Cattanach 1980:fig. 66
-1280	1	Bichrome on lower lining wall, pottery design (nested triangles) on pilaster	Fetterman and Honeycutt 1989:36, fig. 29
-1280	1	Horizon scene with bird and mountain sheep on the boundary between red and white and a textile representation in white field above	Nordenskiöld 1990; Fewkes 1909:52
-1280	1	Horizon scene with textile representations in white field above	Fewkes 1911:plate 13a; Malville and Munson 1998
-1260	1	Horizon scene with terraces in white field above	Author site visit, 5/2005; Utah State site form

Table 12.3. Pottery/textile imagery in architectural murals through time. Shaded cells indicate periods during which the textile source of the analogous pottery design is attested.

Source Imagery (from Textiles)	1020–1060	1060–1100	1100–1140	1140–1180	1180–1225	1225–1260	1260–1280	Total
Coiled basketry band design	1				2			3
Coiled basketry texture		1						1
Non-loom band design			2		1	1		4
Plain-tapestry band design			4		1	3	1	9
Plain-tapestry band inside coiled basketry texture						2		2
Twill-rib (striped-twill) texture design				1				1
Twill-tapestry band inside coiled basketry texture					1			1
Twill-tapestry band						2	3	5
Indeterminate textile imagery			1	1				2
Total	1	2	8	2	5	6	4	28

chronological pattern also holds for the pottery-band mural paintings. Table 12.3 summarizes Northern San Juan pottery-band murals according to their date and the weaving process that was the ultimate source of the mural design. The shaded areas represent time periods during which the sources of the mural imagery are attested in basketry or warp-weft weaves and in pottery designs (after Ortman 2000:table 6). Because no murals occur in periods represented by the unshaded cells, these data are consistent with the expectation that pottery-band murals followed stylistic developments in both pottery decoration and textile design.

This pattern raises the question of whether the mapping was actually from textiles to buildings or whether buildings were decorated with pottery designs that in turn derived from textiles. Regardless of the answer, the mapping was clearly directional, with imagery projected from actual containers (pots and baskets) to architectural spaces. I believe the latter situation is more likely because the walls and floors of buildings share more image-schematic structure with pots than they do with baskets (Table 12.4). Basketry bowls and pottery bowls are both actual containers and have a bowl shape. The walls and floor of a kiva do not make an actual container or present the woven vegetal surface of a basket, but they do create a bowl shape and present a smooth, earthen surface that is parallel to a pottery bowl. Thus kiva walls and floors share more image-schematic structure with pottery bowls than with basketry bowls, suggesting that the mapping was from pottery onto the kiva, with pottery "pre-conceptualized" as a textile. Such "conceptual chaining" is in fact quite common in figurative thought and expression (Kövecses 2002:19). For example, in the expression "he was consumed by a burning passion, and she fed the fire," passion is conceptualized as fire, and fire is in turn conceptualized as an insatiable animal.

Table 12.4. Correspondences among kivas, pottery bowls, and baskets.

Attribute	Kiva Walls and Floor	Pottery Bowl	Basketry Bowl
Bowl shape	X	X	X
Actual container		X	X
Smooth earthen surface	X	X	

The second property, which I call the *superordinate principle*, states that conceptual metaphors exist in the brain at relatively abstract levels of categorization but are expressed at the basic level of concrete mental imagery. Thus, in English, LIFE IS A JOURNEY, but we usually express the concept using concrete images of planes, trains, and automobiles, as in "his career is off-track." This principle is supported by the fact that container imagery occurs in several different architectural contexts, including kiva walls, kiva roofs, and granaries. First, in the case of kiva walls, I have documented twenty cases in which a continuous pottery-band design was painted over a smooth, plastered surface on the interior face of the circular central chamber. These kiva walls, with pottery-textile designs painted on a smooth surface, clearly present the image of a pottery bowl with a geometric band design running parallel to the rim.

Second, the standard way of constructing kiva roofs in the Northern San Juan suggests that such roofs were modeled as coiled baskets. Most kivas in this region have three to eight courses of timbers running between six evenly spaced pilasters inside the round chamber, with the ends of the timbers in each course offset from the course below and above. In some examples, the crib layers form a dome shape, and in others they are stacked vertically. In either case, a flat roof was constructed over the top of the cribbing. It appears from the woven, vegetal, dome-shaped appearance of these roofs that the image presented was that of an overturned coiled basket, mirroring the pottery bowl defined by the kiva walls and floor below.

Third, I have documented four examples of aboveground structures decorated as pottery seed jars on the exterior faces of the preserved walls (Table 12.2, Figure 12.3a-e). These structures blend together attributes of corn granaries and living rooms. All four have small doorways that could be sealed to protect their contents, and one example (Figure 12.3e) also has unsooted walls and is filled with corn cobs, confirming a storage function. However, two other structures (Figure 12.3a, d) have fire pits inside, and a third structure (Figure 12.3c) is unsooted but occurs on the second story of a roomblock for which the upper floors are not preserved. At least one of these structures was clearly designed and used as a corn granary, and the others could have been either granaries that were later appropriated for human activities or habitable rooms that look like granaries from the outside. To better understand these structures, it is important not to overlook the widespread occurrence of the metaphor PEOPLE ARE CORN among maize agriculturalists of the Western Hemisphere, including the Maya (Friedel, Schele, and Parker 1993), Mixtec (Monaghan 1995), Nahua (Sandstrom 1991), Huichol (Schaefer and Furst 1996), and Pueblos

(Ortiz 1969). Given the widespread occurrence of this concept, perhaps the decorated granaries with hearths are metaphorical granaries for people.

Regardless of the functional interpretation of these structures, all four present granary facades, and all four are decorated with pottery-textile imagery arranged in a horizontal band around the preserved exterior walls. These structures are not circular, and because all were built against rock faces in alcoves, none ever had four walls that could have been decorated. Also, the relationship of the mural to the doorway on granary exteriors is different from the relationship of the orifice to the band design on seed jar exteriors. Nevertheless, a band design is horizontal on a jar sitting upright, and only that part of the band that faces a viewer is visible when a jar is viewed from the side. These essential characteristics, in addition to the motifs comprising the band designs, sealable openings, and smooth earthen surfaces, are parallel between seed jars and granaries and therefore suggest these granary facades are decorated as seed jars. Basketry jars with sealed openings have not been found in Ancestral Pueblo sites, whereas pottery jars with lids of pottery or shaped stone are common. This suggests that the mapping was in fact from pottery jars to granaries rather than from basketry jars directly.

Based on this discussion, it appears that the form and decoration of buildings in the Northern San Juan support the superordinate principle because the varied expressions of BUILDINGS ARE CONTAINERS used the concrete imagery of pottery bowls, coiled baskets, and seed jars, in the same way English speakers talk about life using the concrete imagery of planes, trains, and automobiles.

The third property, which I call the *invariance principle,* states that aspects of a source domain that are contradicted by the inherent structure of the target domain are not mapped. This is why TIME IS MONEY; we can spend or waste time, but saved time does not accumulate interest. The pottery-band murals illustrate this property because allover designs, and the specific motifs associated with them, do not occur as mural paintings. The reason for this is that allover designs were mapped onto pottery using the imagery of twill-plaited ring baskets (Ortman 2000:figures 6, 13, 14). These baskets were made by plaiting a square mat of yucca strips and then pressing this mat through a circular hoop, to which the ends of the plaiting strips were fastened. Although the shape of a twill-plaited ring basket does mirror the hemispherical shape of a pottery bowl, such baskets do not have a base and sides corresponding to the walls and floor of a building. In contrast, coiled baskets, an additional source for pottery design imagery, could and often did have a flat base and vertical sides that do correspond to parts of a building.

Based on this differential correspondence between basket and building shapes, one would predict, according to the invariance principle, that the motifs in pottery-band murals would be restricted to those that could be mapped onto pottery via coiled basketry. This is, in fact, what occurs. Motifs such as Dogozshi-style, hatched-ribbon frets (representing interval-shift designs in twill-plaited basketry) and background hachure designs (representing twill-tapestry cotton fabrics with allover designs substituted for the plaited mat of a ring basket) are completely absent from pottery-band murals. In contrast, parallel lines, terraces, and triangles, all of which were mapped onto pottery via coiled basketry, are common in these murals (see Ortman 2000:table 3).

It is interesting to note how specific these restrictions are. Mural 6, from Alkali Ridge Site 11 (Figure 12.2e), consists of a band of closely spaced diagonal lines. Although this mural is poorly preserved, J. O. Brew (1946:141) states that "traces here and there indicated that the diagonal stripes had run all around the kiva." This mural thus consists of a hachure band, which could conceivably derive from the woven texture of a textile produced in a variety of industries, including twill-plaited basketry, twill-tapestry loom weaving, or striped-twill loom weaving. If this design derived from either of the first two options, it would violate the invariance principle. However, this composition most likely represents a striped-twill pattern because the twill ribs in plaited basketry would not parallel the rim of the basket the way the hachure band follows the bench of the kiva, and the hachure is not combined with solid motifs that would indicate an allover twill-tapestry weave. In addition, striped-twill loom weaving had been introduced by the time this kiva was built and decorated, whereas twill-tapestry weaving had not (Ortman 2000:table 2). Thus it appears the design of this mural was imagined by substituting the wefts of a striped-twill weave for the coils of a coiled basket. This mapping is consistent with the invariance principle because it maps loom-based imagery onto the kiva using coiled, not plaited basketry.

There is no physical reason why motifs derived from twill-plaited basketry or twill-tapestry loom weaving could not also have been painted on structure walls, but they do not occur in any of the twenty-six pottery-band murals with classifiable patterns in my database. These specific designs (analogous features 15 and 21 in Ortman 2000:table 6) occur on approximately 25 percent of decorated serving bowls dating between A.D. 1060 and 1280 in the Northern San Juan, so it is unlikely that sampling error is responsible for their complete absence in pottery-band murals (chi-square $P < 0.011$). However, this restriction makes complete sense when it is considered in light of the invariance principle, conceptual chaining, and the specific metaphors involved. If the walls of kivas and granaries were conceptualized as pottery vessels and pottery vessels were in turn conceptualized as textiles, any mappings of pottery designs onto buildings would need to be consistent with the inherent structure of both textiles and pottery. This is in fact what occurs, and the specific restrictions on these mappings are consistent with the invariance principle.

The fourth property, which I call the *constitutive principle*, states that a conceptual metaphor is not just a way of expressing thought but is in fact a conventionalized way of thinking and reasoning. In other words, everyday thinking and reasoning normally occur through the operation of conventional metaphors. This is why it is very difficult to conceive of time without using the framework provided by space or of intellectual argument without the framework of a building. Our literal understanding of concepts such as space and argument are actually quite impoverished.

Metaphor helps us flesh out these concepts so we can think and reason about them in more detail (Lakoff and Johnson 1999). The details of typical kiva roof construction in the Northern San Juan illustrate this principle. Nearly all kivas constructed after A.D. 1100 in this region had six masonry roof support pillars, or pilasters, spaced evenly around the interior chamber. In nearly all preserved kiva roofs, the beams of the first crib layer span the distance between adjacent pilasters, and beams of subsequent crib layers are offset so that the ends of the beams rest on the midpoint of those from the layer below. Two to eight courses of cribbing occur in these roofs, and shredded juniper bark, often referred to as closing material, was also packed between the cribbing beams, in a way reminiscent of the typical two-rod-and-bundle foundation of coiled baskets from the Northern San Juan (Morris and Burgh 1941).

What is striking about these roofs is that the crib layers were not load-bearing. Regardless of whether the crib layers were stacked upright or corbelled to form a dome, the roof itself was flat and supported by vigas that spanned the entire structure and rested on the masonry upper lining wall as well as the uppermost crib layer (Hovezak 1992:41). This is in fact the standard form of kiva roof construction in intact roofs observed by Mark Hovezak (1992) at Square Tower House and Lion House on Mesa Verde and by me during visits to Lewis Lodge, Bannister Ruin, Bare Ladder Ruin, Perfect Kiva Ruin, the Slickhorn Perfect Kiva site, and the Cigarette Springs site in southeastern Utah. Thus the dozens of timbers involved in cribbing a typical kiva were unnecessary from a structural point of view. The flat roof could have been supported completely by masonry, but instead, the design of the typical kiva included a lining of timbers around the upper part of the structure walls, below the roof itself. The occurrence of a cribbed kiva in nearly every house—despite the reliance on wood for cooking, pottery firing, and heating and the slow growth rate of trees in the local environment—clearly indicates that cribbing was a strong architectural convention. It is equally clear that coiled basketry was the source of this convention. Cribbed kiva roofs thus illustrate the constitutive principle because they represent a conventional design rooted in a specific metaphor, despite the fact that there were good economic reasons for designing less expensive roofs.

The fifth property, which I call the *blending principle*, states that two conceptual domains with equal inherent structure can be blended to produce new concepts that are physically impossible but conceptually coherent (Fauconnier 1997; Fauconnier and Turner 1994). This is why you can have a "brainstorming" session with your colleagues, even though a storming brain is literally ridiculous. The connection between thunderstorms and brain activity motivating this concept is electricity, which occurs in the form of lightning in storms and firing synapses in the brain. This correspondence promotes the blending of additional conceptual structure, making it possible to imagine a lightning bolt as a "flash of insight." The occurrence of murals that present pottery designs that are themselves blends of imagery from two different forms of weaving illustrates this principle. For example, on Mural 22 at Roundtree Pueblo (Figure 12.2o), there is an interlocking band design on the lower lining wall of the kiva and framing lines on the pilasters. To understand this composition as an example of blending, we need to consider the derivation of this design from textile imagery and its mapping onto kiva walls.

In pottery, designs such as that on Mural 22 were imagined by blending coiled basketry with loom weaving. The weft threads of a woven article were substituted for the coils of the basket to create a regular, repeating pattern, and the coiled basket onto which the woven article was mapped was acknowledged by creating a framing pattern of thin parallel lines above the band design to represent the surface texture of this basket (see Ortman 2000:632–634). There is a basis for creating this blend on an actual pottery bowl because the shape of a pottery bowl corresponds to that of a basket but not to that of a loom-woven textile. There is also a basis for relating the pilasters of a kiva to the rim area of a pottery bowl because the pilasters are the uppermost smooth plastered surface of the kiva chamber, on which the vegetal, cribbed roof rests. However, there is no corresponding basis for mapping a coiled basket texture directly onto the pilasters because the pilasters do not actually continue the round shape of the lower lining wall below. Thus a putative mapping of a basket directly onto the kiva walls would stop at the bench and not continue onto the pilasters. In contrast, the smooth plastered faces of the kiva pilasters are parallel to the slipped surface of a pottery bowl, so there is an image-schematic basis for continuing the pottery decoration onto the pilasters. This design thus illustrates blending and supports the notion that it is pottery vessels decorated with weaving imagery, and not textiles themselves, that are displayed on these murals.

Finally, the sixth property, which I call the *experiential principle*, states that metaphors are grounded in the direct bodily experiences of individuals in a given cultural context. This is why computer viruses are only possible in a society that knows about both computers and microorganisms. The pottery-band murals are consistent with this principle because several formal and experiential properties of buildings are analogous to those of pottery vessels, and these are as apparent today as they must have been in the past. Table 12.5 lays out a number of these specific correspondences between pottery bowls and kiva walls, coiled baskets and kiva roofs, and seed jars and granaries. These correspondences provided experiential motivation for conceptual relationships between pottery vessels and buildings.

The World Is a Building

Beginning around A.D. 1180, a second major form of wall decoration began to appear in the Northern San Juan. This new style consisted of simple dados, with the lower portion red and the upper portion tan to white, as well as more complex compositions that included sets of projecting triangles and dots running along the boundary between the two colors. The more complex compositions look like abstractions of the horizon, and details such as the crescent moon in the upper field of a mural from Moon House (Figure 12.3f) suggest that a horizon view, with the earth in red and the sky in white, is indeed what they represent. For the sake of

Table 12.5. Correspondences between containers and buildings.

A. *Pottery bowl*	Kiva walls
1. Base	1. Floor
2. Rim	2. Pilasters
3. Hemispherical shape	3. Circular lining wall
4. Clay coils	4. Masonry, mortar
5. Slipped surfaces	5. Plastered surfaces
6. Presents cooked food	6. Contains mature people
7. Interior surface visible	7. Interior face of walls visible
B. *Coiled basket*	Kiva roof
1. Hemispherical shape	1. Domed shape
2. Rod foundation	2. Roof timbers
3. Bundle	3. Closing material
4. Stitching material	4. Yucca bindings
5. Coiling technique	5. Cribbing technique
6. Sides	6. Stacked crib layers
7. Center	7. Roof hatch
C. *Seed ("Kiva") jar*	Granary
1. Base	1. Floor
2. Vessel walls	2. Structure walls
3. Orifice	3. Doorway
4. Lip for lid	4. Coping around door
5. Lid	5. Door slab
6. Holes for cordage to seal opening	6. Loops to seal door
7. Clay coils	7. Masonry, mortar
8. Slipped surfaces	8. Plastered surfaces
9. Contains seeds	9. Contains cobs
10. Exterior surface visible	10. Exterior face of walls visible

analysis, I will call the dados *bichromes* and the more complex compositions *horizon scenes* and will assume that both forms represent abstractions of the landscape. I have identified forty-three landscape murals of these two types across the Northern San Juan, and once again, patterns in this corpus of imagery are consistent with a metaphor interpretation, in this case THE WORLD IS A BUILDING.

The *superordinate principle* is supported because landscape murals were painted on walls of many different kinds of buildings, including kivas, great kivas, and rooms. In other words, several different kinds of buildings were decorated to express the concept that the world is a building. The *invariance principle* is also supported because landscape murals were almost always painted on interior walls (Table 12.6). A person cannot be physically outside the horizon, and thus it makes more sense to paint horizons around spaces people can actually be inside. Only five of the forty-three landscape mural compositions occur on building exteriors. Four of these are simple bichromes, and only one building with an exterior landscape mural does not also have one on its interior (the granary at Polychrome House, Mural 25). Given

Table 12.6. Contexts of landscape murals in the Northern San Juan.

	Exterior Wall		Interior Wall		
Structure Type	Bichrome	Horizon	Bichrome	Horizon	Total
Ground-floor room	2	1	4	4	11
Second- or third-story room	1	–	3	6	10
Granary	1	–	–	–	1
Kiva	–	–	3	16	19
Great Kiva	–	–	–	2	2
Total	4	1	10	28	43

these data, it is highly unlikely that landscape murals were painted randomly with respect to building interiors versus exteriors (chi-square P < .001).

Given that buildings had been conceptualized as containers prior to the appearance of landscape murals in the Northern San Juan, we might also expect to see murals that blend container and landscape imagery. This blending does in fact occur and is most obvious in thirteenth-century kivas that present landscape imagery above pottery-band designs. Mural 24, in a kiva at Fishmouth Canyon Ruin (Figure 12.3g), depicts the sun and moon on opposite walls above the pottery band; and Mural 27, in Kiva E at Long House, depicts zoomorphs and anthropomorphs directly above and below a pottery band executed in red pigment (noted by Cattanach [1980:67] but not shown on Figure 12.2p because they are not discernible in the source image for this drawing). Also, the mural at the Painted Kiva site (Figure 12.3h) combines a pottery band on the lower lining wall with a horizon scene on the pilasters, where the walls and roof of a kiva come together (Figure 12.4). Given that the roof of this kiva was also cribbed, the kiva presents the imagery of an upright pottery bowl and an overturned coiled basket as a microcosm of the world, as indicated by the horizon scene on the pilasters, where the pottery bowl earth and basket sky join together. The dots running along this junction may also correspond to rim ticking or stitching on pottery bowls and baskets, respectively, and lead one to wonder whether the dots on horizon scene murals more generally represent the "rim" of the world. Rina Swentzell (1990) provides ethnographic support for this notion that both the kiva and the world could be modeled as a paired bowl and basket.

The notion that the sky half of the world could be conceived of as a woven, textile-like object is also supported by thirteenth-century compositions that combine landscape and textile imagery (Figure 12.3). For example, Mural 30, inside the third story of a rectangular tower at Cliff Palace (Figure 12.3i), and Mural 29, in the second story of a rectangular tower at Spruce Tree House, both depict a textile in the upper field of a horizon scene. Archaeoastronomers have argued that the Cliff Palace room in particular was an observatory and that the textile in the "sky" portion of the horizon scene was a mnemonic for modeling lunar and solar cycles (Malville and Munson 1998; also see Newsome 2005). If so, we have an example

Scott G. Ortman

Figure 12.4. Decorated kiva from site 42SA9310, southeastern Utah. Photo by Scott Ortman.

of an ancient astronomer using the imagery of weaving on a wide, upright loom—a concrete, rhythmic, mathematical process—to model the back-and-forth movement of the sun and moon as they rise and set on the horizon during the year.

Upright looms were set up inside buildings, where the frame was attached to a ceiling beam above and loops were set into the floor below (Kent 1983:fig. 58). The loom thus spanned the distance between the floor and ceiling of the room, and the tension of the warp threads literally pulled the ceiling and floor toward each other. Thus, in a world conceived metaphorically as a building, the earth and sky could be connected by a loom, in which case the sun and moon, represented by the shuttle, would literally weave together the floor and roof of the world through their cyclical, back-and-forth motions with respect to the horizon. This is a clear illustration of the *constitutive principle*: a theory that accounts for observable cycles of the sun and moon using the imagery of weaving.

The notion that landscape murals often decorated spaces used for calendrical observation is supported by the fact that nine of the seventeen landscape murals painted inside rectangular rooms occur in second- and third-story structures in cliff dwellings (Table 12.6). This is despite the fact that ground-floor rooms were more common in these sites originally, and a lower proportion of upper-story rooms has been preserved in these sites than is the case for ground-floor rooms. These upper-story rooms would have received direct sunlight earliest or latest in the day, when the sun was closest to its rising or setting position on the far horizon. This suggests that an upper-story room with a landscape mural and a window, door, or

Table 12.7. Correspondences between buildings and the world.

Building	World
1. Made of earth, stone, plants, water	1. Consists of earth, stone, plants, water
2. Stone walls	2. Mountains on horizon
3. Vegetal ceiling	3. Sky is lightweight
4. Earthen floor	4. Soil on surface of the earth
5. People live inside	5. People live within
6. Entrance	6. Passage between worlds
7. Upright loom	7. Earth and sky are woven together
8. Movement of shuttle on loom	8. Motions of sun and moon
9. Cotton on loom	9. Clouds/water connect earth and sky
10. Cotton and plaster are white	10. The cloudy sky is white
11. Mortar and adobe are red	11. Mesa Verde loess soil is red

peephole that let in direct sunlight when the sun was low on the horizon could substitute for an actual panoramic horizon view in settings where such a view was not obtainable.

Looms were not used to weave obvious containers like baskets, but they were used to create clothing in which people could be wrapped. Thus fabrics contained people in the same way pots and baskets contained corn (recall PEOPLE ARE CORN), and therefore it seems likely that Ancestral Pueblo people of the Northern San Juan included loom weaving in a "container" category. If so, a total of eight compositions blend container (pottery, basketry, and loom weaving) and landscape imagery. These compositions make a strong case that, during the thirteenth century, Ancestral Pueblo people of the Northern San Juan imagined the world as consisting of containers in addition to imagining it as a building. These blended compositions also support the *directionality principle* because landscape, pottery, and textile imagery are all apparent on buildings, but I have never seen landscape mural imagery painted on pottery or woven into a textile. If we remember that we are talking about mental imagery and not its expression on actual objects, this pattern suggests that conceptual projection was from smaller, more concrete objects to larger, more abstract phenomena.

Finally, the *experiential principle* is supported by two patterns. First, landscapes and buildings share numerous formal and perceptual properties (Table 12.7), and these correspondences provide an experiential motivation for conceptualizing the world as a building. Second, compositions that blend container and landscape imagery follow the advent of landscape murals in the Northern San Juan. Table 12.8 arranges specific expressions of the conceptual metaphors I have proposed for this region according to the date of their first appearance in the archaeological record. The table shows that expressions of pottery bowls and coiled baskets mapped onto the kiva occurred as early as A.D. 1020, but expressions of containers mapped onto the world did not occur in mural painting prior to A.D. 1225. Weaving and building interiors had been associated experientially since the introduction of the upright

Table 12.8. Historical development of metaphorical expressions in the Northern San Juan.

	Time Period (years A.D.)					
Expression	980–1020	1020–1060	1060–1100	1100–1140	1140–1180	1180–1225	1225–1280
Coiled and plaited basketry mapped onto pottery							
Pottery bowl and coiled basketry mapped onto kiva							
Non-loom weaving mapped onto pottery							
Loom weaving mapped onto pottery							
Seed jar mapped onto granary							
Buildings mapped onto world							
Pottery, basketry, and loom weaving mapped onto world							

loom around A.D. 1100, but the use of loom weaving, basketry, and pottery in landscape metaphors does not appear to have taken place until after buildings began to be mapped onto the world, as indicated by the appearance of horizon scene murals around A.D. 1180. Once this conceptual innovation had occurred, the association of the upright loom with building interiors and prior conceptualizations of buildings as containers appear to have promoted a variety of new metaphors that conceptualized the world using container imagery. Thus the evolution of architectural metaphors in the Northern San Juan was grounded in the history of both conceptual and technological innovation and the concrete experiences of people in this society.

SOURCES IN CHACO?

Alternative forms of wall decoration do occur in the Northern San Juan, and additional metaphors I have not considered were likely also expressed through wall decoration in this region. In addition, I stress that I have not conducted an exhaustive study of mural decoration beyond the Northern San Juan, and thus I cannot at this point trace the history of any of the metaphors discussed here across the Greater Southwest. Nevertheless, it is clear from this analysis of the most common forms of wall decoration in the Northern San Juan that architectural metaphors known to these people included BUILDINGS ARE CONTAINERS, THE WORLD IS A BUILDING, and THE WORLD CONSISTS OF CONTAINERS. Knowing this, the final question I address in this chapter is whether any of these concepts could have originated in Chaco Canyon and diffused to the Northern San Juan along with other, better-documented aspects of Chacoan influence.

The Chaco Phenomenon is the label archaeologists give to the most extensive and complex sociopolitical entity of Ancestral Pueblo history. It was centered in Chaco Canyon, a valley in the desolate San Juan Basin of northwestern New

Mexico (Lekson 2006; Mills 2002). The hallmark of the Chaco Phenomenon was great-house architecture, formalized in massive public works projects at great houses like Pueblo Bonito in the tenth century A.D. (Lekson, Windes, and McKenna 2006; Windes and Ford 1992). Some characteristics of great-house architecture in Chaco Canyon include monumental scale; multiple stories; core and veneer walls; suites of large, interconnected rooms; aboveground kivas; and construction in large, pre-planned stages (Lekson 1986).

By the middle of the A.D. 1000s, smaller versions of great houses began to appear in communities far removed from Chaco Canyon itself, including the Northern San Juan (Lipe 2006; Van Dyke 1999; Varien et al. in press). The central question raised by these outlying great houses is what sort of Chacoan influence they represent. To this end, a variety of models have been proposed to explain the widespread distribution of great-house architecture (see recent summaries by Kantner and Kintigh 2006; Mahoney and Kantner 2000; Mills 2002; and Van Dyke 1999). In the final section of this chapter, I consider, first, whether any of the architectural metaphors I have reconstructed could have originated in Chaco Canyon and, second, whether any of these metaphors were actually expressed in outlier great houses of the Northern San Juan. I argue that the answers to these questions shed significant light on the nature of Chacoan influence in the region.

Joan Mathien (2003) recently summarized wall decoration in Chaco Canyon itself and found that the most common decorations in the canyon are representations of hands, sandals, people and animals, and isolated geometric designs. Such designs appear to be much more common in Chaco Canyon than they are in the Northern San Juan. In addition, pottery-band murals are completely absent in documented Chaco Basin wall decoration. A composition from the interior of Room 106 at Chetro Ketl is the only example vaguely reminiscent of such murals (Lekson 1983; Brody 1991:plate 11), but it does not appear to present the room it adorns as a pottery vessel because it only occurs on one wall instead of running around the interior of the room. Patricia Crown and W. H. Wills (2003) suggest a possible symbolic connection between pottery cylinder jars and kivas based on evidence of periodic repainting and refiring of jars and periodic rebuilding of kivas. But even if both types of object were renewed cyclically, it would not indicate that kivas were conceptualized as cylinder jars. At best, it would indicate that both were considered ritual objects that had cyclical "lives." Thus there is no evidence that buildings were conceptualized as pottery vessels in Chaco Canyon.

In addition, it appears the most common method of kiva roof construction did not express basket imagery. In great-house kivas, the evidence suggests that roofs were normally flat, with two vigas spanning the maximum chamber diameter and framing the roof hatch (Lekson 1986:32-34). Partially preserved wainscoting or bench backing has been found rising from the bench surface in several great-house kivas, but this wattle framework appears to have been covered with daub rather than being left exposed (Lekson 1986:54-59). Victor Mindeleff (1989:126-127) describes such a plaster-covered wattle framework in a historic Hopi kiva. It is intriguing that painted, plastered baskets have been recovered from Chaco great houses (Judd 1954:321), but this does not support the notion that the kiva roof or the sky were conceptualized as woven objects in Chaco great-house kivas.

The roofs of most small-house kivas in Chaco Canyon also appear to have been flat. Small-house kivas most often had four pilasters, two opposite each other just north of the maximum diameter of the structure and two placed on either side of and immediately adjacent to the southern recess or ventilator opening (Truell 1986:181-183). It appears that the primary viga rested on the widely spaced pilasters, thus spanning the maximum east-west diameter of the structure and providing a brace on which the ladder could rest. A second viga rested on the pilasters framing the southern recess and provided support for secondary beams resting on the southern wall of the recess or on the primary viga in the center of the structure. So even though cribbed roofs were constructed in some Chaco great-house kivas (Lekson 1986:32) and small-house kivas (Truell 1986:182), it appears safe to conclude that Chacoan builders did not normally conceptualize kiva roofs as coiled baskets, as people in the Northern San Juan appear to have done.

Although no evidence suggests that BUILDINGS ARE CONTAINERS originated in Chaco Canyon, it is possible that THE WORLD IS A BUILDING originated there. Mathien (2003) found that bichromes like those of the Northern San Juan were painted on the interior walls of kivas and great-house rooms in Chaco Canyon. In fact, horizon scenes, such as the example from LA 17360 (Doyel, Simmons, and McAnany 1989; Brody 1991:figure 49), appear to occur earlier in the basin surrounding Chaco Canyon than they do in the Northern San Juan. Thus conceptualization of the world as a building could have originated in the Chaco Basin and diffused to the Northern San Juan. However, the earliest landscape murals in the Northern San Juan date to the late 1100s, by which time Chaco Canyon no longer functioned as a regional center. This suggests that even if THE WORLD IS A BUILDING spread to the Northern San Juan from the Chaco Basin, this diffusion would have taken place during the post-Chaco period, not during the heyday of Chaco Canyon and the regional system.

Finally, I know of only one mural from the Chaco Basin, broadly defined, that blends landscape and container imagery. This mural occurs in a kiva dating to the late occupation of Salmon Ruin and consists of a horizon scene with a series of terraces running just above the boundary between the red earth and white sky in one section (Smith 1982:figure 5). Although Salmon was built during the heyday of the Chaco Phenomenon and is a prototypical example of an outlying Chaco great house, the late occupation at this site occurred almost a century after the collapse of the Chaco Phenomenon and appears to have involved extensive remodeling by people not closely affiliated with Chacoan culture (McKenna and Toll 1992). Thus no good evidence suggests that THE WORLD CONSISTS OF CONTAINERS was invented in the Chaco Basin either.

Although I am not aware of a single Chaco Basin kiva that was decorated as a pottery bowl, such compositions occur in three of the four decorated kivas in outlier great houses in my Northern San Juan database, including a kiva at Haynie

Ruin, several kivas at Lowry Ruin, and a kiva at the Hedley Site Complex. Lowry Ruin continued to be used in the post-Chaco period, but one of the kivas decorated with a pottery-band mural at this site was intentionally filled and a new one built on top of it around A.D. 1120 (Ahlstrom, Breternitz, and Warren 1985:table 1; Martin 1936). Thus pottery-band murals must have been painted at this site during the Chaco period. The pottery-band mural from the Hedley Site Complex (Ortman et al. 2000:135–141) occurs on the original walls of an aboveground kiva adjacent to the Main Ruin Great House (field notes on file, Crow Canyon Archaeological Center). Although this structure was rebuilt during the 1200s, the original kiva was probably contemporaneous with the early occupation of Lowry Ruin because of the shared presence of rare architectural attributes such as interpilaster shelves (Martin, Roys, and von Bonin 1936:42). Finally, the landscape mural on a kiva in the Bluff Great House has been dated to the post-Chaco period, based on associated pottery and radiocarbon dates (Cameron and Lekson 2000; Cameron 2002).

The evidence reviewed in this final section suggests that, at a minimum, BUILDINGS ARE CONTAINERS was not expressed in Chaco Canyon. It also seems highly unlikely that this metaphor could have originated in Chaco because kivas in the Northern San Juan were decorated with pottery-band murals before, during, and after the Chaco period, whereas such murals do not occur at all in Chaco Canyon architecture. Further, the fact that a local metaphor was expressed inside Northern San Juan great houses in use at the height of the Chaco Phenomenon argues that Chacoan influence did not extend to this specific cultural concept. Thus architectural metaphors lend support to emulation models of the Chaco Phenomenon in the Northern San Juan and suggest that the builders of most great houses in the region were influenced by Chaco Canyon but were not forced to abandon previous architectural metaphors.

I hope this study illustrates the benefits metaphor analysis can bring to the archaeological study of cultural cognition, the spread of material culture traits, and the problem of Chacoan influence in particular. In the specific situation discussed here, it is undeniable that architectural details of Chacoan great houses spread to outlying communities ringing the San Juan Basin. However, cultural practices can spread for a variety of reasons: because people with the practice migrate to a new area, because the practices are perceived as prestigious through association with their inventors, because they produce better-engineered tools and buildings, or because worldview concepts expressed by the practice are also spread. Methods appropriate for investigating the first three of these processes are well established, but we have lacked appropriate methods for investigating the invention and diffusion of concepts, which often lie beneath the surface of practices, using archaeological data. I believe metaphor analysis can help us fill this gap and determine whether concepts diffused along with behavioral practices in a given case. It seems to me this is a critical step in evaluating the nature of the Chaco Phenomenon and in learning more about the cultural dimensions of Pueblo prehistory in general.

Acknowledgments. I would like to thank Laurie Webster and Maxine McBrinn for inviting me to participate in the Southwest Symposium; Winston Hurst, Dale Davidson, Jerry Fetterman, Jim Hampson, and Sally Cole for sharing information on decorated buildings; Darrick Mowrey for drafting Figure 12.1; and Scott Evans for rendering the line drawings in Figures 12.2 and 12.3. Michelle Hegmon, Randy McGuire, Elizabeth Newsome, Laurie Webster, and an anonymous reviewer provided helpful comments on an earlier draft.

REFERENCES CITED

Ahlstrom, Richard V.N., David A. Breternitz, and Richard L. Warren
    1985   Archival Excavation: New Tree-Ring Dates from Lowry Ruin. *Kiva* 51(1):39–42.

Blier, Suzanne Preston
    1987   *The Anatomy of Architecture: Ontology and Metaphor in Batammaliba Architectural Expression.* University of Chicago Press, Chicago.

Bloomer, W. W.
    1989   *Moon House: A Pueblo III Cliff Dwelling Complex in Southeastern Utah.* Unpublished master's thesis, Department of Anthropology, Washington State University, Pullman.

Brew, John O.
    1946   *Archaeology of Alkali Ridge, Southeastern Utah.* Papers of the Peabody Museum of American Archaeology and Ethnology 21. Harvard University, Cambridge, Mass.

Brody, J. J.
    1991   *Anasazi and Pueblo Painting.* University of New Mexico Press, Albuquerque.

Cameron, Catherine M.
    2002   Sacred Earthen Architecture in the Northern Southwest: The Bluff Great House Berm. *American Antiquity* 67(4):677–695.

Cameron, Catherine M., and Stephen H. Lekson
    2000   *Preliminary Report on the 1998 Field Season at the Bluff Great House.* Manuscript on file, Southwest Heritage Foundation, Bluff, Utah.

Cattanach, George S.
    1980   *Long House, Mesa Verde National Park, Colorado.* Publications in Archeology 7H. National Park Service, Washington, D.C.

Cowgill, George L.
    1993   Distinguished Lecture in Archaeology: Beyond Criticizing New Archaeology. *American Anthropologist* 95:551–573.

Croft, William, and D. Alan Cruse
    2004   *Cognitive Linguistics.* Cambridge University Press, Cambridge.

Crown, Patricia L., and W. H. Wills
    2003   Modifying Pottery and Kivas at Chaco: Pentimento, Restoration, or Renewal? *American Antiquity* 68(3):511–532.

Davis, Irvine
    1959   Linguistic Clues to Northern Rio Grande Prehistory. *El Palacio* (June):73-84.

Doyel, David E., Alan H. Simmons, and P. McAnany
    1989   A Painted Kiva Near Chaco Canyon, New Mexico. In *From Chaco to Chaco: Papers in Honor of Robert H. Lister and Florence C. Lister*, ed. Meliha S. Duran and David T. Kirkpatrick, 87-102. Papers of the Archaeological Society of New Mexico 15. Archaeological Society of New Mexico, Albuquerque.

Fauconnier, Gilles
    1997   *Mappings in Thought and Language.* Cambridge University Press, Cambridge.

Fauconnier, Gilles, and Mark Turner
    1994   *Conceptual Projection and Middle Spaces.* Report 9401, UCSD Department of Cognitive Science, University of California, San Diego, La Jolla.

Fetterman, Jerry, and Linda Honeycutt
    1989   *The 1987 Mesa Verde Plaster Recordation Project.* Report Submitted to Mesa Verde National Park, Colo. Woods Canyon Archaeological Consultants, Yellow Jacket, Colo.

Fewkes, Jesse W.
    1909   *Antiquities of the Mesa Verde National Park: Spruce-Tree House.* Bureau of American Ethnology Bulletin 41. Smithsonian Institution, Washington, D.C.
    1911   *Antiquities of the Mesa Verde National Park: Cliff Palace.* Bureau of American Ethnology Bulletin 51. Smithsonian Institution, Washington, D.C.

Friedel, David A., Linda Schele, and Joy Parker
    1993   *Maya Cosmos: Three Thousand Years on the Shaman's Path.* W. Morrow, New York.

Gibbs Jr, Raymond W.
    1994   *The Poetics of Mind: Figurative Thought, Language, and Understanding.* Cambridge University Press, Cambridge.

Gunckel, L. W.
    1892   Discoveries in a Rich Field. Chapter 10 of "In Search of a Lost Race. The 'Illustrated American's' Expedition, Sent to Explore the Ruined Pueblos of the Southwest." *The Illustrated American* (August 6):559-563.

Harrington, Carobeth Tucker
    n.d.   *Southern Tiwa Katcinas.* John P. Harrington Papers, National Anthropological Archives, Smithsonian Institution, Washington, D.C. (Microfilm edition: Reel 36, Frame 0902-0930).

Harrington, John P.
    1916   *Ethnogeography of the Tewa Indians.* Twenty-Ninth Annual Report, Bureau of American Ethnology. Smithsonian Institution, Washington, D.C.

Hovezak, Mark J.
    1992   *Construction Timber Economics at Sand Canyon Pueblo.* Unpublished master's thesis, Department of Anthropology, Northern Arizona University, Flagstaff.

Judd, Neil M.
    1954   *The Material Culture of Pueblo Bonito.* Smithsonian Miscellaneous Collections 124, Washington, D.C.

Kantner, John W., and Keith W. Kintigh
    2006   The Chaco World. In *The Archaeology of Chaco Canyon, an Eleventh-Century Pueblo Regional Center*, ed. Stephen H. Lekson, 153-188. School of American Research Press, Santa Fe.

Kent, Kate Peck
    1983   *Prehistoric Textiles of the Southwest*. University of New Mexico Press, Albuquerque.

Kövecses, Zoltán
    2002   *Metaphor: A Practical Introduction*. Oxford University Press, Oxford.

Lakoff, George
    1987   *Women, Fire, and Dangerous Things: What Categories Reveal about the Mind*. University of Chicago Press, Chicago.
    1993   The Contemporary Theory of Metaphor. In *Metaphor and Thought*, 2nd ed., ed. Andrew Ortony, 202-251. Cambridge University Press, Cambridge.

Lakoff, George, and Mark Johnson
    1980   *Metaphors We Live By*. University of Chicago Press, Chicago.
    1999   *Philosophy in the Flesh: The Embodied Mind and Its Challenge to Western Thought*. Basic Books, New York.

Lekson, Stephen H.
    1983   *The Archaeology and Dendrochronology of Chetro Ketl, Chaco Canyon, New Mexico*. Reports of Chaco Center 6. Division of Cultural Research, National Park Service, U.S. Department of the Interior, Albuquerque.
    1986   *Great Pueblo Architecture of Chaco Canyon, New Mexico*. University of New Mexico Press, Albuquerque.

Lekson, Stephen H. (editor)
    2006   *The Archaeology of Chaco Canyon, an Eleventh-Century Pueblo Regional Center*. School of American Research Press, Santa Fe.

Lekson, Stephen H., Thomas C. Windes, and Peter J. McKenna
    2006   Architecture. In *The Archaeology of Chaco Canyon, an Eleventh-Century Pueblo Regional Center*, ed. Stephen H. Lekson, 67-116. School of American Research Press, Santa Fe.

Lewis-Williams, J. David
    2002   *A Cosmos in Stone: Interpreting Religion and Society through Rock Art*. Altamira, Walnut Creek, Calif.

Lipe, William D.
    2006   Notes from the North. In *The Archaeology of Chaco Canyon, an Eleventh-Century Pueblo Regional Center*, ed. Stephen H. Lekson, 261-314. School of American Research Press, Santa Fe.

Lister, Robert H.
    1965   *Contributions to Mesa Verde Archaeology: II, Site 875, Mesa Verde National Park, Colorado*. University of Colorado Studies, Series in Anthropology 11. University of Colorado Press, Boulder.

Littleton, C. Scott
    1982   *The New Comparative Mythology*. University of California Press, Berkeley.

Mahoney, Nancy M., and John Kantner
  2000   Chacoan Archaeology and Great House Communities. In *Great House Communities across the Chacoan Landscape*, ed. John Kantner and Nancy M. Mahoney, 1–16. Anthropological Papers 64. University of Arizona Press, Tucson.

Malville, J. McKim, and Gregory E. Munson
  1998   Pecked Basins of the Mesa Verde. *Southwestern Lore* 64(4):1–35.

Martin, M.
  2004   Personal communication regarding site 5MT9541, from Soil Systems, Inc., field notes, Phoenix, February 27.

Martin, Paul S., Lawrence Roys, and Gerhardt von Bonin
  1936   *Lowry Ruin in Southwestern Colorado.* Anthropological Series, Field Museum of Natural History 23(1). Field Museum Press, Chicago.

Mathien, Frances Joan
  2003   Pueblo Wall Decorations: Examples from Chaco Canyon. In *Climbing the Rocks: Papers in Honor of Helen and Jay Crotty*, ed. Reggie N. Wiseman, Thomas C. O'Laughlin, and Cordelia T. Snow, 111–126. Papers of the Archaeological Society of New Mexico 29. Archaeological Society of New Mexico, Albuquerque.

McKenna, Peter J., and H. Wolcott Toll
  1992   Regional Patterns of Great House Development among the Totah Anasazi, New Mexico. In *Anasazi Regional Organization and the Chaco System*, ed. David E. Doyel, 133–146. Anthropological Papers 5. Maxwell Museum of Anthropology, University of New Mexico, Albuquerque.

Mills, Barbara J.
  2002   Recent Research on Chaco: Changing Views on Economy, Ritual, and Society. *Journal of Archaeological Research* 10(1):65–117.

Mindeleff, Victor
  1989   *A Study of Pueblo Architecture in Tusayan and Cibola.* Reissue of 1891 ed. Smithsonian Institution Press, Washington, D.C.

Monaghan, John
  1995   *The Covenants with Earth and Rain: Exchange, Sacrifice, and Revelation in Mixtec Sociality.* University of Oklahoma Press, Norman.

Morris, Earl H., and Robert F. Burgh
  1941   *Anasazi Basketry: Basketmaker II through Pueblo III: A Study Based on Specimens from the San Juan River Country.* Carnegie Institution of Washington Publication 533. Carnegie Institution, Washington, D.C.

Morris, J. N.
  1991   *Archaeological Investigations on the Hovenweep Laterals.* Four Corners Archaeological Project Report 16. Complete Archaeological Service Associates, Cortez, Colo.

Newsome, Elizabeth
  2005   Weaving the Sky: The Cliff Palace Painted Tower. *Plateau* 2(2):28–41.

Nickens, Paul R.
  1981   *Pueblo III Communities in Transition: Environment and Adaptation in Johnson Canyon.* Memoirs of the Colorado Archaeological Society 2. Colorado Archaeological Society in cooperation with the University of Colorado, Boulder.

Nordenskiöld, Gustav
1990   The Cliff Dwellers of the Mesa Verde, Southwestern Colorado: Their Pottery and Implements, trans. D. L. Morgan. Reprinted by Mesa Verde Museum Association. Originally published 1893, P. A. Norstedt and Söner, Stockholm.

Ortiz, Alfonso
1969   The Tewa World. University of Chicago Press, Chicago.

Ortman, Scott G.
2000   Conceptual Metaphor in the Archaeological Record: Methods and an Example from the American Southwest. American Antiquity 65(4):613–645.

Ortman, Scott G., Donna M. Glowacki, Melissa J. Churchill, and Kristin A. Kuckelman
2000   Pattern and Variation in Northern San Juan Village Histories. Kiva 66(1):123–146.

Parker Pearson, Michael, and Colin Richards
1994   Ordering the World: Perceptions of Architecture, Space and Time. In Architecture and Order: Approaches to Social Space, ed. Michael Parker Pearson and Colin Richards, 1–37. Routledge, London.

Pope, Maurice
1999   The Story of Decipherment. Thames and Hudson, New York.

Rohman, Peter
2003   Site 5MT5498. In The Mid-America Pipeline Company/Williams Rocky Mountain Loop Pipeline Archaeological Data Recovery Project, Northwestern New Mexico, Western Colorado, and Eastern Utah, Volume III, Colorado Technical Report, comp. John C. Horn, Jerry Fetterman, and Linda Honeycutt, 12-1 to 12-136. Woods Canyon Archaeological Consultants, Yellow Jacket, Colo.

Sandstrom, Alan R.
1991   Corn Is Our Blood: Culture and Ethnic Identity in a Contemporary Aztec Indian Village. University of Oklahoma Press, Norman.

Schaefer, Stacey B., and Peter T. Furst
1996   People of the Peyote: Huichol Indian History, Religion, and Survival. University of New Mexico Press, Albuquerque.

Smith Jr., Howard N.
1982   Kiva Wall Paintings at Salmon Ruins, New Mexico. In Collected Papers in Honor of John W. Runyan, ed. Gerald X. Fitzgerald, 79–92. Papers of the Archaeological Society of New Mexico 7. Archaeological Society of New Mexico, Albuquerque.

Smith, Watson
1952   Kiva Mural Decorations at Awatovi and Kawaika-a. Papers of the Peabody Museum of American Archaeology and Ethnology 37. Harvard University, Cambridge, Mass.

Stirling, Matthew W.
1942   Origin Myth of Acoma and Other Records. Bureau of American Ethnology Bulletin 135. American Ethnology Bureau, Washington, D.C.

Swentzell, Rina
1990   Pueblo Space, Form, and Mythology. In Pueblo Style and Regional Architecture, ed. N. C. Markovich, W.F.E. Preiser, and F. G. Sturm, 23–30. Van Nostrand Reinhold, New York.

Truell, Marcia L.
    1986   A Summary of Small Site Architecture in Chaco Canyon, New Mexico. Part II of *Small Site Architecture of Chaco Canyon*, by Peter J. McKenna and Marcia L. Truell. Publications in Archaeology 18D, Chaco Canyon Studies, National Park Service, Santa Fe.

Van Dyke, Ruth M.
    1999   The Chaco Connection: Evaluating Bonito-Style Architecture in Outlier Communities. *Journal of Anthropological Archaeology* 18:471–506.

Varien, M. D., Scott G. Ortman, Susan C. Ryan, and Kristin A. Kuckelman
    In press Population Dynamics among Salmon's Northern Neighbors in the Central Mesa Verde Region. In *Chaco's Northern Prodigies: Salmon, Aztec, and the Ascendancy of the Middle San Juan Region after A.D. 1100*, ed. Paul F. Reed. University of Utah Press, Salt Lake City.

Windes, Thomas, and Dabney Ford
    1992   The Nature of the Early Bonito Phase. In *Anasazi Regional Organization and the Chaco System*, ed. David E. Doyel, 75–86. Anthropological Papers 5. Maxwell Museum of Anthropology, University of New Mexico, Albuquerque.

13

LIFE'S PATHWAYS

Geographic Metaphors in Ancestral Puebloan Material Culture

Kelley Hays-Gilpin

Recognizing the cultural importance of metaphors helps archaeologists and art historians understand how shared ideas facilitate interaction among social groups, past and present. Metaphors describe one thing in terms of another. We usually think of metaphors as verbal expression, but visual metaphors are just as frequent and important and are sometimes amenable to archaeological analysis. Particular expressions and contexts of metaphors should help us trace migration, pilgrimage, and the spread of religious systems across time and space. Metaphors may also provide evidence for transformations and innovations in ritual practice, iconography, and graphic expression in particular times and places.

To study metaphors in the archaeological record, the first task is to recognize material expression of important metaphors and symbols. Ethnography provides the best evidence, but in the absence of texts, one can investigate "natural symbols" and proposed universal metaphors, at least as hypotheses. The second and more difficult task is to find distinctive contexts, combinations, and expressions of such concepts. Third, we must discover how these expressions are patterned in time and space. I would like to suggest two geographic metaphors that are differentially patterned in the Puebloan region: the Pueblo banding line, with a "line break" or "breath gate" in pottery and baskets as a metaphor for women's lives, and the concept of roads converging on center places as metaphors for social organization and community histories.

In addition, Scott Ortman (2003, Chapter 12, this volume) has described a Tewa-centered basket-bowl pair as a sky-earth cosmogram. I have not found this metaphor expressed at Hopi in general, but individual Hopi clan traditions and the traditional histories of other Pueblos should be explored to see if this concept is expressed and if it useful for tracing clan histories. For example, if sky and earth are described as a basket and bowl in some clan histories, songs, or rituals, this might suggest origins for those clans that are shared or derived from Tewa groups. Some metaphorical expressions may be differentially expressed in Pueblo languages and cultures because of the individual histories of different peoples who came together over the last few thousand years to become a heterodox composite of clans, sodalities, dual divisions, villages, and language groups. Some commonly recurring metaphors probably reflect an ancient substrate of belief still held in common throughout Greater Mesoamerica. Still others may indicate ancient, common origins in pan-American and Asian shamanistic traditions, ideas about landscape and cosmology that arise from shared experiences in the natural world (natural metaphors) and the neuropsychological structures and processes shared by all anatomically modern humans.

THE LINE BREAK

Kenneth Chapman and Bruce Ellis surveyed line break features in a 1951 article entitled "The Line-Break, Problem Child of Pueblo Pottery." The line break appears earliest in seventh-century (possibly earlier) basketry in the Canyon de Chelly area (Figure 13.1). It next appears in Chaco Canyon on a small number of pottery vessels and is widespread in the Pueblo world by A.D. 1300 (Figure 13.2). This feature has a particular distribution in time, space, and media. It has different contexts in different Pueblo communities, past and present. Particular ethnographic meanings of the line break suggest it has something to do with emergence and migration, birth, women's reproduction, and craft production. Chapman and Ellis recognized a pattern, posited that the pattern was meaningful, but drew few conclusions about what that meaning might be. More than fifty years later, the line break has been considered something of an unsolved mystery, to which I propose a partial solution: the Pueblo line break on basketry and pottery vessels connects two important metaphors into one context when expressed as BODIES ARE VESSELS and LIFE IS A JOURNEY.

BODIES ARE VESSELS may be a universal metaphor, based on shared physical experience of bodies as containers for food, water, babies, and more abstract concepts such as soul, spirit, or life force. This metaphor is often expressed in the reverse as VESSELS ARE BODIES. Effigy vessels and the application of features that represent breasts to pottery vessels can express this metaphor visually by making vessels into bodies (see David, Sterner, and Gavua 1988 for an African example). Naming vessel

Figure 13.1a and b. Four unfinished burden baskets with deliberate breaks in the banding line, Canyon del Muerto. American Museum of Natural History, Division of Anthropology, catalog numbers 29.1/8840–8843 (see also Morris and Burgh 1941:figs. 14, 28). Photos by Kelley Hays-Gilpin.

Figure 13.2. *Homolovi Polychrome bowl with interior and exterior (in mirror) broken banding lines. Homolovi Polychrome is a type in the Winslow Orange Ware series.* © *The Field Museum, catalog number 72443. Photo by Kelley Hays-Gilpin.*

parts with terms such as lip, neck, shoulder, and belly expresses this metaphor verbally (for example, Bunzel 1929:13 for Zuni).

Linguists George Lakoff and Mark Johnson (1980) proposed that LIFE IS A JOURNEY is a universal conceptual metaphor. Whether this is true is not of interest here. Rather, I am interested in culturally distinct ways of expressing this metaphor. The particular Puebloan expression of this metaphor might be phrased best as LIFE IS A PATHWAY. The geographic component of this metaphor, life's journey symbolized by a footpath or roadway, is an important concept to Pueblo people today and perhaps to Native Americans generally. Many examples of the deployment of the terms "road" or "path" as symbols for Indian lives can be found in popular culture as well as in the traditions of individual cultures, for example, the intertribally negotiated title for the Museum of the American Indian exhibit *All Roads Are Good* (Smithsonian Institution 1994). Life's roads and paths are manifest in ritual lines of pollen and cornmeal, foot racing, and the depiction of footprints and animal tracks. For example, Hopi elders serving as "Katsina fathers" make roads for the katsinas to follow, and certain ritual practices are said to make roads for rain clouds to follow from their mountain homes to dry fields. Roads of cornmeal are particularly important in life-cycle events, such as baby naming (Bradfield 1995:29) and marriage (Parsons 1939:362). At death, a cotton thread with a feather serves as a "road" for the deceased's "breath body" (Bradfield 1995:40). I suggest that the broad line painted around the rim of some pottery vessels may express the same conceptual metaphor at a personal or individual scale and evoke the body-as-vessel metaphor at the same time.

Ethnographic Evidence

Ruth Bunzel (1929:69) translated the Zuni word for the line break, *onane*, as "the road," representing in particular the life of the potter: "When I finish it, I shall finish my road"—that is, "end my life." Potters at Santa Ana told Kenneth Chapman that "the break formerly was an intimate and personal affair to the potter, which

Life's Pathways

had to do with the well-being of her family—its continuation and health." Jemez potters said the line break "was a women's matter" (Chapman and Ellis 1951:277-278). Elsie Clews Parsons (1939:91) reported that Hopi potters of childbearing age made a line break to avert difficult labor and the possibility of stillbirth. Alexander Stephen translated a Hopi term as "breath gate" (but did not provide the Hopi term; Stephen cited in Patterson 1994), in which the line represents the path and the break is a gate or opening for the breath. George Wharton James (1901:194) connected Hopi coiled basket finishing techniques to pregnancy as well: unmarried women left the foundation material exposed, called the "flowing gate." Married women of childbearing age cut the foundation material but did not stitch over it, called the "open gate." Widows and postmenopausal women cut and covered the end of the last coil, called the "closed gate." Alexander Stephen's 1890 manuscript likewise connects the line break on pottery to women and childbearing: "If the woman who decorates the vessel is old and past the child-bearing period, she paints a completely surrounding band; if she has had a child recently or expects to ever have a child, the band is not quite completed, she leaves a small space of a quarter or half an inch unpainted. Young unmarried girls are not permitted to use this surrounding band in their pottery decoration" (quoted in Patterson 1994:35).

The ethnographic pattern converges on the idea that LIFE IS A PATHWAY. Additional aspects of life's path can be represented visually by a circle, a spiral, a "gate" through a boundary of some kind, and a maze, as in Piman "man in the maze" baskets and Hopi petroglyphs that consultants identify with migration stories (Figure 13.3). At least some Pueblos associate the broken banding line with women's reproductive status and capacities. By using this feature on pottery and basketry containers, they link LIFE IS A PATHWAY to BODIES ARE VESSELS. In turn, women's bodies may be viewed as vessels that bring forth blood, water, and new lives the same way that containers crafted by women hold and bring forth food and water.

Archaeological Evidence

How does the archaeological record reflect the history and context of the line break? The earliest deliberate line break in Chapman and Ellis's survey appears on a few coiled baskets from Canyon del Muerto that date to the Basketmaker III period, circa the A.D. 500s-700s (Morris and Burgh 1941:figs. 14, 28) (Figure 13.1). I have found no convincing earlier examples. A close look at other Basketmaker III coiled baskets with woven-in colored decoration reveals a plausible technological source for the line break. The weaver worked outward from the center in a spiral fashion. To make the framing line for a banded design, the weaver stitched colored splints until she reached the place where she began. She was now working on the coil above the previous one, leaving an unavoidable jog in what would otherwise be a perfect circle. In most baskets of this era, there is no deliberate opening. The colored splints meet corner to corner, suggesting, if not actually effecting, a break. These jogs appear on both the lower and upper framing lines. Weavers could have

Figure 13.3. Pathways in petroglyphs. (above) rectilinear spiral with attached figure from La Cienega, New Mexico. Photo by Kelley Hays-Gilpin; (left) labyrinth petroglyphs near Shipaulovi, Second Mesa, Arizona (adapted from Parsons 1936:fig. 516); (below) petroglyphs from Wupatki National Monument interpreted as migration story by Hopi consultants. The spiral refers to a pathway to or from a middle place. The animals on the right represent clans. Photo by Kelley Hays-Gilpin.

hidden this little jog by incorporating it into one of the three to five spokes of the design that radiate out from the inner framing line to join the outer framing line below the rim, but they rarely or never did. Usually, they left it visible. Rarely, they enhanced it.

All the examples of baskets with a deliberate and enhanced line break come from a single cache of unfinished burden baskets from a juvenile burial in Mummy Cave, Canyon del Muerto (Morris and Burgh 1941:figs. 14, 28). Morris and Burgh thought they might be the work of a single weaver. On three of the four baskets, when stitching the two colored coils of the lower framing line, the weaver switched back to undyed splints before completing each coil, deliberately creating a line break much wider than a natural jog occasioned by the coiling technique. This break appears on the part of each basket that would rest against the lower back of the person carrying it and would therefore have been hidden from view while the basket was in use.

It is easy to imagine how one would transfer this broken banding line to pottery: one simply does not paint a complete line in the borders of the pattern. But the earliest pottery painters did not do that. The earliest painted pottery in the Four Corners area dates from the Basketmaker III time period as well. Vessels were made by coiling the clay in a spiral fashion, then scraping and smoothing away the coil joins. The fact that a spiral motion for building a vessel was selected by potters already familiar with coiled basketry is interesting. Painted designs on early pottery appear to derive from coiled basketry as well, at least in terms of using a center-focused radial design with small repeated geometric units (Figure 13.4; see Morris and Burgh 1941 for basketry patterns). Bowl rims were often painted with a solid black line, as in tray baskets of the period, but no line break is necessary because in painting there are no technological constraints on making a complete circle.

The line break first appears on pottery in the Pueblo II–Pueblo III period in the San Juan Basin, including Chaco Canyon. Whether this use of a line break derives from basketry or not is debatable, but I suggest that we are seeing similar expressions of a shared metaphor, regardless of whether there is a historical, technological connection. A long temporal gap argues against such continuity, but the context and position of the banding line on pottery suggest there may be a connection. The line is always in the same position on pottery and on coiled baskets—as a broad banding line, a thin framing line, a rim coil, or some combination. This is an example of what Ortman (2000) calls the invariance principle: a feature mapped from one medium to another will appear in the same structural position. Because baskets and pottery vessels often have similar shapes and are used for containers, the banding line could have been transferred easily from basketry, as source domain, to painted pottery, the target domain. But it did not transfer in all times and places, and in the Basketmaker period and the later Pueblo II–III periods, its use was extremely rare.

The line break is rare but present on Red Mesa, Puerco, Escavada, Reserve, and later Cibola White Ware types that typically have banded designs. The line

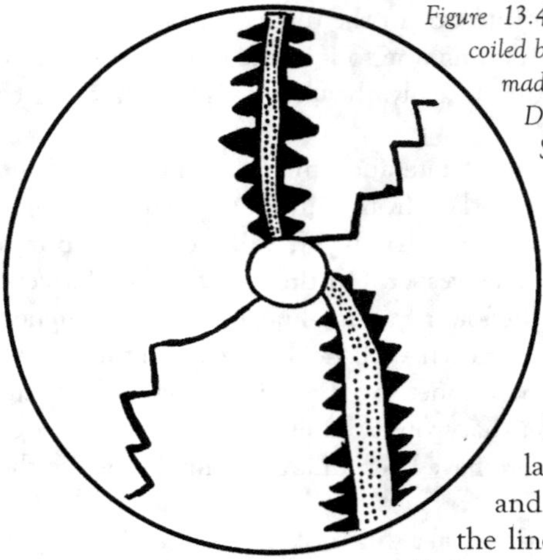

Kelley Hays-Gilpin

Figure 13.4. *Early painted pottery with design based on coiled basket. La Plata Black-on-white, almost certainly made sometime between A.D. 620–700. Prayer Rock District, Broken Flute Cave, Pithouse 6. Arizona State Museum catalog number A-14399. Drawing by Kelley Hays-Gilpin.*

break first became a common feature on Gallina Black-on-white pottery of the late 1100s and early 1200s in northern New Mexico (Chapman and Ellis 1951). It appears frequently in the late 1200s in the Hopi, Little Colorado, and Zuni areas. By the 1300s and 1400s, the line break was very widespread in almost all the pueblos—on Jeddito Yellow Ware from the Hopi Mesas, Winslow Orange Ware (Figure 13.2) from the Lower Puerco to the Middle Little Colorado, Gila and Tonto polychromes from central Arizona, Zuni glaze types such as Pinnawa Glaze-on-white and Kechipawan Polychrome, and Rio Grande glaze ware and biscuit types. It was apparently so important at Hopi that the Smithsonian collections contain a Jeddito Black-on-yellow bowl with a line break scratched into what was a complete banding line until after the bowl was fired (Figure 13.5). The maker or a user apparently had second thoughts about the closed line and added the feature later.

The line break appears on historic painted pottery with the greatest frequency in the Keresan-speaking pueblos, especially Cochiti; somewhat frequently at Hopi (including Arizona Tewa) and Zuni; and occasionally at Tewa-speaking San Ildefonso. An example from Santo Domingo appears in Figure 13.6. An appliquéd fillet with a line break was frequent on Taos and Picuris utility ware from 1500 on (Chapman and Ellis 1951). Navajo and eastern Apache utility pottery has a "necklace" with an indented texture reminiscent of a basket coil, as well as a line break. Many researchers draw a connection between the line break on pottery and features of Navajo baskets, sand paintings, and bordered loom-woven textiles. In all these media and language groups, across nearly 2,000 years, is meaning shared as well as form? Archaeologists typically avoid the question of symbolic meaning, and for good reason. We cannot know for certain what people were thinking. But we can make some more and less plausible interpretations. All I intend here is to present what I view as a plausible interpretation.

The parallels between signaling "three life stages" with a particular coil finish in Hopi coiled basketry and a banding line in pottery confirm a conceptual connection between the two kinds of containers. In light of the Hopi explanation for the line break, it is worth thinking about the context of the Mummy Cave baskets that seem to bear the earliest recorded line breaks: they were unfinished when deposited

Life's Pathways

Figure 13.5. Banding line on Jeddito Black-on-yellow bowl from Homol'ovi I with post-firing line break scratched in. The vessel appears to have been painted by a beginner. Control of lines, proportions, and spacing are comparatively poor. Department of Anthropology, National Museum of Natural History, Smithsonian Institution, catalog number 156725. Photo by Peter Pilles.

as offerings with the dead body of a child. The baskets are very similar to each other in layout, color, materials, and technique but are different sizes and have different designs. If we can speculate about metaphors here, what about unfinished baskets and the unfinished life of a child? Perhaps several family members each made an offering that encoded tribute to an unfinished life.

If the broken banding line began as a metaphor for "life's path," if baskets were metaphors for people, or both, then crossover from basketry into other media, such as pottery and textiles, should be no surprise. Nor should we be troubled by the notion that interaction at the level of the individual and family unit might have spanned centuries and language groups, spreading particular graphic expressions of metaphors to other times and places.

Perhaps the spiral at the heart of the coiled basket is the heart of the "life pathway" metaphor. This can be tested to some extent by looking at the contexts and meanings of spirals in still other media and discussing them with Native speakers of various southwestern languages. Hopi identification of spirals in petroglyphs as "migration symbols" (Figure 13.3) certainly fits the "life's pathway" metaphor. This connection invites us to look for the LIFE IS A PATHWAY metaphor in other contexts.

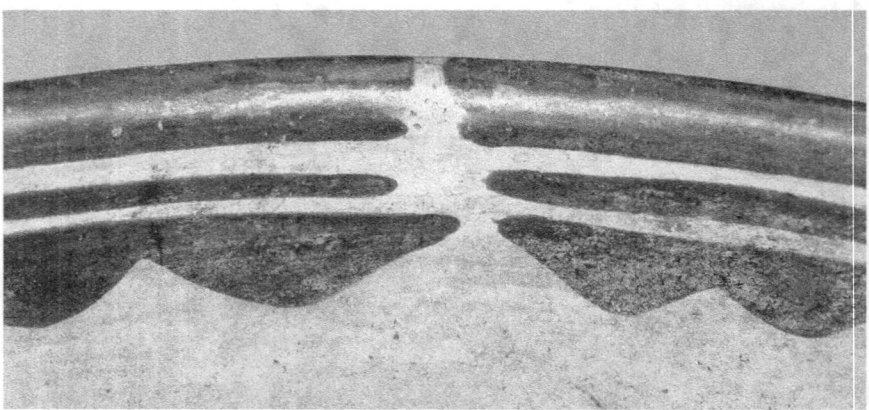

Figure 13.6. Close-up of triple line break at the rim of a bowl from Santo Domingo, probably early twentieth century. Amerind Foundation catalog number 251. Courtesy, Amerind Foundation, Dragoon, Arizona. Photo by Kelley Hays-Gilpin.

Social Scales

Broken banding lines and ceramic vessels as symbols of women's lives and bodies appear to refer to individual and family levels of social scale. A few other studies have worked at this scale, including Hannah Huse's (1976) search for individual potters in fourteenth-century Hopi vessel assemblages from Earl Morris's excavations at Kawayka'a on Antelope Mesa and work on Mesoamerican figurines by Ann Cyphers Guillén (1993), Rosemary Joyce (2000), and others. Archaeologists studying religion and ideology usually work at broader social scales, such as community, regional, or language group scales. Recently, archaeologists and Native American historians and cultural specialists have collaborated to bring archaeology and ethnography together to investigate clan migrations and the sources and transmission of ritual practices—processes important at larger social scales (Bernardini 2005; Colwell-Chanthaponh 2003; Ferguson and Loma'omvaya 1999; Ferguson, Colwell-Chanthaponh, and Anyon 2004). Exploration of geographic metaphors such as roads, center places, and a world axis, which operate at the level of intercommunity and human-supernatural relationships, can contribute to these efforts as well.

ROADS AND CENTER PLACES

If roads and paths are important in one domain, as in the Pueblo line break, then metaphor theory would predict their appearance in other domains as well. As in Mesoamerica and northern Mexico, some Pueblo rituals emphasize the sun's daily and seasonal journeys across the sky and its posited journeys through the underworld at night. The Milky Way is sometimes said to be a pathway. Stories and ritual performances trace pilgrimage and migration routes in detail and sometimes refer to routes and sites along them as trails and "footprints of the ancestors" (Colwell-Chanthaponh 2003; Ferguson and Loma'omvaya 1999), recalling the Mesoamerican convention of depicting footprints when describing a journey in Aztec codex painting (e.g., Boone 2003:169), seen also in Teotihuacan mural painting (e.g., de la Fuente 2001:figs. 6.11, 14.4-5). Thinking about the social and spiritual meanings of roads and pathways invites archaeologists to think more broadly about depictions of footprints in Puebloan rock art, as well as actual sandals and sandal effigies (often called "lasts" [see, e.g., Wetherill 1897], but stone and wooden figures of sandals almost certainly did not function as lasts).

Archaeological evidence of roads and pathways sometimes appears "on the ground" and indicates that prehistoric roads were about more than moving people and cargo from one place to another. Some have suggested that because many Chacoan roads are discontinuous and do not always take the easiest route over difficult terrain, they might best be interpreted as metaphorical or symbolic expressions rather than actual trails followed by traders, builders, and pilgrims (Roney 1992). Whether roads referred to paths taken by heroes, supernaturals, the dead, or the Sun or other celestial personages may perhaps never be known, but detailed fieldwork tracing their actual physical layout is indispensable for understanding them, as is tribal consultation and ethnography. Because they are writ large on the landscape and their construction must have required participation by many individuals working together, Chacoan roads probably refer to larger-scale social groups, such as ritual sodalities, mobile family groups such as the lineage components of groups Hopi people now call "clans," and residential communities. They may simultaneously symbolize connections among cosmological layers, natural forces, and the groups of people who built and used them.

The arrangement of Pueblo roads and pathways also implies the concept of a middle place, such as the emergence place, and the concept of a final migration destination. Oral traditions recall individuals, clans, or small groups of people who travel far away from their place of emergence or birth, have adventures, and return to their middle place. These are not only stories about the past but charters for future behavior. Physical representation of the middle place, whether plaza, shrine, kiva, or *sipapu*, always has an important ritual role (Swentzell 2001).

One kind of middle place is nearly universally understood as an axis mundi, or world tree, connecting upper and lower worlds of a tiered universe. Recognizing material expressions of the axis mundi concept has been covered in great detail by those exploring the archaeology of shamanism the world over (Pearson 2001:69-70). The Pueblo *sipapu* and kiva ladder broadly fit this theme. Again, what should interest archaeologists are the particular expressions and uses made of these concepts, not the near universality of a tiered universe and world tree concept or whether the shamanic worldview is common to all or most hunter-gatherers, to all or most Native Americans, and so on. In spite of a broadly shared worldview, some communities encourage individual shamanic movements between worlds and some, such as the Hopi, do not, at least not in historic times. The Hopi concept of an underworld that reverses the conventions of this world in dynamic, complementary, interpenetrating dualities (summer/winter, left-handed/right-handed, dead/living, katsinas/humans, and so on), the emergence/migration/return-to-center theme, and the roles of ritual practitioners in the hydrological and solar cycles would be fruitful schemata to seek in material culture as well as in oral traditions.

Acknowledgments. I extend my thanks and congratulations to the organizers of and participants in the 2004 Southwest Symposium. I floated some of these ideas at the 2003 Society for American Archaeology annual meeting in Milwaukee and at the Vías del Noroeste Segundo Coloquio Internacional in Real de Catorce, San Luís Potosí, and would like to thank their organizers as well. As always, I am deeply indebted to the curators and collections managers of many museums for collections access, including the Amerind Foundation, American Museum of Natural History, Arizona State Museum, Chicago Field Museum of Natural History, Harvard Peabody Museum, and Museum of Northern Arizona.

REFERENCES CITED

Bernardini, Wesley
    2005   *Hopi Oral Tradition and the Archaeology of Identity.* University of Arizona Press, Tucson.

Boone, Elizabeth Hill
    2003   Glorious Imperium: Understanding Land and Community in Moctezuma's Mexico. In *Moctezuma's Mexico: Visions of the Aztec World,* rev. ed., ed. David Carrasco and Eduardo Matos Moctezuma, 159–173. University Press of Colorado, Boulder.

Bradfield, Maitland
    1995   *An Interpretation of Hopi Culture.* Published by the author, Duffield, Derbyshire, England. Reprinted and revised from the author's 1973 publication, *A Natural History of Associations: A Study in the Meaning of Community,* Duckworth, London.

Bunzel, Ruth L.
    1929   *The Pueblo Potter: A Study of Creative Imagination in Primitive Art.* Columbia University Press, New York.

Chapman, Kenneth M., and Bruce T. Ellis
    1951   The Line-Break, Problem Child of Pueblo Pottery. *El Palacio* 58(9):251–289.

Colwell-Chanthaponh, Chip
    2003   Signs in Place: Native American Perspectives of the Past in the San Pedro Valley of Southeastern Arizona. *Kiva* 69:5–29.

Cyphers Guillén, Ann
    1993   Women, Rituals, and Social Dynamics at Ancient Chalcatzingo. *Latin American Antiquity* 4(3):209–224.

David, Nicholas, Judy Sterner, and Kodzo Gavua
    1988   Why Pots Are Decorated. *Current Anthropology* 29(3):365–389.

de la Fuente, Beatriz (editor)
    2001   *La Pintura Mural Prehispánica en México: Teotihuacan*, Volume 1. Instituto de Investigaciones Estéticas, Universidad Autónoma de México, México.

Ferguson, T. J., Chip Colwell-Chanthaponh, and Roger Anyon
    2004   One Valley, Many Histories: Tohono O'odham, Hopi, Zuni, and Western Apache History in the San Pedro Valley. *Archaeology Southwest* 18(1):1-14.

Ferguson, T. J., and Micah Loma'omvaya
    1999   *Hoopoq'uaqam niqw Wukoskyavi (Those Who Went to the Northeast and Tonto Basin): Hopi-Salado Cultural Affiliation Study*. Report on file at the Hopi Cultural Preservation Office, Kykotsmovi, Ariz.

Huse, Hannah
    1976   Identification of the Individual in Archaeology: A Case Study from the Prehistoric Site of Kawaika-a. Ph.D. dissertation, Department of Anthropology, University of Colorado, Boulder. University Microfilms, Ann Arbor.

James, George Wharton
    1901   *Indian Basketry*. Privately published by the author, Pasadena, Calif.

Joyce, Rosemary
    2000   *Gender and Power in Prehispanic Mesoamerica*. University of Texas Press, Austin.

Lakoff, George, and Mark Johnson
    1980   *Metaphors We Live By*. University of Chicago Press, Chicago.

Morris, Earl H., and Robert F. Burgh
    1941   *Anasazi Basketry: Basketmaker II through Pueblo III: A Study Based on Specimens from the San Juan River Country*. Carnegie Institution of Washington Publication 533. Carnegie Institution, Washington, D.C.

Ortman, Scott
    2000   Conceptual Metaphor in the Archaeological Record: Methods and an Example from the American Southwest. *American Antiquity* 65(4):613-645.
    2003   Using Cognitive Semantics to Relate Mesa Verde Archaeology to Modern Pueblo Languages. Paper presented at the Fifth World Archaeological Congress, Washington, D.C.

Parsons, Elsie Clews
    1939   *Pueblo Indian Religion*. University of Chicago Press, Chicago.

Parsons, Elsie Clews (editor)
    1936   *Hopi Journal of Alexander M. Stephen*, 2 volumes. Columbia University Press, New York.

Patterson, Alex
    1994   *Hopi Pottery Symbols*. Johnson, Boulder. (Based on the work of Alexander M. Stephen.)

Pearson, James L.
    2001   *Shamanism and the Ancient Mind: A Cognitive Approach to Archaeology*. AltaMira, Walnut Creek, Calif.

Roney, John R.
    1992   Prehistoric Roads and Regional Integration in the Chacoan System. In *Anasazi Regional Organization and the Chaco System*, ed. David E. Doyel, 123-131. Anthropo-

logical Papers 5. Maxwell Museum of Anthropology, University of New Mexico, Albuquerque.

Smithsonian Institution
   1994   *All Roads Are Good: Native Voices on Life and Culture.* Smithsonian Institution Press in association with the National Museum of the American Indian, Smithsonian Institution, Washington, D.C.

Swentzell, Rina
   2001   Centers in the Pueblo World. In *The Road to Aztlan: Art from a Mythic Homeland*, ed. Virginia M. Fields and Victor Zamudio-Taylor, 310–317. Los Angeles County Museum of Art, Los Angeles.

Wetherill, Richard
   1897   Sandal Stones. *The Antiquarian* 1:248.

14

THE DYNAMIC NATURE OF CULTURAL IDENTITY DURING THE FOURTEENTH AND FIFTEENTH CENTURIES IN CENTRAL NEW MEXICO

Suzanne L. Eckert

Architectural, ceramic, kiva mural, and faunal data from two sites along the Lower Rio Puerco in central New Mexico indicate that fourteenth- and fifteenth-century residents of the region were struggling with two contradictory aspects of identity. On the one hand, residents of the region had adopted a new ritual system that focused on village-wide social integration. On the other hand, social groups with different migration histories into the villages were emphasizing their unique heritage. I argue that these seemingly contradictory behaviors reflect the dynamic nature of identity and the attempts made by people to negotiate their place in a new social landscape affected by immigration and population aggregation.

The Lower Rio Puerco region (Eckert 2003; Eckert and Cordell 2004; Roney 1996) is located west of Albuquerque in central New Mexico (Figure 14.1). During the Pueblo IV period (A.D. 1300–1500), the local population nucleated into two large pueblos, Pottery Mound and Hummingbird Pueblo. Current data (Eckert 2003) suggest that Hummingbird Pueblo had two occupational components: an early component dating to A.D. 1250–1300 and a late component, A.D. 1300–1400+. Pottery Mound had only one occupation, A.D. 1350–1450+. Pottery from both these villages suggests technological and decorative influence from the Western Pueblo

Suzanne L. Eckert

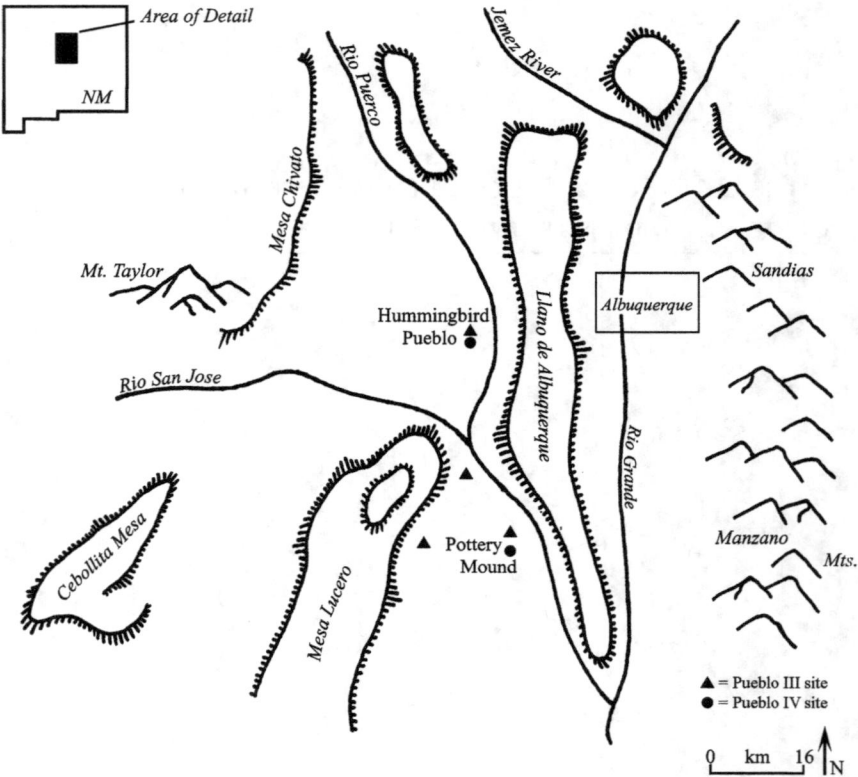

Figure 14.1. Map of the Pueblo Southwest showing the location of Hummingbird Pueblo and Pottery Mound in the Lower Rio Puerco study area.

and Rio Grande regions (Eckert 2003). Especially significant during the 1300s is the introduction of glaze technology into the study area, which quickly replaced the previous black-on-white traditions (Eckert 2003; Eckert 2006b). The shift from carbon- and mineral-painted, white-slipped pottery to glaze-painted, red-slipped pottery was a dramatic transition in terms of both decorative and technological style (Eckert 2006a; Eckert 2006b).

RITUAL AND SOCIAL INTEGRATION

Various researchers have made a connection between the spread of red-slipped, glaze-decorated vessels and the adoption of a new ritual system during the fourteenth century (Crown 1994:108; Graves and Eckert 1998:279; Spielmann 1998). To explore this possibility in the Lower Rio Puerco area, I examined changes in

The Dynamic Nature of Cultural Identity during the Fourteenth and Fifteenth Centuries

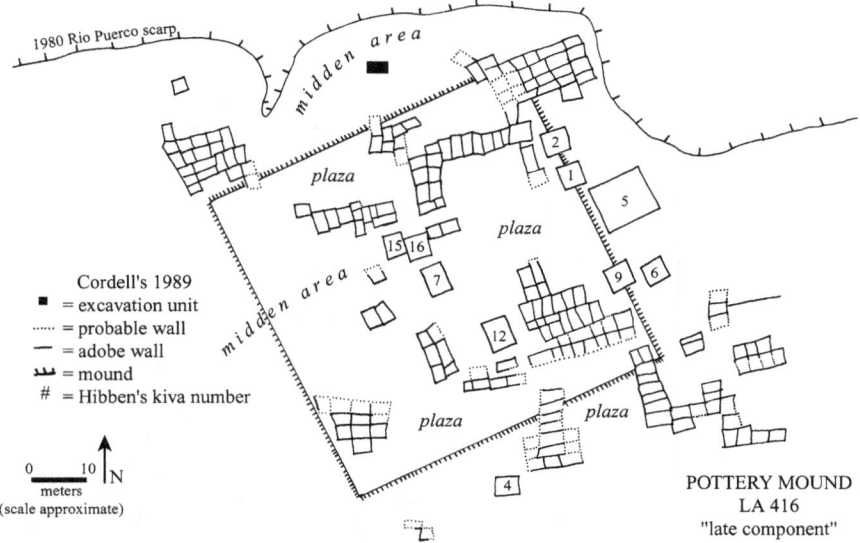

Figure 14.2. Map of Pottery Mound (after Eckert 2003:32).

non-ceramic material culture that occurred at the same time as the introduction of glaze technology into the study area. Architectural data from Pottery Mound (Figure 14.2) and Hummingbird Pueblo (Figure 14.3) show that both sites have plaza spaces and rectangular kivas. These architectural features represent new ceremonial structures in the Lower Rio Puerco area during the 1300s. Prior to this time, plazas were absent in the study area, and kivas were round (Eckert 2003). The presence of these new structures at both villages reflects new ceremonial spaces in the study area and implies potential changes in the local ritual system.

Faunal data from the study area (Table 14.1) suggest that residents of the area began to incorporate feathers from various bird species into rituals during the 1300s and that this pattern continued into the 1400s (Clark and Eckert 2004; Eckert 2003). There are no perching birds or raptors in the thirteenth-century avifauna assemblage from the study area. In the fourteenth- and fifteenth-century assemblages, however, raptors make up the majority of wild bird species, although perching birds and waterbirds are also present. The importance of birds, especially feathers from raptors and perching birds, in modern Pueblo ritual has been noted by various Southwest ethnographers (Bunzel 1932; Parsons 1925, 1936; Stephen 1936). In the archaeological record, birds and feathers are portrayed on rock art but never in a hunting context (Schaafsma 1980). Further, birds—including raptors, roadrunners, parrots, turkeys, waterfowl, and hummingbirds—portrayed on kiva murals at Pottery Mound are always shown in a ritual context, sitting either on or around masked dancers (Crotty 1990; Emslie and Hargrave 1978; Hibben 1975). Again, there are

273

Suzanne L. Eckert

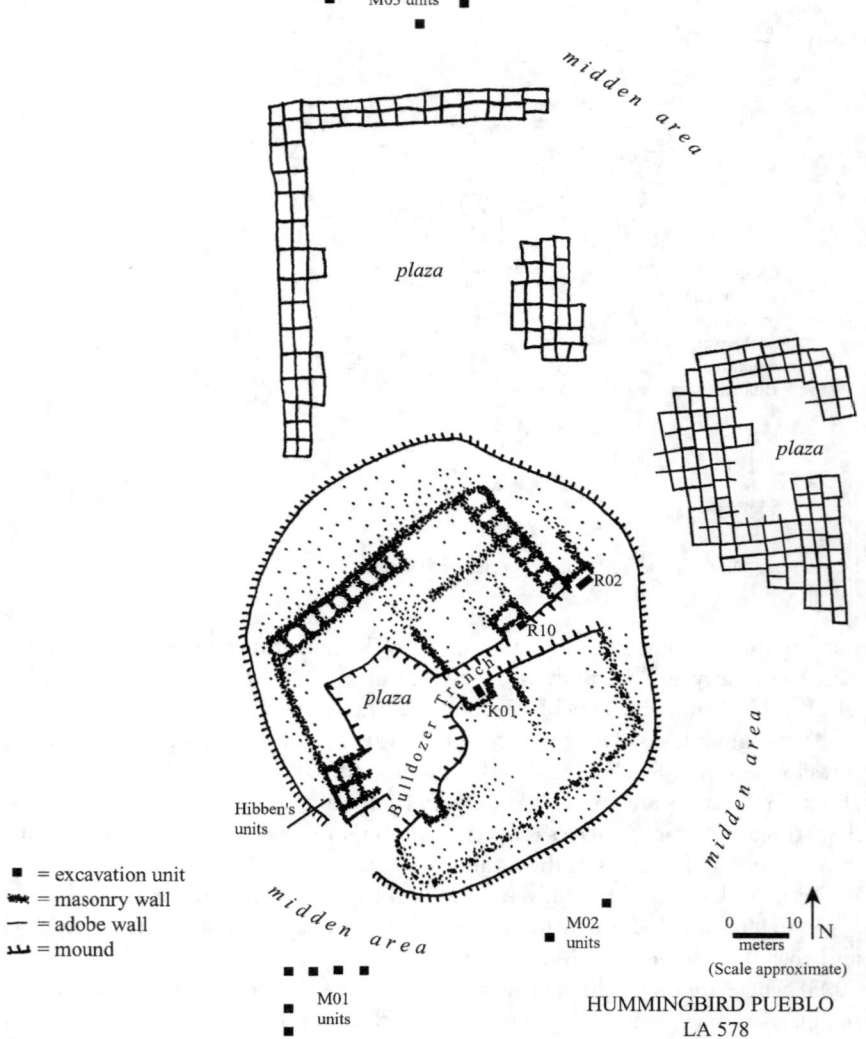

Figure 14.3. Map of Hummingbird Pueblo (after Eckert 2003:33).

no portrayals of birds being consumed for food. Combined, these data suggest that the collection of nonfood bird species began in the study area during the fourteenth century, probably in association with new ritual practices adopted at this time.

A new suite of icons also appears in the study area during the fourteenth century that is associated with both glaze-decorated pottery and kiva murals (Figure 14.4). The vast majority of icons identified on pottery are on glaze-decorated pottery;

Table 14.1. Major avifauna taxa during the 1200s, 1300s, and 1400s in the Lower Rio Puerco Area (from Eckert 2003).

	Turkeys (%)	Water Fowl (%)	Perching Birds (%)	Raptors (%)
Major avifauna taxa in the 1200s (from Hummingbird Pueblo, early occupation)				
NISP	89	11	0	0
MNI	67	33	0	0
Major avifauna taxa in the 1300s (from Hummingbird Pueblo, late occupation)				
NISP	80	2	2	16
MNI	43	14	n/a	43
Major avifauna taxa in the 1300s and 1400s (from Pottery Mound)				
NISP	86	1	6	7
MNI	77	4	4	15

NISP = Number of individual specimens; MNI = Minimum number of individuals

no icons were identified on the thirteenth-century white wares produced in the region (Table 14.2). The introduction of a new suite of motifs associated with glaze-decorated pottery indicates the presence of a new iconic system in the Lower Rio Puerco area during the fourteenth century. The most common icons recorded on sherds include eyes, snakes/lightning, and birds, with more than one incident of serpents, masked figures, stars, feathers, clouds, and dragonflies also recorded (Eckert 2003). This new iconic system is also present on kiva murals at Pottery Mound (Crotty 1995; Hibben 1975), further supporting the idea that a new ritual system, of which glaze-decorated pottery was but a part, was introduced into the study area. Iconic motifs on kiva murals are more detailed than those on pottery, allowing researchers to identify birds to species, specific ceremonial personages, and the use of specific ritual paraphernalia including decorated pottery, prayer sticks, spears, shields, and animal skins (Crotty 1990, 1995; Emslie and Hargrave 1978; Hibben 1975).

Patricia Crown (1994) considers the common icons identified on pottery in the Lower Rio Puerco area as part of an iconic system concerned with fertility, weather control, and community well-being. She argues that this iconic system was associated with the spread of the Southwest Regional Cult, an ideology and ritual system that integrated disparate groups. All common icons crosscut most fourteenth- and fifteenth-century glaze-decorated ceramic types in the study area (Table 14.2) (Eckert 2003). In other words, potters, regardless of their group affiliations, were choosing from the same suite of motifs. This suggests that these icons were not related to signaling group identity but rather may have been associated with concepts of universal concern, such as rain, fertility, or group well-being. The katsina religion, which is part of the Southwest Regional Cult as defined by Crown (1994), is specifically focused on masked dancers believed to be katsina spirits (Adams 1991; Crown 1994). It has been argued that the katsina religion, which swept across the Pueblo world during the fourteenth century, was focused on village-wide social integration (Adams 1991; Crown 1994). Kiva murals at Pottery Mound, as well as ceramic

Suzanne L. Eckert

Figure 14.4. Interiors of four Pottery Mound Polychrome bowls and one bowl fragment from Pottery Mound showing examples of icons found on fourteenth- and fifteenth-century pottery in the study area (after Eckert 2003:102). Stippled areas represent red paint.

iconography from both Pottery Mound and Hummingbird Pueblo, portray masked figures that have been recognized as part of katsina ceremonialism. The similarities between many of the portrayals of masked dancers on kiva murals at Pottery Mound and modern Pueblo katsinas argue strongly in favor of the presence of the katsina religion at this village.

IMMIGRATION AND GROUP IDENTITY

Does the adoption of glaze-painted pottery by all residents of the Lower Rio Puerco area, along with a new ritual system focused on social integration, mean families in the region gave up their identities based on unique social and migration histories?

The Dynamic Nature of Cultural Identity during the Fourteenth and Fifteenth Centuries

Table 14.2. Icons recorded on sherds from Hummingbird Pueblo and Pottery Mound.

Ceramic Type	Serpent	Mask	Eye	Star	Snakes/Lightning	Bird	Feather	Dragonfly	Cloud
Ceramic types dating to the 1200s									
White wares	–	–	–	–	–	–	–	–	–
St. Johns types	–	–	–	–	–	–	–	–	–
Ceramic types dating to the 1300s and 1400s									
Western Pueblo glaze ware, local copies	–	–	20	–	9	–	–	–	–
Early Rio Grande Glaze-on-red	2	2	32	5	89	15	1	6	9
Early Rio Grande Glaze-on-yellow	–	1	10	–	23	1	1	–	6
Early Rio Grande Glaze-on-polychrome	–	–	19	2	39	4	–	–	2
Intermediate Rio Grande Glaze	–	–	2	1	–	1	–	1	1
Hummingbird Red-on-buff	–	–	1	–	1	–	–	–	–
Pottery Mound Polychrome	–	1	5	–	3	2	–	1	1
Hidden Mountain Polychrome	–	–	4	–	4	1	–	–	–

Among various historic Pueblo groups, such histories play an important role in group identity. To explore this question at Pottery Mound and Hummingbird Pueblo, I examined the co-occurrence of technological and decorative styles on pottery.

Four technological styles were identified, based on differences in surface treatment and temper choice, in the fourteenth- and fifteenth-century ceramic assemblage (Table 14.3). I believe these technological styles represent communities of practice as envisioned by Miriam Stark (2006). Communities of practice are social networks in which potters learn their craft from other women in the community. These communities are defined by a shared history of practice, not by spatial constraints. As a result of migration, marriage, and other forms of social interaction, multiple communities of practice can exist within a given village, and a single community of practice can crosscut multiple villages. Patterns in local pottery styles result from potters making different decisions throughout the production process but using a similar set of tools and techniques available to all potters within an area. Some of these decisions are conscious and may reflect potters' decisions to ally themselves with specific social or economic groups. But many of these decisions are unconscious and reflect the general context of socialization and cultural reproduction.

In my dissertation (Eckert 2003), I trace the four technological styles, or communities of practice, to different regions of origin: specifically, the northern portion of the study area, the southern portion, and the Zuni and Hopi regions. I argue that residents of Pottery Mound and Hummingbird Pueblo were disparate social groups from these four areas. If folks were using their regions of origin as a form of identity,

Suzanne L. Eckert

Table 14.3. Communities of practice based on technological styles.

Region of Origin	Temper	Slip
Southern Lower Rio Puerco	rock	self
Northern Lower Rio Puerco	sherd	thin or self
Zuni	sherd	thick
Hopi	untempered	self (or thick?)

I expect these communities of practice to co-occur with decorative style-visual differences on pottery that could have been used to emphasize differences between these groups. Using ceramic types as a reflection of a suite of different decorative attributes, including slip color and design style, I found a co-occurrence of some types with technological styles (Table 14.4). Specifically, at Hummingbird Pueblo, people from Zuni produced pottery types that were visually distinct. Similarly, at Pottery Mound, groups from both Hopi and Zuni were producing visually distinct types.

Although it appears that some potters in the Lower Rio Puerco area chose to use their products to emphasize a social identity that included a unique migration history, different potter communities were reaffirming such social boundaries on at least two different levels. At both Hummingbird Pueblo and Pottery Mound, immigrant potters from the Zuni area used white and buff slips that would have been noticeably different from the more typical red slip, even at a distance. Vessels slipped in white or buff could have signaled the potter's identity from across a room, kiva, or plaza space. Because of this public distinctiveness, it seems reasonable that the scale of social boundary maintenance emphasized by these slip colors would have been below the scale of the village but above the scale of the immediate family—possibly at the scale of the lineage, sodality, or other social grouping that divided villages between immigrant and local groups.

At Pottery Mound, some potters chose to decorate the interior of their bowls with a unique combination of decorative attributes, including a yellow-buff slip, distinct design style, and specific icons. For reasons discussed elsewhere (Eckert 2003), I believe at least some of these potters were immigrants from the Hopi area. Whether these potters were immigrants or not, only people within the immediate vicinity of a bowl would have noticed the decoration on the interior. As such, the interiors of bowls would have signaled group affiliation to people who were probably members of the same intimate social group. Decorations on the interior of the vessels may have served to remind members of their group obligations and to reaffirm their group's unique heritage.

Two other lines of evidence from the study area suggest that kin-based social units recognized, and possibly emphasized, their unique social and migration histories. First, village layout at both Pottery Mound (Figure 14.2) and Hummingbird Pueblo (Figure 14.3) suggests spatial segregation of social units. The layout of both sites is the result of multiple construction events rather than a single planned building episode. Hummingbird Pueblo has three roomblocks, each focused on its own

The Dynamic Nature of Cultural Identity during the Fourteenth and Fifteenth Centuries

Table 14.4. Communities of identity based on co-occurrence of technological and decorative traits.

	Northern Lower Rio Puerco (%)	Zuni (%)	Southern Lower Rio Puerco (%)	Hopi (%)
Hummingbird Pueblo, late occupation				
Locally produced Western Pueblo types	–	100	–	–
Glaze-on-red	45	22	33	–
Glaze-on-polychrome	24	36	40	–
Red-on-buff	–	100	–	–
Pottery Mound				
Locally produced Western Pueblo types	–	100	–	–
Glaze-on-red	31	4	65	1
Glaze-on-polychrome	–	9	89	2
Pottery Mound Polychrome	5	–	94	2
Hidden Mountain Polychrome	–	100	–	–

plaza. Pottery Mound has at least eleven roomblocks laid out in a dispersed fashion with little evidence of a formal plaza space, although there is a central open space ringed by kivas. If the roomblocks within each village were contemporaneous, village layout would allow residents of each roomblock to exist as discrete spatial and social units. Historical accounts suggest that these social units would probably have been kin-based and may have been the result of different families moving into the villages at different times (Mindeleff 1891; Parsons 1940). Second, Helen Crotty (1990) found that kiva murals at Pottery Mound express themes that range from elaborately dressed dancers, to military capability, to the exhibition of valuable possessions. She argues that the display of material wealth reflected in the Pottery Mound murals was the result of rival lineages within the village vying for social and political dominance.

DISCUSSION AND CONCLUSION

I began this discussion by arguing that glaze-decorated pottery was adopted as part of a new ritual system and may have been used to help integrate disparate social groups by signaling village-wide participation in this system. I then argued that certain decorative attributes on glaze-painted pottery were used to emphasize social boundaries between groups with different migration histories. This complex and seemingly contradictory patterning in the ceramic assemblage reflects the complexity of Pueblo potters' identities during the fourteenth and fifteenth centuries.

On one hand, the social makeup of the Lower Rio Puerco population consisted of disparate social groups with unique migration histories. These migration histories would have been reflected in the daily practice of residents in any number of ways. Groups with different social histories may have had different linguistic traditions.

Suzanne L. Eckert

Different migration histories may have been incorporated into oral traditions describing the origins of different family groups. Origins in different regions may have been reflected through different ways of doing numerous daily activities, from making tools, to forming a ceramic vessel, to building or remodeling a roomblock. Further, ideological differences concerning the ritual cycle, marriage practices, or social etiquette may also have divided groups. At the same time, different migration histories would have potentially been the source of important exchange networks, marriage pools, and esoteric knowledge. These differences would only have become important sources of identity once disparate groups began living together. Although some aspects of social practice may have been negotiable, other aspects would not have been. Potters and their associated social groups would have wanted to reaffirm their identity by keeping core practices that reflected "who they were." Part of this reaffirmation would have come from visual reminders on pottery.

On the other hand, regardless of their migration histories, residents of both villages in the Lower Rio Puerco area were struggling with the same issues: how to negotiate their identity within the new social context of aggregation and immigration, environmental concerns stemming from being agriculturalists in an arid environment, how to keep the cosmos in balance, and daily domestic concerns over sickness, childbirth, marriage, and death. It appears that residents of both villages readily adopted a new ritual system, aspects of which were focused on integrating diverse groups of people. By focusing on the shared concerns of all residents and incorporating different ceremonial practices into a whole, this new ritual system would have provided an arena for participants to negotiate new and old social identities. By producing pottery with the same suite of icons, similar colored slips, and glaze paint, potters from diverse backgrounds would have been able to create a visual sense of unity and oneness.

Although the newly adopted ritual system may have provided mechanisms for social integration, these mechanisms may not have been strong enough to overcome the various concerns of the specific individuals and separate immigrant groups who settled in the region. The practice by potters of signaling a common belief and participation in a shared ritual system by using similar decoration on the exterior of their bowls while continuing to signal social boundaries between groups with different migration histories on the interior may reflect this tension between incorporation and segregation that has been noted in modern Pueblo society. The complete abandonment of the region suggests that the particular combination of ritual activities adopted by residents of the area was eventually unable to overcome other sources of tension.

The relationship among immigration, ritual, identity, and material culture is complex. It is the result of decisions made by individuals in an attempt to navigate the multiple social dynamics of daily living. The fourteenth and fifteenth centuries were a time of social, political, and ideological uncertainty in the Pueblo Southwest. It was not until later in the protohistoric period that many groups began to "settle down" and define the regional identities that exist today. Part of this identity would have been the formalization of a ritual system. Prior to this time, many villages were established that created different combinations of ideology and ritual to cope with the social stresses brought on by disparate groups living together. For as many villages as were successful in this endeavor, at least as many others were not successful. It is these latter villages, as well as the ones that eventually became the villages of today, that we must investigate if we are truly to understand the complexities of human behavior.

REFERENCES CITED

Adams, E. Charles
    1991   *The Origin and Development of the Pueblo Katsina Cult*. University of Arizona Press, Tucson.

Bunzel, Ruth L.
    1932   Introduction to Zuni Ceremonialism. In *Forty-Seventh Annual Report of the Bureau of American Ethnology*, 467–544. Government Printing Office, Washington, D.C.

Clark, Tiffany, and Suzanne L. Eckert
    2004   The Ritual Importance of Birds in 14th Century Central New Mexico. Poster presented at the 69th Annual Meeting of the Society for American Archaeology, Montreal.

Crotty, Helen K.
    1990   Protohistoric Anasazi Kiva Murals: Variation as a Reflection of Differing Social Contexts. Paper presented at the 55th Annual Meeting of the Society for American Archaeology, Las Vegas, Nev.
    1995   *Anasazi Mural Art of the Pueblo IV Period, A.D. 1300–1600: Influences, Selective Adaptation, and Cultural Diversity in the Prehistoric Southwest*. Unpublished Ph.D. dissertation, Department of Art History, University of California, Los Angeles.

Crown, Patricia L.
    1994   *Ceramics and Ideology: Salado Polychrome Pottery*. University of New Mexico Press, Albuquerque.

Eckert, Suzanne L.
    2003   *Social Boundaries, Immigration, and Ritual Systems: A Case Study from the American Southwest*. Ph.D. dissertation, Department of Anthropology, Arizona State University, Tempe. ProQuest, Ann Arbor.
    2006a   Black-on-White to Glaze-on-Red: Migration, Ritual and Exchange in the Middle Rio Grande. In *The Social Life of Pots: Glaze Wares and Cultural Transformation in the Late Precontact Southwest*, ed. Judith A. Habicht-Mauche, Suzanne L. Eckert, and Deborah Huntley, 163–178. University of Arizona Press, Tucson.
    2006b   The Production and Distribution of Glaze-Painted Pottery in the Pueblo Southwest: A Synthesis. In *The Social Life of Pots: Glaze Wares and Cultural Transformation in the Late Precontact Southwest*, ed. Judith A. Habicht-Mauche, Suzanne L. Eckert, and Deborah Huntley, 34–59. University of Arizona Press, Tucson.

Eckert Suzanne L., and Linda S. Cordell
    2004   Pueblo IV Community Formation in the Central Rio Grande Valley: Albuquerque, Cochiti, and Lower Rio Puerco Districts. In *The Protohistoric Pueblo World*, A.D. 1275–1600, ed. E. Charles Adams and Andrew I. Duff, 35–42. University of Arizona Press, Tucson.

Emslie, Steven D., and Lyndon L. Hargrave
    1978   An Ethnobiological Study of the Avifauna from Pottery Mound, New Mexico. Paper presented at the 43rd Annual Meeting of the Society for American Archaeology, Tucson, Ariz.

Graves, William, and Suzanne L. Eckert
    1998   Decorated Ceramic Distributions and Ideological Developments in the Rio Grande Valley, New Mexico. In *Migration and Reorganization: The Pueblo IV Period in the American Southwest*, ed. Katherine Spielmann, 263–284. Anthropological Research Papers Series 51. Arizona State University, Tempe.

Hibben, Frank C.
    1975   *Kiva Art of the Anasazi at Pottery Mound*. KC Publications, Las Vegas, N.M.

Mindeleff, Victor
    1891   A Study of Pueblo Architecture in Tusayan and Cibola. In *Eighth Annual Report of the Bureau of Ethnology, 1886–87*, 13–228. Government Printing Office, Washington, D.C.

Parsons, Elsie Clews
    1925   *The Pueblo of Jemez*. Yale University Press, New Haven, Conn.
    1940   Relations between Ethnology and Archaeology in the Southwest. *American Antiquity* 5(3):214–220.

Parsons, Elsie Clews (editor)
    1936   *The Hopi Journal of Alexander M. Stephen*, 2 vols. Columbia University Press, New York.

Roney, John R.
    1996   The Pueblo III Period in the Eastern San Juan Basin and Acoma-Laguna Areas. In *The Prehistoric Pueblo World* A.D. 1150–1350, ed. Michael Adler, 145–169. University of Arizona Press, Tucson.

Schaafsma, Polly
    1980   *Indian Rock Art of the Southwest*. School of American Research, Santa Fe, and University of New Mexico Press, Albuquerque.

Spielmann, Katherine A.
    1998   Ritual Influences on the Development of Rio Grande Glaze A Ceramics. In *Migration and Reorganization: The Pueblo IV Period in the American Southwest*, ed. Katherine A. Spielmann, 253–261. Anthropological Research Papers 51. Arizona State University, Tempe.

Stark, Miriam A.
    2006   Glaze Ware Technology, the Social Lives of Pots, and Communities of Practice in the Late Prehistoric Southwest. In *The Social Life of Pots: Glaze Wares and Cultural Transformation in the Late Precontact Southwest*, ed. Judith A. Habicht-Mauche, Suzanne L. Eckert, and Deborah Huntley, 17–33. University of Arizona Press, Tucson.

Part III

New Research from Northern Mexico: Borders, Contacts, Landscapes, and History

15

AVANCES DEL NORTE DE MÉXICO
(NEW RESEARCH FROM NORTHERN MEXICO)

Un Introducción

Eduardo Gamboa Carrera

Editors' note: *We present the original Spanish version of this introduction, followed by an English translation.*

En un esfuerzo por difundir los avances del conocimiento sobre las culturas prehispánicas que habitaron el noroeste de México, La oficina en Chihuahua del Instituto Nacional de Antropología e Historia en México (INAH) inicio en el año de 1994 La Conferencia "Arqueología de la Frontera Norte de México." Incluía estudios realizados por arqueólogos mexicanos en los actuales estados fronterizos de Baja California, Sonora y Chihuahua. También asistieron arqueólogos de otros estados del noroeste mexicano como Durango, Coahuila y Nuevo León. Así mismo, la oficina incluyo oportunistamente a un numeroso grupo de arqueólogos norteamericanos que interesados en estudiar el fenómeno "Paquimé" habían coincidido en Casas Grandes, con los arqueólogos mexicanos durante largas temporadas de campo y decidieron sumar esfuerzos para llevar a cabo dicha conferencia. Así, con la participación de investigadores del INAH, de profesores de prestigiadas universidades americanas de Nuevo Mexico, Utah, Oklahoma, Texas, y la Universidad Nacional Autónoma de México, se establecieron temas de discusión y se presentaron ponencias acerca de los avances de las investigaciones en la región.

Ocho años después la Séptima Conferencia de Arqueología de la Frontera Norte, coincidía con la celebración del IX Southwest Simposyum, ambos comités organizadores acordaron sumar esfuerzos y empatar ambos eventos en la Ciudad de Chihuahua en Enero de 2004 bajo la temática de las relaciones entre Mesoamerica y el Gran Suroeste. Las ponencias de esas sesiones se comentan brevemente a manera de introducción en el presente texto.

Iniciamos con la lectura titulada "La Pacificación de la Región Chichimeca" por Martha Monzón Flores (Capítulo 24) es un relato de hechos reales, acaecidos a lo largo del siglo xvi que ubican localmente y dan coherencia al empleo del concepto "Región Chichimeca." Una porción del norte de México, que fue habitada por grupos nómadas durante el posclásico represento para los conquistadores españoles grandes dificultades para su dominación y por ende para su pacificación. Las riquezas minerales descubiertas motivaban el avance de la colonización, sin embargo hubo que enfrentar a grupos bélicos que confederados defendían su territorio, La Gran Chichimeca. Los arqueólogos extendieron este concepto hacia el pasado inmediato, el posclásico prehispánico, y hoy en día se emplea frívolamente como una referencia probada.

Bajo diferentes perspectivas los arqueólogos mexicanos han realizado grandes esfuerzos para explicar la evolución de los sistemas culturales de la región. Este texto amalgama una magnifica muestra de la diversidad de estudios con este propósito. Algunos desde una perspectiva filosófica ponen a prueba la valides de los conceptos. La Gran Chichimeca por ejemplo es un concepto que a la luz del dato arqueológico no existe, no se convalida científicamente es una metáfora, sin embargo hoy en día hay grandes debates en torno a la generalización del uso del concepto por parte de un grupo de la comunidad científica. Francisco Mendiola Galván (Capítulo 16) manifiesta esta problemática, quien, sigue a Pierre Bourdieu, asume la urgente necesidad de la vigilancia epistemológica, sobre todo ante la inexistente crítica epistemológica de la presente realidad arqueológica del norte mexicano.

Otro buen ejemplo de esta convalidación epistemológica de conceptos la encontramos en las reflexiones de M. Nicolás Caretta, quien nos habla de "La Percepción de las Guerras en la Visión Arqueológica" (Capítulo 23). Pone de manifiesto el empleo frívolo de conceptos que al contrastarse bajo las técnicas de la arqueología y la antropología para convalidar su aplicabilidad no siempre arroja buenos resultados.

"Todos los Rumbos, Todas las Direcciones: El Paisaje Prehistórico de Nuevo León" de Moisés Valadez Moreno (Capítulo 21) expone como desde la prehistoria la cuidadosa selección de lugares e imágenes pintas y grabados sobre la roca, permite suponer la función simbólica a través del cual, aún siendo sociedades igualitarias, los pretéritos grupos indígenas de Nuevo León, restringían el uso de espacios, el significado de los símbolos y el control sobre las relaciones sociales y creencias religiosas, tanto al interior de la comunidad como hacia grupos vecinos, integrando un mundo omnidireccional, donde cada imagen y cada roca, cada elemento y cada actividad de la vida cazadora recolectora, aparentemente debían interactuar de manera simbólica con los elementos y fuerzas de la naturaleza, para conformar un paisaje dinámico y sagrado que a través de tradiciones de rituales y ceremonias, cíclicamente reforzaban sus tradiciones.

Avances del Norte de México

También se puede observar a lo largo de la lectura de Leticia González Arratia sobre la contribución Walter W. Taylor en 1937 a la arqueología de Coahuila (Capítulo 22) que el arte rupestre es una tradición que ha ido tomado un lugar importante, como dato arqueológico, para probar algunas ideas difusionistas que ya desde los años treinta, se orientaban a la busqueda del petroglifo "roseta" que marcara el punto más al sur de los norteños y el mas norteño de los sureños. O como la lectura de "La Historia Épica de los Toltecas Chichimeccas y Purépechas en las Tierras de los Pueblos Antiguos" (Capítulo 17), realizada por Patricia Carot y Marie-Areti Hers, acerca de las huellas de un mega puente montado sobre las semejanzas y diferencias en el tiempo y en el espacio de tradiciones distantes. Desde Michoacán hasta Arizona, desde la retracción de la frontera mesoamericana hasta la conformación de los pueblos del suroeste norteamericano. Y el documento de Arturo Guevara Sánchez (Capítulo 18) que resalta la consideración de atributos y tradiciones en el estudio del arte rupestre estableciendo con ello un mapa de rutas de difusión a través del altiplano central durante el posclásico tardío.

Un elemento mas para la consideración de contactos entre el Suroeste del los Estados Unidos y Mesoamerica es el intercambio de turquesa. Phil C. Weigand (Capítulo 19) pone de manifiesto a través de la lectura de su ponencia que la minería y el intercambio de turquesa fueron dos actividades claves para apreciar las conexiones socioculturales entre el núcleo de Mesoamerica, en el sur, y el ahora suroeste de Estados Unidos en el norte. La turquesa fue una material tan valiosa que no es lógico que la minería y el intercambio no tuvieran efectos sociales.

Por último la ponencia "Geografía Cultural del Conjunto de Casas Acantilado en el Noroeste de la Sierra Madre Occidental, Chihuahua, México," realizada por Eduardo Gamboa Carrera y Federico J. Mancera-Valencia (Capítulo 20). Siguiendo a Sauer y a la escuela holandesa de los estudios de la geografía cultural, en donde el estudio de los paisajes culturales, implica la descripción explicativa de los hechos de la ocupación del área considerada; unidades ecogeográficas y el descubrimiento de la composición y significado de los agregados no geográficos que reconocemos de forma ambigua como áreas culturales. De esta forma, se produce un conocimiento más preciso de la relación de la cultura y de los recursos que son puestos a disposición de la cultura. Por ende se pueden distinguir desarrollos culturales, paisajes culturales, regiones culturales, extensiones y territorios del sistema regional de Casas Grandes. El modelo se aplica para la definición de la extensión de la provincia serrana de Paquimé, a los datos del estudio del sistema regional de asentamientos de Casas Acantilado en la Sierra Madre Occidental en Chihuahua, México.

NEW RESEARCH FROM NORTHERN MEXICO: AN INTRODUCTION

In 1994 the Instituto Nacional de Antropología e Historia en México (INAH) in Chihuahua organized the conference "The Archaeology of the Northern Borderlands of Mexico" to share recent knowledge about the pre-Hispanic cultures of northwestern Mexico. The conference included research by Mexican archaeologists working in the border states of Baja California, Sonora, and Chihuahua and was also attended by archaeologists from other states in northern Mexico, including Durango, Coahuila, and Nuevo León. INAH also invited numerous North American archaeologists interested in the study of the Paquimé phenomenon whose fieldwork at Casas Grandes coincided with that of Mexican archaeologists and who wished to join forces with their Mexican colleagues. With the participation of investigators from INAH and faculty from prestigious American universities in New Mexico, Utah, Oklahoma, and Texas, as well as the Universidad Nacional Autónoma in Mexico City, themes for discussion were established and papers presented about recent research on investigations of the region.

When the Seventh Conference on the Archaeology of the Northern Borderlands coincided with the observance of the Ninth Southwest Symposium, the committees decided to combine both events in the city of Chihuahua, Mexico, in January 2004, under the overarching theme of relationships between Mesoamerica and the Greater Southwest. In this introduction I comment briefly on the papers presented in the two Mexican sections of the symposium, "Identity and Culture," moderated by Alejandro Martinez Muriel, and "Contact and Commerce," moderated by Joaquín García-Bárcena González.

"Pacification of the Chichimec Region" by Martha Monzón Flores (Chapter 24) provides an account of historical sixteenth-century events that were locally situated and gave rise to the concept of the Chichimec region, that part of northern Mexico inhabited by nomadic groups during the Postclassic period. These groups presented great difficulties for domination and, in the end, pacification by the Spanish conquerors. Motivated by the region's mineral riches, the Spanish colonization effort encountered a united bellicose group prepared to defend its territory, the Gran Chichimeca. Archaeologists have since extended the Gran Chichimeca concept to the immediate past and the pre-Hispanic Postclassic. Today the term is often employed as a general referent for the region.

Mexican archaeologists have made great strides in explaining the evolution of cultural systems in northern Mexico through the use of various perspectives. The contributions of the Mexican authors in this book highlight the diversity of these studies. Some authors bring a philosophical perspective to test the validity of their concepts. The Gran Chichimeca, for example, is a concept that, in the light of archaeological facts, does not exist; nor can it be scientifically confirmed as a metaphor. Even today there is great debate among a segment of the scientific community regarding its generalized use as a concept. Citing the work of Pierre Bordieu, Francisco Mendiola Galván (Chapter 16) addresses this problem and urges greater vigilance in applying epistemological criteria to the archaeology of northern Mexico.

Another example of the epistemological validation of concepts is offered in the reflections of M. Nicolás Caretta, who speaks of "Warfare in the Archaeological Vision" (Chapter 23). As he notes, archaeologists need to take warfare more seriously and be more multidisciplinary in their search for material correlates.

In "All Routes, All Directions: The Prehistoric Landscape of Nuevo León" (Chapter 21), Moisés Valadez Moreno examines the settings for painted and engraved rock art images and the symbolic function of rock art among past societies of Nuevo León. The restricted use of space, significance of the images, and control of social relations and religious beliefs within these communities and with neighboring groups are considered. Valadez Moreno argues that to integrate their omnidirectional world, where every image and rock and every element and activity of hunter-gatherer life required symbolic interaction with the elements and forces of nature, people cyclically reinforced their traditions through the use of rituals and ceremonies that conformed to their dynamic and sacred landscape.

Archaeologists on both sides of the border have long been interested in tracking the southernmost point of the northerners and the northernmost point of the southerners. In "Epic of the Toltec Chichimec and the Purépecha in the Ancient Southwest" (Chapter 17), Patricia Carot and Marie-Areti Hers trace the footprints of a far-ranging cultural system and explore similarities and differences in space and time among distant traditions extending from Michoacán to Arizona, as well as the expansion and retraction of the Mesoamerican boundary and the ebb and flow of social relations between groups in northern Mexico and the U.S. Southwest. Leticia González Arratia's chapter on Walter W. Taylor's contribution to the archaeology of Coahuila (Chapter 22) illustrates that rock art assumed a place of importance along with other archaeological data for testing ideas about diffusion. In a similar vein, Arturo Guevara Sánchez (Chapter 18) uses attributes and traditions from the rock art of Durango to develop a map of diffusion routes through the central altiplano during the Late Postclassic.

Another element used to illustrate contacts between the southwestern United States and Mesoamerica is turquoise. In Chapter 19, Phil C. Weigand argues that the mining and exchange of turquoise were key elements of sociocultural relations between Nuclear Mesoamerica in the south and the southwestern United States in the north. In his view, turquoise was such a valuable commodity that it is senseless to discuss the mining and exchange of the mineral without also considering its many social implications.

Finally, Eduardo Gamboa Carrera and Federico J. Mancera-Valencia, in "The Cultural Landscape of Cliff Houses in the Sierra Madre Occidental, Chihuahua" (Chapter 20), apply the work of Carl Sauer and the Holland school of cultural geography to the Casas Grandes regional system of Chihuahua, Mexico. The Casas Grandes cultural landscape and its ecogeographical units are explored, as are the composition and significance of the geographical aggregates that identify the region as a cultural area. The authors identify the cultural developments, landscapes, and territories that comprise the Casas Grandes regional system and apply their model to both the mountainous province of Paquimé and the regional cliff-house settlements of the Sierra Madre Occidental.

16

IMAGINARY BORDER, PROFOUND BORDER

Terminological and Conceptual Construction of
the Archaeology of Northern Mexico

Francisco Mendiola Galván

In *The Sociologist's Position*, Pierre Bourdieu states that reality is the sum of its relations and that banishing the idea of its transparency is indispensable to the study of the social realm (Bourdieu, Chamboderon, and Passeron 1975:37–38). Preconceptions are barriers, and false constructions are unconscious and uncontrollable pre-constructions to the essence of sociological discourse. These preconceptions incite one to believe that facts should correspond with certain images arising from language, the primary instrument in the construction of the world. If not subjected to methodical criticism, they fall victim to our tendency to accept such pre-constructed ideas as facts of common language. This rigorous definition is useless, and possibly even deceptive, if the principal unifier has not been critiqued. For this reason, epistemological vigilance is needed to avoid the corruption of ideas stemming from these preconceptions.

Why have I begun in this manner? Because certain names and terms that have been applied and are still utilized in the study of the spatial-cultural reality of northern Mexico have yet to be subjected to epistemological critique. They are defined as preconceptions because they have yet to be assessed in terms of how their reality is perceived, an ontological view tied strongly to epistemology and the construction of knowledge. My present objective is not to enter into a critique of the terminological and conceptual construction of concepts such as Arid America (Aridoamérica), Oasis America (Oasisamérica), Northwest (Noroeste), La Gran Chichimeca, and northern Mexico but to focus on elements that justify the need to carry out fundamental theoretical and epistemological reflections on the distinctive names these places have received within anthropological and historical discourse, especially archaeology.

The borders are understood and managed as the sum of interactions in equilibrium or dispute between terminological and conceptual spaces that relate to the physical territories between what is known today as the southwestern United States (the Southwest) and northern Mexico. Arid America, Oasis America, the Northwest, and La Gran Chichimeca are understood to be territories within these two bordering nations. As archaeologists, we move in an imaginary frontier that conforms to the imaginary borders produced by each of the names and terms used to designate the territories of this great region north of Mesoamerica and south of the United States. These are invented and artificial borders in terms of the profound border that encompasses the diverse real borders. They are also ethnocentric and neocolonial elements of the political and ideological environment. These borders, together with the imaginary ones, generate ambiguity and constrict the region—the archaeological northern Mexico located between Mesoamerica and the Southwest. Elements of these profound borders do not appear in the discourse of archaeology because it is generally a given that "archaeology should not be political or ideological but purely scientific." This positivist vision prevails as an inherent and essential part of contemporary archaeology, a position that accepts preconceptions as spontaneous, revealed between the imaginary borders. The data and justification needed to sustain and develop these preconceptions academically and politically, economically and ideologically, can be found within archaeology's own positivist discourse.

THE TERMINOLOGICAL AND CONCEPTUAL CONTEXT OF ARCHAEOLOGICAL INVESTIGATION IN NORTHERN MEXICO

To approach the precontact period in ancient northern Mexico, it is necessary to understand the historiography of the terms and concepts that have been used in archaeological investigation. It is with this aim that I explore some general trends from the end of the nineteenth century to the present and examine some of the theoretical and methodological pressures, on the one hand, and ideologically political and institutional pressures, on the other. This task does not require a culture-historical division of Mesoamerica, the Southwest, and northern Mexico; that would be irrelevant. The challenge for future investigations is to understand the north not only from the Mesoamerican perspective but also from its own northern viewpoint, at the same time considering its own northern dynamics from a solid terminological and conceptual base.

The pre-Hispanic past of the great region known as northern Mexico and the southwestern United States is shared by both nations, now divided by a river. This is the same region that bore past witness to a series of sociocultural processes by groups that existed prior to the arrival of the Europeans and the conquest. Cultural aspects were shared, and material evidence of relations and interactions between these groups has been substantiated along the breadth and length of the territory. Following the conquest, the northern frontier of New Spain was, for 300 years, a vast territory that proved difficult to conquer and colonize. In 1810 this part of northern Mexico became independent, and in 1848 the territories of Texas and New Mexico were lost and became part of the southern United States.

According to Beatriz Braniff (2001a), by the end of the nineteenth and beginning of the twentieth century, North American ethnologists and archaeologists had begun calling this region the Southwest, a term that initially centered exclusively on those areas inhabited by the ancestors of the Pueblo Indians (Zuni, Hopi, and others). Later, Alfred Kroeber (1928), faced with the existence of diverse sedentary and nomadic groups from areas beyond what was then termed the Southwest, expanded the concept of what is now called the Greater Southwest and extended the region southward to the Tropic of Cancer in Mexico. It is here that the term "Greater Southwest" becomes interesting because, according to Braniff (1997:74), as Kroeber's particularist diffusionism indicates, our North American neighbors found "similar cultures north of present-day Mexico City . . . and territorially extended the term, calling it the 'Greater Southwest.' Following this, Paquimé and a large part of the region also came to form part of the 'Southwest,' even though we in Mexico consider it to lie within the northern part of Mexico."

In 1943 the German ethnologist Paul Kirchhoff proposed and developed the term and concept "Mesoamerica" to describe the period of Spanish conquest in the sixteenth century. This work was driven by a need to classify the cultural traits distributed and shared among distinct cultures over a large area, or cultural super-area (Kirchhoff 1960). The introduction of the term "Mesoamerica" in the mid-twentieth century solved, to a degree, the cultural complexity of historic central and southern Mexico. Nevertheless, in this same article Kirchhoff used certain ethnocentric and schematic terms to characterize groups of "inferior" cultivators from North America in his discussion of the "basic unity of *inferior cultivators* within the hunter-gatherer culture of northern Mexico" (italics added; Braniff 2001a:1). These groups had, in the words of Kirchhoff (1960:2), a "culture not only superficially but basically similar" to that found in the "super-areas" of the Greater Southwest established by Kroeber, referred to by Kirchhoff as Arid North America. Following a series of linguistic discussions of these Mesoamerican groups by Kirchhoff (1960:6-7), an important issue arose from his study: not the definition or concept of Mesoamerica but the formulation of questions regarding what had taken place to the north of Mesoamerica. This adjoining territory was occupied by hunter-gatherers, the so-called inferior cultivator groups, whose greater mobility had generated insecurity in Mesoamerica through their invasions from the north.

Kirchhoff (1954) also tried to answer questions regarding events that had occurred to the north of Mesoamerica. Kirchhoff intended to repeat his ordering model, this time focusing on the area located to the north of the Mesoamerican cultural super-area. He underscored the existence of two groups, hunter-gatherers and cultivators, noting that this region was not a single culture area. He proposed the terms Arid America for the former and Oasis America, tied to Mesoamerica, for the latter, abandoning the terms "Southwest" and "Greater Southwest." Henceforth, he used these terms only in a geographical sense (Kirchhoff 1954:550). Distinguishing between hunter-gatherer and agricultural groups was not a simple thing for Kirchhoff because, as noted by Braniff (2001a:2), "neither were clearly nomadic, nor clearly sedentary," a situation Kirchhoff recognized as a problem of classification. The view of the north originated from Mesoamerica, through the colored lenses of Oasis America and Arid America and also La Gran Chichimeca, a term I discuss later.

Charles Di Peso (1974) was the first to use the term "La Gran Chichimeca" in archaeological studies. He considered this territory to encompass all that had developed in the north in the area beyond Mesoamerica and north of the Tropic of Cancer to the 38° N parallel. This area is characterized by a generalized aridity,[1] one of the most important characteristics of its natural environment. Within this great area were the Chichimeca groups, understood to be hunter-gatherers, barbarian agriculturalists, and civilized agriculturalists.

Braniff, drawing from Di Peso's important work, has encouraged reflection on and an elaboration of the term "La Gran Chichimeca." This has resulted in a large number of studies that have analyzed and interpreted the term using direct and indirect archaeological evidence and colonial sources. Braniff has brought the basic elements for understanding this large region within reach of students, at the same time questioning some of the aforementioned terminology, such as Southwest and northern Mexico, which she views as limited and subjective in scope (Braniff 2001a:2-3).[2] Braniff has proposed a return to terminology that combines an indigenous conception of the world (Chichimecatlali, land of the Chichimecas, also known as Teotlalpan Tlacochcalco Mictlampa, northern lands and their inhabitants of northern origin) and Spanish thought (such as the conquered territory remaining in northern New Spain that was inhabited by northern indigenous people, not Mesoamericans), worlds of thought that clearly recognize a Gran Chichimeca (Braniff 2001a:4-5; 2001b:7). It is also recognized, however, that the center of New Spain was the same as Mesoamerica. As such, the term "La Gran Chichimeca" also possesses undeniable ethnocentric connotations and, in this sense, exists at the same level of terminological and conceptual elaboration as Mesoamerica, Oasis America, and Arid America.

FRONTIER IMAGERY: TERMINOLOGICAL AND CONTEXTUAL AMBIGUITY AND RESTRICTION OF THE ARCHAEOLOGY OF NORTHERN MEXICO

In 1990, I pointed out that the Mexican state of Sinaloa is not just a northern territory but also a Mesoamerican one (Mendiola Galván 1990). This situation had been recognized but not completely defined by the spatial-cultural thinking of the

1930s, when contacts and interactions between the cultures of the southwestern United States and Mesoamerica were being considered. I hesitate to ask about the limits of this interaction between the desert cultures and those of Mesoamerica and at what point this interaction disrupted the cultural ambiguity of historical and anthropological investigation of the archaeology of Sinaloa. This situation epitomizes at a regional level the phenomenon of "sandwich," which can be presented schematically as "between and within Mesoamerica" or "between and within the southwestern United States and/or the Sonoran Desert." In this case, a sandwich can be viewed as a "phenomenon that paralyzes Sinaloa in its anthropological investigation and therefore confines it to constant ambiguity and to an outdated history and archaeology" (Mendiola Galván 1990:2, 4, 9-10).

For years it has been thought that this same situation applied at a macro level to the archaeology of northern Mexico and its terminological and conceptual realm. This is complicated not only by the large size of the area, within which archaeological investigation has not been a constant (in contrast to the southwestern United States and Mesoamerica), but also by the high degree of theoretical and epistemological complexity implied by the terminological and conceptual analysis of the region. The ambiguity of these concepts in the archaeology of northern Mexico, with its imaginary borders of Oasis America and Arid America, should place it beyond negative connotations, a challenge for archaeological investigation. As noted by Carlos González Herrera (2003), absolute, airtight explanations, those lacking cracks or doubts, are riskier than ambiguity because they are part of observable behavior within the scientific field of archaeology.[3] Ambiguity itself is not a desirable element, however. The terminological and conceptual restriction of northern Mexican archaeology can be likened to a force shield shaped by the Southwest and Mesoamerica, one constrained by archaeological investigations of the north without considering relations not just between the Southwest and Mesoamerica but also between the southern United States and central and southern Mexico. For this, greater investigation and reflection are required to recognize the existence of these imaginary and profound borders.

Braniff (2001c) has brought to the table a discussion of terms that preceded La Gran Chichimeca. In spite of the academic push to discard the terms "Southwest" and "northern Mexico," "Oasis America" and "Arid America," these terms continue to be used in archaeological and ethnohistorical investigations in northern Mexico. At the heart of this methodological critique and epistemological reflection are two lines of analysis and discussion that in principle agree with the idea of a historical dimension of space in archaeological investigation. First, one must recognize that the north is not a unified entity and has been defined more by what is absent than by its particularities (Hers and Soto 2001:38-39). Second, one must be aware of the influence of the concepts of Mesoamerica and the Southwest or Greater Southwest on archaeological interpretations of northern Mexico.

The first line of analysis and discussion relates to whether the general inertia of archaeological investigation in northern Mexico and Mesoamerica has prevented, until now, the dismantling of the concept that northern Mexico is a unified area. The fact that northern Mexico represents more than half of the national territory and its spatial immensity encompasses great cultural and natural diversity should make it anything *but* a unit. Nevertheless, the north is so strongly considered a unit of central Mesoamerica that it is granted barely part of a room in the Museo Nacional de Antropología in Mexico City. The north is also defined more for what it lacks than for its inherent elements. It is viewed as a "timeless Chichimeca universe," with little understanding of its non-agricultural heritage. Defined not only by its lack of Mesoamerican monumentality, the north is also a testament to the novo-Hispanic notion of the desert. This was the end of the world for the Jesuits in the seventeenth century, an eternal desert space that inhibited civilized life (Rozat 1992:30). For archaeological studies, the paradigm of the novo-Hispanic notion of the desert must be countered with a view that strips away the idea of the desert as an empty and wanting place and incorporates into its definition the concept of general aridity (Cordell 1984, cited by Mendiola Galván in press).[4] The unity of this region is imaginary. It is the concept of Mesoamerica that permeates all interpretations of this region: its space, territory, culture, academic structure, and scientific tradition.

The second line of analysis, closely tied to the first, relates to an understanding of the conceptual preeminence of the U.S. Southwest (Greater Southwest) and Mesoamerica over northern Mexico, the latter restricted in its terms and concepts and, in this sense, open to future interpretation. To guide this analysis, I propose three lines of discussion:

1. Until now, Mesoamerica has been the usual point of departure for referring to, describing, analyzing, explaining, and conceptualizing northern Mexico, which has always been obscured by the former. This is what we might call "the Mesoamerican conscious and unconscious." The archaeology of northern Mexico is what it is because it is consistently referred to, consciously or unconsciously, in terms of Mesoamerica. Consider two examples. A study of Mesoamerican influences at Paquimé is an example of the *conscious* approach, something real, true, and indisputable, whereas the study of a seasonal camp of hunter-gatherers in the desert is often discussed, *unconsciously*, in relation to the abundance and monumentality of Mesoamerica. These biases are largely a result of the fact that the vast majority of archaeologists working in the northern desert of Mexico were trained both academically and professionally in Mesoamerica. (This question relates to scientific tradition, specifically to archaeological tradition, as proposed by Vázquez León [1996:9].) A similar situation has influenced the perspective of archaeologists from the southwestern United States toward northern Mexico as a result of the fact that a voluminous body of archaeological data has been generated in the U.S. Southwest over decades of investigation, compared to northern Mexico, where far less work has been done.

2. We must consider how Kirchhoff's idea of the "high cultures" of Mesoamerica and his notion of the "poverty" of archaeological contexts in northern Mexico, divided and fractured into Arid America and Oasis America, have contributed

to an increase in subjectivity in the northern region and fed an ethnocentric vision.

3. We should also consider how the terminological and conceptual restriction that has characterized interpretations of northern Mexico is related to the historical, political, and ideological environment stemming from Mexico's loss of New Mexico and Texas in 1848, when border tensions began. In this case, "scientific" vision translates as "neocolonial forms of civilizing classification" in academic planning, as expressed by González Herrera (see note 3). Something similar occurred as a result of the pressure Mesoamerica exerted on northern Mexico. As Guillermo Bonfil Batalla (1990:223) has noted, "The only possible exit, arduous and difficult without a doubt, but the only one, is for Mexico to develop the historical will to formulate and undertake our own project of civilization." It is this civilizing character of Mesoamerica, affirmed in the pure sense by Kirchhoff, that is understood in northern Mexico and managed as a homogeneous unit, subjected and manipulated in a uniform manner to this same process of civilization. Mesoamerica imposes itself in a certain sense as a neocolonial form in the classification of civilization. Braniff (2001b:9), in *La Gran Chichimeca: El Lugar de las Rocas Secas*, has applied the term "Northwest" as a reaction against the term "Southwest," noting that the latter term is only 150 years old. This does not solve the problem of the ambiguity, narrowness, and emptiness of the terminology and concepts of northern Mexican archaeology, however. Instead, a deeper epistemological reflection is needed, one that abstains from a war between terms and concepts, as clearly the road does not lie there.

FINAL COMMENTS

Archaeological investigations in northern Mexico should be developed parallel to epistemological and ontological reflections that nurture an equilibrium between what is studied in Mesoamerica and in the southwestern United States. This should be done without integrating in the historiographical sense that which has occurred in specific archaeological regions and sites in northern Mexico. First, we need to recognize that a thorough investigation of most of this area is lacking. Today as never before, there is a growing and clear interest among national and international institutions in archaeological investigations of cultural origins and developments and in the interactions, transformations, and permanency of various groups. These synchronic and diachronic visions can interrelate well with other disciplines. Nevertheless, future studies must ensure that interpretations of northern Mexico as an object of historical analysis and discussion, together with its anthropology and especially its archaeology, are approached with epistemological vigilance. It is possible to banish the preconceptions and transparency of the sociocultural reality of the region and to eradicate the empty terminology and concepts that have prevented this remarkable area from being systematically studied. This could mark the end of imaginary borders and allow us to reach an equilibrium between existing and new knowledge.

NOTES

1. Generalized aridity refers to the types of climate, vegetation, and fauna and does not necessarily mean a sandy desert. Federico Mancera-Valencia (2002:17) indicated that aridity is scientifically defined in Mexico by the dry characteristics found in those climates and is understood to be both arid and semiarid.

2. Marie-Areti Hers and Dolores Soto (2001:39) noted that Beatriz Braniff "supports the accepted concept of the Gran Chichimeca . . . ahead of other, more central, concepts such as Kirchhoff's Arid America and Oasis America."

3. Noted by Maestro Carlos González Herrera in one of the preliminary versions of the project of investigation by Francisco Mendiola (October 11, 2003).

4. Linda Cordell (1984) identified aridity as the common denominator of various ecosystems that comprise La Gran Chichimeca.

REFERENCES CITED

Bonfil Batalla, Guillermo
    1990   *El México Profundo, Una Civilización Negada*. CONACULTA, Grijalbo, México.

Bourdieu, Pierre, Jean-Claude Chamboderon, and Jean-Claude Passeron
    1975   *El Oficio de Sociólogo*. Ed. Siglo 21, Buenos Aires.

Braniff, Beatriz
    1997   Paquimé: Pequeña Historia de las Casas Grandes. En *Papeles Norteños*, Beatriz Braniff, coordinadora, 71–106. Colección Científica 363. Instituto Nacional de Antropología e Historia, México.
    2001a   El Norte de México y La Gran Chichimeca. Ponencia presentada en la lineal de la Sociedad Mexicana de Antropología, Agosto.
    2001b   Introducción. En *La Gran Chichimeca: El Lugar de las Rocas Secas*, Beatriz Braniff, coordinadora, 7–12. CONACULTA. Jaca Book, México.
    2001c   La Gran Chichimeca. En *Arqueología Mexicana* 9(51):40–45. INAH-Raíces, México.

Cordell, Linda S.
    1984   *Prehistory of the Southwest*. Academic, New York.

Di Peso, Charles C., John B. Rinaldo, and Gloria J. Fenner
    1974   *Casas Grandes, a Fallen Trading Center of the Gran Chichimeca*. Eight volumes. Amerind Foundation, Dragoon, Ariz., and Northland, Flagstaff, Ariz.

Hers, Marie-Areti, and Dolores Soto
    2001   La Obra de Beatriz Braniff y el Desarrollo de la Arqueología del Norte de México. En *Nómadas y Sedentarios: Homenaje a Beatriz Braniff*, 37–53. Universidad Nacional Autónoma de México, México.

Kirchhoff, Paul
    1954   Gatherers and Farmers in the Greater Southwest: A Problem in Classifications. *American Anthropologist* 56(4, part 1):529–560.
    1960   Mesoamérica, sus Límites, Composición Étnica y Caracteres Culturales. En
    [1943]   *Tlatoani*, 1–15. Suplemento 3 de la Sociedad de Alumnos de la Escuela Nacional de Antropología e Historia, México.

Kroeber, Alfred L.
1928   Native Culture of the Southwest. *University of California Publications in American Archaeology and Ethnology* 23, 375-398. University of California Press, Berkeley.

Mancera-Valencia, Federico J.
2002   Pedagogía e Historia de las Ideas de la Naturaleza de Chihuahua. Ponencia al 1er Foro de Investigación sobre Cultura Regional del Norte de México, México.

Mendiola Galván, Francisco
1990   Historia Prehispánica y Arqueología de Sinaloa. Ponencia presentada en el Seminario Alfonso Caso. La Época Final del México Antiguo, Siglos XIII al XVI. Museo Nacional de Antropología, julio. INAH, México.
2003   La Arqueología en Chihuahua: Antropología de Unas Tradición Científica que se Debate Entre Mesoamérica, Norte de México y Southwest. Proyecto de tesis de maestría, Escuela Nacional de Antropología e Historia de Chihuahua, Chihuahua, México.
in press   La Noción de Desierto en el Contexto de la Gran Chichimeca. Una Primera Aproximación Desde la Arqueología del Norte de México. (Entregado para su publicación al Comité de Publicaciones del Centro INAH, 2003).

Rozat, Guy
1992   El Desierto, Morada del Demonio. Bárbaros, Viciosos y Censores Jesuitas. En *Trace* 22, 24-30. Centre Français d'Etudes Mexicaines ed Centraméricaines (CEMCA), México.

Vázquez León, Luis
1996   *El Leviatán Arqueológico. Antropología de una Tradición Científica en México.* Research School CNWS, Leiden, The Netherlands.

17

EPIC OF THE TOLTEC CHICHIMEC AND THE PURÉPECHA IN THE ANCIENT SOUTHWEST

Patricia Carot and Marie-Areti Hers

Archaeologists have long been intrigued with relationships between Mesoamerica and the southwestern United States (for an overview of this subject, see Cordell 1997; McGuire 1993; Willcox 1986). Emil Haury's (1945, 1976) studies at Snaketown, Arizona, highlighted interactions between the Hohokam Culture and western Mexico, particularly the Chupícuaro Culture. J. Charles Kelley (1966) later identified shared iconographic elements of Hohokam and Chalchihuites ceramics (see also Braniff 1995).

Recent archaeological investigations in Michoacán[1] and the Sierra Madre Occidental[2] have allowed us to confirm and expand these hypotheses. They have also introduced new elements to our understanding of interactions between the ancient Purépecha (Tarascan) and Chalchihuites cultures, as well as these groups' mutual

---

For a preliminary version of this chapter in Spanish, see Bonfiglioli, Gutiérrez, and Olavaria (2006:47-82). This research was conducted with the support of the Consejo Nacional de Ciencia y Tecnología (CONACYT, proyecto U40611-S) and the Programa de Apoyo a Proyectos de Investigación e Innovación Tecnológica of the Universidad Nacional Autónoma de México (PAPIIT, proyecto IN308602).

participation in establishing a long-lasting bridge with southwestern communities. (Purépecha is the name applied to the indigenous group that inhabits the central portion of Michoacán and is also the name of their language. Since the colonial period, these people have also been referred to as the Tarascans.) Finally, these investigations have revealed what these Mesoamericans received as a result of their contacts with far northern lands. They indicate that this bridge should be viewed as one of mutual cultural involvement rather than of unidirectional Mesoamerican influence, as usually perceived (e.g., see Kelley 1986 and Schroeder 1966; for a critical review of this unilateral diffusion interpretation, see McGuire 1980).

The contraction of the Mesoamerican northern frontier hundreds of miles to the south in the ninth century A.D. involved the return of the Uacusecha (a group of the ancient Purépecha) and the Chalchihuites (ancestors of the historic Toltec Chichimec; see Hers 1989a) to their respective ancestral lands. In the *Relación de Michoacán*, the Uacusecha are identified as the noble lineage that led the groups that returned from the north and founded the Tarascan Empire. (Uacusecha means "Eagle Knights" in the Purépecha language.) Our recent studies support the early hypotheses of Jesse Walter Fewkes (1893), Konrad Preuss (1998), and Eduard Seler (1998), who recognized a kindred relationship among peoples seemingly unrelated in time and space: the ancient Mexica, the modern Cora, Huichol, and Mexicanero of the Sierra Madre Occidental, and the Pueblo Indians of the southwestern United States (Figure 17.1).

Recent archaeological investigations have led to three important conclusions. First, they have allowed us to identify the Mesoamerican actors in this northern epic or saga. In the case of Michoacán, we are talking about a group of the ancient Purépecha known as the Uacusecha. In the case of the bearers of Chalchihuites Culture, we are dealing with the ancestors of the historic Toltec Chichimec, when they still occupied the legendary lands of Chicomoztoc. Second, we now believe the respective destinies of these groups were intertwined within the confines of the Sierra Madre Occidental and that together they explored the faraway lands of the Southwest. Finally, we acknowledge the contributions of ancient Southwest cultures to these northern Mesoamericans.

To summarize our hypotheses, we present a table divided horizontally into three sections (Figure 17.2). The upper row of this table is devoted to the long Purépecha history. Based on recent investigations in the Zacapu region (the north-central part of the state of Michoacán), we accord a much greater time depth to Purépecha history than traditionally granted. The middle row of the chart represents Mesoamerican expansion in the southern half of the western Sierra Madre, corresponding to the modern states of Jalisco, Zacatecas, and Durango. This gave way to the Chalchihuites Culture of the Toltec Chichimec, which, together with other peoples, founded Tula in the ninth century. The bottom row relates to the immense territory of Arizona, New Mexico, Colorado, and Utah, which shares many common features. Our southwestern research focuses primarily on the Hohokam core area during the Colonial and Sedentary periods.

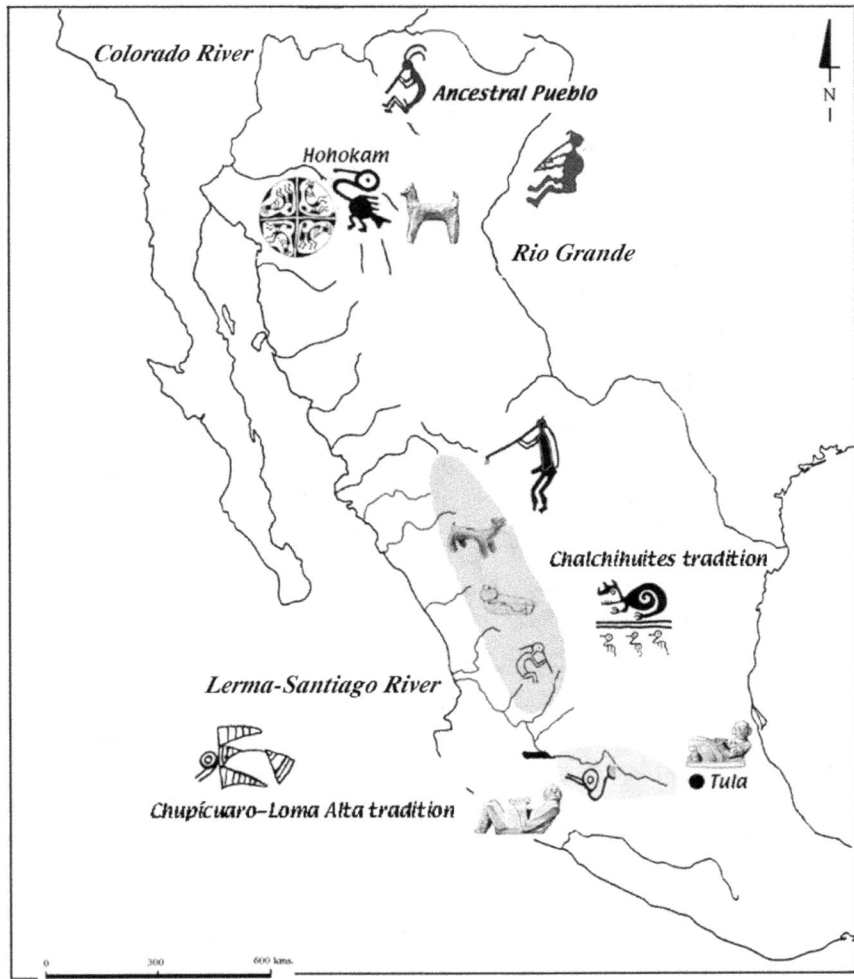

Figure 17.1. Region referred to in the text as the Northwest, consisting of northwestern Mexico and the southwestern United States.

Vertically, the table is divided into three major chronological stages. These are separated by two periods of considerable change, the first occurring in the sixth century, the second in the ninth century. The curved path of footprints represents an ancient bridge of shared influences between Mesoamerica and the ancient U.S. Southwest, an intricate universe of ideas and beliefs expressed through rituals and images. This bridge is somewhat analogous to the colonial Camino Real, except that the former was not sponsored by a dominant power and led to the Salt-Gila

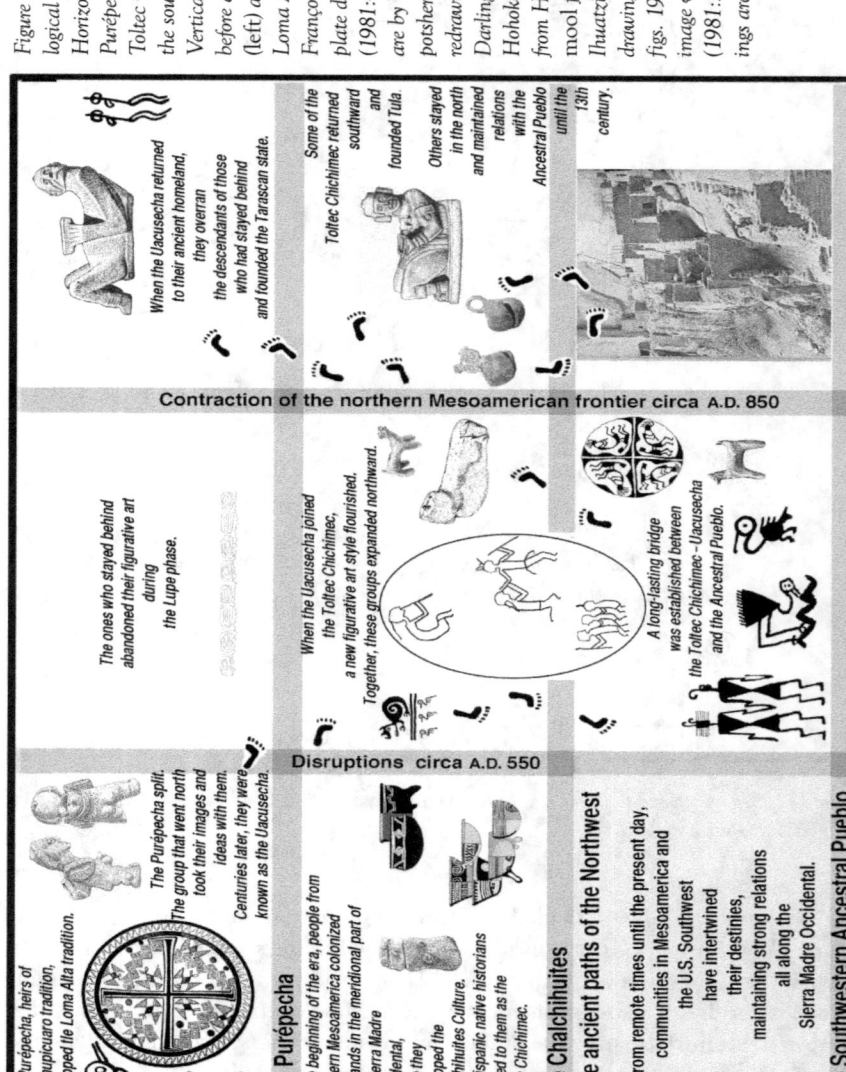

Figure 17.2. Cultures and chronological stages discussed in the text. Horizontal lines demarcate the Purépecha, the Chalchihuites or Toltec Chichimec, and cultures of the southwestern United States. Vertical lines define periods before and after circa A.D. 550 (left) and A.D. 850 (right). Loma Alta–phase drawings by Françoise Bagot, except for the plate drawing, from Lumholtz (1981:418). The two figurines are by Veronica Hernández. The potsherd from La Quemada is redrawn from Jiménez Betts and Darling (2000:fig. 10.10). The Hohokam elements are taken from Haury (1976). The chac mool figures from Tula and Ihuatzio are Ignacio Cabral's drawings from Gendrop (1970: figs. 190, 231). The Betatakin image was digitalized from Noble (1981:58). All remaining drawings are the work of the authors.

Figure 17.3. Partial view of the Loma Alta altar showing some of the sculptures. At left, an anthropomorphic figure. At right, a large fishlike slab. Photo by Patricia Carot.

Basin of modern Arizona rather than along the Rio Grande Valley of New Mexico. In the tenth century this inland route was replaced by a coastal one until the end of the sixteenth century, when it was revived by colonial forces (see Riley 2005).

THE PURÉPECHA OF THE LOMA ALTA PHASE

Our story begins in Michoacán at the beginning of the long Purépecha sequence, which is marked by three major stages (Michelet 1992). The first, the Loma Alta phase (100 B.C.–A.D. 550/600), was characterized by excellent artistic achievements—particularly in ceramics, sculpture, and architecture—and a distinctive funerary complex. In ancient West Mexico, this phase was contemporaneous with the well-known Shaft Tomb and Guachimontones complexes. The second stage, the Lupe phase (A.D. 600–850), evinced a total break with this ancient tradition. The third stage, represented by the Palacio and Milpillas phases (A.D. 950–1450), is marked by a period of resettlement, the presence of northern elements, and a deliberate will to reconnect with the past. As we shall see, this latter stage coincided with the return of the Uacusecha people and culminated in the rise of the Tarascan Empire, later destroyed by the fierce Nuño Beltran de Guzmán.

The Loma Alta phase was defined at the site of Loma Alta, a funerary island and important ceremonial center located in the middle of Zacapu Lake, which

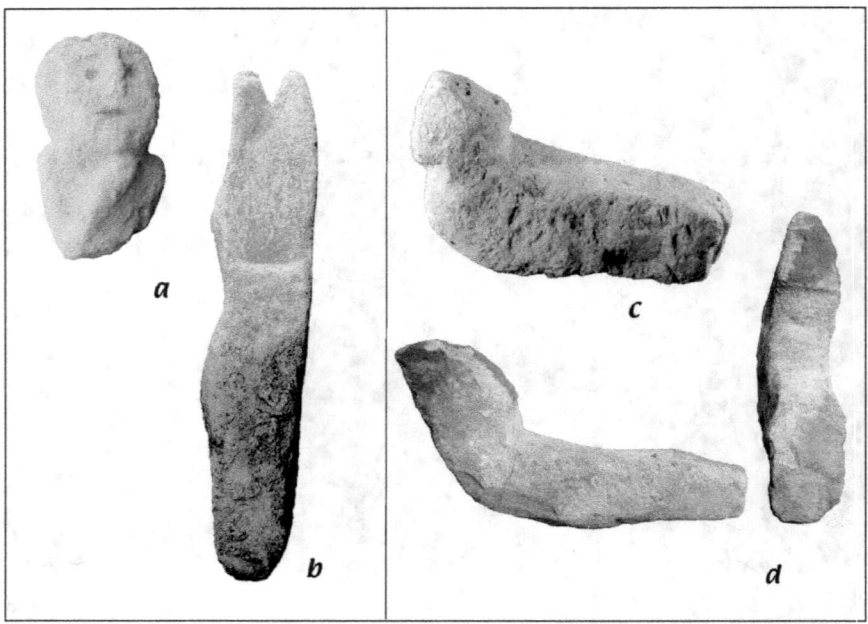

Figure 17.4. The two sculptural traditions of the Loma Alta phase of the Purépecha Culture and the Alta Vista–Vesuvio phase of the Chalchihuites Culture. (a and b) from Loma Alta; (c and d) from Cerro del Huistle. Photos by Patricia Carot and Marie-Areti Hers.

was artificially drained about 1900. An important feature of this initial phase is the distinctive iconographic repertoire used to decorate polychrome ceramics. This figurative tradition was inherited from the Chupícuaro-Morales tradition (300–100 B.C.; see Braniff 1998) and reached its artistic peak during the Loma Alta phase. It was never surpassed in terms of its technical elaboration, its painters' virtuosity, or its diversity of more than forty represented motifs. This style, which constituted an artistic language full of rich symbolic meaning, suddenly appeared in Chalchihuites and Hohokam ceramics around A.D. 600, the same time it disappeared from Michoacán at the end of the Loma Alta phase.

Loma Alta ceremonialism is eloquently represented by an exceptional discovery made at the site, a set of forty sculptures placed in a four meter–diameter pit in the middle of an altar (Figures 17.3 and 17.4). These stone images belong to a vast pan-Mesoamerican sculptural tradition but particularly resemble ones found in the Chalchihuites area. The sculptures, many of which were ritually broken or "killed" prior to burial, were deposited during a solemn ritual that marked the dramatic end of this period but also clearly expressed the will to break away from the image cult (Carot 1997, in press). This break can also be seen in the sudden abandonment of all figurative expression in painted ceramics during the subsequent Lupe phase.

Within this set of sculptures, two different traditions can be distinguished. The first group, executed in delicate and detailed carving, represents a great diversity of deities, including some of the most important figures in the Mesoamerican pantheon. One recognizes the old god of fire, Curicaueri, who is identical to contemporaneous Teotihuacán representations of the same god, Huehueteotl. One also finds Tlaloc, the rain god, with his goggled eyes and incised teeth. Other statues represent unique images, such as the unusual naked figure of a bearer (*mecapalero*) who carries a jar on his back and various phallic sculptures, one of which is anthropomorphized.

The second sculptural tradition is indicative of a true stone cult. More than half of the buried sculptures are stones selected for their original shapes, which evoke natural forms such as fish, snakes, a coyote, a dog, a wing, a half moon, or a human leg. The stones are barely retouched, and only certain elements, such as eyes or teeth, were added to emphasize that they are sculptures, not just simple stones. This ancient cult gains additional relevance and meaning when one recalls that for the Tarascans and Coras, those peculiar shaped stones represented the ancestors (Corona Nuñez 1957; Lumholtz 1981). Zacapu means "place of many rocks, place of origin," and, as we shall discuss, those groups that had gone north later returned to Zacapu. That is, they came back to the place their ancestors had left centuries before, to their place of origin, where their history began.

Another feature of the Loma Alta phase is its unusual repertoire of funerary practices involving the secondary treatment of burials. These include cremating bones, grinding the ashes to dust, whitening the ashes with lime, and placing the ashes in urns. Ceramic offerings originally associated with these burials were ritually broken, and some sherds were used as secondary offerings when the urns were deposited. Notably, the closest similarities that have been found to such practices are again with the Hohokam Culture. Two urns containing contents similar to those from Loma Alta were also found at the Hervideros site in Durango, Mexico. Other distinctive rituals of the Loma Alta phase include flesh-removing practices, dismemberment, sacrifice by cardiectomy (removal of the heart), and what appears to be a cult of head trophies, a trait that appears centuries later among the Chalchihuites (Carot 2005; Hers 1989a; Pereira 1996, 1999).

This phase is also characterized by monumental architecture. In the middle of the ceremonial island of Loma Alta was constructed a monumental 60 m × 40 m rectangular platform with a sunken patio 24 meters square and 2 meters deep, contemporaneous with those from the neighboring state of Guanajuato. Two other important ceremonial structures are known from the site: a circular enclosure 26 meters in diameter and an unusual semi-subterranean structure 5 meters square with a fire pit at the center. This latter structure, referred to as the Fire God House, is the first pithouse reported in the region or elsewhere in Mesoamerica. With its slab-lined sunken walls and central square fire pit, it resembles pithouses of the southwestern United States. Curiously, this structure can also be compared to the *tukipa*, the sacred ceremonial place of the Huichols.

Figure 17.5. Fragment of a ritual vessel from Loma Alta decorated with post-firing painting in the stripped investment technique. Drawing by Françoise Bagot.

Another important discovery at the site was an exceptional ritual vessel that combines the visual language of Teotihuacán with a local technique, the so-called Cheran-style stripped investment (Holien 1977). In this technique, often confused with pseudo-cloisonné, the motifs are incised through layers of different-colored clay surfaces (Figure 17.5). This vessel offers persuasive testimony of the presence of Teotihuacán ceremonialism in the early traditions of the Purépecha and suggests the training of Purépecha scholars at Teotihuacán. The vessel depicts a human figure wearing the paraphernalia of a Teotihuacán priest, most notably the dorsal disc, or *tezcacuitlapilli*, a power insignia par excellence. This insignia endured for centuries not only in Michoacán (Noguera 1944; Pereira 1999) but also in the Chalchihuites Culture, the southwestern United States, at Tula and related Chichén Itzá, and even later at Paquimé. At Teotihuacán, cultural interaction with the Purépecha is demonstrated by the presence of objects from the West, particularly Cheran-style pottery vessels, placed as offerings in some burials (Carot 2005; Gómez 2002).

THE INCIPIENT CHALCHIHUITES: THE CANUTILLO PHASE

About A.D. 100, when the Morales (Guanajuato) and Loma Alta (Michoacán) phases were developing, the Mesoamerican frontier underwent its first great expansion northward in three wide swaths extending toward the northeast in the Sierra Gorda and the Potosí Plateau, toward the central north (the modern states of Guanajuato and Querétaro), and toward the northwest. This expansion followed the same U-shaped curve that marks the courses of the Lerma-Santiago rivers to the west and the Moctezuma-Pánuco rivers to the east and is a product of the arid conditions of the central plateau (Braniff et al. 2001:fig. 3). The northwestern zone, in which we are most interested here, was the territory of the so-called Chalchihuites Culture. In its initial Canutillo phase (ca. A.D. 50–550, based on radiocarbon dates from Kelley and the Cerro del Huistle site [Hers 1989a:fig. 3]), the Chalchihuites Culture flourished and extended along the eastern flank of the Sierra Madre Occidental between the Grande de Santiago and the Mezquital rivers, an area that corresponds to the modern states of Zacatecas and Jalisco. In essence, this culture seems to have originated as a colonizing movement.

The place or places of origin of the peoples who participated in this journey are still to be resolved, as are the reasons that drove them to abandon the land of their ancestors and explore and conquer new territories. It is probably no coincidence that this first great Mesoamerican expansion occurred at a time when the central valleys were experiencing major territorial resettlements and deep cultural transformations as a result of the eruptions of the volcanoes Popocatepetl and Xitle and the rise of Teotihuacán as a major ceremonial center (as witnessed by its monumental pyramids during the Tzacualli phase).

The archaeological evidence, including the presence of tripod vessels of composed silhouette and incised decoration, points to the central valleys as a source for the participants' origin. One also recognizes in some geometric motifs an inheritance from the Chupícuaro Culture and elements of the succeeding Morales phase in Guanajuato. Finally, a certain style of resist-decorated pottery is very similar to that found in the Jalisco Heights.

Following this initial stage, the essential traits of the culture prevailed, including the splitting off of the great majority of the population into small villages. Paradoxically, this dispersal was marked by a surprising unity, reflected archaeologically by a settlement pattern dominated by defensive systems and the presence of common architectural forms or ceramic types, among other aspects. One of the most powerful factors underlying this unity seems to have been the presence of great pan-regional sanctuaries, such as the one at La Quemada. Another aspect of the culture that is particularly relevant to our argument is the deliberate iconophobia characterized by a complete absence of figurative elements that prevailed during the initial Canutillo phase. Instead, all decoration was reduced to geometric motifs, dominated by the stepped scroll (*xicalcoliuhqui*).

THE U.S. SOUTHWEST PRIOR TO A.D. 600

By this time, some communities of the U.S. Southwest had been in contact with southern peoples for centuries. Although these contacts are still far from adequately understood, the remarkable linguistic unity of the Uto-Aztecan languages suggests millennia of population movements and cultural transformations (Hill 1992; Hill and Hays-Gilpin 1999; Valiñas Coalla 2000). The corn-bean-squash triad, introduced into the Southwest from Mesoamerica sometime prior to the beginning of the first millennium B.C. (Cordell 1997:124-126), also supports southern connections. Relatively little is known, however, about the peoples who occupied the immense territory between the U.S. Southwest and Nuclear Mesoamerica during these remote times. All we do know is that they did not participate in the Mesoamerican world.[3] Much remains to be learned about Mesoamerican influences on southwestern ceramics during the initial phases of the Hohokam, Mogollon, and Basketmaker-Pueblo cultures, prior to the Chalchihuites' expansion into Durango.

As these investigations develop, rock art offers a particularly eloquent source of information. It provides our earliest indication of exchange networks between northwestern Mexico and the southwestern United States—or, as we refer to this region here, the Northwest—long before the Toltec-Purépecha journey north (Hers cited in Braniff et al. 2001:66).

THE SIXTH-CENTURY DISRUPTION

During the second half of the sixth century A.D., dramatic events marked the end of the Teotihuacán world. These events must have affected the entire Mesoamerican universe, particularly in the realm of ideas. As noted earlier, the ancestors of the Purépecha were one of the groups in contact with, and under the religious sway of, the grand metropolis of Teotihuacán. These ties were shaken by profound transformations and internal disruptions, including the rise of a triumphant religious iconoclastic movement, which probably led to the migration or expulsion of those who refused to forsake their sacred images. These migrants traveled toward the land of the Chalchihuites, where they profoundly influenced local religious conceptions and attitudes toward images. It was at this time that the Chalchihuites, following a long period of iconophobia and strictly geometric art, initiated a new phase of intense figurative creativity. Here we focus on two developments: evidence for a religious disruption in the Purépecha world between the Loma Alta and Lupe phases (ca. A.D. 550) and the appearance of Purépecha elements among the Chalchihuites of the Alta Vista phase (ca. A.D. 550-850).

The Purépecha Disruption

We have noted that a major closing ceremony took place on the Loma Alta island, at which time ancient sacred stone images were ritually broken and placed in

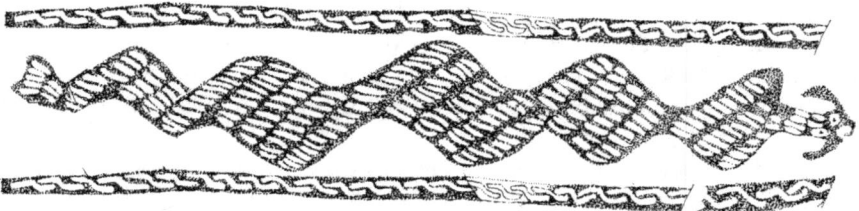

Figure 17.6. The Bird-Serpent, Loma Alta phase, site of Loma Alta. Drawing by Françoise Bagot.

a pit in the middle of an altar, together with the previously mentioned Purépecha-Teotihuacán ritual vessel. This disruption, both real and symbolic, corresponded to the end of the Loma Alta tradition and a figurative language that had flourished for centuries. Evidence of this disruption is reflected in the architecture, when all the structures, including the great sunken patio, were completely filled and sealed. This period coincided with a climatic phenomenon that lowered the level of Zacapu Lake. As new areas of land emerged, they were immediately occupied, as evident at the ceremonial and funerary site of Guadalupe, built on a low butte that emerged at the same time, three kilometers south of the site of Loma Alta.

Despite these disruptions, the Loma Alta site and its surroundings continued to be used. The ceremonial center grew eastward as fill accumulated in areas where the surrounding marsh had dried up. At the same time, at the foot of the island a well was "killed" by placing at its bottom, before filling and sealing it, an arrangement of stones and offerings of ritually broken water-jar necks and painted and incised ceramics. One of these ceramics, decorated in a negative technique with a bird-beaked and feathered-body aquatic serpent, bears an ancient image of the Bird-Serpent, which recurs throughout the history of this Northwest region (Figure 17.6). This motif also resembles the pan-Pueblo plumed water-serpent deities, *Paalölöqangw* of the Hopi (Whiteley 1998:193), *Kolowisi* of the Zuni, and *Awanyu* of the Tewa.

Thus a number of elements provide evidence of major changes and disruptions in both the cultural and climatic realms. During the succeeding Lupe phase, those Purépecha people who remained in the region abruptly transitioned from a centuries-old figurative design system to an austere period of image rejection, which coincided with the appearance of elements related to the art of war (Pereira 1999).

The Intertwined Destinies of the Chalchihuites and the Purépecha-Uacusecha

The Loma Alta ideology did not disappear. Rather, its images and rituals moved north. At the site of La Quemada, recently discovered ceramics provide evidence of ties between Chalchihuites and Purépecha-Uacusecha groups. Ceramists at La Quemada employed a Purépecha technology, including a negative polychrome technique, that was distinct from the older local Chalchihuites negative technique, no longer in use by the sixth century. La Quemada ceramics are also decorated with mixed motifs from Loma Alta and Chalchihuites iconographies (Braniff et al. 2001:247, fig. 3).

The fact that such an eloquent fusion of ritual visual languages occurred at La Quemada, the largest of the Chalchihuites sanctuaries, is not surprising. (For additional discussion of the La Quemada site and its place in Chalchihuites Culture, see Hers 1998, 2002, 2005.) Purépecha migrants, defenders of an ideology expressed through a vivid corpus of images, were apparently well received by the La Quemada faithful. In fact, at the time of the Purépecha disruption (ca. A.D. 550), the Chalchihuites community was undergoing a period of spiritual innovation, evidenced by the flourishing of figurative art following centuries of a strictly geometric tradition. In regional centers as well as humble villages, decorated ceramic types were revived. Through the use of diverse techniques practiced since earlier times, an original iconographic corpus began to flourish (Kelley and Kelley 1971). A new figurative style of rock art also echoed the same corpus of images (Hers 2001).

Negative polychrome ceramic plates that strongly express this religious Purépecha-Chalchihuites symbiosis have been found only at La Quemada, but additional evidence of this symbiosis can be seen within the confines of the north. The most obvious element is the mythological human-serpent figure, which emanated from Loma Alta art and appeared in Chalchihuites iconography, where it became one of its predominant designs (Figure 17.7).

Other probable testimony of the Purépecha Culture's contribution to the Chalchihuites is found in the Sierra del Nayar (the southern part of the Sierra Madre Occidental). Here, two *chac mool* sculptures flanked a temple stairway at the Cerro del Huistle, a small Chalchihuites site we will return to later. This *chac mool* figure appears linked to a northern oracle tradition, yet a Purépecha signature is reflected in the curious combination of different techniques used to carve the sacred image. In the first example (Figure 17.4c), the stone carving, although crude, clearly depicts the typical reclining *chac mool* posture as well as two actions typically attributed to his character: the receiving of offerings on his body, now transformed into a ceremonial table, and the opening of his mouth to transmit the divine word. In the second example (Figure 17.4d), the native stone of the sculpture is nearly untouched, and the natural shape barely alludes to the same figure of the *chac mool*. With just a few strokes, the general square form was modified to evoke the bent body and erect head of the *chac mool*. What we consider the neck was carved by abrasion to distinguish the head as the most active part of the figure, as if the intention was not to impose upon the surface a precise form but rather to liberate the force or being already present in the stone. Thus at the entrance to this small temple are two different conceptions of the same sacred image existing side-by-side. As discussed earlier, this is similar to the two sets of sculptures buried at the Loma Alta altar.

Figure 17.7. Human-serpent composite figures from (a) Loma Alta, drawing by Françoise Bagot, and (b) the Chalchihuites area, adapted from Kelley and Kelley (1971:pls. 19a, 22a, 25f, 27d).

The Purépecha's presence seems to have had an additional impact on these northerners' lives. A short time after the flourishing of figurative art, beginning in A.D. 600, the Chalchihuites people experienced profound changes: they again embarked on their ancestors' march northward and colonized hundreds of square kilometers of Durango's Sierra Madre Occidental, considerably extending their territory to the high Conchos River Basin (Barbot and Punzo 1997; Berrojalbiz in press a and b; Hers 2005; Hers and Soto 1995; Hers, Soto, and Polaco 1998; Punzo Diaz in press a and b; Tsukada in press; for a discussion of the impact of the Teotihuacán population diaspora on Mesoamerican expansion in Durango, see Flores, Hers, and Porcayo in press). Accompanying the Chalchihuites on this great epic were Purépecha migrants. This helps explain the presence of a distinctive funerary ritual at Hervideros, one of the major Chalchuites sites in Durango, where the Tepehuanes and Santiago rivers meet in the high Nazas Basin. Here were found urns filled with finely ground ashes, similar to the cremation urns found at Loma Alta in its initial phase, as described earlier.

Much remains to be understood about interactions between the Purépecha and Chalchihuites, but we now have greater insight concerning one aspect of their common history: how they joined forces to colonize the Durango mountain range and establish strong bonds with territories even farther north, in Arizona and New Mexico, during the seventh to ninth centuries A.D.

THE NORTHERN ROAD

Once again, a comparison can be made with colonial history. Just as post-conquest Nahuatl and Tarascan communities participated in the Spanish colonization of northern New Spain without loss of their respective identities, so, many centuries earlier, did the Chalchihuites and the Uacusecha-Purépecha come into contact with far northwestern communities without losing aspects of their respective cultures. In the following discussion, we first identify certain recognizable Purépecha and Chalchihuites elements in the pre-Hispanic cultures of the U.S. Southwest, then examine some elements that moved in the opposite direction into the Mesoamerican region. Finally, we suggest some ways in which the nature of these cultural interactions can be understood.

The seventh century in the U.S. Southwest was marked by the emergence of localized architectural and ceramic traditions that archaeologists refer to as the Hohokam, Mogollon, and Anasazi or Ancestral Pueblo.[4] As relationships intensified among northern Mesoamerican and southwestern communities between A.D. 600 and 850, it is likely that the older trails were used again, the same ones traveled long before. As a number of authors have noted (e.g., Haury 1976; Kelley 1966; Kelly 1943; Nelson 1986; Schroeder 1966), it is among the Hohokam Culture that these contacts with Mesoamerican groups are most evident. Much of this evidence is based on the pioneering excavations at Snaketown (Gladwin et al. 1965; Haury 1976), the Grewe site (Woodward 1931), and Hodges Ruin (Kelly 1978). Since then, Hohokam archaeology has expanded considerably (Crown 1991; Doyel 1991). However, until now, those sites have produced the most relevant collections to document the Mesoamerican connection (McGuire 1993:100).

Purépecha Iconography and Rituality among the Hohokam

Evidence of Hohokam and Mesoamerican cultural relationships, principally with the Chupícuaro tradition, was first identified by Emil Haury (1976) and later substantiated by Beatriz Braniff (1995) on the basis of materials from the Morales phase. Now we are better able to specify the nature and chronology of these ties. These interactions did not occur directly with the Chupícuaro but through the intermediary of the Loma Alta tradition, the immediate inheritor of the Chupícuaro-Morales tradition.

The influence of the old Purépecha iconography on Hohokam Culture is striking. Of the forty motifs identified from Loma Alta, twenty-six are present in Hohokam ceramics, compared with only fourteen in the Chalchihuites corpus (Carot 2001; see also Teague 1998:178, fig. 8.3). Furthermore, this repertoire was expressed with the same mastery as seen in the Loma Alta style, using swift and sure strokes and painting in a schematic but expressive manner. The designs are displayed on the interiors or exteriors of the ceramics, sometimes both, and appear in free arrangement, friezes, or quartered composition, as in the old Chupícuaro ceramics. In some cases, a single figure fills the entire space.

Among the animal designs, one can identify aquatic birds with open wings and large beaks, ducks or geese, serpents and caimans, deer, and squirrels. The human figures generally appear as lines of dancers, each with well-marked body movements and frequently schematized in simple undulated and vertical linear silhouette. This unique manner of depicting the dance is characteristic of both the Loma Alta style and Hohokam ceramics and rock art (Bostwick 2002). Among the geometric designs, the stepped scroll, or *xicalcoliuhqui*, prevails. It is also very common in Chalchihuites and Hohokam iconography, as pointed out by Braniff (1995) in her important study of northern iconography. We have already noted the similarities between certain funerary customs of the Purépecha and Hohokam, including cremation and the breaking of offerings. We also recall the unique case of the sunken Fire God House from the ceremonial architecture at Loma Alta and its resemblance to southwestern pithouse forms.

The Chalchihuites and the Hohokam

It has long been proposed that the fourfold division of the interior decoration of Hohokam ceramic plates was inherited from the Chalchihuites. This inheritance involved not only particular motifs (Kelley 1966:102) but also a true Mesoamerican cosmovision, with gods and colors associated with each of the cardinal directions.[5] Additional evidence of this relationship is seen in the mirrors with mosaics (Carot 2005; Woodward 1941) and the so-called pseudo-cloisonné decoration (Hers 1983). The strong similarities between anthropomorphic and zoomorphic figurines the Chalchihuites inherited from the ancient Morales phase can be underscored here as well.

Another Hohokam element widely considered to have originated in Mesoamerica is the ball game—its general conception, not the particular floor plan of the ballcourts. In this respect, investigations recently conducted in Durango have confirmed the importance of this practice, as expressed by the presence of numerous small ballcourts at major sites and in the most humble villages (Berrojalbiz 2005, in press b; Hers 1989b, in press c; Kelley 1991). Additionally, copper bells appeared early among the Chalchihuites, by the seventh or eighth century (Hers 1990), and from the ninth century onward were emblematic of trade relations between the Southwest and Mesoamerica.

Patricia Carot and Marie-Areti Hers

The Flute Player Route

The most innovative aspect of our study of Mesoamerican and southwestern relationships pertains to the contribution of the U.S. Southwest to Mesoamerica, which has been little considered. Earlier studies of this cultural bridge incorrectly viewed it as a unilateral movement of influences from south to north. In the rock art of the Sierra Madre Occidental, however, we can clearly see what these Mesoamericans received from their far northern neighbors. In this respect, the image of the flute player stands out as a symbol par excellence of economic and ritual relations between these widespread communities. We now know that this versatile figure is found in rock art from the Grand Canyon to the Lerma-Santiago Basin. Over this wide territory, the flute player's music was heard and his heroic deeds commemorated.

This character, popularly but erroneously referred to today as Kokopelli (Hers 2001, in press b; Malotki 2000), appears in the U.S. Southwest during the sixth century. He is found in the lively scenes of Hohokam ceramics and rock art, as well as in the territory of the northern Ancestral Pueblo Culture. A.D. 600 was a time of great social fluidity and interaction, when iconography expressed alliances in ethnically diversified settlements. This was also when this well-known figure appeared in diverse forms in the Pueblo rock art style (Cordell 1997:249). About this same time, the flute player and other important southwestern motifs were carved and painted in many places along the Sierra Madre Occidental. Thus just as the Chalchihuites and Purépecha made themselves present in the far north in the context of Hohokam cultural florescence and the beginnings of Pueblo Culture, so too did the ancestors of the Pueblo Indians leave their mark in northern Mesoamerican lands.

What was the nature of this interrelationship? To answer this question, we must reopen a debate that has been trapped between two sterile extremes: isolationism versus a centralizing view of a radiating Mesoamerica. The isolationist tendency, which ignores the possible impacts of Mesoamerican cultures on the Southwest, seems to correspond to a defensive attitude, as if recognizing the importance of this impact would undermine the relevance of the achievements of southwestern communities. This view also seems to reflect a certain ignorance of Mesoamerican archaeology in the southwestern academic world, comparable only to the ignorance that prevails among Mesoamericanists relative to the Southwest.

Contrasting with this isolationist view are numerous interpretations based on an image of Nuclear Mesoamerica as a civilizing force that radiated toward simpler northern populations, creating pale copies of their southern prototypes in an area subject to the needs of the great centers of civilization.[6] From Charles Di Peso's diffusionist interpretations for Paquimé to the more recent world system model applied to the Greater Northwest, this centralism obscures the already scarce information we have about the people who interacted with the ancient Southwest—the Chalchihuites peoples of northern Mesoamerica. Chalchihuites iconography itself suffers from this centralist prejudice because it is usually presented as a product of illiterate artists who copied models from the Mesoamerican pantheon, albeit poorly (see, for example, Kelley and Kelley 1971:31).

The origin of the problem lies in a view that considers the Mesoamerican universe profoundly different from that of the U.S. Southwest, a world of pyramids and palaces associated with societies marked by social, economic, political, and religious elites that ruled over large cities and developed state formations versus essentially egalitarian rural communities in the peripheral regions. But another Mesoamerica existed as well, the northern one, which shared many of its religious values, cosmovisions, traditions, and techniques with Nuclear Mesoamerica but lacked its great cities and states. The main limitations to sociopolitical state formation were its vast and sparsely populated territory, which was continually expanding and threatened by war—both wars of resistance and latent harassment from local non-Mesoamerican groups and threats from nomads who occupied the bordering lands in the arid east. Internal conflicts must have been constant in a society of colonizers in which warriors held the prevailing status.

The importance of warfare is reflected throughout the Chalchihuites territory by the presence of diverse defensive systems, strictly adapted to the topography of each locale. Such systems were responses not to the dangers of territorial conquest but to the threat of sudden and fatal attacks directed toward plundering and a quest for captives, some destined for ritual sacrifice (Hers 1989a:chapter 4). Under such circumstances, the coercive force of any potential elite would find its power drastically diminished if it were deemed incapable of efficiently protecting its subjects. Thus it is not surprising that even the major sites have failed to produce evidence of a highly differentiated elite, in terms of either funerary apparel or residential space. Nor has any kind of territorial supremacy been documented at a regional scale beyond the narrow spatial limits of immediate protection.[7]

Diverse Chalchihuites communities developed forms of sociopolitical and economic organization that were essentially egalitarian but certainly not simple, based more on the force of consensus than of coercion and structured according to lineage hierarchies and their alliances within the same settlements and at a regional level. Viewed in this perspective, the Chalchihuites world would have been as complex and difficult for outsiders to comprehend as, for example, historic Hopi society. At all levels, Chalchihuites life was marked by a tension between alliances within each settlement or region and by hierarchical segmentation organized by delimited kinship units and religious or military societies. This tension between unity and segmentation was eloquently expressed in the architecture and rock art. Indeed, residential spaces were clearly segmented around patios or familial courts. In rock art, the recurring aspect was the abundance, in the same locations, of social-marker shields, each one unique, as if to say "we are here together, but we respect our differences."

The Chalchihuites therefore shared essential traits with ancient southwestern communities. They developed an "egalitarianism" that is difficult to comprehend from our Western reality, one that defies the simplicity of our categories, for example, for the great Hohokam irrigation networks or the monumental constructions of the Chaco world. The cultures of northern Mesoamerica and the ancient Southwest were continually at the mercy of precarious agriculture in difficult and unpredictable climatic conditions. It was the strength of their social ties that allowed them to defy the region's territorial immensity and maintain unity at some level despite migrations, colonizing expansions, and the hazards of wars and droughts.

Had the distance between Nuclear Mesoamerica and the Southwest not been so great or the intermediate territories not been colonized by the Chalchihuites, the relationships between both universes would have been very different and closer to models proposed in the past, which emphasized their deep disparities. Nevertheless, a great spatial interval still remains to be documented in the modern states of Chihuahua and Sonora, between the northernmost Chalchihuites communities located at the southern limit of the high Conchos Basin (for example, the site of Loma San Gabriel on the Florido River) and Hohokam, Mogollon, and northern Ancestral Pueblo lands. As has recently occurred in Durango, it is expected that future investigations, particularly rock art research, will reveal evidence of the routes by which people, ideas, and goods traveled through Chihuahua and Sonora (see Guevara Sánchez, Chapter 18).

Chalchihuites rock art testifies to what this far northern territory might have signified to northern Mesoamericans. By studying the distributions of these rock art sites, spaced twenty or thirty kilometers apart, we can document the daily stages of the journeys along the route. In addition to the flute player, the rock art of northwestern Mexico and the U.S. Southwest shares other motifs, including women with the characteristic Pueblo butterfly hairdo, whose presence at sites in Durango may indicate that women also participated in these expeditions (Braniff et al. 2001:245-248). Representations of "exotic" animals such as the buffalo and pronghorn enabled travelers to evoke their faraway lands, where heroes undertook great deeds as merchants, explorers, pilgrims, and warriors.

The bow and arrow must have been one of the most significant technological contributions of the ancient Southwest to the Chalchihuites; the weapon is later known and depicted in Nuclear Mesoamerica by Chichimec archers. The image of the archer is present in Hohokam ceramics during the period that concerns us here (Haury 1976:figs. 12.87, 12.92). The Chalchihuites also adopted this theme in their rock art, recording their new acquisition (Figure 17.8).

In the Chapalagana Basin of the southern Sierra Madre Occidental, at a site with engravings associated with the occupation of the Cerro del Huistle, we find even richer evidence of what the north may have meant to those who visited this sanctuary. Before we examine this evidence, recall that the Huistlenians were representative of areas in which Chalchihuites settlements did not grow beyond the level of villages and hamlets but who nevertheless were able to organize their defenses in an autonomous way. Yet despite the apparent simplicity of their material culture, they did not live an isolated existence. Without depending on any regional center for their security, they participated in extensive exchange networks for valuable goods,

Figure 17.8. Figures with bows and arrows on ceramics and rock art. (a) Hohokam Sacaton Red-on-buff pottery, adapted from Haury (1976:fig. 12.92u); (b) Chalchihuites rock art from Durango, drawing by Marie-Areti Hers.

including marine shells, green amazonite, turquoise, and copper bells. In their ceramics, lithic industry, and architectural materials and forms, they demonstrated a thorough participation in the Chalchihuites Culture (Hers 1992, 1998, 2005).

On the side of a long cliff covered by hundreds of motifs, the Huistlenians selected an isolated panel to summarize their history in the north, grouping three scenes and incorporating an irregularity in the rock's surface.[8] At the lower end of the panel, three individuals walk in a line upstream, toward the north. This is the Mesoamerican convention for migration. It is probable that the Huistlenians participated in the great territorial expansion that occurred around A.D. 600 in Durango's Sierra Madre, as part of a Chalchihuites colonizing movement from the southern part of their territory 400 kilometers to the north. In the middle of the rock panel, a principal figure, wearing a headdress and holding a dart or cane, subdues another figure by the head in a conventional gesture of conquest. We know warriors played an important role in many aspects of Chalchihuites life and that warfare found its religious justification in human sacrifice. Above this conquest scene, a narrow cornice interrupts the smooth rock surface, spanning its entire width. We believe that when this panel was composed, the artists intentionally included this natural irregularity in their discourse. Indeed, had they wished to exclude it, there would have been sufficient space below to compose the three scenes without recourse to a scaffold. This inclusion of natural elements in the composition is a common aspect of Chalchihuites rock art and that of many other cultures. The convention was probably used here to distinguish the two lesser scenes, with their apparently historic content, from the personage who dominates the panel to underscore his non-mundane character or the different space of his actions.

Above the transverse line, we recognize the flute player. Perhaps the panel can be translated in this way: "We migrated to the north, we conquered, and in this manner, we got to know the flute player world." Obviously, there are many questions about this story. Nevertheless, the rock art panel suggests the importance the Huistlenians attributed to their adventures in the far north and their participation in the mythic and ritual universe associated with the flute player. Studies of Chalchihuites rock art now in progress, including documentation of the diverse forms in which the flute player appears, will allow us to better understand the significance of the flute player to the Chalchihuites. For now, the fact that this versatile figure was shared by so many communities over such immense distances and across so many centuries evokes the mythical character of Poseyemu-Montezuma-Jesus, so distinctive of the Pueblo world (Parmentier 1979).

Various hypotheses can be proposed to explain such intense contacts between these remote areas: commerce in precious goods, such as green stones (amazonite, turquoise); pilgrimages to large sanctuaries, such as those of La Quemada or Cruz de la Boquilla (near Sombrerete, Zacatecas), where a network of causeways seems to have channeled the flow and ritual movements of the faithful; expeditions to sacred places, such as those that mark the extensive sacred geography of the modern Huichol; war adventures; migrations. But the data are still missing to establish accurate hypotheses. Whatever happened, we do know that beyond its diversity, the sociopolitical and religious organization of these peoples was connected through the ancient trails of the Greater Northwest and shared a central element: a force capable of resisting considerable territorial resettlement. This force proved vital to the Chalchihuites in the face of dramatic circumstances that marked the ninth century.

THE NINTH-CENTURY DISRUPTION

Wars, starvation, droughts? The reasons behind the generalized contraction of the northern Mesoamerican frontier in the ninth century to the limits that prevailed in the sixteenth century are still debated. About A.D. 850, much of the Chalchihuites territory in the modern states of Zacatecas and Jalisco was abandoned. Some of the population may have gone to the north to the Sierra Madre of Durango, where a Chalchihuites enclave persisted for some time. Others may have taken refuge in the mountain range known today as the Great Nayar. Others went south, back toward their original ancestral lands (Braniff and Hers 1998; Carot 2005; Hers 2002).

Historical sources from the sixteenth century preserve the memory of these migrations when the so-called Chicomoztoquenses, or natives of Chicomoztoc, abandoned the north and resettled among peoples who had not participated in the colonization and loss of this area. These historical references are distorted by a confusion that has prevailed until now concerning these northern immigrants. Commonly, all Chichimec groups have been viewed as nomadic non-Mesoamerican tribes, similar to those who dominated the north from the thirteenth century and violently resisted Spanish conquest. This point of view, however, ignores recent progress in northern Mesoamerican archaeology, which allows us to differentiate between nomadic Chichimecs and Mesoamerican ones, those people who left the north, who are referred to in the sources as Chicomoztoc (Seven Caves) for their place of origin.

When they returned to the south, not all of these northern Mesoamericans were well received. Their arrival marked significant changes. Among the various Chichimec groups who emerged from the northern Chicomoztoc, two stand out in the tradition transmitted by Sahagún's informants: the Toltec Chichimec and the Michoaques, the latter referred to as the Uacusecha in the *Relación de Michoacán*. These groups have also been documented by recent archaeological investigations.

Similar phenomena occurred in both cases. From the north came the bow-and-arrow peoples, strongly organized warriors ready to adapt to migration and take over new territories, migrants able to impose their way of worshipping the gods with human sacrifices and *tzompantli*, or skull racks. These people built singular cloisters and gathered warrior assemblies through rituals ordered by the celestial bodies. Their oracles were held in great esteem, including one character, sculptured in the *chac mool* form, who received the offerings of the faithful and expressed through his mouth the divine will. In this way, the fates of both groups were repeatedly intertwined, first during their epic adventure in the far northern lands of the ancient Southwest and later during their reincorporation into Nuclear Mesoamerica.

THE SOUTHWARD RETURN OF THE NORTHERN MESOAMERICANS

As we have pointed out, the return of the northerners described by Indian informants in historical sources is recognized archaeologically by a suite of coherent elements related to religious and military power: the *chac mool*, the hall cloister, and the *tzompantli*. Significantly, both the Uacusecha and the Toltec Chichimec expressed this same complex of ritual elements. (For a synthesis of this northern legacy, see Hers 2002:53.) Furthermore, in both cases the figure of the flute player has recently been recognized, tangible evidence of the inheritance these northerners preserved from their heroic deeds in the Greater Northwest (Hernández Díaz 2006).

The return of the Toltec Chichimec took place in the Tula region, where other groups of northerners from the central north (the modern states of Querétaro and Guanajuato) had migrated long before. For this reason, while the multiethnic city of Tula flourished under the rule of the Toltec Chichimec warriors, its northern inheritance was diverse and decisive in its power equilibrium. It is in this perspective that Tula's attempts to recover parts of the lost north by establishing precarious settlements in Querétaro, Guanajuato, and San Luís Potosí can be understood (Braniff et al. 2001:106–112; Braniff and Hers 1998).

Two or three centuries after the northward migration of the Uacusecha, the return of these northern peoples seems to have occurred in several stages and various regions. From the Lerma corridor to the Zacapu region, archaeological evidence documents a group of powerful and strongly organized immigrants who intruded on southern lands and began occupying different areas until their return to the region from whence their ancestors had departed in the sixth century A.D. At San Antonio

Carupo and Nogales on the south slope of the Lerma corridor, they established new settlements and raised ceremonial constructions with the innovative hall-cloister form related to Chalchihuites architecture (Faugère-Kalfon 1996; Pereira, Migeon, and Michelet 2005). By the tenth century they had returned to the Zacapu region and founded the first settlement at the edge of the Zacapu Basin during the Palacio phase. Later, during the Milpillas phase, as large establishments flourished amid the barren and well-protected badlands of the Zacapu region, they undertook rituals that underscored their faraway origins in Michoacán (Carot 2001:131). This effort to reveal their roots and return to their origins is eloquently expressed in the famous negatively decorated polychrome Tarascan ceramics, which mimic those of the old Loma Alta phase, so well imitated that they have produced chronological confusion among archaeologists (Carot 2005; Caso 1930).[9] Finally, these northerners established themselves in Purépecha country, where they created a powerful state, the so-called Tarascan Empire, that soon opposed the Mexica Empire. The *Relación de Michoacán* identifies these people as Chichimecs (in other words, northerners) but also clearly recognizes them as affiliated with local inhabitants. Indeed, these sources emphasize that the newcomers, the Uacusecha or Eagle Knights, shared the same Purépecha language and pantheon as those who had remained in Michoacán (Franco Mendoza 2000).

THE NORTH IN THE LAST CENTURIES BEFORE THE SPANISH ARRIVAL

About the time the Chicomoztoc peoples arrived in Nuclear Mesoamerica and consolidated their political power, the Hohokam tradition with its Mesoamerican legacy evolved on its own, reaching its greatest achievements and influencing the flourishing Classic Mimbres art. Through this intermediary, Mesoamerican heritage from the first millennium persisted into Casas Grandes world imagery (Brody 2004:81–86; Moulard 2002:185–197).

By about the eleventh century, new contributions from the U.S. Southwest appeared in the Chalchihuites enclave in Durango. Among these developments, the cliff dwellings are the most evident, dispersed throughout the Sierra Madre in diverse forms and with varying functions (Lazalde 1984, 1987; Punzo in press a; Hers in press a).[10] At the same time, this enclave, isolated for a while from the south and abandoned by the northern Mesoamericans, reestablished its bonds with Nuclear Mesoamerica through the coastal route. Indeed, between A.D. 950 and 1250 in the coastal plain, the Aztatlán expansion occurred, moving the Mesoamerican frontier hundreds of kilometers to the north, from the Piaxtla to the Fuerte rivers. As such, this coastal route was consolidated long before it was traveled by the first Spanish expeditions to the lands of Cibola.

Meanwhile, in the Southwest the so-called Chaco Phenomenon occurred, characterized by the splendor of its constructions and its network of roads extending throughout the territory. Echoes of the old bonds with the Chalchihuites can be recognized in the esteem for copper bells and turquoise held by the participants in this complicated political and religious system. Pilgrimages seem to have played a central role in this formidable integration system (Cordell cited in Braniff et al. 2001:102). It is reminiscent of the great pan-regional sanctuary at La Quemada, also marked by an extended grid of causeways (Nelson 1995).

Toward the thirteenth century, considerable changes occurred in the Greater North, both in Mexico and the U.S. Southwest. The inland route was disrupted when the Tepehuanes, originating from Sonoran lands, occupied the eastern valleys of the Durango mountain range formerly abandoned by the Mesoamericans (Berrojalbiz 2005, in press a and b). On the Pacific Coast another Mesoamerican retreat took place, and Culiacán became the last great urban center along this coastal route. Meanwhile, high in the Sierra Madre of Durango, the Acaxees and the Xiximes, who later confronted the Spaniards and were drastically decimated, are considered the descendants of the Chalchihuites Culture (Punzo 1999, in press a).

In the U.S. Southwest another great cultural and territorial resettlement took place, which constitutes the roots of the historic Pueblos and the O'Odham. The so-called Southwest Regional Cult focused on agricultural fertility rituals and addressed the integrative needs of communities facing migration and ethnic division (Crown 1994). Eventually, this gave way to a flourishing figurative style in ceramics and mural painting (e.g., Hibben 1975:9-66) in which motifs appear that were originally Mesoamerican and were later introduced into the Southwest (Crown 1994:217-225; see also Weigand 2004). The Mesoamerican origins of these motifs can be precisely identified. The majority appear in Chalchihuites rock art, dated between A.D. 600 and 850 (Hers 2005), and include the famous horned serpent, which later appears in the rock art of Chaco Canyon in the Southwest (Crown 1994:220).

To the south in Paquimé, the memory of the Toltec warriors is recognizable in the *tezcacuitlapilli*, or dorsal copper shields, similar to those carried by Tula warrior figures known as the Atlantes, and in the series of human skulls suspended for exhibition. By this time, the bond uniting the Southwest and Mesoamerica no longer passed through the inland Chalchihuites road. Rather, the prevailing route was now the coastal road dominated by the city of Culiacán, which led inland north to Paquimé.

CONCLUSIONS

Relationships between the U.S. Southwest and Mexico were not developed by the great state formations of Teotihuacán, Tula, or Tenochtitlán but rather through the mediations of diverse communities of northern Mesoamerica. Like the ancestors of the Pueblo Indians, these communities developed a sociopolitical and economic organization that was essentially rural and egalitarian, based on maize agriculture in lands constantly threatened by the adversities of drought. Their complex religious and ceremonial lives enabled them to preserve their identities across an immense territory, the boundaries of which fluctuated according to the hazards of war and migrations and within which sacred geography and great pilgrimages played a predominant role.

A century ago, some of the great pioneers in anthropology recognized affinities between the ancient Mexica, the inhabitants of the Great Nayar, and the Pueblo Indians. A century later, archaeology is able to confirm these astute observations and document the long history of the Northwest, when the Toltec Chichimec and the Uacusecha crossed destinies in the Chalchihuites territory of the Sierra Madre Occidental and developed strong bonds in the faraway lands of Arizona and New Mexico. This remote epic did not entirely disappear, as these peoples inherited in many ways the cultural legacy of the northerners.

At the time of the conquest, the Mexicas (Aztecs) were proud to have originated from Chicomoztoc and saw themselves as descendants of the Toltec Chichimec. Despite many differences between the Mexicas and their mythical ancestors, they preserved in their religious life essential elements of their northern roots. As we pointed out in our introduction, comparisons of the ancient Mexicas and modern Huichols, Coras, and Mexicaneros by Eduard Seler and Konrad Preuss that seemed so audacious at first are now supported by a historical basis that can be traced back to the northern Chalchihuites. Indeed, these people inherited a similar Toltec Chichimec background.[11]

Except in the case of the Mexica, a deep misunderstanding of the northern epic we have synthesized here still prevails. Indeed, in an obvious reference to their Toltec Chichimec ancestry, the Mexica chose the north side of the principal pyramid to erect the Casa de las Aguilas (House of the Eagle Knights) at the center of the most sacred place in Tenochtitlán. The layout and decoration of this singular construction follow the model of the Toltec Chichimec cloister, found, for example, at La Quemada and Tula. Symmetrically, on the south side of the pyramid they constructed a temple inspired by the Teotihuacán model. In this way, the Mexica expressed the complex cultural confluence characterizing the origins of their world.

After centuries of conquest among peoples who best resisted and defended their own cultures, other descendants of the long history reconstructed here also stand out: the modern Cora, Huichol, and Mexicanero communities of the Sierra Madre Occidental and the Pueblo Indians of Arizona and New Mexico, particularly the Hopi. Certain Chalchihuites sculptures eloquently reveal the legacy of this ancient shared history, such as the anthropomorphic phallus carrying a vulva on its neck, similar to images about the underworld referenced in Hopi and Huichol traditions (Aedo 2003). (For another recent essay that convincingly compares the Chalchihuites, Huichol, and Pueblo worlds and demonstrates how the theme of southwestern U.S.–Mesoamerican relations can be revitalized, see Faba and Fauconnier in press.). Centuries ago, the precious green stones and copper bells and the paths of the legendary flute player were largely usurped by the routes of gold, silver, and the cross. Because of their deep roots in a common past, however, the ways of the Northwest are still alive and in constant transformation.

Epic of the Toltec Chichimec and the Purépecha in the Ancient Southwest

Acknowledgments. We express our gratitude to Randall McGuire, who read an earlier draft of this chapter and helped us get to this final draft.

NOTES

1. The Michoacán and Loma Alta projects were conducted between 1983 and the present by the Centre Français d'Etudes Mexicaines et Centraméricaines (CEMCA), with funding from the Ministère des Affaires Etrangères and the Centre National de la Recherche Scientifique and with the collaboration of the Subdirección de Laboratorios y Apoyo Académico of the Instituto Nacional de Antropología e Historia (INAH) and the Instituto de Investigaciones Antropológicas of the Universidad Nacional Autónoma de México (UNAM). For publications resulting from this work, see Carot (1998, 2000, 2001, 2005).

2. The Hervideros project was conducted between 1993 and the present by the Instituto de Investigaciones Estéticas of UNAM, with funding from the Consejo Nacional para la Ciencia y la Tecnología (the 0451-H9108 and 3286-H9308 projects), and the Dirección de Asuntos del Personal Académico (Project IN402494) of UNAM, in collaboration with the Instituto de Investigaciones Antropológicas (UNAM), CEMCA, and la Subdirección de Laboratorios y Apoyo Académico of INAH. For a publication resulting from this work, see Hers (2005).

3. See Hers (cited in Braniff et al. 2001:113, note 1; in press c) for reasons we consider the hypothesis of an intermediate Loma San Gabriel Culture in the Sierra Madre of Durango untenable.

4. Although the term "Ancestral Pueblo" is often used as a synonym for the Anasazi Culture, this disregards the multiple ancestral origins of modern Pueblo groups (Brody 2004: xiv), including Hohokam cultural affiliation (McGuire 1993:99).

5. Kelley (1966:98, 109) associated the four directions with a fire god, a sun god, twin war gods associated with a Quetzalcoatl concept, and a rain/fertility cult. His hypotheses were partially upheld in a later ceramics study (Kelley and Kelley 1971). Although that publication is a major source of information, a more systematic study of Chalchihuites iconography is still needed, one less tied to the idea that this culture is merely a pale reflection of Nuclear Mesoamerican models.

6. For example, Phil Weigand (2001) interprets the Chalchihuites as intermediaries between a valued raw material—turquoise—in the Southwest and the needs of the elite in Nuclear Mesoamerica. Recent archaeological fieldwork in Durango raises serious doubts about this hypothetical turquoise route (Hers cited in Braniff et al. 2001:125–130).

7. Ben Nelson (1995) believes La Quemada was supported by an extremely reduced rural population forced to raise the citadel's monumental constructions through the coercive and brutal force exercised by the local nobility, which was sustained by human sacrifice. The role of human sacrifice can be interpreted in a totally different way, however, such as a privileged way to channel and control warrior violence in societies lacking state coercive force, as masterfully studied by René Girard (1983). It is in this sense that the *tzompantli*, or skull racks, of the small Huistle village are interpreted (Hers 1989a).

8. Françoise Fauconnier is preparing a monograph on the Las Adjuntas rock art site (Faba and Fauconnier in press).

9. This attitude of Tarascan ceramists toward the art of their ancestors can be compared with the revival of Classic Mimbres art by the elite of Casas Grandes as a way to assert affiliation with prestigious ancestors (Moulard 2005:73).

10. These numerous constructions in rocky shallow caves, often located in the least accessible cliffs, lack the characteristic T-shaped doorways so common in the Southwest and adopted by the inhabitants of the Chihuahua mountain range associated with Paquimé.

11. The Aztec people in their original lands of Aztlán in northwestern Mesoamerica should not be confused with the Mexicas of the Aztec Empire. The first group played some part in the history synthesized here. The participation of the second in the history of the Southwest would be an anachronism (McGuire 1980).

REFERENCES CITED

Aedo, Angel
    2003   Imágenes de la Sexualidad y Potencias de la Naturaleza: El Caso de las Esculturas Fálicas Chalchihuiteñas de Molino, Durango. *Anales del Instituto de Investigaciones Estéticas* 25(82):47-72. Universidad Nacional Autónoma de México, México.

Barbot, Christophe, and José Luis Punzo
    1997   Antiguos Caminos en el Noroeste Durangueño: Supervivencia de una Tradición Prehispánica. *Trace* 31:22-34. Centre Français d'Etudes Mexicaines et Centraméricaines (CEMCA), México.

Berrojalbiz, C. Fernando
    2005   *Los Paisajes Prehispánicos del Alto Río Ramos, Durango, México*. Ph.D. dissertation, Universidad Nacional Autónoma de México, México.
    In press a   Desentrañando un Norte Diferente: Los Tepehuanes Prehispánicos del Alto Río Nazas. In *Asentamientos y Movimientos de Población en la Sierra Tepehuana desde la Prehistoria hasta Nuestros Días*, ed. Chantal Cramaussel. Simposio Internacional, Santa María Ocotán, Abril del 2000, El Colegio de Michoacán, Zamora.
    In press b   *Paisajes y Fronteras de Durango Prehispánico*. Universidad Nacional Autónoma de México y Universidad Juárez del Estado de Durango, México.

Bonfiglioli, Carlo, Arturo Gutiérrez, and María Eugenia Olavaria (editors)
    2006   *Las Vías del Noroeste, 1: Una Macrorregión Indígena Americana*. Instituto de Investigaciones Antropológicas, Universidad Nacional Autónoma de México, México.

Bostwick, Todd W.
    2002   *Landscape of the Spirits: Hohokam Rock Art at South Mountain Park*. University of Arizona Press, Tucson.

Braniff, Beatriz
    1995   Diseños Tradicionales Mesoamericanos y Norteños. Ensayo de Interpretación. In *Arqueología del Occidente y Norte de México: Homenaje a J. Charles Kelley*, ed. Barbro Dahlgren and Ma. de los Dolores Soto de Arechavaleta, 181-209. Instituto de Investigaciones Antropológicas, Universidad Nacional Autónoma de México (UNAM), México.
    1998   *Morales, Guanajuato, y la Tradición Chupícuaro*. Colección Científica 373. Instituto Nacional de Antropología e Historia, México.

Braniff, Beatriz, Linda S. Cordell, María de la Luz Gutierrez, Marie-Areti Hers, and Elisa Villalpando C.
    2001   *La Gran Chichimeca: El Lugar de los Rocas Secas*. CONACULTA, México, and Jaca, Milan.

Braniff, Beatriz, and Marie-Areti Hers
  1998   Herencias Chichimecas. *Arqueología* (segunda serie) 19:55-80. Dirección de Arqueología, Instituto Nacional de Antropología e Historia, México.

Brody, Jerry J.
  2004   *Mimbres Painted Pottery*, rev. ed. School of American Research Press, Santa Fe.

Carot, Patricia
  1997   A Propos de la Découverte d'un Lot de Sculptures sur le Site de Loma Alta, Zacapu, Michoacán. *Trace* 31:64-69. Centro de Estudios Mexicanos y Centroamericanos, México.
  1998   Cronología de la Ocupación en Loma Alta, Zacapu, Michoacán, o los Antecedentes de la Cultura Purhépecha. In *Antropología e Interdisciplina, Homenaje a Pedro Carrasco, XXIII Mesa Redonda de la Sociedad de Antropología*, Volume 2, 45-63. Sociedad Mexicana de Antropología, Instituto de Investigaciones Antropológicas, UNAM, México.
  2000   Las Rutas al Desierto: de Michoacán a Arizona. In *Nómadas y Sedentarios en el Norte de México: Homenaje a Beatriz Braniff*, ed. Marie-Areti Hers, José Luis Mirafuentes, Ma. De los Dolores Soto, and Miguel Vallebueno, 91-112. Instituto de Investigaciones Antropológicas, Estéticas, e Históricas, Universidad Nacional Autónoma de México, México.
  2001   *Le Site de Loma Alta, Lac de Zacapu, Michoacán, Mexique.* BAR International Series 920. Archaeopress, Oxford, and Paris Monographs in American Archaeology 9, Paris.
  2005   Reacomodos Demográficos del Clásico al Posclásico en Michoacán: El Retorno de Los que se Fueron. In *Reacomodos Demográficos del Clásico al Posclásico en el Centro de México*, ed. Linda Manzanilla, 103-121. Instituto de Investigaciones Antropológicas, Universidad Nacional Autónoma de México, México.
  In press   Cuando se Abandonaron las Imágenes Sagradas: Un Ritual de Clausura del Siglo VI en Loma Alta (Zacapu, Michoacán). In *Imagen, Símbolos y Metáforas del Poder en Mesoamérica*, ed. Guilhem Olivier. Instituto de Investigaciones Históricas, Universidad Nacional Autónoma de México, México.

Caso, Alfonso
  1930   Informe Preliminar de las Exploraciones Realizadas en Michoacán. *Anales del Museo Nacional*, 4a época 6(2):446-452. México.

Cordell, Linda
  1997   *Archaeology of the Southwest*, 2nd ed. Academic, New York.

Corona Nuñez, José
  1957   *Mitología Tarasca.* Fondo de Cultura Económica, México.

Crown, Patricia L.
  1991   The Role of Exchange and Interaction in Salt-Gila Basin Hohokam Prehistory. In *Exploring the Hohokam: Prehistoric People of the American Southwest*, ed. George J. Gumerman, 383-416. University of New Mexico Press, Albuquerque.
  1994   *Ceramics and Ideology: Salado Polychrome Pottery.* University of New Mexico Press, Albuquerque.

Doyel, David
    1991   Hohokam Exchange and Interaction. In *Chaco and Hohokam: Prehistoric Regional Systems in the American Southwest*, ed. Patricia L. Crown and W. James Judge, 225–252. School of American Research Press, Santa Fe.

Faba, Paulina, and Françoise Fauconnier
    In press   Las Adjuntas: Arte Rupestre Chalchihuiteño y Cosmovisión Huichola. In *Las Vías del Noroeste: Hacía Una Perspectiva Sistémica de una Macroregión Indígena Americana*, ed. Carlo Bonfiglioli, Arturo Gutiérrez, Marie-Areti Hers, and María Eugenia Olavaria. Coloquio Internacional (Real de Catorce, Febrero de 2004). Instituto de Investigaciones Antropológicas, Universidad Nacional Autónoma de México, México.

Faugère-Kalfon, Brigitte
    1996   *Entre Zacapu y Río Lerma: Culturas en una Zona Fronteriza*. Cuadernos de Estudios Michoacanos 7. Centro de Estudios Mexicanos y Centroamericanos, México.

Fewkes, Jesse W.
    1893   A Central American Ceremony Which Suggests the Snake Dance of the Tusayan Villagers. *American Anthropologist* 6(3):285–303.

Flores, Daniel, Marie-Areti Hers, and Antonio Porcayo
    In press   Sobre el Trópico en un Mar de Lava: Análisis Astronómico, Arqueológico e Iconográfico en el Septentrión Mesoamericano. In *Las Vías del Noroeste: Hacía Una Perspectiva Sistémica de una Macroregión Indígena Americana*, ed. Carlo Bonfiglioli, Arturo Gutiérrez, Marie-Areti Hers, and María Eugenia Olavaria. Coloquio Internacional (Real de Catorce, Febrero de 2004). Instituto de Investigaciones Antropológicas, Universidad Nacional Autónoma de México, México.

Franco Mendoza, Moisés (coordinator)
    2000   *Relación de las Ceremonias y Ritos y Población y Gobierno de los Indios de la Provincia de Michoacán*. Facsimile reproduction of 1541 manuscript. C IV 5 de El Escorial. El Colegio de Michoacán A. C. Gobierno del Estado de Michoacán, México.

Gendrop, Paul
    1970   *Arte Prehispánico en Mesoamérica*. Trillas, México.

Girard, René
    1983   *La Violencia y lo Sagrado*. Editorial Anagrama, Barcelona.

Gladwin, Harold S., Emil W. Haury, E. B. Sayles, and Nora Gladwin
    1965   *Excavations at Snaketown: Material Culture*. University of Arizona Press, Tucson.

Gómez, Sergio
    2002   Presencia del Occidente de México en Teotihuacán: Aproximaciones a la Política Exterior del Estado Teotihuacano. In *Ideología y Política a Través de Materiales, Imágenes y Símbolos*, ed. Maria Elena Ruiz Gallut, 563–625. Memoria de la Primera Mesa Redonda de Teotihuacán, CONACULTA, Instituto Nacional de Antropología e Historia (INAH), México.

Haury, Emil
    1945   The Problem of Contacts between the Southwestern United States and Mexico. *Southwestern Journal of Anthropology* 1(1):55–74.
    1976   *The Hohokam: Desert Farmers and Craftsmen. Excavations at Snaketown, 1964–1965*. University of Arizona Press, Tucson.

Hernández Díaz, Veronica
2006   Imágenes en Piedra de Tzintzuntzán. Anales del Instituto de Investigaciones Estéticas. Universidad Nacional Autonóma de México, México.

Hers, Marie-Areti
1983   La Pintura Pseudocloisonné, una Manisfestación Temprana en la Cultura Chalchihuites. In *Anales del Instituto de Investigaciones Estéticas* 53:25-39. Universidad Nacional Autónoma de México, México.
1989a *Los Toltecas en Tierras Chichimecas*. Cuadernos de Historia del Arte 35. Instituto de Investigaciones Estéticas, Universidad Nacional Autónoma de México, México.
1989b ¿Existió la Cultura Loma San Gabriel? El Caso de Cerro Hervideros, Durango. *Anales del Instituto de Investigaciones Estéticas* 60:33-57. Universidad Nacional Autónoma de México, México.
1990   Los Objetos de Cobre en la Cultura Chalchihuites. In *Un Hombre, un Destino y un Lugar: Homenaje a Federico Sescosse*, ed. José Guadalupe Victoria, 45-60. Gobierno del Estado de Zacatecas, México.
1992   Colonización Mesoamericana y Patrón de Asentamiento en la Sierra Madre Occidental. In *Origen y Desarrollo en el Occidente de México*, ed. Brigitte Boehm de Lameiras and Phil C. Weigand, 103-136. El Colegio de Michoacán, Zamora.
1998   La Sierra del Nayar en el Contexto del Septentrión Mesoamericano. In *Estudios sobre Arte; Sesenta Años del Instituto de Investigaciones Estéticas*, ed. Martha Fernández and Louise Noëlle, 45-55. Universidad Nacional Autónoma de México, México.
2001   La Música Amorosa de Kokopelli y el Erotismo Sagrado en los Confines Mesoamericanos. In *Amor y Desamor en las Artes*, ed. Arnulfo Herrera, 293-336. XXIII Coloquio Internacional de Historia del Arte del Instituto de Investigaciones Estéticas, Jalapa. Universidad Nacional Autónoma de México, México.
2002   Chicomoztoc, un Mito Revisado. *Arqueología Mexicana* 10(56):48-53. Julio-Agosto. Serie Historia de la Arqueología en México 5. INAH y Editorial Raíces, México.
2005   Imágenes Norteñas de los Guerreros Tolteca Chichimecas. In *Reacomodos Demográficos del Clásico al Posclásico en el Centro de México*, ed. Linda Manzanilla, 11-44. Instituto de Investigaciones Antropológicas, UNAM, México.
In press a   Durango y Sinaloa: Estado Actual de la Cronología de la Ocupación Mesoamericana. In *Cronología Historiográfica del Occidente*, ed. Beatriz Braniff. Centro de Estudios Antropológicos del Occidente Nogueras, Universidad de Colima y Centro INAH Colima, Colima.
In press b   La cultura Chalchihuiteña: Un Antiguo Camino de Tierra Adentro. In *Caminos y Puentes en la Nueva España*, ed. Salvador Alvarez, Chantal Cramaussel, and José Omar Moncada Maya. Instituto de Geografía, Universidad Nacional Autónoma de México, México, and El Colegio de Michoacán, Zamora.
In press c   La Sierra Tepehuana: Imágenes y Discordancias sobre su Pasado Prehispánico. In *Asentamientos y Movimientos de Población en la Sierra Tepehuana desde la Prehistoria hasta Nuestros Días*, ed. Chantal Cramaussel. Simposio Internacional, Santa María Ocotán, Abril del 2000. El Colegio de Michoacán, Zamora.

Hers, Marie-Areti, and Dolores Soto
　1995　Arqueología de la Sierra Madre Durangueña: Antecedentes del Proyecto Hervideros. *IV Congreso Internacional de Historia Regional Comparada* 1:69-89. Universidad Autónoma de Ciudad Juárez.

Hers, Marie-Areti, Dolores Soto, and Oscar J. Polaco
　1998　Reactivar la Arqueología Durangueña. *Hervideros*, un proyecto en curso *Transición*. Instituto de Investigaciones Históricas, Universidad Juárez del Estado de Durango, Durango.

Hibben, Frank C.
　1975　*Kiva Art of the Anasazi at Pottery Mound*. KC Publications, Las Vegas, Nev.

Hill, Jane H.
　1992　The Flower World of Old Uto-Aztecan. *Journal of Anthropological Research* 48(2): 117-144.

Hill, Jane H., and Kelley Hays-Gilpin
　1999　The Flower World in Material Culture: An Iconographic Complex in the Southwest and Mesoamerica. *Journal of Anthropological Research* 55:1-37.

Holien, Thomas
　1977　*Mesoamerican Pseudo-Cloisonné and Other Decorative Investments*. Ph.D. dissertation, Department of Anthropology, Southern Illinois University, Carbondale.

Jiménez Betts, Peter, and J. Andrew Darling
　2000　Archaeology of Southern Zacatecas: The Malpaso, Juchipila, and Valparaiso-Bolaños Valleys. In *Greater Mesoamerica: The Archeology of West and Northwest Mexico*, ed. Michael Foster and Shirley Gorenstein, 155-180. University of Utah Press, Salt Lake City.

Kelley, J. Charles
　1966　Mesoamerica and the Southwestern United States. In *The Handbook of Middle American Indians*, Volume 4, *Archaeological Frontiers and External Connections*, ed. Gordon Ekholm and Gordon R. Willey, 95-110. University of Texas Press, Austin.
　1986　The Mobile Merchants of Molino. In *Ripples in the Chichimec Sea: New Considerations of Southwestern-Mesoamerican Interaction*, ed. Frances Joan Matthien and Randall H. McGuire, 243-269. Southern Illinois University Press, Carbondale.
　1991　The Known Archaeological Ballcourts of Durango and Zacatecas. In *The Mesoamerican Ballgame*, ed. Vernon L. Scarborough and David R. Willcox, 87-100. University of Arizona Press, Tucson.

Kelley, J. Charles, and Ellen Abbott Kelley
　1971　*An Introduction to the Ceramics of the Chalchihuites Culture of Zacatecas and Durango, Mexico: Part I: The Decorated Wares*. Mesoamerican Studies 5. University Museum, Southern Illinois University, Carbondale.

Kelly, Isabel
　1943　West Mexico and the Hohokam. In *El Norte de México y el Sur de Estados Unidos. Tercera Reunión de Mesa Redonda sobre Problemas Antropológicos de México y Centro América*, ed. Rafael García Granados, 206-222. Sociedad Mexicana de Antropología, México.

1978   The Hodges Ruin: A Hohokam Community in the Tucson Basin. *Anthropological Papers of the University of Arizona* 30. University of Arizona Press, Tucson.

Lazalde, Jesús F.
1984   Patrones de Asentamiento Tipo "Cliff Dwellers" en el Norte de México. *Pantoc* 7:89–107. Instituto de Investigaciones Antropológicas, Universidad Autónoma de Guadalajara, Guadalajara.
1987   *Durango Indígena: Panorama Cultural de un Pueblo Prehispánico en el Noroeste de México.* Impresiones Gráficas México, S.A., Gómez Palacio, Durango.

Lumholtz, Carl
1981   *Unknown México: A Record of Five Years' Explorations among the Tribes of the Western Sierra Madre, in the Tierra Caliente of Tepic and Jalisco, and among the Tarascos of Michoacán.* Facsimile of the 1902 edition with an introduction by B. Hinton. 2 volumes. Río Grande Press, Glorieta, N.M..

Malotki, Ekkehart
2000   *Kokopelli: The Making of an Icon.* University of Nebraska Press, Lincoln.

McGuire, H. Randall
1980   The Mesoamerican Connection in the Southwest. *Kiva* 46(1-2):3–38.
1993   The Structure and Organization of Hohokam Exchange. In *The American Southwest and Mesoamerica: Systems of Prehistoric Exchange*, ed. Jonathan E. Ericson and Timothy G. Baugh, 95–119. Plenum, New York.

Michelet, Dominique
1992   El Centro-Norte de Michoacán: Características Generales de su Estudio Arqueológico Regional. In *El Proyecto Michoacán, 1983–1987: Medio Ambiente e Introducción a los Trabajos Arqueológicos*, ed. Dominique Michelet, 9–52. Cuadernos de Estudios Michoacanos 4. CEMCA, México.

Moulard, Barbara L.
2002   *Re-creating the Word: Painted Ceramics of the Prehistoric Southwest.* Schenk Southwest, Santa Fe.
2005   Archaism and Emulation in Casas Grandes Painted Pottery. In *Casas Grandes and the Ceramic Art of the Ancient Southwest*, ed. Richard F. Townsend, 66–97. Art Institute of Chicago, Chicago.

Nelson, Ben A.
1995   Complexity, Hierarchy, and Scale: A Controlled Comparison between Chaco Canyon, New Mexico, and La Quemada, Zacatecas. *American Antiquity* 60(4): 597–618.

Nelson, Richard S.
1986   Pochteca and Prestige: Mesoamerican Artifacts in Hohokam Sites. In *Ripples in the Chichimec Sea*, ed. Frances Joan Matthien and Randall H. McGuire, 154–182. Southern Illinois University Press, Carbondale.

Noble, David Grant
1981   *Ancient Ruins of the Southwest: An Archaeological Guide.* Northland, Flagstaff.

Noguera, Eduardo
1944   Exploraciones en Jiquilpan. *Anales del Museo Michoacano*, 2ª época: 3:37–54. Morelia.

Parmentier, Richard J.
  1979 The Mythological Triangle: Poseyemu, Montezuma, and Jesus in the Pueblos. In *Handbook of North American Indians*, Volume 9, *Southwest*, ed. Alfonso Ortiz, 609-622. Smithsonian Insitution Press, Washington, D.C.

Pereira, Gregory
  1996 Nuevos Hallazgos Funerarios en Loma Alta, Zacapu, Michoacán. In *Las Cuencas del Occidente de México: Época Prehispánica*, ed. Eduardo Williams and Phil Weigand, 105-129. El Colegio de Michoacán, Zamora.
  1999 *Potrero de Guadalupe: Anthropologie Funéraire d'une Communauté Prétarasque du Nord du Michoacán, Mexique*. BAR International Series 816, Oxford.

Pereira, Gregory, Gerald Migeon, and Dominique Michelet
  2005 Transformaciones Demográficas y Culturales en el Centro-Norte de México en Vísperas del Posclásico: Los Sitios del Cerro Barajas (Suroeste de Guanajuato). In *Reacomodos demográficos del Clásico al Posclásico en el centro de México*, ed. Linda Manzanilla, 123-153. Instituto de Investigaciones Antropológicas, Universidad Nacional Autónoma de México, México.

Preuss, Konrad Theodor
  1998 Paralelos entre los Antiguos Mexicanos y los Actuales Indígenas Huicholes. In *Fiesta, Literatura y Magia en el Nayarit: Ensayos sobre Coras, Huicholes y Mexicaneros de Konrad Theodor Preuss*, ed. Jesús Jáuregui and Johannes Neurath, 99-104. Instituto Nacional Indigenista y Centro Francés de Estudios Mexicanos y Centroamericanos, México.

Punzo Diaz, José Luis
  1999 *La Mesa de Tlahuitoles en lo Alto de la Sierra Madre Occidental de Durango: Apuntes para la Historia Antigua Xixime*. Ph.D. dissertation, Escuela Nacional de Antropología e Historia, México.
  In press a Una Larga Secuencia de Ocupación Mesoamericana en la Sierra Xixime. In *Asentamientos y Movimientos de Población en la Sierra Tepehuana desde la Prehistoria hasta Nuestros Días*, ed. Chantal Cramaussel. Simposio Internacional, Santa María Ocotán, Abril del 2000. El Colegio de Michoacán, Zamora.
  In press b La Ruta de las Praderas en Época Prehispánica. El Caso del Abrigo de Piedra de Amolar 1, Durango. In *Las Vías del Noroeste: Hacía una Perspectiva Sistémica de una Macroregión Indígena Americana*, ed. Carlo Bonfiglioli, Arturo Gutiérrez, Marie-Areti Hers, and María Eugenia Olavaria. Coloquio Internacional (Real de Catorce, Febrero de 2004), Instituto de Investigaciones Antropológicas, Universidad Nacional Autónoma de México, México.

Riley, Carroll
  2005 *Becoming Aztlan: Mesoamerican Influence in the Greater Southwest, A.D. 1200-1500*. University of Utah Press, Salt Lake City.

Schroeder, Albert H.
  1966 Pattern Diffusion from Mexico into the Southwest After A.D. 600. *American Antiquity* 31(5):683-704.

Seler, Eduard
  1998 Indios Huicholes del Estado de Jalisco. In *Fiesta, Literatura y Magia en el Nayarit: Ensayos sobre Coras, Huicholes y Mexicaneros de Konrad Theodor Preuss*, ed. Jesús Jáuregui

and Johannes Neurath, 63-98. Instituto Nacional Indigenista y Centro Francés de Estudios Mexicanos y Centroamericanos, México.

Teague, Lynn S.
1998   *Textiles in Southwestern Prehistory*. University of New Mexico Press, Albuquerque.

Tsukada, Yoshiyuki
In press   Estudio Comparativo de dos Grandes Asentamientos Chalchihuiteños en Durango: Molino y Hervideros. In *Asentamientos y Movimientos de Población en la Sierra Tepehuana desde la Prehistoria hasta Nuestros Días*, ed. Chantal Cramaussel. Simposio Internacional, Santa María Ocotán, Abril del 2000. El Colegio de Michoacán, Zamora.

Valiñas Coalla, Leopoldo
2000   Lo que la Lingüística Yutoazteca Podría Aportar en la Reconstrucción Histórica del Norte de México. In *Nómadas y Sedentarios en el Norte de México: Homenaje a Beatriz Braniff*, ed. Marie-Areti Hers, José Luis Mirafuentes, Ma. de los Dolores Soto, and Miguel Vallebueno, 175-207. Instituto de Investigaciones Antropológicas, Instituto de Investigaciones Estéticas, Instituto de Investigaciones Históricas, Universidad Nacional Autónoma de México, México.

Weigand, Phil C.
2001   El Norte Mesoamericano. *Arqueología Mexicana* 9(51):34-39. Instituto Nacional de Antropología e Historia, Editorial Raíces, México.
2004   Los Antecedentes Mesoamericanos de los Murales Kiva de los Hopis de Awatowi, Norte de Arizona: Análisis y Escenario. *Relaciones* 100:313-340. El Colegio de Michoacán, Zamora.

Whiteley, Peter M.
1998   *Rethinking Hopi Ethnography*. Smithsonian Institution Press, Washington, D.C.

Willcox, David R.
1986   A Historical Analysis of the Problem of Southwestern-Mesoamerican Connections. In *Ripples in the Chichimec Sea*, ed. Frances Joan Matthien and Randall H. McGuire, 9-44. Southern Illinois University Press, Carbondale.

Woodward, Arthur
1931   The Grewe Site, Gila Valley, Arizona. *Occasional Papers of the Los Angeles Museum of History, Science and Art* 1, Los Angeles.
1941   Hohokam Mosaic Mirrors. *Los Angeles County Museum Quarterly* 1(4):7-11.

18

Mesoamerican Influences in the Imagery of Northern Mexico

Arturo Guevara Sánchez

This chapter examines symbolic imagery from archaeological sites in northern Mexico, primarily the state of Durango, where painted figures found on large rocks may have formed parts of sanctuaries. Images attributed to a group of hunter-gatherers known as the Zacateco appear to show Mesoamerican influences. Other imagery suggests distinct influences from the southwestern United States via Paquimé in Chihuahua. Some influences may have been brought to Durango by traders traveling between Mesoamerica and Paquimé (see also Weigand 1997).

EXAMPLES FROM DURANGO AND COAHUILA

Communication between northern Mexico and the Chalchihuites area dates from Preclassic times, with the exchange of turquoise from the southwestern United States to Tula passing through the modern states of Durango and Zacatecas (Weigand 1997:28). With deviations to the east, this route was maintained until the Late Postclassic period. A sanctuary of basalt rocks occurs in San Quintín Canyon, Durango, at the edge of a great rocky outcrop known as La Breña. Here is found a dartlike petroglyph commonly associated with the cult of Ehécatl, the Mesoamerican god of

Arturo Guevara Sánchez

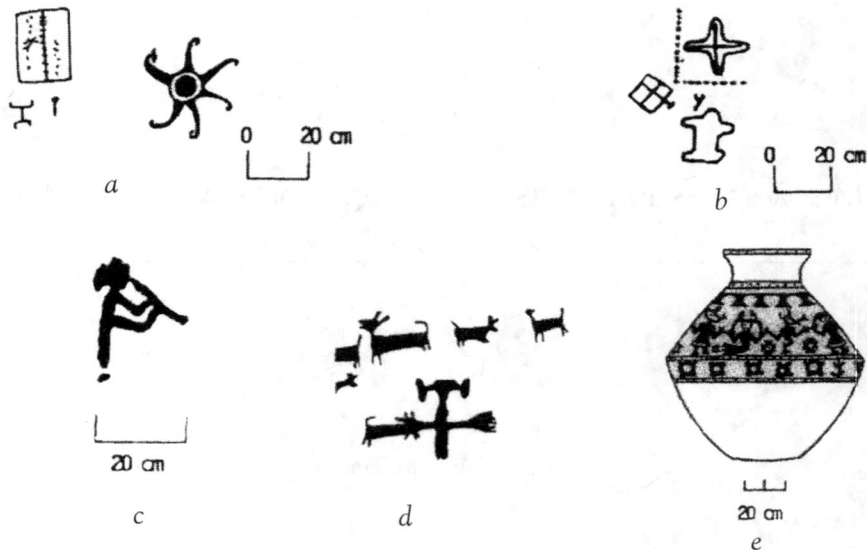

Figure 18.1. (a) Engraving associated with the Ehécatl, the wind spirit in central Mexico, from San Quintín Canyon, Durango; (b) cruciform figure from a site in the Sierra Madre of Durango; (c) figure of Kokopelli from Piedra de Amolar, adapted from Punzo Díaz (1999); (d) butterfly-style hairdo found at Tepehuanes, adapted from Lazalde Montoya (1987); (e) jar from La Ferrería, Durango, depicting a figure with only one leg, adapted from Guevara Sánchez (in press).

wind (Figure 18.1a). The Zacatecos people carefully carved the figure into the wall of the site, which at the time formed part of the territory of Nombre de Dios.

Some of the Mesoamerican travelers who left the Chalchihuites area probably headed north, which would explain the diffusion of these rock art designs. This appears to have been the case at Site 8 in the Sierra Madre, cited in the work of Jesús Fernando Lazalde Montoya (1987:144), an amateur archaeologist who has undertaken investigations in the state of Durango. Designs on some of the rock paintings resemble those found on ceramics from Paquimé. These include a design with a rectangular base divided by diagonal lines that may represent the ball game and a cruciform design associated in central Mexico with representations of precious materials, usually gold (Figure 18.1b) (León Portilla 1997:18). Other meanings may also exist for these figures, such as their association with Venus in the southwestern United States.

Another interesting case involves the image of the flute player known in the U.S. Southwest as Kokopelli (Punzo Díaz 1999:51), or Kokolipau. This figure appears at many archaeological sites in the region, including Piedra de Amolar 1 (Figure 18.1c), where it co-occurs with other figures.

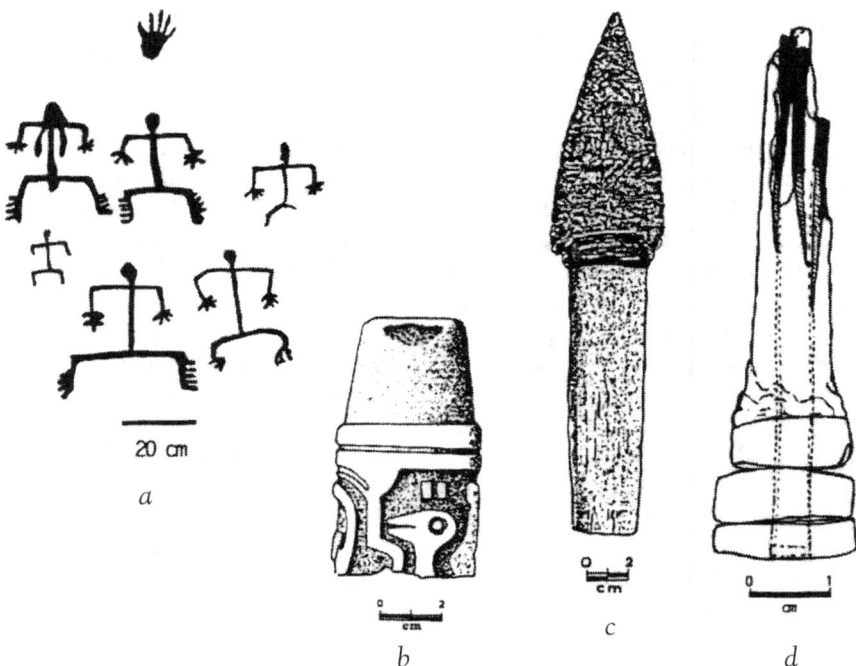

Figure 18.2. (a) Dancers with braids and leather anklets similar to those worn by some Pueblo groups in the southwestern United States, adapted from Lazalde Montoya (1987); (b) polychrome sherd from the coastal cultures, found at La Ferrería, Durango, adapted from Guevara Sánchez (in press); (c) hafted knife from Candelaria Cave, adapted from Aveleyra Arroyo de Anda, Maldonado-Koerdell, and Martínez del Río (1956:fig. 13); (d) spear guard from Candelaria Cave, adapted from Aveleyra Arroyo de Anda, Maldonado-Koerdell, and Martínez del Río (1956:fig. 43).

J. Charles Kelley (1976:30) reported the presence of a cult that worshipped Tezcatlipoca among the Chalchihuites culture. Evidence of this cult may be present at La Ferrería in Durango and at the archaeological site known at Schroeder (Guevara Sánchez in press). This may be the same deity some nomadic groups from northern Durango associated with whirlwinds that appeared on the plains. This deity is commonly depicted with only one foot and may have been venerated to avoid potential danger. Designs corresponding to such a personage appear on the ceramics of La Ferrería. In these designs, the individual appears to float on air. The single-legged figure that appears on some jars from La Ferrería (Figure 18.1e) may be related to Cachiripa, the indigenous name for the spirit associated with whirlwinds, which Pablo Martínez del Río (1954) considered to have Zacatecos roots.

Some of the rock art imagery found in the foothills may have been inspired by ceremonies practiced in the southwestern United States. For example, a painting at the site known as SM2, documented by Lazalde Montoya (1987), depicts a group of human figures dancing. Some of these figures have long braids and appear to wear anklets or leather bands around their ankles (Figure 18.2a), a style still practiced by some Pueblo tribes.

Another site in the region of Guatimapé, Durango, is El Molino. This place must have been of considerable importance to the people of La Ferrería and was used by Kelley (1997) as the final phase name of his chronology. From approximately A.D. 1350–1400, this region saw strong influences from the Pacific Coast. A trade route from the coast connected the coastal regions of Sinaloa with central Durango, through which Mesoamerican groups traveled to La Ferrería and surrounding settlements. Copper objects produced by West Mexican techniques have been found at these sites, as well as spindle whorls and painted objects similar to those described by Gordon Ekholm (1942:89) from Guasave. Although La Ferrería has been intensively looted, pottery sherds of a type known as Amole Polychrome have recently been found (Guevara Sánchez in press) (Figure 18.2b). These could have arrived at the site by way of the route that connects the coast with El Molino and La Ferrería.

In the area surrounding El Molino in central Durango is a cave known as the Cave of Monos, which depicts a battle scene. Painted by an indigenous group, the mural shows a group of indigenous people quarreling with another group that includes a number of horsemen. This painting, which we call "The Battle Mural," documents an attack by Europeans against an indigenous group in which the former emerged victorious. Significantly, between the figures another figure can be seen dancing in an animated manner. The individual is adorned with large feathers that hang from both arms horizontal to the body (Guevara Sánchez 2002:102). Similar figures are found in the cave paintings of Sonora. These may correspond to some indigenous dances from the southwestern United States in which dancers imitate the movements of birds.

This Battle Mural also contains the figure of a person wearing a headdress similar to those worn by some Pueblo katsinas. Both the birdlike dancer described earlier and this figure appear dressed to participate in some type of ritual designed to influence the course of events. This may be another influence brought to Durango over trade routes from the southwestern United States.

Near the highway that runs from Durango to El Zape is a small archaeological site with rock engravings located in Tepehuanes country on the banks of Potreros Creek. Based on the designs, the site appears to have been occupied by people of the Zacatecos Culture, an influential Mesoamerican group. Between the engraved figures is the representation of a funerary bundle, approximately oval in form. Also recognizable are the straps used to wrap the body. The most interesting aspect of this image, however, is the head, which is outside the bundle, separate from the body, and adorned with a *copilli*, or feathered crown, a symbol of royalty in central Mexico. This provides further evidence of Mesoamerican influence in the designs of this region. This site on Potreros Creek was probably occupied by an indigenous group that had seen this symbol used as a mark of power and superior ancestry by members of another culture and placed it on the body of one of their dead leaders.

Not far from the Tepehuanes River in Durango is the small town of El Zape. Here is found a shelter with high, vertical walls where some type of solar ritual was held. Jaime Ganot Rodríguez and Alejandro Peschard Fernández (1997:237-242), physicians and dedicated avocational archaeologists, have studied this ceremonial site and identified a solar alignment on the spring equinox.

This area is also known for its many exceptional rock art depictions recorded by J. Alden Mason (1961). Engravings at one rockshelter, referred to as Las Pitarrillas by the local community, are very well preserved. They consist mostly of small rectangles with patterns at their centers, some with fringes extending from the central designs. One hypothesis, which will be tested in another study, is that the patterns represent cloaks used by a group of Zacatecos, with each design associated with an extended family or clan.

Approaching the Tepehuanes River and close to the previous site is Site RT4, following the nomenclature of Lazalde Montoya. In addition to other engravings, this site includes two important images that appear to represent funerary bundles. Above them occur antlers of a ceremonial nature that appear to represent an elaborate headdress. These headdresses would have been of great ritual importance for hunter-gatherers of the region, and their rock paintings depict figures wearing such headdresses.

Within this collection of Tepehuanes sites is one known as Site 1. Here is found a depiction of a person with a hairstyle typical of a Hopi woman (Guevara Sánchez 1999:147) (Figure 18.1d). This suggests influence from indigenous Pueblo groups in present-day Arizona and New Mexico.

Nearby, in the lake region of western Coahuila, are the important burial sites of Candelaria and Neblina caves, which contained some remarkable features. In the former were found hafted knives (Figure 18.2c) attached to the left arms of the interred in a manner reminiscent of the famous Atlantes statues of Tula (Acosta 1961:224). A sheath (Figure 18.2d) was also found that protected the spears used in ceremonies of self-sacrifice. These may be the work of members of the Zacatecos Culture, although this research is still in progress.

FINAL CONSIDERATIONS

In this preliminary study I have highlighted a number of Mesoamerican influences in northern Mexico, focusing on those found in cave rock art. Although I have limited my discussion to the Late Postclassic period, earlier periods may also show important influences.

One possible trade route, perhaps the most important in the study area, was the one that connected the coastal region with the site known as El Molino. Interactions between these areas must have been intense because they left their mark

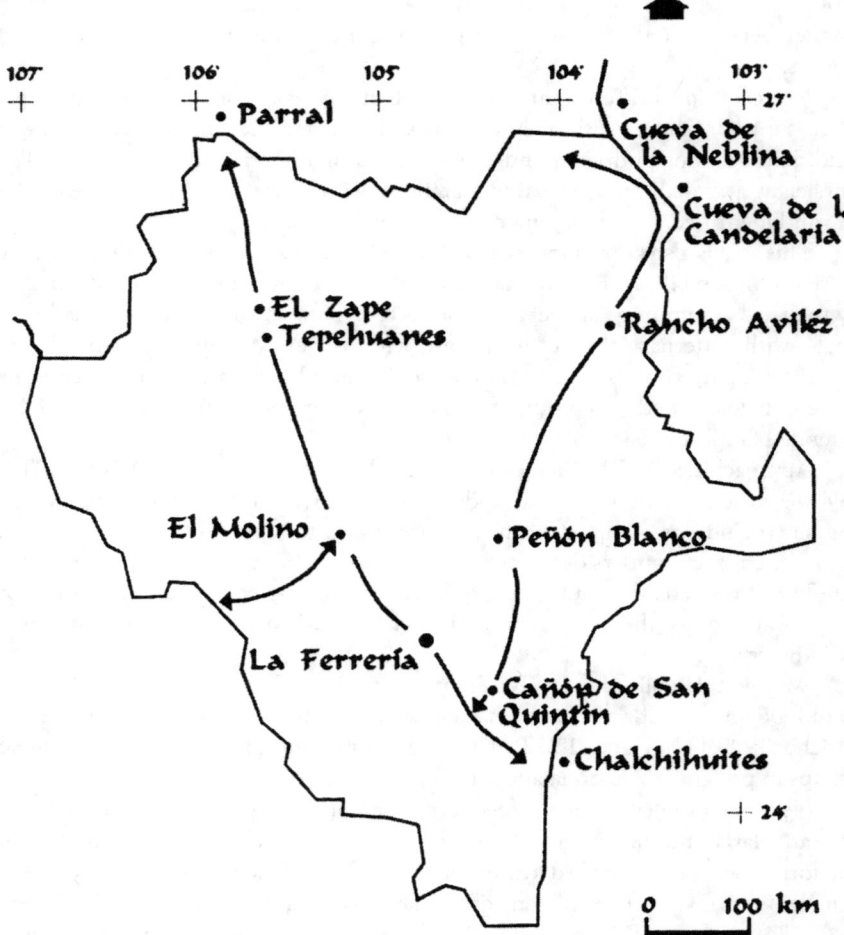

Figure 18.3. Major pre-Hispanic trade routes in the modern state of Durango, northern Mexico.

on trade and cultural patterns, as evidenced by the many influences adopted by the more receptive groups. Another trade route appears to have passed through the Chalchihuites area, extending through Durango in a diagonal direction toward the Tepehuanes region and El Zape. This route would have passed near present-day Parral in the state of Chihuahua. A third route would have entered San Quintín Canyon, continuing through Peñón Blanco, Rancho Aviléz, and Candelaria and Nebilina caves, eventually heading toward the site of Paquimé (Figure 18.3).

The tracing of these routes through the state of Durango has just begun. More sites must be located to identify these routes with greater precision. For now, we must rely on the isolated, albeit interesting, data already collected. Still to be undertaken is a review of the region between the Chalchihuites area and Paquimé, which will be of considerable interest for the cultural study of northern Mexico.

REFERENCES CITED

Acosta, Jorge R.
    1961   La Indumentaria de las Cariátides de Tula. In *Homenaje a Pablo Martínez del Río en el Vigésimoquinto Aniversario de la Primera Edición de Los Orígenes Americanos*, ed. Ignacio Bernal, Jorge Gurria, Santiago Genovés, and Luis Aveleyra, 221-228. Instituto Nacional de Antropología e Historia (INAH), México.

Aveleyra Arroyo de Anda, Luis, Manuel Maldonado-Koerdell, and Pablo Martínez del Río
    1956   *Cueva de la Candelaria*, Volume 1. Memorias del Instituto Nacional de Antropología e Historia 5, México.

Ekholm, Gordon
    1942   *Excavations at Guasave, Sinaloa, México*. Anthropological Papers of the American Museum of Natural History 38(2). American Museum of Natural History, New York.

Ganot Rodríguez, Jaime, and Alejandro A. Peschard Fernández
    1997   *Aztatlán: Apuntes para la Historia y la Arqueología de Durango*. Secretaría de Educación, Cultura y Deporte, Gobierno del Estado de Durango, Durango.

Guevara Sánchez, Arturo
    1999   Atavíos Identificables en el Arte Rupestre del Norte-Centro. *Arqueología* 22:137-156. Dirección de Investigación y Conservación del Patrimonio Arqueológico (DICPA), INAH, México.
    2002   Un Sitio con Arte Rupestre del Estado de Durango. In *Ensayos de Antropología e Historia de Durango*, 99-107. Preprensa Digital, Durango.
    In press Estudio y Conservación del Sitio Arqueológico de La Ferrería, Durango. Gobierno del Estado de Durango, Durango.

Kelley, J. Charles
    1976   Alta Vista: Outpost of Mesoamerican Empire on the Tropic of Cancer. In *Las Fronteras de Mesoamérica*, ed. Jaime Litvak King and Paul Schmidt, 21-40. XIV Mesa Redonda de la Sociedad Mexicana de Antropología, Tegucigalpa.
    1997   La Cronología de la Cultura de Chalchihuites. In *Aztatlán: Apuntes para la Historia y la Arqueología de Durango*, ed. Jaime Ganot Rodriguez and Alexander Alberto Peschard Fernandez, 207-218. Secretaría de Educación, Cultura y Deporte, Gobierno del Estado de Durango, Durango.

Lazalde Montoya, Jesús Fernando
    1987   *Durango Indígena*. Talleres de Impresiones Gráficas México, S. A. de C. V. Gómez Palacio, México.

León Portilla, Miguel
    1997   Oro y Plata de Mesoamérica Vistos por Indígenas y Europeos. *Arqueología Mexicana* 5(27):16-25. CONACULTA-INAH, Editorial Raíces, México.

Martínez del Río, Pablo
    1954   *La Comarca Lagunera a Fines del Siglo XVI y Principios del XVII*. Publicaciones del Instituto de Historia, Primera Serie 30. Universidad Nacional Autónoma de México, México.

Mason, J. Alden
    1961   Some Unusual Petroglyphs and Pictographs of Durango and Coahuila, Mexico. In *Homenaje a Pablo Martínez del Río en el Vigésimoquinto Aniversario de la Primera Edición de Los Orígenes Americanos*, ed. Ignacio Bernal, Jorge Gurría, Santiago Genovés, and Luis Aveleyra, 295-310. INAH, México.

Punzo Díaz, José Luis
    1999   *La Mesa de Tlahuitotes en lo Alto de la Sierra Madre de Durango: Apuntes para la Historia Antigua Xixime*. Tesis para optar por el grado de Licenciado en Arqueología, Escuela Nacional de Antropología e Historia, México.

Weigand, Phil C.
    1997   La Turquesa. *Arqueología Mexicana* 5(27):26-33. CONACULTA-INAH, Editorial Raíces, México.

19

TURQUOISE

Formal Economic Interrelationships between
Mesoamerica and the North American Southwest

Phil C. Weigand

No society in the history of humankind has valued the mineral turquoise more than the ancient Mesoamericans. Massive use of turquoise eventually supplanted jade as the most common and widespread gemstone within that ecumene. As a mineral with such a high profile, its acquisition and procurement, from initial mining to eventual use for prestigious artifacts, deserve much more systematic study and documentation than has been the case to date. What follows is a summary from the perspective of procurement and distribution between the southwestern United States and the rest of Mesoamerica farther south.

TURQUOISE IN THE ANCIENT MESOAMERICAN WORLD

As mentioned, no other mineral was valued as highly by the ancient Mesoamericans as turquoise. By the Postclassic period (beginning about A.D. 850–900), it was in common use throughout the entire macroregion. Previously, we estimated that between one and two million individual pieces of turquoise have been found in the southwestern United States and Mexico, including poorly provenienced materials extant in many museum and private collections (Weigand and Harbottle 1993;

Phil C. Weigand

Harbottle and Weigand 1992; Weigand 1993). Several hundred thousand pieces of turquoise were found at Chaco Canyon alone. With new finds in Guerrero and Oaxaca (Sue Scott, personal communication, 2007), this estimate is probably conservative but nonetheless in the general ballpark. Since the classic study by Pogue (1972), researchers have recognized a crucial fact: whereas the major centers of turquoise procurement were in the southwestern United States and the northernmost reaches of Mexico, the major centers of consumption were in western, central, and southern Mexico. Undeniably, this can mean only one thing: turquoise was an export item from the former areas to the latter ones.

To examine this assertion and gain a better understanding of the role of turquoise in the economies of these two large regions, I consider three topics: (1) the demand for and high value of the mineral, (2) a geographic plot of the areas of demand and highest value versus the natural distribution of the mineral, and (3) the social structures that facilitated the flow of turquoise from its sources to the final points of major consumption.

Demand and Value

The first occurrences of turquoise in Mesoamerica are indeed quite early, although the mineral appears neither frequently nor in large quantities. During the Formative and Classic periods (ca. 2000 B.C. to A.D. 100, and A.D. 100 to 650/700, respectively), jade and malachite were far more popular and widespread. The best-attested early occurrences of turquoise come from the Mezcala region of Guerrero (Rosa María Reyna, personal communication, 2007) and Chalcatzingo in Morelos (Grove 1987). Both sites date to around 600 B.C. Vaillant (1930) reported a small number of turquoise pieces from Zacatenco in the central Valley of Mexico, dating to about 1800 B.C., although this material has never been sufficiently analyzed. At our ongoing excavations at Guachimontones, Jalisco,[1] we have found five pieces of turquoise, although offerings from looted tombs sometimes number in the hundreds of pieces. All this material from western Mexico appears to date from the first century A.D. or slightly earlier.

During the Classic period the distribution of turquoise broadens considerably, although it is still relatively rare. Reyna reports more material from Mezcala, dating about A.D. 600; Felipe Rodríguez (personal communication, 2007) reports turquoise from Quintana Roo in the Mayan area at about the same time. Our work in central Jalisco has located other small amounts from this period as well. For the period A.D. 500–900, Hers (1989) and Kelley (2002) report larger amounts of turquoise from sites of the Chalchihuites Tradition of northernmost Jalisco and southern and western Zacatecas. In this area, thousands of pieces of turquoise have been recovered through excavations at a number of different sites over the past three decades. By far, most of this material came from the status burials encountered at Alta Vista (Zacatecas). Aside from turquoise debris, most of the artifacts are tesserae. Interestingly, many of these mosaic blanks were cut into standardized sizes and display beveled edges, apparently the earliest appearance of turquoise with such characteristics in North America. It is important to note that turquoise was imported into these regions largely as uncut raw material.

During the Epi- and Postclassic periods (A.D. 650/700-900 and 900-conquest, respectively), the distribution of turquoise witnessed a geometric increase in quantity and was found literally in every corner of western, central, and southern Mesoamerica. It was even for sale in the marketplace of Tlatelolco, the twin city of the Culhúa Mexica capital at Tenochtitlán. According to the Florentine and Mendoza codices, discussed later in more detail, turquoise figured as tribute from three provinces within the regions dominated by the Culhúa Mexica, even though none of the three had direct access to turquoise outcrops. Extremely elaborate masks, shields, inlaid jewelry, necklaces, hairpieces, bracelets, and other objects—made from turquoise tesserae, plaques, pendants, and beads—have been found in almost every new excavation in Jalisco, Michoacán, Querétaro, Guanajuato, Hidalgo, México, Puebla, Tlaxcala, Oaxaca, Guerrero, Veracrúz, Chiapas, Campeche, Tabasco, and Yucatán. All of this material had to be imported. Sue Scott's upcoming monographs on turquoise artisanry will be important new contributions concerning the vast amount of new or newly rediscovered material (from forgotten collections) within Mesoamerica.

In central Mexico, as elsewhere, turquoise was a marker of very high status and was utilized during important social occasions and ceremonies. The turquoise diadem, or crown, was the highest symbol of noble rank. Words of wisdom were analogically likened to turquoise; it was the mineral most befitting the gods, especially those of the Quetzalcoatl set, and stood for general symbols of fertility in humans and of agriculture, rainfall, maize grains, the realm of the sky, and themes of renewal of all sorts. It is possible that set measures of turquoise, such as cotton mantas and cacao beans, served as special-purpose currencies. The penetration of turquoise, as a mineral, into the symbol sets and prestige structures of Mesoamerica was thorough. As mentioned, no other societies, before or after, have valued turquoise as much as those of ancient Mesoamerica. Thus it is a crucial commodity to investigate if we are to understand the social and symbolic world of what was once Mesoamerica.

In what was to be a fatal gesture, Moctezuma II sent Hernán Cortéz a gift of an elaborate turquoise mosaic mask of Quetzalcoatl, along with other valuables including those of gold, prior to Cortez's arrival in Tenochtitlán, the Culhúa Mexica capital. Well before that encounter, however, gifts of turquoise were routinely exchanged by noblemen and kings. From Sahagún's Florentine Codex, written in the mid-1500s, comes this example: "And then the rulers of Anauac, Xicalanco, Cimatlán, and Coatzacualco [cities on the western fringe of the Mayan world] reciprocated [to the gift-bearing Culhúa Mexica pochteca] with large green stones, the well colored precious green stone which today we call the finest emerald-green jade . . . and turquoise mosaic shields" (Anderson and Dibble 1950-1982, Book 9:18-19).

Given the fact that no turquoise deposits are found anywhere near this area, this passage is of much interest. The Maya and their immediate neighbors, like the rulers of Xicalanco, must have originally obtained their turquoise through trade from the north, only then to have worked it into elaborate artifacts they gave to the merchant representatives of the northern rulers. People of slightly lower status also had access to turquoise, as well as the obligation to give it as gifts to those of similar or higher ranks. The pochteca merchant class, which was not of noble status, was obliged to host numerous and elaborate ceremonial feasts, during which opulent gifts were given: "And the aged merchants received the people [high-status guests] with flowers, with tubes of tobacco, paper garlands, with turquoise mosaics, and fine maguey fiber plumage glistening with flecks of mica" (Anderson and Dibble 1950-1982, Book 9:38).

When noblemen gave these elaborate feasts for one another, turquoise figured not only as an item to be given away but also as part of the dress of their "bathed" slave servants (those chosen to serve the noble guests): "He [the noble host] put on the heads of the bathed ones that [which] were know[n] as the *anecuyotl* . . . a turquoise device made [also] with feathers" and "He [the host] tied 'shining hair strands' about their temples, which were decorated in this way: alternating [strips of] turquoise [and] gold, reddish coral shells, [and] black [obsidian?] mirror stones" (Anderson and Dibble 1950-1982, Book 9:60).

Even the higher-status artisans, such as the *amanteca* (feather workers), had the right to include turquoise as part of their ceremonial ornamentation: "Then he [a high-status *amanteca*] placed on his radiating ornament of turquoise, his feather staff, his shield, his rattles, and his foam sandals" (Anderson and Dibble 1950-1982, Book 9:84). These quotes are just a small sample of the large offering of historical sources concerning the status and ceremonial use of turquoise within Mesoamerica. Such references number in the hundreds.

Clearly, the consumption and circulation of turquoise in the Mesoamerican world had become extremely complex in the course of just a few centuries. For the Culhúa Mexica, the entymology of the Nahuatl word for turquoise—*teotlxiuitl*, combining the suffix *teotl*, meaning "god" or "of god," with the root *xiuit*, meaning turquoise as a mineral—attests to the esteem in which it was found (Anderson and Dibble 1950-1982, Book 11:223-224).

The Natural Distribution of Turquoise

There are two great hearths of turquoise deposits in the New World: (1) the Bolivian-Peruvian–northern Chilean copper belt and (2) the arid and semiarid regions of northernmost Mexico (Baja California, Sonora, Chihuahua, San Luis Potosí, Zacatecas, and Coahuila) and the southwestern United States (California, Arizona, Nevada, New Mexico, and Colorado). There are minor outcrops in Arkansas and Virginia, but these do not appear to have been used in pre-Columbian times. Although they were quarried, the deposits found closest to the center of

Mesoamerican civilization in Mexico are of relatively poor quality, soft, and prone to lose their color once exposed to air and light. Some of the turquoise is almost powdery. On the Lombard gemological scale for turquoise, the material from these nearby areas rates a classification of 1–4 (out of 10), with some material from the Mazapil area (Zacatecas-Coahuila border) at 5. This was not the material wanted by the great mosaic-making artisans farther south. They wanted and obtained the harder, higher-grade material from farther north, material that did not lose its coloration over time and ranked 6–9 on the Lombard scale.

In this vast area of northern Mexico and the southwestern United States, Acelia García and I have surveyed, mapped, and collected samples from forty-nine different turquoise outcrop zones. Representative samples were analyzed by neutron activation analysis (NAA) at the Department of Chemistry, Brookhaven National Laboratory (BNL), by Garman Harbottle, Edward Sayre, and Ronald Bishop, with grants from the BNL and the National Science Foundation. The mineral collections are now part of the archaeological collections of the Museum of Northern Arizona in Flagstaff. Some of these deposits have hundreds of natural outcrops, whereas others have but a few. The Grass Valley of central Nevada is an example of the former.

Indeed, central and western Nevada represent the mother lode of turquoise in North America, with a small number of commercial operations still functioning. At the other extreme is Canyon Creek on the San Carlos Apache Reservation in Arizona, with just a few sparse deposits, although these mines saw historic use by the Zuni, Navajos, and Apaches. Most outcrop zones have several dozen different deposits. Of the forty-nine outcrop zones, we found evidence of ancient mining activities at twenty-nine. The most important of these are at Halloron Springs in southern California, where the greatest turquoise pit of all, the Toltec Mine, is located. Here and nearby have been found sherds of Hopi Black-on-yellow varieties, this being one of the few localities that have produced artifacts other than mining tools, such as stone picks and hammers. Whereas much of the excavation at the Toltec Mine is historic, the roots appear pre-Hispanic. Over 100 other pits are found in the immediate area, although not all of them were used in pre-contact times. Pickings today are slim. Nearby, at the southernmost tip of Nevada, is the Hopi Mine, now called the Iron Gate, near Searchlight. The gate was erected during the 1940s to keep the Hopis out. Interviews established the presence of Hopi miners at this site and at close-by outcrops during the nineteenth century. The pre-Hispanic artifact cover strongly implies a much longer period of use.

Another important complex is located in the Courtland-Gleason area of southeastern Arizona. At Turquoise Mountain about a dozen more or less intact ancient mines remain, although all of these have received recent attention by miners. The best-preserved mines are chambered and complex, although none is too safe. The Goshert family are the current owners of this complex and have unsuccessfully tried to interest the state of Arizona in preserving the ancient mines as a cultural resource. Many other areas that produced large amounts of turquoise in Arizona have been destroyed or heavily altered by modern open-pit copper mining enterprises, such as those at Morenci, Bisbee, Superior (or Sleeping Beauty), and Mineral Park (or Kingman). All these areas had ancient mining activities and were sampled by us as thoroughly as possible thanks to the courteous cooperation of the respective mining companies.

Located in northern New Mexico is perhaps the best-known ancient turquoise mining complex: Mount Chalchihuitl and its neighboring outcrops in the general Cerrillos area. The great pit and adjoining mines found there were probably first opened during the heyday of Chaco Canyon. Nearby San Marcos Pueblo is one of the largest ruins of the Anasazi tradition and may have directed some of the mineralogical activity there after the Chacoan period ended. The Cerrillos district was claimed in later times by Santo Domingo Pueblo. Many mines there also produce lead. Other districts in New Mexico with excellent evidence of ancient mining are the Jarill Mountains, Azure and New Azure, White Signal, and Old Hachita. The latter's ancient turquoise mines have been destroyed by a new open-pit copper mine, but we examined them in detail just prior to the destruction and recorded a central area consisting of two dozen boot-shaped pits, some over five meters deep, and numerous smaller pits.

It was from many of these aforementioned deposits that the most easily obtained high-grade turquoise was mined. As demand increased, however, newer deposits in more remote areas entered into production, at least on a small scale, such as those in Nevada and Colorado. The increase in demand seems related to the emergence of the post–Chaco Canyon world in the southwestern United States, when, for the first time, there was a generalized demand for turquoise throughout that zone, accompanied by an even heavier demand in the core of the Mesoamerican civilization.

We have identified more than 200 unquestionable ancient turquoise mines in our surveys. But there is firm evidence from the historical record, as well as from informants, that many more mines existed prior to the new phase of turquoise mining that began in the mid-twentieth century and the development of massive open-pit copper mines. It appears, then, that most ancient mines have been either destroyed or heavily altered by contemporary mining. We believe the 200 we have documented are but a fraction, perhaps just 10 percent, of those that must have existed in the southwestern United States at one time. Based on our surveys and interviews plus the historical record, we believe that, conservatively, at least 1,000 mines, excavated into hard-rock deposits over an 800-year span, is a probable number. An upper estimate would be twice that number.

The Trade Structure

As mentioned, we have used NAA to chemically identify turquoise sources. We formed "provenience postulates" for turquoise sources, wherein the amount of variation found in a particular source can be statistically determined to cluster and be noticeably or marginally different from the amount of variation in other sources. Although our techniques and methods of statistical analysis have been criticized, impartial and independent reworking of the techniques and statistics has affirmed that provenience postulates for turquoise do exist. As we stated long ago, though, these are not like types of pigment. Sources, therefore, do indeed have "fingerprints," which can be compared to NAA profiles established from artifacts recovered in excavations or museum collections. Even without the NAA data, the evidence for systematized and extensive trade of turquoise continues to mount. Dismissing the NAA database in no way modifies the rest of the evidence for a systematized trade in turquoise.

The comparisons between artifacts and sources sometimes gives us exact matches, other times only approximate ones. Sometimes there are matches of neither kind, indicating that we have not located all the pertinent sources or that some sources may have been exhausted or destroyed by subsequent mining activities. To date, we have analyzed more that 2,000 samples, roughly two-thirds of which are from source samples. In this fashion, we have identified artifacts made from the turquoise of the general Cerrillos area at Chaco Canyon; a multitude of sites in the general Cerrillos area itself; the Tucson Basin; the highlands of Nayarit, including Ixtlán del Río; the highland lake districts of Jalisco, notably Las Cuevas and Zacoalco; Alta Vista and La Quemada/Tuitlán in Zacatecas; and faraway Chichén Itzá (Yucatán). By A.D. 1000 turquoise was apparently in systematic use from one end of the ecumene to the other. Most of these sites date to the Mesoamerican Epi- or Early Postclassic period, at least in part, thus strongly suggesting that by about A.D. 1000 a systematized trade network for turquoise was in operation. This may be the inception of turquoise's entrance as a commodity into the Mesoamerican trade structure.

Exchange for turquoise, which apparently started slowly, nonetheless illustrates a geometrical progression in utilization and popularity. The first truly identifiable peak coincides with the rise and apogee of Chaco Canyon and the Late Epi- and Early Postclassic social systems of Mesoamerica. Cerrillos turquoise, of fine to excellent quality in hardness and color, seems featured, although it was certainly circulating before A.D. 1000.

The key to understanding, at least in part, the extension of systematized acquisition patterns for this particular mineral may reside in the massive mining operations that characterize the Chalchihuites region of Zacatecas. This is the largest single mining complex yet documented for Mesoamerica and the southwestern United States. Although no turquoise was mined there, various blue-green stones, including malachite, azurite, and cuprite, were recovered. The Chalchihuites mining operation apparently began about A.D. 400, if not a little earlier, peaking around A.D. 700–800, as our research (Weigand 1968, 1993) and that of Vincent Schiavitti (1994) shows. There are over 800 chambered mines in the immediate area, some of which have over a kilometer of interior tunnels and one of which has three kilometers of tunnels. Thus just before the big boom in turquoise acquisition and popularity, the Chalchihuites area was producing experienced miners and minerologists, as well as an apparent lust for blue-green stones. This may have played a role in the development of more formalized turquoise mining farther north. It seems no coincidence that the Chalchihuites area is one of the first regions in Mesoamerica to have a large collection of turquoise; clearly, they were both miners and traders for exotic minerals. Prior to Chaco Canyon, it was probably the Hohokam of Arizona who served as some of the contacts for turquoise acquisition in the far north. How turquoise passed from the north to the south and what went back in return is still a subject of considerable debate. A variety of models have been suggested, none of which has received much common accord. Still to be debated are the sociological impacts the immersion of the southwestern United States within the Mesoamerican trade structure implies.

Concerning turquoise per se, the technology of beveled edges on tessarae blanks, which in turn had rather standardized sizes, appears first in Mesoamerica and subsequently in Chaco Canyon. Prior to Chaco Canyon, as mentioned, it appears as if most turquoise exported south was in raw form. By making beveled tessarae blanks, people at Chaco Canyon may have increased the value of their product while at the same time accepting Mesoamerican standards of measurement for this commodity. This is a hypothesis for further analysis and discussion.

In the post-Chaco Canyon world in the southwestern United States, toward the end of the Early Postclassic period farther south, the demand for turquoise increased once again. This time, part of the increase may be explained by the more generalized use of turquoise in the far north, accompanied by still further increases in demand in the south. In the north, at Paquimé, although fewer pieces of turquoise were found than at Chaco Canyon (Di Peso, Rinaldo, and Fenner 1974), far more sources are indicated by NAA, including some in Nevada. Given Paquimé's extensive contacts with other regions, the 5,000 turquoise pieces recovered may not truly indicate the extent of the flow of turquoise through that system, either through trade or political gift giving. Clearly, this later geometrical increase in demand was reflected by an increase in the number of sources exploited. To draw an analogy: when prices for oil first skyrocketed during the 1970s, a series of rich but hard to reach sources entered into production, such as the north shore of Alaska and the North Sea.

It is interesting that turquoise was not acquired by the organizations of royal merchants, neither those of the Culhúa Mexica (Anderson and Dibble 1950-1982) nor of the Purépecha of Michoacán (Craine and Reindorp 1970; Pollard 1993). As mentioned, the Culhúa Mexica acquired their turquoise either through tribute from areas that themselves had to import the mineral or through acquisition systems that predated the ascendancy of their particular political economy. The same can be said about the Purépecha, although here turquoise does not even appear as tribute. Thus systematic turquoise acquisition predated the formation of the royal trading organizations of the two dominant political economies of the Mesoamerican ecumene north of the Isthmus of Tehuantepec. In addition, there appears to have been a lineal distribution of turquoise objects during this post-A.D. 1000 period. Turquoise artifacts are found in very large quantities along the Pacific Coast, through the highland lake districts of Jalisco, and along the Rio Lerma. This suggested corridor followed closely the route postulated for the development and distribution of the Aztatlán horizon style, although the spread of this style has usually been seen as a south-to-north phenomenon. Thus the massive flow of turquoise in the opposite direction may help explain the dynamics of the horizon's three-century existence. Indeed, the systematic trade for turquoise may be one of the explanators for the very existence of the horizon style. This is probably the main route turquoise traveled to the western and northern parts of central Mexico. Given that turquoise was also very important in Oaxaca, this was probably not the only such route. Another, which bypassed the western Mexican highlands, possibly followed the Pacific littoral farther south to reach Oaxaca, Guerrero, and Chiapas. By the Late Postclassic period the turquoise artisanry of the Mixteca superseded every other region, as Sue Scott's (2006) ongoing studies continue to show.

CONCLUSIONS

To understand relationships between the ancient sociocultural systems of the southwestern United States and those of the rest of Mesoamerica to the south, quantitative approaches offer one avenue. This we have attempted to accomplish through extensive surveys for turquoise outcrops and mining activities, examinations of artifact collections from excavations and museums, and NAA studies of both sources and artifacts. Although this study is not complete, I believe we have demonstrated the need for a macroeconomic consideration for the comparative study of the Mesoamerican ecumene, including the southwestern United States. Even without the NAA study, there are far too many similarities in the social and economic roles played by turquoise in all these regions to be explained away as coincidence, including the sheer quantity of northern turquoise encountered in the south. The information we have collected is helping us understand another element that was crucial in defining the character of the overall Mesoamerican trade structure. The pre-Hispanic southwestern United States participated in this structure for at least a 700-year period and perhaps longer.

Acknowledgments. The collaboration of Garman Harbottle of the Brookhaven National Laboratory was essential to the progress of this investigation. Pedro Armillas, J. Charles Kelley, and Charles Di Peso encouraged us to follow through with our initial interests in turquoise, and ancient mining in general, and bring them to a more scientific conclusion. Armillas considered this project another example of landscape archaeology. Kelley and Di Peso thought it would be important in helping define the nature of the northern frontier of Mesoamerica and its relationships with the ancient societies of the southwestern United States. We hope we have lived up to their expectations, at least in part. Funding for this research came from the National Science Foundation, Brookhaven National Laboratory, and, most recently, the Colegio de Michoacán.

NOTES

1. This research is part of the "Proyecto Arqueológico Teuchitlán" headed by the author and co-sponsored by the Colegio de Michoacán, the Secretaria de Cultura del Estado de Jalisco, and the Municipio de Teuchitlán, Jalisco.

REFERENCES CITED

Anderson, Arthur J.O., and Charles E. Dibble (translators)
    1950-   *The Florentine Codex: General History of the Things of New Spain, Books 9 and 11,*
    1982   by Bernardino de Sahagún. University of Utah Press, Salt Lake City.

Craine, Eugene R., and Reginald C. Reindorp (translators and editors)
    1970   *The Chronicles of Michoacán* (1541). University of Oklahoma Press, Norman. (Original title *Relación de las Ceremonias y Ritos y Población y Governo de Michoacán*. Manuscript C.IV.5. IV del Escorial, Real Biblioteca, Madrid.)

Di Peso, Charles C., John B. Rinaldo, and Gloria J. Fenner
    1974   *Casas Grandes, a Fallen Trading Center of the Gran Chichimeca*. 8 volumes. Amerind Foundation, Dragoon, Ariz., and Northland, Flagstaff, Ariz.

Grove, David
    1987   *Ancient Chalcatzingo*. University of Texas Press, Austin.

Harbottle, Garman, and Phil C. Weigand
    1992   Turquoise in Pre-Columbian America. *Scientific American* 266(2):78-85.

Hers, Marie-Areti
    1989   *Los Toltecas en Tierras Chichimecas*. Cuadernos de Historia del Arte 35. Instituto de Investigaciones Estéticas, Universidad Nacional Autónoma de México, México.

Kelley, J. Charles
    2002   Mesoamerican Colonization of Zacatecas-Durango. In *Homenaje al Dr. John Charles Kelley*, ed. Ma. Teresa Cabrero, Jaime Litvak King, and Peter Jimenez, 83-98. Instituto de Investigaciones Antropologicos, Universidad Nacional Autonoma de Mexico, Mexico City.

Pogue, Joseph
    1972   *The Turquois: A Study of Its History, Mineralogy, Geology, Ethnology, Archaeology, Mythology, Folklore, and Technology*. Rio Grande, Glorieta, N.M. (Originally published in 1915 in Memoirs of the National Academy of Sciences 12, Part 2, Memoirs 2 and 3. National Academy of Science, Washington, D.C.)

Pollard, Helen P.
    1992   *Tariácuri's Legacy: The Prehispanic Tarascan State*. University of Oklahoma Press, Norman.

Schiavitti, Vincent
    1994   La Minería Prehispanica de Chalchihuites. *Arqueología Mexicana* 1(6):48-51.

Scott, Sue
    2006   La Mascara de Malinaltepec y sus Compañeras. Paper presented at the symposium Las Sociedades Complejas del Occidente de Mexico en el Mundo Mesoamericano. El Colegio de Michoacán, La Universidad de Guadalajara, La Secretaria de Cultura de Estado de Jalisco, and El Instituo Nacional de Antropología e Historia, Guadalajara.

Vaillant, George
    1930   *Excavations at Zacatenco*. Anthropological Papers of the American Museum of Natural History 32(1), New York.

Weigand, Phil C.
    1968   The Mines and Mining Techniques of the Chalchihuites Culture. *American Antiquity* 33(1):45-61.
    1993   *Evolucion de una Civilizacion Prehispanica: Arqueologia de Jalisco, Nayarit y Zacatecas*. El Colegio de Michoacán, Zamora.

Weigand, Phil C., and Garman Harbottle
    1993   The Role of Turquoise in the Ancient Mesoamerican Trade Structure. In *The American Southwest and Mesoamerica: Systems of Prehistoric Exchange*, ed. Jonathon E. Ericson and Timothy G. Baugh, 159-177. Plenum, New York.

20

THE CULTURAL LANDSCAPE OF CLIFF HOUSES IN THE SIERRA MADRE OCCIDENTAL, CHIHUAHUA

Eduardo Gamboa Carrera and Federico J. Mancera-Valencia

This study examines cultural landscapes in the highland catchment area of the Río Papigochic and its tributaries, the Río Chico and the Río Tutuaca, in the Sierra Madre Occidental in the northeastern part of the state of Chihuahua. The central part of the project is in the municipality of Madera in that state (Figure 20.1). In general, the ecosystems of the Huápoca and Sírupa canyons and the highland catchment area of the Papigochic are very fragile, and conservation of the region's immense biodiversity is important. Among other considerations, the region is a migratory bird route and is important for the hydraulic recharging of areas of the Chihuahuan semidesert ecosystem.

Humans have inhabited the canyons of this region for thousands of years. Among the most significant traces left by humans are the cave sites, or cliff dwellings, earthen architectural structures built in rocky shelters. These complexes have been identified as part of the Casas Grandes Culture, although the reach of this influence has yet to be established. More than 150 cliff dwellings have been recorded in this part of the Sierra Madre, representing one of the most dispersed and extensive populations in northern Mexico. Given their natural and cultural characteristics, these resources are unique not only for Mexico but also in terms of the

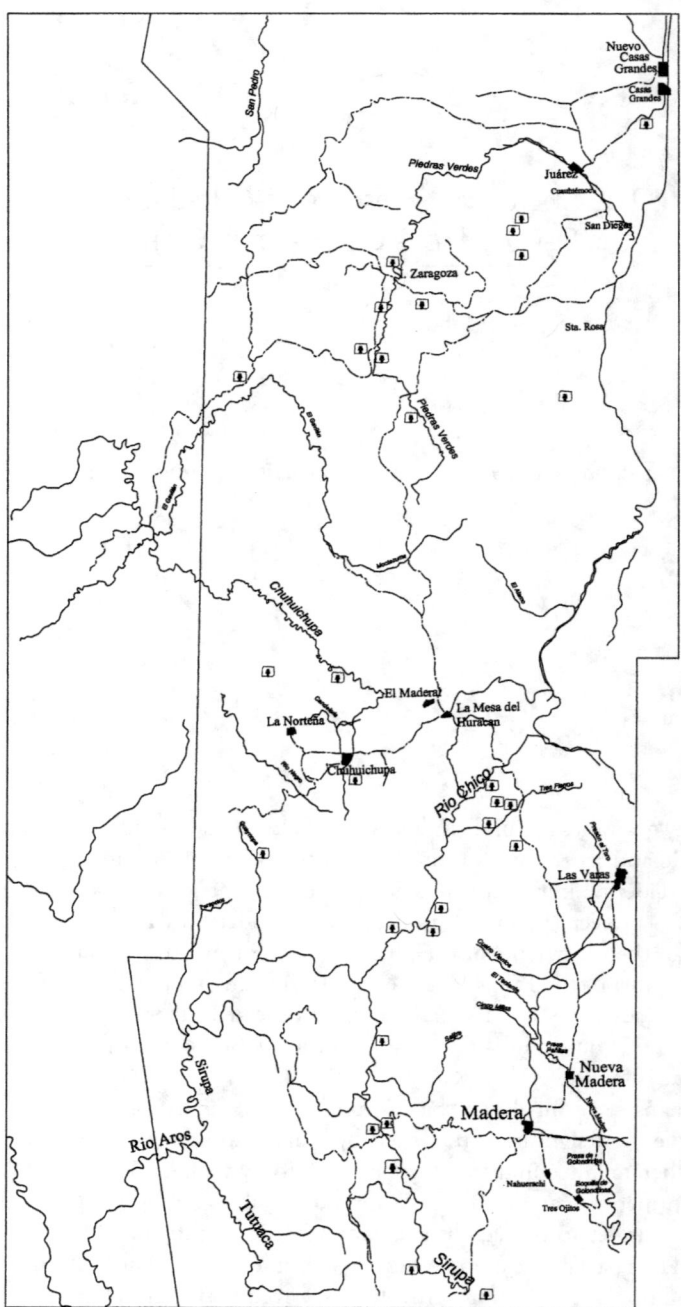

Figure 20.1. Map of northeastern Chihuahua, showing the distribution of cliff-house sites.

cultural diversity of the southwestern United States. These sites possess aesthetic and scientific value, yet they remain largely unknown to researchers studying the archaeology of the Southwest.

Through the project "Sites of the Highland Province of Paquimé," the Instituto Nacional de Antropología e Historia (INAH) has begun to document and preserve sites in the mountains of Chihuahua. An inventory of the cultural resources of the Madera region was undertaken in 2003. This first phase of this project, "Integral Conservation of the Madera Region," was made possible by a grant from the J. M. Kaplan Foundation and the support of the World Monuments Fund and the Wilson Fund to help preserve the cultural heritage of Mexico.

Thus far, archaeological excavations have been undertaken in the mountain basin of the Río Papigochic and in the Sírupa and Huápoca areas, a region nearly 120 kilometers in length. The cultures of this region have been investigated, and an inventory of archaeological sites has been completed. One component of the project has been the implementation of a conservation program within the city of Madera, a community committed to managing these sites and the natural landscape (Gamboa Carrera 2001).

At some cave sites, including Cueva de Ranchería and Cueva de Apache in Sírupa Canyon and Cueva Grande and Conjunto Huápoca (the Huápoca Complex) in Huápoca Canyon, architectural measurements and conservation projects have been undertaken. These efforts have included the documentation of these cultural properties, including the archaeological materials within their immediate boundaries. This has been done using specialized archaeological techniques, facilitating the interpretation of cultural activities associated with the excavated material. These techniques were also utilized for the present study.

THE CULTURAL LANDSCAPE AS INTERPRETIVE MODEL

The concept of landscape was initially documented through the field of geography. The German geographer A. Hommeyerem introduced the word "landscape" (*die landshaft*)[1] to scientific and geographic discourse. This term was understood to mean the sum of all areas as observed from a higher vantage point and as represented by their association with and situation from nearby mountains, forests, and other significant features on earth (Mateo 1982). More pragmatic definitions of landscape also exist and serve as points of reference for regional studies, making it easier to order the descriptive data. These have been applied in a homogeneous manner to the concept of region, without any sense of classification or categorization of the physical elements of terrestrial space. Even simpler definitions exist for commercial use, as advertisements for tourist programs or to promote views of a supposedly pristine nature (Mancera-Valencia 2002:92).

Geographer Pierre Gourou (1984) considered landscapes "united to man's interventions. . . . From their first examination—be it through direct observation or by means of maps or aerial photographs (and satellite images)—landscapes show correlations between their elements. Dwellings are grouped at the foot of the mountains, at the top of a hill, the edge of a river or near its confluence with another. . . . Open landscapes are accompanied by villages."[2] Gourou (1984:12) developed three questions essential to the analysis of any landscape: (1) Why is a landscape as it is as opposed to taking another form? (2) How is human presence evident on the landscape? (3) Through what technical means of production (techniques of exploitation or subsistence) and interactions between humans and the organization of space were these cultural landscapes developed?

In this manner, Gourou confirmed that "[m]an, maker of landscapes, exists solely because he is a member of a group, which combines differing techniques." He concluded that "all humans are subjected to the techniques that make them civilized. Savages do not exist" (Gourou 1984:12). As such, landscapes are seen as natural "complexes" not because of the implications, retrospections, interactions, and interrelations within them but because of their human implications. Whereas the ideas, use, and management of nature have brought about human actions to justify and satisfy their needs, nature is analyzed in history as a line of historical-cultural geography (Mancera-Valencia 2002:96).

Carl O. Sauer of the North American school further developed this line of thought, granting new dimensions to the anthropology and archaeology of landscapes (Mancera-Valencia 2002:96). Sauer (1925) interpreted landscapes as made up of a distinct association of forms, both physical and cultural. Without reference to Sauer, Gourou (1984:15) confirmed that "[e]very human landscape is a conglomerate of problems. . . . None of them can be seen as simple. The landscape is a handful of problems. Luckily! What enrichment to think that before our eyes exists an imprint, revelation, survival, and the almost forgotten memory of successive and diverse civilizations, all of which is to be explained, and that resolved problems will themselves establish new ones."

It was Sauer who stimulated the resurgence of the concept of landscape from a human perspective and emphasized its geographical and archaeological complexity: "The transformation of the natural landscape in the cultural landscape provides a satisfactory working program, by which the assemblage of cultural forms in the area comes in for the same attention as that of the physical forms" (Sauer 1931:622). The process Sauer referred to is cultural geography, in which the study of cultural landscapes "seeks to determine the successions of culture that have taken place in an area. . . . The major problems of cultural geography . . . lie in discovering the composition and meaning of the geographic aggregate that we as yet recognize somewhat vaguely as the culture area, in finding out more about what are normal stages of succession in its development, in concerning itself with climactic and decadent phases and thereby in gaining more precise knowledge of the relation of culture and of the resources that are at the disposal of culture" (Sauer 1931:624; see also Mancera-Valencia 2002:97).

The international French-Holland school developed by Jean Tricart and J. J. Killian (1982) integrated the natural and cultural landscapes, giving them meaning within the study of economic development. In this view, ecogeography implies a methodological integration of morphogenesis (dynamic processes related to the origin and history of the topography, also known as dynamic geomorphology) and pedogenesis, a science that studies how the surface of the lithosphere and its resulting resources were modified.

This focus requires knowledge of the physical medium, its description as well as its dynamics. Processes that allow for the formation and evolution of a model of the topography and soil follow, in a majority of cases, relative and differing rates of change in accordance with the climatic characteristics, geology, and the history of human activity. All of these imprint their own characteristics upon the landscape. This notion of a morphogenesis-pedogenesis balance allows for the identification of geodynamics and the processes of evolution. "Ecogeographic units" can be identified and analyzed in terms of their base rock, topography, and soil units; and topographical changes can be studied in terms of fractures and changes in altitude, relief formation, hydrology of the slopes, and development of the resulting layers. To these ecogeographical units are tied the vegetation and faunal habitats, which constitute integral and holistic units, the biophysics of the landscape. This process of integration is now aided by geographic information systems and the support of site work and remote sensing (Bocco 1998).

Through this naturalistic approach to analyzing the landscape using ecogeography, proposals for its intervention have been formulated. This chapter attempts to achieve this aim and considers that just as there are no humans outside of nature, there are also no humans outside of culture.

As an example, consider Figures 20.2 and 20.3. (To interpret the figures correctly, picture Figure 20.2 as an overlay of Figure 20.3.) Figure 20.2 is a 10.8 kilometer topographical cut along the Río Sírupa in which different ecogeographical units can be seen, including particular sociocultural aspects of the region's cultural landscape. Figure 20.3, based on the same profile as shown in Figure 20.2, is divided into two sections. The upper one shows the distribution of cultural archaeological materials identified during excavations at cliff-dwelling sites in the Río Sírupa region. The lower section presents the different layers of the cultural landscape.

This interdisciplinary approach, which we refer to as archaeogeography, is in accord with ecogeographical diversity, which establishes the complex cultural landscape derived from the particular sociocultural aspects of these regions. We have applied this procedure to five areas in the region: sections of the Garabato, Venado, Embudo, and Conjunto Huápoca drainages and the previously mentioned Río Sírupa (Figure 20.4).

As an interpretive model of archaeological complexes, such as the cliff dwellings, the cultural landscape requires indicators that allow for their interpretation and analysis. Here we propose some indicative principles to facilitate interpretation of the cultural landscape:

1. Explain the appropriation of ecosystems through the use and management of natural resources: water, earth, flora, fauna, topography, and so on. These

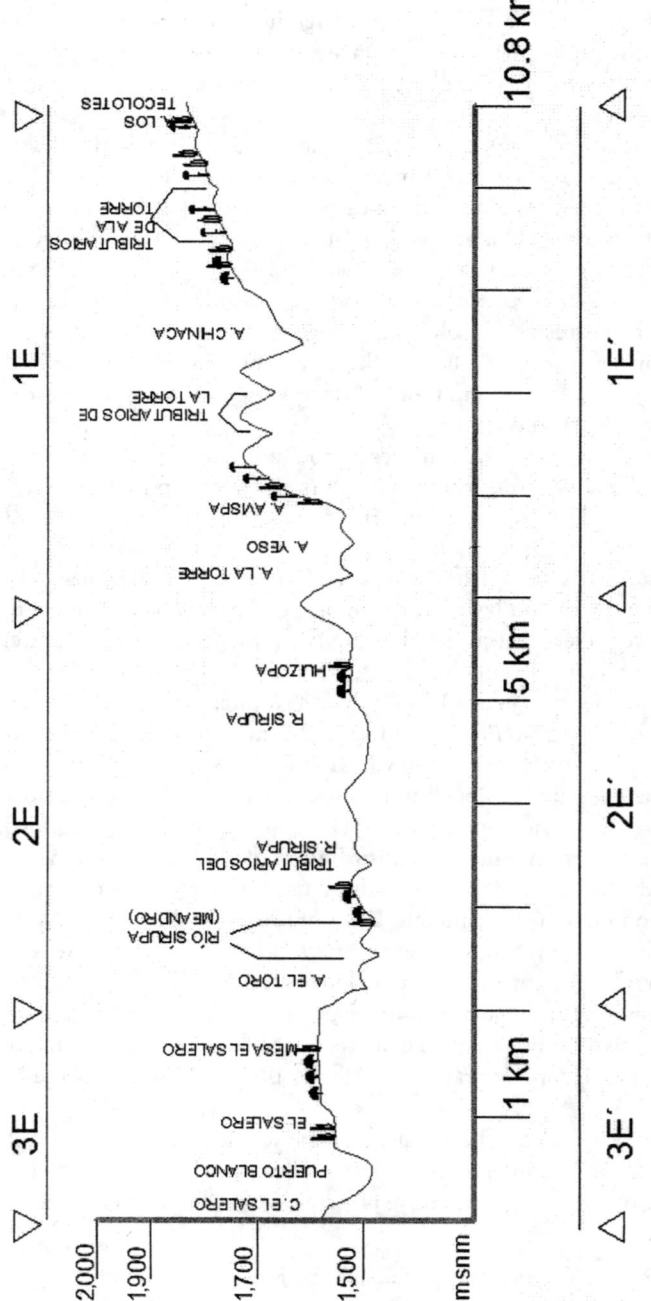

Figure 20.2. Profile of a 10.8-kilometer cut along the Río Sirupa, showing ecogeographical units.

3E	2E	1E
Ceramics, wood, palm, palmilla, textile, carrizo, agave, thorns, ears of corn, chilicotes, suckers, cane, prickly pear, capulín, tejocote (Mexican hawthorne), tomatillo, peanut, fish vertebrae, deer antlers, chamois, leather bags, pipe, and tobacco.	Wood, ceramic material, carrizo, agave, thorns, palmilla, palm, ears of corn, tejocote (Mexican hawthorne), tomatillo, yucca seeds, tascate, textile, fish vertebrae, rabbit bones, deer antlers, chamois, leather bags.	Wood, rodent bones, ears of corn, rocks, corn cane, turpentine, bird feathers, lithics, ceramic clay, rabbit bones, tomatillo.

3E'	2E'	1E'
Mesas and V-shaped valleys; intermontane areas with forest cover of oak, desert scrub, and succulent plants. Activities of gathering, hunting, agricultural terracing, and production of lithics and other tools.	Alluvial and floodplain systems with formation and displacement from escarpments and cliffs. Forests and aquatic vegetation. Agricultural activities such as irrigation, and fishing, hunting, and gathering.	Mountainous system with V-shaped gullies or valleys with pronounced slopes, intermontain areas dissected by escarpments or cliffs covered with oak, mixed or forest cover, desert scrub with succulent plants and grasses. Agricultural activities of terracing and construction of water control features, combined with hunting, gathering, and fishing.

Figure 20.3. *Profile of the same cut along the Río Sirupa shown in Figure 20.2, showing the distribution of archaeological cultural materials identified from excavations in the cliff dwellings (upper section) and features of the cultural and natural landscape (lower section).*

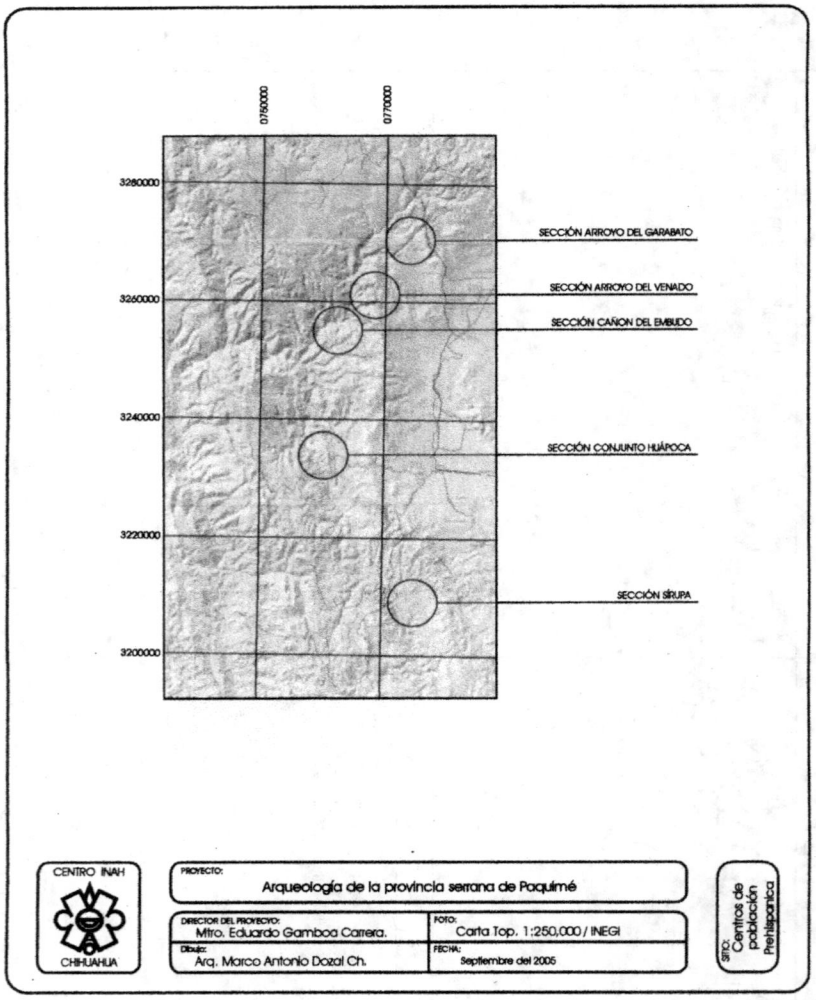

Figure 20.4. Areas of Chihuahua where authors have applied the cultural landscape methodology.

constitute the material resources that satisfied the needs of the people who inhabited these cliff-dwelling complexes and who derived from them the cultural elements that gave rise to regional identity.

2. Generate knowledge about how the ecosystem was appropriated, how natural resources were used and managed, and how they satisfied peoples' needs.

3. Explain the forms of social organization, social cohesion, and formalized institutions developed for the use and management of the natural resources and for control of the region.

4. Examine the ritual and symbolic processes of language and identity associated with the natural resources and the region. These processes constituted the ideological and subjective satisfaction of the needs system as a planned and civilized complex of the mountain territory.
5. Interpret the sacred spaces and times linked to elements of the ecosystem and its biological rhythms.
6. Define the limits, borders, and regions of the natural environment used to establish geopolitical control of and human vigilance over the space through time.

In this manner, "the cultural landscape or occupied areas allow objective and subjective articulation of the complex relationship between culture and nature, and illustrate the dynamics of society and the implications of human occupation and settlement through the territory and history, as influenced by the pressures and/or disadvantages of the ambient environment and the socioeconomic forces, both of which arise from internal and external needs" (Mancera-Valencia 2002:60). This interpretive model of the cultural landscape can be evaluated by its universal applicability, its representativeness in terms of the defined geocultural environment, and its capacity to demonstrate a region's essential and distinct cultural elements. Because of this, and in accordance with the sites' subjective and objective dimensions, cultural landscapes can be considered complexes of cultural heritage.

PRELIMINARY FINDINGS AND INTERPRETATIONS

Our analysis of the cultural geography of the cliff dwellings of northeastern Chihuahua has generated several preliminary observations about ties between this cultural region and the Casas Grandes Culture:

1. These mountain sites were closely aligned with the regional system in which Paquimé functioned as the ritual city. Iconographic elements recorded during our archaeological investigations relate to the cult tradition of the feathered serpent and the *guacamaya* (macaw).
2. A communication system based on watchtowers and roads integrated the system regionally, allowing for its sociocultural appropriation.
3. The recorded cliff-house sites conform to an architectural system similar to that at the archaeological site of Paquimé. Installations and architectural finishes have the same proportions as construction systems at Paquimé. This includes the materials and techniques of construction, as well as the design of doors, floor layouts, passages, plazas, and levels and the uses and functions of these spaces.
4. These data suggest that the cliff-house occupation was tied to the Casas Grandes regional system and was based on the exploitation of natural resources, such as water and soil related to the construction of terraces (*trincheras*).

The occurrence of these sites in zones of ecological transition, such as oak, oak-pine, and mixed forests, demonstrates the complex articulation between culture and nature.

5. Parallel to these conclusions, the spatial construction of sites in the area was based on the satisfaction of ideological beliefs, needs, rituals, festivals, and language, among others, as shown in Figures 20.2 and 20.3.

6. The presence of facilities such as granaries for the storage of agricultural produce suggests a socioeconomic system based on centralization and distribution. This would have allowed for productive control not only over time but also over space, that is, the use and management of the natural resources.

NOTES

1. In Dutch: *landskip*; in English: landscape; in French: *paysage*; in Spanish: *paisaje*.

2. Editors' note: The Gourou quotations in this chapter were excerpted from a Spanish publication and subsequently translated into English by a Mexican translator for our chapter. We lack the page numbers for these quotations.

REFERENCES CITED

Bocco, Gerando
  1998 Naturaleza y Sociedad: Escalas de Espacio y Tiempo. *Ciencias* 51:54–59. Facultad de Ciencas de la Universidad Nacional Autónoma de México, México, Julio-Septiembre.

Gamboa Carrera, Eduardo
  2001 Proyecto de Conservación Integral de la Región Madera. Resumen ejecutivo. Noviembre. Instituto Nacional de Antropología e Historia–Centro Regional Chihuahua. Chihuahua, Chih., México. Manuscrito.

Gourou, Pierre
  1984 *Introducción a la Geografía Humana*. Alianza Editorial 228, Madrid, Spain.

Mancera-Valencia, Federico J.
  2002 *Agua y Cultura: La Construcción de los Paisajes Culturales de Chihuahua*. Fondo Estatal para la Cultura y las Artes "David Afaro Siuqueiros." Informe final, Inédito.

Mateo, J.
  1982 *Geografía de los Paisajes*, ed. André Voisin. Empresa Nacional de Producción y Servicios del Ministero de Educación Superior, Habana, Cuba.

Sauer, Carl O.
  1925 *The Morphology of Landscape*. University of California Publications in Geography 2(2), Berkeley.
  1931 Cultural Geography. In *Encyclopaedia of the Social Sciences*, Volume 6, comp. Edwin R.A. Seligman, 621–624. Macmillan, New York.

Tricart, Jean, and J. J. Killian
  1982 *La Ecogeografía y la Ordenación Territorial del Medio Físico*. Anagrama, Barcelona, Spain.

21

All Routes, All Directions

The Prehistoric Landscape of Nuevo León

Moisés Valadez Moreno

The first humans to occupy the diverse territories of Nuevo León encountered an environment in the process of change. They coexisted with the last Pleistocene species in northeastern Mexico, including the bison and mammoth. Much later, the marked climatic changes of the initial Holocene led to a considerable reduction in plant species. This impacted the population of herbivores, whose numbers had already declined before the reduction in forage, and even more dramatically the carnivores, including humans, who depended on the former for their subsistence. The human ability to adapt to an omnivorous diet, however, proved so successful that from the arrival of indigenous peoples to Nuevo León around 12,000 years ago until their historic disappearance, they were able to sustain a lifeway based on the procurement of raw materials and the hunting, fishing, and gathering of various species. At no time did these societies find it necessary to implement artificial techniques to accelerate the biological cycle of plants and animals. In Nuevo León the development of agriculture and the domestication of animals were never requirements for survival, as occurred in areas farther south.

This condition of maintaining the same resource base through time permitted these indigenous societies to navigate their lives and the natural world through myths, rituals, and ceremonies that structured their social relationships. These patterns persisted for generations until their voices were silenced by immigrants speaking a strange tongue who proclaimed themselves—without permission or consideration—masters of all lands, plants, animals, and people in the region and the places inhabited by their ancestors.

Hispanic colonists never understood the indigenous forms of organization in the region. Instead, they imposed their way of life on the local population and opted for violent seclusion in missions, *encomiendas* (grants of Indian land and labor), and prisons, where indigenous people were sometimes sold as slaves for work in the mines as far away as the booming city of Zacatecas (Del Hoyo 1979, 1985). In contrast to other parts of Mexico, the lack of an indigenous population in Nuevo León for more than a century led to the gradual negation of the native culture at a regional level. Numerous arguments justifying this ethnic genocide still appear in contemporary history textbooks (De León 1961:40).

Nevertheless, the cultural complexity achieved by the indigenous societies of Nuevo León over 12,000 years is recorded in some documentary references, and the significance of their cultural tradition can be inferred from the material remains described in various archaeological studies. To date, archaeological investigations have verified the existence of almost a thousand temporary occupation sites in caves, rockshelters, and open-air locations, ranging in size from a few meters to several kilometers. These have been recorded in all ecosystems, including valleys, plains, and alluvial fans, hilltops and slopes, canyons and ravines, and the margins and banks of rivers and intermittent streams (Rivera Estrada 1996, 1997, 1998, 1999, 2000, 2001; Valadez Moreno 1993a, 1994, 1995, 1997a, 1998, 1999a, 1999b, 2000, 2001a, 2001b, 2001c, 2002a).

These investigations have resulted in the recording of over 25,000 archaeological remains, including materials of stone, bone, shell, wood, clay, and vegetal fiber. Morphotechnological and functional analyses of these materials have identified such artifacts as choppers, scrapers, projectile points, brushes, gouges, polishers, perforators, necklace beads, pendants, pipes, smoothers, incising plates, vessels, and grinding tools for the preparation of plant materials and pigments. Hundreds of hearths, fire pits, and human burials have also been found, as well as numerous cave paintings and thousands of rocks carved with petroglyphs. I discuss the rock art in greater detail in the next section.

Chronologically, this abundance of cultural material is assigned to the following periods:

- Period I (ca. 12,000–9000 B.P.): characterized by tools and expedient artifacts such as unifaces with reworked edges (flat scrapers), flat tabular bifaces, elongated knives, small gouges in a diamond form, and lightly retouched flakes.

- Period II (ca. 9000–7500 B.P.): represented by disc-shaped bifaces, unifacial and bifacial gouges of the Clear Fork type, and pendunculate-shaped projectile points of the Lerma and Plainview-Golondrina types.

- Period III (ca. 7500–5000 B.P.): notable for its scarcity of archaeological materials, with only a few unifacially and bifacially reworked flakes found; gouges continue, and elongated projectile points with a triangular and lanceolate form appear.
- Period IV (ca. 5000–1000 B.P.): projectile points of triangular, amygdaloidal, and pendunculate forms of the Shumla, Matamoros, Tortugas, Abasolo, Nogales, Catán, NL 2 Rana, NL 4 Pinitos, NL 5 Cataara, NL 8 Icamole, NL 12 Anacua, and NL 15 Rinconada types are common. Also found are choppers, simple scrapers, and bifaces of diverse forms, scrapers of the Coahuila type, grinding instruments, gouges, necklace beads and shell pendants, bone strikers and spatulas, stone pipes, and plates incised like amulets.
- Period V (ca. 1000 B.P. to time of Spanish contact): crude artifacts absent, scrapers of the Coahuila type and gouges continue, and arrow points of the Starr, Fresno, Harrel, and Toyah types and grinders proliferate.
- Period VI (time of Spanish contact to the end of the nineteenth century): represented by projectile points and scrapers manufactured from metal and glass, shell buttons, and small, rough ceramic vases.

ROCK ART

Various studies have discussed these peoples' settlement patterns, religion, shamanism, burials, linguistic traits, and ethnicity (Reyes Trigos and Valadez Moreno 1996; Valadez Moreno 1993b, 1997b, 1999c, 1999d, 1999e, 2001d, 2002b; Valadez Moreno and Reyes Trigos 1997). What stands out is the large number of engraved and painted stone symbols and markings in the region. At first glance, the characteristics and distribution of this rock art appear abstract and without order. A closer look at the location, orientation, and types of elements at each site, however, reveals their intentional placement on prominent vertical and horizontal rock outcrops and an orientation toward geological forms or features on the landscape.

This ordering of space, in which each symbol or group of symbols, each site or group of sites, has a predetermined position in relation to the surrounding landscape, denotes an omnidirectional sense reflected not only in the cave paintings but also in activities, behavior, and objects—including the types of dwellings, encampments, roasting features, and seasonal rounds. Rock art was used to define territories and delimit sites and to identify special places on the landscape, such as peaks, cardinal points and elevations, and points on the horizon that marked the rising and setting of the sun on predetermined dates, such as solstices and equinoxes.

In reality, such observations did not demand complex calculations or a precision characteristic of agricultural groups. Through the use of simple sums and multiples of numbers, people could keep track of the passage of days, the moon's cycle, the growth of plants, and animals' gestational periods and identify the right time to move a seasonal camp or to celebrate important events and ceremonies.

The highest concentration of cave sites in Nuevo León is found in the east-central and northern parts of the state. The cave iconography of this region exhibits four principal themes:

- Places devoted to special features on the landscape. Related images include angular, undulating, or curved lines resembling the tops, peaks, or profiles of hills or mountain ranges.
- Sites dedicated to the recording of celestial events. Images at these sites include straight or crossed lines or lines intersecting circles that coincide with the cardinal directions, or simple circles, series of circles, and lines connecting or hanging from circles that represent the sun, moon, or stars or the passage of comets and shooting stars. These sites are usually on hilltops where the night sky can be observed or at locations where the rising and setting of the sun are marked by hills to the east and west.
- Sites devoted to the veneration of water and hunting. Here are found series of straight, horizontal, and vertical lines, parallel lines, and sinuous or zigzag lines indicative of rain, lightning, or riverbeds and creek beds through which water flows. Such images are commonly found at the junctions between hills, along drainages and rivers, and at springs where the rocks come into contact with water. Also found are depictions of deer horns and tracks, atlatls, projectile points, and series of dots similar to numerical beads. The latter may have been used to keep track of the phases of the moon and the gestational periods of deer (Murray 1982, 1986, 1992, 1993, 1994, 1999).
- Sites with representations of ritual objects and mythical people. Engraved images related to these themes include handled knifes, psychoactive plants such as peyote, anthropomorphic figures with the hands, feet, or bodies of mythical beings, and individuals with special attributes. Their presence suggests the observance of various kinds of rituals (cf. Valadez Moreno 1997b). The most frequent locations for these images are the slopes and tops of low hills or the walls of shelters and caves.

Although the deer horns, numbered beads, and atlatls described earlier are associated with hunting, a connection with the veneration of water may also be assumed, symbolizing the veneration of life. The search for places located at the junctions of hills, where water runs, may symbolize the feminine part from whence fluid runs after the source is broken and life is born. The chronicles relate that when a boy was born, he was carried to a nearby creek to be washed as his first contact with the exterior world. The image of the deer antlers may symbolize the two hills or rocks where water crosses. The beads might have been used to calculate the gestational cycle of the doe. Other symbols have been found for which the meaning has not been identified, but they may have a relationship to rain phenomena.

The atlatl denotes the instrument with which the deer were hunted, but it could also symbolize the virility of the hunter as a complement to the feminine part, from which runs water. In this way, rain and hunting were combined in a complex relationship that sustained the region's hunters and gatherers. The rain assured numerous plant species the following season, which in turn sustained the herbivores, such as the deer, and the carnivores, including humans. The representations of peaks or hills may have served as a virile complement to the feminine geography, combining metaphors in the landscape. This is further suggested by the fact that many hills of curved form have been given feminine names.

In social terms, these petroglyph and cave painting sites can be divided into public and private spaces. The first, as the name implies, were places of easy access to the open sky, where groups of individuals could witness astronomical phenomena or ceremonies, rituals related to the themes of water and hunting, and other celebrations, such as puberty, initiation, war rites, marriages, peace pacts, and alliances. Individuals may have come together in such places at special times to observe the changes of the seasons or to perform ceremonies, and they may have recorded these events in symbolic rock art. Private spaces, in contrast, are small spaces in separate zones only marginally related to the landscape, where individuals, alone or in the company of a guide or master, may have undertaken rites of passage related to elements of the natural world.

The careful selection of these places and images in accordance with the type of landform suggests that these rock art sites may have functioned as symbolic refuges for these egalitarian societies. A determined sector of the population may have been able to limit the use of these spaces as well as the meanings of the symbols and to control social relations and religious beliefs, both within the community and with neighboring groups.

The petroglyphs and cave paintings were applied to clear limestone walls or to rocks strongly resistant to oxidation by natural agents. This created a visual contrast between the painted or engraved images and the surfaces that formed the support. Even if the walls or rocks met these criteria and the site was easily accessible, the location might still be rejected if the rocks did not project toward a natural feature or if the site's orientation did not meet the thematic criteria mentioned earlier. In that case, the location was ruled out as a place to integrate the omnidirectional world, where each image and rock, every element and activity in the lives of these hunter-gatherers, interacted symbolically with the elements and forces of nature to conform to a sacred and dynamic landscape cyclically reinforced through ceremony and ritual.

REFERENCES CITED

De León, Alonso
    1961   Relación y Discursos del Descubrimiento, Población y Pacificación de Éste Nuevo Reino de León; Temperamento y Calidad de la Tierra. In *Historia De Nuevo León, con Noticias sobre Coahuila, Tamaulipis, Texas y Nuevo México, Escrita en el Siglo XVII por el Cap. Alonso De León, Juan Bautista Chapa, y el Gral. Fernando Sánchez de Zomora*, estudio preliminar y notas de Israel Cavazos Garza, 2–119. Biblioteca de Nuevo León, Gobierno del Estado de Nuevo León, Centro de Estudios Humanísticos, Universidad Autóma de Nuevo León, México.

Del Hoyo, Eugenio
 1979   *Historia del Nuevo Reyno De León (1577-1723)*, 2nd ed., ed. Al Voleo. México.
 1985   *Esclavitud y Encomiendas de Indios en el Nuevo Reyno De León, Siglos XVI-XVII*. Archivo General Del Estado De Nuevo León, Monterrey, México.

Murray, William B.
 1982   Calendrical Petroglyphs of Northern Mexico. In *Archaeology in the New World*, ed. Anthony F. Aveni, 195-204. Cambridge University Press, Cambridge.
 1986   Numerical Representation in North American Rock Art. In *Native American Mathematics*, ed. Michael P. Closs, 45-70. University of Texas Press, Austin.
 1992   Antlers and Counting in Northeast Mexican Rock Art. In *American Indian Rock Art*, Volume 15, ed. Kay Sanger, 71-79. American Rock Art Research Association, Whittier, Calif.
 1993   Counting and Skywatching at Boca de Potrerillos, N.L., Mexico. In *Archaeoastronomy in the 1990s*, ed. Clive Ruggles, 264-269. Group D Publications, Loughborough, England.
 1994   Seasonality and Time Reckoning among the Hunter-Gatherers of Northeastern Mexico and South Texas. In *Time and Astronomy at the Meeting of Two Worlds*, ed. S. Iwaniszewski, A. Lebeuf, A. Wiercinski, and M. S. Ziolkowski, 207-220. Warsaw University Press, Warsaw.
 1999   San Bernabé: Lugar De Cazadores. In *Expresión y Memoria: Pintura Rupestre y Petrograbado en las Sociedadaes del Norte de México*, Volume 16, ed. Carlos Viramontes Anzures and Ana María Crespo Oviedo, 45-46. Instituto Nacional de Antropología e Historia, México.

Reyes Trigos, Claudia, and Moisés Valadez Moreno
 1996   Identificación Geográfico-Lingüística de los Grupos Indígenas del Noroeste de México (Siglos XVI-XIX). *Tercer Encuentro de Lingüística en el Noroeste*, Tomo I, Volumen 2, 575-594. Universidad de Sonora, Hermosillo, México.

Rivera Estrada, Araceli
 1996   Proyecto: Registro y Catalogación de Sitios Arqueológicos en el Extremo Sur de Nuevo León. Informe Técnico 1995. Archivo Técnico de la Coordinación Nacional de Arqueología, Instituto Nacional de Antropología e Historia (INAH), México.
 1997   Proyecto: Registro y Catalogación de Sitios Arqueológicos en el Extremo Sur de Nuevo León. Informe Técnico 1996. Archivo Técnico de la Coordinación Nacional de Arqueología, INAH, México.
 1998   Proyecto: Registro y Catalogación de Sitios Arqueológicos en el Extremo Sur de Nuevo León. Informe Técnico 1997. Archivo Técnico de la Coordinación Nacional de Arqueología, INAH, México.
 1999   Proyecto: Registro y Catalogación de Sitios Arqueológicos en el Extremo Sur de Nuevo León. Informe Técnico 1998. Archivo Técnico de la Coordinación Nacional de Arqueología, INAH, México.
 2000   Proyecto: Registro y Catalogación de Sitios Arqueológicos en el Extremo Sur de Nuevo León. Informe Técnico 1999. Archivo Técnico de la Coordinación Nacional de Arqueología, INAH, México.
 2001   Proyecto: Registro y Catalogación de Sitios Arqueológicos en el Extremo Sur de Nuevo León. Informe Técnico 2000. Archivo Técnico de la Coordinación Nacional de Arqueología, INAH, México.

Valadez Moreno, Moisés
1993a Informe Técnico de la 1ª Temporada del Proyecto, Catalogación e Identificación de Sitios Arqueologicos en la Parte Norte de Nuevo León. Archivo Técnico de la Coordinación Nacional de Arqueología, INAH, México.
1993b Datos Etnohistóricos y Etnogricos de las Sociedades Indigenes que Habitaron Nuevo León. *Revista Deslinde*:39-40, 124-136. Facultad de Ilosofía y Letras de la Universidad de Nuevo León, Monterrey.
1994 Informe Técnico de la Iiª Temporada del Proyecto, Catalogación e Identificación de Sitios Arqueologicos en la Parte Norte de Nuevo León. Archivo Técnico de la Coordinación Nacional de Arqueología, INAH, México.
1995 Informe Técnico de la Iiiª Temporada del Proyecto, Catalogación e Identificación de Sitios Arqueologicos en la Parte Norte de Nuevo León. Archivo Técnico de la Coordinación Nacional de Arqueología, INAH, México.
1997a Informe Técnico de la Viª Temporada del Proyecto, Catalogación e Identificación de Sitios Arqueologicos en la Parte Norte de Nuevo León. Archivo Técnico de la Coordinación Nacional de Arqueología, INAH, México.
1997b Practicas Shamánicas y el Mitote Indígena en Nuevo León. *Revista De Humanidades: Tecnológico De Monterrey* 3:191-199. División de Ciencias y Humanidades, Instituto de Estudios Superiores de Monterrey, Monterrey.
1998 Informe Técnico de la Iª Temporada del Proyecto, Arqueología En Nuevo León. Archivo Técnico de la Coordinación Nacional de Arqueología, INAH, México.
1999a Informe Técnico de la Vª Temporada del Proyecto, Catalogación e Identificación de Sitios Arqueologicos en la Parte Norte de Nuevo León. Archivo Técnico de la Coordinación Nacional de Arqueología, INAH, México.
1999b Informe Técnico de la Iiª Temporada del Proyecto, Arqueología En Nuevo León. Técnico de la Coordinación Nacional de Arqueología, INAH, México.
1999c *La Arqueología De Nuevo León y el Noreste*. Universidad Autónoma de Nuevo León, Monterrey.
1999d El Piloncillo, La Caña de Azúcar y Los Cambios Ecológicos Culturales en el Valle de Mina, Nuevo León. *Revista De Humanidades: Tecnológicos De Monterrey* 6:225-241. División de Ciencoas y Humanidades, Instituto Tecnológico de Estudios Superiores de Monterrey, México.
1999e Plantas Aluncinógenas y Medicinales Utilizadas por las Sociedades Pretéritas del Noreste. En *La Medicina Tradicional en el Norte de México*, ed. Silvia Ortiz Echaniz, 115-124. Colección Científica, Serie Antropología Física, 1ª Edición. INAH, México.
2000 Informe Téchnico del Análisis de los Materiales Colectados en la 1ª Temporada del Projecto, Arqueología en Nuevo León. Archivo Téchnico de la Coordinación Nacional de Arqueología, INAH, México.
2001a Informe Técnico del Análisis de los Materiales Colectados en la Vª Temporada del Proyecto, Catalogación e Identificación de Sitio Arqueologicos en la Parte Norte de Nuevo León. Archivo Técnico de la Coordinación Nacional de Arqueología, INAH, México.
2001b Informe Técnico de la Iiiª Temporada del Proyecto, Arquelogía En Nuevo León. Técnico de la Coordinación Nacional de Arqueología, INAH, México.
2001c Informe Técnico de la Ivª Temporada del Proyecto, Arquelogía En Nuevo León. Técnico de la Coordinación Nacional de Arqueología, INAH, México.

2001d Expiración, Luto y Defunción. Evidencias Sobre Prácticas Mortuorias Entre los Antiguos Norestense. *Revista De Humanidades: Tecnológico de Monterrey* 10:121-131. División de Ciencias y Humanidades del Instituto Tecnológico de Estudios Superiores de Monterrey, México.

2002a Informe Técnico del Análisis de los Materiales Obtenidos en la Iiª Temporada del Proyecto, Catalogación e Identificación de Sitio Arqueologicos en la Parte Norte de Nuevo León. Archivo Técnico de la Coordinación Nacional de Arqueología, INAH, México.

2002b Vinateros y Talladores: Dos Pervivencias Indígenas de Nuevo León. *Revista De Humanidades: Tecnológico De Monterrey* 12:249-258. División de Ciencas y Humanidades del Instituto Tecnológico de Estudios Superiores de Monterrey, México.

Valadez Moreno, Moisés, and Claudia Reyes Trigos

1997 Distribución Étnico-Lingüística de la Población Indígena Norestense. *Revista De Humanidades: Tecnológico De Monterrey* 2:133-153. Departamento de Ciencias y Humanidades, Instituto Tecnológico de Estudios Superiores de Monterrey, Nuevo León, México.

22

CONTRIBUTIONS OF WALTER W. TAYLOR TO THE ARCHAEOLOGY OF COAHUILA, 1937–1947

Leticia González Arratia

The first archaeological project developed, organized, and designed for the state of Coahuila in northern Mexico was the U.S. National Museum's Coahuila Expedition, directed by Walter W. Taylor.[1] The project required several seasons of fieldwork, followed by a long period of inconclusive analysis. The focus of this chapter is Taylor's site work in northeastern Coahuila.[2] The geographical point of reference is the settlement of Cuatro Ciénegas, Coahuila, where Taylor established his base camp and planned his surveys and excavations.

The work can be divided into three stages, which collectively became known as the Coahuila Project (Taylor 1988:19). The 1941 field season, Taylor's third visit to Coahuila, can be distinguished by the intensity and goals of his fieldwork. The three stages of work are:

- Stage 1. Pre-Coahuila Project
    Summer 1937: Reconnaissance of the area north of Cuatro Ciénegas to locate archaeological sites.
    Summer 1939: Reconnaissance of the area west and south of Cuatro Ciénegas to locate archaeological sites.

- Stage 2. Development of the Coahuila Project
  January–May 1941. Excavation of previously recorded caves or shelters considered to have been used as habitations in the mountain drainages near the Valley of Cuatro Ciénegas.
  June 1941. Reconnaissance of additional sites west and northeast of the Valley of Cuatro Ciénegas. Surface material was collected, and several burial shelters were excavated.
- Stage 3. Post-Coahuila Project
  September 18 to November 16, 1947. Reconnaissance in other parts of Coahuila for sites analogous to the Cuatro Ciénegas sites (Taylor 1947).

THE YEARS 1937–1938

In 1937 Walter W. Taylor undertook his first fieldwork in the deserts of Coahuila in northern Mexico. That same year he also began his second semester of postgraduate work at the University of New Mexico, where he studied with Leslie Spier (Taylor 1988:1). At that time the area closest, and to some degree most similar, to Coahuila, about which Taylor already possessed some knowledge, was the Big Bend area of Texas. Taylor's methodological approach, which he viewed as "one of the most productive in archaeology," was to proceed from the known (the archaeology of Big Bend, Texas) to the unknown (the archaeology of Coahuila, Mexico) (Taylor 1988:6).

On his first trip to the state of Coahuila, Taylor used the settlement of Monclova, Coahuila, as his point of departure and headed eastward toward Cuatro Ciénegas and from there to points north (Taylor 1937:45). He visited twenty shelters or caves during that visit but no open-air sites. Although not all of the sites exhibited archaeological evidence, each eventually received a reference number consisting of the prefix CM and a consecutive number.[3] Taylor's northernmost site was approximately eighty miles south of the Río Bravo, or the Rio Grande, as it is known in the United States.[4] He hoped to find ceramics that could be used to determine the approximate age of the sites, a goal that was never achieved.[5]

Despite the informality of his fieldwork, lack of knowledge about the archaeology of Texas and Coahuila, and lack of experience in collecting and recording surface artifacts, Taylor produced three papers about his recent experiences after his return to New Mexico, one of which was published that same year (Taylor 1937).[6] In all three papers he expressed a similar sentiment: that "the cave culture of Coahuila, Mexico, may be considered *much like*, but not *identical with*, the cave culture of West Texas. The similarities indicate a unity which binds the areas together in one problem. The differences point to the fact that the material culture changes as it proceeds south and to the possibility that there were associations and *influences* acting upon Coahuila from directions other than the north" (emphasis added).[7]

This quotation incorporates three theoretical problems Taylor worked on throughout his life but never resolved: (1) how to conceptualize the similarities between the cultures of Coahuila and West Texas without losing sight of their differences, (2) how to identify a cultural continuum and at the same time differentiate phases or periods within this continuum, and (3) how Mesoamerican influences affected the cultures of Coahuila, given the proximity of the state's southern border to the northernmost part of this region.

One of Taylor's major objectives was to "clarify the origin and position of the Texas cave material and its relations, if any, to cultures in Mexico. Such a continuous link between the American Southwest and the southern portions of the Mexican plateau would be of the utmost value, should it be demonstrated."[8] All evidence pointed to the existence of a route or corridor extending between the Mexican central high plateau, with its great pre-Hispanic cultures, and the southwestern United States—a route that crossed the great Chihuahua Desert, the prevalent environment of Coahuila.

Following this expedition, Taylor enrolled in a doctoral program at Harvard (Euler 1997:23). At the end of 1938, he began to analyze the archaeological material collected by Edward Palmer in 1880, which was curated at Harvard's Peabody Museum. Palmer had collected the material from the burial caves of the Comarca Lagunera, 300 kilometers southwest of Cuatro Ciénegas. This work fit Taylor perfectly. He revealed his enthusiasm in a letter to his friend Albert Schroeder: "I came here hoping but did not dare hope too much that they would do that very thing."[9]

THE YEAR 1939

In June 1939 a determined Walter W. Taylor returned to Coahuila to continue his reconnaissance of the region and its archaeological features. He spent thirty-two days surveying the region west and northwest of Cuatro Ciénegas and southward to a point halfway along the road between San Pedro and Cuatro Ciénegas (Taylor 1988:4).[10] During this time he discovered three of the four caves with deposits (CM-24, Burro Gordo, or Fat Burro Cave; CM-28, El Nopal, or Nopal Shelter; and CM-37). He interpreted these sites as "habitations" and excavated them in 1941 as part of the U.S. National Museum's Coahuila Expedition.

The nature and quantity of archaeological sites Taylor recorded and his analyses of the pictographs, flaked stone artifacts, and ceramics influenced his decision to excavate several of these caves the following year.[11] He hoped to correlate the ceramics chronologically with the material from the caves to verify that the caves' early inhabitants were of considerable antiquity and associated with other pre-Hispanic settlements. He proposed a post–A.D. 700 date for the initial occupation of these sites.[12]

After completing his reconnaissance work in Coahuila, Taylor went to Chaco Canyon where he met Frank D. Setzler, head curator of the Smithsonian Institution, who was in residence there (Taylor 1973:220 n. 120). He maintained correspondence with Setzler and later obtained academic endorsement from the Smithsonian

Institution to obtain the necessary permissions from the government of Mexico to formally undertake archaeological work in Coahuila. He also began to search for financial support and received a donation of $2,500 at the beginning of 1940 from a wealthy friend (Taylor 1988:4).

THE YEAR 1941

With his two principal problems—financial support and academic endorsement—resolved, in 1940 Taylor began making preparations for his next field trip. He decided to focus his doctoral thesis on the excavations in Coahuila. Taylor arrived at Cuatro Ciénegas on Christmas Day 1940, together with his wife, Lyda, and Albert Schroeder, who had been invited to collaborate as his assistant.[13] Excavations commenced on January 4, 1941 (Taylor 1988:5). From January to May, Taylor excavated several sites he had recorded during previous trips. The month of June was devoted to surface surveys and the excavation of sites known to contain burials.

Excavation of the Cave Habitations

The first caves Taylor excavated were Burro Gordo and El Nopal.[14] Later, he moved on to the famous cave La Espantosa. Because of its extensive features, large size, deep deposits, and relative density of artifacts, La Espantosa became Taylor's prototype site and principal point of reference for interpreting the archaeology of central Coahuila and the pre-Hispanic societies that inhabited the area.

Taylor's experiences in 1939 had led him to believe he would encounter primarily artifacts of stone. Contrary to expectation, he recovered great quantities of wooden, fiber, and leaf artifacts from the caves. No ceramics were found. The most significant strata revealed the presence of two kinds of objects Taylor believed were of considerable antiquity: certain types of woven sandals and an incised rock fragment (Table 22.1).

The objects that drew Taylor's strongest attention were the sandals made of fibers and leaves. He noted to Setzler that "our definite sandal stratigraphy is still intact and really a beautiful example of mutually exclusive superposition . . . something to dream about!"[15] His interest in the sandals and the potential they held for his studies continued until his death and was the focus of his only publication dedicated entirely to the material culture of Coahuila (Taylor 1988).

Taylor did not limit his thinking to the chronological aspects of the sites or the material culture of the pre-Hispanic inhabitants of the Coahuila caves and their significance. He also continued to elaborate on an idea that was manifested in 1937 and that appears to have excited him even more, given the emphasis he placed on it in a letter to a friend. After three months of excavation, he described his ideal site "where a stratigraphy exists that shows an association between our crude nomadic culture and that of the people of a higher culture, who manufacture the ceramics

Table 22.1. Taylor's proposed relative chronology of cultural materials from the Coahuila Caves.

Oldest	Most Recent
Certain sandal types	Increasing quantities of agave-processing waste
Incised rock	Pictographs
Large quantities of animal bones	*Yahuales* (a type of curved machete)
Lesser quantities of agave-processing waste	Minor quantities of animal bones
Lesser presence of sotol ovens	Increasing evidence of sotol ovens

to the south in the Valley of Mexico."[16] Despite this interest, nothing he found during the remainder of his fieldwork near Cuatro Ciénegas that year supported his theory of an encounter between local nomadic groups and sedentary people from Mesoamerica.

Based on his knowledge of material from the burial caves of La Laguna gained during his research in the collections of the Peabody Museum, Taylor recognized a discrepancy regarding the location of this type of site: "Caves that demonstrate occupation have been reported in the southern part of the Coahuila border with Zacatecas."[17] This location corresponded not to Cuatro Ciénegas but to the burial caves of La Laguna. Taylor seems to have considered a regional change in his area of study: "[W]e desire and pray to find a site that furnishes us with relative stratigraphy and establishes the missing link between the cultures of the United States and the high cultures of Mexico." He ended with the affirmation, "for this [is the reason] we are here."[18] Possibly for this reason, after his return to the United States, he began to reexamine the material from the burial caves of La Laguna in the archives of the Smithsonian and the Peabody Museum (González Arratia 2006).

Survey Activities and the Excavation of Burials

After completing excavations of the habitation caves of Cuatro Ciénegas, Taylor dedicated a week to finding sites "more prominent to the region," which he appears to have learned about from his Mexican workers. He dedicated another week to excavating previously located burial sites. As a result of this survey and his decision to allow his reference numbers to be used for sites in Coahuila investigated by others, the catalog of sites increased from CM-64 to CM-101.[19] With that, he concluded his 1941 field season.[20]

CHARACTERISTICS OF THE LOCAL PRE-HISPANIC CULTURE

Taylor interpreted the local pre-Hispanic population as composed of small groups of nomads who subsisted by gathering fruits and hunting animals. This type of "savage" life (a term used by Taylor) encouraged mobility from one place to another in accordance with the seasons of the year. In Taylor's view, the numbers

377

of individuals who composed these groups must have been small. This would have enabled them to distribute themselves over the length and breadth of the region and to repeatedly occupy the same localities and caves. Taylor saw this as one plausible explanation for the great accumulation of artifacts and sediments found in La Espantosa Cave. In Taylor's opinion, "[N]omadism grants the form and nature of the cultural material."[21]

Prior to Taylor's work, the German geologist and archaeology enthusiast Frederico Müllerried had traveled to the region east of Monclova in 1926 and discovered the remains of pre-Hispanic occupation on the surface. Combining his field observations and a sophisticated analysis of the flaked stone material with ethnohistoric research and his knowledge of geology, Müllerried arrived at many of the same interpretations as Taylor. Although Müllerried's results were published in 1934, Taylor apparently did not consult them (González Arratia, document in preparation).

DATING THE SITES

The temporal nature of the material Taylor discovered in his excavations, the depth of the deposits in La Espantosa (2.5 meters), and the color of the sediments deposited directly on bedrock suggested a change in climatic conditions. Nevertheless, Taylor did not reconsider his theory regarding the age of the occupation, which he believed had begun about A.D. 500, according to a letter he wrote to a friend during the excavation. In 1940 a proposed date of about A.D. 700 was published (McGregor 1940:254). Taylor later proposed a terminal date of A.D. 1700 to mark the end of the occupation.[22]

TAYLOR'S ARCHAEOLOGICAL ANALYSIS AND DOCTORAL THESIS

Taylor had entered into an agreement with the U.S. National Museum and the Instituto Nacional de Antropología e Historia (INAH) to write a report that detailed his site work and included an analysis of the artifacts obtained during his excavations. While beginning this work at the U.S. National Museum, he encountered a burial bundle that had originated in one of the caves explored by Edward Palmer at La Laguna (Taylor 1968). For a number of reasons, the burial had been sent to the U.S. National Museum in 1880 (González Arratia 2006). Thus in addition to analyzing the material from his own excavations, he also studied this other material (Taylor 1968).

At the start of 1942, Taylor received a scholarship from Harvard University that required him to move back to Cambridge, Massachusetts, to serve as Alfred Tozzer's graduate assistant. While at Harvard, he reexamined Edward Palmer's collections and continued his study of the artifacts from Cuatro Ciénegas.[23]

So overwhelmed was Taylor by the quantity of archaeological material recovered from his expeditions in Coahuila that he decided to change the focus of his

Contributions of Walter W. Taylor to the Archaeology of Coahuila, 1937–1947

Table 22.2. Summary of Taylor's fieldwork in Coahuila, 1937–1947.

Site Numbers Registered, by Year	Number of Sites Registered	Time in the Field
1937: CM-01 to CM-20	20	1 month
1939: CM-21 to CM-63	43	1 month
1941: CM-64 to CM-101	38	6 months
1947: CM-102 to CM-115	14	2 months
Total	115	10 months

dissertation.[24] The threat of induction into the United States Army probably added to his tension and sense of urgency about finishing his doctorate. Certainly, he would have been unable to finish his dissertation as quickly as he did if he had stayed with his original theme.[25] Instead, he chose a topic of theoretical discourse, which resulted in a work that came to occupy a seminal place in the history of archaeology, *A Study of Archaeology* (Taylor 1973). During the war Taylor was wounded and taken prisoner by the Germans. He returned to the United States in 1945 and continued work on his dissertation, which was published in 1948.

POST–COAHUILA PROJECT: THE 1947 SURVEY

In 1947, although he had still not completed a report on his 1941 excavations, Taylor decided to undertake another field season in Coahuila. His goal was to find new sites to excavate and "to bridge the gap between the 1940–41 diggings around Cuatro Ciénegas and the sites excavated by Kelley at Presidio, Texas (Junta de los Ríos), and those in the Big Bend and Trans-Pecos region of Texas" (Taylor 1947). In the absence of publications that clearly explain his approach, we must read between the lines to infer his philosophy and hypotheses stemming from the material excavated in the caves La Espantosa and Burro Gordo. From an interpretative perspective, his original hypothesis and point of departure in 1939, which anticipated similarities between the sites at Big Bend and those of Cuatro Ciénegas, did not come to fruition.

During his 1947 trip, Taylor added fourteen new sites to his inventory (CM-102 to CM-115), none considered worthy of excavation. Sometime around December 1947, he wrote a brief report to INAH in Mexico City that described each site in detail (Taylor 1947).

During his ten-year love affair with Coahuila, Taylor traveled extensively through the mountains of central and northwestern Coahuila, an area comprising approximately one-quarter of the state. Considering that Coahuila is the third-largest state in the Republic of Mexico, with an area of 151,571 square kilometers, this is a region of considerable size. Table 22.2 provides a summary of the amount of time Taylor spent in the field and the number of sites visited and recorded during his three trips.

CONCLUSION

Walter W. Taylor's contributions focused above all else on an extended exploration of the caves and rockshelters in the mountains of Coahuila, especially certain drainage systems. His excavation of habitation and burial sites brought to light the diversity of archaeological artifacts typical of the region and the desert in general. This in itself earns him the distinction of pioneer archaeologist of Coahuila.

Taylor integrated the sites and materials others recorded in Coahuila into his own studies, resulting in an inventory of the first 115 sites recorded in the state. The types of artifacts and raw materials he documented—including pictographs, remnants of human bone tissue, abundant textiles, baskets, vegetable food remains, wooden tools, and other organic materials, along with lesser quantities of flaked stone tools—confirmed the importance of plant-based materials for pre-Hispanic societies of hunter-gatherers. Taylor's work also revealed the absence of pre-Hispanic agriculture in central and northwestern Coahuila (Taylor 1972).

Although other professional archaeologists and semiprofessionals, including Müllerried in 1926 and Mason in 1936, studied sites and archaeological material from Coahuila before him, Taylor is the only investigator who maintained continuity in his fieldwork and a focus on the archaeology of Coahuila. He dedicated a decade to this research and analysis and nearly a year of his life to fieldwork over four different periods. Between 1937 and 1949, Taylor combined his extensive and varied field experience with an analysis of curated artifacts, including those from La Comarca Lagunera in southwestern Coahuila. This enabled him to develop an empirical, rather than a systematic, approach to his investigations—"the culture of the caves," in the terminology of that era. He compared his finds with material from Big Bend in Texas and with La Comarca Lagunera in southwestern Coahuila, a region unfamiliar to Taylor, although relatively close (approximately 300 km) to his area of investigation. He also compared similarities and differences between regions—not just between sites—and explored a theoretical problem that transcended these desert societies: the influence or presence of a Mesoamerican culture alien to the realm of hunter-gatherers.

Through his decade of work, he was able to differentiate for the first time two archaeologically homogeneous zones in the region: central and northern Coahuila and the area of La Comarca Lagunera. He believed the cultural base reflected by the habitation caves of Cuatro Ciénegas differed from that found at La Laguna. Taylor noted that in the latter area, "definite suggestions of 'high culture' influences are present. Agriculture, pottery, cotton and loom-weaving, sandal types, the elaboration of netting techniques, all point to extra-Coahuila sources, specifically to Zape, the cave-house people of Chihuahua, and the culture found in the vicinity of Durango City which, in turn, leads on to Chalchihuites and the so-called Toltec periphery."[26]

Although he lacked fundamental evidence, Taylor may have felt pressured to identify the presence of agriculture in the La Comarca Lagunera area from the extended range of artifacts considered indicators of Mesoamerican influence.

Doubts still remain, however, as to whether plants were cultivated in pre-Hispanic times in this part of Coahuila (González Arratia 2000:44). Nevertheless, loom-woven textiles are present and also small quantities of cotton objects. Taylor concluded that "the Laguna District does not contain a typical Coahuila cave culture but represents a very vital area of cultural transition and cross-influence."[27]

Walter W. Taylor's greatest shortcoming was his lack of publications. The quotations in the preceding two paragraphs come from unpublished correspondence from 1948. Taylor expressed these same ideas publicly in 1961 in a paper presented before the Mexican Society of Anthropology, cited in the bibliography of that report.[28] By 1955 radiocarbon dating suggested much greater antiquity for the occupations of his excavated caves. Although Taylor's fundamental premises remain intact, this dating has led to a reconsideration of the chronology of the hunter-gatherer occupation in the region. The discovery and exploration of Candelaria Cave in La Comarca Lagunera by Mexican archaeologists and anthropologists in 1953 and the subsequent analysis and publication of its findings (Aveleyra Arroyo de Anda, Maldonado-Koerdell, and Martinez del Rio 1956) brought to light materials similar to those investigated by Taylor from Edward Palmer's explorations and reinforced Taylor's position in respect to this region (González Arratia 2000:55).

NOTES

Editors' note: Some quotations attributed to Taylor in this chapter are verbatim quotations from Taylor's writings in English. Others are Spanish translations of his writings that were translated back into English by a Mexican translator for this publication. The quotations cited in notes 7, 8, 9, 15, 25, and 26 are verbatim quotations. The other quotations deviate from Taylor's original wording. The abbreviation WWTP refers to the archives of the Walter W. Taylor Project, National Anthropological Archives, Smithsonian Institution, Washington, D.C.

1. Walter W. Taylor undertook his archaeological research in Coahuila as part of a major investigation related to the history of archaeology in that state, from the perspective of constructing archaeological knowledge. Taylor expressed his feelings about the project in a letter to Frank D. Setzler dated November 22, 1943 (WWTP). The former U.S. National Museum is now the National Museum of Natural History of the Smithsonian Institution.

2. Later, around 1958, Taylor presided over additional site work in northeastern Coahuila in the area of Presa de la Amistad, near the city of Acuña, Coahuila. The actual site work and analysis of archaeological materials were undertaken by Alberto González Rul from the Instituto Nacional de Antropología e Historia (Taylor 1958; Taylor and González Rul 1960; González Rul 1990).

3. During this period, sites CM-1 to CM-20 were registered.

4. Walter W. Taylor, *Plano Maestro de Coahuila* (WWTP), n.d.

5. Walter W. Taylor, *A Preliminary Report on Sites in Coahuila, Mexico*. Typewritten manuscript (WWTP), n.d.

6. The other two papers are Walter W. Taylor, ibid., and *A Report on a Short Reconnaissance in Coahuila, Mexico*, both typewritten manuscripts (WWTP), n.d.

7. Taylor, *A Preliminary Report*.

8. Ibid. In 1937 the term "Mesoamerica," coined by Paul Kirchhoff, still had not come into common usage to describe the "high cultures" of central and southeastern Mexico. It was not popularized until his 1943 article, "Mesoamerica."

9. Letter from W. W. Taylor to Albert Schroeder, November 1, 1938 (WWTP).

10. Letter from W. W. Taylor to J. Alden Mason, October 3, 1939 (WWTP).

11. Letter from W. W. Taylor to Robert Stewart, January 22, 1940 (WWTP).

12. Letter from Taylor to Mason.

13. Letter from W. W. Taylor to Albert Schroeder, August 25, 1940 (WWTP).

14. Walter W. Taylor, Day Book, Coahuila Expedition, 1940–1941 (WWTP).

15. Letter from Walter W. Taylor to Frank M. Setzler, May 4, 1941 (WWTP).

16. Editors' note: We lack a source for this quotation.

17. Letter from Walter W. Taylor to Harold H. Swift, March 21, 1941 (WWTP).

18. Ibid.

19. Although the sites CM-88, CM-89, CM-90, CM-91, CM-93, CM-94, CM-97, and CM-100 were not discovered by Taylor, his consecutive numbering system was retained.

20. Letter from Walter W. Taylor to Frank M. Setzler, June 1, 1941 (WWTP).

21. Letter from Taylor to Swift.

22. Ibid.

23. Walter W. Taylor, typewritten memorandum to the Peabody Museum, February 23, 1942.

24. Letter from Walter W. Taylor to H. C. Wood, May 14, 1942 (WWTP).

25. Letter from Walter W. Taylor to Frank D. Seltzer, August 13, 1942 (WWTP).

26. Letter from Walter W. Taylor to Donald J. Lehmer, March 13, 1948 (WWTP).

27. Ibid.

28. Walter W. Taylor, La Posición Cultural de la Comarca Lagunera en el Norte de México. Paper presented in 1961 at the Ninth Roundtable of the Mexican Society of Anthropology, Chihuahua (WWTP), 1.

REFERENCES CITED

Aveleyra Arroyo de Anda, Luis, Manuel Maldonado-Koerdell, and Pablo Martinez del Rio
    1956   *Candelaria Cave*, Volume 1. Memorias del Instituto Nacional de Antropología 5, México.

Euler, Robert C.
    1997   Walter Willard Taylor Jr., 1913–1997. *SAA Bulletin* 14(4) (September):23.

González Arratia, Leticia
    2000   *Museo Regional de La Laguna y la Cueva de la Canderlaria*. Instituto Nacional de Antropología e Historia (INAH) y Adopte una Obra de Arte, México.
    2006   *La Exploración de Edward Palmer de Varias Cuevas Mortuorias en Coahuila en el Siglo XIX*. Collección Regiones, CONACULTA-INAH, México.

González Rul, Francisco
    1990   *Reconocimiento Arqueológico en la Parte Mexicana de la Presa de la Amistad*. Serie Arqueología, Colección Científica 203. INAH, México.

Kirchhoff, Paul
    1943   Mesoamérica. *Acta Americana* I:92–107.

McGregor, John C.
1940   Notes and News. *American Antiquity* 5(3):253-254.

Taylor, Walter W.
1937   Report of an Archaeological Survey of Coahuila, Mexico. *New Mexico Anthropologist* 2(2):45-46. Department of Anthropology, University of New Mexico, Albuquerque.

1947   *Summary Report of the Archaeological Reconnaissance of Coahuila, Mexico, 1947.* Archivo Técnico, INAH, México (Eight typewritten pages, twenty-seven photographs.)

1958   Archaeological Survey of the Mexican Part of the Diablo Reservoir. In *Appraisal of the Archaeological Resources of Diablo Reservoir, Val Verde County, Texas,* ed. J. A. Graham and W. B. Davis, 87-89. Report of the National Park Service by the Inter-Agency Archaeological Salvage Program, Field Office, Austin, Tex.

1968   A Burial Bundle from Coahuila, Mexico. In *Collected Papers in Honor of Lyndon Lane Hargrave,* ed. Albert H. Schroeder, 23-56. Papers of the Archaeological Society of New Mexico 1. Museum of New Mexico, Albuquerque.

1972   The Hunter-Gatherer Nomads of Northern Mexico: A Comparison of the Archival and Archaeological Records. *World Archaeology* 4(4):167-178.

1973   *A Study of Archaeology.* Southern Illinois University Press, Carbondale. Originally published in 1948 as Memoir of the American Anthropological Society 69, Menasha, Wis.

1988   *Contributions to Coahuila Archaeology with an Introduction to the Coahuila Project.* Southern Illinois University at Carbondale, Center for Archaeological Investigations, Research Paper 52, Carbondale.

Taylor, Walter W., and Francisco González Rul
1960   An Archaeological Reconnaissance Behind the Diablo Dam, Coahuila, Mexico. *Bulletin of the Texas Archaeological Society* 31:153-165. Austin.

23

ARCHAEOLOGY AND PHYSICAL ANTHROPOLOGY

A Reflection on Warfare in the Archaeological Vision

M. Nicolás Caretta

In Mexico the relationship between archaeology and physical anthropology has operated as an arrangement between separate disciplines rather than as an interdisciplinary one. This relationship has been constrained in the fields of demography, health, disease (the latter badly interpreted and in some cases exaggerated or invented), and particularly death and violence, including human sacrifice, cannibalism, and warfare. Focusing on this latter point, in this chapter I argue that Mexican archaeologists have failed to adequately consider the importance of warfare in their interpretations and that physical anthropologists have inadequately contributed to interpretations of war and violence in Mexican archaeology.

The world has constantly been immersed in wars and the threat of moving troops, displacements, and banishments. Historians have taken the lead in studying these conflicts, their characters and shifting territories, and the disruptions caused by external influences. In times of peace, historians and archaeologists have worked together on questions related to technological advances, culture change, the conquest of nature, and, more recently, gender relations. In recent years the topic of violence among worldwide prehistoric populations has received increasing attention (e.g., Ferguson 1984; Haas 1990; Keeley 1996; Lekson 2002). Despite the scarcity of archaeological clues and the problems with interpreting the evidence, it is now accepted that prehistoric societies were not always peaceful.

The prehistoric past was not an event that occurred at a specific moment. It was characterized by different technological, cultural, and economic stages. This diversity is a result of the different physical and social environments within which these civilizations developed. Social scientists who think the world became more advanced only with the advent of writing commit a major methodological mistake. Societies that expressed their histories through oral traditions also reached a high level of sophistication. This is apparent in the archaeology of the Middle East, where the earliest writing appeared. Numerous important developments preceded the advent of writing: the "invention" of agriculture, appearance of urban cities, rise of dynasties and elites, long-distance trade, and complex religions. The roads to power and conflict were not inevitable (Keeley 1996:23).

An understanding of conflict becomes more nuanced when we consider prehistoric non-western, non-state-level societies, especially hunting-and-gathering groups that lived without agriculture and survived on what nature offered—hunting wild animals, fishing, collecting shellfish, gathering greens, roots, and fruits. Because of their low population size, which remained relatively steady over the millennia, these groups were often envisioned as brotherly, calm, and philanthropic, lacking conflicts or problems—in short, as living in a "Christian paradise."

Many scholars undervalue the role of warfare in prehistory, considering it only a minor activity. At the other extreme, warfare is often exaggerated, with the strategies of some groups compared to those of the Romans. At one extreme, "primitive groups" are perceived as pacifists (the idea of the "noble savage" and probably the Pax Mesoamericana derive from this). At the other, they are envisioned as "war machines," like the gladiators. Yet ethnography reveals the importance of war as a social, political, and economic condition among non-state-level societies. Archaeological evidence of warfare includes fortifications, weapons, and, for physical anthropologists, osteological evidence of massacres. These factors only tell us that violence occurred, however. The reasons behind these skirmishes are much more difficult to glean from the material evidence. Battlefields are anonymous, and their landscapes appear peaceful today. Some have been turned into golf courses. Only rarely do tombs and graves survive the passage of time. The number of recovered human burials is miniscule compared to the size of original populations. For this reason, demographic reconstruction is difficult, and controversies arise.

In the earliest Sumerian city-states in Mesopotamia (ca. 3000–2500 B.C.), the Sumerians waged war and massacred each other, fought for territory, took each other captive, and stole each others' wealth. In addition to the discovery of fortifications in such cities as Uruk, we also find panels with scenes alluding to war, sculptures of prisoners and soldiers, insignias, and so on. In Lagash is found the "vulture stone," which narrates the victory of the sovereign of Lagash over the neighboring city of Umma in the year 2450 B.C. References to combat, battles, vengeance, captivity, and banishments occur in abundance in religious documents and epics, such as the Epic of Gilgamesh, the Odyssey, the Bible, the Koran, and *The Art of the War* by Tsun Tsu. These few examples are enough to make my point.

Indeed, warfare is more ancient in Mesopotamia than in any other city-state. Violence and warfare go along with human society, although the scales and manifestations vary. Yet despite the fact that many sites contain archaeological evidence supporting an interpretation of war, relatively few sites have yielded the human remains or other elements that provide evidence of these massacres.

Warfare was as present in the New World as anywhere else, although neither Rousseau nor Montesquieu and his followers would be pleased to hear this. New World societies did not develop an alphabetical writing system to tell about their stories. Instead, their representational system was a pictographic, iconographic, and sculptural system that functioned as a mnemonic device and support mechanism for oral traditions, as in the case of Mesoamerican societies. Battles were represented in various ways by the Classic-period Maya and reached their apogee during the Postclassic with the Mexicas (Aztecs).[1] These two groups provide the clearest examples, but this does not exclude groups—state-level societies or not—from other regions of Greater Mesoamerica. Nor does this pattern have definite temporal limits. The depiction of people with armaments (bows, arrows, atlatls, shields) does not necessarily mean warfare is represented. The figures represented could be hunters instead. Representations of warriors and deities with armaments could represent religious scenes, mythic battles, or rituals related to hunting.

The presence of warrior imagery raises questions about the existence, function, significance, and scale of these wars. The question arises: Where are all the dead people or other material indicators that could provide evidence of these wars for Mesoamerican archaeologists? What do physical anthropologists have to say about this matter?

Before discussing the Mesoamerican situation further, I should point out that only in the southwestern United States have these kinds of battles and other acts of violence been interpreted at various levels and archaeological scales (LeBlanc 2000; see also Lekson 2002). Although it might be possible to project these same ideas onto societies of northern and central Mexico, these inferences cannot move beyond assumptions without supporting data. Archaeological interpretations of conflict rely on the preservation and interpretation of artifactual and human remains. Unfortunately, the preservation and deterioration of organic material, especially bone, in archaeological contexts is problematic. The necessary physical evidence for interpreting warfare at archaeological sites is often lacking.

One oft-cited recent Mexican example of human remains resulting from warfare is the group of primary burials found by Cabrera and collaborators (1991) in the Temple of Quetzalcoatl in Teotihuacan, dating to A.D. 200. Because of the context in which they were found, however, these bones suggest a ritual treatment commonly found in other civic-religious structures. Not even Epiclassic sites such as Xochicalco, which contain fortifications used during these violent epochs, have produced human remains that substantiate these battles (González Crespo et al.

1995; Hirth 1995). More than one investigator has proposed a warfare model for the archaeological site of La Quemada in Zacatecas (Armillas 1964; Nelson 2000; Weigand 1975). These proposals are based on La Quemada's resemblance to Tula, as well as the presence of coyote and eagle war symbols and roads that would make warfare more effective, as in the Roman style (Trombold 1991). Although some of the human remains recovered during archaeological investigations in San Luis Potosí, Zacatecas, Durango, and Jalisco have been primary burials, the vast majority are secondary burials, which usually show evidence of ritual treatment (Pickering 1985; Pijoan and Mansilla 1990). Most of these human remains are long bones (mainly femurs), skulls, and jawbones with evidence of cut marks, muscle dismemberment, and perforations (Holien and Pickering 1978; Pickering 1985; Pijoan and Mansilla 1990), and some show signs of postmortem treatment. The site of Cerro del Huistle produced not only burials with signs of fleshing and perforations but also sixty skulls that may have comprised a *tzompantli*, or skull rack (Hers 1989). Many of these elements were no doubt related to ritual processes, similar to the Flowery Wars (Guerras Floridas) and sacrifices of the Postclassic in the central plateau. To our eyes, these were violent acts. To those societies, they were ritual ones.

Even though these actions may seem inhuman and savage to the western mind, they are not sufficient to prove the existence of large-scale wars (Nelson 2000). The topic of cannibalism cannot be avoided, whether the practice served as a form of ritual activity, violent social restraint, or vengeance (Turner and Turner 1997). Does archaeology have the means to investigate these conflicts? Can archaeological methods reconstruct scenarios of conquest and violent invasion? As a human science, it is difficult for archaeology to avoid the historical and cultural contexts in which the discipline developed. A vision of history based on warlike conflicts has influenced numerous concepts and explanations. Western history has recorded continual invasions: Celtic looters traveling through Europe, Germanic villages fighting against the Roman Empire, Viking plundering, Arab invasions, nomadic incursions, the Hundred Year War, the Balkan war (with its coined term, "Balkanization," now frequently used by archaeologists), and so on.

From an archaeological perspective, the burning of villages, whether by internal or external agents, can be one form of evidence of warfare and strife (Chavaillon 1996:189-190). Nevertheless, we cannot assume that all burning was intentional. Fire was also used to eradicate diseases and insect pests. Intentional "peaceful" burning versus fires caused by vandals can be difficult to distinguish. Spanish ethnohistorical sources discuss "barbarian" societies of Mexico that conducted great massacres to worship their "pagan" deities. They also discuss "savage" people of the north who attacked not only Spanish conquerors but also local villagers. Although these are valuable documents, they are biased and propagandistic, written to justify the conquerors' actions. Others are filled with misinterpretations and exaggerations by the Spaniards, who praise their own deeds of conquest and denigrate the culture of the "Other."

Archaeology tends to project its own vision of the world into the past. One way or another, whether European or American, twentieth or twenty-first century, armed conflicts of the past have influenced archaeological interpretations. Changes in material culture are interpreted as intrusive, with modifications attributed to migrants and "foreigners."[2] If the term "warfare" is generally understood to mean conflicts accomplished by groups of armed individuals, then how should we interpret mortal encounters between individuals, band raids between neighbors, ambushes, or assassinations? Should we consider human sacrifice an act of war, an act of violence, a religious component of a ritual, or all of these?

To incorporate such acts into the definition would widen the concept considerably and permit us to examine ancient societies from a new point of view. We must avoid thinking about pre-Hispanic groups as idyllic societies and try to envision what kinds of violence may have been practiced, bearing in mind that what we now consider violence may have been viewed differently by these groups. Nevertheless, expanding the view of violence does not avoid all problems because there will always be those who conceive of pre-Columbian groups as inhabitants of an Eden, living in total harmony with nature, or, at the other extreme, as terrible warriors engaged in endless battles.

In addition to violent acts based on vengeance, conquest, or robbery, Mesoamerica also witnessed ritual wars intended to demonstrate the bravery of their participants. These conflicts were more like games of sport that followed a series of pre-established rules. Participation in the Flowery Wars, for example, led to either prestige or death for the warrior. This type of warfare required not only ritual preparation but also great bravery and skill. Magic was commonly invoked to explain supernatural abilities. These ritual battles had important social and economic ramifications. Ritual sacrifice, the ball game, and even birth were all considered forms of battle. Although it may seem contradictory to us, ritual wars were regulated acts that followed ethical modes of behavior.

Archaeologists are prisoners of their times. Whether they like it or not, they project their own vision of the contemporary world and their culture onto their work. This may vary with one's situation, intellectual training, age, experience, and philosophical approach. Terms such as "Balkan" or "Taliban" are often used today in vague, uncontextualized forms. Perhaps the terrorist attack of September 11, 2001, in the United States will leave its mark on future interpretations of archaeological data, so that past conflicts will be interpreted as terrorist attacks. Or perhaps they will be compared to *Star Wars* or *The Lord of the Rings*.

I do not deny the existence of warlike periods or highly pacifist societies. My argument is that our inferences need to be based on well-interpreted empirical data rather than a priori assumptions. Much of my quarrel lies with the fact that Mexican archaeology is insufficiently multidisciplinary and fails to incorporate other areas of knowledge. Mea culpa. To conclude, I direct three questions to Mexican physical anthropologists: Why have you permitted archaeologists to let their imaginations flow as they please? Why have you not participated more actively in fieldwork, the excavation process, and the recovery of human remains? And why have you been content to accept a secondary role in archaeology, analyzing only what others excavate? Your input is crucial to the understanding of warfare in pre-Hispanic Mexican societies.

Acknowledgments. This essay is dedicated to Dr. R. Van Zantwijk.

NOTES

1. For state-level societies such as the Maya and the Mexica (Aztec), there were several types of wars, including the "Flowery Wars." This is one reason we must take care when applying similar models to state- and non-state-level societies.

2. We tend to rely on anthropological frameworks for interpreting violent behavior in hunter-gatherer societies and tribal villages. Keeley's (1996) excellent study, *War before Civilization*, compares warfare in prehistoric and historic societies and leaves little doubt about the presence of violent executions and warfare in small-scale societies.

REFERENCES CITED

Armillas, Pedro
 1964 Condiciones Ambientales y Movimientos de Pueblos en la Frontera Septentronal de Mesoamérica. In *Homenaje a Fernando Marquez-Miranda*, 62–82. Universidad Complutense de Madrid, Seminario de Estudis Americanistas, Madrid.

Cabrera, Rubén, Saburo Sugiyama, and George L. Cowgill
 1991 The Templo de Quetzalcoatl Project: A Preliminary Report. *Ancient Mesoamerica* 2(1):77–92.

Chavaillon, J.
 1996 *L'Age d'Or de l'Humanite*. Odile Jacob, Paris.

Ferguson, R. B. (editor)
 1984 *Warfare, Culture, and Environment*. Academic, Orlando, Calif.

González Crespo, Norberto, Silvia Graza Tarazona, Hortencia Vega, Pablo Meyer, and Giselle Canto
 1995 Archaeological Investigations at Xochicalco, Morelos: 1984 and 1986. *Ancient Mesoamerica* 6(2):223–236.

Haas, Jonathan (editor)
 1990 *The Anthropology of War*. Cambridge University Press, Cambridge.

Hers, Marie-Areti
 1989 *Los Toltecas en Tierras Chichimecas*. Instituto de Investigaciones Estéticas, Cuadernos de Historia del Arte 35. Universidad Nacional Autónoma de México, México.

Hirth, Kenneth
 1995 Urbanism, Militarism, and Architectural Design: An Analysis of Epiclassic Sociopolitical Structure at Xochicalco. *Ancient Mesoamerica* 6(2):237–250.

Holien, Thomas, and Robert B. Pickering
  1978   Analogues in a Chalchihuites Culture Sacrificial Burial to Late Mesoamerican Ceremonialism. In *Middle Classic Mesoamerica: A.D. 400–700*, ed. Esther Pasztory, 145–157. Columbia University Press, New York.

Keeley, Lawrence H.
  1996   *War before Civilization*. Oxford University Press, Oxford.

LeBlanc, Stephen
  2000   Regional Interaction and Warfare in the Late Prehistoric Southwest. In *The Archaeology of Regional Interaction: Religion, Warfare, and Exchange across the American Southwest and Beyond, Proceedings of the 1996 Southwest Symposium*, ed. Michelle Hegmon, 41–70. University Press of Colorado, Boulder.

Lekson, Stephen H.
  2002   War in the Southwest, War in the World. *American Antiquity* 67(4):607–624.

Nelson, Ben
  2000   Aggregation, Warfare, and the Spread of the Mesoamerican Tradition. In *The Archaeology of Regional Interaction: Religion, Warfare, and Exchange across the American Southwest and Beyond, Proceedings of the 1996 Southwest Symposium*, ed. Michelle Hegmon, 317–340. University Press of Colorado, Boulder.

Pickering, Robert B.
  1985   Human Osteological Remains from Alta Vista, Zacatecas: An Analysis of the Isolated Bone. In *The Archaeology of West and Northwest Mesoamerica*, ed. Michael S. Foster and Phil C. Weigand, 289–325. Westview, Boulder.

Pijoan, Carmen, and Josefina Mansilla
  1990   Mesoamérica y Norte S. IX–XII. *Seminario de Arqueología "Wigberto Jiménez Moreno,"* ed. Federica Sodi Miranda, 467–478. T. I-II. Museo Nacional de Antropología e Historia, Instituto Nacional de Antropología e Historia, México.

Trombold, Charles D.
  1991   Causeways in the Context of Strategic Planning in the La Quemada Region. In *Ancient Road Networks and Settlement Hierarchies in the New World*, ed. Charles D. Trombold, 145–168. Cambridge University Press, Cambridge.

Turner, Christy G., II, and Jacqueline A. Turner
  1997   El Canibalismo Prehistórico en el Suroeste de Estados Unidos. In *El Cuerpo Humano y su Tratamiento Mortuorio*, ed. Elsa Malvido, Grégory Pereira, and Vera Tiesler, 241–255. Serie Antropología Social, INAH, México.

Weigand, Phil
  1975   Possible References to La Quemada in Huichol Mythology. *Ethnohistory* 22(1):15–20.

24

Pacification of the Chichimeca Region

Martha Monzón Flores

They do not exist. They died because they did not fit into a world whose rationality was beyond their comprehension, and because they could not "stop being" indigenous, nomads and barbarians, according to the classification granted to them by their conquerors (Valdés 1995:17).

To the Spanish conquerors, northern New Spain represented a difficult problem in terms of domination and control. Spaniards began moving north after the conquest of the Basin of Mexico in 1521, with the aim of exploring and expanding the area of domination. Not until 1541, however, when a fierce attack occurred against the Cazcanes in the Mixtón War, did confrontations intensify, foretelling the war and bloodshed to come.

Numerous battles were fought from that time until 1590–1592 to solidify the territory already in Spanish possession and to exert control over the region's rich resources and resident population. Between 1590 and 1592, a peace agreement was signed by the indigenous and Spanish parties, and the town of San Luis de la Paz was founded in commemoration of the event.

From the time of the arrival of the missionaries, whose work was not always successful, to the present, many historical accounts have been written about these incidents. The legal status of *los indígenas*—the indigenous people—before the introduction of the so-called New Laws by the Spanish Crown is a common topic of discussion at conferences and scientific meetings.

Despite continual confrontations between both parties and assaults and robberies in the villages, Spanish wagons and influence continued to follow the trajectory of the "silver route," with subsequent loss of human life and economy. This situation is illustrated in the Map of the Villas of San Miguel and San Felipe, prepared in 1580 at the request of King Felipe II (Nieto 1995). Its painter masterfully captured the region, its inhabitants, and the social situation, as well as the geography, flora, and fauna, much of which is still recognizable today. He also presented scenes that portray the tensions in the area. Various indigenous people are shown, some individually, others strategically grouped, with their bows and arrows pointed toward the roadways, natural passes, and plains. The map also depicts friars and Spanish assassins, cattle and horses killed by arrows, the shadowy images of Spanish soldiers guarding the road, and an Indian executed by hanging.

Spanish actions were dictated by current events, sometimes planned, other times unforeseen, and were not always appropriate. The Spaniards eventually prevailed in spite of this, largely as a result of the military pressure they were able to exert on the Indians. The latter lacked the means to obtain additional assistance, which undermined their resistance. In contrast, Spanish soldiers received continual support from the Crown.

In 1561 Don Alonso de Zorita brought before King Felipe II of Spain a document in which he outlined a plan of action that could be implemented to pacify the area of conflict. Don Alonso, who held the title of lawyer (*licenciado*), had arrived in New Spain in 1556 following a long career as a public official, first with the High Court of Granada and later with the High Courts of Santo Domingo and Guatemala. Upon his arrival he was appointed judge of the High Court of New Spain in Mexico City and became representative to Viceroy Don Luis de Velasco (Ahrndt 2001:18; see also Vigil 1987; Zorita 1963).[1]

The Crown had previously sent the viceroy its so-called New Laws, which, among other provisions, ordered a reduction in the amount of tribute or taxes, made the *encomiendas* (grants of Indian land and labor) nonhereditary, and prohibited exploitation of the Indians. These new statutes were at odds with the private interests of New Spain, especially those individuals who amassed their wealth by exploiting the Indians, such as the head *encomenderos* (grantees) of Martín Courts. This led to a period of transition and instability between the High Court and the viceroy (Ahrndt 2001:19).

To create a more even balance among members of the High Court and to generate support for approval of the laws mentioned earlier, the viceroy requested the allocation of additional judges, a petition accepted by the Crown. For this reason, Judge Zorita was sent to New Spain. From the first, he openly supported the decisions of the viceroyalty, and the two men later developed a strong personal friendship (Ahrndt 2001).

Judge Zorita also relied on assistance from the Franciscan missionaries, with whom he shared many philosophical beliefs. Those beliefs, developed during his academic years in Salamanca, gave his character a strong humanistic aspect. This is clear in his earliest writings as a lawyer working on behalf of the poor of Granada—in particular, his offer of a dignified treaty to the indigenous people that generally coincided with the statutes set by the New Laws (Ahrndt 2001).

Zorita's ideas and actions were attacked by other members of the Royal High Court, especially the royal commissioner, Gerónimo de Valderrama. He was criticized as much for his unconditional support of the viceroy as for his openness regarding protection of the Indians. The situation became so tense that the judge, who was experiencing health problems, requested a return to Spain. The viceroy persuaded Zorita to remain in his position, but when the former died in 1564, Zorita was left without official protection (Ahrndt 2001:21).

In 1561, five years before leaving New Spain, Zorita prepared a document in which he addressed the pacification of the Chichimeca area. The concrete actions outlined in his proposal were intended to achieve quick resolution of the armed conflict that characterized Indian-Spanish relations at the time. His proposal included these provisions:

- Establish new Spanish towns in the north.
- Appoint a governor and a captain in each town to maintain order.
- Nominate a legal body to include mayors, managers, and justice and council officials.
- Obey the High Court of Mexico.
- Set aside areas for churches, monasteries, hospitals, town halls, prisons, plazas, and public spaces.
- Provide financial support from the Royal Revenue Office for salaries of Spanish officials and the civilian population.
- Distribute fields and ranch land.
- Bestow grants from Crown lands or mines on Spanish soldiers who protect the friars.
- Settle the Indians peacefully in towns.
- Keep Indian and Spanish towns separate.
- Protect Indian towns from outside intruders.
- Assign the Franciscan Order responsibility for converting and educating the natives.
- Prohibit the establishment of an archdiocese for twenty years, and bar other religious orders from the region.
- Recognize peaceful Indians as citizens of the Royal Crown of Castille, and ensure that they are not subject to the *encomienda* system, sold, pressed into debt or servitude, or alienated by title or any other manner. Exempt the Indians from tribute for ten years, after which time their tax should be moderate and should take into account the amount they have earned from their land.

- Protect the rule, rents, and duties of Indian lords, *caciques* (leaders), and principals; prohibit wrongs against them, and give them preference in the division of lands.
- Include friendly and cooperative Indians in the division of lands.
- Exempt the Indians from tithes.
- Implement a duty in place of the tithe, a portion of which is intended for the church.
- Provide support to the church in the form of ornaments, wine, candles, and oil.

Zorita's proposal established the offices of governor and captain, provided salaries for Spanish officials and civilians, and limited the number of friars who could work in each community. It also identified the benefits that would result from each of these points, both for the Crown and to secure the peace (Vigil 1987:220; Zorita 1963, 1971). Regrettably, Zorita's ideas were never implemented. Further, they contributed to the military strength of opposition groups, which confederated themselves into a grand alliance. The result was a fierce battle in 1561 on the Spanish mining frontier, initiated by the Spanish. Other battles followed, jeopardizing the economic activities of the region even before the attacks of the Chichimecas became relentless (Powell 1984:86; see also Powell 1952).[2]

Viceroy Don Gastón de Peralta, Marquis of Falces, in command from 1566 to 1567, tested various strategies for peace, but without positive results. Eventually, he organized a large-scale war to establish command over the territory, with the aim of breaking the indigenous groups' military might (Powell 1984:86). Viceroy Martín Enríquez, whose command during 1568–1580 succeeded that of Peralta, continued this policy. Clashes continued, each more damaging to the opposition and the civilian population. To avoid being victims of war, people migrated to areas that offered greater security (Powell 1984:87).

In time, it became evident that the decision to confront the resistance through war had led only to increased Spanish uncertainty and a lack of capacity to capitalize on victories, spurred by an increase in Chichimeca attacks. This led to a notable decrease in the production of silver. Given that silver production sustained the economy of the entire region, the negative effects of its decline were felt quickly (Powell 1984:87).

Captain Pedro de Ahumada was charged with establishing peace during this period. In a wise military move, he became more familiar with the territory and the Chichimecas' travel routes and held a number of meetings with opposition leaders, offering them gifts in return for promises of peace. His actual intent, however, was to invade the areas controlled by the indigenous resistance (Powell 1984:94). This strategy proved beneficial to the Spaniards because one of their major obstacles to dominance was ignorance of the territory the Indians moved through so easily, especially areas of rough terrain difficult to access with Spanish horses.

This campaign led to the decline of the indigenous alliance for two reasons. First, it enabled the Spaniards to penetrate settlements that, until now, had been dominated by the Indians. Second, as a result of meetings with indigenous leaders, the Spaniards were able to sign a peace treaty with the Tepehuanes, thus dividing the Native confederation. This successful military campaign gave the Spanish Crown relative control over the conflict (Powell 1984). Despite the success of the campaign, government indecision and dissent regarding the best way to bring peace to the region allowed Spanish incursions and attacks on the Natives to continue.

The next three viceroys, who governed from 1585 until the end of the century, sought to further pacify the northern territory. Realizing that the existing strategies were ineffective, they began to promote changes in government policy meant to secure a long-lasting peace.

Alonso Manrique de Zuñiga, Marquis of Villamanrique and the seventh viceroy, began his term of office in 1585 by ordering an end to the "war of blood and fire" and initiating a new policy with the aim of ending the conflict through negotiations between the parties (Powell 1984:93). His drastic but necessary measures were intended to halt the excessive abuse of indigenous groups by prohibiting the illegal sale of Indian slaves and the liberation of captives for the protection of religious communities. He consolidated the war administration, lowered its costs, reduced the presidio system, and relocated soldiers who caused friction on the frontier (Powell 1984). Just as the friars used goods to convert those under their protection, Zuñiga also promoted the exchange of peace for clothing, food, land, agricultural equipment, and other goods, He achieved these initiatives through negotiations with the main Chichimeca chiefs and loyal government mediators, including Rodrigo del Río, Miguel Caldera, Francisco de Urdiñola, and Gabriel Ortiz Fuenmayor (Powell 1984:196; see also Powell 1977).

Viceroy Don Luis de Velasco II continued these peace initiatives through persuasion, enticement, and conversion by offering religious gifts. He achieved these ends principally through the work of the Franciscan missionaries and the defensive colonization of the area. As the result of negotiations with Tlaxcaltecan leaders, 400 Tlaxcaltecan families were persuaded to move north and help the rebels make the transition from nomadic to sedentary life. Velasco also appointed government officials to the jurisdiction of Nueva Galicia to secure the release of Chichimecas detained by soldiers, traded as slaves, or held in the military reserves. Negotiations with the Chichimeca groups concluded in March 1591 (Powell 1984).

Viceroy Velasco completed this process by signing a peace treaty and initiating various actions to fulfill the document. They included these measures:

- Establish captain-protectors, headed by Miguel Caldera as chief justice and superintendent (Powell 1977), and equip Caldera with appropriate assistants.
- Strengthen the bureaucratic system.
- Dispense food rations and gifts of clothes, various types of implements, games, reading handbooks, and tobacco from the Royal Revenue Office.

- Provide housing financed by the government.
- Bestow ceremonial rewards on religious days.
- Buy, build, or rent shops.
- Give gifts from the private stores of the captain-protectors.
- Appoint assistants—teachers, known as *labradores*—to help former soldiers cultivate the land.
- Grant disposition to Christianize the Indians.
- Send southern Indians from Tlaxcala to settle the frontier.

Notably, these proposals closely coincided with those put forth by Judge Alonso de Zorita in 1561. This time, however, they proved effective.

FINAL CONSIDERATIONS

The measure of time is relative. Events that result from human action can be prolonged or shortened depending on the circumstances. The rhythm of the calendar can seem routine, or it can disrupt us severely. The fifty years of fighting associated with the pacification process in the Chichimeca territories resulted in a long period of death and destruction for both parties. Ultimately, this translated into a relative victory for the Spaniards, but one that led to the complete destruction of several Native ethnic groups and the loss of an important part of Mexico's historical and racial heritage. Contemporary Mexicans are generally unaware of these cultures, whose customs, languages, religions, festivals, traditions, thoughts, and dreams have been lost to time.

Only cultures documented in the chronicles are still known to us today, but these accounts are strongly influenced by their authors' western thinking. Archaeological evidence also offers mute testimony of the presence of these groups at a given time or place.

The period from the beginning of the Mixtón War in 1541 to its conclusion in 1592 saw fifty years of military incursions that severely undermined the indigenous population. Comparing Zorita's proposal to the measures finally taken to end the persecution, we can see that the former contained legal policies intended to convince the Indians to accept their new situation. Zorita's proposal also provided for the establishment of new towns led by authoritative Spanish bodies, consisting of a head governor followed by captains, mayors, managers, justice officials, a council, and, finally, civilians, each intended to fulfill a specific role to ensure order and justice. Zorita also proposed to keep indigenous and Spanish towns separate to avoid abuses by both parties and to maintain control over access into the towns to discourage intruders. He also provided for public and private spaces, as needed, to ensure a town's optimum functioning. To bolster the economy, he requested the support of the Royal Revenue Office to provide reasonable salaries for officials, the extension of taxes, and the payment of tithes. Finally, he emphasized the role of the indigenous people as citizens of the Royal Crown of Castille and granted preferential status to local *caciques*.

The resolution of 1592, in contrast, created the role of captain-protectors and their respective assistants, supported by the Royal Revenue Office, to stimulate and compensate the indigenous population. The bureaucratic structure of the time was strengthened with the goal of obtaining optimum efficiency from the new settlements. Financial aid was provided for houses and shops, and instruction was given to former soldiers to help with the development of agricultural projects. In actuality, a paternalistic program was implemented that led to the underdevelopment that has characterized the Native population for over 500 years.

Both proposals relied on missionaries to evangelize the Indian population. Zorita included only the Franciscans in his proposal and added an assurance that no archdiocese could be established for at least twenty years. Both proposals arranged for the transfer of Indian allies, principally the Tlaxcaltecans, to the north to demonstrate the advantages of peaceful life to the Chichimecas.

Zorita's proposal reflected a genuine understanding of the indigenous problem and offered specific requirements and actions to secure the peace. Ultimately, the resolutions implemented in 1592 differed little from those initially proposed by Zorita (Keen cited in Zorita 1963:50). By resurrecting many of Zorita's ideas, subsequent viceroys established a relative peace. Had Zorita's ideas been implemented at the time of their writing in 1561—twenty years after the first uprising and around thirty years before the peace was secured—numerous battles would have been avoided. Within that thirty-year period, thirty-three Spanish incursions and thirty-five attacks by the Chichimecas were recorded. Doubtless, many others are unchronicled by history.

TIMELINE OF SIXTEENTH-CENTURY EVENTS IN THE CHICHIMECA REGION, FROM 1529 TO THE SIGNING OF THE PEACE TREATY IN SAN LUIS DE LA PAZ IN 1592[3]

1529–1536	Nuño de Guzman moves to the north and west. The province of Nueva Galicia is established. Rebels are subjected to torture and punishment, including mutilation of limbs (Galaviz de Capdevielle 1967).
1531	Uprising of Teulteco Indians as a result of the cruel treatment they received from Nuño de Guzmán and Juan de Oñate. This leads to the deaths of a large number of Spanish soldiers, although the Indians are ultimately defeated (Galaviz de Capdevielle 1967).
1537	Uprising of Guaxicar Indians against Governor Diego Pérez Torre. This bloody battle takes place in northeastern Guadalajara, with the ultimate defeat of the indigenous groups (Galaviz de Capdevielle 1967).
1538–1542	Vázquez Coronado arrives in Sinaloa, Cibola, and Quivira and begins to exterminate the Indians (Powell 1984).
1539	Rebellion of the Indians of Guaynamota and Guasamota in the mountains of Nayarit, where churches and chapels are burned. The rebellion

	expands to include the Cazcanes of Juchipila, Tlaltenango, Nochistlán, and Teocaltiche (Galaviz de Capdevielle 1967).
1541–1542	The Mixtón War. Following the previously mentioned rebellion, Captain Miguel de Ibarra tries to establish dialogue with the Indians to make a pact and appease them. The Cazcanes do not accept this effort and initiate a struggle against the invaders in Juchipila. Rebellions are simultaneously carried out in Xalpa, Tlaltenango, and other places. The rebellion spreads throughout the entire region wherever the Natives are willing to rise up and fight. The arrival of Pedro de Alvarado fortifies the Spaniards, but the Cazcane, Zacateco, and Tecuexe fighters are determined and eventually force his defeat. Alvarado dies in battle. As the insurrection spreads to Michoacán and Mexico City, the Spaniards intensify the fighting, leading to the killing, punishing, mutilating, and enslaving of many Indians. In spite of their resistance and fierce battles, the Chichimecas are eventually defeated. Many choose to plunge to their deaths in ravines rather than surrender (Galaviz de Capdevielle 1967).
1542	Juchipila is founded as a result of the previously mentioned battle and surrender of the Indians (Galaviz de Capdevielle 1967).
1542–1550	Hernán Pérez de Bocanegra undertakes military incursions and establishes mills and inns at Apeseo and Acámbaro Gto (Powell 1984).
1549	The mines of Zacatecas became a focal point for the Spaniards, who implement even crueler strategies to subdue the rebel groups (Powell 1984).
1550	The discovery of gold, silver, and other minerals makes the Spaniards resolve to avoid another war like the Mixtón War (Powell 1984).
1550	Between Morcilique and the rivers of Tepezala, the Zacateco Indians attack and kill a group of Tarascan merchants bound for Zacatecas. At the same time, the Guachichiles, Guamares, and Zacatecos carry out attacks in diverse parts of Zacatecas, San Miguel, and San Felipe. Based on official documents and the opinions of chroniclers, Powell assigns the beginning of the Chichimeca War to this year and notes that this successful battle was a continuation of the Mixtón War (Powell 1984).
1551	The Guachichiles attack caravans laden with merchandise extracted from the mines of Zacatecas, killing slaves, Indians, and merchants. The Guamares and Copuces in Guanajuato attack cattle ranches and the town of San Miguel (Powell 1984).
1551	Sancho de Cañego, the mayor of Zacatecas, and Baltasar Temiño de Bañuelos, one of the town's founders, retaliate against the Chichimecas who assaulted the merchant Medina (Powell 1984).
1551–1552	Expeditions are mounted by Hernán Pérez de Bocanegra and Gonzalo Hernández de Rojas as a result of battles against the Chichimecas in Zacatecas (Powell 1984).
1552	An expedition is mounted by Lic. Herrera, who confronts, captures, and hangs Chichimecas (Powell 1984).
1552–1554	Attacks intensify on caravans from Zacatecas (Powell 1984).
1553	Gonzalo Hernández de Rojas confronts Chichimeca bandits (Powell 1984).
1555–1560	The town of San Miguel suffers successive attacks (Powell 1984).

Pacification of the Chichimeca Region

1557	Nicolás de San Luis Montañez defeats and captures the Chichimeca leader Maxorro and undertakes battles against indigenous groups in San Miguel, San Felipe, Xichú, San Francisco, and Río Verde (Powell 1984).
1559	Otomí chiefs Juan Bautista, Valerio de la Cruz, Juan de Austria, Nicolás de San Luis, Diego Atexcoatl, Antonio Luna, and Diego de Tapia initiate war against the Chichimecas in San Miguel, San Felipe, Xichú, Río Verde, Nueva Galicia, Celaya, and Valle de Gueychapa (Powell 1984).
1560	Pedro de Ahumada Sámano and Jerónimo Mercado Sotomayor are rewarded for mutilating Guachichiles in such a way that they can no longer use a bow and arrow. They receive orders, authority, and the necessary equipment to capture the Guachichiles Chichimecas (Powell 1984).
1561	The Great Chichimeca uprising begins, and the Confederation of Chichimeca Tribes is established (Powell 1984).
1561–1562	The town and presidio of San Felipe are founded to defend against the Guachichiles (Powell 1984).
1562	Destructive Chichimeca attacks ensue from the founding of Spanish towns in locations well suited for strategic attacks (Powell 1984).
1563	Hernando Martell establishes Santa María and San Juan de los Lagos to defend against Chichimeca raids (Powell 1984).
1563–1565	Chichimecas are on the brink of war in Pénjamo, where farms are burned and many individuals are killed, including Spaniards, Indians, mulattoes, blacks, mestizos, and converted Indians (Powell 1984).
1565–1567	Captain Rodrigo del Río de la Loza undertakes a Spanish expedition with the support of Mexicans and Tarascans (Powell 1984).
1568–1569	Chichimecas attack Comanja and murder the Spaniards who lived in this mining settlement, resulting in its abandonment (Jiménez 1944).
1568–1580	The fourth viceroy of New Spain, Martín Enríquez de Almanza, attempts to pacify the Chichimecas through slavery and force (Powell 1984).
1569	Groups of Chichimecas attack settlements near Guadalajara, killing hundreds of Indians allied with the Spaniards (Jiménez 1944).
1569	The port of Robledal near Guadalajara is attacked, after which the mayor initiates persecution of the Indians (Jiménez 1944).
1570	By order of the High Court of Nueva Galicia, the town of Jerez is founded by Pedro Caldera, Pedro Carrillo, and Martín Moreno to protect the town of Zacatecas (Powell 1984).
1571	Two indigenous groups threaten the Spanish town of San Juan Bautista de Caropa and cause its abandonment (Jiménez 1944).
1573	Chichimecas attack and martyr Franciscan friars in the port of Fraile. The crucifix of one of the friars is venerated as Lord of the Conquerors (Jiménez 1944).
1574	Chichimecas attack settlements near Guadalajara, Zacatecas, San Martín, Sombrerete, and other sites in Nueva Galicia, murdering Spaniards and pacified Indians (Powell 1984).
1574	Charcas and Tepezala are founded through the efforts of Juan Bautista Orozco as part of a strategy to advance toward the Chichimeca territories. Under his command, eighty Chichimecas chiefs are captured and punished (Powell 1984).

1575	Chichimecas attack Aguascalientes and kill nearly the entire population. Guachichiles in Saltillo rebel against Captain Francisco de Urdiñola. Attacks by the Pames intensify in northeastern Querétaro and the Valley of Maxcala (Powell 1984).
1575	The town of León is established in the Huiascatillos Valley by Dr. Juan Bautista Orozco by order of the viceroy to pacify the rebels of nearby Comanja and Guanajuato. The city of Aguascalientes and its presidio are founded by order of Dr. Jerónimo de la Cueva. To protect itself from the Copuces, Guajabanes and its allies establish two other presidios, one north of Querétaro in Jofre and the other in Palmar de Vega (Powell 1984).
1576	Assaults and attacks result in the abandonment of mines, fields, and ranches. An uprising occurs near San Juan del Río in the province of Xilotepec (Powell 1984).
1576–1578	A presidio is founded in the Maxcala Valley in northeastern Querétaro (Powell 1984).
1577	Intense attacks occur on the fort near Pénjamo (Powell 1984).
1578	Saltillo is established to contain and attack the Guachichiles (Powell 1984).
1578–1579	Garrisons of soldiers are sent to the province of Pánuco (Powell 1984).
1578–1585	Chichimecas attack and damage the presidio of Tamaos and two other presidios in Tampico (Powell 1984).
1580	Commerce in and trafficking of enslaved Chichimecas intensifies (Powell 1984).
1580–1585	Martín Enríquez intensifies battles against the Chichimecas (Powell 1984).
1580–1585	An intensification of the Chichimeca threat results in stronger alliances among Indian tribes (Powell 1984).
1581	Priest Juan de Cuenca is assassinated in Comanja, Guanajuato (Jiménez 1944).
1581–1583	Soldiers are recruited to double the military forces against the Guachichiles (Powell 1984).
1582	Towns to the south of Querétaro and San Juan del Río are abandoned as a result of hostilities by the Pames (Powell 1984).
1583	Rebellion of Zuaques and Ocorinis in Sinaloa results in the murder of two friars and fifteen Spaniards and the burning of the town (Galaviz de Capdevielle 1967).
1584	Chichimecas attack the convent and mines of Nahuipan, burning haciendas and killing Spaniards (Huerta 1966).
1584	To exploit the nearby mines at Huaynamota, Spaniards settle the area without consent of the Natives. They are attacked and murdered (Huerta 1966).
1585	The viceroyalty orders the enslavement and punishment of Chichimecas, resulting in robberies and killings (Powell 1984).
1585	Chichimecas use horses in their attacks, increasing the danger on the road and to the settlements (Powell 1984).
1586	A presidio with four soldiers is established in Xichú to halt the depredations of the Guachichiles Indians (Powell 1984).

1586	Priest Espino is murdered in Arroyo de la Loza, Guanajuato (Jiménez 1944).
1586-1589	A surge in rebellions by Guachichiles and Páchos, headed by Cilavón and Zapaliname, against Saltillo, Mazapil, and Matehuala (Galaviz de Capdevielle 1967).
1588	Chichimeca attacks at Yuiririapúndaro. Despite peace pacts, conflicts continue in some places (Powell 1984).
1588-1589	Uprising in Villa de Santiago. After several confrontations, the Chichimecas are defeated by Francisco Urdiñola (Galaviz de Capdevielle 1967).
1590	Chichimeca rebellion in Tamaulipas, and new insurrections by groups already pacified (Galaviz de Capdevielle 1967).
1590	An armory is established in the royal warehouse of Zacatecas to equip soldiers against the Chichimecas (Powell 1984).
1590-1595	A presidio with six soldiers is established in Atotonilco to protect the route to Zacatecas (Powell 1984).
1591	Tlaxcaltecan Indians are transferred to the Chichimeca frontier in San Luis de la Paz, Zacatecas, Colotlán, and Saltillo to establish eight new towns.
1591-1601	Uprising of Acaxeés against church doctrine results in the destruction of churches and the deaths of five Spaniards. Attacks on the military camps of Topia and San Andrés. Demolition of Las Virgenes (Huerta 1966).
1592	San Luís Potosí is founded by F. P. Tapia, Nicolás de Arnaya, and Juan de Oñate (Jiménez 1944).
1592	A presidio is established in San Andrés in the eastern mountains to protect against Indian hostilities (Powell 1984).
1592	Rebellion of Tepecanos, Usiliques (Huicholes), and Zacatecas in San Andrés and San Luís Potosí. Mayor Miguel Caldera, engaged in exploring mines in Potosí, receives news of a Chichimeca uprising. Finally, the indigenous groups are pacified (Galaviz de Capdevielle 1967).

NOTES

1. Editors' note: For accounts in English about Alonso de Zorita's remarkable life and career, see Benjamin Keen's introduction in Zorita (1963) and Vigil (1987). We have added these references to the text as warranted.

2. Editors' note: For writings in English by Philip Powell about the Chichimec Wars, see Powell (1952, 1977). We have added these references to the text as warranted.

3. Editors' note: This timetable of the Chichimec uprising and Spanish incursions originally appeared in the author's manuscript as two separate lists. At the suggestion of a reviewer, we combined them into a single list to provide a more holistic view of the conflict.

REFERENCES CITED

Ahrndt, Wiebke
    2001   *Edición Crítica de la Relación de la Nueva España y de la Breve y Sumaria Relación Escritas por Alonso de Zorita*. Colección Obra Diversa. Instituto Nacional de Antropología e Historia (INAH), México.

Galaviz de Capdevielle, María Elena
    1967   *Rebeliones Indígenas en El Norte del Reino de la Nueva España: Siglos XVI and XVII.* Colección Clásicos de la Reforma Agraria. Editorial Campesina, México.

Huerta, María Teresa
    1966   *Rebeliones Indígenas en El Noreste de México en La Época Colonial.* INAH, México.

Jiménez, Wigberto
    1944   La Colonización y Evangelización de Guanajuato en El Siglo XVI. *Cuadernos Americanos* 13(1), Año III. México.

Nieto, Luis Felipe
    1995   El Camino Real de Tierra Adentro. In *Primer Coloquio Internacional, Valle de Allende, Chihuahua,* 36-53. INAH, México.

Powell, Philip W.
    1952   *Soldiers, Indians, and Silver.* University of Calfornia Press, Berkeley.
    1977   *Mexico's Miguel Caldera: Warrior and Peacemaker on North America's First Frontier, 1548-1597.* University of Arizona Press, Tucson.
    1984   *La Guerra Chichimeca (1550-1600).* Lecturas Mexicanas 52. Fondo de Cultural Económica-Secretaría de Educación Pública, México.

Valdés, Carlos M.
    1995   *La Gente del Mezquite: Los Nómades del Noreste en La Colonia.* Colección Historia de los Pueblos Indígenas de México. Centro de Investigación y Estudios Superiores en Antropogía Social-Instituto Nacional Indigenista, México.

Vigil, Ralph H.
    1987   *Alonso de Zorita: Royal Judge and Christian Humanist, 1512-1585.* University of Oklahoma Press, Norman.

Zorita, Alonso de
    1963   *Life and Labor in Ancient Mexico: The Brief and Summary Relation of the Lords of New Spain.* Translated and with an introduction by Benjamin Keen. Rutgers University Press, New Brunswick, N.J.
    1971   Breve Relación de Los Señores de la Nueva España. In *Colección de Documentos Para la Historia de México,* comp. Joaquín Garcia Icazbalceta, 333-342. Facsimile edition of the 1877 second edition. Porrúa, México.

Contributors

Karen R. Adams
Crow Canyon Archaeological Center
Cortez, Colorado, USA

M. Nicolás Caretta
INAH Zacatecas
Zacatecas, Mexico

Patricia Carot
Instituto de Investigaciones Estéticas, Universidad Nacional Autónoma de México
Mexico City, D.F., Mexico

John P. Carpenter
INAH Mexico
Mexico City, Mexico

Contributors

Jeffery J. Clark
Center for Desert Archaeology
Tucson, Arizona, USA

Linda S. Cordell
School of Advanced Research
Santa Fe, New Mexico, USA

William E. Doolittle
University of Texas
Austin, Texas, USA

Suzanne L. Eckert
Texas A&M University
College Station, Texas, USA

Gayle J. Fritz
Washington University
St. Louis, Missouri, USA

Eduardo Gamboa Carrera
INAH Chihuahua
Chihuahua, Mexico

Leticia González Arratia
Centro INAH Coahuila
Coahuila, Mexico

Arturo Guevara Sánchez
Centro INAH Chihuahua
Chihuahua, Mexico

Robert J. Hard
University of Texas at San Antonio
San Antonio, Texas, USA

Kelley Hays-Gilpin
Northern Arizona University and Museum of Northern Arizona
Flagstaff, Arizona, USA

Marie-Areti Hers
Instituto de Investigaciones Estéticas, Universidad Nacional Autónoma de México
Mexico City, Mexico

Amber L. Johnson
Truman State University
Kirksville, Missouri, USA

Steven A. LeBlanc
Peabody Museum, Harvard University
Cambridge, Massachusetts, USA

Patrick D. Lyons
Arizona State Museum, University of Arizona, and
Center for Desert Archaeology, both Tucson, Arizona, USA

Jonathan B. Mabry
City of Tucson, Cultural Resources and Historic Preservation
Tucson, Arizona, USA

A. C. MacWilliams
University of Calgary
Calgary, Alberta, Canada

Federico J. Mancera-Valencia
Centro INAH Chihuahua
Chihuahua, Mexico

Maxine E. McBrinn
The Field Museum
Chicago, Illinois, USA

Francisco Mendiola Galván
Centro INAH Chihuahua
Chihuahua, Mexico

William L. Merrill
National Museum of Natural History
Washington, D.C., USA

Martha Monzón Flores
Centro INAH Guanajuato
Guanajuato, Mexico

Scott G. Ortman
Crow Canyon Archaeological Center, Cortez, Colorado, and
Arizona State University, Tempe, Arizona, USA

John R. Roney
Bureau of Land Management (retired)
Albuquerque, New Mexico, USA

Guadalupe Sánchez
Subdirección de Laboratorios y Apoyo Académico, INAH
Mexico City, Mexico

Moisés Valadez Moreno
INAH Monterrey
Monterrey, Nuevo León, Mexico

Bradley J. Vierra
Statistical Research, Inc.
Albuquerque, New Mexico, USA

Laurie D. Webster
University of Arizona
Tucson, Arizona, USA

Phil C. Weigand
Centro de Estudios Arqueológicos, El Colegio de Michoacán
Michoacán, Mexico

Index

Page numbers in italics indicate illustrations.

Abasolo points, 367
Acaxees, 323, 403
Acoma, creation story, 227-28
A47-02, 43
A47-04, 43
Agave cultivation, 28
Agency theory, 148
Agriculture, 89, 164, 170, 172; climate and physiography, 39-40; in Desert Borderlands, 25, 28; early/incipient, 36-37, 55-57; Late Archaic, 73-80; and migration, 30-31; modeling intensification of, 96-98; niche filling, 65-66, 109; San Juan Basin and northern Rio Grande Valley, 73-81; in southern Chihuahua, 35, 42-45, 46, 47, 48; spread of, 107-8, 109; transition to, 7-9, 26, 27, 29-30, 64-65, 90, 91-92, 94-96, 98-101, 102-3; and Uto-Aztecan speakers, 116-17, 158, 172-73(n1). *See also* Farming techniques/systems
Aguascalientes, 157, 402
Agustín points, 160, 167
Ahumada Sámano, Pedro de, 396, 401
Ak chin farming, 59, 60
Albumin Mexico (AL*Mexico), 124
Albuquerque, 79, 114
Alkali Ridge site, pottery-band murals at, *232*, 239
Almagre points, 160
Alta Vista, turquoise in, 344-45, 349
Alta Vista phase, 310
Alta Vista-Vesuvio phase, sculpture, 306
Altithermal, 63, 158
Alvarado, Pedro de, 400

Amanteca, 346
Amaranth, 27, 28, 41, 72, 73, 75, 79, 132(n20)
Amole Polychrome, 338
Anacua points, 367
Anatolia, 119
Ancestor cults, 307
Ancestral Puebloans, 12, 190, 316, 318, 325(n4); architectural metaphors, 151, 229, 237; buildings as containers, 232-41; world as building in, 241-46
Apaches, 264, 347
Aquatic resources, hunter-gatherer use of, 97, 98, 99, 102, 104-5n4
Archaeoastronomy: Cliff Palace murals, 243-44; Nuevo León rock art, 367, 368
Archaeobotanical evidence, Late Archaic, 28-29

409

Index

Archaeogeography, 12
Archaeological sequences: durations of, 94-96, 104; regularity of, 101-2; transition to agriculture, 98-100
Archaic period, 111, 123, 149; agriculture and, 8-9; plant husbandry during, 27-28; projectile points, 159-65; in southern Chihuahua, 47-48. *See also* Late Archaic period; Middle Archaic period
Architecture, 7, 307; as metaphor, 151, 227-29, 230-50; in Lower Rio Puerco, 273, 274, 278-79
Arid North America: cultural events in, 293-94; as term, 295, 298(n1)
Arizona, 108, 157; Archaic projectile points in, 161-62, 163, 164; early maize farmers in, 126-27, 128; turquoise in, 346, 347-48. *See also various regions, sites by name*
Arizona Tewa, 195-96, 197, 264
Armijo-Concho points, 161
Armijo points, 161, 162, 164
Armijo Tank Shelter, 162
Arnaya, Nicolás de, 403
Arroyo de la Loza, 403
Artifacts, 150, 187; as cultural indicators, 167-68; iconological style, 212-13; Nuevo León, 366-67; social identity, 210-11, 277-78
Astronomy, 266
Atexcoatl, Diego, 401
Athapaskan speakers, mtDNA data from, 121, 122
Atlantes, 323, 339
Atlatl Cave, 161
Atlatls, 165, 168, 368
Axis mundi, 267
Aztatlán expansion, 322
Aztecs, 324, 326(n11)
Azure (New Mexico), 348

Baja California, 165, 285, 288, 346
Bajada point, 162
Ballcourts, Hohokam, 315
Balleza, Río, 37
Ball game, 336, 389

Balsas, Río, 36, 39
Bands, hunter-gatherer, 211
Bannister Ruin, 240
Bare Ladder Ruin, 240
Barrier Canyon Archaic style, 112
Basin and Range Province (Chihuahua), 26, 37-38, 166; *cerros de trincheras* in, 41, 45; D-shaped terrace sites in, 42-44
Basketmaker II, 57, 108, 114, 130(n2), 131(nn3, 4, 5), 159, 164, 166; population and trait differences, 110-12, 121, 123-24, 125, 128, 131(nn5, 7). *See also* Eastern Basketmaker II; Western Basketmaker II
Basketmaker III, 112, 130(n2), 261, 263, 264
Basketry, 169, 171, 236, 248; Basketmaker II, 111, 113, 169; line break motif in, 257-58, 259, 263, 264; as migration evidence, 165-66; kiva as metaphor for, 237, 240, 242(table); and pottery designs, 238-39, 241
Bat Cave, 41, 166, 213; dart points in, 160-61, 162, 215-17; maize dates from, 163-64
Bat Cave points, 160, 161, 164
Battle Mural, 338
Beans, 27, 79, 116, 166, 167, 169, 170
Belize, 166
Bell-shaped pits, 64
Big Bend area, 374, 379, 380
Binford, Lewis, 104n3; on frames of reference, 92-93
Birds: in Lower Rio Puerco sites, 275(table), 276; in Pueblo ritual, 273-74
Bird-Serpent, *311*
Birth rates, 65
Bisbee, 348
Black Mesa, 162
Blending principle, 240-41
Bluff Great House, 231, 249
Bodies, as vessels, 258, 260, 261
Boomerang Shelter, 123

Borders, archaeological epistemology and, 292, 297
Bow and arrow, 164, 318, *319*
Buildings, 250; as containers, 231-41; world as, 241-46, 248-49
Burials: Basketmaker II, 111, 112, 171, 307, 388; Basketmaker III, 263, 265; Chalchihuites, 344-45; Coahuila cave sites, 339, 377, 378; Late Archaic, 74, 127; low desert, 113-14
Buried Dune site, 161, 164-65
Burro Gordo, 375, 376, 379
Butterfly hairdo, 336, 339

Cachiripa, 337
Cahitan language/speakers, 171, 172
Caldera, Miguel, 397, 403
Caldera, Pedro, 401
Calendrical observations, landscape murals as, 243-45
Caliente Arroyo, 46
California, 122, 160; Proto-Uto-Aztecans in, 64, 156, 157; turquoise in, 346, 347; Uto-Aztecan speakers in, 115, 171
California Penutian, 122
Campeche, 345
Canals, 25, 55, 57, 166, 170
Candelaria Cave, 339, 340, 381
Candelaria style rock art, 128
Cañego, Sancho de, 400
Cannibalism, 388
Canutillo phase, 309
Canyon Creek (Arizona), 347
Canyon de Chelly, 123, 258
Canyon del Muerto, 123, *259*, 261, 263
Carrillo, Pedro, 401
Casa de las Aguilas (House of the Eagle Knights), 324
Casas Grandes regional system, 12, 285, 287, 288, 289, 322; cave sites, 355-57, 363-64
Cataara points, 367
Catán points, 367
Cave of Monos, 338
Cave sites: in Chihuahua, 40, 46, 49; in Coahuila, 374, 375, 376-81; in Nuevo León, 368-69

410

Index

Cazcanes, and Mixtón War, 393, 400
Ceramics. *See* Pottery
Ceremonial centers: Guadalupe, 311; La Quemada, 309, 325(n7); Loma Alta, 305-6
Cerrillos mines, 348, 349
Cerro de Huistle, 306, 309, 312, 388; rock art at, 318-20
Cerro Juanaqueña, 26, 41, 44, 126
Cerro La Noria, 45
Cerro las Flojeras, 45
Cerro Prieto de Santa Bárbara, 45
Cerros de trincheras: Early Agricultural sites on, 26-27, 49, 126-27; in Chihuahua, 41, 44-45, 48
Chac mool sculptures, 312, 321
Chaco Canyon, 161, 246; architecture as metaphor, 151, 229, 249; kiva architecture in, 247-48; line break in, 258, 263; maize ubiquity in, 78-79; turquoise in, 344, 348, 349, 350
Chaco Phenomenon, 246-47, 249, 267, 322-23
Chalchihuites culture, 304, 306, 307, 309, 310, 315, 326(n10), 335, 336, 337; and Chaco Phenomenon, 322-23; colonization and migration by, 319-20; Mesoamerican influence, 316-17, 324; migrants, 321-22; mining, 349-50; and Paquimé, 340-41; and Purépecha, 301, 311-14; sociopolitical organization, 317-18
Chalchihuitl, Mount, 348
Channel Islands, 160
Chapalagana Basin, exchange networks, 318-19
Charcas, 401
Chenopods-amaranths (Chenoams), 27, 28, 72, 73, 75, 79
Chetro Ketl, 247
Chiapas, turquoise in, 345, 351
Chichén Itzá, 308, 349
Chichimeca, 12, 296, 318, 322; concept of, 286, 288, 294; migration of, 320-21; pacification of, 393-403

Chichimecatlali, 294
Chichimeca War, 400-401
Chicomoztoc, 302, 324; migration of, 320-22
Chihuahua, 6, 12, 108, 126, 163, 165, 220, 285, 287, 288, 346; Archaic period in, 47-48; *cerros de trincheras* in, 44-45; cultural landscapes in, 355-64; D-shaped terrace sites, 42-44; early agriculture in, 26-27, 35, 36-37; early farming sites in, 127, 128; maize agriculture in, 36, 40-41, 46, 61, 158; rock art in, 112, 128
Chihuahuan Desert, 37, 40
Chiricahua points, 160-61, 162, 163-64
Chiricahua stage, 163-64
Chupícuaro tradition, 309, 314
Chuska Mountains, 79
Cibola, 399
Cibola White Wares, line break motif on, 263-64
Cienega Creek site, 163, 165
Cienega phase, 127, 164
Cienega point, 164
Cienega Valley, 113, 127
Cigarette Springs site, 240
Cilavón, 403
Circle, symbolism of, 261
Clans, 267; Hopi, 116, 195
Classic period (Mesoamerica), turquoise in, 344
Clearwater site, 161, 162, 164-65
Cliff dwellings, in Sierra Madre Occidental, 12, 287, 289, 355-57, 363-64
Cliff Palace, murals in, 233, 243-44
CM-24, 375
CM-37, 375
Coahuila, 160, 285, 287, 288; rock art, 289, 339; Walter Taylor's expeditions to, 373-81; turquoise in, 346, 347; and West Texas, 12-13
Cochiti, 264
Codexes, 267
Collier Dunes site, 162
Colorado, turquoise in, 346
Colorado Plateau, 63, 64, 164, 166, 168, 169; Archaic projectile points on, 162, 163; early agriculture on, 29, 36, 71-80; prehistoric polities on, 115-16; rain-fed farming on, 59-60
Colorado River, 170
Colotlán, 403
Columbia Plateau, 156
Comanja, 401, 402
Conceptual projection, 228; buildings as containers, 232-41
Concho, 115
Concho points, 161
Conchos River Basin, 37, 313, 318
Confederation of Chichimeca Tribes, 401
Conjunto Huápoca, 357
Constitutive principle, 239-40, 244
Constructing Frames of Reference (Binford), 92
Contracting stem points, 160-61, 167, 171
Copilli, 338-39
Copper, copper artifacts, 315, 323, 338, 348
Copuces, 400, 402
Cora, 115, 121, 302, 307, 324
Cordage: Basketmaker, 111, 131(n6); as migration evidence, 165, 166; and social identity, 11, 213-15
Cordova Cave, 166, 213
Corn. *See* Maize
Coronado, Francisco Vásquez de, 399
Cortaro bifaces, 113, 164-65, 168
Cortéz, Hernán, Moctezuma II's gifts to, 345
Cottonwood Canyon, 123
Courtland-Gleason area, 347
Coxcatlán phase, 160
Cradleboards, 111
Creation story, Acoma, 227-28
Cremations, 165, 307, 313-14, 315
Crop complexes, 56, 64
Crosses, in rock art imagery, 336
Cruz de la Boquilla, 320
Cucurbita. *See* Squash
Cuenca, Juan de, 402

411

Index

Cueva, Jerónimo de la, 402
Cueva de Apache, 357
Cueva de los Indios (C75-01), 42
Cueva de Ranchería, 357
Cueva Grande, 357
Culhúa Mexica, turquoise use, 345-46, 350
Culiacán, 323
Cultigens, 165, 166-67
Cultural systems, northern Mexico, 286, 288
Culture, and ethnicity, 192, 193
Culture history, 186; linguistic models of, 155-56
Curicaueri, 307
Cylinder jars, 247

Dancers, rock art imagery of, 337, 338
Dart foreshafts, 159
Dart points, hafting designs, 159-65
Datil points, 162, 163
Decoration, of buildings, 231-50
Decorative space, organization of, 191
Defensive systems, Chalchihuites, 317, 326(n10)
Deities, sculptures of, 307
Devil's claw (*Proboscidea parviflora*), 28
Diet, and fertility, 65
Diffusion, 156, 287, 293; and agricultural adoption, 27, 109; of crops, 64, 114, 169
Directionality principal, 233
Dogs, burials of, 111, 113-14
Dropseed, 28, 72, 76
Drought, and water-table farming, 62-63
Dry farming, 38, 58, 62
D-shaped terrace sites, in southern Chihuahua, 26, 27, 42-44, 48
Durango, 12, 45, 285, 288, 302, 307, 323, 325(n6), 388; Chalchihuites culture in, 313, 314, 320, 322; Proto-Uto-Aztecan in, 157, 158; rock art, 318, 336, 336-41; trade routes in, 339-40

Early Agricultural period, 9, 35, 166; in Chihuahua, 40-44; definition of, 36-37
Early Formative period, 166
Early Mesoamerican Crop Complex, 56, 57
Early Postclassic period, 349
Early Southwestern Crop Complex, 56
Eastern Basketmaker II, 111-12, 122, 125, 128, 129, 130, 131(n3)
Ecology, and agricultural intensification, 96-98
Economic networks, 211-12, 213
Effigies, 258, 267
Egalitarianism, Chalchihuites-Southwest, 317-18
Ehécatl, rock art associated with, 335-36, 336
Elko Contracting Stem points, 160, 167
El Molino (Durango), 338, 339-40
El Nopal, 375, 376
El Paso, 127
El Zape, 339
Empire points, 162, 163
Enculturationist perspective, 147, 185, 186; culture and ethnicity, 189-91; social distance, 197-98; stylistic variation, 192-93
Energy efficiencies, farming techniques, 60-61
En Medio Shelter, projectile points from, 161, 162
Enríquez de Almanza, Martín, 396, 401, 402
Epiclassic period (Mesoamerica), 345, 349, 387
Epistemology, of northern Mexican archaeology, 291-93
Espino, Padre, 403
Ethnic groups, 148, 168
Ethnic identity, 147, 148; creation of, 193-94; social interaction and, 198-99
Ethnicity, 147, 149; Arizona Tewa, 195-96; and culture, 192, 193; diacritica of, 196-97; social construction-

ist model of, 194-95; social distance, 197-99; style and, 189-90
Exchange, 287, 310; and identity formation, 186, 188-89; long-distance, 12, 287; northern Mexico-U.S. Southwest, 318-19
Expanding stem points, 161-63
Experiential principle, 241

Farmers: pre-pottery-making, 112-13; spread of, 108-10, 130; Western Basketmakers as, 110-11. *See also* Forager-farmers
Farming techniques/systems, 28; early, 55-61; risks and, 62-63; San Juan Basin and northern Rio Grande Valley, 74, 75, 77, 81; Tarahumara, 38-39. *See also* Agriculture
Fat Burro Cave, 357. *See also* Burro Gordo
Feathers, in Pueblo ritual, 273-74
Fertility rates, 65
Fiber, 111; as migration evidence, 165-66
Field cache sites, San Juan Basin, 73, 74, 75-76
Fire, 57, 388
Fire God House (Loma Alta), 315
Fishmouth Canyon Ruin, murals in, 233, 243
Floodplain sites, 127, 172
Floodwater farming, 28, 56, 58, 62; Colorado Plateau, 74, 80; productivity of, 59, 60
Florida, Río, 37
Flowery Wars, 389, 390(n1)
Flute player, 316, 321, 336; Chalchihuites rock art, 319-20
Footprints, as journey symbols, 267
Forager-farmers, 41, 111; adoption of crops, 27, 29, 30-31, 64, 129; maize adoption, 71-72. *See also* Hunter-gatherers, hunting-gathering
Formative period (Mesoamerica), 344

412

42SA9310, decorated kiva at, 244
Fraile, 401
Frames of reference, 92-93
Franciscans, 395, 399, 401
Fremont, 123
Fresnal Shelter, 213; cordage from, 214-15; fiber and cultigen remains, 165-66; projectile points from, 215-17; sandals from, 219-20, 221
Fresno points, 367
Funerary complex, 339; Purépecha, 305, 307, 313-14

Gallina Black-on-white, 264
Ganóchi Cave (A33-02), 46, 47, 48, 49
Gate, symbolism of, 261
Gatecliff Contracting Stem points, 160, 167
Genetic evidence, 132(nn13, 14, 15, 16, 19); Uto-Aztecan speakers, 117-18, 120-25
Glaze ware pottery, 264, 279; icons on, 274-75; ritual system, 272-73
Gourds, bottle, 27, 166, 167, 170
Granaries, decorated, 237-38
Gran Chichimeca, La, 3-4, 12; concept of, 13, 286, 288, 294
Grand Gulch, 123
Grasses, plant husbandry of, 27, 28
Grass Valley (Nevada), turquoise from, 347
Great Basin, 63, 108, 111; agriculture in, 170, 172; mtDNA data from, 121, 122; projectile point types, 160, 167; Proto-Uto-Aztecans in, 64, 156, 171
Great Chichimeca uprising, 401
Greater Southwest, 3, 293; and Mesoamerica, 287, 288, 316-20
Great houses, 231; Chacoan, 247-48; outlier, 248-49
Great Nayar, 320, 324
Greece, genetic patterns in, 118-20, 132(nn13, 14)
Green House, murals in, 233
Grewe site, 314

Ground stone tools, and agriculture, 28, 29
Guachichiles, 400, 401, 402, 403
Guachimontones complex, 305, 344
Guadalajara, 399, 401
Guadalupe, 311
Guajabanes, 402
Guamares, 400
Guanajuato, 307, 309, 321, 345; rebellion in, 400, 402, 403
Guasamota, 399
Guasave, 338
Guatemala, 166
Guaxicar Indians, 399
Guaynamota, 399
Guerrero, 36, 166; turquoise in, 344, 345, 351
Guilá Naquitz, 39
Guzman, Nuño de, 399
Gypsum Cave points, 160, 167

Habitation sites, 126; Late Archaic, 73, 74-75, 76, 77-78; maize adoption and, 78-80
Habitus, 193-94
Hafting designs, dart points, 159-65, 167-68
Hall cloister, 321, 322
Halloron Springs, 347
Harbison Cave, 162
Harness Cave, 231-32
Harrel points, 367
Hastqin site, 162
Haynie Ruin, 231, 232; decorated kiva at, 248-49
Hedley Site Complex, 231, 249
Hernandez de Rojas, Gonzalo, 400
Hervideros site, 307, 313-14, 325(n2)
Hidalgo, 345
High Court, and New Laws, 394, 395
Histories, migration and social, 276-77
Hodges Ruin, 314
Hohokam culture, 12, 57, 115, 122, 131(n11), 307, 316, 318, 319, 322, 350; Mesoamerican interactions, 302, 304; Purépecha iconography and ritual and, 314-15

Hokaltecan languages, 165
Hokan speakers, 122, 171
Homol'ovi, ceramics from, 191, 260, 265
Hopi, 115, 116, 151, 169, 191, 258, 260, 262, 324, 347; line break motif, 261, 264; and Lower Rio Puerco pueblos, 277, 278; mtDNA data, 121, 122; Tewa and, 195-96; underworld concept, 267-68
Hopi Mine, 347
Hopi-Tewa, 195-96, 197, 264
Hoy House murals, 233
Huápoca Complex, 357
Huaynamota, 402
Huehueteotl, 307
Huiascatillos Valley, 402
Huichol, 115, 121, 237, 302, 307, 320, 324, 403
Human remains, 387. See also Burials, Trophy heads
Human-serpent figures, 312, 313
Hummingbird Pueblo, 150; architecture, 273, 274; pottery from, 271-72, 277-78; village layout, 278-79
Hunter-gatherers, hunting-gathering, 8, 57, 81, 93, 104(n3); adoption of agriculture, 26, 63, 95-96; in Coahuila, 377-78; duration of, 94, 102; in Mexico, 98-101; north of Mesoamerica, 293-94; in Nuevo León, 12, 286-87, 365-66; plant husbandry of, 27-28; social identity of, 149, 210-11, 213; social organization of, 209-10; subsistence strategies, 29, 30, 89, 90-91, 96-98, 104-5(n4)
Hunting, rock art devoted to, 368

Iatiku, 227-28
Ibarra, Miguel de, 400
Icamole points, 367
Iconography, 322, 323; Chalchihuites, 309, 316-17, 318, 325(n5); Lower Rio Puerco, 274-76, 276, 277(table), 280; northern Mexican, 335-41; in Nuevo León cave sites,

413

Index

368-69; Purépecha, *311, 313*, 314-15
Iconological style, 149, 212-13, 219
Identity, 159, 277; ethnic, 193-94; markers of, 279-80; negotiation of, 11, 186; social, 145-52, 209-11, 271; social construction of, 194-95, 280-81
Incised rocks, 376
Indigenous peoples: legal status of, 394-95; Spanish era subjugation, 393, 396-403
Interactionist perspective, 147, 148, 185, 187; exchange and, 186, 188-89
Intermarriage, Hopi-Tewa, 195-96
Invariance principle, 238, 242
Iron Gate Mine, 347
Irrigation, 38, 58, 71, 170; early, 25, 55; productivity, 59, 60; Proto-Uto-Aztecans, 158, 166
Isochrestic style, 149, 212, 213; in cordage and sandals, 219, 220-21
Ixtlán del Rio, turquoise in, 349

Jalisco, 157, 302, 388; Chalchihuites Culture in, 309, 320, 344-45; turquoise in, 349, 351
Janos, 41
Jarill Mountains, 348
Jeddito Yellow Ware, line break motif, 264, *265*
Jemez, line break motif, 261
Jemez Cave, 28, 77, 80-81
Jerez, 401
Jofre, 402
Joint Casas Grandes Expedition, 6
Jornada Basin, 165
Journey, 260; symbolism of, 266-67
Juan Bautista, 401
Juan de Austria, 401
Juchipila, 400

Katsina religion, icons of, 275-76
Keresan language/speakers, 115, 116, 264

Keystone Dam site, 160
Kingman, turquoise from, 348
Kivas, 267; as architectural metaphors, 227-29; birds in murals, 273-74; in Chaco Canyon, 247-49; as container metaphors, *232*, 236, 237, 239, 240-41; landscape murals in, 243-46; Lower Rio Puerco, 274-75
Knobby Knee Stockade, *232*
Kokopelli. *See* Flute player

LA 6444, 73
LA 6448, 73
LA 70667, 75
LA 81172, 75
LA 107577, 77
LA 110946, 77
Labor requirements, of farming, 60, 61
La Breña, rock art, 335-36
La Cienega rock art, 262
La Comarca Lagunera, 375, 380-81
La Espantosa cave, 376, 378, 379
La Ferrería, 337, 338
Laguna Salada site, 161
Lakes: of emergence, 228, 229; salt, 37
La Laguna caves, burials from, 377, 378
Landscape(s), 11, 12, 368; modeling archaeological, 357-59; Northern San Juan murals, 241-46, 248-49; Río Papigochi, 359-64
Langtry points, 160, 167
Language, 150, 197; and agriculture, 7, 57, 108. *See also* Proto-Uto-Aztecan speakers/language; Uto-Aztecan speakers/language
La Plata Black-on-white, 264
La Playa, 113, 114, 126, 127
La Quemada, 304, 309, 320, 324, 325(n7), 349, 388; Purépecha ceramic iconography, 311-12
Las Cuevas, 349
Las Pitarrillas, 339
Las Virgenes, 403
Late Archaic period, 8, 9, 36, 71; *cerros de trincheras*, 126-

27; in Chihuahua, 26-27, 41, 42-44, 46; San Juan Basin and northern Rio Grande Valley, 28-29, 72-78; social identity, 210-11
Late Holocene, 158; projectile point technology, 164-65, 168
Late Mesoamerican Crop Complex, 56
Late Southwestern Crop Complex, 56
Leapfrogging, 109
Legal status, of Mexican Indians, 394-95
León, 402
Lerma area, 321-22, 351
Lerma points, 366
Lewis Lodge, 240
Life: as journey/pathway, 260-61, 265
Line break: ethnographic interpretation, 260-61; in pottery and basketry, 257-60, 263
Linguistics, 57, 169; and culture history, 155-56. *See also* Proto-Uto-Aztecan language/speakers; Uto-Aztecan language/speakers
Lion House, 240
Literature, Mexican and U.S., 4-5
Little Colorado River, 114, 161, 264
Loma Alta, 315, 325(n1); as ceremonial center, 305-6; closing ceremony, 310-11; sculpture from, *306*, 306-7, 312
Loma Alta phase, 304, 305-8
Loma San Gabriel, 318
Looms, landscape metaphors and, 244, 245-46
Long House, kiva murals, *232*, 243
Los Pilares site, 45
Los Pozos, 26, 127
Lower Pecos, 47
Lower Rio Puerco. *See* Rio Puerco, Lower
Lowry Ruin, 231, *232*, 249
Luna, Antonio, 401
Lupe phase, 305, 306, 311

414

Index

McEuen Cave, 113, 164
Madrean Evergreen Woodland, 38
Maize, 59, 61, 63, 170, 172; in Bat Cave, 163-64; in Chihuahua, 40-41, 42, 45, 46, 47; climate settings for early, 39-40; diffusion of, 114, 129, 156; domestication and adoption of, 7, 8, 36; and early agriculture, 90, 126, 132(n20); early dates on, 25, 26, 28, 49, 166-67; migration of, 27, 30-31, 64; people as metaphor, 237-38; projectile points associated with early, 160, 161-62; and Proto-Uto-Aztecans, 158, 169; in San Juan Basin and northern Rio Grande Valley, 71-81
Maize stalks, 61
Map of the Villas of San Miguel and San Felipe, 394
Marriage, Hopi-Tewa, 195
Marriage groups, hunter-gatherer, 211, 212, 213
Marsh Pass, 123
Martell, Hernando, 401
Martín Courts, 394
Masked figures, 273, 275, 276
Matamoros points, 367
Matehuala, 403
Maxcala Valley, 402
Maximal band, 211
Maxorro, 401
Mayans, 115, 121, 126, 237, 387; turquoise use, 344, 346
Mazapil area, 347, 403
Maze, 261, 262
Mercado Sotomayor, Jerónimo, 401
Merchant class, 346
Mesa Verde, 116, 240, 243-44
Mesoamerica, 1, 13, 64, 157, 293, 314, 319, 375, 389; and Greater Southwest, 287, 288, 302-5, 310, 316-20, 322-24; metaphors, 258, 267; northern frontier of, 302, 309, 317, 320-21; and northern Mexico, 296-97; projectile point hafting technology, 160, 167; Sinaloa

as, 294-95; spread of farmers from, 108-9; turquoise in, 289, 343-46
Metaphors, 151; in archaeological record, 257-58; architectural, 227-29, 230-50; body as vessel, 259-60; life as journey, 260-61, 264-65; people as corn, 237-38; properties of, 229-30; roads and paths as, 266-67
Metates, 61
Mexicas (Aztecs), 324, 326(n11), 387
Mexicaneros, 302, 324
Mexico, 160, 165, 121; cultural epistemology, 291-92; northern, 293, 295-97; pre-pottery farming in, 125-26; transition to agriculture in, 98-101
Mexico, Basin of, 63, 166, 344, 345
Mezcala region, 344
Michoacán, 36, 301, 302, 325(n1), 345, 400
Michoaques (Uacusecha), 321
Middle Archaic period, 8, 9, 36, 47, 63; projectile points, 163-64; in southern Chihuahua, 26-27, 42-44, 45, 46, 48-49
Middle East, genetic evidence in, 118-20
Middle Holocene: projectile points from, 162, 168; Sonoran Desert during, 158, 172. *See also* Middle Archaic period.
Middle place, 262, 267-68
Migration, 129, 170, 310, 319; and agricultural adoption, 7-8, 9, 26, 27, 29, 30-31, 63, 64, 103, 109, 169; artifacts as evidence of, 159-66, 167; of Chalchihuites people, 313-14; Chicomoztoque-nenses, 320-21; and cultural traits, 155-56, 190; to Lower Rio Puerco, 271, 279-80; in Neolithic Greece, 118-20; in northern Mesoamerica, 320-22; in oral tradition, 266-67, 276-77; of Uto-Aztecan speakers, 9, 108,

114-28, 146, 150, 158; and village layout, 278-79
Milagro site, 26, 127
Milky Way, as pathway, 266
Milpillas phase, 305, 322
Mimbres art, 322, 325(n9)
Mineral Park, turquoise from, 348
Mining: Spanish, 394, 396, 400, 402; turquoise, 348, 349
Missionaries, 393, 395, 399, 401
Mitochondial DNA (mtDNA), 118; Uto-Aztecan speaker migration, 120-24
Mixe speakers, 121
Mixe-Zoquean, 115
Mixtecs, 121, 237, 351
Mixtón War, 393, 398, 400
Moctezuma II, turquoise gifts, 345
Mogollon, 113, 115, 122, 318
Mogollon Highlands, 163, 166, 168, 169; artifact style and social group in, 213-20
Moon House, murals in, 233, 241-42
Morales phase, 309, 314
Morenci, 348
Moreno, Martín, 401
Mortality rates, 65
Mortuary practices, Basketmaker, 111
Mosaics, Hohokam, 315
Müllerried, Frederico, 378
Mummy Cave, baskets from, 263, 264-65
Murals, 267, 338; basketry-based, 238-39; landscape, 241-46; pottery-band, 232, 232-36, 237, 240-41, 248-49; Pottery Mound, 273-74, 275-76

Nahua speakers, 115, 121, 237
Nahuipan, 402
Native American Graves Protection and Repatriation Act, 145
Navajo, 264, 347
Navajo Reservoir, 78
Nayarit, 157, 349; rebellion in, 399-400
Neblina cave, 339, 340

415

Index

Neolithic, farmer migration during, 118-20, 132(nn15, 16)
Neutron activation analysis (NAA), turquoise sources, 347, 348-49, 350, 351
Nevada, 170; turquoise in, 346, 347
New Archaeology, 186, 189
New Azure, turquoise in, 348
New Laws, 394, 395
New Mexico, 108; Archaic projectile points, 161, 162, 164, 165, 293, 297; hunter-gatherer social identity, 210-11; turquoise in, 346, 348
New Spain, northern frontier, 293, 294
Nicolás de San Luís. See San Luis Montañez
Nobility, Mesoamerican, 346
Nochistlán, 400
Nogales (Lerma region), 322
Nogales points, 367
Nomadic groups, 12, 317; in Coahuila, 377-78
Nombre de Dios, 336
Nopal Shelter, 375
Norogachi, 46
Northern Mexico, 335, 344; and Mesoamerica, 293, 295-97; U.S. Southwest exchange, 318-19
Northern side-notched point, 163
Northwest Mexico, 3, 397
Nueva Galicia, 397, 399, 401
Nuevo León, 285, 288, 289; artifacts in, 366-67; hunter-gatherers in, 12, 286-87, 365-66; rock art, 367-69
Numic speakers, 115, 122, 123, 159, 167

Oak Man, 227
Oasis America, as term, 294, 295
Oaxaca, Valley of, 63, 160, 166; early maize in, 36, 39; turquoise in, 344, 345, 351
Ochre/hematite, in early farmer burials, 112, 113
Ocorinis, 402
Ojala Cave, 77

Old Hachita, turquoise in, 348
Olivella rectangular beads, 171
Oñate, Juan de, 399, 403
Opata, 115, 172
Oral tradition, 386; of journeys, 266-67; of middle place, 267-68; migration and social identity, 276-77, 279-80
Orozco, Juan Bautista, 401, 402
Ortiz Fuenmayor, Gabriel, 397
Oto-Manguean speakers, 108-9, 115, 121
Otomí, 401

Pachos, 403
Pacification, of Chichimeca, 393-403
Painted Kiva site, murals at, 233, 243
Paiute, 121, 122, 170, 172
Palacio phase, 305, 322
Palmar de Vega, 402
Pames, 402
Panama, maize domestication in, 36
Panic grass, Sonoran (*Panicum sonorum*), domestication of, 28
Papigochic, Río, cultural landscape of, 355-57, 359-64
Palmer, Edward, 375, 378
Paquimé, 5, 12, 285, 287, 288, 289, 296, 308, 323, 335, 336, 350; and Chalchihuites, 340-41
Parral, D-shaped terrace sites near, 42, 43, 44
Pathway(s), 262; life as, 260-61, 265-66; symbolism of, 266-67
Peace agreements, 393, 403
Peace treaties, 395, 397-98
Pecos Valley, projectile points, 160
Pelona points, 160, 162, 167
Pénjamo, 401, 402
Peñon Blanco, 340
Peralta, Gastón de, 396
Pérez de Bocanegra, Hernán, 400
Pérez Torre, Diego, 399
Perfect Kiva Ruin, 240
Petran Montane Conifer Forest, 38

Petroglyphs, 262, 287
Physical anthropology, and archaeology, 385, 389-90
Picuris, 264
Piedra de Amolar rock art, 336
Pilgrimages, 320, 323; in oral tradition, 266-67
Pima, 121
Piman speakers, 115, 171, 172; genetic data, 121-22, 124
Pinitos points, 367
Pinto points, 161, 162, 167
Pithouses, 113, 131(nn4, 6), 315
Pit structures, decorated, 231-32
Plainview-Golondrina points, 366
Plant use, 61, 90, 117; hunter-gatherer, 96-101, 102; husbandry of, 27-28, 44, 57, 62, 64, 170, 172
Platforms, Loma Alta, 307
Platform shelter sites. See D-shaped terrace sites
Playa farming, 74
Plazas, Lower Rio Puerco, 273
Pochteca, 346
Population aggregation, 150, 271; and social identity, 280-81
Population density, 7, 65, 104(n3)
Population growth: southern Chihuahua, 47-48; transition to agriculture, 65-66
Poseyemu-Montezuma-Jesus, 320
Postclassic period (Mesoamerica), 345
Pottery, 7, 36, 63, 308, 322, 325(n9), 336, 337, 338; architectural metaphors for, 232-41, 242(table), 247, 248-49; Chalchihuites, 309, 325(n5); effects of enculturation on, 190-91; line break in, 257-58, 263-64, 265, 266; Purépecha iconography, 311-12, 315; social identity and, 271-72, 274-76, 277-78, 279(table), 280
Pottery Mound, 150; kiva murals, 273, 273-74, 274, 275; pottery from, 271-72,

416

276, 277–78; village layout, 278, 279
Practice theory, 9–10, 149; structure-agency dichotomy, 193–94
Pre-pottery Formative, 112–13, 127
Presidio (Texas), 379
Presidios, establishment of, 403
Prestige goods, distribution of, 188–89
Projectile points, 209; Basketmaker II, 111, 113; iconological style, 212–13; and identity, 159–65, 167–68, 215–17; Middle and Late Archaic, 42, 43, 44, 45, 46, 47, 63, 64; Nuevo León, 366–67; Proto-Uto-Aztecans and, 150, 171
Projecto Arqueología de Chihuahua, 6
Proto-Maya, 116
Proto-Mixe-Zoque, 116
Proto-Numic speakers, 167
Proto-Tepiman, 157
Proto-Uto-Aztecan (PUA) language/speakers, 116, 158, 172; early agricultural terms in, 57, 169; migration, 63, 64, 150; origins of, 156–57; projectile points, 159–65, 167, 168
Pseudocloisonné, 315
PUA. *See* Proto-Uto-Aztecan language/speakers
Publication, Mexican-U.S., 4–5
Puebla, turquoise in, 345
Pueblo IV period, 271; icons, 274–75; ritual system, 273–74; social stratification and prestige goods, 188–89
Pueblo Southwest, 237, 293, 311, 324; in fifteenth century, 150–51; line break motif, 257–61, 263–64; roads and pathways in, 266–67
Purépecha, 12, 287, 289, 302, 310, 350; and Chalchihuites culture, 301, 311–14; and Hohokam culture, 314–15; Loma Alta phase, 305–8. *See also* Tarascans

Querétaro, 309, 321, 345, 402
Quetzalcoatl, and turquoise, 345
Quintana Roo, turquoise in, 344
Quivira, 399

Radiocarbon dates, 50(n1), 63, 165; associated with Archaic projectile points, 160–61, 162, 163, 164; for Chihuahua sites, 41, 42, 44, 45, 46, 49
Rain-fed farming, 56, 58; productivity of, 59–60
Rana points, 367
Rancho Aviléz, 340
Rebellions, indigenous people, 399–403
Rejogochi, 46
Ricegrass, Indian, 28, 72, 73, 76
Rinconada pints, 367
Río de la Loza, Rodrigo del, 397, 401
Rio Grande Pueblos, 115, 264
Rio Grande Tewa, 228
Rio Grande Valley, 114; early agriculture in, 80–81; Late Archaic sites in, 28–29, 72, 76–77; projectile points, 160, 168
Rio Puerco, Lower, 264; icons, 274–75; ritual system, 273–74; social identity on, 271–72, 279–80
Rio Puerco, Upper, early agriculture in, 78
Ritual, 339, 368, 388, 389; red-slipped glaze ware and, 272–73; and social integration, 151, 280, 281
Ritual systems, 280, 321, 322, 388; Lower Rio Puerco, 271, 273–74; Nuevo León rock art, 368–69
River's Edge sites, 79
Roads, symbolism of, 266–67
Robledal, 401
Rock art, 12, 262, 289, 316; Basketmaker II, 112, 128; Chalchihuites, 319, 319–20; La Breña, 335–36; northern Mexico, 310, 318, 335–41; Nuevo León, 367–69

Rockshelters, 26; in Coahuila, 374, 380; with D-shaped terraces, 42–44. *See also* Cave sites
Roofing, kiva, 237, 240, 247–48
Roosevelt Red Ware, 151, 191, 264
Roundtree Pueblo, pottery-band designs in, 232, 240–41
Royal Revenue Office: town establishment, 398–99
RT4 (Durango), 339
Runoff farming, 58, 59, 60, 75

Sacrifice, human, 325(n7), 389
Salado polychrome pottery, 151, 191, 264
Salmon Ruin, 248
Saltillo, 402, 403
Salutatory jumps, 109
San Andrés, 403
San Antonio Carupo, 321–22
Sandals, 267, 376; Basketmaker II, 111, 113, 169; as evidence of migration, 165, 166; ichonological and isochrestic style, 212, 217, 218, 219, 217–20, 220, 221
San Felipe, 401
San Ildefonso, line break motif, 264
San Jose phase, 162
San Jose points, 161, 162
San Jose–Pinto points, 161
San Juan Anthropomorphic rock art, 112, 128
San Juan Basin, 162; architecture as metaphor, 151, 229; buildings as containers, 232–41; early agriculture in, 73–76, 78, 79–80; great house architecture in, 247, 248–49; Late Archaic sites in, 28–29; line break motif in, 263–64; world as building in, 241–46
San Juan Bautista de Caropa, 401
San Juan de los Lagos, 401
San Juan del Río, 402
San Luis de Paz, 393, 403
San Luis Montañez, Nicolás, 401

417

Index

San Luis Potosí, 321, 346, 388, 403
San Marcos Pueblos, 348
San Martín, 401
San Miguel (Guanajuato), 400
San Pedro, Río, 37
San Pedro Cochise, 112, 113, 127-28
San Pedro phase, 64, 127, 163, 164, 169-70
San Pedro point, 163, 164
San Quintín Canyon, 335-36, 340
Santa Ana, line break motif, 260-61
Santa Cruz Bend site, 127
Santa Cruz River, 63, 162-63
Santa Fe, 77
Santa Isabel, 42
Santa Isabel, Río, 42
Santa María, 401
Santo Domingo, 264, 266, 348
Sayles, E. B., 1
Scalps, scalping, Basketmaker, 111, 131(n7)
Schroeder site, 337
Sculpture, Purépecha and Chalchihuites, 306-7
Sedentism, 7, 26
Semidesert Grassland, 37-38, 41
Serpents, horned/plumed, 311, 323
Shabik'eschee Village, 79
Shaft Tomb complexes, 305
Shipaulovi, petroglyph near, 262
Shoshone, 170, 122
Shoshonean wedge, 171
Shumla points, 367
Side-notched points, 163-64
Sierra del Nayar, 312, 320
Sierra Madre Occidental, 37, 38-39, 49, 171, 301, 302, 316, 323, 336; Chalchihuites culture in, 320, 324; cliff dwellings in, 12, 287, 289, 326(n10), 363-64; cultural landscapes in, 355-64; maize from, 40-41; Proto-Uto-Aztecans in, 157, 158
Sierra Tarahumara, 26, 38-39, 40, 46, 48-49
Silver production, 394, 396

Sinaloa, 158, 164, 294-95, 338, 399, 402
Sirupa Canyon, 357, 359
Site 423-158, 73
Sitio Pienso (A47-05), D-shaped terrace at, 42, 43-44
Skulls, display of, 323
Slavery, of Chichimecas, 401, 402
Sleeping Beauty mine, 348
Slickhorn Perfect Kiva site, 240
SM2, rock art at, 337, 338
Snaketown, 314
Social boundaries, organization of decorative space, 191
Social constructionist model, 194-95
Social distance, 185; and ethnic identity, 197-99
Social groups, 159, 187, 267; exchange as marker, 188-89; membership identity, 196-97; and pottery technology, 277-78; social identity and, 211, 279-80
Social identity, 9-11, 145; in archaeology, 146-52, 209-11; in artifact technology, 213-22, 277-78
Socialization, and ceramic decorative styles, 190-91
Social markers, 148-49, 150
Social networks, and social identity, 150-51
Social organization, hunter-gatherers, 209-10
Social scale, metaphors for, 266
Social units, and village layout, 278-79
Soda Dam lake, 77
Solar ritual, 339, 367
Sombrerete, 401
Sonora, 6, 61, 126, 128, 158, 285, 288, 346; Archaic points in, 163, 164; Uto-Aztecan speakers in, 108, 157
Sonora, Río, Tepiman speakers, 157
Sonoran branch (Uto-Aztecan), 157
Sonoran Desert, 157, 158
South America, 36
Southern Tiwa, 228

Southwest, 344; and Mesoamerica, 302-5, 310, 317-19, 322-24; as term, 293, 295, 297
Southwest Regional Cult, 275, 323
Sowérare Cave (A32-02), 46
Spanish, 366; and Chichimec pacification, 393-403; on nomadic groups, 12, 388
Spirals, 261, 262, 265
Spruce Tree House, 243
Square Tower House, 240
Squash (*Cucurbita*), 27, 28, 72, 73, 75, 76, 79; spread of, 166-67, 169
Starr points, 367
State formation, Mesoamerica, 317
Stone cult, Loma Alta, 307
Stone Pipe site, 127
Storage pits, 25-26, 74
Straight-stem points, 163
Structuration theory, 193
Structure-agency dichotomy, 192; practice theory, 193-94
Style, 187; enculturationist perspective, 189-91, 192-93; iconological and isochrestic, 149-50, 212-13
Subsistence strategies, and agricultural adoption, 89, 90-91, 96-98
Sun, journey of, 266
Superior, turquoise from, 348
Superordinate principle, 237, 242
Swallow Cave, 40, 46

Tabasco, 36, 345
Tahue, 172
Takic language/speakers, 115, 171
Tamaos, 402
Tamaulipas, projectile point types, 160
Tampico, 402
Tanoan language/speakers, 115, 116, 117, 229; mtDNA data, 121, 122-23
Taos, 264
Tapia, Diego de, 401
Tapia, F. R., 403
Tarahumara, 38-39, 115, 121, 171

Index

Tarascan Empire, 302, 305, 322. *See also* Purépecha
Tarascans, 307, 322, 325(n9), 401
Taylor, Walter W., 1; Coahuila Expedition, 373-81
Tecuexe, 400
Tehuacan Valley, 40, 160
Temiño de Bañuelos, Baltasar, 400
Tenochtitlán, 121, 324
Teocaltiche, 400
Teotihuacán, 267, 307, 308, 309, 310, 324, 387
Teotlalpan Tlacochcalco Mictlampa, 294
Tepecanos, 403
Tepehuanes, 157, 323, *336*, 338, 397
Tepezala, 401
Tepiman languages/speakers, 115, 157, 171
Terraced hills. *See Cerros de trincheras*
Terraces. *See Cerros de trincheras*; D-shaped terraces
Terrestrial model densities, 97
Teutelco Indians, 399
Tewa, 258, 264; ethnic identity of, 195-96; kiva as metaphor, 228-29
Texas, 47, 165, 293, 297, 374
Textiles: and landscape metaphors, 243-44; and pottery metaphors, 233, 236, 238-39, 240-41
Tezcacuitlapilli, 308, 323
Tezcatlipoca cult, 337
Tiwa, kiva as metaphor, 228-29
Tlaloc, 307
Tlatelolco, 121, 345
Tlatenango, 400
Tlaxcala, turquoise, 345
Tlaxcaltecans, 397, 403
Toltec Chichimec, 12, 287, 289, 321; and Chalchihuites culture, 302, *304*, 324
Toltec Mine, turquoise in, 347
Tonto Basin, 190
Topia, 403
Tortugas points, 367
Toya points, 367
Trade: Southwest-Mesoamerican, 315, 325(n6), 335; turquoise, 335, 346, 350-51

Trade routes: northern Mexican, 338, 339-41; southwestern U.S.-Tula, 335-36; turquoise, 350-51
Trails, symbolism of, 267
Tribute, turquoise as, 345
Trophy heads: Loma Alta, 307; Western Basketmaker, 111, 131(n7)
Tucson Basin, 164, 349; Early Agricultural period in, 36, 55, 63, 127, 128, 166
Tula, 302, 308, 388, 321, 324
Tularosa Basin: artifact styles in, 213-22; fiber and cultigens in, 165-66
Tularosa Cave, 41, 166; artifact styles in, 213, *218*; projectile points, 216-17
Turquoise, 335; Chalchihuites culture, 323, 325(n6); long-distance exchange of, 12, 287, 289; in Mesoamerica, 343-46; natural distribution of, 346-48
Turquoise Mountain, 347
Tzompantli, 321, 388

Uacusecha (Eagle Knights), 302, 205, 321, 322, 324
Underworld: Hopi concept of, 267-68; kiva as microcosm of, 227-28, 229
Upper Rio Puerco. *See* Rio Puerco, Upper
Uprisings, of indigenous peoples, 399-403
Urdiñola, Francisco de, 397, 402, 403
Urique, Rio, 38, 46
Usilique, 403
Utes, 170
Uto-Aztecan language/speakers, 57, 156, 157, 170, 310; and agriculture, 7, 116-17, 169, 172-73(n1); artifacts as indicators of, 159-67; genetic evidence for, 120-25; migration of, 9, 30, 108, 114-28, 146, 150; outside Southwest, 171-72; spread of, 108, 109, 130

Valderrama, Gerónimo, 395
Valerio de la Cruz, 401
Velasco, Luis de, II, 394, 397-98
Ventana Cave, 169-70
Venus, 336
Veracrúz, 166, 345
Vessels, bodies as, 258, 260, 261
Villa de Santiago, 403
Villages, 79, 80, 271, 388; early 25-26, 125-26
Violence: in archaeological record, 385-86, 387, 388, 389, 390(nn1, 2)
Visual metaphors, 151

Walls, decorated, 231-50
Warfare, 317, 319, 338, 385, 389, 390(n1); in archaeological record, 386-88; pre-Hispanic, 13, 286, 288-89; Spanish era, 393, 396-97, 398, 399-401
Warriors, 323; bow-and-arrow, 319, 321
Washo, 122
Water, as rock art theme, 368
Water control features, 57, 90, 166
Water-table farming, 28, 58, 59, 62-63, 80, 81
Wattle frameworks, in great house kivas, 247-48
Wave of advance theory, 109, 110
Weaving: great house kiva roofs, 247-48; and world metaphors, 245-46; and pottery metaphor, 233, 236, 238-39, 240-41
Weirs, 57
Western Basketmaker II, 108, 125, 129, 130, 131(nn3, 7, 8); cultural traits, 111-12, 113, 114; as migrant farmers, 110-11, 128; mtDNA data from, 123-24; projectile points, 163, 164; and San Pedro traits, 169-70
West Texas, and Coahuila, 12-13, 374-75
Westwater 5 Kiva Ruin, *232*
White Dog phase, 169. *See also* Western Basketmaker II

419

Index

White Signal, turquoise in, 348
Winslow Orange Ware, 191; with line break, 260, 264
Women, and line break motif, 258-59, 261
World tree, 267
Wupatki National Monument, rock art, 262

Xalpa, 400
Xicalanco, 346
Xichú, 402
Xilotepec, 402
Xiximes, 323

Yucatán, turquoise in, 345

Yuirirapúndaro, 403
Yuman languages/speakers, 122, 124, 131(n11), 157

Zacapu Basin, 322
Zacapu Lake, 305-6, 311
Zacapu region, 302, 307, 321, 322
Zacatecas, 12, 157, 302, 388, 400, 401, 403; Chalchihuites culture in, 309, 320; turquoise in, 335, 344, 346, 347, 349-40
Zacatecos, 400; rock art and pottery, 335-36, 337, 338-39

Zacatenco, 344
Zacoalco, 349
Zapaliname, 403
Zapotecs, 121
Zorita, Alonso de, 394, 395-96, 398-99
Zuaques, 402
Zuni, 347; early canals in, 55, 71; line break motif, 260-61, 264; and Lower Rio Puerco, 277, 278
Zuñiga, Manrique de (Marquis of Villamanrique), 397
Zuni glaze wares, 264
Zuni speakers, 115, 121, 122, 124, 131(n11)

www.ingramcontent.com/pod-product-compliance
Lightning Source LLC
Chambersburg PA
CBHW071227070526
44583CB00017B/2078